Bureaucratic Decision
A Complicated Process

Dr. R.P. Balwan
(Swami Gyananand Saraswati)

ATLANTIC
PUBLISHERS & DISTRIBUTORS (P) LTD

Published by

ATLANTIC

PUBLISHERS & DISTRIBUTORS (P) LTD

7/22, Ansari Road, Darya Ganj, New Delhi-110002
Phones : +91-11-40775252, 40775214, 23273880, 23275880
Fax : +91-11-23285873
Web : www.atlanticbooks.com
E-mail : orders@atlanticbooks.com

Branch Office: Chennai
Phones : +91-44-48531784, 28291383
E-mail : chennai@atlanticbooks.com

Printed & bound in India by Atlantic Print Services

"Your right is to work only and never to the fruit thereof. Do not be the cause of the fruit of action, nor let your attachment be to inaction."

—*The Bhagavad Gita*, 2.47

Dedication

To my mother Smt. Narayani Devi and father Sh. D.R. Balwan, who taught me honesty, integrity, commitment to hard work, being self reliant, empowerment of disadvantaged, necessity of being resilient, and everything I needed to be a successful *Karamyogi*.

"The unreal has no existence, and the real never ceases to be; the reality of both has thus been perceived by the seers of truth."

—*The Bhagavad Gita*, 2.16

Foreword

The executive branch is one of the three pillars (legislature and judiciary are the other two pillars) of democratic governance system. In Indian governance, All India Services (AIS), specifically Indian Administrative Service, Indian Police Service, and Indian Forest Service, are critical part of the executive branch. These three services, however, have their roots in the colonial regime of the British Empire. The adaptation of these services as per the social and cultural environment and the expectations of the citizens of independent India have been debated for decades. The main issue of the debate has been the transformation of the attitude of the members of the services from "rulers" to "public servants". The answer and interventions to this question are not simple; and it is almost impossible to find the correct answer and required interventions using the tools of the dominant paradigm of scientific approach.

In the scientific approach, search for answers is deliberate, systematic, and structured, and it is not supposed to take the beliefs around them granted. Hence, this approach is termed as objective and neutral. However, in this approach, real-life processes are externalized into measurable and comparable objects through transparent and replicate modes of transformation. The objectivity, therefore, is based on the conversion of real-life processes into theoretical objects, and neutrality is based on the process of disconnecting the observers from their social and cultural environments. However, these processes introduce their own subjectivity. Hence, the objectivity and neutrality are maintained and used to convince people at the expense of shirking social responsibility. In essence, the scientific approach is also a social construct, and it will be better that the users of scientific knowledge are made aware of its connections to social and cultural environment.

The dominant scientific view of reductionism has been challenged by the Quantum Theory. As per this theory, even the sub-atomic particles (electrons, protons, and neutrons) cannot exist in isolation and do not have properties independent of its environment. All these particles can be understood as interconnections/relations between different particles. As per Bell's experiment, due to non-local connections, the two particle-system is an indivisible whole even if particles are far apart. Bohm, in S-Matrix theory, suggested "unbroken whole" or "each part, in some sense, contains the whole" which is similar to Rumi's philosophical view—an individual is not a single drop in an ocean but contains the whole ocean in a drop.

In essence, the decision-making process of the members of the AIS cannot be understood by separating them from their social, cultural, political, and organizational environment. In this book, the author has made an excellent attempt to provide glimpses of various environmental factors that affect the decision making of the members of the AIS. The contents and the quality of the book are enriched by an outstanding experience and impacts of the author. The author, Dr. Balwan, has 35 years of experience as a bureaucrat. His experience includes capacity building of disadvantageous social groups, strengthening and empowerment of village institutions, administration of natural resource management and environment protection, and policy analysis, formulation, and coordination. He is highly regarded for his exemplary work to save Aravalli Ecosystem even at the cost of his career and threats to his life. He took *Sanyas Diksha* (sainthood) immediately after taking voluntary retirement. The book is a true reflection of the author's deep understanding, knowledge, analytical skills, experience from inside and outside of the executive branch, and the challenges faced during the decision making in the AIS.

In conclusion, I would like to highlight two specific features of the book. First, the book takes a holistic and systematic view to conduct comprehensive analyses of the issues related to the decision making by the members of the AIS. In this process, it includes individual, group, and system's variables, and keeps the analyses very simple and easy to follow. The author has examined the relationships between all these variables. Second, the book includes a very rich and unique primary data set—data on 262 variables from 283 respondents who are the members of AIS. I hope, the book and the data set will motivate many scholars to move the frontier of research on decision making by the members of executive branch in India as well as other countries.

Shashi Kant
Professor, Forest Resource Economics and Management
Institute for Management and Innovation
University of Toronto Mississauga
University of Toronto

Appraisal Letter

Rationale for Changing the Bureaucratic Structure

In my over thirty-five years of public service, I have not seen such an in-depth analysis of the governmental decision-making process in India, and one that included inconvenient issues such as self-promoting behaviour, hidden motives behind decision-making, disregard to efficiency, productivity and achievement of goals, insensitivity to public service, focus on individual gain rather than the public good, and unbridled and shameless continuity of outdated mindsets. The findings by the author confirm my fear and beliefs about the inefficacy of the present governing system in India—a system, which has its origin in pre-independence era to serve the interest of the then imperialist power—to fulfil people's aspiration in the 21st century.

By providing a historical perspective of the then prevailing governing systems in India and by delving into the origin and continuity of the All India Services, the author presents a strong rationale for re-structuring the current decision-making process with a particular focus on reforming the dominant and redundant bureaucratic structure. The process has to shift in favour of decisions that would benefit the billion plus Indians from decisions that predominantly focus on benefiting the self-aggrandizing few thousands of bureaucrats, who often come across to common man as arrogant and egoist '*Sahibs*'. There are enough evidences in the book that indicate the mindset of All India Service officers, still entrenched into pre-independence era. Most of them, particularly in the Indian Administrative Service, continue to behave and work like erstwhile '*Gaura Sahibs*'.

The author has extensively demonstrated with facts that the persistence of old outlook in bureaucracy is a serious obstacle in the progress of the country. He talks about a number of contemporary issues associated with the present bureaucratic system: manipulation of decisions, amenability of service members to political and other pressures, focus on individual gain rather than collective welfare, demoralisation of subordinates, loss of innovativeness, and so on. It is disheartening to see that the status, power, influence, and prestige become key motivators for service members rather than the honesty, hard work, work ethics, and developmental activities.

The author deserves appreciation for his bold approach in this extraordinary research work. What makes this work unique and creditable is that the primary information comes directly from horse's mouth. The All India Services officers, who are also the part of the problem, have voluntarily shared their perceptions and thoughts. The issues have been presented in a straightforward plain language without mincing unpalatable words. In my view, retirement from active service and the detachment from societal activities have helped the author to reflect back into the functioning of service members including the need to call a spade a spade. More importantly, he has made immense efforts to present the findings to a broader audience through this book by incorporating his own candid perspective.

I believe that the real value of this work lies in its potential to instigate a debate on the effectiveness of current bureaucratic system in addressing the prevalent socio-economic problems. Some service members may not be happy or agree with the findings. Others may be prompted to look into their own behaviour, which they are not generally able to comprehend when in power. I feel that the various issues raised and solutions proposed in this book should be thoroughly discussed in diverse forums. This book can also be a useful reference in developing suitable policies. I strongly feel that this is a must-read book for all people whether in service or outside of service.

Jagdish Prasad Yadav, Ph.D.
IFS (Retired),
Education Sector Advisor, Canada

Preface

While working as a Scientific Officer/Scientist in the Department of Atomic Energy, I developed a great reverence for the All India Services. Later on, when I joined the All India Services, I felt like flying on pinnacles and soon during training rediscovered that we are the legacy of the Imperial British era. While working in the Haryana Cadre and various positions at Center, I got plethora of opportunities to study the behavior of these super elites from closest range. I have a deep rooted interest to study 'individual's orientation' and the system, where different variables are operating on them. During scintillating experience and first-hand interaction with politicians and super powerful elites, I rediscovered that AISO are super actors and the greatest politicians. They are the masters of wind to churn every opportunity in their favor to serve their self-goals.

With passage of time as my interactions with the AISO increased, my obsession to study their cognitive psychology and behaviour multiplied. Vainly in search of solutions, I unsettled the dust of various libraries for many years. I was elated in real sense after 9 months of rigorous hard work in libraries, when Dr. Pritam Singh approved my questionnaires with some modifications. Retrieval of information from the AISO is one of the most difficult tasks on the earth. My efforts of couple of years saw the sunlight, when feeding of desired information was completed in Statistical Package for the Social Sciences for Windows (SPSS) software on PC.

Data Analyses and research findings are purely neutral to any service or person, and strictly based on results/findings of the research; any member of any service should not perceive about it. Research is a search for appropriate variables and the web of their interrelationship. Its findings are explained by narrative of appropriate order based on reliable statistical results. Some individuals may find different statistical results depending on the accuracy of used statistical instruments, but in research work factual findings have to be presented.

Vedic Period onwards indigenous system of administration had been sustainable for thousands of years. During Medieval Period system of administration was altered to individual oriented. Imperial Colonial Period expressed the culmination of policy of repression and ruthless exploitation of indigenous people to serve the Imperialistic interest in England. Repression of Indian subcontinent was reflected in recruitment in England. Constitutional autocracy was not differing the '*tota daclo*' from Asian despotism. For over two centuries, Colonial rulers administered and ruled India through the imperial bureaucracy to protect their throne in England. The All India Services were the time-tested system of exploitation and ruling from remote to serve the interests of select few at top. Thus, because of their origin, the All India Services are exploitative and self-goal oriented.

Great concerns were expressed and voices were raised during the independence movement against the agencies of repression and suppression. Even after that about 3 million Colonial officials were permitted to stay on their posts at the time of independence, with the expectation that they will change themselves. Indian bureaucracy remained preoccupied with retention of power and purse for self-goal maximization. Slow and sure degradation in bureaucratic system has made it mystery and secret sacrilege for protection of own deeds or misdeeds or misdemeanor.

Colonial Civil Administration in India was through All India Services Officers. District was basic unit and District Collector was the 'alter ego' of the Viceroy at the top, and the same was accepted in the independent India also. Centralisation in decision-making was its key feature. Heaven borne and pampered AISO steel frame to enslaves the Indians from their childhood. Elite class stratification in services with own separate career prospectus generates conflicts in the bureaucratic system. Public servants with political support start behaving as *de facto* rulers in an autocratic manner with eyes on self-goal maximization only.

The AISO idolize authority. Public faith has turned into materialism, materialism into passive obedience, and obedience into self-goals. Self-goals turn state into individual fiefdom for self-career and perpetuation. The AISO are symbol of status, ego, arrogance, and power based politically dominated class in itself. Bureaucrats are power elites everywhere in the world, so India cannot be an exception.

The AISO have outlived their utility. Present bureaucratic system has become heaven for ill motivated and corrupt persons. For common public it has become circuitous to scale the cliffs of decision in bureaucratic system. The new image of the All India Services is as the self-satisfied glorious innovator, egoist, elitist, groupist, authoritarian, power crazy, monopoliser, status hungry, perk jerker, and decision dodger.

Politics is the unsanctioned or illegitimate use of power to achieve unsanctioned or illegitimate ends. It is a way to exploit the formal system. People love to use politics for own goal maximization. No system in the world is free from politics of pressure, so is in India. Under political pressure goal revision leads to goal enlargement, which leads to goal displacement, and goal succession imprisons the decision-making process. Collective goals emerge as a result of voluntary trading and contracting between the All India Services Officers and politicians. Goals continuously change, when individual improves own benefits. By such change, public goals are toppled in power struggle; and the political relations and success modify individual officer's behaviour. Utility and futility of goals motivate individual to generate more and more political patronage and hence, role of political pressure continues to increase with passage of time. Such systems/processes of political patronage/obligation/nexus have become heaven for corrupt officers.

Stratified Indian Society is entrenched with institutionalised inequalities. Colonially created imperialistic institution cannot remain on original terms, but has to be readjusted to be in harmony with new changing socio-economic-political situations. The AISO have become necessary evil to create an elite class among the services.

If something can go wrong it will go wrong. The All India Services have regulated to multiply only subordinates not rivals. The AISO have reached the pinnacles of their incompetence, but still they are undoubtedly 'the best' to rule the country by virtue of their training and location in power hierarchy. In comparison with private sector technocrats, Public Sector Undertakings, specialist, and rest of the bureaucrats, the AISO are undisputedly the best. In India, ours experiences with railways, postal and communication, doctors, engineers, scientists, and specialists show that bureaucracy operates in similar way in all the departments through power elites with foundation in self-goals. Civil Services operate through elitist foundation and resilience. Garrison of politically picked up persons uphold the crown for British and now holding it for the politicians.

Terms such as bureaucrat, public servant, government servant, political administrator, civil servant, and civil administrator have different meanings in reference to different works; here these terms have been used interchangeably to cover the All India Services Officers posted in different positions and at different locations. Terms such as public administration, bureaucratic system, and civil administration have also been used interchangeably to indicate the government administration, where the All India Services Officers are located and take decisions.

The AISO are located on all pivotal positions in public administration. By their location, they have insured that performance is relegated to oblivion. Complete bureaucratic system has been molded around self-goals. Behavior of individual AISO is a matter of concern for public as complete decision-making process revolves around them. It works in both ways—the behaviours of the AISO and in turn public and politician also influence forcefully behaviours of individuals and services in due course of time.

Issue of political pressure is as old as human civilization. In any organization, pressure moves things in desired direction in turn outcomes that motivate pressure exerter to accelerate it with continual efforts. Pressure is a compulsory compulsion of every organisation. Activities under pressure are not carried out according to rules, regulations, and procedures. They are considered to be brought under influence or an attempt to influence the outcome of decision to meet their self/own goals or interests from public administration at the cost of public. Illegitimate political pressure is the pressure, which violates the well laid down rules, regulations, and procedure of the bureaucratic system. Whereas, legitimate political pressure is the overriding pressure asserted in normal administration by in-charge Centre or State Minister/Chief Minister/Prime Minister, through formal line of command, which is in consonance with the laid down rules.

Bureaucratic system is the biggest cause to invite and sustain the political pressure. System boundary is such that political pressure continuously percolates and submerges/mingles to propel it. Political pressure has become the integral part of it and its sustainability revolves around it. Different causes of political pressure have been studied and the results indicate that the most important causes and genesis ooze from the system itself.

Perhaps this research is first of its kind, where we have studied the AISO's behaviour, biographic orientation, locus of control, motivation, life style orientation, cultural aspects, conflict management, risk taking behaviour, innovations, and work place environment of AISO in decision making process under political pressure. We have selected 22 modes of political pressure and our results indicate five most commonly used modes which are crucial. Fifteen most important reasons to accept political pressure have been studied and ten sources of political pressure (PM/CM to village level) have been analysed to find out intensity of pressure from these sources.

For sake of convenience of software, USA/UK English has been used. Where so ever word 'he' has been used as neutral to both genders. 'He' also denotes 'she'. After data analysis on SPSS, in exhibits all the values have not been shown due to limitation of space and clarity, only highest values or relevant figures have been indicated at places according to requirement of that variable. Language has been kept simple for the convenience of common people.

It is not possible for me to acknowledge and enumerate each and every source of help that I have received during the research work. But, it was not possible to complete this task without the support provided by the library at MDI, Gurgaon. Really, it is a wonderful library. I am grateful to Dr. Pritam Singh (ex-Director, IIM Lucknow) and Professor Kaleem Mahammed Khan for providing support in research work. I am grateful to all the All India Services officers, who spared their valuable time to reply the long questionnaire. I am thankful to members of my family, who have allowed me and helped me for continuous long hours of work and particularly my daughter Indu Baalvan and son Akshu Balwan who helped me a lot in this endeavour. Finally, my sincere thanks are to the Atlantic Publishers and Distributors Pvt. Ltd. for publishing the book on time.

Dr. R.P. Balwan, IFS Retired
(Now, Swami Gyananand Saraswati)
E-mail: swamigy07@gmail.com

Contents

Part Two: Individual Variables in Decision under Political Pressure in Bureaucratic System

Part Three: Group Variables Impact on Decision under Political Pressure

Abbreviations

ACF	Assistant Conservator of Forests
ACR	Annual Confidential Report
ACP	Assistant Commissioner of Police
ACS	Additional Chief Secretary
ADGP	Additional Director General of Police
ADGF	Additional Director General of Forests
AIS	All India Services
AISO	All India Services Officer/s
APA	Annual Performance Appraisal
APCCF	Additional Principal Chief Conservator of Forests
AS	Additional Secretary
BC	Backward Castes
BDPO	Block Development and Panchayat Officer
BLP	Block Level Politicians/ Block Samiti Chairperson/Members
CDP	Conflict in Decision Process
CCF	Chief Conservator of Forests
CF	Conservator of Forests
Cb.S.	Cabinet Secretary
CM	Chief Minister of State
Cm.M.	Communication Media (print or visual or any other or all kinds of media)
Com.	Divisional Commissioner or Commissioner
CS	Chief Secretary
DC	Deputy Commissioner /Collector
DCF	Deputy Conservator of Forests
DGF	Director General of Forests
DGP	Director General of Police
DGP(HOP)	Director General of Police (Head of Police Department)
DIGF	Deputy Inspector General of Forests
DIGP	Deputy Inspector General of Police

DLP	District Level Politician / Zila Parishad Members/ Chairperson
DM	District Magistrate
DMP	Decision-Making Process
DP	Decision Process
DRDA	District Rural Development Agency
DS	Deputy Secretary
DSP	Deputy Superintendent of Police
et al.	et alia meaning 'and others' 'other authors'
etc.	et cetera meaning 'and the other things' or 'and the rest'
FCA	Forest Conservation Act (1980)
FIR	First Investigation Report
FRH	Forest Rest House or Rest House (including any government rest house)
HF	Hidden Financiers
HOD	Head of Department
IAS	Indian Administrative Service
ICS	Indian Civil Service
IFA	Indian Forest Act (1927)
IFS	Indian Forest Service
IGF	Inspector General of Forests
IGNFA	Indira Gandhi National Forest Academy, Dehradun
IGP	Inspector General of Police
IPS	Indian Police Service
JTS	Junior Time Scale
JS	Joint Secretary
LBSNAA	Lal Bahadur Shastri National Academy of Administration, Mussoorie
Mins.	Center or State Minister
MLA	Member Legislative Assembly
MLC	Member Legislative Council
MP	Member of Parliament
NCR	National Capital Region, New Delhi
NIC	National Information Center
OBC	Other Backward Castes
PAR	Performance Appraisal Report
PB	Power Brokers /Touts / Musclemen
PCS	Provincial Civil Services
PFS	Provincial Forest Services

PLPA	Punjab Land Preservation Act (1900)
PM	Prime Minister
PP	Political Pressure
PPS	Provincial Police Services
PCCF	Principal Chief Conservator of Forests
PCCF(HOF)	Principal Chief Conservator of Forests (Head of Forests Department)
PS	Principal Secretary
RFO	Range Forest Officer or Sub Divisional Level Officer
SC/ST	Scheduled Caste/Scheduled Tribe
SDM	Sub Divisional Magistrate (Civil)
SDFO	Sub Divisional Forest Officer
SHO	Station House Officer
SP	Superintendent of Police
SSP	Senior Superintendent of Police
SPSS	Statistical Package for the Social Sciences
SAPNPA	Sardar Vallabhbhai Patel National Police Academy, Hyderabad
STS	Senior Time Scale
UPSC	Union Public Service Commission
VH	Village Heads
VLW	Village Level Workers
w.e.f.	With Effect From
WLPA	Wild Life (Protection) Act (1972)
w.r.t.	With Respect To

Note: Regional Officers with reference to the All India Services officers for this book are considered as Divisional Commissioner, Inspector General of Police or Deputy Inspector General of Police and Conservator of Forests, respectively. This may be different/variable for different States in the Union of India.

List of Figures

List of Exhibits (Tables)

List of Charts

List of Annexures

You brood of vipers! How can you speak good, when you are evil? For out of abundance of the heart the mouth speaks. The good man out of his good treasure brings forth good, and the evil man out of his evil treasure brings forth evil. I tell you, on the day of judgment men will render account for every careless word they utter; for by your words you will be justified, and by your words you will be condemned. —Mathew 12.34-37.

Dishonesty in business or uttering of lies causes inner sorrows.—Adi Granth, Maru Solahe, M. 3, p. 1062.

Part–One
Bureaucracy Historical and Research Perspectives

"Your right is to work only and never to the results thereof. Do not consider yourself to be the cause of the results of your actions, nor let your attachment be to inaction." *The Bhagavad Gita* 2.47.

"Since I have craving for the results of actions, actions do not taint Me. Even he who thus knows Me, in reality, is not bound by actions." *The Bhagavad Gita* 2.14.

Unit 1

Bureaucracy in Historical and Research Perspectives

"Democracy arises out of the notion that those who are equal in any respect are equal in all respects; because men are equally free, they claim to be absolutely equal." —Aristotle

"That government is the strongest of which every man feels himself a part."—Thomas Jefferson

"Only way to do great work is to love what you do."—Steve Jobs

- *Introduction*
- *Bureaucracy in the Perspective of Literature*
- *All India Services Historical Perspective*
- *Conceptual Perspective for Research Study*
- *Research Inevitability for All India Services*
- *Need for Research to Study Political Pressure*
- *Research Study Objectives*
- *Sampling Technique and Data Collection*
- *Questionnaire Formulation and Testing*
- *Research Data Processing and Analyses*
- *Research Variables and Hypothesis Testing*

This unit starts with the introduction of research work. Bureaucratic administration as mentioned in ancient literature to the present day has been succinctly mentioned. The All India Services in historical perspective has been introduced. Then various aspects related to research work have been mentioned. Towards the end, research variables and hypothesis introduction has been mentioned.

1.1. Introduction

Bharatvarsha had been the cradle of one of the earliest and oldest civilizations in the world. The ancient kingless state of *Vrishnis* was administrated through *samitis* of select people. During ancient times, highly powerful persons like *Nahush* and *Pururva* ruled over the entire earth.[1] References are available that *Rigvedic* administration was triumvirate; *Senani* (Commander-in-Chief), *Purohita* (adviser) and *Gramani* (village head), which slowly evolved to *Sarvaraja* with 18 *ratnins*[2] (*mantrins, amatyas, sachivas, parishadas, arthkarinsand dharmikas,* etc.).

In the north-west parts of Bharatvarsh, *Kshatrapa* or *satrap* administrative pattern was in vogue. Later on, *Kushanas* introduced *dandanayaka* and *baladhikrita* designations. Gupta administration used a title like *maharajadhiraja paramabhattaraka* and *paramadaivatta* with officials like *kumaramatya* (Prince as minister attached to Royal), province head as *uparika*, district heads as *vishayapati. Vithis* and *manadalas* were smaller administrative units. *Prambhattarka maharajadhiraj* designation evolved during Delhi Sultanate and Mughal into *calipha* or *zillillah* to *hazrati-padshah-zill-i-Ilahi* and they followed the policy of recruiting indigenous persons at lower levels with a limited opportunity of promotions; at the same time, all higher positions were kept with foreigners. Revenue collection was a major focus for that village-level heads were termed as *muqaddam* or *lambardar*.

One of the oldest and richest civilizations of the world, corroded, shattered, and ruled by few foreign aggressors for the centuries together, because of its inherent internal fighting and conflicts. Foreigners crossed oceans and mountains for business, in turn; they ruled the mighty *Bharatvarsha* (*vishawaguru* or *sone ki chidiya*) over centuries. They had used the vision and farsightedness while establishing and consolidating their grip and complete control over the Indian administrative system.

The colonial rulers established the Imperial Services (bureaucratic system) as a mechanism to rule the Indian soils. Imperial Civil Service (ICS), Imperial Forest Service (IFS), and Imperial Police Service (IPS) were established to serve the imperial interests in England. These Crown services were established exclusively for the British people to rule the Indian masses perpetually, with the purpose to consolidate and expand the land under the control of the Crown. The Indians took a very long time to reckon with their fallacies. After decades of struggle and insurmountable pressure, the Indians were allowed to compete for these services. Rest is history with a lot of meanderings in itself.

Later on, under political pressure from Independence Movement, these services were renamed as Indian Administration Service (IAS), Indian Forest Service (IFS), and Indian Police Service (IPS) along with some other services. During the Second World War, recruitment and training for these services got a severe jolt. In the post-war era, the British Crown has not shown any serious concern for these services. Remotely controlled officers of these services governed the operations in India to serve the imperialist rulers in England. Remotely located imperialistic rulers achieved their objectives of revenue collection and wealth maximization; retention of strategic powers, maintaining law and order to serve self-ends. Subordination of administration was to meet the selfish needs and greed of the rulers.

---

1. Vedic literature provide detailed account of areas ruled by those rulers of that primitive times.
2. List of *ratnins* ....The *Taittriya Samhita* 1.8.9.1 and The *Taittryiya Brahmin* 1.7.3.1 The *Satpatha Brahmin* 5.3.1.1.

Political leadership in India identified the five major objectives in 1947, to cover social, political, and economic dimensions of life in India. These were (a) establishment of Parliamentary type of democracy, (b) formation of a federation, the constitution, making both Centre and States, autonomous in their respective sphere of operations, (c) setting up self-sufficient, self-reliant economic systems, (d) promotion of social justice, and (e) goals and value-oriented public administration.

Civil Administration in India was through All India Services Officers; the district was a basic unit and District Collector was the 'alter ego' of the Viceroy at the top, as it was accepted in independent India also. Centralisation in decision-making was its key feature. Indian Civil Service members as a rule manned all the leadership positions, at all levels and all sectors of administration. The administration was based on a system of rules, procedures and regulations. Secretariat got the role of policymaking and executive for the operational and implementation responsibility. An unusual feature was included in the Indian Constitution (Articles 308, 310, 311, 312 and 313) regarding provisions containing definite guarantees and safeguards for these most powerful elites of the society.

Stratified Indian Society is entrenched with institutionalised inequalities. India is particularly committed to the economic and social development of the disadvantaged sections of society and this end policy of positive discrimination is enshrined in the Constitution of India. Socio-economic planning is the preferred mode of development, which is in the hands of All India Service Officers. Decades after independence socio-economic-political scenario have undergone a sea change at the district level, which seems to be irreversible. A colonially created imperialistic institution cannot remain on original terms but has to be readjusted in harmony with emerging new socio-economic-political situations. Civil services of this land have been steadily losing the trust and confidence of the common man (Sh. S.R. Maheshwari).

Sh. Navanit Sinha has described All India Services, "To some who may call these services an evil, these now have become a necessary evil. India has been ruled by the largest and one of the most organized, All India Services that ever established anywhere. The sheer size of these services needed to rule India and the enormity of its tasks have reinforced the tendency towards having a highly organized and stratified structure of authority for a sound all-round development of India. Being par excellence, these services were rendering main support to British Imperialism for a century and a half that it endured. They did bring a measure of order and peace, if not prosperity, to the areas where anarchy had long hold sway. Even though primarily being—a garrison of picked up men—, with the mission of upholding the Crown, they did still possess the tradition of strength and efficiency with aloofness, exclusion and class consciousness".

The All India Services Officers could not correct their behavior by learning from their inherent mistakes. The result has been that bureaucratic patterns of actions, such as impersonality of rules and centralization of decision-making have been established in such a way that they have become a part of the reinforcing equilibrium. The new image of the All India Services as the self-satisfied glorious innovator, egoist, elitist, groupist, authoritarian, power crazy, monopolizer, status hungry, perk jerker, and decision dodger. Bureaucrats are power elite everywhere, so India cannot be an exception. For their decisions, it is commonly whispered in the corridor of power. 'You show me a person, I will quote the rules and deliver the decision to serve the clientele needs'. Bureaucrats have outlived their utility. Public administration has become a heaven for ill-motivated and corrupt persons. This reflects the crux of our problem in our bureaucratic system.

"To be king of Indian heap, it is not enough to be best that you are. You cannot seed your field and reap what you have sown. You must scale those cliffs of bureaucracy, you must be prepared to be scratched by those thickets of regulations, and you must be prepared to re-energise the patches where politicians have sucked out fertility. When you talk to insiders in any Indian industry, they will tell you how every number one has emerged from the scrimmage after nibbling rivals, bending the rules, cozying up to the right politician or *babu,* and paying off or edging out the inconvenient official. The public face of an Indian businessman as-role-model is drastically different from the wheeling-dealing he indulges into best his peers. It is almost as if the role model holding that trophy of achievement is cut out, hiding from us his other-self. The simple truth is that beyond a certain point, liberalization has not changed things. And it never will, as long an entrepreneur has to cozy up with official and the politician."[3]

All India Services Officers are devoid of human values and equity since their origin in the Colonial era. "In various parts of the underdeveloped world, the prospectus for economic growth will not become particularly bright until there are some rather profound changes in human motivation and values and social-political structure" B.B. Khare (1974). These officers cannot deliver efficient and effective development for the prosperity of the masses. The All India Services Officers by their origin are exploitative, parasitic, and self-goal achievers in the bureaucratic system.

1.1.1. What is political pressure?

Management literature viewed politics as an unsanctioned or illegitimate use of power to achieve unsanctioned or illegitimate ends, it indicates informal, parochial, and selfish individual behavior to exploit the formal authority [Mayes 1977, Murray 1980, Mintzberg 1983, and Enz 1988]. In public administration, political power on occasions is discussed as a legitimate power and by virtue of their position in the hierarchy, the politicians enjoy full authority over the decision-making process. In the case of All India Services also, a politician is invariably located above these officers in the respective departmental hierarchy, so politicians enjoy a supreme position to control the bureaucratic system.

Politics is the fact of life, so political pressure is the necessary evil in the bureaucratic system. People love it, to use this for own goal maximization. It is not possible that any system can be free from politics and pressure tactics. Individuals make groups, groups make class, the class makes services, and services make systems with different values, goals, and interests. Marshall and Cooper (1979) defined pressure as "Pressure—a problem, something you find difficult to cope with, about which you feel worried or anxious." Asha Bhandarker (1985) observed "Pressure—as a problem, something you find difficult to cope with, about which you feel worried or anxious or tense. Pressure can be positive or negative or both." Political pressure for us is the unauthorized demand problem in public administration to which the AISO finds it difficult to find a solution as prescribed in rules, procedures, and regulations to arrive at a decision.

Political pressure is the compulsory compulsion of the bureaucratic system. Activities under political pressure are not carried out according to rules, regulations, and procedures, it is considered to be brought under the influence or an attempt to influence the outcome of a decision to meet their self/own goals or interests from public administration at the cost of the public. Illegitimate political pressure is the pressure, which violates the well laid down rules, regulations, and procedures of

3. *Business Today*, 'Mourn the Indian Way' editorial, Vol. 10, No. 13, July 7-July 21, 2001 (Living Media India Ltd. New Delhi).

the bureaucratic system. Whereas, legitimate political pressure is the pressure asserted in normal administration by the in-charge Center or State Minister/Chief Minister/Prime Minister, through a formal line of command, which is in consonance with laid down rules.

The exertion of political pressure by politicians on All India Services Officers requires an attempt to use an inherent political power base to influence the goals, interests, criteria, and processes used for decision making for distribution of advantages and disadvantages within the department in the desired direction. Government resources are limited and there is ever-increasing huge demand from different quarters, which forces politicians to exert pressure on bureaucrats with the highest intensity and extensively over the bureaucratic system. In government bureaucracy, any gains by any one group will be at the expense of others only. Everyone cannot remain, gainer, all the time. Today's gains are tomorrow's loss, but no one is interested in knowing the fate of that tomorrow.

1.1.2. Term bureaucrat

Public servant, government servant, political administrator, civil servant, and civil administrator have different meanings in references in different works, here these words have been used interchangeably to cover the All India Services Officers located in different positions and at different locations. Word public administration, bureaucratic system, and civil administration also have been used interchangeably to indicate the government administration, where these All India Services Officers are located and take decisions.

Analyses of prevalent workings in the bureaucratic system remind us of following well-established laws in public administration, which are true to the All India Services Officers also.

Murphy's Law (1956)

- If something can go wrong, it will. (AIS will go wrong)
- When left to themselves, things always go from bad to worse. (So, as Indian Bureaucracy and All India Services) Parkinson's Laws (1957)
- Officials multiply subordinates, not rivals. (AISO wants the whole country as subordinate to them only, no rivals, please)
- Officials make work for each other. (Different services, fight with each other)
- Delay is the deadliest form of denial. (That is the ultimate decision) Peter Principle (1969)
- In a hierarchy, every employee tends to rise to his maximum level of incompetence. (All India Services tends to be) Greshnan's statement
- Trivial matters are handled promptly—important matters are never solved
- Peter Drucker (1980), "Malperformance is increasingly being taken for granted."

1.1.3. Chapterisation (Units Introduction)

The present book has been divided into five parts. Part I deals with bureaucracy historical and research perspectives with one unit in it. Unit 1 deals with historical and research perspectives, comprising the introduction, historical perspectives of the bureaucracy, and the All India Services in India. It also explains the conceptual perspective of the research study, the inevitability of studying the All India Services Officers. Process of instrument/questionnaire formulation, testing, sample design, and study is followed by research data processing by using different statistical tools for analyses. Research variables and hypothesis testing has been covered in this unit.

Part II comprises the individual variables in the decision-making process under political pressure in a bureaucratic system with five units in it. Unit 2 pertains to the individual ALSO decision-making process, influences, decision constraints, and bureaucratic decision evaluation along with a summary of important variable evaluation (as an exception included in this unit) that has been mentioned in it. Unit 3 research results mention the impact of political pressure on the AISO orientation and role of individual biographic characters in the decision-making process along with the conceptual framework. Unit 4 explains how the locus of control in the AISO has a relation with career, efficiency, reward, advancement, growth-related perceptions, the role of internality and externality in the decision-making process to cope with political pressure. Unit 5 on motivation comprises the concept of power, motives, status base, policy, needs, equity, and expectation play role in the decision-making process under political pressure. Unit 6, we have studied the AISO lifestyle orientation role in handling pressure in the decision-making process.

In Part III, we have studied group variables influence on the decision-making process under political pressure with four units in it. Unit 7 Concepts of officers behavior, various variables interaction, value and attitude role in handling political pressure and officers behavior amenability as part of system (so included in this Unit as group variable) to accept political pressure have been studied. Units 8 involves the study of the AISO risk-taking under political pressure in the decision-making process. Unit 9 how innovations including different influence styles bring changes in the bureaucratic system under political pressure. Unit 10 Sources of conflict and different approaches adopted by the AISO management of conflict in the decision-making process.

Part IV comprises the system-related variables to study the dynamics of political pressure in the decision-making process and it includes the six units. Unit 11 we have studied ten major sources (PM/CM down to village level political workers) of political pressure being exerted on the AISO decision-making process. Unit 12 different types of political pressure being exerted on 76 different pressure points/pressure areas on the AISO has been researched and intensity has been studied. Unit 13 different modes and forms of political pressure being exerted on the AISO decision-making process and its impact has been studied. Unit 14 mentions why or what are reasons (as part of bureaucratic system so included in this part) for accepting political pressure by the AISO in the decision-making process. Unit 15 studied the role of prevalent bureaucratic culture role in the acceptance of political pressure in the decision-making process by the AISO. Unit 16 research results on the study of workplace environment of the AISO and the impact of political pressure on the decision-making process.

Part V regarding what can be done to improve our system for managing bureaucracy in India. Recommendations mentioned in Unit 17 as Strategies for future management.

1.2. History of Administration

History of administration comprises bureaucracy and administration in historical perspectives of literature and history of the All India Services.

1.2.1. Bureaucracy and Administration in Historical Perspectives

Indian Sub-Continent: One of the oldest civilisations on earth, the Saraswati-Indus River Valley civilisation excavations suggest that people at the time had a highly organised administrative set up with provision for law and order and protection from external aggression through police and military. The literature on the *Sapt-Sindhu* region shows well-organised secular political units.

The Devine Kingship finds mention in *Aitterya Brahman* (1.14), *Tattaraiya Brahman* (1.59), *Satpath Brahman* (12.9.3.3 and 5.4.2.8). The *Aitterya Brahman* (8.12), how the king was elected or selected is debatable according to different researchers. Various scriptures mention officials associated with the administration as *Senani*,[4] *Senapati* of the *Aittereya Brahmina*, *Purohit*[5], *Gramini*[6]. Popular bodies for administration were *Sabha*[7] and *Samiti* gatherings of elders to discuss the matter of social interests. In some places Vedic literature described the non-monarchical form of governance, reference had been found about the kingless state of *Vrishnis*.

Later on, the head of the State was called *Samraja* or *savraja* (*the Rigveda* 3.55.7; 3.56.5 and 4.21.1) and was synonymous with righteousness. Eight *Viras* or heroes found mention in some literature. Title as *Rajadhiraja* (*Taittraiya Aranyak* 1.31.6) and *Maharaja rajadhirraja* found in *Texila* records. *Sthapati* mentioned in the *Athar Veda* might have been Chief Judge at that time. *Ratnins* list find mention in the *Taittraiya Samhita* and the *Taittraiya Brahman* include *Raanaya* (king clan), *Purohit* (adviser), *Mahishi* (first wife of a king), *Vavata* (favorite wife of a king), *Parivarikti* (discharged wife of a king), *Senani* (commander-in-chief of the army), *Suta* (charioteer), *Gramini* (village head), *Kshattri* (chamberlain), *Samgrahitri* (treasurer), *Bhagadhugha* (tax collector or food distributor), *Akshavapa* (head for sports), the order of precedent varies in the literature. *Samgrhitri*, *bhagadugha*, *suta*, *gramini*, and *kshatri* were probably entrusted with public duties. *The Taittriya Samhita* also mentions *dutta* (messenger or envoy) and *prahtas* (spy).

The science of governance with the enunciation of duties and functions of the various organ of administration has been described through the *Rigveda*, the *Yajurveda Samhitas* (the *Kath Samhita*, 17.9, the *Satpath Brahman,* 8.6.1.21) and the *AtharVeda*, the *Taittraiya Brahman*, the *AtharVeda* (8.5.5), the *Chhandogya Upanishad* (5.3.1), the *Upnishads, the Aitarya Brahman, the Satapatha Brahmana,* the *Maityayi. Samhita* (2.8.10) *Gautam Sutra* (11.12), the *Bagwadgeeta, Arthsastra of Kautlaya, Mahabhasya of Pantjali, Manu Samiriti, Shukraniti, Yaghvalikaya Samiriti, Narad Samiriti, Brihspati Samiriti, Harshcharit* of Ban, *Asthadhyayi* of Panini, and *Rajtarngani* of Kalhan etc. The civil administration is as old as human civilisation. After *Bharatvarsha*, the Chinese are considered one of the pioneers in evolving the well-established bureaucracy and civil services. When we go through the *Vedic* literature, we come across different duties (word *Dharma* mentioned as duty) that had been assigned to various functionaries and levels of hierarchy under the king.

The bureaucratic system in India evolved, refined, and redefined under the wisdom of sages and kings through the ages. The *Ramayana* and the *Mahabharata*, great epics of this land had detailed descriptions pertaining to the duties and work of civil administration through various functionaries. If we neglect the process and science of public administration, all virtues will decline in society

4. Leader of army (the *Rigveda* 7.20.5, the *RigVeda* 9.1 and 10.84.2) *Kath Samhita* 17.9, the *Satpath Brahman* 8.6.1.21, in the *Aiterya Brahmin* this official is named as *Senapati*. The Mahabharata *SabhaParva* 86.29.30, *Kautalya Arthsastra* 2.30.
5. The *RigVeda* 1.44.10.12, and 3.2.8; the *Aitterya Brahmin* 8.24. Adviser to king in administration
6. Village head, the *RigVeda* 10.62.11; the *Taittairya Samhita* 2.5 and 4.4, and 7.4; the *Taittaraiya Brahmin* 1.1.4.8. Position of *Graminis* included in *ratnins*. The *Prashna Upanishad* mentions *adhikritas* as village head and identical to *gramikas* of Bimbisara, who have eighty thousand in number.
7. *Samiti* defined as Assembly of *Rastra* (national) whole community or people and *Sabha* as association of Rulingfolk or advisory body to rule. There are variations of views regarding this.

[*Mahabharat, Shantiparva* 63.78]. Knowledge empowers ruler to be proficient in administration and to keep their subjects happy [*Sukarniti*, 6.7]. The Ramayana and the Mahabharata epics mention 18 offices of state[8].... 1. *Mantri* (chief councilor), 2. *Yuvrajas* (crown prince), 3. *Purohita* (chief priest), 4. *Chamupati* (commander in chief), 5. *Dvarpala* (chamberlain), 6. *Antaravesika* (overseer of haerm), 7. *Karagaradhikari* (prison head), 8. *Dravya-samchayakrit* (chief steward), 9. *Krotya krityeshu chariham viniyojakah* (chief executive officer for the transaction of public business), 10. *Pradeshta* (chief judge), 11. *Nagaradhaksha* (city prefect or chief for law and order and civil defense), 12. *Karyanirmana* (Chief Engineer), 13. *Dgarmadhyaksha* (chief justice), 14. *Sabhadhyaksha* (Assembly President), 15. *Dandapala* (chief criminal judge), 16. *Durgapala* (warden of Forts), 17. *Rashtrantapalaka* (warden of marches), 18. *Atavipalaka* (Chief Conservator of Forests). Art of public administration has been continued from the *Aittraiya Brahman* and the *Satapatha Brahman*.

Literature mention public administration procedure and implementation of civil and criminal law in the *Sukarniti, Brhispatiniti, Gautmaniti, Apastamba, Vashishthaniti, Bodhyana, Jainism* and *Buddhist Sutras, the Jatakas* and *Milinda Panha* works. According to the prevalent concept of that time, king was the servant of the state and paid by the public, the duty of the king was to protect his subjects. The *Dasa-purusa-rajya* mentioned in the *Satpatha Brahmana* point towards the occurrence of hereditary rule.

Monarchical to republican state existence with separate administration systems evolved through Nandas and Mauryas elucidated as *matsyanyaya* king council comprises crown prince, *amatyas*, *sachivas* and 18 officers with the concept of *sarvabhauma*. Provincial unit heads known as *kshatrapa*, who was king personal nominee. Village unit was *gramani*, whereas, head of ten villages called as *dasagrama*, twenty as *vimsatipa* and hundred as *gramasodadhvaksha* and head of 1000 villages as *adhipati*. The administration was based on *dharma*. *Mantra parishad* and *sabha* for administration and king visited daily *mantragriha* or Council Hall for consultation. Administration comprises *mantrins*, *amatyas* and *sachivas*, *parishadas*, *arthakrins*, *dharmikas* to help *Parishad* and *sabha*.

The *Astadhyayi* of *Panini* mention *ayukta*[9] and *niyukta*[10] and *adhyakshas*[11] heads of departments and the number mentioned was about 25 in *Arthsashtra*. Ministers forming council and department heads known as *tirthas* and then *amatyas*[12] and *sachivas* were in a line of administration, *thirthas* were assisted by *ayuktas* and *niyuktas*. *Panini* mentioned republic states as *ganas*[13] and *sanghas* (Mahabharata republican as *ganas* and sovereignty of many confederations as *sanghas-gana*). Old literature has references to elected king among *Kathas, Kathoi* and *Kathians*. *Lichchavis* have 7707 knights and a Parliament of 500 *rajas* (kings). Bimbisara founder of real *Maghadan* have an efficient administrative setup, Kingdom was called *Rastra* made up of different countries (*desas*) or *janapadas* or *vishayas*.

8. *History of India Administration*, Vol. 1, by B.N. Puri, Bhartiya Vidhya Bhawan, Bombay.
9. II.3.40 engaged in routine work. Kautalya (I.15) *ayukta-purushas*.
10. Or *koshtakshas* IV.4.69 employed in royal store house.
11. VI.2.67 mention *asavadhyaksha* and *gavadhyaksha*.
12. In Pali *amachcha* (Jataka I.262) described as kings' intimate friend may corresponding to *amatya*.
13. *Gana* signify form of government, parliament or senate and *sangha* may be union of independent states for set purpose for infinite period.

The tradition of the *Mahasammata Suggand* tradition mentioned in the *Pancha-guru-jatka* suggests an elective king and council of ministers. Chankaya composed great work *Arthsashtra* for different aspects of administration with a detailed division of work for each level of administration. The Kautalya approach of public administration was for public welfare through public officials known as *gopas* and *sthunikas*. Kautilya's *Arthasastra*, was the legendary work (literature), where well-prescribed duties (*dharma*) were laid down for the bureaucratic system towards subordination and administration of law.

According to *Arthsashtra*, king vow (*varata*) was constant activity in the welfare of people (*uthanam*), his religious ceremony was the administration work (*karyanussasanam*), and his charity (*dakshina*) was equality of treatment for all. *Mantrins* was a higher body and *mantriparishad* seemed to be the second body to help the king. Besides this, other positions find mention were *amatya* (administrative and judicial appointment), *senapati* (commander-in-chief of the army), *yuvaraja* (crown prince), *purohita* (priest), *davuvarika* (warden of the palace), *antarvamsika* (overseer of harem), *prasastri* (in-charge of munitions), *samahartri* (chancellor of the exchequer), *sannidhatri* (high treasurer), *pradeshtri* (superintending official of multifarious functions), *nayaka* (lead vanguard army), *paura* (superintendent of the capital city), *vyavaharrika* (city judge), *karmantika* (superintendent of manufacturers), *mantra-parishadadhyaksha* (secretary to the council of ministers), other *adhyakshas* (head of departments), *dandapalas* (wielder of a rod), *antapalas* (warden of frontiers), *atavikas*.

The Ashoka's and Gupta's period rock edicts and inscriptions throw light on methods of public administration during that time. During the period of the great Ashoka, public administration was carried out through *Mahamantras*, *Pradesikas*, *Rajukas*, *Mahamandlesvaras*, *Rajansthniyas*, *Uparikas*, and *Vishayapatis,* with province, districts, and sub-district as the territorial unit of administration. The Great Ashoka worked day and night for the welfare of his subjects. He was always available for public affairs, as mentioned in rock edicts that "at all hours and all places; whether dining, or in the *Raniwasa*, or in his bedroom, or in my closet, in my carriage, or in the palace gardens; the official Reporters should report to me on the people's business, and I am ready to the people's business in all places" [Rock Edict VI].

After centuries drift, First AD onwards *Huns* and *Sakas* aggression show its impact with changes in designations as kingdom of *Vidharbha* find mention of slightly different terms as, *achiradhishthita* for a ruler, *strategos* for governor, *meridarch* for district officers and *kharoshti* as records maintainer. During the Gupta period designations evolved as *uparika* (royal prince) was equated with *sthapati-samraj* of earlier times. Other functionaries were called as *dutaka* (officer to sanction grants), *sandhivigrahika* (minister in-charge of peace and war), *mahadandnayaka* (leader of forces), *vishayapati* (provincial or district heads). *Vishayapati* headquarter was called *adhishathana*, his office named as *adhikarana* and subdivision called as *vithi* or *mandala*, whereas in-charge of *vithis* was called as *ayukataka*, who was assisted by *kutumbin's* or *mahattaras* below him.

In south India, royal administration functionaries were akin to north India with some difference and some of the designations mentioned were as '*mahamatra*' (official commissioned for a special task), '*bhandagarika*' (in-charge of stores or granary), '*heranika*' (treasurer), '*mahasenapati*' (chief of army), '*lekhpala*' (document drafter), '*nibandhakaras*' (to register necessary documents), whereas a province called as *'aharas'* and its head as *'mahabhojas'* and *'maharathis'* and village unit was *'gramas'* headed by *'graminis'* and town were called *'nigmas'* headed by *'njgamsabhas'*.

King Harsha also carried out people-oriented administration through couriers. *Mudra raksha* of Vishakhdutt, *Mrichchaktika* of Sudraka, *Harishcharita* of Bann, and *Rajtarngani* of Kalhana threw light on the contemporary style of administration prevalent during those times. With the passage of time administration functionaries designations changed and Harischarita (Baan Bhatt) and Chinese pilgrim Hiuen-tsang records mention king named as *pramabhattarka maharajadhiraj*, provincial heads were designated as *lokpalas* (*goptrins* of earlier times) or *samantas* or *mahasamantas*. Other officials were designated as *mahasandhivigrahadhikrita* (high minister for peace and war), *sandhivigrahaka* (in-charge of peace and war), *mahabaladhikrita* (head of forces), *mahapratihara* (head of palace guards), *mahakshapatalika* (chief accounts officer), *mahapramatra* (spiritual counsellor), *daussadhasadhanika* (village heads), *katuka* (civil justice), *lekhaharaka* (letter carrier), *sarvagatah* (for spying), *lekhaka* (writers), *dutaka* (conveyer of royal grants), *bhogpati* (tax collector), and *chatas* (policemen).

The powers of the king were not absolute; there were various checks on the authority of the monarch. The ruler had to abide by the law laid down in the *Shashtras* or customs of the country. The *Shashtras* were regarded as the constitution of the country. King was not above the law; a story was mentioned by the Hiuen-Tsang about the King Bimbisara that to prevent frequent fires in the capital. The king passed an ordinance that, if a fire will break out in anybody's house, that person will be exiled to forests. One day, a fire broke out in Royal Palace. The king said to his Ministers, "I must be exiled to forests." To maintain the law, the king gave up the government and retired to forests. In *sachivayath-tantra* form of government, real power was vested in the hands of the Council of Ministers as mentioned in *Mudra Raksha*. Different *Puranas* were composed for the common person, even for those who cannot understand the intricacy of the system of public administration. Many books on the art of public administration were composed during the period of the King Bhoj of *Dhara*.

In north India, plates inscriptions found of some Hindu kings mention hierarchy as *maharaja* (king), *maharajputra* (crown prince), *mahamatya* (prime minister), *mahapurohita* (royal preceptor), *dharampradhana* (head of the department of religion), *mahapradhanarthalekhi* (chief scribe), *sandhivigrahika* (minister of peace and war), *pratihara* (chief warden), *dushtasadhya* (mentor of criminals), *mahasamanta* (general), *akshapatalika* (record keeper), *pramattavara* (judge), *asavasadhanika* (horses head), *bhandagarika* (treasurer), *gramvasi* (village dwellers), etc.

Scanning medieval period literature, one finds that the Delhi Sultanate attention was more of central, and provincial and local bureaucracy was drawn from foreign for higher positions and indigenous for lower positions. Head or king mentioned as *Calipha* or *Kalipha*, and his lieutenants as *khutba*, minister (*wazir*), head of administrative bureaucracy (*wazir-ut-tanfidh*), finance dealings (*diwan-i-wizarat*) who was assisted by *naib-wazir* and deputy as (*mustaufi-i-mumalik*) general auditor, accounts general (*diwan-i-wizarat*), state diplomatic administrator (*diwan-i-risalat*), chief secretary (*dabir-i-khas*), dealing royal proclamation (*diwan-i-insha*), official dealing army matters (*diwan-i-arid* or *arz*), minister of wars (*naib-i-arz-i-mumalik*), minister of local government (*naib-i-diwan-i-insha*), chief *qazi* (*sadr-us-sudar*), governor with full powers (*imarat-i-khassah*), commander of guards (*jandar*), prime minister (*ala-dabir*), chief secretary (*amirul-umara*), chief dignitary of royal house (*vakil-a-dar* and *amir-i-hajib*), royal kitchen (*sharab-khanah*), commander of military expeditions (*khasahajibs*), religious head (*ulemas*), master of horses (*amir-i-akhur*), taster of food (*chasnigir*), runner in front of royal cavalcade in loud voice (*naqibs*), royal body guard (*jandar* and *silahdars*), in charge of royal library (*kitabdar*), in-charge of royal wardrobe (*sn-jamdar*), keeper of royal writings (*dawatdar*), royal intimate personal attendant (*aghachi*), treasurer (*khazinahdar*), person responsible for royal arms (*qurbeg*), official responsible for lightings (*mabhaladhar*), official responsible for accounts (*malik* or *khan* or *mutasarrif*), chief of accounts (*muta-sarrif*), accounts auditors (*diwani-i-wizarat*), administrator (*nadins*), letter drafter (*dabir-i-khas*), personal writer (*khas-nawis*), revenue officer (*diwan*), village headmen (*muqaddam* or *mukhiya*), and village accountant (*patwari*).

Before the aggression of Mughals in south India, Yadava kings of southern India divided (kingdom) *desas* into *khampa-nakas* (a term for administrative divisions), and designated as sub-king (*mahamandalesvara*), lords (*manneyas*), minister (*kandharadeva*), in-charge of income (*sunkhadhikarin*), high minister (*mahapradhana*), army head (*senapati*), head of 6000 villages (*dandanayaka sarvadhikarin*), head of the group of 140 villages (*manneya*), larger than 1600 villages (*vishaya*), provincial heads (*dandanayaka*), feudatory chiefs and provincial heads were called *sarvadhikari*, military chiefs (*nayakas* or *samantas*) and their estates were called *nayak-sthalas* or *nayaka-sthala-vrottis* and system was known as *nayamkara* system. *Lenkas* head of 18 villages (like *nayaka*) were hereditary in character and get their maintenance called *lenka*. Other functionaries were the bearer of the betel bag of a king (*adapam*), holder of a large fan (*alavattam*), and bodyguards (*anga-rakshaka*). Districts were called *nadus* or *kurram* and smaller areas as *sthala* (10 to 60 villages). More than two *nadu* (districts) were called *vadi* or *bhumi*. Head of a township (*pattana-svami*) and officer under governor was called *heggade* or *heggade-karana*, accounts keeping head (*sakala-karna-dhipa*), village policemen (*talari*), village tax collector (*kolakandru*), treasury keeper (*hiriyabhandari*), treasury inspector (*koshadhyaksha* or *manikya-bhandarada-adhyaksha*), chief justice (*pradvivaka* or *dandnatha*), and military officers (*senadhipati* and *sahinis*).

Sher Shah Suri managed administration through *parganas* and *sarkars* with the help of *shiqqdars* (revenue official) and *munsif* (judicial official). Later on, the official hierarchy of administration was through *Mansabdar, faujdars* and *Amirs,* paid by commission or through *jagirs*. Big hereditary *Zamindars* were appointed as *jagirdars, izatdar,* and *taluqdars* for revenue administration. Civil administration had been described in the *Akbarnama* and *Aine-i-Akabari*. Abul Fazal had described ways and means for political administration and implementation of the law.

In the Mughals period *padshah* or *badshah* or *hazrati-padshah zilli-Ilahi* was the head king or emperor and *vakil* was another highest position higher than *wazir*. Other designations were governor (*atalik*), head of the administration (*khan-khanam*), minister of supplies (*khan-i-saman*), prime minister (*vakil-i-mutlaq*), the person presiding over finance department (*diwan-i-ala*), two of his subordinates in-charge of salaries (*diwan-i-tan*) and in charge of state lands (*diwana-i-khalsa*), in charge of royal expenditure (*khan-i-sama*), paymaster of general empire (*mir-i-bakshi*) in-charge of public charities and endowments (*sadr-i-jahan* or *sadr-i-sudar*), auditor of income and expenditure (*mustaufi*). Provinces were called *subahas* and province head as *siphahsalar subahdar* or *nazim* and governors were called *mansabdar*. *Aatalia* was de-facto governor. Other functionaries were record keeper of farmers (*waqia navis*), in charge of the secretariat (*mushrif*) *diwan* of crown look after the transfer and postings of *subahdars*, *faujdars*, *amins*, *diwani* officials were revenue collector (*kroris*), *musharifs*, *daroghah* and *tahsildars*, *khazanchis*, *sazawals* (agent for compelling payments) and *mutaliba* (loan recovery).

Bureaucracy Viewed by Western World: In the Western part of the world, Mill (1861) viewed bureaucracy as rule by the officials. Civil Services Reform of 1870 invested continental counterpart control in British bureaucracy. Hegel considered bureaucracy a universal class with the general interest of the state. Marxist enunciated that state reflect the economically determined power relationships existing in a given society at a given point of time. Bureaucracy, he considered, as an economically dominant class as an agent of the government in controlling the power of the purse.

Bureaucracy is the instrument of the ruling class; it strove for the power of its own. "The general spirit of bureaucracy is secret, mystery, safeguarded inside itself by hierarchy and outside by its nature as a closed corporation. Thus, the public will, political spirit, and political mentality appear to bureaucracy as a betrayal of its secret. The principle of its knowledge is therefore authority, and its mentality is the idolatry of authority. But within the bureaucracy, the spiritualism turns into crass materialism, the materialism of passive obedience, faith in authority, the mechanism of fixed and formal behavior, fixed principles, attitudes, traditions. As far as an individual bureaucrat is concerned, the aim of the state becomes his private aim, in the form of a race for higher posts of careerism" Marx (1843).

Later on Marx (1871) observed that in a classless society there would be no place for appointed officials, executive powers be vested with the people themselves. Bureaucracies acquire unlimited power for the preservation of its independence as an instrument of administration. Mosca called bureaucracy a power-based political dominated class, which monopolizes power and enjoy advantages that power brings. Emotional confabulations generate pressure in such a political organization.

Bureaucracy is a class of power-elites, exercise control over society to meet their own goals or ideology or a combination of both. In a bureaucratic system, a strong social and economic base for the support for modern bureaucratic organization remained more or less non-existent. Gradually, technological changes took place all over the world. The industrial renaissance in Western world faced a new set of problems. Therefore, different philosophies, as an approach, a thought, or schools were woven into an integrated fabric, came to be called a theory. Studies were carried out on individual productivity and performance.

Max Weber (1864-1920), a German social scientist is considered the father of the bureaucratic concept. He identified personal prejudices, caprices, favoritism, nepotism, inefficiency, ad-hoc-ism, arbitrary authority, discrimination, and incompetence as an essential part of the bureaucracy.

F.W. Taylor (1856-1915) worked on economic incentives, which work as motivators for better productivity. Henry Gantt, Frank, William Gilbertli, Harrington Emerson and Taylor carried out time and motion studies to standardise the operations to lay down performance level for various incentive schemes. Later on Taylor propounded functional supervision or line and staff theory for better performance, which was labeled as a motivational approach, behavioral approach.

Fayol (1841-1925), a French engineer, was first to state functional breakdown of administrative activities. Gulick and Urwick work acknowledged the specialisation, coordination, and rational assignment of duties—as basic elements of bureaucracy. Mooney and Reiley (1931) regarded co-ordination as the mother principle for bureaucracy. Scott and Mitchell suggested division of labour or specialisation. During this period classical organisation theory came under, criticism from Simon, Smithburg, Thompson and Othem. After the Hawthorne experiment emphasis was laid down, on behavioural considerations. A large number of persons worked on this aspect—just to name—Mayo, Roethlisberger and Dickson, Whitehead, Lippin and White, Coch and French Jr. et al. their emphasis was on human behaviour.

A large number of persons worked on psychological and material inducement, its relationship with authority, organisation structure, communication, leadership style, performance, etc. Some of the studies can be named—Moreno's socio-metric studies, Lewis's group dynamics, Maslow's hierarchy of needs, McGreger's Theory X, and Theory Y, Argyris's problem as personality development and Likert's system, etc. The system approach (Kast and Rosenzwerg) is characterised by patterns of authority, power, and status. Anything going wrong in the system, we have to examine the operation of a system to find out what is wrong with the system. Katz and Kaliri's open system receives shocks and influence from their environment.

Carzo and Yanouza's gave three kinds of subsystems—technical, social, and power. The social subsystem goes into group dynamics and individual behavioural traits for the social satisfaction of its members. Power influences the decision-making process. Power holders enjoy a status in accordance with their ability, to carry out orders according to their wishes. Various systems are complex and the government organisation is a very complex system. Sachuin Homans, Likert and Kahnsek et al. brought out various models for studying them. Major findings are (a) success of a change in one subsystem cannot be ensured unless its impact on another subsystem is considered. (b) A network of activities interactions and sentiment leads to the development of external and internal systems, which affect the functioning. (c) Key individuals are called link-pins, all there are overlapping and interlocking role sets, individuals perform their roles.

Bureaucracy was thought of as a body of public officials as an integral part of the ruling class for public administration. Max Weber clarified the conceptual knowledge of organization, power, authority, and administration along with organization behavior. A person in a position of power will carry out his own will despite resistance. Authority gives imperative control; it demands the power to command it. He elaborated on the charismatic authority, traditional authority, and legal authority types. Weber's concept of bureaucracy is based on eight principles of rational-legal authority and five concepts of legitimacy. Weber's rational bureaucracy was based on precision, reliability, discipline, speed, continuity, discretion, and operational uniformity. He rejected the principle of decision making, which differed from case to case.

Modern View on Bureaucracy: Marx (1972, 1969 and 1964) and Durkheim (1951) studied the societal structure, industrialization, and individual experience of alienation with their cause and effect relationship. Marx's concepts of alienation have an impact on individuals and provide a sense of powerlessness and isolation (Blauner, 1964). Man evolved through his work and alienation has caused extensive damage according to Marx's views. In Durkheim's (1951) 'anomis' concept, traditional rules and norms of behavior are broken down and individuals are left without moral guidance in pursuit of their goals (Asha Bhandarkar 1985, Dubrevil 1971, Cohen 1959, 1955, Faris 1944, Faris et al. 1938).

N.C. Roy in his publication *The Civil Service in India* has done structural analysis. L.S.S. Omalley in his work *Indian Civil Service* had romanticized the Indian Civil Service. Bureaucracy is a class of power-elites exercise control over society to meet own goals or ideology or a combination of both. *The Men who Ruled India* by Philip M. Woodruff had dwelt on achievement by ICS for British Crown. When political masters (minister) were unable to distinguish between political and administrative functions, it is difficult to keep away civil servant from political pressure. It has been observed that All India Services Officers accumulate power and try to control the actions of their leadership.

Taub R. (1969) had romanticised the Colonial Civil Services. Heginbotham presented colonial legacy survival through difficult times. Braibanti extensively described the traditions of the civil servants. Weiner, Brass, Rudolph, Moris, Jones, Kothari, Kochanek, Hanson, Alavi, Bettleheim, Sen, and Moore have done work pertaining to the bureaucratic system. Bradford Spangenberg in his research work *British Bureaucracy in India* (1976) observed that ICS officers had an obsession with status and promotion. The presence of imperialism on Indian soil had been the biggest impediment for rational thinking. Civil servants and the public both were influenced by adulation to rulers, which moved them in direction of cherishing individual goals. Subramaniam (1977) thought-provoking view and concept of persistence of colonial administration is the continuance of derivative power.

"Concurrent with Marxian alienation, Fromm (1964) and the existentialists (Friedenberg) foresees the rise of psychological alienation, which deprives people of the capacity to accept or become aware of their own feelings and respond to their own needs. Both kinds of alienation probably parallel to one another create anxiety, low self-esteem, and intolerance of positive growing qualities (Friedenberg 1973). The result is the creation of the 'ressentiment' individual, characterized by a certain mental attitude, caused by systematic repression of certain normal human feelings, leading to value delusions resulting in the emotions of revenge, hatred, malice and envy (Friedenberg 1973)" Asha Bhandarker 1985.

The growth of the bureaucratic structure and ICS correspond with the growth of the nationalist movement, which was expanded and monopolized to crush that movement. The bureaucratic system continued to tighten its grip over the Indian masses to maximize the exploitation and retention of imperialism. Griffiths in his work *British Impact on India* had appreciated Indian bureaucracy as the most powerful and closely-knit bureaucracy in the world. This very bureaucracy was the foundation for an expansion of British imperialism. John Strachey contested this bureaucracy with full force in his work *The End of Empire*.

A strong social and economic base for the support for the modern bureaucratic system remained more or less non-existent in India. The caste-ridden stratification of Indian society is increasingly reflected in the administrative behavior of the All India Services. The increasing clout of provincial services has been threatening the political and administrative importance of the All India Services. The basic character of Indian society is reflected in the political administration, and a particular class-supporting politician in power may get linkage and benefits from the All India Services Officers.

Affairs in the Union of India are run by the monolithic All India Services. With few officers at the top in the hierarchy, who respond to problems, challenges, and political pressure with unanimity. Efficiency in essence was a mythical rationale used originally by the British to justify their monopoly of higher positions. The "efficacy" of British officials became a racist desideratum for the exclusion of Indians, who were branded as inefficient and incompetent, no matter how well they might perform in the bureaucratic system. With the passage of time, the attribution of efficiency to British official no longer feasible for the exclusion of Indians from the administration (B. Spangenberg 1976). The same approach is now dominantly used by the All India Services Officers towards officers of other services, who consider them akin to '*Bura Sahib*' of the colonial era. History is repeating in itself with the elitist concept of the All India Services, which is bound to recoil over the passage of time to over through the colonially created exploitative bureaucratic system.

Bertalanffy, inventor of General Systems theory, presented the integration of several levels of the system, Scott and Mitchell's view on individual attitude and motives interact and influence each other and every individual has to perform an assigned role. Polsby 1963, Wolfinger 1971, Steven Lukes 1974, Gaventa 1980 and Saunders 1980 have carried out some research work pertaining to the decision process and power operation in an organization. The dearth of research work regarding the behavior and working of the All India Services Officers have been demanding further research in the coming future.

The contingency approach seeks to understand the interrelationships within and among subsystems to define patterns of relationships and configurations of variables and suggest leader actions most appropriate for specifications. Kelly studies are related to behaviour and attitudes of a person, the organization's effect on his perceptions, feeling actions and low individual behaviour affects the achievement of Organisation goals. Lundberg studied the goal achievement, efficiency, and environmental dependencies of bureaucracy. P.M. Jackson (1983) in his work of *The Political Economy of Bureaucracy*, put forward various theories of bureaucratic behaviour.

Indian bureaucracy is widely covered; a lot of literature is being published on various aspects related to the delivery of goods and services by the All India Services Officers. Prof. S.R. Maheshwari has published work on the functioning of the bureaucracy. C.P. Bhambhri (1971) published his work on *Bureaucracy and Politics in India*. Armstrong J. (1973) dealt with the behaviour patterns, norms, and values based on positions, traditions, method of work, process, and administrative culture. T.N. Chaturvedi (1988) wrote on *Politics, Bureaucracy, and Development: Some Issues*.

Rajni Kothari has written about muddling in bureaucracy and its impact on people. Dr. Pritam Singh and Asha Bhandarkar (1990) work on transformational leadership has analysed the state of Indian bureaucracy and its adverse impact on corporate growth. B.B. Mishra (1977) has brought out an analysis in the development and history of the bureaucracy in India more particularly the All India Services during the colonial era. Role played by bureaucrats in India in its development has been analyses by K. Mathur (1991). Politician and civil servant relationship have been expressed by S.C. Vajpayi and P.K. Kaul (1993).

Dr. P. Singh and Dr. Asha Bhandarker (1994) by their research in 'I.A.S. Profile: Myths and Realities' brought out new realities about the working, functioning, performance, ambiguity, career, and image of the Indian Administrative Service officers in India. Subash Sharma (1992) carried out an empirical study on the decision-making style of I.A.S. officers.

1.2.2. The All India Services in Historical Perspective

Queen Elizabeth on 31.12.1600 granted a charter to East India Company for quite trading without land wars in India. Person transecting business was called 'Factor' and trading station as 'Factory'. Agent of Surat was designated as President in 1616. Royal Charter of 1661 authorized the Company to appoint Governors to Presidencies to perform judicial functions within limits of their towns. The business was transacted by a majority of votes through the council. Employees' categories were 'Apprentices', 'Writers', 'Factor' and 'Merchants'. Regular services with specified salary and conditions of tenure were introduced in 1674.

A new mode of selection was introduced in 1714. Political power and authority without any responsibility came to trader servants after the Battle of Plassey in 1757. Robert Clive was said to have received a kickback of 234000 pounds. After getting the *Diwani* rights of Bengal in 1765, covenanted servants of the Company took over the administration of revenue. Warren Hastings in 1772, established civil and criminal courts in each district of Bengal and direct collection of revenue and administration of justice. During 1775, twenty-six *faujdari thanas* were established. The Regulating Act (1773) prohibited the company officers from revenue collection and judicial administration, except participating in commercial activities. Company covenanted servant called Collector was given executive powers to collect revenue. Warren Hastings took direct responsibility of civil administration and gave power of civil courts to the collectors of the districts.

Board of Commissioners started controlling political and financial affairs through Pitt's India Act (1784). Cornwallis restructured administration on a functional basis and excluded Indians from the process. He brought all public functions under the direct control of the state and organized hierarchical functioning in departments through his own servants. Cornwallis in 1792 changed the administration process of law and order started the Europeanization of Civil Services. He appointed *darogas* as in charge of *thanas* or police stations, and this continued up to 1814. Cornwallis was the first person to eliminate community participation in local administration. European covenanted servants of the company replaced all offices of any consequence under the control of the Indians. Collectorship was allowed only after 12 years of service.

In 1800, commission was appointed for the availability of teak in Malabar forests and in 1805 Forest Committee was constituted. East India College started at Hertford in 1805, was shifted to Haileybury in 1809, to impart training to the civil servants. On 10.11.1806, Madras Presidency appointed the first Conservator of Forests to organize teak production for the Navy. Office of Divisional Commissioner was created in 1829. Later on, the office of Superintendent of Police was designated as Inspector General of Police. Sir Chares Napier took effective steps towards the establishment of a modern police force on the Bombay pattern.

After 1833, limited competition and written test for admission to the Haileybury College were introduced. Dispatch 44 of 10.12.1834, debarred the distinctions on the basis of race or religion and test of qualifications be adopted for appointments to posts. In 1847, Bombay appointed Conservator of Forests. Necessary provisions were made for recruitment through open competition examination by the Act of 1853. Indians were allowed to compete with Europeans and British Parliament confirmed it in 1853. The first such examination was held in 1855. In 1853, George Clerk appointed Superintendent of Police in each district in Bombay. Regular Conservator of Forests was appointed in Madras in 1856. On 3.8.1855, Lord Dalhousie, Governor-General promulgated promulgation towards forest conservancy for the whole country.

In 1856, Brandis, a trained forest officer was appointed Superintendent of Forests in India. Macaulay was of the view that Indian of distinction merit can serve imperial interests with Western knowledge and the English outlook. The principle of open competition was reaffirmed by the statute of 1858. Government of India Act 1858 transferred civil services to the Crown. In

1859 controversial Collector-Magistrate system was accepted as part of district administration. Bureaucrats developed a dichotomy between sustained imperial interests and supremacy of law. The civil services operated through its elitist foundation and resilience.

"We have traced the growth of new India, developed by British capital, enriched by British commerce, and fostered British education. We have watched the rise of new ambition among those children of new India, who owe most to British rule. We have seen how the appeasement of this ambition, at first could no bigger than a man's hand, has gradually become the most prominent of Indian problems. We have traced constitutional changes by which our statesmen endeavored to meet its complexities" (S. Verney Lovett).

Police Act of 1861 based on the report of Police Commission 1860, proposed a well-organized police force. Gradually, provincial police force headed by Inspector General of Police under whom Deputy Inspector General of Police worked. As a follow up of dispatch from Governor-General, dated 1.11.1864, Forest Administration was organized in Government of India and first Inspector General of Forests was appointed as head of Forests Department. In 1877, the Madras Government created a cadre of unconverted Assistant Superintendent of Police.

The Aitchison Commission observed that most of the senior police officers were drawn from the army. In 1869, Forest Service was reorganized into hierarchy of Conservator of Forests, Deputy Conservator of Forests, and Assistant Conservator of Forests, and regular Forest Service was started in 1870. In 1878, Forest School was inaugurated at Dehradun. Lord Lytton created the aristocratic statutory services in 1879. Provincial Forest Service was started in 1891. Hutchins in his work *The Illusion of Permanence* had opinioned that the British were attracted to India: "The prospect of aristocratic security at a time when England itself was falling prey to democratic vulgarity."

Through resolution dated 4.11.1886, commission was constituted under Sir Charles Aitchison as President. The commission submitted its report on 23.12.1887. The Government of India considered it, and through resolution dated 21.4.1892, created Imperial Services and Provincial Services. Indian repression was reflected in recruitment in England for these Imperial Services. Officers for Imperial Services were recruited in England, where it was difficult for Indians to compete. The first open competition for police was held in 1893 in England.

"They hoped to bend the principle of autocracy derived from Moghul emperors and Hindu kings with the principle of constitutionalism derived from the British Crown and Parliament; to create a constitutional autocracy which differing *toto caelo* from Asiatic despotism, should bind itself to govern by rule" (Lord Minto, 1907 cited in a report on Constitutional Reforms). He thought that moderate and aristocratic elements will side with the British and power balance will remain with them.

Forests Service was reorganized into Imperial Forests Service by the resolution of 1896. In 1905, post of Chief Conservator of Forests in each province was created. Orders of 1905 incorporated wide-ranging changes in police administration, recruitment, training, and working, divided the imperial and provincial branches, and recruitment for the imperial branch started through open competition in England. In 1910, the Board of Forestry was set up under the President-ship of the Inspector General of Forests. In 1914, Forest Research Institute main building was opened. 1915 number of Indian officers recruited in England for Imperial Civil Service, Imperial Forests Service, and Imperial Police Service was negligible to very small. In 1915, there were two Indians in the Imperial Forest Service out of 228 officers, 10 Imperial Police Service out of a cadre of 737, and 63 Imperial Civil Service out of 1342. In 1917, efforts were made to increase the Indian association in administration. After the Government of India Act 1919, Indian politicians emphasized gaining control over the All India Services Officers.

"India is an integral portion, and it may be said one of most important portions of the Mighty British Empire. Its destinies have been confided to the guidance of an alien race, whose function it is to arbitrate between a multitude of conflicting or antagonistic interests, and its government is conducted in the name of a monarch, whose throne is in England. The executive that represents her imperialism in India is an executive directly responsible, not to any local authority, but to the sovereign and to the British Parliament," Lord Dufferin wrote in 1917.

Simon Commission mentioned the following All India Services in India:

- Indian Civil Service
- Indian Forest Service
- Indian Police Service
- Indian Education Service
- Indian Veterinary Service
- Indian Medical Service and
- Indian Service of Engineers.

Provincialisation of All India Services was considered a form of Indianisation. Based on Islington Commission, the Government of India on 1.12.1920 changed the name of services as Indian Police Service and Indian Forest Service. Due to pressure exerted by the freedom movement number of Indians recruitment increased in these services. During 1922, the Indian Civil Service had 11% Indians, the Indian Police Service has 9.5% Indians, and Indian Forest Service has 15% Indians. European civil servants considered this Indianisation as a serious threat for them.

Demand for complete provincialisation of services was strong from the Indian politicians. Hailey policy of replacement helped in the reconcilement of demand for complete Indianisation. After the Legislative Assembly resolution dated 11.2.1922, the percentage of Indians was increased in All India Services to meet the demand of Indianisation. MacDonnel Committee recommended that going against the recruitment of Indians more than a fixed percentage is not possible. Lee Commission, 1923, observed that All India Services (ICS, IPS, and IFS) would continue to operate in their reserve field.

Colonial ruler for 150 years administered and ruled India through All India Services. Attempts were made to reduce the number of All India Services after 1925; existing members were allowed to continue to enjoy rules and conditions prescribed under All India Services. Training for Indian Forest Service was commenced at Dehradun from October 1926, instead of United Kingdom. Recruitment to Provincial Forest Service was ceased from 1926. 1935 Act and after its demand for full autonomy, politicians viewed the location of All India Service officers as an invasion of their autonomy. Indian Forest College was stated in Dehradun in 1938 to impart training to forest officers.

Control and method of recruitment to All India Services was discussed in Conference on 21 and 22.10.1946, under the Chairmanship of Home Minister, Sardar Vallabhbhai Patel and as follow up circular dated 12.11.1946, a draft scheme was revised through an executive order. Indian Administrative Service and Indian Police Service were constituted as All India Services. Again, at a cabinet meeting on 30.04.1948, special protection for All India Services was on agenda. Again, Sh. Patel dominated in discussion to protect these services. The Constituent Assembly debated on Articles 308-13 of the Constitution on 7 and 8.09.1949, and approved it after considerable discussions. One remaining article (314) was discussed on 10.10.1949.

Sh. Sakshena regarded ICS, as 'the steel frame which enslaved us, are heaven-born and pampered'. Recruitment to these services will be made through the UPSC, based on an annual Competitive Examination of very high standards. Officers of these services should be free from political control, contented, and having a sense of security. "It was also decided that only a maximum of 25% of superior posts (Cadre posts) should be thrown open to the State Civil/Police Service Officers of outstanding merit as against the maximum of 20% of the superior posts in the I.C.S./I.P."

"In pursuance of the above-mentioned decision, the two All India Services were formed and they were put on a statutory basis under the Indian Civil Administrative Service Cadre Rules, 1950, the I.P. (Cadre) Rules, 1950 and Indian Administrative and Police Services (Pay) Rules, 1950. The All India Services Act, 1951, passed by the Parliament, under Article 312(1) of the Constitution of India, empowers the Government of India to make, after consultation with State Governments, rules for the regulation of recruitment and conditions of service of the persons appointed to an All India Service. The All India Services Act 1951 was amended in 1963 enabling the constitution of the Indian Forest Service[14] with effect from 1.7.1966.

Civil services in India emerged from the Macaulay Report of 1854 are a product of elitist outlook and goal maximization for self and master. Systems of classes in civil services, with their own separate career prospectus, generate conflicts in the bureaucratic system. Politically public service of appointed officials starts acting as rulers or functions as a social class of power elites, whose decisions are being influenced by considerations other than the impersonal framework of rules. Independent India inherited a colonial concept and structure of All India Services.

Institutions of All India Services do not fit into our newfound independence and invited criticism from states. The All India Services Officers mobilized political support to retain the supreme position in the hierarchy. All India Services Act, 1951, was enacted and came onto force w.e.f. 29.10.1951. The first batch of regular recruits was trained at Metcalfe House, Delhi in 1949, Staff College Shimla functioned for a while in 1950. Then during 1959, the government merged these two institutions and shifted to Mussoorie. National Academy of Administration was renamed as LBSNAA in 1972. IPS officers get their training at Central Police Training College, Mount Abu, which was shifted to Hyderabad and named as Sardar Vallabhbhai National Police Academy. Krishamachari Report 1962 examined the process of recruitment, training and working to streamline the working of the All India Services. The All India Services Act was amended in 1963 and Indian Forest Service was revived again. Indian Forest Service officers were trained at Indian Forest College at Dehradun, which was renamed as Smt. Indira Gandhi National Forest Academy 1987 onward.

14. The All India Services Manual, Part I, 5th Ed., DOPT, Government of India, 1984.

Pt. Jawaharlal Nehru as the first Prime Minister of India regretted his failure to change and replace colonially created All India Services, later on, his daughter, Smt. Indira Gandhi also expressed the same opinion, 'had occasion to regret that her father had not seized the opportunity to overhaul our administration' (P. Singh, 1981). It has become job toughest in India to bring any kind of reorientation in colonially nourished All India Services and their work mechanism. In spite of the number of Administrative Reform Commissions, up to now, there have not been any systematic efforts to explain, why colonially created structures have been continuing with full immunity to distort and destroy the Indian public mental and psychological fabrics.

Indian bureaucracy is the class of power-elites, exercising own control supremacy and hegemony over Indian society to meet own goals or ideology or combination of both. A strong social and economic base for the support for modern bureaucratic organization remained more or less non-existent in India. It has been the misfortune of our country, that highly selfish bureaucrats are ruling us nexus with elected politicians. Change of designation and inserting new layering in the AISO has been a common phenomenon. After the implementation of different pay commissions (now 7th Pay Commission), the AISO changed the nomenclature of posts such as; CCF to PCCF, then APCCF, Principal Chief Conservator of Forests and now new designation of PCCF (HOF), in IAS Secretary to Principal Secretary then Financial Commissioner and now Additional Chief Secretary; similarly, police IGP to Additional DGP, now DGP (HOP). Laws of dynamism are operational in bureaucracy also.

1.3. Rationales for Research Study

The most important aspect of the present study is the impact of political pressure on the All India Services Officers and its ultimate bearing on the decision-making process, which have been left out till now. Significant research work has not been carried out in this sphere. Personal orientation (21 variables) of All India Services Officers and the relationship of different personality variables with the handling of political pressure in the decision-making process. Locus of control (30 variables) and its relationship with the decision-making process under political pressure has been studied. Impact of political pressure in the decision-making process and relation with the AISO behaviour (12 variables), motivation (10 variables), lifestyle orientation (nine variables), culture (13 variables double raking 13+13), conflict handling (seven variables), risk management (six variable), innovation (10 variables), and workplace environment (seven variables) relationship with different variables have been studied. The All India Services Officers motivation orientation in the decision-making process under political pressure has been studied.

In our research, we have carried out research on different sources of political pressure working on the decision-making process of All India Services Officers. We have studied such ten major sources of political pressure and its relationship with the decision-making process. There can be a number of areas in a bureaucratic system, where political pressure can be exerted; we have studied 15 such major areas comprising 76 different situations pertaining to the decision-making process of All India Services Officers. Most important 22, forms and modes of exerting political pressure have been studied in the decision-making process. Why All India Services Officers accept the political pressure, major 15 reasons for acceptance of political pressure have been studied in present research work. Present research work has been very exhaustive and lengthy, but we have tried to cover maximum aspects pertaining to All India Services Officers, which may be related to the decision-making process under political pressure. This is rare and in-depth insider research work of its kind in the history of the All India Services.

1.3.1. Conceptual Perspective for Research Study

Political pressure has its impact on the decision-making process of the All India Services Officers, which has been studied in our research. These officers are mostly located as the head of the organization, it may be small or big, at the district level, or state level, or regional level, or national level, or it may be at the international level (sometimes). According to their locations, we have studied the problem in the conceptual framework of behavioral theories with reference to hierarchy levels, departmental structure, and departmental goals assigned to them. We have refocused our study, around their departmental or ministerial boundaries. We have studied and described the department, environment interface, interdepartmental relations, and analytically described the public administration in general, a bureaucratic system in particular under which these AISO are working.

The present study has described the emergence of specific forms of economic organization and behavior of economic decision-makers in that institutional structure. Our study disentangled the paralleling requirements for differentiation and integration of the bureaucratic system. Various processes that tend to elaborate or change departmental form or state of various concepts, which are interwoven with public administration system include power, authority, status, the role of position, motivation, task, perceptions, value, culture, locus of control, conflict, innovations, exchange, bargaining, ubiquitous, system, change, restructuring/de-layering of departments.

The All India Services Officers take a decision as an individual leader in a given departmental hierarchical structure. The processes of information dissemination and analysis to reach a decision under various constraints have been studied with reference to individual behavior. In the public administration system, dominant inbuilt uncertainties generate conflicts; the All India Services Officers have to resolve internal and external conflicts at the time of decision-making. Conflict resolution follows Ando's (1979) theory of adjustment, if the capability of individuals and organizations to comprehend, describe and respond to their environment is without limit, then their behavior reflects nothing but their goals and the characteristics of their environment. If any change occurs in the environment, such a change will be reflected in the behavior of the concerned decision-makers instantaneously and completely. In such a situation, individual may decide to do nothing so that risks can be minimized.

Self-goals mostly influence the outcome of the decisions, in such situations, choices are computed and exercised, by these officers as directed by the most motivating factors of the outcome. Rationality in decision-making or choices, therefore, involves internal consistency. "A person's choices are considered rational in this approach if and only if, these choices can all be explained in terms of some preference relation consistent with the revealed preference definition, that is if all his choices can be explained as futile choosing of the 'most preferred' alternatives with respect to a postulated preference relation" (Sen 1976).

An individual is assumed to be always acting to maximise own utility. The All India Services Officers behave and make choices and decisions based on individual aspiration levels, which are revised in the light of one's success or failures in attaining them. The decision-making process or search procedure for a solution involves setting out a limited number of alternative solutions (the limitation is determined by the decision and time constraint in producing them and computational limitations of the decision-maker in comparing them).

Problems are recognised and solved by individuals, not by organisations. Individual officers with a different specialism and demographic background will identify different problems, or see a different facet of the same problem, or they will give a different definition of a similar problem (Deaborn and Simon). Problems are structured in line with individuals' values, prejudices, and beliefs. Decision-maker does not have to be thought out from scratch on each occasion, previous experience and organisation history is used to filter out alternative considerations. In this process, individual effort to involve the team in the decision-making process, team efforts to solve the problems have been studied in the context of behavioural theories.

Individual behaviour under political pressure vis-à-vis departmental and service behaviour have been considered with its linkage to well-established behavioural theories. Revisions of goals, goal enlargement, goal displacement, and goal succession process reshape the decision-making process under influence of political pressure. The collective goals emerge either as a result of voluntary trading and contracting between individuals, who have different personal goals. Goals will change when an individual sees scope for improving one's benefits by means of goal change, dominate-goal is toppled in the power struggle. In any government departmental structure, the number of relationships and interrelationships available at any point of time, in actuality modify individual All India Services Officers behaviour, from formal relationships, non-formal and informal relationships, tend to develop in the process.

Future shape of bureaucratic system, individual and departmental behavior is the matter of great concern for our nation. The bureaucratic decision is being viewed in the continuation of motivation, individual orientation, cultural, environmental, and behavioral leadership theories. Utility and futility of present bureaucratic system to serve the need of a nation, after all, whose purpose these All India Services Officers serves, public or bureaucrats or its masters? Whole resources of the country are at their (AISO) command, resource allocation, and distribution of welfare largesse, vis-à-vis relation of such powers with the decision-making process to own advantage.

The process of bureaucratic control on pivotal positions is used as the process of bargaining. Continuous modifications and the coalition of politicians and All India Services Officers proving to be an effective tool for own interest maximization. Community relations, social environment, cultural setting, and population changes are an indicator of relationship with individual behavior and decision-making process of All India Services Officers. Different counter demanding situations regulate departmental goals and infuse dynamism in goals. Departmental goals are being converted into individual goals under various kinds of pressures and temptations. Individual behavior is goal-directed and that individual, when making rational choices between competing goals, always chooses that alternative that best serves the individual's own best interests (P.M. Jackson).

Role-played by competition, bargaining co-operation and coalition on the process of decision-making require in-depth studies. Departmental goals are being used to serve vested interests/ individual interests. The control has been passed into the hands of a select few All India Services Officers, who are perpetuating themselves. These elites have gained full control over the complete public administration system. Rules and regulations are manipulated under political pressure to meet individual officers' own needs and blame is passed on the politicians. Theories of playing safe or distorted decisions are destroying the public administration and are regularly misused by the bureaucrats. The complete decision-making process and decision-maker bend to serve the clientele needs to churn out tailor-made policy/law/decision for them. Individual considerations get over-riding priority at the time of decision-making. Blockage and leakage in communication mismatch the codebooks to serve the interest of clientele.

The All India Services Officers try to evade and deviate in conforming and observance of authority (politicians). The role of the hierarchy, social standards, individual perceptions, economic security, and status in the delivery mechanism of authority requires further conceptualization. In the present bureaucratic process, authority, power, and status have fused together. The concept of authority, power, and status proves the relevance of the Wolfe statement, "Power induce force on another person towards, movement or change in a given direction with a given behavior region, at a given time". Politicians have contested and cornered the power, in this process ethics and goals have been lost.

External forces and pressures are relevant in self-goal continuation related to an individual location. According to Brown's theory, uncertainties wield the power, which can influence the outcome of any decision. Whereas the 'garbage-can model' argues that individuals face situations over which they often have only modest control. Solutions and problems are not matched up but are instead thrown together independently. In the process, the social structure of the department influences the decision-making process. All India Services Officers forcefully use the role of domination and manipulation. As we travel deep inside the conceptual framework of behavioral theories, we may observe that status has become end in itself, status is creating social distances, these status-oriented All India Services Officers put maximum emphasis on position, rather on justice, equity and acts.

Administrative relationships of authority (politician), status, and power generate stresses and strains on the decision taken by the All India Services Officers in the process of its exercise. The concept of power has explanatory value in determining the final outcome of any relationship of exchange or negotiation, be it the level of individual or collective. Proper understanding of bureaucratic system operation provides us a realistic view. The problem of equity or unfairness dominates in the decision-making process. Society has to pay a financial cost for All India Services Officers status orientedness. These officers have been preoccupied with differential distribution of power among themselves only. Power is frequently used to prevent things, which are not favorable to them. Which in turn invite conflicts in various levels of hierarchy or interdepartmental. There is a strong need for a shift from negative power for self-use to power as an organized, creative energizer for the system.

The problem of political pressure in the bureaucratic decision-making process has been studied in the theoretical framework of government departments with a view on behavioral aspects. A large number of variables in a bureaucratic system may directly or indirectly be related to the decision behavior, only a limited number of variables, which were considered to have a significant association with the decision-making process, have been studied at length. Motivated facilitation of different interactions among people, which are working towards blockage of communication system has a premeditated impact on the decision. Communication system manipulated to own advantage has an impact on the behavior of the All India Services Officers and decision-making process vis-à-vis, in turn, has an impact on the people.

It is true that All India Services Officers receive the best-desired training for motivating and leading the people. However, most of the government departments are conflict-ridden, where they are posted as leaders (heads). Conflict management either it is functional or dysfunctional has it's bearing on the decision. While arriving at a decision, All India Services Officers make efforts to find out ways and means to resolve such conflicts according to the mode of political pressure and source of political pressure. Politicians exert pressure on vast areas in accordance with their own interests, which vary with time and space. In our study, we have studied important areas in the bureaucratic system, which cause maximum difficulty to All India Services Officers. Reasons for accepting political pressure have been studied to establish a relationship with the decision-making process. There is an urgent need to bring a change in the colonially created bureaucratic system. People must be facilitated in the decision-making process to incorporate change if needed. Administrative leadership has to be restructured/reshaped in such a way that people are willing to accept the change. We have endeavored to study all these related issues in the conceptual framework of the behavior theories.

1.3.2. Research Inevitability for the AISO Study

Colonially created unequal All India Services have been ruining and hampering the psychological growth of the nation continuously at a steady pace. Rationale and need for continuing such an imperialistic administrative structure in India force us to rethink. Continuance of such a layered and structured services framework based on the principle of self-goals maximization deserves detailed analyses. When Indian masses are the victims in the hands of colonially created services, still perpetrators of injustice are exclusively occupying top positions, denying equity to others. Need of time to study futility of manners and methods by which these officers have usurped the whole system to own advantage.

Every one cry from rooftops regarding pervasive political pressure in the bureaucratic system, we have to find out such pressure is flourishing on the whims of politicians or these elite officers have invited/created political pressure to monopolize self-goal attainment. Who is the real gainer from the extent of such pressure? Though politicians redirect people pressure on the All India Services Officers, in the process, these power elites have developed a system, where each and every benefit only flows to meet their own self-needs. Political pressure has become subservient to bureaucrats. We have studied the extent of this pervasive political pressure in the decision-making process. Different modes and forms used for exerting political pressure have been studied.

Interested parties mobilize the political pressure to meet their own needs in violation of set norms and laws. Politicians exert political pressure when they visualize that the All India Services Officers will accept such political pressure. Acceptance of political pressure by individual officers is the process of bargaining to maximize own goals at the cost of others. If no one accepts the political pressure and every officer work according to set norms and rules (do not appear to be possible), all the problems of the bureaucratic system will be solved automatically. No politician can afford to waste energy and time for pursuing unfruitful pressure on the All India Services Officers. Public allege that the All India Services with colonial culture and traditions, imperialistic thinking, exploitative attitude, and perception of self-maximization motivate them to search for political pressure.

Biographical characters of the All India Services Officers do influence the acceptance of political pressure in the decision-making process. What are the motivators for the All India Services Officers, what force them to approach politicians? The cultural milieu of services and prevalent AISO workplace environment, how during the decision-making process they swing in the search for political pressure. The AISO behavior with the politicians towards acceptance of political pressure in the decision-making process is related to individual personality up to what extent. In what way, the AISO lifestyle orientation has an association with the acceptance of political pressure while taking a decision. Creativity, innovations, conflict, and risk management in the decision-making process by AISO are crucial to deciding about the acceptance of political pressure. Factors and reasons responsible for the acceptance of political pressure in decisions need to be delineated. Need for research pertaining to various prevalent modes of political pressure exerted in different areas of bureaucracy to get the preferred decision. Prime Minister at the top to village level most common sources of political pressure cannot be ignored to study the behavior of the All India Services Officers in the decision.

A large number of persons have carried out research work pertaining to the All India Services, but most of them remained concerned to glorify traditions, structure, composition, and history of these most powerful officers. Romanizations of colonial services have been mainly done to help and support the All India Services officers so that they can retain their grip and advantage in the bureaucratic system. Fair systematic scientific introspection has been due for a long.

Imperialist structure placed generalists on the top and technical experts on the tap. To meet the vested interest of exploitation and subjugation, the whole imperial structure celebrated generalist control and continuity, which was devoid of innovations and creativity. The British want mobile elites, who can deal ruthlessly with Indian kings and rulers on one side and exploit masses on other hand to enrich the coffers of the Imperial Crown. All comforts and facilities these bureaucrats enjoyed were made available at the cost of the Indian masses. These comforts stimulate the feeling in these All India Services Officers to ruthlessly suppress Indians so that they can continue to avail their perquisites and enjoyment.

"ICS had contained some outstanding individuals, but it is a symbol of inequality, casteism, and amateurish dilettantism in our administration.... The tradition may have been appropriate to a colonial regime when functions of government were limited and comparatively simple; with the increasing complexity of functions and technical nature of many of the problems faced, the continuance of this tradition is bound to affect the successful conduct of our attempts at planned development" (H.K. Pranjape, 1966).

"The reason why the ICS (now IAS) survived, indeed prospered, and despite increasing hostility needs explanations. Why did that institutional form persist despite opposition? Two aspects of an answer to the question are explored here: first IAS people had a major say in all attempts for administrative reforms during periods, and second, there was never sufficient political clout from political leadership at the center for radical reform of existing administrative framework" (D.C. Potter, 1986).

In the process, politicians and bureaucracy blame each other to pass on the blame to nowhere, and reforms got lost in papers only. Administrative reforms suggested by Gorwala (1951), Appleby (1953), Chanda (1958) and Krishanamachari (1962) remained in files only. In the process, Indian Administrative Service officer's mobilized support and structure, so that, the imperial system is not changed, but they updated and expanded colonial manuals to suit them in changed situations with a higher share of cake for themselves exclusively.

"It can further be postulated that if the strengths of the current Indian Administrative Service are in heritage from the British past, so too deficiencies are not altogether the fault of post-independence Indian bureaucracy. All the major deficiencies highlighted in Appleby's study show affinity with and derivation from the British tradition. The practices so often causing delay and frustration during the British period are identical with those exposed by Appleby as responsible for post-independence perplexities in India, excessive references passing to and fro among the departments, the accompanying accumulation of files, and the concurrent failure to formulate crucial decisions" (B. Spangenberg 1976).

The present system of "The filing system and the related business of work done through hierarchical movement of papers. The time required for answering letters is much too long... reference is sent on its usual course downward to subordinate personnel charged to examine everything critically in terms of precedent and [of] possible ill consequences."[15] A system of no responsibility and accountability is highly suitable for elite Indian Administrative Service officers. Lack of initiative and unnecessary paperwork is reminiscent of the British era, retained to hide own inefficiency, deficiencies, and failures.

During the past on different, occasions, a number of changes have been suggested by different persons, one thing has been common, any proposal which diminishes the power and position of Indian Administrative Service officers never saw the light of the day. Different political leaders demanded relief from the Indian Administrative Service officers' invasion of state power. But no one suggested an alternate system, which can sustain the bureaucratic system to run the administration. Politicians never pressurized hard to abolish the All India Services. The pre-eminent position of generalist officers in central and state deserve to be rethought, all Class-I officers from all the services should have access to middle and top management posts in the secretariat in their respective areas of competence and strength. Technical and specialist services are in existence for a long, they must be given fair chance to man these posts. The doors of senior management should be opened to all sectors of civil services. The All India Services officers invariably erroneously advocated that their elitist supremacy and dominance is required to be maintained.

"The agency of IAS initiative in blocking such reforms succeeded because there was not the political will to force them through against such powerful resistance. In the absence of that IAS was safe" (D.C. Potter). Political timings were not proper and political liking got changed in due course of time under political compulsions. Like bureaucracy, politicians also show first interest in protecting their own chair or vote bank or winning elections. In Pakistan on 20.8.1973, Prime Minister Bhutto implemented, what the Administrative Reforms Commission pointed out in India. The Jana Sangh Party promised to tone up the civil service by stopping political interference in administration and Samyukta Socialist Party promised to abolish the post of Collector.[16]

On many occasions in the past, many retired civil servants eloquently advocated regarding the need for change in All India Services, "Colonial system has to be completely changed before any marked improvement in the implementation of the government policies can be expected"

15. Paul Appleby, *Re-examination of India's Administrative System,* New Delhi, Government of India.
16. Balraj Madhok (1967) and Madhu Limmaye (1967). (As cited by Potter in his book.)

(B.N. Mullick, 1971). Like K.K. Dass (1975), many wrote number of pages, but no one dares to bring out a revolutionary change in the system demanded by the situations. In the words of K. Rajan (1982), IAS stands for Incompetent Arrogant Sahibs in administration, but they are highly competent in mobilizing political support to retain their power. IAS legitimacy in all levels, pervasive control over the whole administrative setup, guaranteed their safety in the bureaucratic system. Any change in the All India Services structure has never been an election issue for any political party. IAS lobby works hard passively to protect their position.

Imperial colonial rulers have left its scars on post-imperial independent India, it is historical that how political leadership discerns and fashion them after chiseling. The social scientist only revolved around 1947 as a date, no research work has been carried out on the impact of imperial services on public psychology and society and societal system.

The British know that aristocratic and moderate elements were with them in ruthless suppression of Indian masses, so as now, neo rich (including part of the upper-middle class also) and progressive persons are always with the power holders (chair of power). Dominating a sense of retaining and continuing what they have, forces them to obey everything to any non-sense, illegal, and immoral order to meet their own goals. "The native bourgeoisie of the colonial period was born under Western domination with four original sins. It was derivative, imitative, lopsided, and frustrated" (V. Subramaniam, 1996).

1.3.3. Need for Research Study on Political Pressure

Indian economy is one of the largest and most important economies of the world. The whole economy and economic superstructures are under the tight grip of Indian Bureaucracy (mainly the All India Services Officers). The All India Services Officers are occupying most of the vital positions in our system. These low paid, the super-powerful elite's invariably dictating the outcome of every decision-making process. In turn, self-goal directed decisions are imposed on our society, industry/business/corporate sector, and common person. The decision may be related to any of the areas, e.g. entry of multinational companies, liberalisation of the economy, growth of the industrial sector, import of new technology, up-gradation of existing institutions, new innovations in technology, rural development, scientific development, infrastructure development (transportation, health, education, power or any other sectoral development), it may be related with the launching of a satellite, to digging of a pond at the village level—all such policy decisions are invariably taken by these super-elite officers of the All India Services, located at various places in the bureaucratic system.

What is the role of various types of pressures and pulls on the decision-making process? How far political pressure regulates the decisions churned out of the system? How the quality of such decisions is related to their behaviour and piers pressure? What is the role of economic factors in churning out such decisions? What is the cost of the decision-making process? Are decisions are taken to meet the organisation goals? While making a decision, individual choices are influenced by whom and up to what extent? How these individuals reach the decision? What is the quality/type of decision provided and its relationship with the leadership provided? What are motivational factors, which have an impact on the decision-making process? What is the impact of such decisions on development works? Due to such actions/decisions, how social values and perceptions are changed in due course of time?

The entire social fabric is related or revolving around decisions taken by these officers. Because of their presence/control over all the key positions, maybe at the top level, maybe at Prime Minister or Chief Minister Office or village or plant level, any decision coming out of the bureaucratic system is the outcome of their manipulations. It is said that they have specialised in tilting balances in their favour or remote controlling the decisions for their own advantage and to maintain their own assertive role in the power process.

They provide direction and impetus to the Indian Economy for its structural adjustment and movement. They command the resource allocation, distribution of welfare measures, policymaking, resource competition, and resource utilisation. Entire institutional finance and public finance is under their control (directly or indirectly). They have their say in the flow of international finance also. In this process, they influence the flow of corporate finance also. The whole business sector is under the power clutches of the bureaucrats. Today's corporate/business stalwarts or giants maybe tomorrow's non-entity by a single decision or manipulation made by these bureaucrats.

The root cause of the problem lies in the bureaucratic concept of authority, power, and status. The constitution has enshrined the authority to the legislature (politician) and power is vested with the executive organ of the system. Well-established behavioural science theories explain the influence of authority over the decisions. Politics is the process, whereby power is acquired, transferred, exercised upon others to influence their behaviour (R.A. Sharma, 1993). Power is in fact, one's ability to influence others' behaviour. The individual, who influences the behaviour of the other may be located at any level of the hierarchy. This is what these officers are doing in the bureaucratic system.

According to D.M. Wolfe, power is the potential ability of one person to induce forces on another person towards movement or change in a given direction, within a given behaviour region, at a given time. The politicians contest for power, where ethics and national goals have little concern to them. Thus, politicians operate the power, consciously or unconsciously; directly or indirectly. Politicians use force and dominate/prevail over decisions making process to manipulate the policy decisions in their favour. All India Services Officers are status and position conscious, in the process, the status becomes end in itself. In due course of time, the status creates social distances. The position consciousness ruins the quality of decisions. To maintain their own supreme position, the principle of equity and fairness are sacrificed at the altars of favours.

In this process, department goals are sacrificed in the process of goal succession and goal displacement creeps in. In due course of time, the goal becomes the means and means serves as self-goals. Well laid down goals are being used for personal aggrandisement (R.A. Sharma). Personal interests prevail upon their constitutional obligations. This confirms Michel's 'Iron Law of Oligarchy', these elite (All India Services Officers) have gained complete control over the resources and power structures. Decisions are tailor-made to fulfill the need for authority (politician/clientele, etc.) Pressure commands the decision-making process and the social behaviour of such officer's flows in tune with the direction of materialistic pressures.

Sh. Bata K. Day has described the profile and problems of Indian bureaucracy in his article "Beyond Bureaucracy, Beyond Hierarchy" (1992). Some of these issues are relevant for our study, part of it is reproduced here as follows. The portrait of typical bureaucracy in India (as also bureaucrats as a tribe) reveals the following structural-functional as well as behavioural-orientation characteristics:

- "It lives in a sheltered world of its own, largely insulated and quarantined, fractionalised and sectoralised.
- It is elitist and overlordist, groupist and separatist, in approach and attitude; its proclivity.
- Its business is to be busy about its own business, unmindful of others business which, however, remains the rational for its existence.
- It authoritarian, power crazy and monopoliser.
- It is instantiated, aloof and remote from the reality, environment, people and social dynamics.
- It is unresponsive and irresponsible not sensitised enough to empathise.
- It develops strange negative orientation almost raised to level of 'addiction' (both naturally as well as part of cultivated culture) suffering from 'if-you-can-say-no, never-say-yes' syndrome.
- Rule mindedness is an article of faith with to the point of being 'deaf, dumb and blind' when it suits.
- It is precedent worshipper, setting its sight to the dead past, not to the living present, certainly never to the emerging future.
- It is strong hierarchy believer, status hungry and 'perk-jerker'.
- It is decision-dodger, believing in following principles—if you can postpone, don't act now; and tomorrow will take care of today and therefore, wait till tomorrow.
- It believes in the virtue of self-aggrandisement, given to empire building.
- It does not believe in delegation; it pins its faith in concentration; if there is delegation, its operation is so manipulated as to make it nugatory.
- It possesses, in immense measure, 'passing the buck' trait. Its game plan is 'let somebody else be the scapegoat', why you? And hence, it practices the dictum, '*sabko lapet lo*'.
- It is a votary of 'redtapism', with a fabulous 'file fetish' and noting and drafting' as the most favourite pastime, the guiding principles being.
- Delay, as much as you can, hasten slowly if you must.
  - Walk, never run and not even jog.
  - Revise, rewrite, redraft and retype as much as you can that is what you are paid for.
- It is the staunches supporter of the doctrine of 'play safe'-ism, meaning:
  - No extra dynamism
  - No entrepreneurial thrust
  - No discontinuity
  - No futuristic antics.
- 'Conformist' in its action orientation, it believes in
  - Sail with the wind
  - Run with the ball
  - Never get isolated, never be singled out.

- Bureaucracy believes in preservation, reservation and conservation (of self and the system), indulging in
  - No needless heroics
  - No 'self-immolation', no 'martyrdom'.
- It is basically 'no-changer', not 'prochanger', inviting the acronym abominable no man.
- It is impersonal to the point of being nameless, faceless, and soulless, excelling in anonymity and revelling in 'shooting from behind the screen'.
- Bureaucracy preaches 'merit', but practices its opposite, outflanking merit through 'in-law and out-law' mechanism, and nepotistic patronage.
- In bureaucracy's public accountability, there is neither public nor accountability. It is championed overtly, but negative covertly. It is an illusory concept and an illusive phenomenon—more violated than protected.
- Bureaucracy's 'instrumental neutrality' is a clever covers for supreme passivity 'taking no-side' stand being the other name of 'keeping the crucial aside'.
- Bureaucrats in India are intense 'careerist' but paradoxically; there is neither career nor management in bureaucracy in general, as, career for most is left to the 'cruelty of mercy of chance'. In fact, the prevailing ambiance is that career (mis) manages itself! No systematic plan for career development is in evidence anywhere.
- There is neither immediate reward for good work nor instant punishment for the bad, non-ethical action and behavior; thus, good work is at a discount and non-fears the consequences of bad work. Motivation is missing, work culture is negative, and efficiency is the casualty. There is pervasive and permeative frustration in all layers and branches of bureaucracy. Surprisingly, even a large segment of those who enjoy a larger share of the distributive largesse is also equally unhappy and unenthused lack of achievement motivation being a deep-rooted universal phenomenon in Indian bureaucracy."

Indian bureaucracy has lost rationality, efficiency, uniformity, and predictability. In the present-day scenario, non-conformance with rules, nepotism, favouritism, personal interest, inefficiency, and incompetence prevails. Indian bureaucrats take decisions on their whims, fancies, prejudices, caprices, and idiosyncrasies of individuals (R.A. Sharma). In such a bureaucratic setup, incompetent officers enjoy the aura around them with political patronage and good officers struggle to meet frustrating challenges. The system itself is the adversary. The criticism of bureaucracy has received strength because of the fast-changing environment and evils overflowing over it. Bureaucracy has failed to bring a social change as envisaged by the framer of the constitution (S.R. Maheshwari).

Bureaucracy has not kept its pace in learning challenges pertaining to the dynamic environment. Over time, competitiveness has increased and stiff's competition in grabbing and retaining the key positions. The approach and behavior of politicians have undergone a sea change; they have witnessed the authority flowing, and commanding the power at their will. Authority, power, and status have coalesced in the furnace under the pressures of lusts, lulls, and favors. This has enhanced and aggravated the political expectations, which have manipulated over changing government policies/laws. This gave rise to new challenges; inside the cadre's which require learning of challenges pertaining to the internal environment of their cadre's.

Human resource development in the All India Services has assumed new dimensions, which has put pressure on teamwork and quality orientation in demands/expectations. There is constant pressure to improve efficiency and productivity with doses of technological innovations. Bureaucrats have kept themselves on the other side of the court, to play with the game of favors. Training, counseling, career planning, and multi-skilling are the need of the hour. Sycophant, selfish, incompetent, greedy officers, have manipulated the performance review system through politicians and greedy officers. They prevail upon top politicians to churn out the favors for them. Ethics, moral values, culture, organizational commitment, and attainment of goals have melted away/evaporated in the process of own utility maximization.

The private sector has to face new competition due to globalisation and liberalisation of the economy and structural adjustment. An increase in quantum of investment has increased the expectations from the bureaucrats. The process of decision-making is facing tuff competition. The entry of multinational companies have globalised and liberalised the favour money (bribery) to alarming proportions, which has enhanced the economic pressure on these officers through private sectors to get tailor-made policy/decisions. Profit maximisation approach in the corporate sector has been resorted to large-scale tax evasion (income tax, customs duties, excise and Goods and Services Tax, etc.) to boost their image, and enhance the sale.

Private sector or multi-national companies have been exerting frequent pressure to amend the various acts/laws/rules to amend it according to their needs. Economic pressure has been playing a deciding role to get the tailor-made policy, decisions. It may be import/export policy or production regulations or manufacturing or license or labour welfare or labour laws, in every sphere; business houses pressurise through a politician or approach directly for law/rules/regulations passed/approved/amended/revised in their favour. The impact of such decisions on the overall growth of the economy, industrial growth, industrial climate, condition of workers and investors attitude, etc. is not favourable.

Top business house's success stories are often related to bureaucrats-politicians-businessmen nexus and favours. Decisions taken by the All India Services Officers command the direction of the market and economy. The rate of inflation is invariably linked with the type of leadership provided by the ruling party at the Centre and in the States. Policy decisions have serious repercussions for the national and international market. Thus, the whole business system revolves around their decision.

These officers invariably act under piers pressure, so their family attitude, individual lifestyle, and social attributes influence the decision-making process. Physiological needs, safety needs, security needs, stability needs, social affiliation, or belonging needs, self-esteem need (Maslow's need hierarchy) also influence the decision-making process. The degree of job dissatisfaction invariably related to the decreasing or weakening of the satisfiers. Growth in career, job advancement, recognition of achievement, may work as satisfiers or motivator factors. At the same time, any decrease or weakening of maintenance factors (status, relation with piers and politicians) may weaken the great extent of job dissatisfaction.

Officers of the All India Services live in the social crucible, social norms, social structure; prevalent social values have their impact on their behaviour in the decision process. The turbulent environment at home has its relation with their behavioural traits (attitude, perceptions, responses, relation, etc.) and decision at the workplace. Quality of decision taken may be directly related to the environment at home, social environment, and family background, the capacity to resolve conflict, security, job satisfaction, job performance, and issues, related to it. Political and economic pressures generate stress and stains, which has a direct bearing on their behaviour, ethics, and values.

How energetic, outgoing, organizer, bossy, cynical, tolerant, gregarious, responsible, courageous, confident, loyal, selfish, individuality, creativity, sensitivity, feeling for other, and scores of other aspects, were studied. What kind of human these officers are? How people visualize them in a social framework, a study has been carried out to assess them. Attempts have been made to adopt a multidimensional/multifarious approach, to study each and every issue related to our problem with full depth.

Administrative relationships of authority, status, and power generate considerable stresses and strains in the process of its use and exercise. In turn, a decision taken by these officers may be quoted as dimensions to the concept of new values, new social perceptions, and new order to work with. In any given set up number of relationships and interrelationships are working at any time; in actuality, modifications occur therein; and from formal relationships, non-formal and informal relationships tend to develop.

The problem of Indian bureaucracy has been blown out of proportion. Sakina Yusuf Khan Survey results have blamed the system (78%) as an adversary in itself. So many scandals came out; some of those can be listed as Harshad Mehta scam, MS Shoes scandal, The Reliance muddle, The Telecom scandal, The Jain Hawala racket, The Sugar scam, The Bofor gun deal, Fertilizer scam, The Securities scam Foreign Exchange scandal, The ABB loco deal, The Airbus deal, Tehalaka exposure, Kargil defense deals, Vyapam scam, Commonwealth Games, Rafael deal, PMC Bank scam, DHFL and UPPCL EPF scandal, PNB scam, Nirav Modi scam, CBI infighting, Scholarship scams in many States, Lalit Modi IPL scam, etc. list is very long and ever ending as published in media. What type of role these bureaucrats have played? Kind of political leadership and directions provided to the Central and State Investigation agencies invariably will decide the future recurrence of such scandals. All know approach adopted by top-notch senior bureaucrats in these scandals. It is an open secret, no need to further explain about the system, how it works? The crux of the problems is the political pressure exerted on the decision-making process and its impact on the end results (decision churned out).

1.3.4. Research Study Objectives

Key objectives covered under this study are:

1. What are the root causes for growth, perpetration, and sustenance of political pressure in the bureaucratic system?
2. Demographic characters of the individual All India Services Officers influence personal orientation on the acceptance of political pressure in the decision-making process.
3. Locus of control and its relationship with the acceptance of political pressure in the decision-making process.
4. Intrinsic and extrinsic motivators motivate the AISO in acceptance of political pressure.
5. All India Services Officers lifestyle orientation and their association with acceptance of political pressure in the decision-making process.

6. The cultural background of the All India Services Officers and impact of service culture on the acceptance of political pressure in the decision-making process.
7. Behaviour of the All India Services Officers and association with the acceptance of political pressure in the decision-making process.
8. Conflict management by the All India Services Officers in the decision-making process under political pressure.
9. Risk management by the All India Services Officers in the decision-making process under political pressure.
10. Impact of political pressure on innovation and creativity in the decision-making process.
11. An environment of the service they belong to, and the impact of workplace environment in the decision-making process under political pressure.
12. Different sources of the political pressure and intensity of political pressure exerted by them in the decision-making process.
13. Association of different areas in the decision-making process and acceptance of political pressure, the intensity of pressure exerted on the different areas.
14. Most commonly used modes and forms for the exertion of the political pressure in the decision-making process and association with the decision.
15. Reasons and factors, which influence the All India Services Officers for acceptance of political pressure in, decision-making process.

1.4. Research Work Methodology

The research methodology comprises research work organization, sample elucidation, sample dimension, sample structure, sampling technique, the framing of questionnaire/instrument, testing reliability of questionnaire/instrument, justification criteria for sample selection for data collection. After successful data collection, an important task is data feeding for processing, then the use of appropriate tools for statistical analyses and outcome of results help in the testing of the research hypothesis.

Indian bureaucratic set up have long tentacles spread all over the Union of India. The nature of the problem is such that, it is relevant to the whole population of the country. The universe for our study have been the All India Services Officers spread over the length and breadth of the Union of India. Statistically, it is not required to cover the whole universe for the research work. For the present research work, the best option was to contemplate a gradation list of the AISO as published every year during January as a sample universe. Practically, every year in position cadre strength of the AISO changes according to the need of different cadre states (besides regular cadre reviews, ex-cadre posts are created by cadre states). According to published reports as of 1.1.2019, 5205-Indian Administrative Service officers, 4021-Indian Police Service officers, and 2446-Indian Forest Service officers were in position. Our sample comprised; 11672-All India Services Officers who were in position against total sanctioned cadre strength of 14072 in Union of India.

These All India Services Officers are highly mobile due to frequent transfer in their cadres. Besides this, a large number of them proceed on deputation (in different positions) in different organizations and places in India and abroad. Such deputations are all-encompassing across the various sphere of working life, which may be a small non-governmental organization to highflying international organizations. It is of utmost difficulty to get an access to these highly egoist, arrogant, and hypocrite (some individual) officers who lives in ego and with self-concealing as their way of life. The All India Services Officers cherish a tremendous superiority complex. Even if you get an appointment with them, it is a Herculean task to get a reply to the questionnaires. Information gathering from them has been the greatest problem. Fieldwork has been tedious and extremely difficult. It has been a Herculean task to retrieve correct information from these egoists and introvert All India Services Officers'. High mobility and a watertight time schedule have added fuel to the fire.

Samples have been drawn from the three All India Services Officers located at different locations across the different States cadres. To maintain a regional balance, officers from southern, eastern, central, and northeastern cadres have been selected from deputation pool and one-week compulsory training programs. Some field visits were carried out to gather information from officers posted in far-flung areas also. Government of India's compulsory training programs have been most handy for getting readymade sample across cadres and the All India Services Officers from different batches and cadres were at one place and with some spare time also.

A small number of politicians and businesspersons (not part of our sample) were also consulted in our study to find out validation or confrontation with research data or results. Research variables were discussed with some ex-central ministers, ex-state ministers, and a large number of other politicians regarding data validation and to corroborate results.

About 100 officers from each service were considered as an appropriate sample size for research work. For sample stratification, the All India Services officers from different decades of recruitments and with different cadres, such as up to eighties, nineties, late nineties, and after that batches were stratified. A stratified random sampling technique was adopted for the present study for data collection. We have sent 1500 questionnaires by post, in which the response received was very low. 500 questionnaires were delivered to individuals in person. It was observed that in the case of officers posted in Central Bureau Investigation has been most prompt in replying to the questionnaire. Top bureaucrats and very senior officers have been the most difficult respondents and expressed fears to reply questionnaire. In some cases, the author has to meet such respondents more than five times to get the marked questionnaire back. Some questionnaires were also sent to retired All India Services Officers, those who have retired recently. In the case of Indian Administrative Service officers, retired officers were highly scared to reply. Questionnaires did not bear any kind of identification mark, and anonymity was assured and ensured.

Whole society looks for justice towards the All India Services Officers, and administration of the whole country have been entrusted to them, we are unable to appreciate, why they felt threatened by replying to a petty questionnaire, saying that political leadership may get annoyed. Then society can assume that such officers cannot make a decision against the wishes of the politicians in charge of affairs in their respective jurisdiction. Even after years of retirement, they expect to extract some benefits from the politicians, so they did not like to reply to a questionnaire. The author met some of them repeatedly until they refused to reply to the questionnaire.

After sample stratification, demographic composition responses are received and their analysis results are shown in Exhibit 1.1 to establish stratification of the sample. Our total response profile indicates that 28% of Indian Administrative Service officers, 35% of Indian Police Service officers, and 37% of Indian Forest Service officers responded to our questionnaires. Direct personal details were avoided, as the All India Services Officers are highly sensitive and we were aware that inclusion of any such thing was bound to jeopardize research work. However, data pertaining to demographic characters are considered to be mostly speaking about self and might have been explained with respect to self only or nearest to self. Such indirect information is compiled in Exhibit 1.1.

Exhibit Number 1.1: Personal Profile of Sample

Item Name	Details	N	%
Service	Indian Administrative Service	79	28
	Indian Police Service	99	35
	Indian Forest Service	105	37
Cadre	Working in Neighbouring State	51	20.8
	Working in Home Cadre	76	31
	Outside State	118	48.2
Family Economic Background	Poor	22	8.5
	Middle Class	82	31.7
	Upper Middle Class & Above	154	59.7
Martial Status	Separated	5	1.9
	Unmarried	10	3.8
	Married	251	94.4
Sex of the Officer	Female	21	7.8
	Male	247	92.2
Education	Ph.D.	17	6.6
	Management & Related Areas	29	11.3
	Engineer & Technocrats	53	20.6
	Post-graduate	86	33.5
	Graduate	72	28
Place of Birth	Rural	68	25.5
	Urban	128	50.2
	Semi-urban	62	24.3

Our indirect inferences regarding sample profile are self-explanatory in Exhibit 1.1. Our respondents have been highly educated, highly motivated, and financially well-off in their present lifestyle because they are the best-paid and most powerful persons of Indian bureaucracy.

The author organized focused meetings with some of the busy senior bureaucrats, explained to them the questions, requested them to reply to the questionnaire, and provided another person to mark the responses. The author traveled with some bureaucrats to extend some kind of favor for them pertaining to their private works, but these All India Services Officers are so blatant and self-goal driven that, they expected that others should do their work, but they will not reply to the questionnaire in full. One retired officer from the highest position of the State took us five times to his farmhouse with more than 90 minutes drive each time, but he replied only five questions and that also partly. This shows the height of self-centredness dominant among the All India Services Officers even after retirement.

Only some response sheets were made available from the interview method. The discussion method was widely used in training programs and after a long discussion respondent was requested to mark the responses and the author remained there to reply and clarify any kind of doubts or ambiguity in the questionnaire. In some cases, the author met them on a number of occasions to collect questionnaires during and after training programs. This method has been the most successful in retrieving the information.

The questionnaire method was used throughout the research for data collection and e-mail was used just to remind them to send replies to the questionnaire. A questionnaire, interview, schedule, and telephone interview methods were used in different combinations to gather information. The author has put maximum emphasis on the 400-targeted officers, from where we considered reply could come. These expected targets were followed continuously and personal influence and contacts were commonly used to collect the replies. The maximum reply came from officers located in New Delhi or State capitals or from training courses. Reply from the field postings and district headquarters has been minimal. Young officers posted in the various locations at the regional level or down below were most prompt in sending replies and senior-most have been most lackadaisical.

Flexibility has been the essential character of our data collection technique. To make our research highly appropriate and efficient efforts were made to consult selected officers while framing questionnaires and these questionnaires were discussed with a number of All India Services Officers to get their views and test the questionnaires. Small test-sample groups were selected to test the reapplication of the questionnaires. Reapplication-ability has increased the prediction in our study. Data collection was randomized to keep it safe from extraneous factors. Dividing the study into blocks and groups reduced variations.

We have gathered various types of data required for our study from our sample frames. We have studied All India Services Officers family, social, and office environment (setup), under which these officers are working. The impact of political pressure and the relation of various variables (political, economic, social, and individual) with the decision behavior have been studied. Data pertaining to sources of political pressure, areas of political pressure, modes of political pressure, and reasons for accepting political pressure have been collected and studied. The bureaucratic system itself is an adversary to the positive decision-making process; political expectations induce high expectations and pliability in it. Data were collected pertaining to non-conformance to the rules, nepotism, whims, favoritism, personal interests, and related issues pervasive in the system, and its association with pressure and individual behavior was studied.

These officers have been occupying the key positions, which require team innovations to lead their departmental team. Assessment and study of the various variables/attributes related to their decision behavior were studied. Data have been gathered regarding individual behavior related to risk-taking behavior, innovative behavior, style of decision-making, achievement, affiliation, influence, control, extension, dependence, dominance, tolerance, self-control, flexibility, and responsibility variables were processed to know the association with individual decision behavior.

Collection of primary data have been the Himalayan task, most of the data have been collected through direct communication with the respondents. Methods used for this study have (a) interview, (b) schedule, (c) questionnaire, and (d) electronic communication (as supplementary to the questionnaire), etc. The mode of data collection has been changed and modified according to the need of the situation. A situational and flexible approach has been adopted.

Questionnaires or instruments were framed covering various aspects related to our problem. Readily available and well-accepted statistical tools were used to assess various attributes to establish the validity of the study. It was not possible for all the respondents to answer all the questionnaires fully, many parts of the questionnaires were left unmarked, and these data have been processed as we got them. So, the situational and need-based approach according to the availability of time/resources have been used. On average, one hour time was devoted to replying to the questionnaire by each respondent, in one or more sittings/interactions. As discussed with respondents, some of them spent higher energy and time in answering it.

Most of our respondents have been having time constraints and high mobility. For top-level senior officers, it was extremely difficult to spare sufficient time for answering a lengthy questionnaire, in such situations telephone/telefax/E-mail method used to remind them.

1.4.1. Questionnaire Formulation and Testing for Research Work

Available literature was explored and surveyed to find out relevant instruments or questionnaires for the research work. Appropriate instruments for this research were not found anywhere, so it was decided to design new instruments. Need specific instruments were designed for this study; results based on fifteen instruments used for research are presented here. While designing the purpose of the questionnaire of research was kept in mind. Each questionnaire is designed in such a way that it can be administrated to individuals and groups both. Pfeiffer and Ballew's (1988) considerations for the instrument were kept in mind.

The time required for answering all 15 questionnaires was on the higher side. These time considerations have been constraints, because we have to cover the complete research items. We have to cover all the interrelated and interwoven aspects of the decision-making process and behavior of All India Services Officers. Instruments were designed for collecting the data pertaining to different aspects related to the All India Services Officers to extract findings and overview of conclusions. The items included in each questionnaire have been related and interrelated with different aspects pertaining to All India Services Officers' behavior and handling of political pressure in the decision-making process.

Reliability most of the questionnaires have been tested with help of SPSS tools command has been used for scaling to carry out reliability analysis with the split-half model to find out inter-item correlation, covariance with respect to the significance level. Some questionnaires have more than eight items. Factor analyses have been carried out by using the Principle Component Analysis method for extraction along with the Varimax Rotation method to test the significance of the factors. Our results for most of the questionnaires are highly significant.

Individual officer orientation instrument comprises 21 items and each item with two to five options. These 21 items are pertaining to personal characters related to the individual All India

Services Officers' personal details. In this questionnaire, five items are related to personal details, five items to study service, and three items pertaining to All India Services Officers' social-cultural milieu. Five items have been kept regarding the domicile of the individual officers and his family members and similarly, three items related to education have been kept for studies. All these demographic characters in the study were arranged in such a way that individual officer amenability towards political pressure can be studied with respect to the individual earlier background. The All India Services Officers handling of political pressure and association with the decision-making process has been studied. Under these 21 items, mainly 15 characters related to individual officer personal background have been studied.

The instrument for motivation consists of 10 items, four items pertain to extrinsic, and six items related to intrinsic factors. Five factors are motivational and five of them can be considered as hygiene or maintenance factors. Respondents have been asked to rank these according to their priority in the job. Results show the association of these items as significant.

To study lifestyle orientation, author included nine items in the instrument. Respondents were requested to rank the three most interesting areas of their life to studying the cultivated habits of AISO. Five items pertain to enlarging style and four items related to enfolding lifestyle were included in it. The previous instrument of Burks and Weir (1980) for positive habits was studied. Items show good association and relationship is significant. To study the dominant culture of these services and the cultural background in which the AISO take a decision, an instrument of 13 items was devised, respondents have been asked to rank the three most disliked things in AIS to know the irritating aspects of the culture. In the second part of this questionnaire, respondents were requested to evaluate these items of dominant service culture on a five-point scale. Results show association and reliability are significant.

To study the behavior of the AISO, 12 traits related to individual officer behavior in the decision-making process under political pressure were studied. Each respondent has been asked to rank these items in order of importance as an important quality of the AISO. All these items have been discussed with a select group of the AISO and each item utility and relation with decision behavior has been established.

The politicians exert political pressure in the decision-making process, which generate uncertainty, and conflicts in the mind of All India Services Officers. Research on conflict management has been carried out with the help of seven major styles of conflict handling. All India Services Officers have been requested to rank the most preferred style used by them in order of priority in the questionnaire. Associations of different items have been found significant after statistical analysis.

When political pressure is exerted on the All India Services Officers, acceptance or rejection of political pressure creates a certain amount of risk in individual officer mind. Risk management by the AISO was studied with the help of six items in the questionnaire or six different approaches adopted by these officers in handling the risk in decision. The AISO has been asked to rank the order of priority the most preferred choice adopted used in such situations. Research results show a good association with a highly significant correlation ship. Every individual officer possesses a lot of innovations and creativity, and some of them like to use innovations in the decision-making process. Continuous political pressure or negative incidences of political pressure instill fear among the AISO and innovation behavior gets affected adversely. Nine motives for innovation handling have been studied with the help of a questionnaire. Respondents have been asked to rank their preferences for innovation motives and change they bring out in the system in order of priority on nine items instrument. All the items show good association and correlations are significant.

Workplace environment, workplace setting, dominates environment of services, and department, which influences the decision-making process and handling of political pressure in it. For studying the orientation of the AISO in the workplace environment, job orientation a seven-itemized instrument has been devised for the study. The AISO has been requested to reply in yes or no, for these seven items of instrument. Correlation and association instrument items have been significant.

For this research work, different forms or modes of indirect political pressure were enumerated and after discussions with select All India Services Officers, only 22 important modes of indirect political pressure were retained for study. These 22 modes of political pressure have been randomly arranged in a questionnaire, and respondents have been asked to rank the seven most important modes or forms of indirect pressure, which they come across in the decision-making process. Nine items have been pertaining to the bureaucratic system, five modes relate to social power groups, five items concerning to political parties and three modes through power agents have been studied. All items show good association and significant correlation.

Acceptance or rejection of political pressure by an individual officer is situational and invariably influenced by the different factors and reasons prevalent in the bureaucratic system and related to self. A long list of such factors was discussed with the select group of the All India Services Officers and out of those factors only 15 reasons have been retained for study. All India Services Officers have been asked to evaluate these factors on a five-point scale based on their experience in accepting or rejecting the political pressure in the decision-making process. Items show good association and correlations are significant.

Instruments on the locus of control framed by Rotter (1954, 1966), Mirels (1970), Levenson (1972, 1981), and Archer (1979) were studied with respect to internal, external, powerful others, and chance. The present locus of control questionnaire has been adapted from Udai Pareek[17] (1997) and modified according to the need of the present research work. Ten items each for internality, externality for others, and externality by chance have been kept for study. Further, these items have been classified as; two items for a general locus of control, three items for success and effectiveness in a decision, one item each for influence, acceptability, career, advancement, and rewards. Factor analysis was also carried out, besides other tests. Correlation and association results have been significant.

The biggest and longest questionnaire has been pertaining to pressure points or areas on which political pressure is exerted. A large number of areas were studied and discussed. Ultimately, 15 most important areas were retained where political pressures have been exerted mostly. Each pressure point has been dealt with in detail with five sub-points, except in recruitment, which has six sub-points. Thus, these pressure points have been sub-divided into 76 variables for research to study the intensity of political pressure on each and every point. Respondents have been asked to evaluate the intensity and frequency of each pressure point on a five-point scale in an

17. Udai Pareek, *Training Instruments for Human Resource Development*, 1997.

instrument, as they experience in the decision-making process. Results are significant and show a good association.

Different direct sources of political pressure were enumerated and discussed with the select group of All India Services Officers. From a long list of such direct sources of political pressure only ten most important sources of political pressure, which are frequently exerted on the decision-making process by the All India Services Officers, have been randomly arranged. Respondents have been asked to evaluate 10 direct sources of political pressure on a five-point scale in the devised instrument. The relationship of these 10 direct sources of political pressure with the 15 areas of pressure was also studied through a separate questionnaire. The intensity of pressure on each variable has been studied. Factor analysis has been carried out. Correlation and association of these items have been significant.

We received 290 replies from the All India Services Officers. These instruments have been considered useful for generating sufficient data for research work. Instruments were designed in such a way that it reduces the psychological threat to any individual. Respondents have been requested to send it by ordinary post. All the responses received were pooled and randomly mixed, these pooled data do not attribute opinions to any specific individuals. The anonymity of the respondents has been ensured and maintained at all levels.

Feelings of threatening were prevalent among a large number of respondents. Such feelings can be attributed to the low rate of return for questionnaires. Behavior-related items for assessment and action planning were included in the instruments. To assure confidentiality, any kinds of identity marks were not attached to any instrument and at anywhere in the instruments. Instruments were designed according to research need; any kind of data overload was avoided.

Some of the respondents have attributed the questionnaire as lengthy. Some of them raised the question, why so much information is sought. Another group of officers expressed fear that it may be leaked to their disadvantage to the politicians. Some of them felt threatened, that they can be victimized. Some of them felt threatened that information provided in the questionnaire can be disclosed to the politician. In turn, a politician can victimize them in the future. Others said that it is such secret information that they cannot furnish it. Some of them simply refused to answer. Few of them asked why individual variables have been kept. They advised to carry out research without individual variables. Some of them advised keeping pressure areas up to ten items only, instead of 76 in the present questionnaire. Some of them asked, what they would get in lieu of responses provided by them (self-benefits maximization). The author has to face enumerable questions from the All India Services Officers, most of which were pertaining to the behavior of the individual officer.

Some of the All India Services Officers have been casual in marking; whereas the score table was printed in front of each question. Some of the responses have been left blank or unmarked. Some of them gave the same ranking to many responses/items. Some of them replied to a few responses and left many more un-responded. Some of them wrote descriptive/narrative notes also. Few of them wrote, "do not understand" and left the question un-responded.

In the case of modes of political pressure, some respondents ranked one to all items, instead of ranking only seven items; whereas some of them repeated the same rank to many items. Some of them gave wrong responses also, they have not thought about the response, what they are marking. Some of them underlined the responses; at the same time, they have underlined two responses. Whereas the last item has been left un-marked at places, it has been assigned the last rank automatically.

1.4.2. Research Data Processing and Statistical Tools Used for Analysis

Responses data received through questionnaires were entered in the datasheet of Statistical Package for the Social Sciences and processed in the same software on PC/laptop. The SPSS for Windows was used for all statistical calculations along with Windows and MS Office for research work in the study. Processing of data comprised of editing, coding classification of primary data according to variables suitability. Data have been computed with help of windows-based software to find out statistical relationships and testing of each hypothesis. Mean, mode, median, range, standard deviation, standard error, variations, skewness or kurtosis has been worked out for all the variables by the SPSS software. Major data analysis has been carried out for each variable by using cross-tabs, which have provided us percentage analysis for the All India Services, Indian Administrative Service Officers, Indian Police Service Officers, and Indian Forest Service Officers respectively. Results provided analysis for Chi-square, Pearson's correlation, and Spearman correlation values along with their level of significance. Statistical analysis provided results for Phi, Lambda, Gamma, Kendall Tau, and other coefficients. Only relevant values have been shown in exhibits/tables and charts to avoid overload of excessive data also to save space.

Exhibit Number 1.2: Statistical Tools Used for Analysis

Unit	Variable Details	Statistical Tools Used
Unit 2 to 10, 15 and 16	Individual Orientation characters, Locus of Control, Behaviour, Motivation, Life Style Orientation. Culture, Conflict Resolution, Risk Management, Innovations and Work Place Environment	Mean, Median, Mode, Standard Deviation, Frequency Analyses, Pearson Chi-square Analyses, Pearson's Correlation, Spearman Correlation, Box's Test, Lavene's Test, F-Ratio, Equality Covariance matrices, Rho and Cramer's Test, Manova and CrossTabs in SPSS for Percentage Analyses.
12 & 14	Areas of Political Pressure and Reasons for Accepting Political Pressure	Mean, Median, Mode, Standard Deviation, Frequency Analyses, Ranking, Pearson Chi-square Analyses, Pearson's Correlation, Spearman Correlation, Manova and CrossTabs in SPSS for percentage analyses.
11	Sources of Political Pressure	Besides above tools, Factror Analyses, Kouser-Meyer-Olkins (KMO measure), Barlets Test, Eigen Value (R. Matrix), Kaiser Criteion, Varimax Rotation Methods, etc.
13	Modes of Political Pressure	Independent Sample T-test besides tools used in unit 2 to 10.

Scale reliability analyses have been carried out with split half and Guttman models to find out inter-item correlation and covariance significance. 262 Hypotheses have been tested for 262 variables through various parametric and non-parametric statistical methods: such as Chi-Square, Pearson's correlation, Spearman correlation, multivariate analyses of variance (MANOVA), analyses of variance (ANOVA), Correlation, sign test for paired data, the Mann Whitney test, Wallis test, Kouser-Meyer-Olkin (KMO Measure) test, Barlet's test, Eigenvalue, Kaiser Criterion, rank correlation, General linear Model for multivariate, GLM-repeated measures, T-test and factor analysis, etc., Box's Test, Lavene's test, Rho and Cramer's (relevant methods have been selected for each questionnaire). These statistical tools have tested the validity, association, correlation, and significance of different variables used in the study. Standard deviation, central tendency, dispersions, and ranges of dispersion have been produced only where the need was felt (Exhibit 1.2). A rank correlation test has been used to test the relationship between variables.

During the study, an ordinal scale has been used for the ranking of items in questionnaires. In scaling techniques to represent the variables, interval and graphic rating scales have been used as a measure of evaluation. Likert type of summated scales has been used for many questions/ instruments. Variables evaluated by respondents have been analyzed with appropriate statistical methods.

1.5. Research Variables and Hypothesis Testing

Political pressure, its nature, and extent of exertion have a serious relation with the decision behavior of the All India Services Officers. The present study has covered modes of political pressure used on the All India Services Officers, and sources of political pressure mostly operating on these officers pertaining to different areas or points in the decision-making process at various levels in the public administration. Reasons, factors, or causes motivating the All India Services Officers to accept the political pressure and dimensions of such pressure have been studied. Different economic variables, social variables, individual variables, variables pertaining to individual personality, which have direct bearing and impact on individual behavior have been studied. The decision-making behavior has been studied with reference to the kind of constraints and variables vis-à-vis the type of behavior reflected by an individual officer.

1.5.1. Variables

1.5.1.1. Independent Variables: Independent variables or causal variables are presumed cause of change in the dependent variable, and are determinant in the All India Services Officers behavior in the handling of political pressure in the decision-making process. The impact of below mentioned independent variables has been studied on the decision-making behavior of the All India Services Officers under political pressure. Personal and work-related variables have been studied as independent variables.

1.5.1.1.1. Individual Level: Personal characters operating in All India Services Officers personal profile consisting of personality and individual officer details such as:

Related to service: Type of service they belong, method of recruitment, length of service, position (level) in the hierarchy, a cadre of the officer.

Social and cultural background: Community background of the officer, regional background of the officer, and economic background of the officer.

Personal background of the officer: Marital status, sex, a profession of spouse, number of children, and attitude of family members.

Education related: Education of the self, spouse, and parents.

Domicile related: Officer own place of birth, spouse, parents, place of residence of parents, and place of education after high school.

Locus of control: Internality, externality for others, externality for chance, success or effectiveness, influence, acceptability, career, advancement, and rewards in handling political pressure in the decision.

Reasons/factor for accepting the pressure: 15 variables mostly pertaining to individual and some to group and service (explained with system variables).

Individual officer behavior in the decision: 12 variables pertaining to behavior traits (explained with group variables).

1.5.1.1.2. Group Level: Behavior of officers in-group, when individual officer behavior operates in a group, it may be more than sum total of individual actions.

Innovation traits: Nine variables pertain to individual innovations in the decision.

Conflict management: Seven variables in conflict handling in the decision-making process.

Risk management: Six variables for individual risk management indecision.

1.5.1.1.3. Bureaucratic System Level: At the bureaucratic system level, individual and group behavior variables work together on the decision-making process.

Bureaucratic culture: 14 variables are pertaining to individual and service culture in the decision-making process.

Workplace environment: Seven variables related to individual behavior in decisions pertaining to the workplace environment.

Some of the variables pertaining to the job can be counted as independent variables also.

1.5.1.4. Dependent Variables: Dependent variables or caused variables are affected by an independent variable. These variables are operational in terms of political pressure; these variables are affected by some of the other factor/s.

Sources of political pressure, modes of political pressure, areas, and points of political pressure reflect individual officer interests over those of individual variables.

Sources of political pressure: Ten variables, which exert political pressure on the decision-making process of the All India Services Officers.

Modes of political pressure: 22 variables, the forms, and modes exerting political pressure in the decision-making process of the All India Services Officers.

Political pressure points or areas: 15 major areas, where political pressure is exerted, 76 variables were kept to study the intensity of political pressure exerted in the decision-making process on the All India Services Officers.

Associations among independent and dependent variables have been studied.

1.5.2. Research Hypothesis

"Bureaucratic Decision: A Complicate Process" (Political Pressure and its Impact on the Decision-Making Process of the All India Services Officers) have been studied with the help of a number of hypotheses and sub-hypotheses. Our research data have been planned in such a way that every variable has been studied as a research hypothesis, and the same has been tested by the statistical methods. Total 262 (+23 variables ranked differentially) hypotheses pertaining to 262 variables have been tested in the present research work, along with below-mentioned 21 important hypotheses also.

1. Personal characters of an individual All India Services Officers influence the handling of political pressure in the decision-making process.
2. Motivating factors in a job prioritize political pressure and influence the decision-making process of the AISO.
3. Lifestyle orientation of an individual AISO related to decision-making behavior.
4. The handling of political pressure is likely to be influenced by goals perused in the cross-cultural milieu by the individual officer.
5. The AISO adopts a situational approach in the handling of conflict in the decision-making process caused by political pressure.
6. Computations of constraints and choices in the decision-making process are related to individual officer risk-taking behavior.
7. Hierarchical position of an individual AISO influence the innovations pursued under political pressure in the decision-making process.
8. The workplace environment in the decision-making process decides the attitude of an officer towards handling political pressure.
9. Individual officer goals priority is related to political pressure handling in the decision-making process.
10. The extent of political pressure acceptance is linked with location, the importance of the post, power enjoyed by the officer.
11. Individual officer behavior attributes influence political pressure handling in the decision-making process.
12. Different pressure groups exert indirect political pressure on an individual officer, the kind and importance of pressure mode determine the outcome of any decision.
13. Acceptance of political pressure in the decision-making process by an individual officer is influenced by the personal motives and values pursued by the officers.
14. The locus of control of an individual officer determines the handling of political pressure in the decision-making process.
15. Politician frequently exerts pressure on different decision-areas in the bureaucratic system. The intensity of political pressure exerted on an individual officer is according to political interests pursued by the politicians.
16. The capacity of any source of pressure to exert direct political pressure on an individual officer to get the desired decision is related to the position enjoyed by that source in the power hierarchy.
17. Flexibility in-service conditions (in promotions, transfers, postings, tenure, career progression, and opportunities to pursue self-seeking goals) influences the individual decision behavior.

18. The relationship of the politician with the individual officer is related to the compromising behavior of each other, the strength of such a relationship will be proportional to the aggrandizement of mutual interests/goals. A stronger relationship will have a higher negative impact on the outcome of the decision.
19. The All India Services Officers show a strong desire to maintain the status, status creates social distances; this has an impact on the social behavior of an individual.
20. Yielding behavior with respect to political pressure is related to the economic social and family background of an individual officer.
21. Performance review by a politician is used as a tool to influence the decision, individual utility is positively related with the decision behavior.

"It is always easier to fight for one's principles than to live up to them."—Alfred Adler

Part–Two
Individual Variables in Decision under Political Pressure in Bureaucratic System

"Wiseman possessing equipoise mind, renouncing the results of all actions and free from shackles of birth, attains the blissful supreme state." *The Bhagavad Gita* 2.51

Unit 2

Decision-Making Process of Bureaucracy

"One's own self is the friend of the soul by whom the lower self (consisting of the mind, senses and body) has been conquered; even so the very self of him who has not conquered his lower self behaves antagonistically like an enemy."[1] *The Bhagavad Gita* 6.6.

"Donotfollowwherethepathmaylead. Goinsteadwherethereisnopathandleaveatrail."
—Ralph Waldo Emerson

- *Decision-Making Process of the All India Services Officers*
- *Influences on the Decision-Making Process*
- *Government Decision System*
- *System Decision Constraints*
- *Decision Evaluation*
- *Evaluation of Political Pressure Impact on Decision*

This unit covers the decision-making process in public administration and its constraints. Political, bureaucratic economic, and individual officer self-goals influences on the decision are described. Decision evaluation comprises the impact of political pressure on the decision-making process of the All India Services Officers.

1. VI.6. *The Bhagavad Gita*.

2.1. Decision-Making Process of the All India Services Officers

The All India Services Officers in the decision-making process under political pressure have to make a choice from adherence to bureaucratic system rules, regulations, and procedures or twist the system according to politician's expectations to meet individual goals. The choice is between merit-based objectivity and politically propelled desires for subjectivity. The decision-making process under political pressure is a dilemma as it causes the inconsistency between adherence to the current system or adherence to individual politician desired expectations. Individual All India Services Officer arrives at decisions according to their own choices, which are influenced by individual perceptions, beliefs, and past experience in doing so. In every decision, individual All India Services Officer receives, perceives, screens, processes, interprets, and evaluates the information to develop alternatives according to own preferences in the decision-making process to arrive at a decision. The bureaucratic decision-making process mainly comprises the following nine steps:

(a) **Problem:** In this stage, individual All India Services Officer will try to define and delineate the extent of political pressure with respect to present position in the bureaucratic system and future implications in his own career. An individual officer will gather information for the consequences of accepting or not accepting political pressure. Individual All India Services Officer feels competent to handle it and focus on the decision problem rather than the people and system.

(b) **Intensions:** Individual officer analyses soul-searching, cognisant and self-centered intensions pertaining to the problem, in this stage analyses politicians' intensions, possible public intensions and search for senior officer's intension pertaining to a specific problem. Individual officer conscious competence feeling will invariably influence the intensions computations in the decision-making process in this stage.

(c) **Options:** Individual All India Services Officer explores all possible options, alternatives, choices, substitutes, and criteria devised by him for the problem. Consequences and outcomes for each option are explored. Individual All India Services Officer interest, values, beliefs, preferences, politician interest, and public interest for all relevant and irrelevant aspects are weighed in this stage.

(d) **Rationality:** Individual All India Services Officer carries out vertical and lateral thinking for various choices available to him along with successive/consecutive comparisons. In this stage, each option is ranked and weighted to reflect the importance of each choice. Then individual officer list out and rationally analyzes the attributes of each option.

(e) **Alternatives:** Individual officer carry out valuations and evaluation of each alternative in a decision. All possible preferences and alternatives are deeply studied with reference to political pressure exerted by a particular politician. Stability for each alternative is developed to avoid difficult tasks and consequences. Then the best choice is selected for further action.

(f) **Conflicts:** Uncertainties, precariousness, and conflicts will be computed in every alternative available for the individual officer in the decision process. The extent of conflicts associated with different alternatives and uncertainties generated by outcomes have to be computed and calculated in a systematic manner to avoid future complications from the decision. Individual officers' inner self will try to avoid conflicts, if not possible, then try to minimize conflicts.

(g) **Decision:** Individual officer after evaluating and weighing each alternative, the best option with the highest value and minimal conflicts is considered for selection. The best option will be according to individual preferences, predilections, orientations, and choices related to that individual personality. Individual decision-making officer learns by self to draw inferences based on readily and instantly available information in his memory. Individual All India Services Officer may increase his commitments to his previous decision in spite of the negative impact. Individual All India Services Officer analyzes the likelihood of occurrence of political pressure based on own analogy.

(h) **Monitoring:** Monitoring is the most crucial part of the decision taken by the All India Services Officers in public administration. An individual officer tries to collect feedback from different sources to know about the reaction of the opposition party politicians, ruling party politicians, prominent political leadership, public, seniors officers and juniors in the bureaucratic system and colleagues, who can influence the future course of events. On many occasions, new decisions have to be taken to neutralize the previous decision to save one's image and service. Monitoring is the essential, indispensable, and obligatory requirement of the decisions taken in public administration.

(i) **Modifications:** In public administration decisions modifications and alteration, aspects are the common and frequently used phenomena, which is not used in the corporate sector. On many occasions individual All India Services Officers selectively leak out the proposed decision and try to assess the feedback from various quarters, realizing the potent danger or public unrest or opposition, they modify decision taken on files, and the final decision coming out is the modified version. Due to the change of political leadership in the state, politicians instruct or influence the All India Services Officers to modify decisions taken by the previous incumbents.

Individual All India Services Officer does not get much time to ponder, deliberate, and evaluate alternatives courses of action. Based on their own perceptions, experience, knowledge, values, attitude, and situations, individual officer explores various options. Individual All India Services Officer decisions are based on situations reasonably optimizing political or public interest, at the cost of someone else. Choices are confined to system parameters and individual officer limitations. Most of the All India Services Officers' decisions are judgmental, spur-of-the-moment, and sentimental rather than based on any model or concept. Individual persons follow intuitive decision-making (W.H. Agor, 1989; H.A. Simon, 1987) and mostly operate independently of rational analysis due to high uncertainty, unpredictable variables facts don't indicate solutions, no time is allowed, alternatives are plausible, and every decision is independent of previous decisions.

Very limited information is made available to the individual officer, which signifies the tremendous role of manipulations in the outcomes. Dimensions of the pressure in the decision comprise the All India Services Officers cognition, thinking, processing of information, perceptions, tolerance to uncertainty, minimizing the conflict and risk, structuring the pressure sources and modes in the system. The individual All India Services Officer has to work with high tolerance towards uncertainty. They have to be logical and rational in thinking. The All India Services Officers have to be efficiency-oriented. They must have the ability to derive a decision with minimal information and the least alternative evaluation. With the passage of time individual All India Services Officers develop the capability to cope with pressure and tolerate uncertainty, play safe, and collect full information about pressure so that they can examine possible alternatives. Innovative All India Services Officers arrive at decisions based on long-range implications and explore creative options.

System abider individual All India Services Officers organize meetings, discussions with seniors and juniors and try to retrieve suggestions. Such an individual All India Services Officer avoids conflict and tries to take acceptance of the politician before taking a decision. Every individual officer arrives at decision at a different time and in a different way, which may be related to one's position, place of posting, relation with senior/junior, the attitude of political leadership, local political leader relationship with the chief and key politician who matters in the system.

2.2. Influences on the Decision-Making Process

Whenever the AISO arrives at any decision, a large number of factors influence such decisions; it is not possible to enumerate every kind of influence, only some important influences on the decision-making process have been elucidated here.

2.2.1. Political Influences on the Decision

Politicians influence the decision-making process and its outcome in different modalities or ways and means. People approach politicians or affected parties mobilize politician support from various sources to exert political pressure on the concerned All India Services Officer to get a decision in their favor. Politicians use force to manipulate decisions in the desired direction by virtue of their controlling-location and holding the top position in the bureaucratic system. In case the concerned officer is not willing to listen, acquiesce, or accede to politician demand, in such situation's politicians attempt to use the power base available to him to get the desired outcome from the decision. Politicians put efforts to influence decision goals; criteria and processes to meet self-needs from the decision-making process. Politicians occupy the top position in the hierarchy, so they manipulate through discretion in the distribution of advantages and disadvantages to the All India Services Officers in the bureaucratic system. In case the concerned officer is not trapped by the lusts for advantages, politicians use the weapon of their public responsibility and accountability to influence the decision. Continuous success in decision manipulations tends to develop politicians-bureaucrats-businessmen nexus. In long run, such nexus spread its roots in the form of politician-criminal-bureaucracy nexus. Such nexus continuously influences the decision-making process of the All India Services Officers.

Politicians' top positions in the bureaucratic system provide him access to every kind of bureaucratic information, withholding key information from decision-maker officer influence the decision outcome. In situations where politicians find individual officers not amenable to political demands, he uses whistleblowing against such persons and spreading rumors pertaining to such officers. To influence the decision on occasions politician, indulge in the leaking of confidential information about decision activities. Politicians exchange favors with individual All India Services Officers for mutual benefits. Politicians carry out intense lobbying for or against any decision alternative or individual to influence the decision. Politicians indulge in spreading information for image building of such All India Services Officers, who oblige them in the decision.

Politicians use fear of transfers as an effective tool to get a tailor-made decision. Those who do not oblige politicians, such officers are frequently shifted on different postings. Those All India Services Officers, who oblige politicians are rewarded with choicest postings. Promotions in the bureaucratic system have used an instrument to the influence decision-making process. Politicians ensure longer tenures for pliable officers and continuously influence the decision-making process. Pliable officers get higher budgetary allocations and desired annual appraisal reports from the politicians, who in turn get tailor-made decisions from them. Politicians commonly protect pliable officers in grievance redressing mechanism. When the public criticize the decisions taken by the All India Services Officers, politicians protect public criticism to pliable officers. When the All India Services Officers deliver decisions according to political desires, the politicians protect such poor performance in the decision. Even politicians do not hesitate to exert pressure on seniors to provide freedom in working to pliable officers. Politician uses his power in resource allocation as media to influence the decision. Individual officer collaborations with politicians have a serious impact on subordinates regarding power and politician connections, politicians extend help to such officers to influence subordinates in the decision.

Politicians do not hesitate to use his nuisance powers, in case the All India Services Officers do not oblige them in the decision. Politicians by-pass the chain of command and interact directly with the desired bureaucratic level to influence the decision. Politicians form coalitions with other politicians or with the All India Services Officers to influence the decisions. In case the outcome of the decision is not desirable, politicians obstruct the decision by excessive adherence to rules or inaction. To get the desired decision politician to start developing contacts outside or down the chain in the hierarchy. When a particular officer or level is not obliging then politicians indulge in complaining to high ups against such officers. To influence a decision in a particular direction, politicians use adherence to merit, ignoring merit, ignoring seniority, and good work as tools to meet own goals. Through manipulations in the administrative process, politicians create individual group conflicts in values, goals, and interests vis-à-vis resource conflict to get the desired decision. Politicians use work allocation and resource distribution as a tool to influence the decision.

Politicians extend gains to individuals at the cost/expense of others, who are not attuned with politicians. Politicians induce ambiguity in the process to influence the outcome of a decision. Politicians show whimsical attitudes towards individual officers, who do not oblige them in the decision process. However, those officers, who oblige politicians in case of any problem to such officers, politicians decrease standards of probity for them. Lack of transparency is used as a tool to get tailor-made decisions to suit the need of authority or clientele. Political expectations from the decision are unlimited and never-ending. Politicians use progress review and performance review as a tool to influence the decision in own favor. The continuous influence of politicians has a serious impact on the leadership style of individual All India Services Officers and decisions taken by him.

The All India Services Officers' desire to retain power forces them to exercise full control over the information and allow filtered and biased information to come out of the system for the furtherance of own interests. In case the politicians fail to add uncertainties, the All India Services Officers cultivate uncertainty to harvest a bumper crop of self-goals. When a political boss is powerful and exercises full control with access to alternate sources of information, an individual All India Services Officer has modest or no control over the situations. Politicians do not bother to evaluate options available to them before exerting pressure or taking decisions. The All India Services Officers use power to cultivate own interest, "can there really be much doubt who governs our complex modern societies? The modern political system is essentially bureaucratic, characterized by the rule of officials" Putnam (1973). Various components of the decision process specify the problems and solutions in the given hierarchical structure of that service.

2.2.2. Influences of Bureaucratic System

The politicians use bureaucratic system variables; some of such variables have been discussed in Part Four of this book. Bureaucratic systems provide power to the All India Services Officers; the desire to maintain individual power influences the decision behavior of the officers. The bureaucratic system provides authority to the politicians and authority plays its role to influence decisions taken in the system. Politicians at the top position in the hierarchy in the bureaucratic system influence the decision-making process. The All India Services Officers are highly status-conscious, desire to maintain status becomes end in itself (the ends justify the means). High-status consciousness influences the decision. Status orientations create social distances in the bureaucratic system or emotional aloofness, that aloofness from masses seriously impairs the decision-making process.

High hierarchical levels orientations of the bureaucratic system influence the decisions, resultant of this, accountability to the decision is got lost in the levels. In bureaucratic system, decisions are goals directed and goals influence the decisions. The bureaucratic system has to pay a social cost for goal-oriented decisions. Bureaucratic systems of controls to retain power by the power holders influence the decision. The relation between power and control over the decision-making process in bureaucracy influence the decision. Our bureaucratic system puts a high emphasis on position rather than acts, which influence the decision negatively. Power holders sacrifice fairness and equity in the bureaucratic system to influence the decision. Excessive position consciousness among the All India Services Officers ruins the decision. Loss of creativity from the process has impaired decision. The bureaucratic system has surrogated power from the decision process.

The bureaucratic system is such that the All India Services Officers invariably play safe in the decision, without any harm to self-relying on the concept that I do not harm you—you should not harm me. Rules, regulations, and procedures looked as if these are made for non-conformance in the decision, commonly said that show me a person, I shall show you the rules. Rules are for fools is the popular 'saying'. The decision-making process is full of nepotism and favoritism, this has eroded public faith from the decision taken by the All India Services Officers, so for every decision public approach politician for his intervention. A bureaucratic system is such that it allows blockage and leakage in communication, which in turn loses the rationality of the decision. This problem of communication-related with status prevalent among the All India Services Officers create distance from the public, who in turn go to a politician for help. The All India Services Officers like to maximize their own needs from political collusion, refrain from collective decision making; in case of failure or brewing problem, the All India Services Officers pass the blame on the system as an outcome of collective decision.

The bureaucratic system itself is an adversary in the process of decision. The present bureaucratic system is dominated by a lack of ethics, declining moral values, neglecting the respect for culture, absence of public service commitment, and public goals among decision-makers in the process. Dominating uncertainty in the bureaucratic system and frequent politically motivated transfers create roles of conflicts among the All India Services Officers and uncertainties carry its harmful impact on the decision. Greater participation in decisions produces a favourable attitude, higher job satisfaction, fewer feelings of threats in service, and higher self-esteem (French and Caplan, 1970). Employee's lack of participation in the decision-making process leads to consistent poor health, strain, and stress (Margolis, 1974). Present day, the All India Services Officers decision has failed to bring out any social change due to its dominant bias.

Past precedents cannot help in case of political pressure, because every situation will rebound in time and space with its own set of outcomes. Individual officer collusion with the politician in terms of benefit maximization increases constraints on the officer in numerous ways. Politicians extend help and patronage; a sense of obligation and commitment prevail on the officer. The All India Services Officers give due weightage to politicians while calculating the alternatives for the decision. Political pressure induces sensitivity in the decision process. Performance satisfaction gets relegated under the sense of security provided by the politician. Ambiguity in policy, rules and law increases the problem of interpreting, distorting, and perceiving goals for maximization of self-interests. Discretion and flexibility in the system is a deliberate attempt to maximize utilities and retain scope for political interference. Means and ends in practice are not distinct; end results for an individual may work as means or inputs for another person (Simon, 1965).

Public goals, government goals, politician goals, political parties' goals, department goals, and individual goals work in a conflicting manner. Goal succession is a common phenomenon (R. Michel, 1911; Merton, 1957; Perrow 1961) in the All India Services also. Goal displacement is accelerated under political pressure; means serve as ends in the process at the cost of efficiency, fairness, and justice in public administration. Goal succession and goal displacement highlight the dynamics of the decision process. The actual outcome of a decision deviates from the expected outcome of the decision in goal dynamics.

"The sequel of an action chosen by one man will be shaped by circumstances, and its circumstances will include the actions chosen now and actions to be chosen in time to come by other men" Shackle (1974). Decisions taken by individual officers have implications for the group. When other officers see that due to collusion with a politician, that officer has attained self-goals. Then others follow it and slowly individual preferences are aggregated into collective likings. Individual officer joins small groups to secure patronage and benefit for themselves in resource allocation. These small groups introduce resource competition among interest groups and motivate others to toe with political pressure to enjoy power. Available discretion in the system of public administration serves individual own interests, where other groups compete for power to protect their interests and in the process falls in line with political pressure.

2.2.3. Economic Influences

The influence of economic variables on the decision-making process cannot be ruled out or ignored. The politicians influence the All India Services Officers and, in turn, they influence all policy decisions, which command the market economy. Politicians are aware that they are for five years period (tenure period of their election), politicians have to spend a lot of money to attain the present position, so politicians also want economic security; hence influence the decision in own favor. Politicians develop their own economic network to save their own interests. Politicians refuse to take cognizance of corruption, rather shield corruption to fulfill own economic interests from the decision-making process.

In public administration decisions, variables are dynamic in nature, consequences of marginal change have serious implications, and conditions of equilibrium are non-maintainable due to externalities and uncertainties involved in the process. Decision-makers were unable to operate under conditions of perfect rationality. Economic interests of pressure groups induce preference ordering in individual officer power and capability to maximize their own utilities. In case stakes are higher, no one is willing to own the responsibility, the most compromising way used is collective decisions, where disagreements and conflicts are diluted and shared by none. The collective choice is the choice of power or authority without an iota of responsibility. The outcome of the decision is directly proportional to the coercive power and position enjoyed by the chairperson. Merit is sacrificed at the altar of collective and individual interests. Decision taker rarely works as a unified body of thoughts. Rationality and fairness of decision is being surrendered under economic influences.

2.2.4. The All India Services Officer Interests and Goals Influence

Individual All India Services Officer has a tendency to look for gratification of personal interests from the decision outcomes. Propelled by feelings of self-interests the Indian Administrative Service officers have managed complete control over resources in the bureaucratic system. The Indian Administrative Service officers have stage-managed the power structure in their own favor to meet self-interests perpetually. In the process, every service and individual officer in different services use goals for personal aggrandizement, and goals serve as a means to meet ends. Bureaucratic system goals are used for personal utility, and respective services, and individuals use goals for own growth maximization in the decision. In this process, the dominant goal might change in the decision-making process and cause goal conflict in the process. Slowly, goal succession and displacement take place in the bureaucratic system. Operational goals to be served emerge from a bargaining process. Expected outcome and actual outcome of decision are in conflict.

Government goals for revenue maximization in some departments end up with wealth maximization for individuals. If the government loses revenue, individual officers and politicians do not feel it as deprivation. The revenue maximization process is invariably used as individual benefits maximization. Government laws are used as a threat to individuals to enhance chances for an accumulation of money for self. Individual All India Services Officers are in search of own economic interests from the decision. Individual officer attitudes, interests, beliefs, motives, past experiences, and personal expectations from the decision influence the outcome of the decision-making process. Individual officer location in the hierarchy, position in power, level of career, time, and kind of decision influence the decision-making process. The size of the outcome, the background of the outcome, and individual utility of outcomes also influence the individual decision.

The individual officer searches for own roles in the decision-making process and analyzes the role played by him for his own utility in long run. Individual officer efficacy and effectiveness influence on the decision-making process is used for self-aggrandizement. The self-capability and self-esteem of any officer influence the decision and handling of political pressure in it. Important steps followed in the process of decision-making influence decision outcomes. In any decision, not all activities or objectives can receive the same attention, which influences the decision. Individual officer intension to resolve a conflict by ordering of objectives in decision sequence influences the decision. In such ordering internal consistency of individuals in decision-making will influence the decision. Individual officer reflexivity in choices in a given situation influences the decision outcomes.

Individual officer ranking of consequences of decision outcomes will influence the decision process. Individual officer rationality in the decision-making process will be according to individual wisdom and individual personality traits will influence the decision and prevail over it. Individual officer sense of obligation to commitments towards self, public, bureaucratic system, and politicians will influence the decision. Individual officer sense of calculated-ness and commitment are invariably used in the decision process.

Individual officers' amount of sensitivity to differences magnitudes towards outcomes influence decision. Individual officer quantum of satisfaction with individual established performance influences the decision. All India Services Officer's sense of perseverance with which individual pursue goals influence the decision. Individual officer positive favorable attitude towards political pressure in decision-making process influence the handling of issues in decision. Individual officer problem imagination and sensitivity for different aspects influence the decision. Creativity and innovation pursued by any individual officer in the decision-making process will influence the decision outcome. Everyone possesses many ideas, but idea fluency is crucial for quick and relevant decisions. Individual officer incubation time influences the decision. Individual officer thinking and illumination about a problem influence the decision-making process.

Individual All India Services Officers located at various levels in the hierarchy have major clustering of decisions at the district level, regional level, and state level. The All India Services Officers' individual decision quality is largely influenced by individual perceptions. The All India Services Officers have an inbuilt advantage in the current state of affairs and desired outcomes from alternative options available to them. Pressure perceptions are also situational and variable according to individual All India Services Officer. Individual All India Services Officer interpretation and evaluation of pressure is invariably is situational to the individual officer. On the spur of time individual, the All India Services Officer develops alternatives based on strength and weakness of time and space with a bearing on the final outcome.

The individual officer with different social, economic, community, and regional backgrounds have different perceptions and attitudes, reflect different preference ordering for alternatives and problems. The problem of political pressure is computed in different lines with individual attitudes, values, perceptions, prejudices, and beliefs. Officer's past experience in handling the pressure becomes handy in responding to the present situation. Once a bad experience officer behaves in a doubly cautious manner, whereas success increases officer confidence in handling the problem.

In the Gestalt concept of perceptions, perception is highly selective to an individual specialism, background, and values. Different officers located in various positions of hierarchy in the same department will have different perceptions about the same problem. Every officer has a limited capacity (located in his past background and experience) to calculate and evaluate the consequences of all possible alternatives courses of actions adopted in process of decision. "Individuals choose their most preferred alternatives from a set of available alternatives and face no barriers such as search and calculating cost in discovering it" P.M. Jackson (1983).

When an officer joins service, his responses will be calculated and related to his socio-cultural-educational background. As the officer grows in the service, computations will be related to the service conditions, experience with a decision in his career, and capability to calculate consequences and probability of future events as the outcome of a decision. Dynamic and uncontrollable decision variables and limited available choices related to a particular service at any point of time are highly unpredictable for the non-programmed decision process of All India Services. Strategic decisions taken by these elite officers shape the process by which they are made. Constraints with the decision process, advantages of alternatives to self-capacity, and capability of an individual officer in computations, behavior towards utility functions, personal goals, and interests, individual aspirations level, experience with success and failures in career, satisfying and maximizing behavior set up an environment for decision process and officer always cope up within personal limitations.

The decision was taken by an officer based on individual officer experience and comparable priorities in the process, better solutions and outcomes may be possible but the approach adopted may affect chances of alternative adoption. Officer may not be fully satisfied with the decision but an individual likes to maximize his own goal and interests. Due to pressure on the decision-process officer, adaptive behavior will be dynamic in nature and ready for mutual adjustments. In the process of adjustment, risk will be minimized and the goal will be maximized. Individual officer response to political pressure will reflect individual goals, which will be characteristic of their service working conditions.

2.3. Government Decision System

The decision process of the All India Services Officers is full of uncertainties and risks, which are unpredictable in nature. The All India Services Officers never know the future repercussions of the decision. Even a highly positive, fair, and a just decision may recoil after a lapse of time and as bad, unfair, and biased decision, or may make out heroic stature of a decision-maker. Really, the All India Services Officers' decisions can take a swing in any direction, highly uncertain future and bloom with risk. The situation is such that no information about the future is available with certainty. The All India Services Officers use this uncertainty to their own advantage for their stability, resourcefulness, and career advancement.

Political uncertainty or pressure group uncertainty, which is located outside the department of the officer, can cause uncertainty inside the department also. Individual officers are sure about their continuance in their positions and they are unable to assess the repercussions of decision or outcome of utility to their goals. The Indian Administrative Service officers, who are located in all crucial positions, make use of uncertainty to their own advantage and get complete control over the public administration to cultivate them. Such monopolization can be reduced only through widening the access of all other services to top positions, so that, they can slow down the monopolization of bureaucracy and work as a buffer in the decision.

In the Union of India, political uncertainty in the decision cannot be reduced or avoided; rather it is bound to increase in the future. Hierarchically structured organizations effectively function in the uncertain environment in which they operate (Wooward, 1958; Burn et al., 1961; Katz, 1966; Thompson, 1967; Lawrence and Lorsch, 1967). How the All India Services Officers arrive at decision in a climate of uncertainty, complexity, and ambiguity? The All India Services Officers can mobilize resources freely and use flexibility and ambiguity of law, rules, and procedure to their advantage. They hide their accountability under prevailing uncertainty and the limitless size of the government. Here vastness of the size of the government helps the All India Services Officers in the decision-making process and problem-solving. On many occasions, ill effects of the decision are spread over and diluted by passing the buck to seniors or juniors or vertical or horizontal or upward or downward or public at large.

The All India Services Officers communicate political pressure in decision upward and downward to dilute the outcomes, they follow the common approach *sabh ko lapete lo, khud bach niklo* (save yourself, pass on the buck to all). Political pressure in the decision and its relation within the department, intra department, and outside department manifest goals and interests. These goals work as a set of contracts for individuals, individual officer negotiations with pressure revolve around own goal possibilities. The behavior of members of any service at any given time and place is the function of the intricate interplay of power struggle and forces working on it. Power bias reveals their behavior and their goals can be inferred from working behavior.

Every decision taken by the All India Service Officers, they evaluate it in terms of opportunities lost by them or chances delayed for them in the attainment of goals, or loss of advantage in career progression, or dislocation and instability due to decision, diminishing in individual utilities and loss of marginal information advantage. On many occasions, the All India Services Officers are under compulsion to take a decision; some decision has to be taken; merits of such decision are immaterial. Number of times the All India Services Officers save themselves by not taking any decision or delay it and wait for new postings. Frequent transfers are handy for the All India Services Officers, they delay decisions for the next incumbent, and anyone never takes controversial decisions. All share responsibility for delay, it means no one is responsible for it. Individual member interactions within the service give the impression of uncertainty and risk involved with the decision. A glaring example of removing encroachments from public property, decisions are delayed forever and no responsibility is fixed, and no one gets penalized.

The All India Services Officers enjoy power and status from this in-built uncertainty or unpredictability. "Great power is wielded by those at a point where the greatest amount of uncertainty is absorbed since they can considerably influence the decisions that will finally be made by others" (Brown, 1970). Political behavior power plays a crucial role in decision constraints. Competing interest groups vie with each other to get control over scarce power resource. Legitimate power located with position and status in the hierarchy regulates the decision process. Power holders manipulate information and push preferred alternatives to harvest their goals and interests from the decision process.

Decision outcome is the optimal and efficient allocation and utilization of men, material, money, and machinery resources at one's command. The beauty of public administration is that organizational goals and efficacy are the causality and invariably replaced by individual goals and interests. An indicator of efficacy is extending to which political goals/master goals are met with success. Output in public administration cannot be measured, they offer services, which are personal state of well-being acts of production and consumption are simultaneous. "Hardness, self-composure, coolness in face of pain and danger, confidence in own decision—these were qualities required by the imperial class, which a growing empire demanded" (Wilkinson, 1964).

The Indian Administrative Service officers' major goal was land and revenue management, different operational goals have replaced it in the name of coordination and they miserably failed in their original assigned goals. The Indian Police Service officers' goal was law and order maintenance, they have failed miserably in it and frequently military services are used for it. The Indian Forest Service officers' goal was sustainable management of natural resources, resources have depleted to an insignificant level, miserable failure in management. Multiplications of operational goals augment bureaucratic inefficiency and goal conflict as a result of allocative inefficiency of demand. Operational goals fail to serve primary goals; operational goals of the present officer are challenged by successor officer goals. With the passage of time, new goals evolutions displace existing goals and the bureaucratic system is challenged. Only Indian Administrative Service officers systematically pursue its goals as they are in a commanding position with respect to resources. Any kind of inefficiency of resources for the Indian Administrative Service officers is shifted and reflected in other services.

Differentiation in the hierarchy has been created to maintain efficacy, itself give rise to sectional interests, each one protects own group needs, goals, and priorities. Each group creates own goals, which serve their own interests. Concept of differentiation (Pfeffer, 1978) powerful (IAS) has accrued power as a result of their proximity and control over resources, system look towards suppliers to gain resources. Differential allocation of jobs confronts subunits (IPS and IFS) in its specialist area with an uncertainty that is critical for government, and it copes in such a way as to buffer other subunits (IPS and IFS) from any resulting instability, then it can (IAS) widely influence decisions even beyond its own competence, Hinings (1974).

Ongoing bargaining and negotiations among the All India services, shifting coalitions of goals, impose their service rationalities on the given decision. The Indian Administrative Service officers make decisions regarding the destiny of the Indian Police Service officers and the Indian Forest Service officers, ultimately, they (IAS) will protect themselves only. At the same time, the Indian Police Service officers and the Indian Forest Service officers want to be involved with the decision process, because they (IPS and IFS) are affected by what is being decided by the Indian Administrative Service officers. They (IPS and IFS) see their chances with the politicians to influence the decision for the protection of their interests. A politician at top of it enjoys the game of power and authority played by the All India Service Officers. This process enhances the possibilities of complex political pressure in the decision process. In such competing interest groups setting, where each group vying for bargaining with a desire to influence the decision, the public interest gets relegated to dark or forgotten and a common person finds no place in it. Respective cadres of their services work as an institution for them and each service officers like to see the power base rolling in their camp only.

Political authorities are fully aware of service conflicts, they use power in the suppression of conflict, and decisions are postponed or never taken to perpetuate the concept of non-decision. Pervasive Indian Administrative Service officers at the top camouflage their interests and goals in such a way that the others do not recognize these. Hearts and minds of political authority are so manipulated and abetted by the hegemony of the Indian Administrative Service officers that they visualize things as desired and shown by the ruling Elite Service clan and their scheme of actions. Public welfare and social upliftment views get relegated, detrimental and hazardous decisions are left unquestioned. Political pressure dimensions infuse diverse interests in the decision process. Powerful political interests force the decision process to make a decision in advance or keep it off the agenda, Pettigrew (1973, 1985, 1987).

Slowly creeping awareness in a society bound to generate conflicts in the larger sections of the society. The genesis of conflict lies in the process of making functional organs of bureaucracy into dysfunctional, with a motive to monopolize the power by the Indian Administrative Service officers. This inherently inequitably power monopolization by the Indian Administrative Service officers has serious ramifications over the society. Exploitative economic interests of various services groups are bound to give rise to inter-service conflicts; in due course of time reflected as an inter-class rivalry. Quinn (1980), Heller et al. (1988) studied the step by step actions progress and sequence in the achievement of goals and objectives in the decision process. Butler et al. (1993) worked on the achievement of coherence intentions by paying attention to inspiration, judgment, and computation factors. The outcome of any decision will have its relation with part four of the book, system-related variables of political pressure operating upon the decision-making process of the All India Services Officers.

2.4. System Decision Constraints

Senior/junior relations, service working environment, performance evaluation, transfer posting policy, promotion policy, punishment policy, rules and regulations, law, rewards, and resource availability create space (leverage) in the decision-making process. The All India Services Officers, who cultivate political connections, for them the outcome of the decision has no negative impact on their performance evaluation. This fact motivates the All India Services Officers to accept political pressure. Where information about the decision outcomes never reaches up to top bosses, this facilitates the acceptability of political pressure for the All India Services Officers.

Choices available in the decision are preferred to own goals/interests, individual All India Services Officer assessment that pleasure of the politician may help him in the achievement of own goals, extended tenure or posting protection help in multiplying rewards, which influence the All India Services Officers to accept pressure in the decision. The Indian Administrative Service officers get a higher degree of support from seniors and colleagues, a higher sense of security influences them to mobilize pressure with higher intensity. On the other hand, in the case of the Indian Forest Service officers, seniors and colleagues are highly critical and non-supportive, which reduce the quantum of pressure mobilization and acceptance by them.

Ambiguity in rules, regulations, procedures, and situational interpretation of the law makes it easy for the All India Services Officers to accept pressure in the decision. Lack of standardization in decision and absence of transparency allow inducement of pressure in the decision. Government bureaucratic system doesn't fix any deadline and time limits for the decisions, the All India Services Officers get plenty of time to manipulate decision suitable according to own needs. Frequent transfers on short tenures have encouraged the All India Services Officers to postpone difficult and risky decisions for the next incumbent. Why I should invite the wrath of the public and politicians by taking any decision; let me enjoy and exploit short tenure to maximize personal benefits. Let the next incumbent take hard decisions and so on continue to linger on.

Transfers are predictable along with the outcome of the decision, then why take any risk in the decision during the short tenure of posting. Public perceptions about bureaucracy go on changing, they perceive that bureaucracy has ignored or failed to protect public interests. The public has started behaving in a manner to exploit the system to their own advantage. Historically time hides merit inside the files, all-around chaotic situations prevail over the system. Seniority-based promotions and career progression generate own type of problems. Non-performer individual All India Services Officers do not take any controversial and challenging decision throughout their service career, but still, they get their promotions in time. Due to this situation, innovative All India Services Officers feel that why they should consider challenging decisions without any gain. Excessive security provided to the All India Services Officers has also killed the innovation and risk-taking in the decision. Rather it has worked in a reverse manner, those who worked and took a decision, suffered due to outcomes of the decision.

Any rationale and a merit-based decision will block supply channels of politicians and senior officers; they eagerly wait for the appropriate moments to harass and surrogate such upright individual All India Services Officer. Those All India Services Officers, who take unrealistic and insulated decisions ensuring that supply channels remain connected up to top-level (vertically and horizontally, omni directions), everyone stands gainer (win-win situation), such officers get unlimited support from all quarters in the system. In spite of all the immoral and unfair practice used in the decision, people call such officers as good officer and shower every undue privilege on such officers. This type of behavior from people motivates pliable officers and coerces upright officers to follow the same kind of flexibility in the decision. The All India Services Officers rarely follow precedents of his predecessor. For an individual officer ghost of his unpleasant past decisions continuously haunt his present choices. Similarly, any kind of past commitments with politicians or commitments committed at the time transfer or posting become a constraint for present options and possibilities in the decision.

The All India Services Officers present cadre state and cultural background and lineage influence the decision-making process, e.g. decision taken by an officer from Haryana will differ from the officer from Nagaland in similarly placed situations, as both will have different perceptions about the same problem, different logic and approach will be adopted in analysis and different rationality in thinking will be used. According to individual background, the All India Services Officers' beliefs, attitude, perceptions, orientation, the importance of rationality, faith in a collective decision, preferences for the abilities in subordinates to solve the problems are related to the All India Services Officers cultural lineages. Probably, an All India Services Officer from Gujarat state will value more collaboration, conventionality, and transparency; whereas an officer from eastern India will believe in accepting the situations as they are, as part of the influence of early life culture.

A public utility must dominate decisions. The All India Services Officers' decisions must be public utility-oriented, consistent with public welfare goals. Decisions must be efficiently and timely delivered and utility for the whole segment of the population. Decisions must protect the rights and liberty of all citizens and impartial in nature. Decisions must protect the interests of underprivileged, under-represented, and lesser powerful persons in society. Decisions taken by the All India Services Officers must be acceptable to the whole society (all societal segments).

2.5. Decision Evaluation

The bureaucratic system has been molded like that at any stage cost of decision making by the All India Services Officers is hidden. If every step-in decision-making process has been defined and certain cost could have been attached to it. Fear of that cost could have put pressure on the mind of the All India Services Officers to adhere to system norms and work on merit. A decision taken by the All India Services Officers may extend benefit the worth of millions of rupees to an individual, but bureaucratic systems do not assign any cost to it. Since no cost has been attached to any step and any stage of the decision-making process in the bureaucratic system, so, every employee behaves casually towards the government and extract maximum for self.

For effective evaluation of the decision-making process, all the variables or factors affecting the speed of decision-making have to be considered and evaluated systematically. Proper evaluation is only possible when the decision-making process is arranged in a sequential nature. The present decision-making process has not incorporated and kept any scope for learning and feedback in the decision. The bureaucratic system has not brought out and delineated decision objectives, which make evaluation impossible. Colonially created bureaucratic system provides a significant role to status in the decision and high-status consciousness does not allow any kind of evaluation to a decision taken by those power holders. The decision-making process must have inbuilt special pressure, values, beliefs, socially acceptable actions for the evaluation. Each and every personal need of the All India Services Officers must be evaluated.

The decision-making process by the All India Services Officers is complex and has a variety of paradigms and perspectives. The process of decision is dotted with question marks, it starts with the problem identification, initiated by a search for solutions and their consequences, computation of alternative choices for a solution with their acceptability and feasibility in conflicting interests. Implementation of the decision is done with authorization and negotiation, which do not allow evaluation. "Decision imply commitment action, there are situations, where actions are taken without decisions having been made", S.J. Miller et al. (1996).

In public administration, it must be the public, who should monitor the decisions in an indirect way. In what way political pressure has influenced the choices made by the All India Service Officers, how they have arrived at decision? How much information is necessary, who influences whom, how disagreements were resolved, what procedures are used (Apple White, 1965). The All India Service Officers are in a position, where they allocate resources, exercise power, distribute welfare largesse, distribute benefits of economic activities, and legal implications to maximize the value of utility functions and policy interpretation for maximization of objective functions. They have to instantly compute how much to appease, how much to manipulate, to what extent to compromise, at what time a decision be announced, what will be the direction of the decision, and choices available at any point if time is given circumstances, etc. Decisions taken in public administration are bound to mold the lives of people living within its sphere, have wider and larger implications on the masses, even if, such decisions are directed for individual interests or goal maximization. Ramifications and implications of the decisions continue to accrue over a long period of time in the future. All these make it difficult to evaluate.

Decision-maker behavior under conditions of uncertainties or certainties will have bearing on the performance of the officer. Various sets of techniques cannot describe the different approaches for the decision process to address the principles and thoughts conflict in the officer behavior. Individual All India Services Officers are motivated, goal-oriented, well-informed, intelligent, strong in computation power, enshrined in power, they can make rational choices among the available alternatives at a given point of time in the decision process. At the same time, the individual officer is actuated by self-interests and maximize own utility functions. Officers are self-goal directed; they devise the most efficient means to optimize their goals in the garb of ensuring political pressure and try to show equilibrium in the system. The individual officer's behavior is goal-directed; when making rational choices between competing goals, or between competing means of achieving these goals, will always choose that alternative that best serves the individual's own interests (P.M. Jackson, 1983; Collard, 1983; Sen, 1976). This makes evaluation a difficult task to undertake.

Rational choice is that, which can "be explained in terms of some preference relation consistent with the revealed preference definition, that is, if all his choices can be explained as the choosing of the most preferred alternatives with respect to postulated preference relation", Sen (1976). Human frailties and demands from both within and outside the department limit the degree of rationality, which can be employed. The decision process of these officers is full of conflicting constraints, much time is not available for the evaluation of alternatives, and comparison, alternate utility choices becomes the limiting factor in the decision. Under mounting pressure, internal consistency of the officers, get reflected in line with inconsistencies and uncertainties preferences get modified accordingly. The choice is between self-interest and public interest, consequences of self-interest are valued higher than the public interest, and officers will go with the self-interests. Self-interests perpetuate due to lack of any evaluation process.

2.6. Political Pressure Impact on Decision: Evaluation and Summary

Swirling of the AISO decisions under political pressure, statistical analyses of different variables and research findings are succinctly summarized 2.6.1 to 2.6.14.7, the full narrative is mentioned in respective Units (here, summary is mentioned as decision evaluation and impact of pressure on the decision outcomes).

2.6.1. Demographic Characters and Impact on Decision

Statistical analyses result for 21 demographic characters, indicating how these variables speculate variance within individual officer behavior and create discontinuities while working in the decision-making process.

2.6.1.1. Type of Service More Amenable to Political Pressure: 46.1% of IAS officers, 29.7% of IPS officers, and 24.2% of IFS officers are amenable to political pressure in the decision-making process. Results are highly significant at a 0.01 level of significance.

2.6.1.2. Method of Recruitment: 69.3% of IAS officers, 68.4% of the All India Services Officers, 74% of IPS officers and 38% of IFS officers are of the view that promoted officers are amenable to political pressure in the decision-making process.

2.6.1.3. Position (Level) in Hierarchy: 66.0% of the IFS officers, 58.1% of the IAS, and 51.6% of the IPS officers think that top-level officers in the hierarchy accept pressure more readily in their decision-making process.

2.6.1.4. Length of Service: 73.3% of the Indian Police Service officers, 67.1% of the Indian Administrative Service officers, and 53.6% of the Indian Forest Service officers are amenable to accept political pressure in decision working in that of the super time scale of pay. Association of the length of service with the decision-making process is significant at 0.003, level of significance in Pearson Chi-Square analyses.

2.6.1.5. Cadre of the Officer: 40.2% of the All India Services Officers, 61.8% of the Indian Administrative Service officers, 49.9% of the Indian Forest Service officers, and 41.4% of the Indian Police Service officers are of the view that officers in outside Cadre State are amenable to accept political pressure in the decision. Our results are highly significant at 0.001, level of significance in Chi-square.

2.6.1.6. Regional Background: 28.4% officers from south India, 25% from north India, 16% from east India, 13.4% from northeast India, and 8.6% from central and west Indians accept political pressure in the decision. Association of regional background with decision-making process is significant at 0.005, level of significance in Pearson Chi-square analyses.

2.6.1.7. Community Background: 52.9% of the Indian Forest Service officers, 42.3% of the Indian Police Service officers, and 38.0% of the Indian Administrative Service officers from the general category are amenable to accept political pressure in the decision. The IAS, IPS and IFS officers think that 57.7%, 54.5% and 42.5% of officers of scheduled castes and scheduled tribes accept the pressure in the decision process. Rho value of –0.2 indicates significant negative relations with 0.01, level of significance.

2.6.1.8. Family Economic Background: In the combined rich and upper-middle-class category, 42.3% of the All India Services Officers, 61.4% of Indian Administrative Service officers, 75.5% of Indian Police Service officers, and 43% for the Indian Forest Service officers accept political pressure in the decision-making process; Pearson Chi-square results are significant with a significance level of 0.000.

2.6.1.9. Marital Status and Sex: 92.2% of respondents say male officers are more prone to accept pressure in the decision. IPS officer's results are 100% with the male.

2.6.1.10. Profession of Spouse: In the combined business and entrepreneur professions category, 51.2% of spouses exert pressure on their sweethearts to accept political pressure in the decision-making process. Among the three All India Services, this combined pressure (business and entrepreneur) exerted in the decision process is 67.1%, on the IAS, 63.4% on the IPS, and 26.1% on the IFS officers.

2.6.1.11. Family Member Attitude: 62.7% of the All India Services Officers, 90.8% of the Indian Forest Service officers, 66.7% of the Indian Administrative Service officers, and 39.6% of the Indian Police Service officers get influenced by the attitude of spouse in acceptance of political pressure which has an impact on the decision taken by them. Pearson Chi-square results are significant with a 0.000, level of significance.

2.6.1.12. Number of Children: The score for the respective three services is 59.8% for the Indian Police Service officers, 42.5% for the Indian Administrative Service officers, and 41.4% for the Indian Forest Service officers.

2.6.1.13. to 2.6.1.15. Education of Self, Spouse, and Parents: Our results are highly significant at 0.001, level of significance in Chi-Square. 33.6% of the All India Services Officers with postgraduate qualifications, 51.3% of the Indian Administrative Service with technical and management qualifications have an impact on the decision by acceptance of political pressure. Educational qualifications of the All India Services Officers show a good relationship with their birthplace; 34.26% of postgraduate are amenable to accept political pressure in the decision process. Results for the postgraduate qualification of spouse and parents indicate that 42.7% and 39.4% of them accept political pressure in the decision-making process.

2.6.1.16. to 2.6.1.20. Domicile of Self, Spouse, and Parents: In the combined urban and semi-urban category 90.2% of the Indian Administrative Service officers, 79.2% of the Indian Forest Service officers, and 67.8% of the Indian Police Service officers from urbanite culture accept political pressure. Pearson Chi-square results are significant at 0.000, level of significance.

Place of birth of parents and amenability to political pressure results indicates that 66.2% of combined urbanite parents influence an individual officer in acceptance of pressure in the decision. Statistically, analyses on Chi-square indicate that results are highly significant with a significance level of 0.001.

Results indicate that 94.4% of the Indian Administrative Service officers, 78.6% of the Indian Police Service officers, and 70.9% of the Indian Forest Service officers feel that urbanite residence of parents makes them accept political pressure in the decision. Chi-Square results are highly significant at 0.001, significance level.

Combine urban and semi-urban results indicate that 80.3% of the Indian Administrative Service officers, 78.5% of the Indian Police Service officers and 70.8% of the Indian Forest Service officers feel that urbanite spouse influences the All India Services Officers to accept the pressure. Pearson's correlation negative value of –0.2 shows is significant at 0.002, level of significance.

Results for combined urban and semi-urban indicate that 92.3% of the Indian Forest Service officers, 91.7% of the Indian Administrative Service officers and 82.3% of the Indian Police Service officers who got their education in urban areas after matriculations accept political pressure and get impact on the decision.

2.6.2. Locus of Control

2.6.2.1. Locus: 46.3% of the Indian Administrative Service officers and 38.1% of the Indian Police Service officers, 27.3% of the Indian Forest Service officers have a general feeling (rank of 4) that they can determine the direction of the decision.

2.6.2.2. Career: 40.3% of the Indian Police Service officers strongly feel that their career depends upon them only; 35.6% of the Indian Administrative Service officers and 31.3% of the Indian Forest Service officers show internality control in career.

2.6.2.3. Efficiency: 34.4% of the All India Services Officers strongly felt that success or failure is related to the efforts mobilized by them, 36.6% of the Indian Police Service officers, 36.6% of the Indian Administrative Service officers and 33% of the Indian Forest Service officers think that same way under internal control.

2.6.2.4. Rewards: 35.9% of the All India Services Officers generally realize that they are responsible for what they are getting out of the system, 40.6% of the Indian Police Service officers, 33.7% of the Indian Forest Service officers and 32.9% of the Indian Administrative Service officers feel this way.

2.6.2.5. Advancement: Internal locus of control, 38.3% of the All India Services Officers strongly thought that their advancement and promotions in their service are related to their own abilities and efforts. 42% of the Indian Administrative Service officers, 39.3% of the Indian Police Service officers and 34.7% of the Indian Forest Service officers strongly felt that capability and own efforts determine their advancements.

2.6.2.6. Acceptability: 38.7% of the Indian Police Service officers, 38.6% of the Indian Administrative Service officers and 36.4% of the Indian Forest Service officers think that they have to strive hard to get their decision accepted in the department.

2.6.2.7. Influence: 52.8% of the Indian Police Service officers, 50.4 of the Indian Administrative Service officers and 38.4% of Indian Forest Service officers strongly think that because of their behavior people accept their influence.

2.6.3. Motivation

2.6.3.1. Economic Security: 70% of the Indian Administrative Service officers, 56.7% of the Indian Police Service officers, 50% of the Indian Forest Service officers consider financial security as an important motivator.

2.6.3.2. Retirement Benefits: 71.4% of Indian Administrative Service officers, 79.5% of Indian Police Service officers, 55.8% of the Indian Forest Service officers feel that retirement benefits motivate them in the decision process.

2.6.3.3. Status and Power: 90% Indian Administrative Service officers, 91.7% Indian Police Service officers, 73.2% Indian Forest Service officers status, power and desire to influence others is the most important factor to accept political pressure in the decision-making process.

2.6.3.4. Chances to Serve People: 44.3% Indian Administrative Service officers, 49.5% Indian Police Service officers, and 45.6% Indian Forest Service officers rank it lower ranks to serve people.

2.6.3.5. Freedom to Do Original Work: 35.7% Indian Administrative Service officers, 42.7% Indian Police Service officers, 20% Indian Forest Service officers show low concern for doing innovative original work.

2.6.3.6. Professional Competence: Mean value 6.96 for the Indian Administrative Service officers, 6.39 for the Indian Police Service officers and 5.41 for the Indian Forest Service officers with a standard deviation of 2.73, 2.71 and 2.80 for respective services show chances to demonstrate professional competence are not significant for the All India Services Officers.

2.6.3.7. Lower Responsibility: 80% Indian Administrative Service officers, 86.9% Indian Police Service officers, 73.4% Indian Forest Service officers do not want to own any responsibility.

2.6.3.8. Prestige and Reputation: 80% Indian Administrative Service officers, 89.7% Indian Police Service officers, 61% Indian Forest Service officers have shown prestige and reputation consciousness prevalent among them, which motivate them to accept political pressure in the decision-making process.

2.6.3.9. Financial and Salary Structure: 80% Indian Administrative Service officers, 78.1% Indian Police Service officers, 45.6% Indian Forest Service officers consider salary structure as a motivator.

2.6.3.10. Career Progression: The mean value is 4.0 for the Indian Administrative Service officers, 4.02 for the Indian Police Service officers and 5.27 for the Indian Forest Service officers with a standard deviation of 1.65, 1.4 and 2.30 for respective services. Timely promotions are significant for the All India Services Officers and any such denial or delay motivates the All India Services Officers to approach politicians to invite political pressure in the decision.

2.6.4. Lifestyle Orientation

2.6.4.1. Family and Close Relatives: 51.4% of the Indian Administrative Service officers have assigned it first preference with the first rank, 57.7% for the Indian Police Service officers and 28% Indian Forest Service officers as 1st rank in second preference shown concern for the family.

2.6.4.2. Occupational Activities: 40% of the Indian Administrative Service officers, 91% of the Indian Police Service officers, and 51% of the Indian Forest Service officers have assigned preference to professional activities and considered occupational activities as immaterial.

2.6.4.3. Socialization: 37.1% of Indian Administrative Service officers have ranked it at number one, 78.4% of the Indian Police Service officers have not shown interest in any such activities and ranked it 6th, 19% of the Indian Forest Service officers have considered it as the first option as third interesting preference.

2.6.4.4. Religion: 97.1% of the Indian Administrative Service officers, 97.9% of the Indian Police Service officers and 92.0% of the Indian Forest Service officers have not assigned any rank to religious activities.

2.6.4.5. Self-Improvement: 20% of the Indian Administrative Service officers have shown first preference with 1st rank, 11% Indian Forest Service officers ranked 3rd in first preference and 20.6% Indian Police Service officers, ranked it 2nd in first preference; to go for the course for self-improvement.

2.6.4.6. Recreation: 40% Indian Administrative Service officers ranked first in third preference; 44.3% Indian Police Service officers given it first ranking in second preference 11.0% Indian Forest Service officers have ranked third in first preference for recreational activities.

2.6.4.7. Friends and Acquaintances: 22.9% of the Indian Administrative Service officers have ranked it a second interesting area with 2nd rank, 44.3% Indian Police Service officers, ranked it first in second preference and 11% Indian Forest Service officers have ranked 3rd in first preference.

2.6.4.8. Reading and Writing: 92.9% of the Indian Administrative Service officers, 81.4% of the Indian Police Service officers, and 63% of the Indian Forest Service officers have not considered these activities in the first three ranks.

2.6.4.9. Spiritual and Physical Fitness: 35.1% of the Indian Police Service officers have considered physical fitness as 2nd interesting area, 14%of the Indian Forest Service officers have shown little interest in third preference and 92.9% of the Indian Administrative Service officers have no interest in their physical and spiritual fitness.

2.6.5. Behaviour

2.6.5.1. Honesty and Integrity: 32.4% of the Indian Administrative Service officers have ranked honesty at last 11th rank, 17.9% of the Indian Police Service officers have assigned honesty 1st rank, 52.4% of the Indian Forest Service officers have assigned it first rank.

2.6.5.2. Professional Competence: 28.8% of the Indian Administrative Service officers have considered this at 6th rank, 25.3% of the Indian Police Service officers have ranked it to last, and 25.2% of the Indian Forest Service officers have assigned it first rank preference in their decision.

2.6.5.3. Good Mannerism: 24.3% of the Indian Administrative Service officers have assigned it 10th rank. 14.7% of the Indian Police Service officers have put it 5th rank and 20.8% of the Indian Forest Service officers have given it 9th rank.

2.6.5.4. Caste/Religion/Region: 75.8% of the Indian Police Service officers and 64.8% of the Indian Administrative Service officers have assigned it 12th rank. 41.0% of the Indian Forest Service officers have considered it at 11th rank.

2.6.5.5. Sympathetic: 49.5% of the Indian Police Service officers and 41.1% of the Indian Administrative Service officers gave it 9th rank and 18.8% of the Indian Forest Service officers at 1st rank for sympathetic manners.

2.6.5.6. Transparency and Straight Forwardness: 25.3% of Indian Police Service officers ranked it 10th, 28.8% of the Indian Administrative Service officers and 17.7% of the Indian Forest Service officers have ranked it 3rd important aspect in the decision.

2.6.5.7. Helping Attitude: 31.1% of the Indian Administrative Service officers ranked it 8th, 23.2% of the Indian Police Service officers ranked 5th and 22.4% of the Indian Forest Service officers have assigned ranked it 4th.

2.6.5.8. Political Affiliation: 25.7% of the Indian Administrative Service officers ranked it 7th, 20.2% of the Indian Police Service officers ranked it 6th and 45.2% of the Indian Forest Service officers have ranked it at 11th rank.

2.6.5.9. Devotion to Duty: 41.1% of the Indian Police Service officers and 32.4% of the Indian Administrative Service officers have given it 1st rank. 17.2% of the Indian Forest Service officers have ranked it 3rd important factor in the decision.

2.6.5.10. Politeness: 33.8% of the Indian Administrative Service officers ranked it 5th, 26.3% of the Indian Police Service officers ranked it 3rd and 22.9% of the Indian Forest Service officers have ranked it 8th.

2.6.5.11. Behaviour with Others: 32.4% of the Indian Administrative Service officers have ranked as 2nd, 33.7% of the Indian Police Service officers have ranked it 4th and 16% of the Indian Forest Service officers have ranked it 5th.

2.6.5.12. Team Work: 24.3% of the Indian Administrative Service officers have given teamwork 4th rank. 20% of the Indian Police Service officers have ranked it 4th. 22.8% of the Indian Forest Service officers have considered it for 9th rank.

2.6.6. Risk Management

2.6.6.1. Affiliation: 33.7% of the Indian Police Service officers and 30.1% of the Indian Administrative Service officers have ranked it at first and 24.3% of the Indian Forest Service officers have assigned it 2nd rank option to approach their friends and seniors in case of risk.

2.6.6.2. Control: 35.1% of the Indian Police Service officers and 26% of the Indian Administrative Service officers with 5th rank think that they seek help from the rules and orders, whereas, 28.2% of Indian Forest Service officers stick to rules and orders.

2.6.6.3. Expert Influence: 50.5% of the Indian Police Service officers refer the matter for expert advice; 41.15% of the Indian Administrative Service officers and 36.9% of the Indian Forest Service officers with a rank of 3rd seek expert help.

2.6.6.4. Dependency: 39.7% of the Indian Administrative Service officers, 29.5% of the Indian Police Service officers, and 31% of the Indian Forest Service officers depend on their immediate seniors in crisis.

2.6.6.5. Extension: 28.8% of Indian Administrative Service officers ranked it 3rd, 47.5% of Indian Forest Service officers ranked it last, 30.5% of the Indian Police Service officers have ranked it at 5th importance.

2.6.6.6. Achievement: 53.8% of the Indian Police Service officers and 42.5% of the Indian Administrative Service officers also have ranked it 6th rank and 37% of the Indian Forest Service officers have indicated the first preference for achievement in the time of risk.

2.6.7. Innovations

2.6.7.1. Expert Influence: 31.9% of the Indian Administrative Service officers ranked it 3rd, 24.2% of Indian Police Service officers ranked 1st and 27.8% of the Indian Forest Service officers have given it last and 9th rank.

2.6.7.2. Custom Influence: 35.65% of the Indian Administrative Service officers and 29.5% of the Indian Police Service officers have ranked it 5th and 15.8% of the Indian Forest Service officers have assigned it 4th rank showing moderate reliance on customary influence in innovations.

2.6.7.3. Imagination: 38.4% of the Indian Administrative Service officers ranked it 6th, 23.1% of the Indian Police Service officers ranked 7th and 24.8% of the Indian Forest Service officers have ranked its 1st rank.

2.6.7.4. Control Influence: 32.9% of the Indian Administrative Service officers and 28.4% of the Indian Police Service officers have also ranked this at 1st rank, 21% of the Indian Forest Service officers have assigned 6th rank.

2.6.7.5. Dependency Influence: 32.9% Indian Administrative Service officers ranked it 2nd, 29.5% Indian Police Service officers ranked it 2nd, 18.2% Indian Forest Service officers ranked it 2nd in showing dependency influence.

2.6.7.6. Confidence Influence: 42.5% of the Indian Administrative Service officers, 31.6% of the Indian Police Service officers support overall rank of 4th and 19.8% of the Indian Forest Service officers have ranked it at 2nd bringing moderate to high reliance on confidence.

2.6.7.7. Achievement Influence: 24.7% of the Indian Administrative Service officers ranked it 7th, 17.6% of the Indian Police Service officers have ranked 8th and 18.8% of the Indian Forest Service officers have ranked it 1st.

2.6.7.8. Affiliation Influence: 28.8% of the Indian Administrative Service officers, 20% of the Indian Forest Service officers have shown 8th rank and 20% of the Indian Police Service officers have assigned 7th rank.

2.6.7.9. Extension Influence: 28.8% of the Indian Administrative Service officers, 20% of the Indian Forest Service officers ranked it 9th and 29.7% of the Indian Police Service officers assigned it 9th rank.

2.6.8. Conflict Management

2.6.8.1. Negotiation: 41.5% of the Indian Police Service officers gave it 1st rank, 25% of the Indian Administrative Service officers have ranked it at first priority and 41.2% of the Indian Forest Service officers have ranked it at 7th priority to oblige politicians in the decision-making process.

2.6.8.2. Withdrawal: 42.6% of the Indian Forest Service officers, 30.6% of the Indian Administrative Service officers and 29% of the Indian Police Service officers ranked withdrawal approach.

2.6.8.3. Resignation: 44.4% of the Indian Administrative Service officers do not like to intervene in the conflicting situation, 25.3% of the Indian Police Service officers have ranked it 3rd and 28.2% of the Indian Forest Service officers have ranked it 4th.

2.6.8.4. Confrontation: 41.1% of the Indian Administrative Service officers and 37.9% of the Indian Police Service officers have ranked this at 7th and 32% of the Indian Forest Service officers have expressed their will at 1st rank.

2.6.8.5. Arbitration: 39.2% of the Indian Forest Service officers, 27.4% of the Indian Administrative Service officers have ranked it 2nd and 23.9% of the Indian Police Service officers have ranked it 7th.

2.6.8.6. Compromise: 27.2% of the Indian Forest Service officers have ranked it 3rd. 26% of the Indian Administrative Service officers and 19.6% of the Indian Police Service officers have ranked 4th rank.

2.6.8.7. Appeasement: 39% of the Indian Forest Service officers have ranked 7th, 31.5% of the Indian Administrative Service officers ranked at 5th and 19.6% of the Indian Police Service officers think it worth 4th rank.

2.6.9. Sources of Pressure and Impact on Decision

2.6.9.1. Chief Minister/Prime Minister: 69.15 of the Indian Administrative Service officers and 69% of the Indian Police Service officers get political pressure for this source frequently sometimes in the decision-making process, whereas 37.54% of the Indian Forest Service officers get political pressure sometimes.

2.6.9.2. Center or State Ministers: 62.5% of the Indian Administrative Service officers get political pressure from Centre or State Ministers always to mostly in the decision-making process. 62.5% of the Indian Police Service officers get political pressure mostly in the decision. 66.7% of the Indian Forest Service officers come across political pressure from the Centre or State Minister sometimes to frequently in the decision.

2.6.9.3. Member of Parliament: 76.3% of the Indian Administrative Service officers get political pressure from Member of Parliament mostly to frequently in the decision-making process. 69.2% of the Indian Forest Service officers and 64.9% of the Indian Police Service officers come across political pressure sometimes to frequently from the Member of Parliament in the decision process.

2.6.9.4. Member Legislative Council/Member Legislative Assembly: 83.1% of the Indian Administrative Service officers get political pressure always mostly from the Member Legislative Council/Member Legislative Assembly in the decision-making process. 76% of the Indian Police Service officers and 79.5% of the All India Services Officers get the political pressure frequently to always from Member Legislative Council/Member Legislative Assembly in the decision. 77.1% of the Indian Forest Service officers get political pressure from Member Legislative Council/Member Legislative Assembly frequently, sometimes, and mostly in the decision.

2.6.9.5. District Level Politician/Zila Parishad Members: 74.9% of the All India Services Officers, 81.6% of the Indian Administrative Service officers and 80.9% of the Indian Police Service officers get political pressure in the decision-making process always to frequently from the District Level Politician/Zila Parishad Members. 68.3% of the Indian Forest Service officers get political pressure mostly to sometimes from District Level Politician/Zila Parishad Members in the decision process.

2.6.9.6. Block Level Politicians/Block Samiti: 57.4% of the All India Services Officers, 70.4% of the Indian Police Service officers, 55.7% of the Indian Forest Service officers and 57% of the Indian Administrative Service officers get mostly to frequently political pressure from Block Level Politicians/Block Samiti, which has an impact on the decision process.

2.6.9.7. Village Heads/Village Level Workers: 61.4% of the All India Services Officers, 62.1% of the Indian Police Service officers, 51.6% of the Indian Forest Service officers and 73.1% of the Indian Administrative Service officers get always to frequently political pressure from Village Level Politicians, which has an impact on the decision process.

2.6.9.8. Power Brokers/Touts/Musclemen: 77.4% of the Indian Administrative Service officers, 71.6% of the Indian Police Service officers, 38.4% of the Indian Forest Service officers and 61.9% of the All India Services Officers get political pressure always to frequently from the Power Brokers/touts/musclemen in their decision process.

2.6.9.9. Communication Media: 79.4% of the Indian Administrative Service officers, 64.3% of the Indian Police Service officers and 54.5% of the Indian Forest Service officers get pressure from communication media mostly to sometimes to pass on the impact on the decision process.

2.6.9.10. Hidden Financier: 84.6% of the Indian Administrative Service officers 72.9% of the Indian Police Service officers and 20.4% of the Indian Forest Service officers get pressure always to frequently from hidden financiers which has an impact on the decision-making process.

2.6.10. Areas/Points of Political Pressure in Decision Process

The highest total score for transfer and posting among all 76 variables indicates that this area gets maximum political pressure to have the greatest impact on the decision-making process.

2.6.10.1. Political Pressure in Transfer Decisions: 70.1% of the Indian Administrative Service officers, 40.6% of the Indian Forest Service officers and 46.1% of total All India Services Officers receive political pressure always to influence the transfers' related decisions. Pearson Chi-square results with a '0.000' level of significance indicate a good association of transfer with the decision-making process.

2.6.10.2. Political Pressure in Postings Decisions: Mean and modal value of 4, clearly indicates that most often political pressure influences the decision pertaining to postings. 37.9% of the Indian Police Service officers, 25.4% of the Indian Administrative Service officers and 21.4% of the Indian Forest Service officers are most often influenced by political pressure while taking decisions for postings.

2.6.10.3. Political Pressure in Recruitment Decisions: Most often and always combined score shows that 70.3% of the Indian Forest Service officers, 67.8% of the Indian Administrative Service officers and 64.5% of the Indian Police Service officers come across political pressure while making decisions for recruitment. Pearson Chi-square results show a good association with the decision-making process at the '0.01' level of significance.

2.6.10.4. Political Pressure in Resource Allocation Decisions: 79.1% of the Indian Police Service officers, 63.3% of the Indian Administrative Service officers and 32.6% of the Indian Forest Service officers come across political pressure rarely to sometimes in decision making for resource allocation. 0.000, level of significance in Chi-square results indicate a good association of resource allocation variable with the decision-making process.

2.6.10.5. Political Pressure in Rewards: 75.9% of the Indian Police Service officers, 61.4% of the Indian Forest Service officers and 57.8% of the Indian Administrative Service officers get influenced frequent to sometimes by political pressure in the decision-making process while distributing rewards. Pearson Chi-square 0.000 level of significance indicates that rewards related decisions are significantly related to political pressure.

2.6.10.6. Political Pressure in Punishment Decisions: 85.5% of the Indian Police Service officers, 76.6% of the All India Services Officers, 72.7% of the Indian Administrative Service officers and 68.3% of the Indian Forest Service officers are influenced by political pressure frequently to sometimes while taking decisions for the punishments. Pearson Chi-square results are significant at 0.003 level of significance, which shows the good association of political pressure in decision with the punishment.

2.6.10.7. Political Pressure in Promotion Decisions: 69.7% of the Indian Police Service officers, 64.3% of the Indian Administrative Service officers and 62% of the Indian Forest Service officers get influenced most often to frequently by political pressure in decisions pertaining to promotions. Pearson Chi-square results are significant at 0.03, a level of significance indicating a good association of political pressure in the decision-making process for promotions.

2.6.10.8. Rule, Regulations and Procedures in Decision: 87.1% of the All India Services Officers, 99.2% of the Indian Police Service officers, 72.5% of the Indian Forest Service officers and 83% of the Indian Administrative Service officers' decisions are getting influenced by political pressure frequently to rarely in the manipulation of rules, regulations, and procedures.

2.6.10.9. Political Pressure in Policy-related Decisions: 77% of the Indian Police Service officers, 48.9% of the Indian Administrative Service officers and 63.9% of the Indian Forest Service officers are influenced by political pressure frequently to sometimes while taking policy-related decisions. Pearson Chi-square results indicate a good association of political pressure in policy with the decision-making process and are significant with a 0.000 level of significance.

2.6.10.10. Political Pressure in Change of Law Decisions: 94.5% of the Indian Police Service officers, 83.9% of the Indian Administrative Service officers, 65.4% of the Indian Forest Service officers and 82.7% of the All India Services Officers are influenced sometimes to frequent by political pressure for decisions pertaining to change of Law and Acts. Results are significant with Pearson Chi-square analyses showing '0.000' level of significance and showing a good relationship of the decision-making process with political pressure for a change of Law and Acts.

2.6.10.11. Political Pressure in Demure in Decision Process: Demur in the decision process has a good association with the decision-making process as shown by the Pearson Chi-square results, which are significant at the '0.000' level of significance. The highest score indicates that 37.4% of the All India Services Officers, 51.2% of the Indian Police Service officers and 33.3% of the Indian Forest Service officers 31.3% of the Indian Administrative Service officers are influenced by political pressure frequently to delay the decision process.

2.6.10.12. Political Pressure in Decisions for Development Works: 57.7% of the Indian Forest Service officers, 21.6% of the Indian Police Service officers and 57.6% of the Indian Administrative Service officers are influenced most often to frequent by political pressure while taking decisions pertaining to development works. Pearson Chi-square results are significant with a '0.000' level of significance. Political pressure for development work shows good association with the decision-making process.

2.6.10.13. Political Pressure in Crime-related Decisions: 62.8% of the All India Services Officers, 75.4% of the Indian Police Service officers and 55.1% of the Indian Administrative Service officers are influenced by political pressure always to most often in crime-related decisions. Pearson Chi-square 0.000 level of significance indicates a good association of political pressure in crime handling with the decision-making process.

2.6.10.14. Political Pressure in Training and Tours Decisions: 50% of the Indian Administrative Service officers and 22.8 % of the Indian Forest Service officers' decisions are influenced always to mostly by political pressure for recommending persons of political choice for tours and training. Pearson Chi-square 0.000 level of significance shows a good association of training and tours with the decision-making process.

2.6.10.15. Political Pressure in Decisions for Social Issues: 65.7% of the All India Services Officers, 74.5% of the Indian Administrative Service officers 70.2% of the Indian Police Service officers and 51% of the Indian Forest Service officers are influenced by political pressure sometimes to frequently while taking decisions for social issues. Results are significant with Pearson Chi-square 0.000 level of significance. This shows a good association of social issues with the decision-making process.

2.6.11. Modes and Forms of Political Pressure in Decisions

Politicians' control over public servants has been ranked as first and abuse of position and authority by the politicians is the second most important mode for exerting political pressure in the decision-making process. Political pressure through member citizenry is the last mode for exerting political pressure. Rankings mean values and standard deviations results for the seven most important modes of political pressure have been discussed below.

2.6.11.1. Politician Control over Public Servants: Our research results indicate that politician control over public servants is the first and most important mode of pressure commonly used by politicians to influence decisions. 62.7% of the Indian Administrative Service officers, 62.5% of the Indian Police Service officers and 58.5% of the Indian Forest Service officers' decisions are influenced by virtue of politician control over them as the major source of political pressure. Pearson Chi-square results show a good association of politician control over the bureaucratic system with the decision process at 0.01, level of significance.

2.6.11.2. Political Pressure by Abuse of Position and Authority: Abuse of position and authority by politicians has been rated as second most common mode for exerting political pressure on the decision-making process by AISO. 93.7% of the Indian Police Service officers, 90.5% of the Indian Administrative Service officers and 59% of the Indian Forest Service officers consider that politicians abuse his position and authority to influence the decision-making process. Abuse of position by the politician in the decision process shows a strong association at the '0.000' level of significance as shown by the Pearson Chi-Square.

2.6.11.3. Political Pressure by Bureaucratic System Seniors: 83.3% of the Indian Forest Service officers, 67.6% of the Indian Administrative Service officers and 64.6% of the Indian Police Service officers' decisions are influenced by political pressure exerted through the bureaucratic system and their seniors. This mode has been ranked third most important mode among all the 22 modes. Pearson Chi-square 0.000 level of significance indicates good association pressure through seniors in the bureaucratic system with the decision-making process.

2.6.11.4. Political Pressure through Power Brokers: 65.2% of the All India Services Officers, 71.1% of the Indian Forest Service officers, 65.6% of the Indian Police Service officers and 58.1% of the Indian Administrative Service officers' decisions are not influenced by political pressure through power brokers. This is having been considered as the fourth most important mode of political pressure exerted on the decision-making process.

2.6.11.5. Political Pressure through Political Groups/Activists: 59.5% of the Indian Forest Service officers, 29.7% of the Indian Administrative Service officers and 34.4% of the Indian Police Service Officers' decisions are influenced by political pressure in the decision-making process through political groups/activists. Political groups and activist mode has got overall fifth rank among all 22 modes of pressure. Pearson Chi-square significance level of 0.000, shows a good relationship of this mode of political pressure with the decision process. The strength of this correlation is shown by the Spearman correlation (Rho) value of 0.2 with a 0.002, level of significance.

2.6.11.6. Political Pressure by Politician Supremacy in Decision Process: 59.1% of the All India Services Officers realize this mode of pressure as an important mode of pressure and ranked it at sixth overall rank. 60% of the Indian Administrative Service officers, 59.5% of the Indian Forest Service officers and 58.3% of the Indian Police Service Officers' decisions are influenced due to politician supremacy in the decision-making process.

2.6.11.7. Political Pressure through Known and Friendly Bureaucrats: Pearson Chi-square results show a good association of this mode of political pressure with the decision-making process at '0.000' level of significance. 46.4% of the Indian Forest Service officers, 40.5% of the Indian Administrative Service officers and 33.3% of the Indian Police Service officers have considered this as an important mode of political pressure used by the politician in the decision-making process which has an impact on decisions taken by AISO.

2.6.12. Reasons for Accepting Political Pressure in Decision

Research results are highly significant with all values of significance are less than 0.05. Strength of associations for different reasons towards accepting political pressure with the decision-making process, is also established by the Rho and R-values, which are highly significant. Out of 15 reasons studied in research seven groups most important reasons are discussed below.

2.6.12.1. Enhancement of Status and Decision: 98.5% of the Indian Administrative Service officers, 98% of the Indian Police Service officers and 67.5% of the Indian Forest Service officers (combine first three score of most important, very important and important) due to their desire for enhancing status they accept political pressure while making decisions. Pearson Chi-square results are highly significant at the '0.000' level of significance. Pearson's correlation and Spearman's correlation of '0.000' level of significance indicate a very strong correlation of enhancement of status with the decision.

2.6.12.2. Proximity to Politician Generate Information for Decision: 58.3% of the Indian Police Service officers, 14.1% of the Indian Forest Service officers and 56% of the Indian Administrative Service officers accept political pressure to develop proximity to a politician, which may generate information having an impact on the decision-making process. Pearson Chi-square results indicate that proximity to politicians generate information has a good association with the decision-making process.

2.6.12.3. Lust to Grab Power and Decision: Pearson Chi-square results show a good association of lust for power with the decision-making process and the results are significant with a 0.000 level of significance. The most important and very important combined evaluation shows that 84.5% of the Indian Administrative Service officers, 64.5% of the Indian Police Service officers and 55% of the Indian Forest Service accept political pressure in the decision-making process due to AISO lust for power.

2.6.12.4. Career Advancement and Decision: Combined score of three ranks; most important, very important and important show that 98.7% of the Indian Administrative Service officers, 99% of the Indian Police Service officers and 77.8% of the Indian Forest Service officers accept political pressure in the decision-making process for self-career advancement. Career advancement shows good association with the decision-making process as demonstrated by the Pearson Chi-square results.

2.6.12.5. To Secure Political Patronage and Decision: 41.7% of the All India Services Officers, 48% of the Indian Administrative Service officers, 20.5% of the Indian Forest Service officers and 56.3% of the Indian Police Service officers consider securing political patronage as the most important factor for acceptance of political pressure, which influences the decision-making process. Results are highly significant and the Pearson Chi-square indicates a good association of political patronage with the decision-making process. Pearson's correlation and Spearman correlation values are significant with 0.000, level of significance, and show good relation with the decision.

2.6.12.6. Security and Stability in Job/Least Disturbances: The All India Services Officers have ranked security and stability at sixth rank among different factors influencing the acceptability of political pressure in the decision. 93.2% of the Indian Administrative Service officers, 63.6% of the Indian Forest Service officers and 62.7% of the Indian Police Service officers consider security and stability in the job as very important in acceptance of political pressure in the decision process.

2.6.12.7. Avoid Conflicts in Decisions: Pearson Chi-square analyses indicate that there is a good association between the decision-making process and avoidance of conflict by the All India Services Officers. 38% of the All India Services Officers, 48.6% of the Indian Administrative Service officers, 21.6% of the Indian Forest Service officers and 44.8% of the Indian Police Service officers consider conflict avoidance as the most important factor for acceptance of political pressure in the decision process.

2.6.13. Cultural Milieu

19.1% of the All India Services Officers have ranked dominant ego and arrogance at first rank. Results of second rank, 14.2% of the All India Services Officers have assigned obsession with status at first rank.

2.6.13.1. Low Salary: 100% of the Indian Administrative Service officers' respondents have not considered low salaries an issue. 15.2% of the Indian Police Service officers and 12% of the Indian Forest Service officers have shown concern for a low salary.

2.6.13.2. Favouritism and Nepotism: 84.9% of the Indian Administrative Service officers and 97.8% of the Indian Police Service officers have not considered it an issue. 35.8% of the Indian Forest Service officers have shown concern for this issue.

2.6.13.3. Ego and Arrogance: 47.9% of the Indian Administrative Service officers, 40.2% of the Indian Police Service officers and 30.1% of Indian Forest Service officers assess this item as a serious problem.

2.6.13.4. Tenure Security: 19.1% of the Indian Administrative Service officers, 7.6% of the Indian Police Service officers and 29.6% of the Indian Forest Service officers have shown concern for this problem.

2. 6.13.5. Careerism: 30.1% of the Indian Administrative Service officers, 31.5% of the Indian Police Service officers and 16% of the Indian Forest Service officers have a feeling for too much careerism is a serious issue.

2.6.13.6. Status: 41.1% of the Indian Administrative Service officers, 42.4% of the Indian Police Service officers and 28.4% of the Indian Forest Service officers have shown status obsession.

2.6.13.7. Self Goals: 68.5% of the Indian Administrative Service officers, 43.5% of the Indian Police Service officers and 19.8% of the Indian Forest Service officers are influenced by self-goals in the decision-making process.

2.6.13.8. Political Interferences: 50.7% of the Indian Administrative Service officers evaluated it fourth problem, 70.2% of the Indian Police Service officers ranked it second, and 42% of the Indian Forest Service officers ranked it first problem of the system.

2.6.13.9. Lack of Devotion to Work: 81.5% of the Indian Police Service officers and the Indian Forest Service officers and 72.6% of the Indian Administrative Service officers do not consider it a problem.

2.6.13.10. Power and authority: 32.1% for the Indian Forest Service officers, 28.8% for the Indian Administrative Service officers and 27.2% for the Indian Police Service officers, who are seized with this issue.

2.6.13.11. Discrimination and Obstruction: 6.8% of Indian Administrative Service officers, 13.6% of the Indian Forest Service officers and 29.3% of the Indian Police Service officers feel this as a problem.

2.6.13.12. Political Opportunism: 44.9% of the Indian Administrative Service officers ranked it sixth, 53.7% of the Indian Police Service officers ranked it sixth and 29.6% of the Indian Forest Service officers have ranked it at fifth rank.

2.6.13.13. Immoral Behaviour: 100% of the Indian Administrative Service officers, 91.3% of the Indian Police Service officers and 85.2% of the Indian Forest Service officers do not consider it as a problem.

2.6.14. Workplace Environment

Mean values are 1.31 to 1.61 and standard deviation from 0.46 to 0.5, this indicates that maximum the All India Services Officers are not satisfied with the workplace environment.

2.6.14.1. Salary: 72.9% of the Indian Police Service officers, 71.6% of the Indian Administrative Service officers and 55.3% of the Indian Forest Service officers shown concern for salary.

2.6.14.2. Chances of Promotion: 54.9% of the Indian Administrative Service officers are satisfied with the present chances of the promotions. 68.9% of the Indian Forest Service officers and 54.9% of the Indian Police Service officers are not satisfied with the present chances of promotions.

2.6.14.3. Nature of Work: 56.3% of the Indian Administrative Service officers, 52.2% of the Indian Police Service officers and 51% of the Indian Forest Service officers feel satisfied with the present work done.

2.6.14.4. Interpersonal Relations: 52.9% of the Indian Administrative Service officers and 50.5% of the Indian Police Service officers are not satisfied with the present interpersonal relations. But the 55.2% of the Indian Forest Service officers feel satisfied with the present state of an interpersonal relationship.

2.6.14.5. Rules of Work: 76.7% of the Indian Police Service officers, 76.4% of the Indian Administrative Service officers and 58.8% of the Indian Forest Service officers feel satisfied with the rules of work.

2.6.14.6. Workplace Setting: 59.2% of the Indian Administrative Service officers and 62% of the Indian Police Service officers are feeling satisfied with the environment and workplace ambiance. But 57% of the Indian Forest Service officers are not satisfied with the working environment and workplace setting.

2.6.14.7. Conformity of Orders: 63.5% of the Indian Administrative Service officers and 60.4% of the Indian Police Service officers do not want confirmation for verbal. But 74.8% of the Indian Forest Service officers want that the superior officer or politicians must confirm any verbal order in writing.

Unit 3

Biographical Orientation and Amenability to Pressure

"Actions arising from clarity lead to efficiency and effectiveness...clarity gives peace of mind, and peace enhances the clarity. Peace of mind and clarity are the results of dedication and self-control of the responsible leader."—G. Narayana

"When one thoroughly dismisses all aspirations of the intellect and is satisfied in the self through the self, then is stable mind." *The Bhagavad Gita* 2.55

- *Individual Orientation*
- *Exploring Oneself in the System*
- *Analyses Results of Biographic Variance*
- *Service-Related*
- *Community, Social and Cultural Background*
- *Personal Characters*
- *Education Characters*
- *Early Background*

In this unit research analyses, results have been presented with respect to the individual officer biographic variables relationship with the decision-making process under political pressure and its impact on the outcome of decisions.

3.1. Individual Orientation

Individual All India Services Officers' biographical characters and personal orientation determines the handling of political pressure in the decision-making process. Individual officer desires induce oscillation in one's life. The amplitude of such oscillation invariably determines the composure and calmness of an individual mind, which decides the direction of individual actions in the decision. Internal discomforts and high oscillations sabotage the decision made by an individual officer. When materialistic temptations in self and family members generate goals of conflict for achievement, the self-destructive process derails the decision process. Failure in self-goal achievement induces failure complex in individual, and individual intensifies the efforts to meet own objectives. Individual officer personal orientation influences the extent and nature of handling of political pressure in the decision-making process.

An individual person is growing in a social system, watching the aura of power and flaunting arrogance of the All India Services Officers. Power and authority induced arrogant behavior of All India Service Officers in society to leave a traumatic impression and experience on an individual person. Thus, every individual person tends to develop own ideas towards power and devise own ways and means to defend self from the arrogance and such abusive power occurrences. Every individual person has inbuilt concern for self, family, service, society, and surrounding environment, where he is living and working. Present states of affairs automatically leave scars on an individual mind, personality, and growth. In the process, individuals find that many people are highly unreliable and the world is full of dangerous people. Individual devises ways and means to defend self only. Most of the persons tend to avoid any kind of trouble threats to self and family.

Individual officers show a desire to retain control over the situations and enhance the chances for self-involvement in the surrounding decisions. Non-fulfillment of desires generates inbuilt resentment in the individual. Any individual does not like unfavorable outcomes and tries to avoid, what to avoid and avoidance or pretension behavior dominant in the circumstances beyond own control. Initially, a person reflects a reactive responsive orientation and then responsive behavior. Ultimately, reactive orientation in an individual person becomes a habit. "Political culture is held to be the pattern of attitude towards the political system and its various parts, and the attitudes towards the role of the self in the system internalized in the cognition's, feeling and evaluations of its population", B.B. Khare (1974).

One has to appreciate the word 'self', every individual carries out computations according to self only, which cognition, in turn, is processed in the background of self-knowledge, situations, and conditions at that time of action. It is self-understanding, which equips an individual officer to deal with prevailing conditions in any decision. Individual self-confidence is crucial for the effectiveness of the individual officer in the decision-making process. The potential effectiveness and individual officer's competence are related to the self (Brockner, 1988).

Individual officers self-nurture the self-esteem in him, try to influence the situations in near surroundings. Self-esteem is a trait reflecting an individual's characteristic, effective evaluation, i.e. self-worth or self-liking, Gist and Mitchell (1992). Individual All India Services Officers handle the political pressure according to own self-esteem, which determines the individual efficacy in the decision-making process. "Self-efficacy refers to beliefs in one's capacities to mobilize the motivation, cognitive resources and courses of action to meet given situational demands," Wood and Bandura (1989).

The self-efficacy of an All India Services Officer will be related to the perceived capability of an individual to perform a given task. Decisions will not be static, new information will lead to a differential performance in the decision. Conceptually (McClelland and Winter, 1969), efficacy has a relation with goals, an individual officer's self-being will have a relation with his decisions and inherent initiative, and actions will be related to compliance achievements. Individual officer approach to solve the pressure problem in the decision will be related to avoidance behavior. An individual officer efficacy is the sense of adequacy and contributes to individual effectiveness in working for task related to own goals.

It is worthwhile and futile to study that, what will contribute maximum to individual efficacy. Different variables for study have been selected keeping this in mind. An All India Services Officer with high self-awareness will manage his strengths and weaknesses in a more effective manner and will produce better results. "Identity crisis has a direct effect on the people of developing areas; they are losing faith in their own potentialities", B.B. Khare (1974). Every individual officer shows serious concern for own identity among various services. Many individuals with proactive orientation feel that they can change things in the bureaucratic system through the decision-making process. Such persons will invariably determine own course of actions in the decision. A proactive person will not wait for any outside help or avoiding the problem, he will solve the problems within the available environmental setup. Individual officers with McCllend (1975) "activity inhibition" will work hard, he will not succumb to immediate gratification to some of his desires, he will be future-oriented and try to deliver a decision in that direction.

3.2. Exploring Oneself in the System

Many All India Services Officers are not aware of what they are, there is a need to explore oneself to study their handling of pressure in the decision. Luft and Ingham 1973, Johari Window can be used for this purpose.

	Known to self	Not known to self
Known to others	ARENA	BLIND
Not known to others	CLOSED	DARK

Arena: Arena is the public self, the officer is known himself and other persons who interacts with him, also know him, e.g. name, age, biographical characters.

Blind: Individual officer behavior and style of working, those others know but the concerned officer himself does not know the self, e.g. mannerism and behavior traits.

Closed: Officer is known to self, but not revealed to others, e.g. juniors standing, hierarchical decision behavior.

Dark: Not known to self and not known to others, inaccessible to both, really hypocrites.

Individual officer behavior in the decision-making process and handling of political pressure is also related to the personal background and factors associated with it. Some of such characters researched are sex of the officer, and marital status of the individual, the profession of the spouse, the number of children, and the attitude of the members of the family. These factors also influence the amenability of political pressure in the decision of an All India Services Officer. In the need of crisis individual officer repose owns faith in the closest member of his family and guidance provided by that factor influence the outcome of decisions taken by an individual officer.

Individual orientation and personal thinking mostly related to individual social-cultural and environmental belongingness, when an individual joins any service. Individual officer economic background and community background to some extent influence the handling of political pressure in the decision-making process. That service training imprints the first impression on the person's mind for future eventualities. Most of the decisions taken by any individual officer will reflect the grooming one has got during the initial period of one's services. When someone grows in a particular service, that service culture, senior's behavior, and dominant service perceptions will decide the behavior of individual officers in the decision-making process. Such characters as a type of service one belong, method of recruitment, the position of individual officer in hierarchical levels, individual officer regional background, and a cadre of the All India Services Officers invariably decide the behavior of an individual officer in the decision-making process.

The Indian education system is frequently blamed for values and ethics inculcated among students, when they were studying in school, college, and university. Type of education and quality of carries its impression on any individual throughout his life. Education is also associated with the place of imparting education and domicile of the individual receiving the education. It is thought that an individual place of childhood carries its imprint throughout his life. Social, economic, cultural, environmental, and religious surroundings leave their imprint on the mind of an individual, which directs individual capacity to make a decision under different situations. In the present study, place of birth of individual officers, place of birth of parents, spouse place of birth, education of self, education of parents, education of the spouse, and place of education after matriculations have been studied. It was presumed that these factors influence the decision-making behavior of All India Services Officers under political pressure.

3.3. Biographical Variance: Results Analyses

Different biographical attributes can speculate variance within a service behavior and create discontinuities in working in the decision-making process. Statistical analysis carried out for all the 21 biographical characters is brought forth (Exhibits 3.1 to 3.15) and has been explained in proceeding paragraphs. The number of missing replies for the variable attitude of members of the family (Exhibit 3.1) may be due to its location in the last in the questionnaire or the All India Services Officers may not like to reply to this item. Every variable is independent, hence described in detail individually.

3.3.1. Service Related

3.3.1.1. Type of Service More Amenable to Political Pressure: Among three All India Services, which service is more amenable to political pressure? This is a highly complex question and interrelated with multifarious and innumerable other factors. Service culture, workplace environment, senior-junior relationships, and uncertainty involved in the decision process influence the acceptability of political pressure. Invariably after every change of political leadership, the first thing the new political party does after assuming a new office is to order a large-scale transfer of the Indian Administrative Service officers at district to secretariat levels followed by other services. Public presume without any prejudice that some of the self-goal oriented AISO are the most pliable officers in the Indian bureaucratic system. Such individual AISO belief is that their survival is up to that time until they are most amenable and suitable for political leadership. Basic behaviour and their internal demand to retain power, maintenance of status, and control over resources force them to maximize the acceptance of political pressure.

Exhibit Number 3.1: Statistical Analysis of Biographical Characters

Biographical Character Name	Total Cases	Valid Cases		Missing Cases		Mean	Median	Mode
		Cases	%	Cases	%			
Service related								
102. Type of service	279	269	96.4	10	10.6	1.78	2	1
103. Method of recruitment	279	271	97.1	8	2.9	1.68	2	2
104. Level in hierarchy	279	269	96.4	10	3.6	1.58	1	1
105. Length of service	279	258	92.5	21	7.5	3.81	4	5
107. Cadre of the officer	279	245	87.8	34	12.2	1.88	2	2
Social and cultural								
106. Regional background	279	268	96.1	11	3.9	3.81	4	5
108. Community background	279	248	88.9	31	11.1	2.2	3	1
109. Family economic background	279	258	92.5	21	7.5	2.38	2	1
Personal								
110. Marital status	279	266	95.3	13	4.7	1.07	1	1
111. Sex of the officer	279	268	96.1	11	3.9	1.08	1	1
115. Profession of the spouse	279	257	92.1	22	7.9	2.39	3	1
121. Number of children	279	252	90.3	27	9.7	2.64	2	2
122. Family member attitude	281	231	82.2	50	17.8	1.7	1	1
Education and domicile								
112. Self-education	279	257	92.1	22	7.9	2.49	3	3
113. Spouse education	279	253	90.7	26	9.3	2.53	3	3
114. Parents education	279	248	88.9	31	11.1	2.36	2	3
116. Own place of birth	279	260	92.5	21	7.5	1.98	2	2
117. Father place of birth	279	258	92.5	21	7.5	1.92	2	2
119. Spouse place of birth	279	254	91	25	9	2.03	2	2
120. Own place of college education	279	253	90.7	26	9.3	2.14	2	2
118. Parents place of residence	279	254	91	25	9	2.05	2	2

Analyses of research data also indicate the same thing as shown in the below-mentioned Exhibit 3.2. Members of IAS and IPS allege each other services members as more amenable to political pressure than their service. But Indian Forest Service officers have not shown much articulation and 34.3% of them accepted against All India Services average of 24.2% as their amenability to pressure. In the perception of IAS and IPS, only 11.5% of IFS officers are amenable to pressure, which is very low or we can say that one out of ten IFS officers is amenable to pressure.

Results indicate that IAS officers are highly amenable to accept political pressure, 46.1% of IAS officers or every second IAS Officer is willing to accept political pressure. 29.7% of IPS officers are amenable to accept political pressure; this percentage is quite low in comparison to the IAS officers. Only 25.3% of IAS officers acknowledged that they are amenable to political pressure, this indicates the IAS officers show concealing or obscure propensity. Perhaps IAS officers are perceived to be highly amenable to accept political pressure, so politicians adopt the line of least resistance and use willing IAS officers to pressurize officers of other services through them. Results are highly significant at '0.01' level of significance (two-tailed analysis) as shown by Chi-Square analysis (Pearson Chi-Square value is 39.328 at 4 degree of freedom).

Exhibit Number 3.2: Type of All India Services Officers More Amenable to Political Pressure

Service Amenability	Item Details	Respondent Service Name			Total
		IAS	IPS	IFS	
IAS	Frequency	19	53	52	124
	% of this frequency	15.20%	43.20%	41.60%	100%
	% of total IAS	25.30%	55.80%	52.50%	46.10%
	% of AIS	7.10%	19.70%	19.30%	46.10%
IPS	Frequency	39	28	13	80
	% of this frequency	48.80%	35%	16.30%	100%
	% of total IPS	52.00%	29.50%	13.10%	29.70%
	% of AIS	14.50%	10.40%	4.80%	29.70%
IFS	Frequency	17	14	34	66
	% of this frequency	26.20%	21.50%	52.30%	100%
	% of total IFS	22.70%	14.70%	34.30%	24.20%
	% of AIS	6.30%	5.20%	12.60%	24.20%
Total	Frequency = N	75	95	99	269
	% of Service & AIS	27.90%	35.30%	36.80%	100%
	Mean value of All India Services				1.97

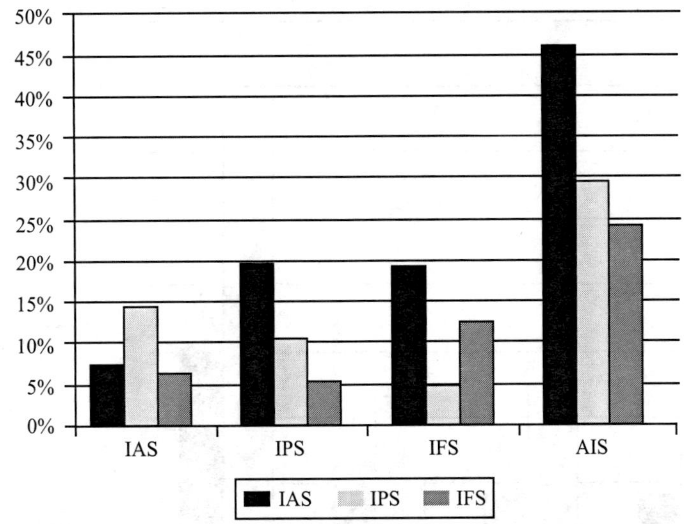

Chart No. 3.1: All India Services Amenable to Pressure

3.3.1.2. Method of Recruitment: 66.66% of the AISO are recruited through open competitive examination conducted by the UPSC and 33.33% of them are by promotion from state feeder services. State service officers become eligible for promotion to the All India Services after eight years of substantive appointment to feeder State Service, subject to availability of vacancies in their quota. During the course of their career, these officers develop and cultivate their political connections for their advancement in service. The dominance of self-goals in the State service officers motivates them towards acceptance of different kinds of external pressure in the decision-making process to accomplish own needs. Perception, attitude, and approach towards political pressure will be variable and related to the individual personality and location in the hierarchy. It is a common belief that promoted officers are more amenable to pressure acceptance than direct recruit officers.

Exhibit Number 3.3: Method of Recruitment More Amenable to Political Pressure

Method of Recruitment	Item Details	Name of AIS in which Respondent have been Borne			
		IAS	IPS	IFS	Total Resp.
Promotes	Frequency count	52	70	63	185
	% within service	69.30%	73.70%	62.40%	68.40%
	% of total	19.20%	25.80%	23.00%	68.40%
Direct recruiter	Frequency count	23	25	38	86
	% within service	30.70%	26.30%	37.60%	31.70%
	% of total	8.50%	9.20%	14.00%	31.70%
Total	Frequency count	75	95	101	271
	% of total	27.70%	35.10%	37.10%	100%

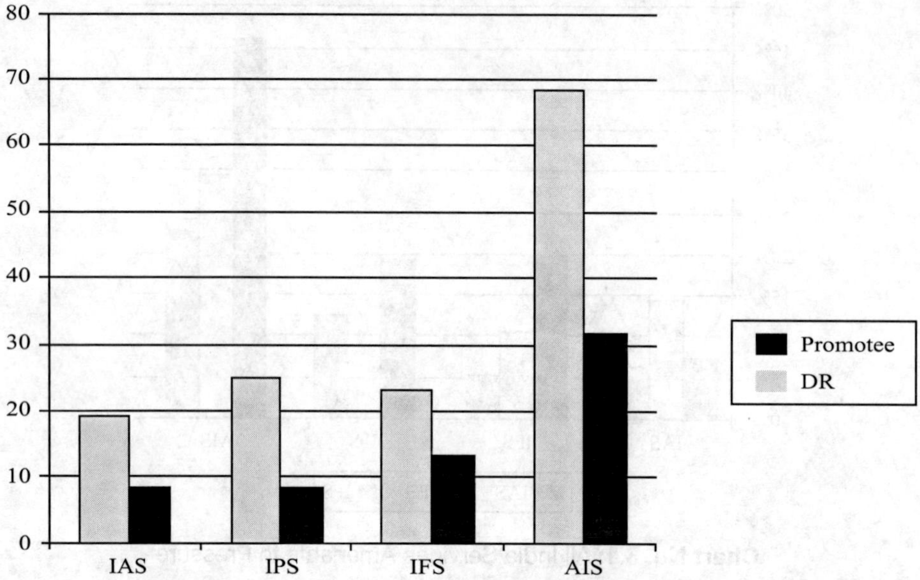

Chart No. 3.2: Method of Recruitment Amenability to Pressure

The All India Services Officers perceptions analyses through results indicate that 68.4% of the All India Services Officers feel that promote officers are more amenable to accept political pressure in comparison to 31.6% of the directly recruited officers. If we study the prevalent situation among various All India Services, 74% of IPS officers feel that promoted officers are more amenable to political pressure acceptance. But among IFS officers' prevalent perception about direct recruit officers is comparatively different than IAS and IPS. 38% of IFS officers feel that directly recruited officers are also amenable to pressure acceptance, which is the highest among All India Services Officers. Some officers have expressed serious concerns that promoted officers have mollified the All India character of the All India Services, by increasing their proportion in these services. Another common accusation alleged against them is that some of the promoted officers have entered state service through inequitable means and when they join the All India Services, this denigrates the overall standard of the All India Services.

3.3.1.3. Position (Level) in Hierarchy: Length of service and location in a hierarchy (position) is related to the performance of an individual All India Services Officer in the decision-making process. Behavioral analysts believe that as officers grow old, their efficiency and performance go down. As the length of service of individual officers increases, a decline in performance has been observed universally. It is believed that as the officers climb the higher ladder of the hierarchy, there is a sharp decline in their performance and productivity. Productivity starts declining with aging and is aggravated by health problems. The All India Services Officers close to their retirement, compromise more with pressure to garner more retirement blues.

The All India Services Officers close to their retirement have a dominant feeling that they have done enough, little or no stimulation is left to overcome the driving force for resisting political pressure. With age officers develop higher patience, coolness and become more disciplined, but have no or little interest in new technology. Elderly officers have less adaptability for change, innovations, and newer techniques. Chances for a change in job got reduced to a minimum after 24 or more years of service. Senior officers have to cope with greater responsibilities at home and their energy gets decimated and compels them to compromise and accommodating behaviour dominate under any kind of political pressure in the decision-making process.

Aggravating health problems reduce their concentration on work and reduced vitality to fight with the ever-increasing demand of the bureaucratic system. Promptness, speed, strength, and agility of the All India Services Officers got decayed in a natural way with increasing age. The All India Services Officers with more than 24 years of service may have higher job satisfaction, become more prone to accepting political pressure. With increasing age tolerance limit also increases, seniors' high tolerance for political pressure, which they pass down below the hierarchy lines to save themselves from political wrath.

Braford Spangenberg[1] mentioned the behaviour of the All India Services Officers during colonial rule: "Higher officials who remained in India beyond the limit of twenty-one years necessary for pension were under no compulsion to complete any further period of service. They might resign or they might take furlough at any time, perhaps thereby seriously embarrassing the Government of India. The weapon employed to obtain desired posts often included a threat of resignation." The politicians can easily calculate and predict the future behaviour of an elderly All India Services Officer, which is a continuance of the colonial era. "Higher bureaucracy in India has failed the country's expectations", Ashok Mukhopdhyay (1994). Our research analyses are shown in Exhibit 3.4 also show similar results.

Exhibit Number 3.4: Which Position in Hierarchy is More Amenable to Political Pressure

Hierarchy Level	Item Details	Service in which Respondent Borne			Total
		IAS	IPS	IFS	
Top level	Frequency = N	43	49	66	158
	% within service	58.10%	51.60%	66.00%	58.70%
	% of AIS total	16.00%	18.20%	24.50%	58.70%
Middle level	Frequency = N	17	32	17	66
	% within service	23.00%	33.70%	17.00%	24.50%
	% of AIS total	6.30%	11.90%	6.30%	24.50%
Lower level	Frequency = N	14	14	17	45
	% within service	18.90%	14.70%	17.00%	16.70%
	% of AIS total	5.20%	5.20%	6.35	16.70%
Total	Frequency = N	74	95	100	269
	% of AIS total	27.50%	35.30%	37.20%	100.00%

58.7% of the All India Services Officers feel that the top level in government administration is amenable to accept political pressure in the decision-making process. Whereas 24.5% of the All India Services Officers feel about the middle level and 16.75% of them realize that the lower level

1. In his book *British Bureaucracy in India*.

in public administration is amenable to accept the pressure. Among different services, 66.0% of the IFS officers, 58.1% of the IAS, and 51.6% of the IPS officers think that top-level officers in the hierarchy accept pressure more readily. For middle-level IPS score is highest to that of 33.7%, thereby indicating that DIGP and IGP level officers approach politicians, carry pressure with them, and ultimately pass on that pressure to a downward direction. Seniors are not supposed to interfere in the working of functionaries below them. The IAS officers have indicated that 18.9% of their own officers accept pressure at a lower level at their own will, which is very close to the total All India Services score. We can draw inferences that Indian Administrative Service officers at a lower level have more lateral movement than the other services.

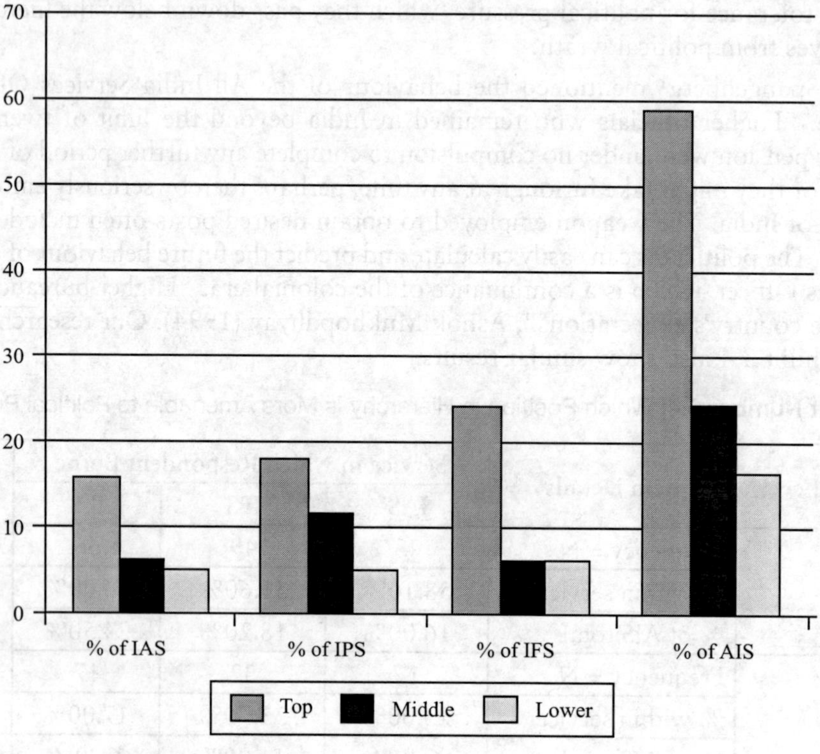

Chart No. 3.3: Hierarchy Level Amenability to Pressure

3.3.1.4. Length of Service: Higher on ladder of career the All India Services Officers climb in their respective services, chances for accepting pressure increases more and more. The individual officer moving ahead on the ladders of a career becomes more reactive towards pressure. All India Services Officers' willingness to accept pressure increases with the length of service, as they cherish more self-goals in it. 45.7% of All India Services Officers think that officers with more than 24 or more years of service are the highest amenable to pressure. This corroborates with the notion that officers at the top position are more prone to accept political pressure readily. The All India Services Officers reaching close to top position become highly vulnerable to pressure due to high position consciousness. Commissioner, Secretary, Additional Chief Secretary, Additional DGP, DGP, Inspector General of Police, Chief Conservator of Forests and APCCF, PCCF are positioned, where All India Services Officers are highly amenable to accept pressure. However, officers in these positions are working as controlling officers and can easily avoid the pressure exerted on them.

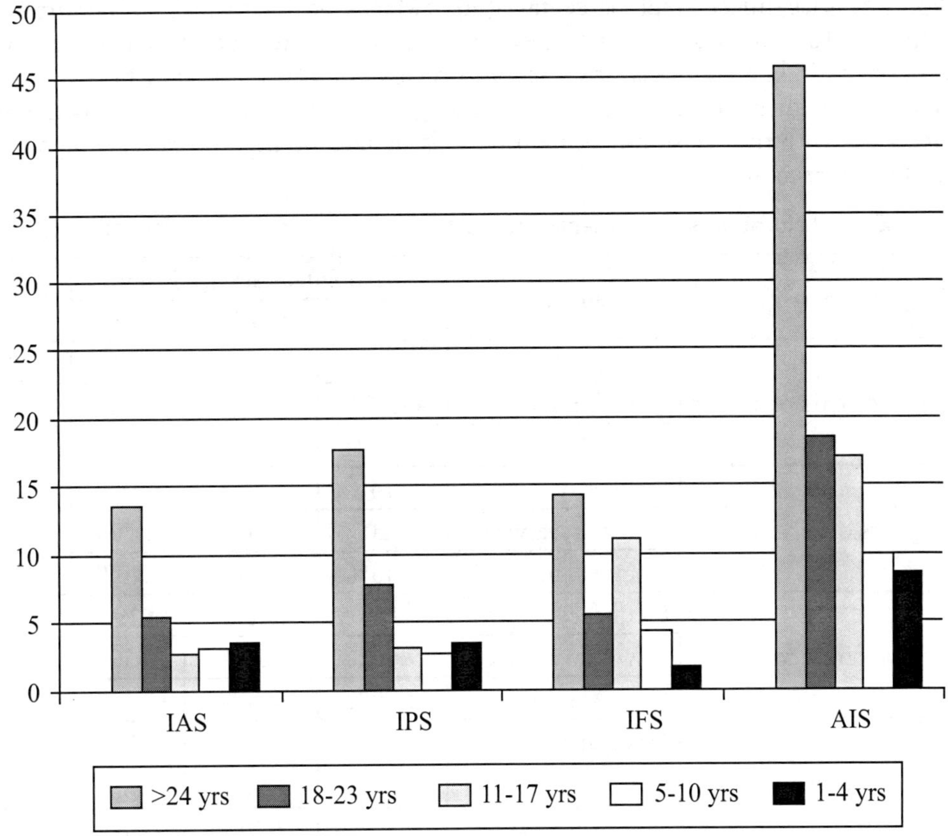

Chart No. 3.4: Length of Service Amenability to Pressure

Maximum pressure acceptance was expected at the implementation level at the district, where stakes are very high. Research results show contrary findings, which can be explained by the behavior of the All India Services Officers. Transfer or posting at a senior level should not be a matter of great concern to any individual officer; as such positions are mostly located close to power holders' headquarters. Research results indicate that as officers move ahead with white hairs, they become more conscious about family and self. Self-goals also multiply with higher experience and lust to fulfill them increases with more acceptance of political pressure.

Young officers with less than five years of service are least willing (8.5%) to make a compromise in the decision process under political pressure. Indian Forest Service officers are the least flexible as indicated by its low percentage. If we study the acceptance of pressure in super time pay scale (i.e. postings after district and above), research results indicate that major pressure is accepted at that level. 73.3% of the Indian Police Service officers, 67.1% of the Indian Administrative Service officers, and 53.6% of the Indian Forest Service officers are amenable to accept political pressure working in that of the super time scale of pay. In the case of officers in the junior administrative scale, amenability to pressure is 30.5% for the Indian Forest Service officers, 9.6% for the Indian Administrative Service officers, and 8.9% for the Indian Police Service officers. In the case of the Indian Forest Service officers' high percentage (30.5%) may be due to a lack of opportunities for promotion after 16 years of service, and they continue to stagnate on that same scale. Invariably in the case of the Indian Administrative Service officers after 16 years, they next promotion in super time scale, higher positions are more satisfying in career advancement. Association of the length of service with the decision-making process is significant at 0.003, level of significance in Pearson Chi-square analyses.

Exhibit Number 3.5: Amenability to Political Pressure with Length of Service

Length of Service	Item Details	Respondent Service Name			Total
		IAS	IPS	IFS	
More than 24 years of service	Frequency	35	46	37	118
	% within service	47.90%	51.10%	38.90%	45.70%
	% in AIS total	13.60%	17.80%	14.30%	45.70%
18 to 23 years of service	Frequency	14	20	14	48
	% within service	19.20%	2.20%	14.70%	18.60%
	% in AIS total	5.40%	7.80%	5.40%	18.60%
11 to 17 years of service	Frequency	7	8	29	44
	% within service	9.60%	8.90%	30.50%	17.10%
	% in AIS total	2.70%	3.10%	11.20%	17.10%
5 to 10 years of service	Frequency	8	7	11	26
	% within service	11.00%	7.80%	11.60%	10.10%
	% in AIS total	3.10%	2.70%	4.30%	10.1
1 to 4 years of service	Frequency	9	9	4	22
	% within service	12.30%	10.00%	4.20%	8.50%
	% in AIS total	3.50%	3.50%	1.60%	8.50%
Total	Frequency	73	90	95	258
	% of AIS total	28.30%	34.90%	36.80%	100.00%

3.3.1.5. Cadre of the Officer: The perceptions of internal threat within the cadre augment the individual/group anxieties among the All India Service Officers. Psychological insecurity in a group/service motivates them to develop collaboration with political authorities. Officers have a fundamental urge to escape restraints, frustrations, and guilt accumulated through their actions and secretly harbored in their imaginations; they find a release of this through indiscriminate use of power by finding shortcomings in helpless subordinates. Many officers allotted to cadre other than the home state, look upon that cadre state as an exile to endure. Some of them consider it as a burden imposed by their luck or circumstances; reluctantly and unwillingly accept it in lieu of promising opportunities available to them in the future.

Individual AISO as part of the All India Services hold common attributes of batch and birth state. Dissimilar individuals from different states in a cadre are more likely to possess diverse abilities and information proves to be more efficient. Mixing of insider and outsider in a cadre of service increases the probabilities for getting better abilities, skills, personalities, options, and perspectives in the decision. The All India Services Officers of a cadre hailing from a diverse cultural background and suppose to assimilate a new culture of cadre to perform effectively. Cadre allocations from one State to another State create cultural differences among the All India Services Officers, and such diversity hinders the process of small in-service group formation.

In a new cadre, All India Services Officers initially face problems in learning and imbibing the new culture of the State. It has been observed that officers working for more than 20 years face problems in cadre culture and are unable to assimilate and live with that culture. On the first available occasion, such officers try to shift from the cadre state. Some members of their family have been observed continuously criticizing and cursing cadre state culture throughout their career. As an end result, most of the All India Services Officers (some stay back) resettle back to the home of their parent state after retirement. This continuous feeling of cultural estrangement reduce their performance in the decision-making process.

An individual All India Services Officer attributes in relationship towards the attributes of people with whom they work. Any difficulty in communication with the sub-ordinates has a serious impact on the All India Services Officers' performance. Cultural differences enhance power conflicts and make membership less attractive. Among the All India Services Officers, the same batch friendship is the most common binding force in that State cadre.

Exhibit Number 3.6: Amenability to Political Pressure and Cadre of the Officer

Cadre	Item details	IAS	IPS	IFS	Total
Home Cadre	Frequency	8	22	46	76
	% in service	11.80%	25.30%	51.10%	31.00%
	% of total AIS	3.30%	9.00%	18.80%	31.00%
Outside State	Frequency	42	36	40	118
	% in service	61.80%	41.40%	44.40%	48.20%
	% of total AIS	17.10%	14.70%	16.30%	48.20%
Neighbour State Cadre	Frequency	18	29	4	51
	% in service	26.50%	33.30%	4.40%	20.80%
	% of total AIS	7.30%	11.80%	1.60%	20.80%
Total	Frequency	68	87	90	245

Study results indications on Chi-square test are highly significant at 0.001, level of significance. Our hypothesis that All India Services Officers working in the home cadre are more prone to acceptance of pressure has been rejected at the degree of freedom of 4 in Pearson Chi-square analysis. Pearson's correlation value of –0.35 and Spearman's correlation value of –0.3 are significant with a 0.000, level of significance.

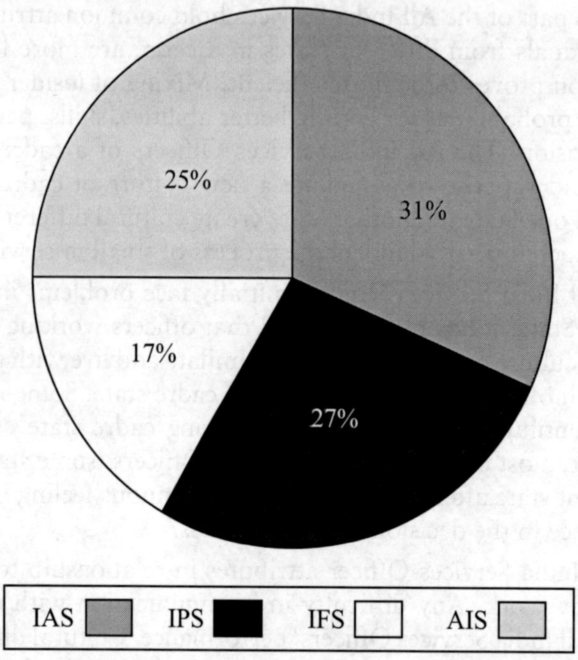

Chart No. 3.5: Outside Cadre and Amenability to Pressure

Results show that 40.2% of the All India Services Officers are of the view that officers from outside cadre state are more amenable to pressure than officers borne in home state (31.0%) cadre. 61.8% of the Indian Administrative Service officers and 41.4% of the Indian Police Service officers are of the view that officers have borne and brought up in other than cadre state are more prone to accept the political pressure than the officers borne and working in the parent state. The Indian Forest Service officers' feelings are different from IPS and IAS, and 51.1% of the Indian Forest Service officers think that officers working in the home state are more amenable to pressure.

3.3.2. Community, Social and Cultural Background

3.3.2.1. Regional Background: The All India Services Officers' regional backgrounds motivate and attract other officers of similar background to stay together. Before recruitment to the All India Services, individual officers have studied and lived in a similar culture prevalent in their respective colleges, universities, and other educational institutions. Dominant social setup enhances small group formation and cohesiveness at initial stages among persons hailing from a similar social background. Regional similarities among the All India Services Officers facilitate and improve interactions among them.

Similarities in food habits, dress codes, living style, and thinking patterns induce the formation of small groups when political pressure is exerted on the individual officer. These small groups do share their political lineage and affiliations to extract maximum utility out of such relations. By and large, the higher the small group formations, the higher are the chances of accepting political pressure in the decision-making process. Frequent transfers, distant locations, and position in the hierarchy with respect to geographical distribution are the hindrances in regional group formations.

It is commonly believed that in case of perceived threats, regional groups extend help to each other. Small groups in services stimulate competition for own goals maximization in the decision process. Information sharing of these small groups is based on regional background across the services, invariably influences the decision. Regional cultural backgrounds of an individual All India Services Officer invariably influence the behavior of the officer in the decision. An individual All India Services Officer's behavior to face the challenges imposed by the political pressure is regulated by the internal conscious pattern of behavior, which is influenced by the officer's regional cultural background.

A study of research data indicates that 28.4% of officers from south India are at the top in accepting the political pressure in a decision, followed by north India 25.0%, east India 16%, northeast India 13.4%, and central and west Indians ranked as least at 8.6% each. In the case of the Indian Police Service officers and the Indian Administrative Service officers, south Indians were ranked the highest amenable to political pressure at 37.9% and 29.7% respectively. In the case of the Indian Administrative Service officers, the north and northeastern region were ranked amenable at 17.6% from each region, followed by west India at 16.2%, which is different from the other two services. The anomalous situation in the case of the Indian Administrative Service officers may be ascribed to differential cultural background or impact of the Indian Administrative Service work culture on these officers. We have to explore the reasons for such deviations. In the case of the IFS officers, the highest amenability of 35.4% has been ascribed to the officers from north India, followed by 18.2% from south India. Reasons for variations can be explained to the IFS work culture prevalent in their department. Association of regional background with decision-making process is significant at 0.005, level of significance in Pearson Chi-square analyses.

Exhibit Number 3.7: Regional Background of an Individual Officer and Amenability to Pressure

Respondent Service Name	AISO Regional Background						Total
	Southern	Northern	Eastern	Western	Central	N/eastern	
IAS frequency	22	13	8	12	6	13	74
% in service	29.70%	17.60%	20.00%	16.20%	8.10%	17.60%	27.60%
% in AIS total	8.20%	4.90%	3.00%	4.50%	2.20%	4.90%	27.60%
IPS frequency	36	19	19	4	7		95
% in service	37.90%	20.00%	20.00%	4.20%	7.40%	10.50%	35.50%
% in AIS total	13.40%	7.10%	7.10%	1.50%	2.60%	3.70%	35.50%
IFS frequency	16	35	16	7	10	13	99
% in service	18.20%	35.40%	16.20%	7.10%	10.10%	13.10%	36.90%
% in AIS total	6.70%	13.10%	6.05	2.60%	3.70%	4.90%	36.90%
Total frequency	76	67	43	23	23	36	268
% total AIS	28.40%	25.00%	16.00%	8.60%	8.60%	13.40%	100%

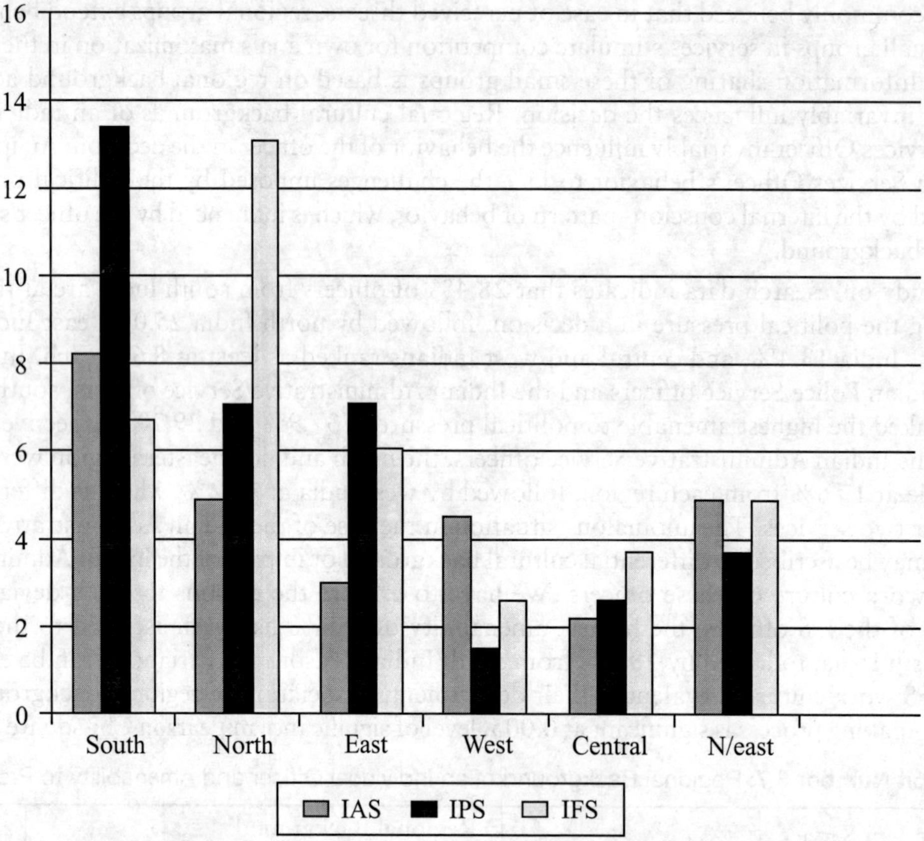

Chart No. 3.6: Regional Background and Amenability to Pressure

3.3.2.2. Community Background: Most of the States are ruled by a few of the most powerful castes/clans in India. So, the political power base has a class/caste bias in the layered and structured system in India. Officers from these communities find it easy to align with them for political patronage. In practice, it has been observed that officers are clearly divided over caste lines. Many of them join their caste associations and actively work for them, while in service. Officers collect subscriptions and donations for their caste groups by using their positions. How these officers can be neutral, how the public can expect neutrality from them? It is natural that they invite political pressure from the political authority for the aggrandizement of self-needs. Feeling of intense competition and strong rivalry has been observed among officers to accept political pressure because of community lineages.

But ultimately mutual economic interests prevail over for own benefits maximization for each other. Ultimately, collectivity turns into economic gains and personal goals. In the social system, affluent sections frequently become part of the pressure groups at ease. They have fear of alienation from privileges. Due to social grooming, the average person is scared of political pressure and their muscle power. Officers from underprivileged sections in the All India Services are engulfed finding out their position and power against someone else when they are under pressure. With pressure in front of their eyes, their nerves quiver, they subside into a queer state of jealousy and avaricious running after power they had enjoyed.

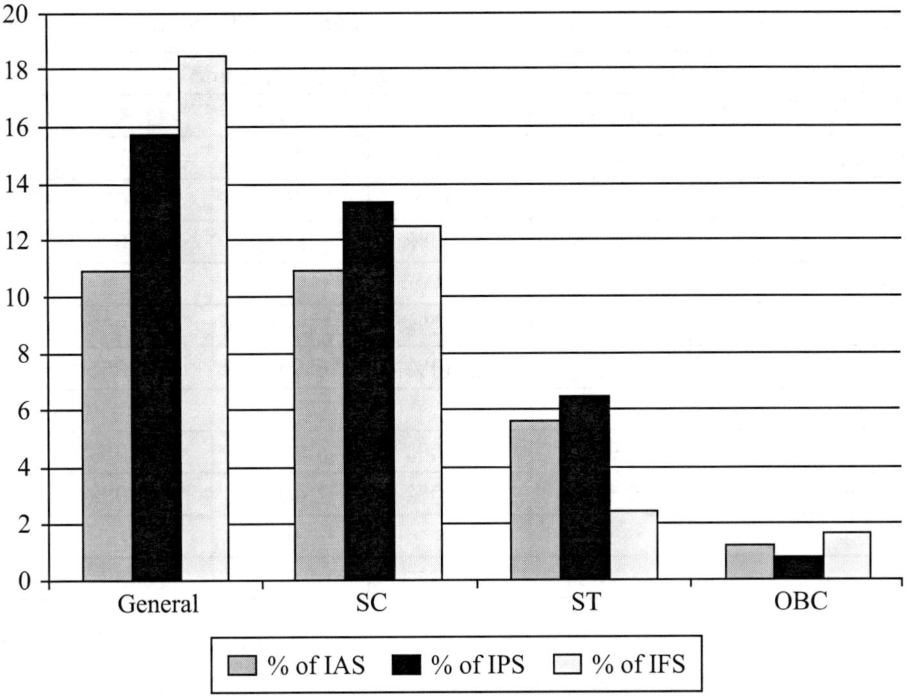

Chart No. 3.7: Community Background Amenability to Pressure

Agglomeration of different private interests gives rise to the formation of pressure groups and these pressure groups have an upper-class bias, who form the core of power (Schattschneider, C.W. Mills, R.P. Wolff). Diverse competing community interests combine to exert political pressure on the All India Service Officers. These interest groups invariably show class bias for the protection of self-goals. Different studies indicate that consanguinity continued to play important role in separating the favored few from the helpless majority of the All India Services Officers, which is a continuation of the East India Company Policy of exploitations. Hypocrisy is rampant in three All India Services at all levels. Clegg (1989), class and social mechanism perpetuate ideological hegemony of status quo, in Hyman and Brough (1975) view "a structure of power relations is fully legitimized by an integrated system of cultural and normative assumptions."

45.2% of the All India Services Officers think that the All India Services Officers from the general category are more amenable to accept political pressure. Results for three services show that 52.9% of the Indian Forest Service officers, 42.3% of the Indian Police Service officers, and 38.0% of the Indian Administrative Service officers from the general category are willing to accept political pressure. The IAS officers think that 57.7% of officers of scheduled castes and scheduled tribes jointly accept the pressure. The IPS officers feel that 54.5% of officers of combine scheduled castes and scheduled tribes accept the pressure. 42.5% of the Indian Forest Service officers feel in that way. Rho value of –0.2 indicates significant negative relations with 0.01, level of significance.

Low social support base and feeling of threatened and insecurity may be responsible for such amenability towards pressure.

Exhibit Number 3.8: Community Background and Amenability to Political Pressure

Respondent Service	AISO Community Background				Total
	General	S.C.	S.T.	O.B.C.	
IAS Frequency	27	27	14	3	71
% within service	38.00%	38.00%	19.70%	4.20%	28.60%
% in AIS total	10.90%	10.90%	5.60%	1.20%	28.60%
IPS Frequency	39	33	16	2	90
% within service	43.30%	36.70%	17.80%	2.20%	36.30%
% in AIS total	15.70%	13.30%	6.50%	0.80%	36.30%
IFS Frequency	46	31	6	4	87
% within service	52.90%	35.60%	6.90%	4.60%	35.10%
% in AIS total	18.50%	12.50%	2.40%	1.60%	35.10%
Total Frequency	112	91	36	9	248
% of caste	45.20%	36.70%	14.50%	3.60%	100%

3.3.2.3. Family Economic Background: 35.7% of the All India Services Officers think that officers from the rich family background are more amenable to accept political pressure in comparison to 8.5% of officers from the poor family background. If we combine rich and upper-middle-class, 42.3% of these, the All India Services Officers accept pressure. These combined results for rich and upper-middle-class background officers for the Indian Administrative Service officers are 61.4%, for the Indian Police Service officers 75.5% and 43% for the Indian Forest Service officers respectively, who are amenable to accept political pressure in the decision-making process, as shown in Exhibit 3.9.

54.4% of the IPS officers feel that officers from the rich family background are more prone to accept political pressure. The analysis makes it clear that even if we combine officers from poor and lower-middle-class family background, acceptability towards pressure is less than 25% in case of any service or combine All India Services. Results are interesting that even this combined percentage is less than half of the percentage for officers from a rich family background. Low scores for officers from poor family backgrounds do not match with the results for SC/ST analysis. Here difference may be due to the reason that the majority of SC/ST officers may not from the rural poor class but the second generation of highly placed officers or beyond, from the financially affluent family background. Pearson Chi-square value of 39.6 with the degree of freedom of 8 and a significance level of 0.000, are significant and show a good association. Spearman correlation value of 0.141 shows correlation and results are significant at 0.02, level of significance.

Exhibit Number 3.9: Family Economic Background and Acceptance of Political Pressure

Respondent Service Name	AISO Family Economic Background					Total
	Rich	U/middle	Middle/C	LMC	Poor	
IAS Frequency	26	20	10	9	10	75
% within service	34.70%	26.70%	13.30%	12.00%	13.30%	29.10%
% in AIS total	10.10%	7.80%	3.90%	3.50%	3.90%	29.10%
IPS Frequency	49	19	6	11	5	90
% within service	54.40%	21.10%	6.70%	12.20%	5.60%	34.90%
% in AIS total	19.00%	7.40%	2.30%	4.30%	1.90%	34.90%
IFS Frequency	17	23	29	17	7	93
% within service	18.30%	24.70%	31.20%	18.30%	7.50%	36.00%
% in AIS total	6.60%	8.90%	11.20%	6.60%	2.70%	36.00%
Total Frequency	92	62	45	37	22	258
% in economic class	35.70%	24.00%	17.40%	14.30%	8.50%	100%

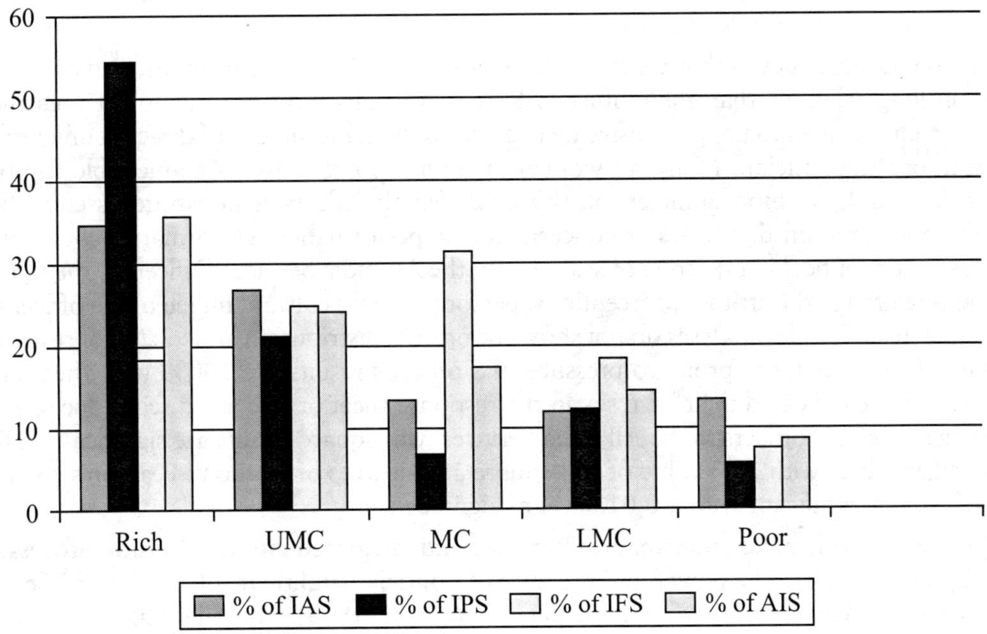

Chart No. 3.8: Economic Background and Amenability to Pressure

Differential results for the IFS officers also remind us again that the nature of the job in the IFS being arduous and difficult, persons from the affluent family background may not be joining the service. A lot of status and power may be a motivating factor for persons from affluent family backgrounds to join IAS and IPS. There can be another reason that officers from a rich family background in IFS may not be interested in challenging field postings, where one has to work under a lot of pressure. Officers from the upper middle class and beyond are comparatively more pliable than officers from the lower middle class and below them. Our results analysis on Chi-square rejects our hypothesis that officers from the poor family background are more prone to pressure acceptance in the decision-making process. An alternate hypothesis is accepted that officers from the progressive family background are more amenable towards acceptance of political pressure in the decision-making process.

3.3.3. Personal Characters

3.3.3.1. Marital Status and Sex: Responses to political pressure in the decision-making process from males and females are akin to motivation, problem-solving ability, and analytical skills. Much difference is not recognized in performance in the decision process. Studies have indicated some differences that females are willing to conform to authority and are conformist, likely to amenable more to pressure. Male members are attributed for their toughness, perseverance, assertiveness, aggression, toughness, and higher ego. On the other hand, female members are known for their collaboration, nurturance, creativity, compassion, and harmony. The All India Services Officers when dealing with the social system, it is expected that they deal with pressure accordingly in different ways. The social system and politicians impose their value system on the decision process. However, in the All India Services roles are not allocated according to sex but invariably there is social role allocation.

It is commonly believed that women officers are more pleasant, courteous, and co-operative to sustain long relations than male officers. Research results indicate it is power regardless of gender, which attempts to use persuasive tactics with politicians instead of direct conflict to invite the wrath of the politician. Men and women in similar power bases are amenable to political pressure in a similar fashion. Some people think that female officers demonstrate lesser confidence in pressure negotiation due to lesser concern for the performance. Performance concerns have been observed identical irrespective of sex, among the All India Services Officers. Amenability to pressure is related to the attitude, perceptions, personality, and cultural milieu of the officer rather than gender bias. Results analyses do not show the normal distribution and 92.2% of respondents say male officers are more prone to pressure. IPS officer's results are 100% with the male. We feel officers have indicated their own sex in the response sheet or one-sided score due to the low percentage of female officers in the All India Services. Chi-square results are significant at 0.000, level of significance with 20.3 value of Chi-square at 2 degrees of freedom. Pearson's correlation value of –0.2 is significant with a 0.01, level of significance.

Qualities of both males and females are valued and integrated into the decision process. How is the response of sex to the power and pressure of politician and their tolerance to it? Separated persons are at greater risk than married persons (Lynch, 1978). Happily married persons are found to be more satisfied in a job than single persons. At the same time, marriage increases the responsibilities, and work becomes more valuable for the family, chances of amenability to pressure increases. After marriage person develops more social connections, these connections become more demanding, higher pressure on decisions increases the vulnerability to pressure. A supportive spouse is perceived to reduce the incidences of tension in the job, then a no supportive spouse (Madalie and Goldbourt, 1976). Happy married life supports the positive outcome from the decision, whereas divorce or tension in family life makes the All India Services Officers more amenable to pressure. Good family relations improve decision quality.

Exhibit Number 3.10: Marital Status and Amenability to Political Pressure

Marital Status	IAS	IPS	IFS	Total
Married Frequency	69	91	91	251
% within service	92.00%	95.80%	94.80%	94.40%
Unmarried Frequency	3	3	4	10
% within service	4.00%	3.20%	4.20%	3.80%
Separated Frequency	3	1	1	5
% within service	4.00%	1.10%	1.00%	1.90%
N	75	95	96	266

It appears that respondents have replied with respect to own position or majority of the All India Services Officers are leading a happy married life.

3.3.3.2. Profession of Spouse: It is commonly believed that a professional spouse will move across the different layers of social strata. This enhances social interaction among various segments of society. Higher mobility of spouse will invite higher chances of external pressure from different sources, which may be directed towards the decision process by the AISO. The profession of the spouse is directly related to the exposure and movements in different circumstances. Homemakers may be busy with more of the aesthetic nature of work and may demand more money for better upkeep of the house. Life partners engaged in business, entrepreneurship, and services would have different friendship circles and certainly, put forward different nature of requests to All India Services Officers to oblige.

Results indicate that 31.4% of entrepreneur spouses are exerting pressure on the All India Services Officers to accept pressure in the decision. If we combine business and entrepreneur professions together, which are alike in nature, we observe that 51.2% of spouses exert pressure on the All India Services Officers in the decision-making process. Among the three All India Services, this combined pressure (business and entrepreneur) exerted in the decision process is 67.1%, on the IAS, 63.4% on the IPS, and 26.1% on the IFS officers. In the case of the Indian Administrative Service officers, 16.4% and the Indian Police Service officers 15.1% of spouses staying at the house do not exert much pressure on their decision process. 56.5% of the Indian Forest Service officers feel that spouse staying at home interfere in the process of decision. This high pressure may be due to the availability of limited avenues for spouses and at the same time indicate less mobility of the Indian Forest Service officers among various strata of society. This also indicates that a very low percentage of spouses of the IFS officers indulge in income-generating activities in comparison to the two services. This may be due to fact that IAS and IPS spouses get higher exposure and chances for earning money through manipulations and twisting in the bureaucratic system, whereas Indian Forest Service officers do not enjoy comparable privileges.

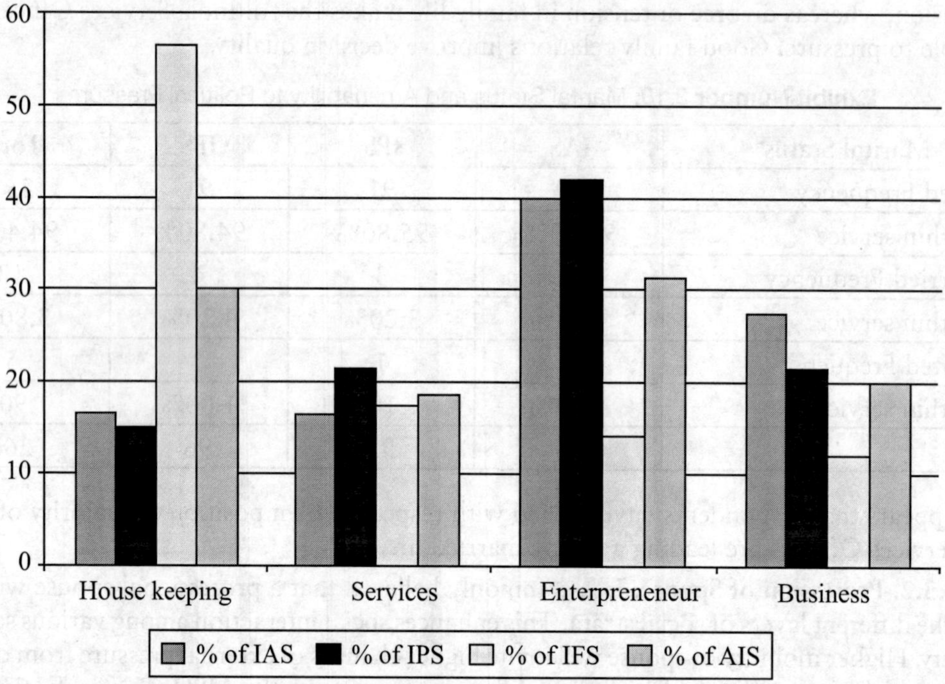

Chart No. 3.9: Amenability to Pressure and Profession of Spouse

3.3.3.3. Family Member Attitude: Members of family exert any kind of pressure on the All India Services Officers decision-making process, who maximizes it? Role conflicts among the All India Services Officers put emphasis on stability and show high concern for spouses and children. It is commonly thought that people approach the All India Services Officers through their near and dear ones, relatives, friends, and acquaintances to get the maximum benefit out of the decision process. Among these sources members of the family are the persons, who have unrestricted and unlimited access to the All India Services Officers. What is the attitude of the family members; it has an impact on the decision.

Our results indicate that 62.7% of the All India Services Officers feel that spouse (wife/husband) attitude is crucial for them to be looked after. Results for three All India Services indicate that 90.8% of the Indian Forest Service officers, 66.7% of the Indian Administrative Service officers and 39.6% of the Indian Police Service officers feel that the attitude of a spouse has an impact on the pressure acceptance behavior. An interesting feature is that brother/sister scores are negligibly low, but in the case of the IPS officers, it is similarly distributed among all the members of the family. This may be due to higher discipline prevalent in police forces; even they can easily oblige all the members. Exceptional high score for spouse (90.8%) among Indian Forest Service officers indicate that they do not have enough to oblige their family members, what so ever resources are available spouse exhaust most of them.

Pearson Chi-square value of 48.9, with 6 degree of freedom is significant with 0.000, level of significance; show good association this variable with the acceptance of political pressure in the decision-making process. Spearman correlation negative value of –0.2 is significant at 0.01, level of significance. The alternate hypothesis is accepted that acceptance of political pressure in the decision-making process is related to the attitude of members of the family of an individual officer.

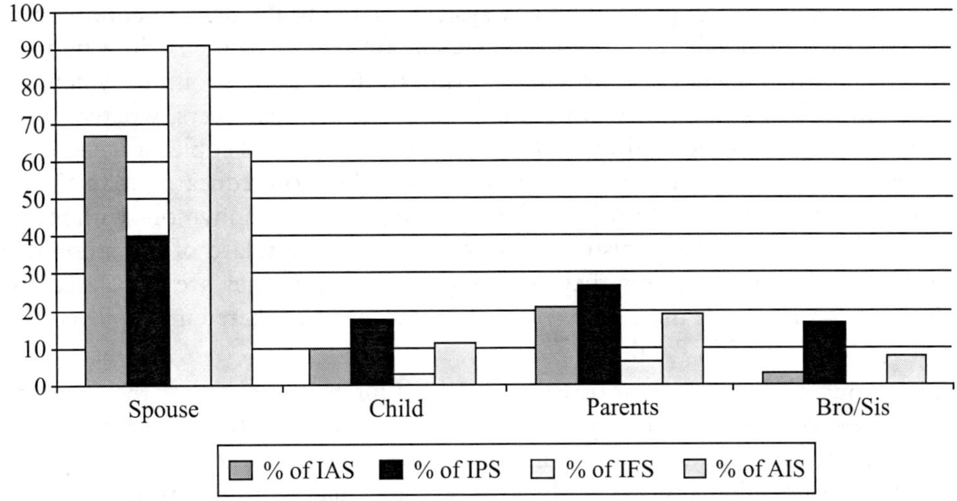

Chart No. 3.10: Family Attitude and Amenability to Pressure

3.3.3.4. Number of Children: It is believed that officers with a higher number of children may have higher material requirements, which may force them to accept pressure more frequently. It appears that respondents have a marked number of children as they have or most of them have a similar number of children. Most of the officers have one or two children, so, 48.4% of them accepted two children as an answer. The scores for the respective three services are 59.8% for the Indian Police Service officers, 42.5% for the Indian Administrative Service officers, and 41.4% for the Indian Forest Service officers. Details results are as shown in Exhibit 3.11.

Exhibit Number 3.11: Family Member Attitude, Profession of Spouse and Number of Children

Factor	Item Details	IAS	IPS	IFS	Total
Profession of Spouse	At House	16.40%	15.10%	56.50%	30.20%
	Services	16.40%	21.50%	17.40%	18.60%
	Entrepreneur	39.70%	41.90%	14.10%	31.40%
	Business	27.40%	21.50%	12%	19.80%
Family Member Attitude	Spouse	66.70%	39.60%	90.80%	62.70%
	Children	9.70%	17.60%	3.10%	11.00%
	Parents	20.80%	26.40%	6.20%	18.90%
	Brother/Sister	2.80%	16.50%	0%	7.50%
Number of Children	One child	8.20%	6.50%	5.70%	6.70%
	2 children	42.50%	59.80%	41.40%	48.40%
	3 children	17.80%	14.10%	20.70%	17.50%
	4 or more	31.50%	19.60%	32.20%	27.40%

3.3.4. Educational Characters

3.3.4.1. Education of Self, Spouse, and Parents—Amenability to Political Pressure: Is amenability to accept political pressure in any system related to the level of education acquired by an officer? Traditional values imbibed by a person are related to the socio-economic status, educational, and development of a particular section of the societal group to which the officer belongs to. Some social groups have more affinity towards political piers, whereas a particular social group may like to keep a distance from the political piers. People, in general, feel that authority flow from the top, and those in power should be more educated than them. This is because, in India, every program flow from the top, and power is synonymous with money. "The character and conduct of the administrators depend upon the standard of education they get in the universities, and type of training they get, people with whom they are associated and moral standards that prevail outside their office rooms. A vast sea of educated unemployed is going to devour our social system," B. Panda (1978).

Results of our study are shown in Exhibit 3.12. Our hypothesis that the acceptability of pressure increases with the increase in qualification has been rejected. Results are highly significant according to Chi-square analysis at less than 0.001, level of significance. 33.6% of the All India Services Officers think that officers with postgraduate qualifications are more amenable to pressure acceptance. Among Indian Administrative Service officers' results are different, may be due to the differential composition of service. With the passage of time more and more engineers and technocrats are joining the Indian Administrative Service, indicating higher internal lust and temptations, which motivate them to accept pressure to meet self-needs. 51.3% of the Indian Administrative Service officers feel that officers with technical and management qualifications are the highest receiver of political pressure. This variable percentage is observed low in Indian Police Service officers and Indian Forest Service officers.

Exhibit Number 3.12: Self Educational Background and Amenability to Political Pressure

Service		Graduate	Technical	PG	Management	Ph.D.	Total
IAS	Frequency	21	24	9	14	6	74
	% within service	28.40%	32.40%	12.20%	18.90%	8.10%	28.80%
IPS	Frequency	21	16	43	6	4	90
	% within service	23.30%	17.80%	47.80%	6.70%	4.40%	35%
IFS	Frequency	30	13	34	9	7	93
	% within service	32.30%	14.00%	36.60%	9.70%	7.50%	36.20%
Total	Frequency	72	53	86	29	17	257
	% of qualification	28.00%	20.60%	33.50%	11.30%	6.60%	100%

Analyses of data for IPS officers indicate a very high score of 47.8% for postgraduate education. Results indicate a matter of great concern; particularly those engineers and technocrat's huge number joining the All India Services are showing self-goal orientation. Similarly, in the case of IFS officers' number of such graduate joining service is limited, but the score of 32.3% of that group indicate that all such officers accept pressure in the decision. Officers with Ph.D. qualification, who are amenable to pressure acceptance score is 6.6%, which is very low. This may be due to the presence of few Ph.D. officers among the All India Services or they are least amenable to pressure.

Exhibit Number 3.13: Relationship of Place of Birth and Educational Background of the AISO

Variable	Education Level		Officer Place of Birth			Total
			Rural	Urban	S/Urban	
Educational background of the officer	B.A./B.Sc./B.Com./Graduate	Count	19	30	20	69
		% of Total	7.569	11.95	7.9681	27.49
	Engineer/B.Tech./Technology	Count	11	22	18	51
		% of Total	4.382	8.76	7.1713	20.32
	M.A./M.Sc./M.Tech./Postgraduate	Count	29	42	15	86
		% of Total	11.55	16.73	5.9761	34.26
	Management Diploma/MBA/CA	Count	2	20	6	28
		% of Total	0.797	7.96	2.3904	11.16
	Ph.D. (Doctor of Philosophy)	Count	4	11	2	17
		% of Total	1.594	4.38	0.7968	6.773
Total		Count	65	125	61	251
		% of Total	25.89	49.8	24.303	100

Educational qualifications of the All India Services Officers show a good relationship with their birthplace. 34.26% of postgraduate are maximum amenable to political pressure acceptance, in that category 16.73% of officers with an urban background are amenable to accept political pressure. Officers with postgraduate qualifications (34.26%) from an urban background (16.76%) have been recorded as most amenable to acceptance of political pressure in the decision-making process. Correlation of educational background and place of birth under Chi-square analysis (N = 251, df = 17.9) are significant at 0.022 level of significance.

To find out co-relationship with the education of spouse and parents and its relation with the acceptability of pressure data have been analyzed. Results are similar to previous analysis; postgraduate qualification of spouse and parents comes out at 42.7% and 39.4% respectively, which motivates individual officers to accept political pressure in the decision-making process. Spouse postgraduate education impact on the acceptability of pressure among the three All India Services observed at 52.7%, 39.7%, and 34.8% for IPS, IAS and IFS respectively. The spouse with a postgraduate qualification and its influence on the decision is highest in the Indian Administrative Service officers and least in the Indian Forest Service officers.

Parents' education and relationship with the acceptability of the pressure in the decision-making process, have been observed as 49.3% and 47.3% for the Indian Administrative Service officers and the Indian Police Service officers. The IFS officers' parents' and spouse education scores are different; it is 38.2% for graduate spouses and 44.7% for matriculate parents. The differential score is consistent with other demographic characters and indicates that to some extent IFS officers' hails from lower-middle-class income groups with parents' education hovering around matriculate. Spouse graduate education for the IFS officers maximizes at 38.2% figure. Details are shown in the below-mentioned exhibit.

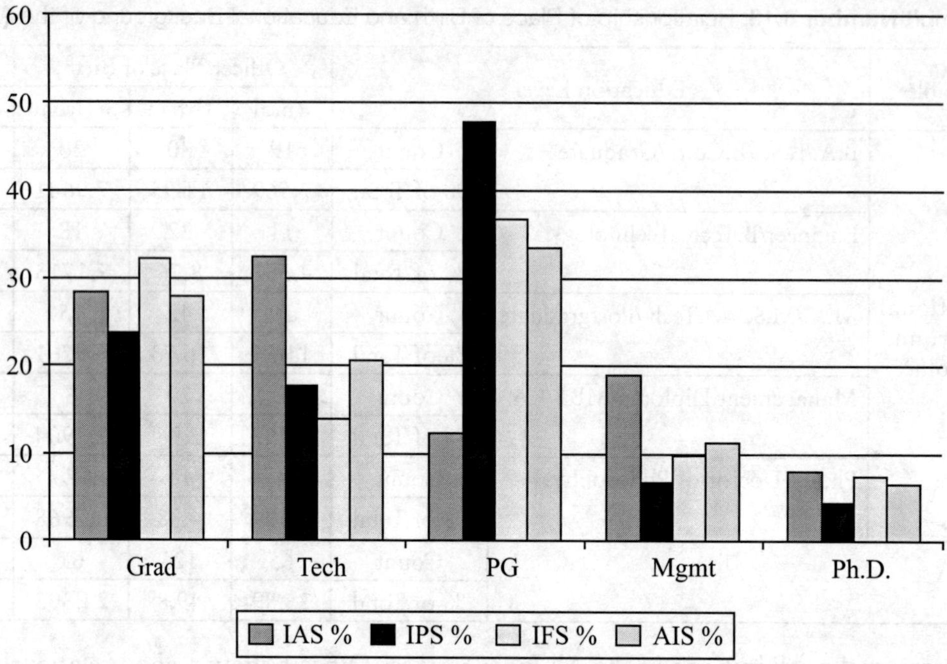

Chart No. 3.11: Educational Background and Amenability to Pressure

Exhibit Number 3.14: Parents and Spouse Education Relation with Acceptability to Pressure

Service Name	Relation with AISO	Item Details	Educational Qualifications				Total
			Ph.D.	P.G.	Graduate	Metric	
IAS	Spouse	% within service	16.40%	39.70%	32.90%	11.00%	28.90%
	Parents	% within service	12.30%	49.30%	28.80%	9.60%	29.30%
IPS	Spouse	% within service	12.10%	52.70%	26.40%	8.80%	36%
	Parents	% within service	11.00%	47.30%	26.40%	15.40%	36.50%
IFS	Spouse	% within service	9.00%	34.80%	38.20%	18.00%	35.20%
	Parents	% within service	10.60%	22.40%	22.40%	44.70%	34.10%
Total	Spouse	% of education	12.30%	42.70%	32.40%	12.60%	100%
		Frequency	31	108	82	32	253
	Parents	% of education	11.20%	39.40%	25.70%	23.70%	100%
		Frequency	28	98	64	59	249

Our hypothesis, acceptability of political pressure increases with the increase in the educational level of parents and spouse is rejected. It is related to the nature of the service and family background of an individual officer. Pearson Chi-square value of 34.8 with 6 degree of freedom and 0.000, level of significance indicates a good association with the decision-making process. Values of R and Rho are 0.3 are significant with 0.000, level of significance. A lot of glamour is associated with the Indian Administrative Service and Indian Police Service as indicated by high scores in comparison to Indian Forest Service, where the score is lower. Education of parents is also lower in the case of IFS officers, which may be due to the difficult nature of the job and more difficult career than the rosy-cozy career of the other two services.

3.3.5. Early Background

3.3.5.1. Domicile of Self, Spouse, and Parents: Place of birth of father, spouse, and own were considered for the study, how energy level, biological rhythm, and temperament are related to political pressure acceptance in the decision process. Does rural/urban background influence to shape the physiological and psychological thought formation among the All India Services Officers? An individual personality formation is considered as the outcome of the early cultural conditioning, family norms, social group influences as experienced by an individual person. Norms, values, attitudes towards political pressure moderate the influence on the decision, as the intensity of ideology fostered in culture, where an officer has spent one's early life.

It is usually thought that officers from rural backgrounds are more amenable to pressure acceptance in the decision-making process. Officers from rural backgrounds are simple and more straightforward in dealing with the pressure in the decision. Persons from rural areas are comparatively less financially sound than their urban counterparts. At the same time, officers from rural areas are less inclined towards materialistic things. Rural people are not so choosy about items of luxury. Rural persons are well connected and respect the values and cherish prolonged relationships even far from distances. An officer from urban areas has comparatively lesser faith in relations and more oriented towards his own goals. Commonly believed that officers from rural backgrounds believe in sustaining political relationships and they are more prone to pressure than officers from an urban background.

50.2% of the All India Services Officers feel that individual officers from the urban background are more amenable to pressure acceptance. If we combine urban and semi-urban, the All India Services Officers feel that 74.5% of urbanite officers take pressure in the decision. 90.2% of the Indian Administrative Service officers, 79.2% of the Indian Forest Service officers and 67.8% of the Indian Police Service officers from urbanite culture accept political pressure in the decision. Pearson Chi-Square value of 30.9 with 4 degree of freedom shows results at 0.000, level of significance.

Place of birth of parents and amenability to political pressure results indicate that 39.5% parentage of urban and 66.2% of combined urbanite parents influence an individual officer in acceptance of pressure in the decision. Statistically, analyses on Chi-square method indicate that results are highly significant with a significance level less than 0.001. Our hypothesis that rural people are more amenable to pressure has been rejected. An alternate hypothesis is accepted that officers from urban areas are more amenable to accept political pressure in the decision-making process.

Exhibit Number 3.15: Early Background and Acceptability of Pressure by the AISO

Factor Name	Domicile	% Within Service of Respondent			Total
		IAS	IPS	IFS	
Own place of birth	Rural	9.90%	32.30%	30.80%	25.50%
	Urban	59.20%	39.80%	53.80%	50.20%
	Semi-urban	31.00%	28.00%	15.40%	24.30%
Father place of birth	Rural	11.10%	34.10%	50.50%	33.70%
	Urban	55.60%	34.10%	32.60%	39.50%
	Semi-urban	33.30%	31.90%	16.80%	26.70%
Spouse place of birth	Rural	9.70%	21.50%	29.20%	20.90%
	Urban	62.50%	47.30%	56.20%	54.70%
	Semi-urban	27.80%	31.20%	14.60%	24.40%
Residence of parents	Rural	5.60%	21.30%	29.00%	19.70%
	Urban	58.30%	53.90%	54.80%	55.50%
	Semi-urban	36.10%	24.70%	16.10%	24.80%
Own education after high school	Rural	8.30%	17.80%	7.70%	11.50%
	Urban	66.70%	46.70%	75.80%	62.80%
	Semi-urban	25.00%	35.60%	16.50%	25.70%

Present-day materialistic demands exercise a great amount of control over personal needs and influence the behavior of a person in his interactions. It is commonly believed that a person living in urban areas may be influenced by new products and develop desires to acquire new things. Temptations and enticements drive parents to pursue All India Services Officers to accept pressure to attain own goals and interests. 55.5% of the All India Services Officers think that urban place of residence of parents motivates officers to accept pressure more frequently. Results indicate that 80.3% of total All India Service Officers respondents, 94.4% of the Indian Administrative Service officers, 78.6% of the Indian Police Service officers and 70.9% of the Indian Forest Service officers feel that urbanite parent's residence make them accept political pressure more commonly. Our hypothesis that rural parentage residence increases the pressure acceptability has been rejected in Chi-square analysis. Results are highly significant at 0.001, significance level. R and Rho values of –0.3 are significant at 0.000, level of significance.

We have seen after the analysis of data that the behavior of spouse influence the process of decision-making and behavior of the All India Services Officers also. By and large spouse dominant over the private and official life of an individual officer. Cultural lineage and environment of her/his upbringing in childhood will regulate one's perceptions, attitude, beliefs, and behavior of the spouse.

It is commonly believed that an urbanite spouse will be more aware of about luxury and consumerism articles. Higher materialistic needs to influence the All India Services Officers to pursue pressure to meet their own needs. Urbanite life-partner is more conscious and assertive than a rural partner. Urbanites are more aware and possess the desired skills for manipulating things to their advantage. Urbanites are more flexible and adaptive; hence quickly change sides to exploit the situation to own advantage. Urbanites are more progressive in thinking and put lesser emphasis on values and ethics. Urbanites have a great instinct for survival amidst adverse situations.

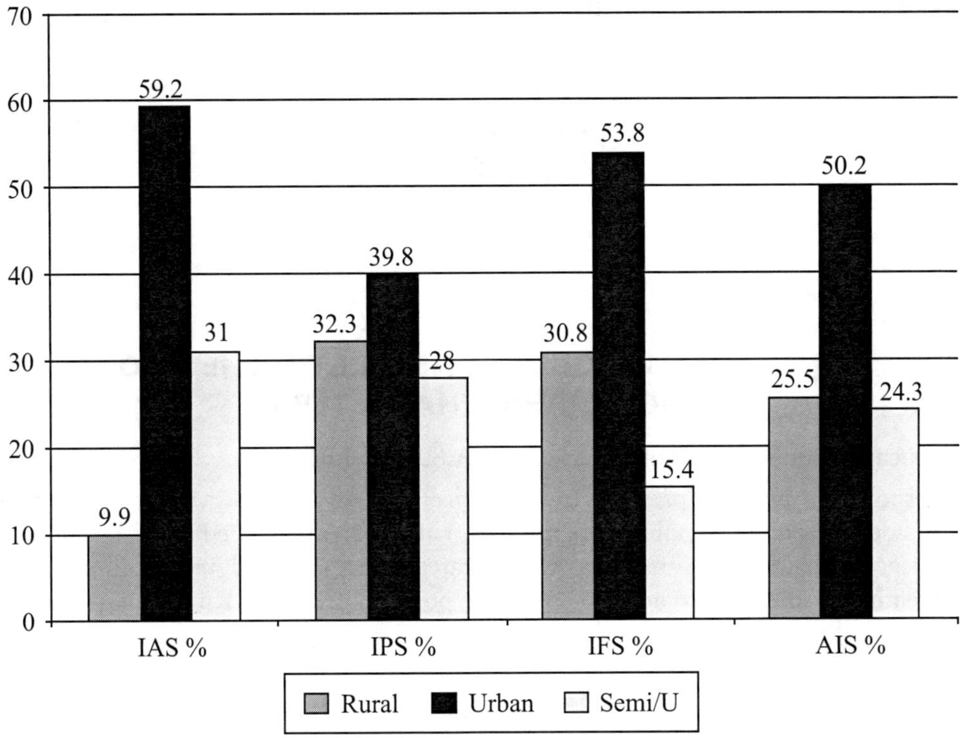

Chart No. 3.12: Own Place of Birth and Amenability to Pressure

54.7% of the All India Services Officers feel that spouse from urban birthplace will enhance pressure acceptability. If we combine urban and semi-urban results indicate that 80.3% of the Indian Administrative Service officers, 78.5% of the Indian Police Service officers and 70.8% of the Indian Forest Service officers feel that urbanite spouse will influence the All India Services Officers to accept the pressure in a decision to meet own needs. Results are significant on Chi-square analysis at 0.006, significance level. Pearson's correlation negative value of –0.2 shows is significant at 0.002, level of significance.

It is commonly believed that many students from rural areas shift to urban areas in search of better education after matriculation. A new place of education brings structural changes in the personality, perceptions, and attitudes of an individual. Urban life induces new desires and needs in the life of that individual person. When such a person joins the All India Services, his behavior will be in between urban and rural candidates. As an All India Services Officers such induced urban background perceptions will influence his interactions and behavior. It is also possible that such officers will develop a higher confidence level in the effective management of pressure to own advantage. 62.8% of the All India Services Officers feel that officers with urban education after matriculation will accept the political pressure more commonly. Again, if we combine urban and semi-urban, 88.5% of total the All India Services Officers, 92.3% of the Indian Forest Service officers, 91.7% of the Indian Administrative Service officers, and 82.3% of the Indian Police Service officers think that in the case officer has got his education in urban areas after matriculations, acceptability to pressure will be more.

ANNEXURE 3.A: QUESTIONNAIRE ON THE AISO BIOGRAPHIC CHARACTERS

101. Indicate Your Service Name: .............I.A.S./I.P.S./I.F.S.

A.1. Response to political pressure by the officers of All India Services may be situational and depends on personal factors related to any individual. We have listed the following categories in various situations. Which **category in your judgment and experience has been more amenable** to acceptance of the political pressure? Kindly, mark **one category** under each situation.

102. Type of service:
(1) IAS (2) IPS (3) IFS

103. Method of recruitment:
(1) Direct recruit (2) Promotes

104. Which level is more amenable:
(1) Top-level (2) Middle level (3) Lower level

105. Length of service:
(1) 1 to 4 years (2) 5 to 10 years (3) 11-17 years (4) 18 to 23 years
(5) more than 24 years of service

106. Officer regional background:
(1) North-eastern part (2) Eastern part (3) Western part
(4) Northern part (5) Southern part (6) Central part of India

107. Cadre of the officer:
(1) Home cadre (2) Outside cadre (3) Neighbour state

108. Community background:
(1) General (2) OBC (3) SC (4) ST

109. Family economic background:
(1) Rich (2) Upper middle class (3) Middle class
(4) Lower middle class (5) Poor

110. Marital status:
(1) Married (2) Unmarried (3) Separated

111. Sex:
(1) Male (2) Female

112. Education of self:
(1) B.A./B.Sc./B.Com./Graduate (2) Engineer/B.Tech.
(3) M.A./M.Sc./M.Tech. (4) Management/M.B.A./C.A./C.W.
(5) Ph.D.

113. Education of spouse:
(1) Matriculate (2) Graduate (3) Postgraduate (4) Ph.D.

114. Education of parents:
(1) Matriculate (2) Graduate (3) Postgraduate (4) Ph.D.

115. The profession of Spouse:
(1) Housekeeping (2) Services
(3) Entrepreneur (4) Business

Rural/Urban background of family members:

116. Own place of birth:
(1) Rural (2) Urban (3) Semi-Urban

117. Father's place of birth:
(1) Rural (2) Urban (3) Semi-Urban

118. Place of residence of parents:
(1) Rural (2) Urban (3) Semi-Urban

119. Spouse place of birth:
(1) Rural (2) Urban (3) Semi-Urban

120. Place of education after High School:
(1) Rural (2) Urban (3) Semi-Urban

121. Number of children:
(1) 1 Child (2) 2 Children (3) 3 Children (4) 4 or more

122. Family member attitude:
(1) Spouse (2) Children (3) Parents (4) Brother/Sister

Unit 4

Locus of Control Oscillations under Pressure

"A liar lies to himself as well as to the Gods. Lying is the origin of all evils; it leads to rebirth in the miserable planes of existence, to breach of pure precepts, and to corruption of the body."—Maharatnakuta Sutra 27, Bodhisattva Sutra's Discourse

"Who has not controlled intelligence and senses can have no purpose; such an undisciplined person cannot think practicality. The insensitive person has no peace and a person lacking peace cannot be happy." *The Bhagavad Gita* 2.66

- *Concept of Locus of Control and All India Services Officer*
- *Analyses of Research Data on Locus of Control*
- *Career Related*
- *Efficiency Related*
- *Reward Related*
- *Advancement and Growth Related*
- *Internality and Externality Related Influence Related*

This concept explains about level up to which, persons perceive that contingencies in decisions may affect the outcomes. Any change in control orientation will bring change in the individual and his immediate surroundings. This unit research data analysis results presented show a relationship to the locus of control variables of individual All India Services Officer and their response in handling political pressure in the decision-making process.

4.1. Concept of Locus of Control and the All India Services Officers

Locus of control construct derives strength from the 'social learning theory' of Rotter (1954). James (1957) developed a construct for 'internal-external locus of control.' The 'internal-external locus of control' concept explains about level up to which, persons perceive that contingencies may affect the outcomes. Rotter's (1966), instrument of internality was found to be laced with multi-dimensionality and mixed locus of control was found in this scale by Guttentay (1972) and Mirels (1970), Singh and Shukla (1986). The multi-dimensional character of Rotter's scale was studied by the Gurin et al. (1969). Govindaraju (1984) proposed probabilistic orientation in the locus of control. A person with internal control perceptions about positive or negative happenings of events thinks that things are being a consequence of own actions and he can control them.

Behavior researchers believe that it is desirable to change a person in the direction of internality. Gist and Mitchell (1992) proposed a model of determinants with three-dimensional efficacy. External determinants are task-related. Performance, ability, and personality are related to internal determinants. Any program towards changing control orientation will bring change in an individual and his immediate surroundings. In internal locus of control, the All India Services Officers will have low perceptions about the contingencies and they feel that actions taken by them will have bearing on the decision outcomes. An officer with internal control will be directed more towards goals and an officer with external control will be more emotional.

According to Lefcourt and Wine (1969), persons with high internal are more sensitive towards information, are better observant, and help in resolving the uncertainties in the decision process. Officers with internal control will demonstrate a better ability to acquire more information regarding political pressure, they will try to understand the pressure and solve it. Franklin (1963) indicated that perseverance and internality show a high and positive correlation. Such an individual All India Services Officer devotes more time in office, he involves himself to find solutions for difficult problems. They derive greater satisfaction in their job and believe in a participatory approach in management. McClelland's achievement motive need is expected to be high in such officers.

Internal control is related with the diverse achievement behavior (Coleman et al., 1966, McGee and Crandall, 1968; Harrison, 1968; Nowicki and Roundtree, 1971; Eppes, 1970; Bertel, 1969), related to conformity (Odell, 1959; McDonald, 1972), and reaction to influence attempts (Biondo et al., 1971, Hjelle et al., 1970, Phares, et al., 1969). Internals defer gratification (Lefcourt, 1976). The All India Services Officers with internality are inner-directed, respect values, maintain personal autonomy, and work with full responsibility when they are involved with political pressure. When pressure is exerted, they try to adhere to such values.

An individual All India Services Officers with internal control generally come from a democratic family background. Persons who have suffered, deprivation, punishments, and overprotection are external (Chavee, 1965; Davis and Phares, 1969 and McDonald, 1971). Temptations are related to the internality according to Frank and Fionda (1968). The relationship of internality and attitude towards the organization, the behavior was found out by Mitchell et al. (1975). Weiner (1974) added stability and variability dimensions to the locus of control. Internality is crucial for the All India Services Officers in deciding standards for their own behavior.

The All India Services Officers, who recognize their own capabilities and actions, experience stress due to failures in managing the political pressure. They consider themselves responsible for such lapses and become self-punitive in the process. High internality observed among the Indian Administrative Service officers can be attributed to their location on top positions in the hierarchy and excellent rapport and support provided by the seniors. Low confidence in a hierarchy, non-supportive seniors, and harshness of the bureaucratic system invariably increase the externality among the Indian Forest Service officers. The Indian Police Service officers enjoy the in-between position.

Performance at work, depression-related anxiety, and their correlation with the locus of control were studied by Jacobs (1976) and Gengh (1974). Externals are less satisfied with their job and get a more alienated work setting than internals. Beliefs in powerful others and others' control were correlated to internal orientation and faith in happiness (Morelli, 1979). Persons resorting to alcoholism scored high chances in an external locus of control, Castor and Parsons (1977). Persons with lower external control react more in problem-solving exercises (Track and Robbins, 1979), whereas the internals were found more task-centered, Anderson (1977). The All India Services Officers with an internal locus of control will show a higher interest in information gathering about pressure before arriving at decision. The All India Services Officers with an external locus of control will accept the pressure and political will and compliant the directions as earliest possible.

The internal or external locus of control indicates the extent to which any person will perceive a contingency relationship between their actions and their outcomes. The officers with high internals think they have control over their destiny and they can control their actions in decisions and outcome from it. The officer's high externals think outcomes are determined by agents or factors extrinsic to themselves such as luck, fate, and powerful others, MacDonald (1972).

People with high perceptions about uncertainties will have an external locus of control. They think that results are attained by chance; events are unrelated to their own behavior and are beyond own control (Rotter, 1975). Persons with higher internality experience less anxiety and stress (Singh and Bhandarkar, 1989). The All India Services Officers with high external locus, seriously lack personal predictability and they will have internal fear for unforeseen political pressure. Decisions taken by them will be affected by the outcome of the political pressure. Such officers believe in immediate gains. They do not try to achieve future goals.

In the present bureaucratic system, the All India Services Officers have a lot of freedom and flexibility to set their goals for performance and at the same time enough opportunities for personal growth. In a bureaucratic system, the location of the All India Services Officers is such that, they can influence important events in their respective sphere of work. Working conditions of the Indian Administrative Service officers allow them to grow their internality continuously. But this is not happening in case all other services. Continuous influence and assertive control of the Indian Administrative Service officers over IPS and IFS officers induce a decreasing trend in their internality, which may be highly detrimental to the decision process at their location. Present studies indicate that externality in the Indian Forest Service officers is the highest among the three All India Services. This can be attributed to non-accessibility to real power or continuous comparatively lower position in process of decision assigned to them. For higher effectiveness and acceptability, it is essential to increase the internality of the Indian Forest Service officers and the Indian Police Service officers through interventions of training, modifying their working conditions, improving the appraisal system, and infusing working freedom.

"Officers with higher belief in chance would not strive for any kind of action, reasoning that things happen by chance or luck or fate. Those with a predominant belief that powerful others are in control would seek to influence those in positions of power to get things done. People holding high internal control belief would strive to get things done through their own effort based on their ability in the contemporary world where a nation is talking about the relevance of promoting innovation and entrepreneurship, scrutinizing IAS officers on this dimension becomes very critical" (P. Singh and Bhandarkar, 1994).

Self-efficacy is an officer is indicative of individual beliefs that he can perform the given task under a given environment. The higher self-efficacy of an officer originates from his confidence in his abilities. An individual All India Services Officers with lower self-efficacy will be easily amenable to pressure or will give up resistance to political pressure in the early stage itself. An individual All India Services Officers with high self-efficacy put efforts to face the challenges, and increase one's efforts when politician give negative feedback. The success of desired outcomes in the process of decision by the All India Services Officers can be attributed to changeable or adjustable efforts put in by an officer. When an individual All India Services Officers get success in managing the political pressure, he will put more effort to gain more mileage out of it.

Any kind of non-fulfillment of goals or failures, an individual All India Services Officers will attribute them to chance, luck, or grace of God. An individual All India Services Officers attributing one's failures to chance were found to be more amenable to various kinds of direct and indirect political pressures. The Indian Administrative Service officers with high internality were observed and they felt that they could successfully influence the results and grounds, both. Slowly, they have exaggerated their belief in their capabilities. They perceive their abilities as a stable and powerful service they belong to. Among the Indian Administrative Service officers, internality has become a service variable. In a bureaucratic system, where the Indian Forest Service officers found that they are powerless to influence the decision outcomes, they attribute such failures to the present bureaucratic system and other people located in the hierarchy. Some of them located away from power attribute failures to fate, destiny, and luck.

Locus of control orientation indicates the All India Services Officers behavior and approach adopted in handling the political pressure, their feelings related to happenings occurring in service and department they work. This indicates concern for the top persons, politicians, senior bureaucrats, and bosses, who exercise control over the decision. The All India Services Officers show tremendous concern for any decision, which has bearing on their effectiveness, promotions, career progression, resource control, rewards acceptability, power allocation, and status distribution in the bureaucratic decision process. Entrepreneur and non-entrepreneurs belief differentiation were studied by Rupkey (1978) and observed that entrepreneurs have higher internality and externality to others.

Continuum of the All India Services Officers Behavior: Questionnaire at Annexure 4.A includes 10 items each for internality, externality for others, and externality by chance. One item's each for influence, accountability, career advancement, and rewards, two items for general, and three items were kept to study the effectiveness of the All India Services Officers in the decision-making process. The All India Services Officers' individual orientation is neither is purely internal or external. It is situational and continues to change as directed by the circumstances and forces operating on an individual All India Services Officer.

Collective orientation and service orientation are also perceived to be being influenced by the events in service career and forces of pressure operating in the decision-making process. Whatsoever be the internality or externality, it has an effect on the determinant of an officer and remolds the behavior of an individual All India Services Officer. The externality of the Indian Forest Service officers can be attributed to human variables and non-human stable dimensions of locus of control. Based on different studies in this area, we can have arranged the following continuum of behavior. Implications of variable determinants can be explained as below, and modified in time perspective of locus of control of different studies. Exhibit 4.1 depicts the peculiarity of locus, its attribution, and AISO behavior.

Exhibit Number 4.1: Continuum of the All India Services Officers Behavior

Peculiarity of Locus	Nature of Attribution	Affected Factor/Agent of Behavior	Behavior of the AISO
i. Internality stability of individual AISO	Stable	Officer capability	Feeling of elite, consider oneself like God, supremacy in system
ii. Externality stability human	Stable	Bureaucratic system	Officer desire to accept different responsibilities
iii. Internal stability in respective service	Stable	Cadre/caste groups/regional grouping	A feeling of service superiority, caste and region groups in particular service
iv. Stability in externality, non-human	Stable	Destiny, God	Assigning decision outcome to destiny, casual behavior
v. Officer with stability in internality	Variable	Attempt and struggle	Persistence and resolution in a decision by an officer
vi. Externality stability, human	Variable	Other services, decisions of others	Weak officer, a decision will be in conformity with pressure
vii. Internality stable in service	Variable	Efforts as a service member	Persistency in that bureaucratic system
viii. Stability in externality, non-human	Variable	Opportunity, chance/luck	Behavior in likelihood feasibility or probability in decision

4.2. Analysis of Research Data on Locus of Control

Data on the locus of control questionnaire were studied to find out the way individual All India Services Officers feel about the things happening in their department with respect to their service and cadre. In their respective departments, how much control they exercise in the decision-making process? Who are the persons, who control the process of decision? Different items on success or effectiveness of the All India Services Officers in their organization have been studied. Acceptability and influence of the All India Services Officers in the decision-making process of their department were considered for research. Data on career advancement and rewards were also studied.

The score and ratio for the internality (I), externality for others (EO), externality by chance (EC), and internality with EO + EC have been studied. The ratio of I/EC is 1.56, which indicates high internality among the All India Services Officers. The ratio of I/EO is 1.12; it is significant that the All India Services Officers show serious concern for seniors and politicians while arriving at any decision. At the same time, a high score on **EO** indicates the dysfunctional dependence of the All India Services Officers on the seniors and politicians. A high ratio of 1.56 for **I/EC** indicates high internality in comparison to belief in happening things by chance. The combined ratio of **I/EO+EC** is 0.65 indicating dominant internal orientation among the All India Services Officers. Results indicate that the All India Services Officers are effective performers; high self-confidence and they mobilize resources to attain the end goals. **Internality means score** for the All India Services Officers is more than 38 indicate that the All India Services officers are not realistic regarding the problems faced by their subordinates but they possess high confidence in themselves, which helps them in achieving goals assigned to them.

P. Singh and A. Bhandarkar's (1994) findings about the locus of control of IAS officers are similar to the results of the present study. "IAS officers are low fatalist and high self-determining in orientation. Such a profile indicates that they are self-confident and believe in shaping their own destiny. (2) They are moderately inner (self) directed. They also believe, to a moderate extent, that many life events are controlled by the situation and also by people in a powerful position. (3) Putting together the above findings, one would notice that two streams of possibly contradictory values operate simultaneously in the minds of the IAS officers, creating dissonance and ambivalence of action. This paradox is likely to result in lower risk-taking behavior, low desire to take charge of the situation, and accommodate and compromising stance with higher and powerful authorities. In addition, the officers with this orientation are likely to follow the beaten track, avoiding confrontation on the issues, taking recourse to rules, regulations, and procedures."

Results for the locus of controls general, career, success, effectiveness, rewards, acceptability, and influence are discussed with details shown in exhibit number 4.9 and statistical analysis in Exhibit 4.2. In general, 30.36% of the All India Services Officers strongly felt (rank of 5) that they are the masters of the situation and they have freedom in decision-making, score for respective services are 46.3% for the Indian Administrative Service officers and 38.1% for the Indian Police Service officers. 27.3% of the Indian Forest Service officers have a general feeling (rank of 4) that they can determine the direction of the decision. This indicates that the IFS officers are enjoying lesser freedom in the decision-making process in comparison to the Indian Police Service officers and the Indian Administrative Service officers. This creates powerlessness among the Indian Forest Service officers, which has an adverse impact on the decision. The general locus of control among the IFS officers in internality is around half, in comparison to the IAS officers; however, both should have similar values. Excessive control exercised by the IAS officers has caused this situation and reduced the internality of the Indian Forest Service officers and the Indian Police Service officers.

35.6% of the All India Services Officers strongly felt that pressure groups and most important persons determine the decision. Every third of the All India Services Officer indicates strong externality for others, indicating an orientation of counter dependence and reliance on the political leadership for the decision. Results for externality for the other three services are 45.8% for the Indian Administrative Service officers, 41% for the Indian Police Service officers, and 34.2% for the Indian Forest Service officers. Similarly, results for externality for luck, 28.9% of the All India Services Officers generally feel that things are beyond their control (rank 4). Results indicate that the All India Services Officers' lower score for externality for luck has a lesser problem in coping with the system frustrations.

Exhibit Number 4.2: Locus of Control for the All India Services Officers, Statistical Analysis

Sr.	Item Name	n	Score	Mean	SD	chi.	Sif.
245	I can largely determine what matters me	267	994	3.78	1.18	29.95	'.000
246	Course of my career largely depends upon me	272	1036	3.81	1.08	13.08	'0.10
247	My success/failure depends on efforts I put in	264	1011	3.83	1.08	6.35	'0.6
254	Successful completion due to my hard work	265	1120	4.23	0.86	5.28	'0.50
260	Success depends on my competence/hard work	254	937	3.69	1.06	10.59	'0.2
264	I am responsible for getting/not getting rewards	261	936	3.4	1.18	7.3	'0.5
267	My promotion depends on my ability and effort	261	986	3.78	1.15	15.5	'0.05
269	I can work hard to get my suggestions accepted	236	913	3.87	0.97	13.8	'0.08
271	I determine what happen me in the department	237	799	3.37	1.32	34.9	'0.000
272	My acceptability depends on my behaviour with them	248	1038	4.19	0.9	12.62	'0.1
	Internality total mean (score = 39)	256	9770	3.4	1.06		
248	Most important persons, control matters here	263	1031	3.92	0.99	25.72	'0.001
249	To large extent my career depends on my seniors	252	942	3.65	1.01	33.98	'0.000
250	My effectiveness determined by senior people	258	915	3.55	1.04	33.45	'0.000
259	Senior person's preference decide rewards	267	914	3.42	1.04	14.89	'0.06
255	Seniors liking influence promotion decisions	274	1046	3.82	0.98	14.66	'0.06
261	I am being liked depends upon my seniors	274	812	2.96	1.18	12.76	'0.1
263	If my seniors do not like me, I probably would not succeed in this department	271	607	2.24	1.14	10.95	'0.2
266	My success/failure depends who work with me	248	602	2.43	1.17	57.24	'0.000
273	My ideas get accepted if I fit in desire of seniors	249	839	3.37	1.23	23.44	'0.003
274	Pressure groups are powerful and control things	261	1028	3.94	1.07	48.4	'0.000
	Externality for Others, Total		8736	3.3	1.08		
251	Service one joins is accidental matter	267	782	2.93	1.26	22.03	'0.000
252	One's career is a matter of chance	266	731	2.75	1.17	23.96	'0.000
253	Success depends upon the chances one gets	266	769	2.89	1.26	78.24	'0.000

Sr.	Item Name	n	Score	Mean	SD	chi.	Sif.
256	Getting rewards in department is matter of luck	273	668	2.45	1.08	48.67	'0.000
257	Success of one's plans is, to large extent a matter of luck	266	594	2.23	1.05	30.45	'0.000
258	Promotion depends on being right place & time	267	713	2.67	1.36	40.4	'0.000
262	It is matter of luck that people listen to me	249	462	1.86	1.08	15.01	'0.05
265	My success or failure is mostly matter of luck	259	484	1.87	0.91	17.25	'0.02
268	Most things are beyond one's control	223	606	2.72	1.15	15.38	'0.05
270	I am acceptable because I am lucky	241	437	1.81	1.02	29.6	'0.000
	Externality for Luck, Total		6246	2.2	1.13		
	Grand total average	281		2.93	1.09		

n = frequency. SD = Standard deviation. chi = Pearson Chi-square. Sif. = Significance level

4.2.1. Career-related Aspects

The All India Services Officers are highly career conscious; locus of control results indicate that 35.6% of the All India Services Officers feel that generally (rank 4) they can play role in shaping their career. It infers that political leadership does not exercise full control as envisaged commonly. In case the All India Services Officers possess the desire to take strong decisions, they can comfortably afford to make merit-based decisions. 40.3% of the Indian Police Service officers strongly (rank 5) feel that their career depends upon them only; if they perform well, they can progress in their career. Among the All India Services Officers, the Indian Police Service officers' highest score shows that being uniformed service, rules and merit is more important than pressure. 35.6% of the Indian Administrative Service officers and 31.3% of the Indian Forest Service officers show internality control in career.

Again, the Indian Forest Service officers are the least secure among the All India Services. To see externality for other services, analyses indicate that 42.7% of the All India Services Officers think generally that their career is safe within the hands of their seniors. 56.1% of the Indian Police Service officers have faith in their seniors, which is highest among the All India Services, may be due to disciplined uniformed service, where line of command prevails over. Sittings on the top of power the Indian Administrative Service officers have great faith in their seniors for their career. As far as concern for others locus is concerned, the Indian Administrative Service officers are fairly sure that once they join IAS, their career is secure and safe with their seniors sitting at the top of government administration.

Only 29.3% of the Indian Forest Service officers indicate faith in their seniors. The comparatively low score on faith towards seniors for career indicates highly pervasive powerlessness among the top hierarchy of the Indian Forest Service officer's cadres. This is the reason that externality for luck replaces the externality for others. Ultimately, frustrations pervade the decision process and the country is the sufferer. The Constitution of India has envisaged the same service conditions for the three All India Services, but executives located close to power have usurped the whole power for them only, resultantly frustration and withdrawal behavior accumulate among other officers like Indian Forest Service officers.

Exhibit Number 4.3: Place of Birth of the Officer and Locus of Control for Career

Locus	Ranking Item	Variable	Birth Place of Officer			Total
			Rural	Urban	S/Urban	
The course of my career largely depends upon me	Hardly feel this way	% within place of birth of the officer		1.59	5	1.98
		% of Total		0.79	1.186	1.98
	Slightly feel this way	% within place of birth of the officer	14.93	11.1	13.34	12.6
		% of Total	3.953	5.53	3.162	12.6
	Somewhat feel this way	% within place of birth of the officer	13.43	19.8	18.33	17.8
		% of Total	3.557	9.88	4.348	17.8
	Generally feel this way	% within place of birth of the officer	34.33	36.5	36.67	36
		% of Total	9.881	18.2	8.696	36
	Strongly feel this way	% within place of birth of the officer	37.31	31	26.67	31.6
		% of Total	9.881	15.4	6.324	31.6
	Total	% within place of birth of the officer	100	100	100	100
		% of Total	26.48	49.8	23.72	100

Exhibit 4.3 analysis results for a variable relationship of a place of birth of officer with locus of control item in course of a career (internality related) analyses show 49.8% urban, 26.48% rural and 23.72% semi-urban AISO feel a place of birth do influence course of a career in service. Data analysis for ranking of options show 37.31% rural background AISO strongly feel, 36.5% of urban background generally feel, and 36.67% semi-urban background generally feel that place of birth does influence the course of the career of officers in service.

4.2.2. Efficiency-related Items in Decision

We have tried to study success and effectiveness in relation to locus of control. The analysis consists of three statements each for internality, externality for others, and externality by chance. One statement each for success, competence, and planning, and hard work was studied in the locus of control. 34.4% of the All India Services Officers strongly (rank 5) felt that success or failure is related to the efforts mobilized by them, 36.6% of the Indian Police Service officers, 36.6% of the Indian Administrative Service officers, and 33% of the Indian Forest Service officers think that same way under internal control. Success for the All India Services Officers is a matter of faith in themselves and their efforts.

The All India Services Officers have high confidence in their abilities and efforts; with hard work they can mobilize the decision outcome to their desired direction. Thus, confidence induces the feeling of success with political pressure and motivates them to achieve own goals under the shadow of pressure. 47.1% of the All India Services Officers strongly felt that due to their detailed planning and hard work they complete their assignments successfully. 54.8% of the Indian Administrative Service officers, 47.5% of the Indian Forest Service officers, and 40.2% of the Indian Police Service officers have belief in their capacity for hard work and meticulous planning in internal control. Here comparatively low percentages for the Indian Police Service officers can be assigned due to prevalent discipline in the police forces, thus the system line of command ensures the success for them.

34.1% of the All India Services Officers show generally faith in their competence. Internal control for competence is marginally low among the Indian Administrative Service officers; this may be due to an assured position in the bureaucratic system. The Indian Administrative Service officers believe more in hierarchy, power, and position than individual competence. Irrespective of the competence and merit of the case, the Indian Administrative Service officers will dominate and prevail over all others in the decision process. The Indian Administrative Service officers show low concern for competence and effectiveness.

The All India Services Officers once complete the UPSC selection process, for the rest of their service, they are assured for career progression. After a long spell of hard work, some of them do not bother to read other than the newspaper to remain aware of political programs. They relegate concern for studying in their unconscious mind, lay to rest their books forever for eternal peace. Excessive security in the career has eaten away and eroded the feeling for competence. Undesirable excessive security in the bureaucratic system has reduced the concern for competence.

Results for externality for others indicate that 35.4% of the All India Services Officers somewhat feel that their effectiveness is decided by their seniors. 33.3% of the Indian Administrative Service officers generally feel, 43.2% of the Indian Police Service officers somewhat way feel, and 35.4% of the Indian Forest Service officers feel in somewhat the manner that their senior officers determine their effectiveness. But it is not true that they have excessive faith in the seniors, in next statement 35% of the All India Services Officers hardly feel that but for seniors help they could have collapsed in career. This indicated that the All India Services Officers could have worked hard without the pleasure of seniors to achieve success.

32.9% of the All India Services Officers slightly feel that team members working with them influence their success or failure. The All India Services Officers thinking that without any external help they can attain targets effectively. The Indian Forest Service officers have demonstrated a greater need for support from the team members, this is due to the highly arduous nature of the job, they perform, and activities are located in far-flung areas. In forestry, a single person cannot sustain the results. The All India Services Officers show low externality for others on most of the statements, they show reliance for the seniors, peers, and political leadership. Reliance on the seniors and political leadership induce dysfunctional dependence on others and mobilize them to accept political pressure in the decision-making process.

Externality by chance or luck among the All India Services Officers has been found to be low. 30.7% of the All India Services Officers somewhat feel that success depends on the chances they come across in the service. The Indian Police Service officers have a slight feeling that success is related to the chances they get, that chance externality is lowest among the Indian Police Service officers in the All India Services Officers. 32.3% of the Indian Forest Service officers generally think that success in the job is related to the chances they get in the decision process. High rankings in chance externality by the Indian Forest Service officers indicate that powerlessness and frustration are common across the ranks and files in this service. The Indian Forest Service officers will be having a serious problem in coping with the unforeseen situations and accumulated frustration arising out from the pressure. The external pressures will impair efficiency and effectiveness. The All India Services Officers have demonstrated a very low rank of hardly for the luck factor alone, indicating that the All India Services Officers do not have dependence or belief in luck rather believe in working hard to meet the needs.

Exhibit Number 4.4: Method of Recruitment more Amenable to Pressure and Success/Effectiveness

Locus	Ranking	Item	Method of Recruitment more Amenable to the Political Pressure		Total
			Direct Recruit	Promotes	
My success/failure depends mostly on efforts I put in	Hardly feel this way	Count	3	3	6
		% within method of recruitment more amenable to the political pressure	3.8	1.65	2.3
		% of Total	1.15	1.15	2.3
	Slightly feel this way	Count	6	21	27
		% within method of recruitment more amenable to the political pressure	7.59	11.5	10.3
		% of Total	2.3	8.05	10.3
	Somewhat feel this way	Count	20	42	62
		% within method of recruitment more amenable to the political pressure	25.3	23.1	23.5
		% of Total	7.66	16.1	23.8
	Generally feel this way	Count	22	55	77
		% within method of recruitment more amenable to the political pressure	27.8	30.2	29.5
		% of Total	8.43	21.1	29.5
	Strongly feel this way	Count	28	61	89
		% within method of recruitment more amenable to the political pressure	35.4	33.5	34.1
		% of Total	10.7	23.4	34.1
Total		Count	79	182	261
		% within method of recruitment more amenable to the political pressure	100	100	100
		% of Total	30.3	69.7	100

Exhibit 4.4 shows locus variable individual success or failure in decision depends mostly on efforts individuals put in relationship with the demographic variable method of recruitment in the AIS, analyses results show 69.7% promoted and 30.3% direct recruited show efficiency of a decision taken by an individual depends on efforts put in by that individual. Statistical analyses ranking show 35.4% direct recruited and 33.5% promoted strongly feel that efficiency officers are related to individual efforts put in by them, whereas the percentage is negligible in slightly and hardly feeling ranking.

4.2.3. Rewards-related Aspects

We have discussed in previous paragraphs that individual needs and goals drive the All India Services Officers to mobilize pressure to meet those self-goals. Rewards are basically the motivator to induce officers to accept pressure to serve own goals. In government administration rewards definition is very extensive and incomprehensible. One item each for internality, externality for others, and externality for chance were studied. In locus of control through rewards, we have tried to study the perceived relationship between the All India Services Officers' actions in decision and outcome of decision for rewards.

35.9% of the All India Services Officers generally realize that they are responsible for what they are getting out of the system, 40.6% of the Indian Police Service officers, 33.7% of the Indian Forest Service officers, and 32.9% of the Indian Administrative Service officers feel this way. Here comparatively lowest value for the Indian Administrative Service officers indicates that they think that by virtue of being a member of the Indian Administrative Service group they are getting rewards without any efforts. Actually, the Indian Administrative Service officers by virtue of their position, they acquire rewards automatically.

Externality for others indicates that 40.1% of the All India Services Officers generally feel that senior person preferences will decide who will be rewarded. 46.3% of the Indian Police Service officers, 37% of the Indian Administrative Service officers, and 36.6% of the Indian Forest Service officers bank upon their seniors. The highest externality among the Indian Police Service officers indicates that for any kind of own benefits they will be first to accept the political pressure in the decision-making process. This also indicates that the Indian Police Service officers are comparatively less satisfied with their job. Externality for luck or chance is highest among the Indian Police Service officers (58.5%) in comparison to the other two services.

Exhibit 4.5 shows locus variables usually individual is responsible for getting or not getting rewards relationship with the demographic variable level in the hierarchy of the AISO in the decision-making process. 58.15% of top level, 25.2% of middle level, and 16.7% of junior level AISO feel what they get or do not get they themselves are responsible for that. At the same time in ranking of responses, 36.31% at the top level and 36.8% at a middle level generally feel but junior level 28.9% feel generally with the same score in somewhat way feeling, two score total of 57.8% at junior level show low confidence in rewards.

Exhibit Number 4.5: Which Level is more Amenable to Political Pressure and Locus in Rewards

Locus	Ranking	Item	Level More Amenable to Political Pressure			Total
			Top Level	Middle Level	Lower Level	
Usually I am responsible for getting/not getting rewards	Hardly feel this way	Count	13	8	4	25
		% of level more amenable to political pressure	8.28	11.8	8.89	9.26
		% of Total	4.815	2.96	1.48	9.26
	Slightly feel this way	Count	22	8	5	35
		% within which level is more amenable to political pressure	14.01	11.8	11.1	13
		% of Total	8.148	2.96	1.85	13
	Somewhat feel this way	Count	37	16	13	66
		% within which level is more amenable to political pressure	23.57	23.5	28.9	24.4
		% of Total	13.7	5.93	4.81	24.4
	Generally feel this way	Count	57	25	13	95
		% within which level is more amenable to political pressure	36.31	36.8	28.9	35.2
		% of Total	21.11	9.26	4.81	35.2
	Strongly feel this way	Count	28	11	10	49
		% within which level is more amenable to political pressure	17.83	16.2	22.2	18.1
		% of Total	10.37	4.07	3.7	18.1
Total		Count	157	68	45	270
		% within which level is more amenable to political pressure	100	100	100	100
		% of Total	58.15	25.2	16.7	100

4.2.4. Advancement and Growth-related Perceptions

Advancement in the service and growth in career is perceived to be one of the biggest and vital motivators for the All India Services Officers. Internal locus of control has been observed to be very high among the All India Services Officers. 38.3% of the All India Services Officers strongly thought that their advancement and promotions in their service are related to their own abilities and efforts. If we see the same thing among various services, 42% of the Indian Administrative Service officers, 39.3% of the Indian Police Service officers, and 34.7% of the Indian Forest Service officers strongly felt that capability and own efforts determine their advancements. Very high internality is observed among the majority of the officers.

At the same time, the All India Services Officers show 37.4% of general feeling indicating high externality for others also. Respective figures for three services towards externality for others are 39.8% for the Indian Police Service officers, 37% for the Indian Administrative Service officers, and

36.6% for the Indian Forest Service officers. High externalities score for the Indian Police Service officers pointing towards the fact that they will be more amenable to accept political pressure in the decision process. Externality for chance is low at 27.5% with slight feelings, whereas IAS and IPS hardly felt in that way.

Here results for the IFS officers are perturbing, 23.8% with a general feeling that getting promotion depends upon the individual being at the right place at right time. This serious situation points towards high stagnation and a prevalent high degree of manipulations in the promotion process for the Indian Forest Service officers. The Indian Forest Service Officers' beliefs in fatalism and luck or God are a matter of great concern, there is an urgent need to initiate a correction in the system, and otherwise, it will seriously impair the decision process. Promotion-related frustration is highest among the Indian Forest Service officers, pointing towards high uncertainty in the decision.

Exhibit Number 4.6: Attitude of Family Members and Locus for Advancement

Locus	Rank	Item	Attitude Family Members				Total
			Spouse	Children	Parents	Brother/Sister	
My promotion in department depends mostly on my ability and effort	Hardly feel this way	% within attitude family members	2.206	0	0	0	1.4
		% of Total	1.395	0	0	0	1.4
	Slightly feel this way	% within attitude family members	10.29	8.7	12.5	0	9.77
		% of Total	6.512	0.93	2.33	0	9.77
	Somewhat feel this way	% within attitude family members	32.35	39.1	30	56.3	34.4
		% of Total	20.47	4.19	5.58	4.19	34.4
	Generally feel this way	% within attitude family members	13.24	26.1	17.5	18.8	15.8
		% of Total	8.372	2.79	3.26	1.4	15.8
	Strongly feel this way	% within attitude family members	41.91	26.1	40	25	38.6
		% of Total	26.51	2.79	7.44	1.86	38.6
Total		Count	136	23	40	16	215
		% within attitude family members	100	100	100	100	100
		% of Total	63.26	10.7	18.6	7.44	100

Exhibit 4.6 analyses for locus variable my promotion in department depends mostly on my ability and efforts relationship with demographic variable family member attitude show 63.26% spouse, 10.7% children, 18.6% parents and 7.44% brother/sister show relation with the advancement in service. Family members' attitude ranking in decision pertaining to advancement, 41.91% spouse feels strongly this way, children 26.1% feels strongly and the same percentage in general or say, 52.2% children feeling show for advancement, whereas parents score is 40% with strongly feeling.

4.2.5. Internality and Externality Acceptability in Decision

The All India Services Officers work in the differential cultural background under a high degree of uncertainty. Cultural diversity and decision variations put a big question mark on the acceptability of the decision and the All India Services Officers themselves by the people and bureaucratic system. One item each for internality, externality for others, and externality for chance were studied to find out the acceptability of the AISO in the decision. Internal locus of control is very high, 32.9% of the All India Services Officers strongly felt that they work so hard that their suggestions are accepted in the department they work with.

38.7% of the Indian Police Service officers, 38.6% of the Indian Administrative Service officers and 36.4% of the Indian Forest Service officers think that they have to strive hard to get their decision accepted in the department. The Indian Police Service officers indicate the highest concern of internality for acceptance, this may be due to the reason that people, in general, raise lesser opposition to their decisions due to fear of rod or uniform or discipline in forces. Even if someone has grudge against the police officer, first he will ensure his safety then only will lodge a complaint or protest. Even politicians have internal restraints for police officers and they refrain from criticizing them in public.

Externality for others indicates that 29.1% of the All India Services Officers somewhat felt that their decisions are accepted if the outcome is suitable to their seniors. 34.4% of the Indian Administrative Service officers generally felt, 33.7% of the Indian Forest Service officers somewhat felt, and 32.9% of the Indian Police Service officers somewhat felt that they have to take decisions in tune with the pressure from the seniors.

Results for Indian Administrative Service officers indicate that they have higher externality for others, which makes them more vulnerable to accept any kind of pressure from the politicians. The Indian Administrative Service officers predominantly live under the feeling that the politicians relate their survival with their acceptability. High consciousness for the power and desire to retain the top position compel the Indian Administrative Service officers to accept any kind of political pressure in the decision. Externality for luck or chance has been observed to be very low among the All India Services Officers. 50.4% of the All India Services Officers hardly believe that the system accepts them due to their luck. The Indian Administrative Service officers show the least externality for the chance and Indian Forest Service officers highest among three of the All India Services on the lowest rank of hardly feelings.

Exhibit 4.7 statistical results for locus variable, 'I can work hard enough to get my suggestions accepted in the department' relation with biographic variable community background show 46.23% general category, 35.85% SC category, 13.68% ST category and 4.2% OBC feel their community background play role in the acceptance of their decision in the system. Analyses of a feeling of community background in the highest score of 33.67% in general category feel somewhat way, 44.74% SC feels strongly, 48.28% ST strongly feel and 55.56% OBC somewhat way feels that hard work pay in the decision. A very low score for OBC may be due to a low percentage of the AISO in services or a low percentage of questionnaire respondents.

Exhibit Number 4.7: I can Work Hard Enough to get my Suggestions Accepted in the Department with Community Background

Locus	Rank	Item	Community Background				Total
			General	OBC	SC	ST	
I can work hard enough to get my suggestions accepted in the department	Hardly feel this way	Count	2		1		3
		% within community background	2.041		1.316		1.42
		% of Total	0.943		0.472		1.42
	Slightly feel this way	Count	7		1	1	9
		% within community background	7.142		1.316	3.448	4.25
		% of Total	3.302		0.472	0.472	4.25
	Somewhat feel this way	Count	33	5	23	7	68
		% within community background	33.67	55.55	30.26	24.14	32.1
		% of Total	15.56	2.358	10.85	3.302	32.1
	Generally feel this way	Count	31	2	17	7	57
		% within community background	31.63	22.22	22.36	24.14	26.9
		% of Total	14.62	0.943	8.019	3.302	26.9
	Strongly feel this way	Count	25	2	34	14	75
		% within community background	25.51	22.22	44.73	48.28	35.4
		% of Total	11.79	0.943	16.04	6.604	35.4
Total		Count	98	9	76	29	212
		% within community background	100	100	100	100	100
		% of Total	46.23	4.245	35.85	13.67	100

4.2.6. Influence in Locus of Control

The All India Services Officers occupy the positions of crucial importance in the hierarchy to reflect their influence on the decision. The All India Services Officers' perception about the need for coercive and persuasive power bases can be seen from the locus of control. One item each for internality, externality for others, and externality for a chance for influence were studied. Internal locus of control for influence has been observed very high among the All India Services Officers. 44.7% of the All India Services Officers strongly felt that they are acceptable in the bureaucratic system due to their behavior with others. 52.8% of the Indian Police Service officers and 50.4 of the Indian Administrative Service officers strongly think that because of their behavior people accept their influence. The Indian Police Service officers show higher internality for influence than Indian Administrative Service officers, this may be due to fear of police among masses force them to accept the influence of the Indian Police Service officers. Power flows from the rod of the Indian Police Service officers.

The lowest internality for influence was observed among Indian Forest Service officers, 38.4% of them generally felt people accept them due to their behavior. Lower internality has been induced due to the continuous feeling of powerlessness generated by sustained coercive power used by the other service officer on them. The Indian Administrative Service officers have a high need for coercive power and their first target to use persuasive-coercive power on the Indian Forest Service officers. The Indian Forest Service officers under continuous powerlessness respond from reactive orientation, the Indian Administrative Service officers react from coercive power bases to influence the Indian Forest Service officers.

Exhibit Number 4.8: Locus for Acceptability and Family Economic Background

Locus	Rank	Item	Family Economic Background					Total
			Rich	Upper middle class	Middle class	Lower middle class	Poor	
My acceptability to others will depend on my behaviour with them	Hardly feel this way	Count	0	0	2	0	0	2
		% within family economic background	0	0	4.65	0	0	0.9
		% of Total	0	0	0.86	0	0	0.9
	Slightly feel this way	Count	3	0	2	1	0	6
		% within family economic background	3.9	0	4.65	2.63	0	2.6
		% of Total	1.29	0	0.86	0.43	0	2.6
	Somewhat feel this way	Count	16	7	8	4	1	36
		% within family economic background	20.8	12.3	18.6	10.5	5.56	15
		% of Total	6.87	3	3.43	1.72	0.43	15
	Generally feel this way	Count	27	28	11	14	4	84
		% within family economic background	35.1	49.1	25.6	36.8	22.2	36
		% of Total	11.6	12	4.72	6.01	1.72	36
	Strongly feel this way	Count	31	22	20	19	13	105
		% within family economic background	40.3	38.6	46.5	50	72.2	45
		% of Total	13.3	9.44	8.58	8.15	5.58	45
Total		Count	77	57	43	38	18	233
		% within family economic background	100	100	100	100	100	100
		% of Total	33	24.5	18.5	16.3	7.73	100

The AISO show moderate externality for others. 34.6% of the All India Services Officers somewhat way felt that their seniors decide their influence on the decision-making process. 38.9% of the Indian Police Service officers, 32.7% of the Indian Forest Service officers, and 31.5% of the Indian Administrative Service officers think that somewhat manner their seniors' liking decides their influence in the system. This indicates moderate externality for others is highest among the Indian Police Service officers, pointing that the Indian Police Service officers use the highest amount of negotiation skills in the decision process. Externality for chance has been recorded very low among the All India Services Officers. 49.2% of the All India Services Officers hardly felt that due to good luck they are acceptable in the decision-making process. The lowest luck externality was observed among the Indian Administrative Service officers, followed by Indian Police Service officers and Indian Forest Service officers.

High internality dominates among the All India Services Officers should induce them to adopt political pressure solving approach. They should have a lesser feeling of stress in the management of the uncertainty in the decision. They should use more motivational behavior inclining towards persuasive power bases with their subordinates. Along with internality, the All India Services Officers have moderate to high externality for others also, which induce low inter-personal faith in them. High externality induces high use of coercive power bases and at the same time makes them more amenable towards acceptance of political pressure.

Exhibit 4.8 results for locus variable 'my acceptability to others will depend on my behaviour with them' relationship with biographic variable family economic background show 33% rich category, 24.5% upper, 18.5% middle class, 16.3% lower and 7.73% poor economic class think that their decision acceptability is related to their economic background. Acceptability of the AISO decision feeling results in various economic backgrounds are 40% rich feels strongly, 49.1% upper class feels generally, 46.5% middle class feels strongly. 36.8% lower class feels generally and 72.2% poor class strongly feels that their decision acceptability depends upon their economic background.

Exhibit Number 4.9: Locus of Control, Highest Percentage Values for the All India Services

Locus of Control Statement	AISO Total				IAS		IPS		IFS	
	N	n	Sc	%	Sc	%	Sc	%	Sc	%
I largely determine what matters me	263	84	4	31.9	5	45.8	4	39.1	4	28.3
My career largely depends upon me	267	95	4	35.6	5	40.3	4	39.6	4	31.3
Success/failure depends on my efforts	259	89	5	34.4	5	36.6	5	36.6	4	33
Successful completion of assignments due to my detailed hard work	261	123	5	47.1	5	54.8	5	40.2	5	47.5
My success to a large extent, depends upon my competence and hard work	249	85	4	34.1	4	33.3	4	34.6	4	34.3
I am responsible for rewards	270	97	4	35.9	4	32.9	4	40.6	4	33.7
My promotion in department depends mostly on my ability and effort	256	98	5	38.3	5	42	5	39.3	5	34.7
I can work hard enough to get my suggestions accepted	231	76	5	32.9	5	38.6	5	38.7	4	36.4
Generally I determine what happen to me in the department	233	67	5	28.8	5	46.8	5	36.8	3	26.3
My acceptability to others will depend on my behaviour with them	244	109	5	44.7	5	50.8	5	52.4	4	38.4
Internality total	281		5	36.4	5	42.2	5	39.8	4	34.4

Locus of Control Statement	AISO Total				IAS		IPS		IFS	
	N	n	Sc	%	Sc	%	Sc	%	Sc	%
Most important persons, control most matters here	258	87	5	33.7	5	50	4	37.1	4	37.4
To large extent my career depends on my seniors	253	108	4	42.7	4	45.8	4	56.1	4	29.3
My effectiveness in department is mostly determined by senior people	254	90	3	35.4	4	33.3	3	43.2	3	35.4
Senior person's preference determine who would be rewarded	269	108	4	40.1	4	37	4	46.3	4	36.6
Being liked by seniors or impression usually influence promotion decisions	262	99	4	37.8	4	37	4	39.8	4	36.6
My liking depends upon my seniors	269	93	3	34.6	3	31.5	3	38.9	3	32.7
If my seniors do not like me, I probably would not succeed	266	93	1	35	1	37.1	1	37.9	1	30.7
My success or failure depends mostly on those who work with me	243	80	2	32.9	2	42.9	2	45.1	3	37.8
My ideas get accepted if I make them fit with the desire of seniors	244	71	3	29.1	4	34.4	3	32.9	3	33.7
Pressure groups are most powerful	256	96	5	37.5	4	41.8	5	44.9	3	31
Externality for Others, total	281		3	35.9	4	39.1	3	42.2	3	34.1
Service one joins is accidental matter	262	79	3	30.2	3	34.2	3	34.1	3	25.7
One's career is a matter of chance	261	100	2	38.3	2	35.6	2	48.9	3	32
Success of person depends upon the chances one gets	261	80	3	30.7	3	35.6	2	37.1	4	32.3
Getting rewards is matter of luck	268	134	2	50.01	2	57.5	2	58.5	2	36.6
Success large extent a matter of luck	261	106	2	40.6	2	46.6	2	39.1	2	37.6
Getting promotion largely depends on being my right place at right time	262	72	2	27.5	1	31.5	1	34.1	4	23.8
It is matter of luck that people listen me	244	123	1	50.4	1	48.4	1	48.8	1	53.1
My success or failure is matter of luck	254	112	1	44.1	1	49.3	1	44.3	1	40.4
Most things are beyond one's control	218	60	4	27.5	4	32.7	4	33.8	3	33.7
I am acceptable to others in my department because I am lucky	236	116	1	49..2	1	54.1	1	51.9	1	43.8
Externality for chance, total mean			2	33.9	2	37.1	2	43.1	2	35.9

N = total responces, n = response for that score, sc = evaluation score, % = % value of score

ANNEXURE 4.A: LOCUS OF CONTROL QUESTIONNAIRE

Given below are some statements indicating the experience of the All India Services Officers in the decision-making process in Public Administration. There are no right or wrong answers. Read each statement, based on your experience in public administration; indicate the extent to which you feel that way, on the five-point scale.

Mark 5, if you strongly feel this way. Mark 4, if you generally feel this way. Marks 3, if you somewhat feel this way. Marks 2, if you slightly feel this way. Mark 1, if you hardly feel this way.

Statements		Ranking Scale				
245.	I can largely determine what matters to me in the department	5	4	3	2	1
246.	The course of my career largely depends upon me	5	4	3	2	1
247.	My success/failure depends mostly on the efforts I put in	5	4	3	2	1
248.	Most important persons, control most matters here	5	4	3	2	1
249.	To large extent, my career depends on my seniors	5	4	3	2	1
250.	My effectiveness in the department is mostly determined by senior people	5	4	3	2	1
251.	Service one joins is to a large extent, accidental matter	5	4	3	2	1
252.	One's career is to be a great extent, a matter of chance	5	4	3	2	1
253.	The success of a person depends upon the chances one gets	5	4	3	2	1
254.	Successful completion of assignments is mainly due to my detailed planning and hard work	5	4	3	2	1
255.	Being liked by seniors or making a good impression usually influence promotion decisions	5	4	3	2	1
256.	Getting rewards in the department is a matter of luck	5	4	3	2	1
257.	The success of one's plans is, to large extent a matter of luck	5	4	3	2	1
258.	Getting a promotion largely depends on being in the right place at the right time	5	4	3	2	1
259.	Senior person's preference determines who would be rewarded in the department	5	4	3	2	1
260.	My success to a large extent depends upon my competence and hard work	5	4	3	2	1
261.	How much I am liked in the department depends upon my seniors	5	4	3	2	1
262.	It is a matter of luck that people listen to me	5	4	3	2	1
263.	If my seniors do not like me, I probably would not succeed in this department	5	4	3	2	1
264.	Usually, I am responsible for getting/not getting rewards	5	4	3	2	1

Statements	Ranking Scale				
265. My success or failure is mostly a matter of luck	5	4	3	2	1
266. My success or failure depends mostly on those who work with me	5	4	3	2	1
267. My promotion in the department depends mostly on my ability and effort	5	4	3	2	1
268. My experience is that most things in a department are beyond one's control	5	4	3	2	1
269. I can work hard enough to get my suggestions accepted in the department	5	4	3	2	1
270. I am acceptable to others in my department because I am lucky	5	4	3	2	1
271. Generally, I determine what happen to me in the department	5	4	3	2	1
272. My acceptability to others will depend on my behaviour with them	5	4	3	2	1
273. My ideas get accepted if I make them fit with the desire of seniors	5	4	3	2	1
274. Pressure groups are most powerful (and control things) in the department	5	4	3	2	1

Unit 5

Motivation (Power, Motives and Status Base) in Decision

"Surely, no one can ever remain inactive for a moment; everyone is dependently motivated to act by the means of the Nature." *The Bhagavad Gita* 3.5

"Motivation is a fire from within. If someone else try to light that fire under you, chances are it will burn briefly."—Stephen R. Covey

"No man should talk one way with his lips and think another way in his heart."—Talmud, Baba Metzia 49

King and members of his jury must not show disrespect to scholars and should never respect offenders, so that, the public has the reliance on ethics. King must gather full information by spying on powerful enemies to rein them.—The Yajurveda 15.1

- *Motives Stimulate Decision*
- *Concept of Power Base as a Motivator*
- *Need as a Motivator in the Decision*
- *Policy as a Motivator in the Decision*
- *Equity Motivate Decision*
- *The Expectation from the System Motivates*
- *Chain Saw Motivation Model*
- *Orbital Motivation Model*
- *Analyses Results of the Motivation of AIS in Decision*

This unit deals with different aspects of motivation and motivator working in public administration while arriving at the decision under political pressure. How extrinsic and intrinsic motives stimulates an individual officer. The concept of different types of power bases operating on the All India Services has been mentioned. The policy, equity, and expectations role in motivation has been described. A new model of motivation as the chain saw model and orbital model has been described, how it operates on All India Service while taking a decision. Research data analyses results for motivation variables have been described.

5.1. Motives Stimulate Decision

A motivated individual officer will deliver high personal efficacy in the decision. The All India Services Officers with high motives (needs) will show a high need for efficiency/excellence towards the achievement of the needs. The power motive will arouse the need to influence others; under extension motive officers will help many individuals to meet their own needs of pursuing goals. The All India Services Officers with achievement motivation will show concern for competition; this will improve the performance of the officer in the decision process. All the All India Services Officers have some innovation, creativity, discretion, liking for status, motivation to use power, the intensity of desires, opportunities, use of them will vary from individual to individual officer. Enjoyment of power related to socio-economic conditions and location in the hierarchy of bureaucratic administration.

Extrinsic factors, as government policies and administration co-ordination, inter-personal relations, working conditions, etc. are related to dissatisfaction within the decision. Status, power, and influence by virtue of being the All India Services Officers, they get more opportunities to serve people to satisfy extrinsic needs. The All India Services Officers get freedom in working so that they can show their professional competence, which serves as an extrinsic motivator to them. The All India Services Officers get timely promotions and chances are better than other services, this career progression, and reputation they enjoy in the society motivate them. The All India Services Officers get sustained motivation in a decision from rewards given by politicians but such rewards are not perceived as equitable. Motivation and sense of competition among the All India Services Officers mutually influence each other. Experience of success in political pressure is sensed as competence by the All India Services Officers. This motivates individual officers to interact with the work environment. Erratic and irregular successes motivate individual All India Services Officer desires for engaging with pressure in behavior with the decision-making process.

Intrinsic rewards are not sustainable in the bureaucratic system as a politician at the top is changed frequently. The need for achievements motivates the All India Services Officers to strive for success and they succeed in the attainment of goals. Financial security, the best salary structure, and availability of such financial benefits after retirement intrinsically motivate the All India Services Officers. The All India Services Officers occupy senior positions where they enjoy lesser responsibilities and accountability in other ways motivates them intrinsically. The All India Services Officers have a strong need for power; the Indian Administrative Service officers indicate the greatest need for power. The Indian Administrative Service officers exert tremendous efforts, so that, the Indian Police Service officers and the Indian Forest Service officers alike rest of the services must behave in the way as desired by the IAS. This very same factor increases dissatisfaction among the IPS and the IFS officers, as their need for power is encroached and usurped by the IAS and they consider it most humiliating and kill the drive for decision among IPS and IFS. "High achievers perform best when they perceive their probability of success as being 0.5, that is where they estimate they have a 50: 50 chance of success" (S.P. Robins).

5.2. Power Base as Motivator

Individual All India Services Officer with power motivation will try to influence others, such officer can incorporate changes to meet and fulfill the need of power motive. Power emanates from control and ownership of means of production, mastery of rules, tasks are fragmented, skills are diverse, and knowledge is differentially confided, held, and valued (OrFE. Claus. 1976). Power provides the ability to get others to do what you want them to do, if necessary, against their will (Weber, 1978). Different bases of power operate for information, expert knowledge, status, prestige in the system, resource control (Pettigrew, 1973), uncertainty control (Crozier, 1964), develop contacts in the higher hierarchy, issue of sanctions, rewards, financial control (Benfari et al., 1986), mobilize politics (Hickson et al., 1986) and many more aspects work in the bureaucratic system.

Differential power is legitimately vested in hierarchy layers, where an individual officer has the temperament and temptation to exercise power for the maintenance of own goals and interests. Slowly realization will come, how long the elite All India Services Officers can retain concentration of potential power, which reduces or limit the capabilities and capacities of their subordinate employees, and how long other departments will accept such a system of regulatory control over them? The larger the gap in power discretion, the sooner realization will come to other departments' employees for control of power by them. Power discretion is bound to deflect and will ultimately harm the monopolizers. Only self-discipline can prolong the position of elite power holders. In the hierarchy of the All India Services, power structures are uneven and concentrate at the district level and secretary level. Individual officers of the elite services develop a tendency to misuse and abuse power and monopolize it solely by them. They devise ways and means to keep other officers away from power, which creep in frustration and powerlessness among the other All India Services members.

Operational distribution of power is such that the Indian Administrative Service officers usurp exclusive formal functioning power of IPS and IFS also and accumulates actual illegitimate power with them by virtue of their location and hegemony. This neglect of authorized power creeps frustration in the Indian Police Service officers and the Indian Forest Service officers and on the other side actual power actuates the Indian Administrative Service officers' behavior in an authoritative manner. Departmental structures, the position of the Indian Administrative Service officers in hierarchy, twisted policy, and rules, due to location and proximity to the politician provide the ability and motivate Indian Administrative Service officers to influence the decision and create uncertainty in the process. The Indian Administrative Service officers approach politicians with a lust to increase uncertainties in the bureaucratic system; to increase their own power, relative to formal assigned power in a hierarchy.

The degree of autonomy of relative power available to the Indian Administrative Service officers is far excessive, in comparison to the Indian Police Service and the Indian Forest Service officers; which make it difficult for the Indian Police Service officers and the Indian Forest Service officers to the maintenance of their power base. This imbalance of power between the All India Services Officers and other services is a major reason for uncertainty in the decision process. This differential power is slowly but surely hurting the system. Strategically in a very well-planned manner, the Indian Administrative Service officers invest all powers to its subunits; secretary/commissioners at the secretariat, at district to Deputy Commissioner/District Magistrate, and down to subdivision to Sub-Divisional Magistrate, etc. They make other departments dependent on their units to create uncertainty at all times, to retain power, they keep their subunits cohesive in nature and illegitimate power overflows from them. Voices of dissent start oozing out. Whenever anyone is marginalized but the internal mechanism of power by the Indian Administrative Service officers and their subunits allow representation to the Indian Administrative Service officers at the top only to silence the conflicting voices.

Lust for **retention of power**, if not now, on some other occasion, after all, it is always with the Indian Administrative Service officers' cadres, keep them united and marginalize the internal dissent voice, so that other service officers do not challenge their misuse of illegitimate power. Due to the well-entrenched position of the Indian Administrative Service officers, other services officers have little scope for resistance and consent for subjugation is taken for granted. Individual officer instances of resistance against their exploitation by the Indian Administrative Service officer's subjugation are dealt as a challenge to whole the Indian Administrative Service and dealt sternly, manipulated, coerced, hoodwinked, cajoled and out of way victimization of such officers throughout their career. The pervasiveness of power relations makes them difficult to resist, resistance serves only to reinforce the existing systems of power (Clegg, 1979; Knight and Morgan, 1991).

Elite services misuse **discretionary power**, they like to sustain their full dominance and in due course to reduce the ability of other services. Accumulated frustration and powerlessness among services, other than Indian Administrative Service will revolutionize the other services for their share of power. Political power is the safest barrier available to other services officers (less powerful) to participate in the decision process, prevent the IAS from invocation all rules and procedures in their favor, and manipulating decisions in their favor behind the scene. Position of dominance, surveillance, and control of the IAS has lineage to colonial rule in Indian historical perspective. Power is used as a convenient, manipulative, and deterministic resource. If politicians delegate their authority to the All India Services Officers, delegation entails rules and regulations. Rules and regulation interpretation necessarily involve discretion, discretion gives birth to negotiated order to self-interests.

Power is used as a means by which legitimacy is created for the incarnation of illegitimate actions. Power is used consciously and deliberately mobilization of resources to pursue self-interests. Power motivates the All India Services Officers to use political pressure to provide legitimate cover to their informal actions to achieve desired results. Power motivates the All India Services Officers to use resources and avoid conflict in the decision to meet self-goals. Political pressure and power influence the process of social inquiry, social justice, and used in an illegitimate manner to attack political opponents as emancipators' tools.

Raven (1959, 1992, and 1993) reviewed his **six power bases** of reward, coercion, legitimacy, expertise, reference, and information to enlarge it to more power bases. Power bases have inherent dichotomy and influence individual officer behavior to accept others' want. Inner fears influence officer behavior in a negative manner under fear of scolding, feeling of disapproval, the extent of criticism, fear of political power, fear of top-notch position, and political influence of political pressure. At the same time, the positive influence of encouragement, individual power, love power, compliments, personal push and pull power, and influence over politicians motivate officer positive behavior. Politicians' **coercive power** of transfer, posting, recruitment, resource allocation, punishment, promotions, and policy control influence the All India Services Officers' emotional need to accept political pressure. Politicians' large mass base, the top position in grievance redressing mechanism, the power to review performance, supremacy in decision-making, and control over bureaucracy provide them persuasive power bases in convincing the All India Services Officers to accept political pressure as a motivator.

The All India Services Officers have developed expertise in using various power bases to own advantage (Figure 5.1), if not for self, then ensure it for their own service enjoyment. Officers of the Indian Administrative Service are in such a position that they misuse power bases more frequently and more discretely than the Indian Police Service and the Indian Forest Service officers. The Indian Administrative Service's complete control over crucial locations and positions motivate their status consciousness to use coercive power. The Indian Administrative Service officers maintain close relations with all sources of political power, which is reflected in the increase in the frequency of coercive power use by heavily penalizing any kind of voice of dissent against them. The Indian Administrative Service officer's personal relationship with political power at an emotional level provides them chances to withhold information and they deprive other services of information by manipulations to pose them as **charismatic power** holders. The All India Services Officers in general and the Indian Administrative Service in particular use **coercive power**, so that others in the system realize their omnipresence and omnipotent elite power.

Coercive Power Base Used	→	Kind of Power
Location and position in bureaucratic hierarchy	→	Prestige and status
Proximity to source of political power/authority	→	Contemplation
Regulating law, rules, regulations and procedures	→	Regulator
Control over bureaucratic promotions, postings and transfers	→	Elite
Final say in resource allocation in system	→	Supremacy/Godly
Destroy challenger/voice raiser by punishments	→	Punitive coercive
Propagate self-success, praise and charisma	→	Charismatic
Cultivate strong political personal relationships	→	Emotional capability
Keeping information close to own positions only	→	Manipulations
Withholding decision information/selective release	→	Secretive

Figure No. 5.1: The All India Services Officers and Coercive Power Base

When the All India Services Officers are in danger or they realize that coercive power will not work effectively to serve their own interests, they use **persuasive power** to prove their competence. The Indian Police Service and the Indian Forest Service officers try to show their expertise and use **expert power**, but the Indian Administrative Service officers behave as super experts to demoralize the opponent's point of view. When this appears to be less powerful, then they use past precedence's and role models cases, and use **referent power**. The Indian Administrative Service officers reward the officer selected by them and reinforce their power among other services. On such occasions, the Indian Administrative Service officers select docile and weak targets and extend some kind of help to demonstrate their **extension power**. The Indian Administrative Service officers in collaboration with political leadership located in the government bureaucracy, exercise full control over information, relevant information about the decision are not passed on to the department. The Indian Administrative Service officers present selective and distorted information to the politician to prove their own **logical power**.

A lot of studies have been carried out on six motives of achievements in organization behavior and dependence has been studied for people behavior (Pareek, 1997). Officers with achievement motives will hope for success but fear avoidance behavior leads to failure. Individual effectiveness with expert **influence motive** will mark an impact on a decision but fear instills impotence.

Motive	→	Approach (hope of)	←	Avoidance (fear of)
Achievement	→	success	←	failure
Expert influence	→	impact	←	impotence
Control	→	order	←	chaos
Extension	→	relevance	←	irrelevance
Dependence	→	growth	←	loneliness
Affiliation	→	inclusion	←	exclusion

Figure No. 5.2: Six Motives of Behavior[1]

5.3. Needs as Motivator

Individuals try to establish, maintain satisfactory and comfortable relationships with people, which meet their interpersonal need for inclusion and affection (Schutz, 1966). Individual All India Services Officer **need of inclusion** motivate officer to take interest in others. Personal relationships with others are goal motivated are not long-lasting in the case of the All India Services Officers. The dominance of **control need** the All India Services Officers like to control the behavior of others, but they do not like to be controlled by others. **Need for love** is not satisfied fully, lack of organism formulate stress among the All India Services Officers, which is maximum among the Indian Administrative Service officers then the Indian Police Service officers and the Indian Forest Service officers. **Power need** among the Indian Administrative Service officers is higher, which motivates them to influence the behavior of others and is compelled to direct others' behavior and decisions.

The All India Services Officers during their initial years of career concentrate more on Maslow's hierarchy of needs, this may be an explanation for low political pressure at that time. Dominant needs for power keep them away from self-actualization. We have studied different needs pertaining decision process by the All India Services Officers in our study. Economic security as a member of the All India Services reflects **security need**. Retirement benefits available in the All India Services are related to the **safety need**. Status, power, and influence enjoyed by the All India Services Officers associated with **esteem need**. Higher chances and opportunities to serve people with the freedom to meet the **belonging need**. The All India Services Officers enjoy the highest freedom in daily working and easily afford to do original work, which will meet their **affiliation and recognition need**. The All India Services Officers through innovative work can easily prove their professional competence to meet **achievement needs**. All India Services Officers occupy the top position in their respective fields; they start working from a pretty senior level, which reduces

1. Adopted from Udai Pareek, 1997 and modified.

the risks and responsibilities comparatively, which in turn fulfill their **need for protection and responsibility**. The All India Services Officers enjoy the highest reputation and prestige in the society, which in turn meet their **social reputation need**. The All India Services Officers enjoy the best salary structure available in the government sector, which motivates and meets their **biological needs**. Promotions to the All India Services Officers are most timely and secured, so their **growth and advancement needs** are met.

Those officers, who show concern for others, his subordinates can assign to his urge for extension motive. The All India Services Officers "motives and values play a significant role in growth process", McClland (1961). Individual officer "Goal being related to the need of more than one individual or one group, and that which cannot be attained by efforts of one individual or group alone" (Sherif and Sherif, 1953). Concern for others would include concern for one's family, and society at large. The individual officer is motivated by self only, common thinking that the All India Services Officers are working for the cause of the nation never holds true even during the colonial imperialistic era. "There is a prevalent idea that men at the 'outposts of empire' are at least able and hard-working. It is delusion...few of them work as hard or as intelligently as the postmaster of a provincial town in England. The real work of administration is done mainly by native subordinates."[2]

Emergent threats after the Hawala, 2G, Rafale, PNB Scam, and Coal scams revelations invited criticisms from the public, politicians, and judiciary. Protest behavior has been rising with increasing security from different services, which is adding insecurity in elite services. Sense of insecurity and defensive behavior reflect the fragility and brittleness pervading in the All India Services. Expanded authority interjects the debate on power. Elitist premonition is that through power-sharing they cannot retain the hegemony for long. We have a serious concern with the prevalent instability of the temper of various services and their hysterical attitude and its incompatibility with public perceptions, how long elitist concept can survive in India.

The All India Services Officers exert high-level efforts based on their ability to satisfy their dominating needs/goals. These needs are attained mostly at the cost of departmental goals or the public at large. What motivates the All India Services Officers in the pursuance of goals to reflect interests in work-related behavior? Any kind of pressure in the decision-making process will satisfy the goals of the politicians, businessmen, or public or vested interests of a particular person or group, who want to maximize own interests from public exchequer or increasing benefits interested party at the cost or from a share of another party.

Such interests on the face of it may be camouflaged, looking as if no one is adversely affected, but consequences in long run recover more than its cost, e.g. encroachments allowed or neglected on public land, people feel they have not lost anything, but long-term consequences have an impact on every citizen. Manipulated production or supply price of a restricted item in collusion with the All India Services Officers, common person perceptions, I have nothing to lose but every citizen pay for it as a social cost. Mr. 'X' criminal is allowed to go scot-free under pressure, the public at large shows no concern but in the long run that becomes threatening to the whole society. Public access in forests is provided and beneficiaries feel happy, but in long run, colossal environmental losses accumulate and threaten the survival of humankind. In public administration, motivating

2. George Orwell in his work *Burmese Days*, p. 60f.

factors are elusive, concealed, covered, and with a long-term gestation period, which influences the decision.

The All India Services Officers in collusion with interested party en-cash it for self and family, but the public does not get air about it. It is difficult to measure the intensity of motivating factors, but the public administration process is also a motivation need/goal satisfying process. Materialistic outlook in society, low salaries of the All India Services Officers, insurmountable and unlimited powers, non-accountability, non-transparency, ambiguity in rules, procedures, and law, give birth to numerous unsatisfied needs. Such unsatisfied needs to generate tension; stimulate drive within individual All India Services Officer to find out search behavior to fulfill those needs and goals. Acceptance of political pressure by the All India Services Officers help in the achievement and attainment of such goals, interests, and needs. The All India Services Officers in collusion with politicians, when both of them needs are compatible both of them attain their needs at the cost of goals of public administration.

Safety and biological needs (lower order) in the All India Services Officers are externally and satisfied (**extrinsic**), examples; pay tenure, service rules, administration, supervision, interpersonal relations, work conditions, security, safety, protection and responsibility, and biological needs. **Intrinsic needs** (higher-order-love, esteem, self-actualization) are achievement, recognition, work itself, responsibility, advancement, growth, job content, esteem, belongingness, affiliation, achievement, and social needs. These needs motivate the All India Services Officers towards acceptance of political pressure and lead to job satisfaction. **Hygiene factors** such as retirement benefits, status, power, prestige, work, responsibility, and salary, etc., motivate the Indian Administrative Service officers more, and for the Indian Forest Service officers and the Indian Police Service officers, hygiene factors accumulate dissatisfaction due to unwarranted suppression on the name of co-ordination from the Indian Administrative Service. Motivational factors as economic security, more opportunities to do original work, higher chances to show professional competence, and timely promotions motivate the All India Services Officers in the decision process. Individual All India Services Officer work and attitude towards decision invariably determine individual officer success or failure in the decision-making process. Intrinsic factors achievement, recognition, the decision itself, responsibility, advancement, and career growth are related to satisfaction with the decision.

5.4. Policy Motivation

In policy matters, only the Indian Administrative Service officers have the chances of success. Decisions and policy pertaining to the Indian Police Service officers and the Indian Forest Service officers at different levels are coordinated/supervised by the Indian Administrative Service group, so the Indian Police Service officers and the Indian Forest Service officers do not get motivated in the decision-making process. High need for power among the Indian Administrative Service officers leads to make them more concerned by prestige, reputation, gaining control over other services rather than concern for effective performance in the decision. The All India Services Officers experience a loss of control over their own behavior that motivations do not diminish. Individual officer tolerates low performance in order to avoid decreasing motivation.

Research works indicate that the interdependence of extrinsic and intrinsic rewards are really happening in work-life (J.B. Miner, 1980). Extrinsic rewards appear to increase intrinsic motivation

(B.J. Collder, 1975). The goals/interests cause internal stimulus in the All India Services Officers, which involve acceptance of political pressure under such situation's decision may be invariably related to goals. Politicians exert a high level of effort until their goals/interests are achieved. Colleagues and seniors provide feedback to the All India Services Officers regarding movements towards goals unable to deter/stop their behavior, whereas individual All India Services Officer own progress towards attainment of goals act as a more and more powerful motivator than that.

Public administration, public welfare policies are difficult and full of ambiguity. Flexibility in policies, availability of space for choices, for the All India Services Officers motivate them to use such space for own goal achievement. When the All India Services Officers visualize that politician of high stature likely to continue to occupy chief key position related to the All India Services Officers interests in the long run. Continual pressure from such sources acts as reinforcement for allurement for personal goal achievement and motivates the All India Services Officers to accept such political pressure for long-run benefits.

5.5. Equity Motivation

"Equity theory recognizes that individuals are concerned not only with the absolute amount of rewards they receive for their efforts but also with the relationship of this amount to what others receive. They make judgments as to the relationship between their inputs and outcomes and the inputs and outcomes of others. Based on one's inputs, such as efforts, experience, education, and competence, one compares outcomes such as salary levels, wages, recognition, and other factors. When people perceive an imbalance in their outcome-input ratio relative to others, tension is created. This tension provides the basis for motivation, as people strive for what they perceive equity and fairness," S.P. Robins (1998). The Indian Police Service officers and the Indian Forest Service officers always think about equity with the Indian Administrative Service officers as the inputs are similar, but outcomes are perceived to be in favor of the IAS.

Research works indicate, "Distributive justice has a greater influence on employee satisfaction than procedural justice, while procedural justice tends to affect an employee organizational and commitments trust in his boss, and intention to quit," S.P. Robins. The All India Services Officers do not share information, how allocation decisions are made by them, and procedures adopted by them are only known to the person, who takes such decisions. The All India Services Officers and politicians do not like to show any procedural fairness towards beneficiaries. Public and employee both perceive the decision as highly unjust and unfair. The All India Services Officers and politicians are the distributor and they distribute whole benefits to themselves only. Relative distribution of rewards among the All India Services influences individual motivation. The Indian Administrative Service officers garner most of the rewards others look towards them like hungry persons and in turn approach politicians for help. Firstly, service members search equity inside their service in own cadre and then they look for what is happening outside their parent cadre, in other states. How the Indian Police Service officers and Indian Forest Service officers visualize equity (Figure 5.3) in their cadre with respect to Indian Administrative Service officers and after that equity in other state cadres is sought.

Service Name	Self Service Inside Cadre	Self Outside Other State Same Service	Other AIS Inside Cadre State	Other AIS Outside State Cadre
IAS	w.r.t. other IAS officers of the state	IAS officers of other cadre states	IPS and IFS officers in own cadre	IPS and IFS officers in other cadre states
IPS	w.r.t. other IPS officers of the state	IPS officers of other cadre states	IAS and IFS officers in own cadre	IAS and IFS officers in other cadre states
IFS	w.r.t. other IFS officers of the state cadre	IFS officers of other cadre states	IPS and IAS officersin own cadre	IPS and IAS officers in other cadre states

Figure No. 5.3: Rewards Motivation and Equity among the All India Services

5.6. Motivation by Expectations from System

If we look into Vroom's (1964) expectancy theory with reference to the All India Services Officers, the strength of tendency of the All India Services Officers to accept political pressure on a decision will depend on the strength of expectation, the decision outcome utility to individual All India Services Officer. When individual All India Services Officer get motivated by accepting political pressure when he is aware that it will help him in his career progression and maximization of own goals/interests. Individual All India Services Officers' performance will be highest to garner more and more rewards. Once an individual All India Services Officer start getting rewards by accepting political pressure, then that officer gets so motivated that, he voluntarily approach politician and educate politician about ways and means for self-goal maximization. In the process, politicians also get motivated through a high amount of illegal attainment of rewards. In the process, personal goals motivate individual All India Services Officers, and politicians tend to develop strong nexus for mutual benefits. Relations transform into sharing, distribution, and maximization of interest and rewards to such an extent that both join together to change and modify whole procedure, policy, and law in favor of own needs goals/rewards. Performance in the decision-making process is related to the loyalty, benefits maximization to seniors and politicians at the top.

It becomes clear to individual All India Services Officers that any amount of increase in efforts, honesty, integrity, and sincerity is not going to improve or get reflected in their Annual Performance Appraisal, postings, and promotions. The All India Services Officers perceive that collusion/friendship/acceptance of political pressure will only help in career progression. Even going on deputation to different places has been related to political connections. It is true that in the case of the Indian Administrative Service officers, where their seniors occupying every position of importance help some Indian Administrative Service officers for assuring good deputation postings for them. Whereas most of the assignments, in turn, serve the long-term objectives of the IAS persons located at that top position. An Indian Administrative Service officer was posted as Deputy Commissioner in the home district of the previous Chief Minster solely on the ground that he was the only available Indian Administrative Service officer in that cadre, who was not willing to accept any kind of political pressure. Sometimes due to compulsions, the ruling party has to post a person whom they do not like. Postings and transfers mainly motivate individual All India Services Officer to accept political pressure; however, individual All India Services Officers has to pay the price of this by doing various jobs against the law for the master politician. At times, most of such benefits, goals, and attainments can be converted into monetary terms also.

5.7. Chain-Saw Motivation Model

What motivates the Indian Administrative Service officers to stand united and always close to a politician? They have understood that any moment they allow any kind of access to power for members of other services, that officer may develop a close relationship with the politician, the Indian Administrative Service officers can lose their grip over power in turn. To retain a strong grip over the whole resources of the country, the Indian Administrative Service officers oblige politicians to the greatest extend, and in turn politicians feel safe to rely on the Indian Administrative Service officers. Members of the Indian Administrative Service officers share common weaknesses of the politicians to exploit politician to serve own goals. Then extend the benefit to members of own service groups and the IAS as a whole service. After that generally, things dry up in the government. This gross monopolization of power by the Indian Administrative Service officers motivates them to accept any kind of political pressure exerted at any level, at any time, and any place. Figure 5.4 of the chain-saw model of motivation shows this. Where Indian Forest Service officers are invariably grinding to break down on the name of performance or evaluation and are the greatest sufferer from the hegemony of the bureaucratic system. Moreover, the Indian Administrative Service officers enjoy the benefits without any responsibility or accountability and Indian Police Service officers occupy positions in-between.

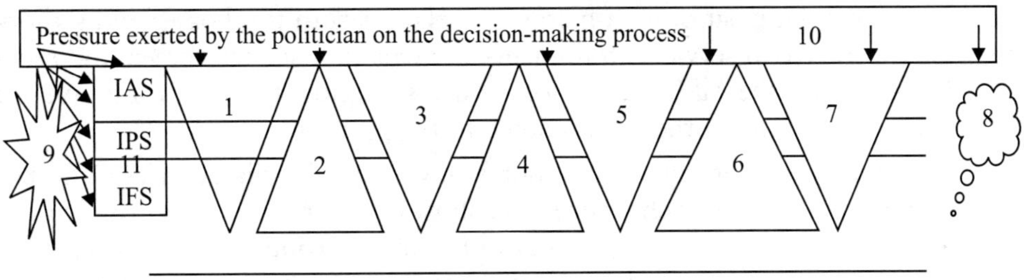

Figure No. 5.4: Chain-Saw Motivation Model of the All India Services Officers

1. Career progression and working freedom in the bureaucratic system.
2. Expected performance from AISO and effectiveness in the decision.
3. Rewards distribution and respect for a position in the hierarchy.
4. Evaluation of the decision and monitoring the implementation of the outcomes.
5. Personal goals/interests/needs attainment from the bureaucratic system.
6. Accountability and responsibility for the decision in the bureaucratic system.
7. Availability of opportunities for AISO in the bureaucratic system.
8. Rolling like a drum and moving like a dry cloud, the government administration system.
9. Handle of the chain-saw within the grip of the politician, who allocate political pressure in the decision-making process.

10. Politician occupying the top position in government administration, they are in a position to send pressure to anywhere in the decision process in the system.
11. Position of the All India Services Officers in the bureaucratic system.

The Indian Police Service officers and the Indian Forest Service officers perceive that they have been left behind in power-sharing, they also try hard to catch up the race for own goal maximization but the Indian Administrative Service officers sitting close to politicians blow the whistle and settle down the race before it gains any momentum.

Performance in public administration is directly related to the availability of opportunities. An individual officer with the highest abilities cannot perform effectively without equity in opportunities. High performance is partially a function of an absence of obstacles that constrain the employee (S.P. Robins, 1998). The Indian Administrative Service officers have maximized the opportunities for them in the system. It is either Government of India postings or State Government, the Indian Administrative Service officers ensure that best opportunities are exclusively reserved for them. The Indian Police Service officers and the Indian Forest Service officers even if strive hard, their fate got sealed, minimum opportunities are left to interact with top politicians and complete control over the process of policy by the Indian Administrative Service as a cadre ensure to strangulate others.

The All India Services Officers' desire to achieve personal goals create willingness among them to accept risk and uncertainty in the decision. Personal goals overwrite the concern for performance, quality, objectivity for which these All India Services Officers are recruited. Sources of motivation vary with time and space; in the same way extent of motivation also depends upon individual officer location, position in a hierarchy, relation with top bosses and seniors, length of service, past experience in service, attainments of goals in a service career, and security in a job, etc. Particularly when the All India Services Officers are close to their promotion; they try to ignore other motivating factors other than related to the promotion.

Materialistic things and new challenges motivate young All India Services Officers. As they grow, they become immune to new challenges and show high concern for security in career. After 24 years of service annual performance appraisal becomes a routine subject matter, so annual performance appraisal consciousness does not motivate them at that level, unlike promotion and self-goals.

Figure 5.5 represents the All India Services Officers decision-making process under political pressure and individual officer motivations. Individual officer behavior and capacity to manage the political pressure on the top of a triangle, motivations provided by the bureaucratic system on one corner, and self-goals on the third corner of the triangle, sandwich the decision-making process in blocks. These blocks make it difficult for a decision to move on any side, even if it is moved; the decision is struck up that place only. Operating forces produce oscillations; blocks are converted into arcs under political pressure (this stage is not shown in the figure). These arcs center lie on the three points of the triangle, continuous moving political pressure, converts arcs into a circular path. Then decision starts moving in a circular way under the forces from the three corners of the triangle. The intensity of the political pressure will determine the motion of the decision. The size of the circle will be related to the group variables, individual variables, and bureaucratic system variables prevalent in the decision-making process. It is more inclined towards public pressure and political pressure; slowly the All India Services Officers lose their control over the decision.

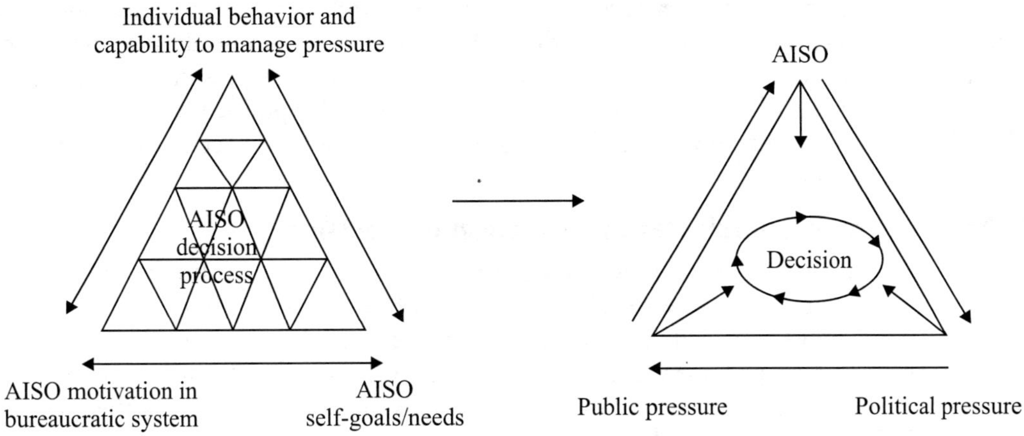

Figure No. 5.5: Triangular Representation of the Decision Process

5.8. Orbital Motivation Model

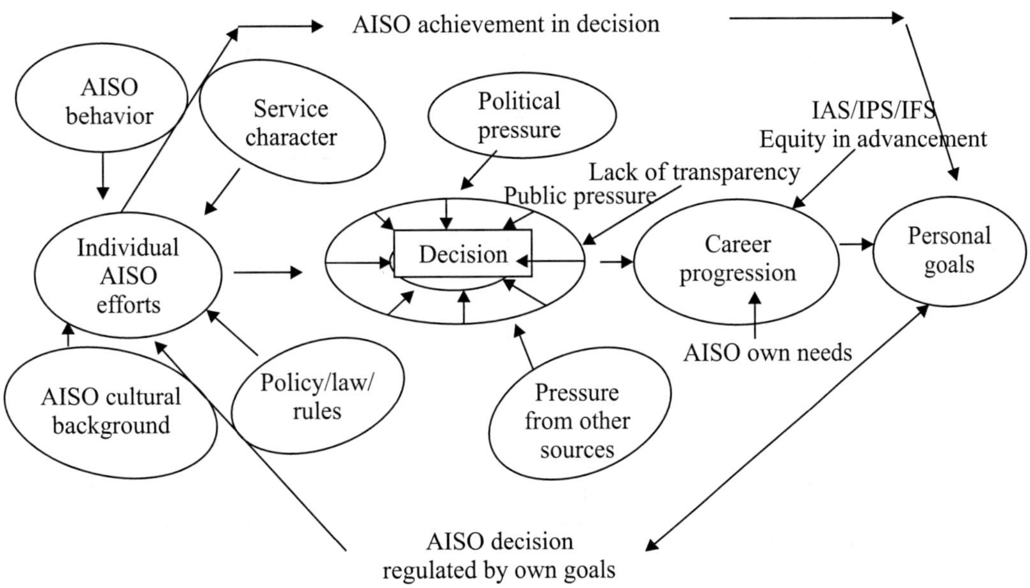

Figure No. 5.6: Orbital Motivation Model of All India Services Officers

The orbital motivation model of the All India Services Officers is shown in Figure 5.6 indicate that every motivation has own orbit and moves in it and ultimately all orbits move around the decision. The first center is the individual officer efforts, around its individual behavior, individual service characters, individual cultural backup, and government policy and procedures move in independent orbits. Individual All India Services Officer is motivated by own achievements in the decision. Decision block under the pressure from different sources itself acquire the orbital shape in the process. Individual All India Services Officer is in search of career progression from such decisions. Through career advancement, individual officer meets own needs and find out equity among the All India Services. This whole process is oriented towards personal goals. Ultimately, decision-making process by the All India Services Officers under political pressure is regulated by the self-goals and needs only. We can say that some of these needs act as hygiene factors for the All India Services Officers.

5.9. Analyses of Research Data Motivation in Decision

Statistical analyses results are shown in Exhibits 5.1 to 5.3. Values for Box's test of equality of covariance matrices are: Box's M = 468.254, F = 7.543, df1 = 55, df2 = 14051, and significance at 0.000, test the null hypothesis that the observed covariance matrices of the dependent variables are equal across groups. Levene's test values are significant if values of significance are less than 0.05. Here except professional competence, where the value is more than 0.05, all other significance values are 0.000. Test of whether the group means are the same as represented by the F-ratio for combined between effects of motivation. The value of this ratio 7.321 to 45.419, whether these values came by chance, '0.000' significance level indicates the likelihood of F-ratio, indicating elimination of any kind of chances criteria. Except for one variable, all significance values are less than 0.05 for other variables, we can say that motivation has a significant effect on the decision-making process of All India Services Officers.

Exhibit Number 5.1: Motivation Factors, a Statistical Analysis

Items Details	Mean				Standard Deviation				F	Sig.
	I.A.S.	I.P.S.	I.F.S.	AIS	I.A.S.	I.P.S.	I.F.S.	AIS		
Timely promotions, career progression	4	4.02	5.2	4.5	1.65	1.4	2.3	1.9	17.479	'0.000
Economic security in services	4.8	4.9	3.9	4.5	1.7	2.2	2.4	2.2	9.101	'0.000
Retirement benefits available	7.4	8.6	6.6	7.5	1.7	1.5	2.6	2.2	17.449	'0.000
Status, power and influence	1.7	1.8	2.9	2.2	1.3	1.4	2.6	2.1	29.055	'0.000
Opportunities and more chances to serve people	7.2	6.9	5.5	6.5	1.4	1.2	2.8	2.2	45.419	'0.000
Opportunity, freedom to do original work	6.7	6.5	5.3	6.1	2.7	2.1	2.8	2.6	9.546	'0.000
Professional competence	6.9	6.3	5.4	6.1	2.7	2.7	2.8	2.8	0.631	'0.533
Less work, little responsibility, no risk	8.3	9.1	7.6	8.3	2.2	1.4	3.1	2.4	33.098	'0.000
Prestige & reputation in society	2.5	2.9	3.5	3.1	1.3	1.2	2.3	1.8	17.46	'0.000
Best salary structure in government	5.2	3.7	5.1	4.6	2.1	1.8	2.4	2.2	7.321	'0.000
df1 = 2 and df2 = 239, F values and significance level in Levene's Test of Equality of Error Variance. Error variance of dependent variable is equal across groups.										
Frequency for I.A.S., I.P.S. and I.F.S. were 70, 82, 90 and 242 for total										

Equality of covariance matrices is checked by Levene's test and significant for variables. Levene's test does not take account of the covariance's and so the variance-covariance matrices are compared between groups, using Box's test. Results are significant as matrices are different from Levene's test. Variations in mean and standard deviation indicate that the All India Services Officers have many motivational factors, which operate upon their behavior in the decision. Box's test of assumption of the equality of covariance matrices tests the null hypothesis that the observed covariance matrices of the dependent variables are equal across the groups of the All India Services Officers. Statistical analyses are significant as significance values are 0.000 less than 0.05, except in the case of chances to professional competence. Tabachnick and Fidell (1996) suggested that larger samples produce greater variance and covariance, so our findings can be trusted.

Exhibit Number 5.2: Rank and Highest Percentage Score of the All India Services in Motivation

Items Details	I.A.S.			I.P.S.			I.F.S.		
	Rk	Top %	IInd%	Rk	%	IInd%	Rk	%	IInd%
Timely promotions, career progression	3	37.1	6/32.9	3	40.2	4/20.6	7	22.1	4/14.0
Economic security in services	6	30.01	5/24.3	5	24.7	7/19.6	1	20.4	2/15.2
Retirement benefits available	7	25.7	9/24.3	10	39.8	9/22.7	9	21.1	8/20.1
Status, power and influence	1	68.6	2/11.4	1	61.5	2/17.7	1	48.5	2/18.1
Opportunities and more chances to serve people	7	44.3	8/22.9	8	49.5	6/40.2	6	17.8	8/14.9
Opportunity, freedom to do original work	8	35.7	9/24.	7	42.7	10/19.8	4	20.1	9/16.1
Professional competence	10	22.9	9/21.4	9	27.1	6/16.7	3	16.3	5/15.3
Less work, little responsibility, no risk	10	50.1	9/14.3	10	44.6	9/29.3	10	50.1	9/13.8
Prestige and reputation in society	2	35.7	1/22.9	1	52.6	2/24.7	1	21.1	2/20.1
Best salary structure in government	3	35.7	4/24.7	4	40.6	2/19.8	4	18.8	8/12.9
Rk = Respondent Ranking, IInd% = Respondent Ranking/Highest percentage score in IInd rank.									

Exhibit Number 5.3: Statistical Analysis for Motivation

Items details	df	Chi-square	Significance	Pearson correlation	Significance	Eta
131. Timely promotions, career progression	18	104.25	0.000	0.227	0.000	0.202
122a. Economic security in services	18	68.16	0.000	–0.163	0.007	0.208
123. Retirement benefits available	18	95.85	0.000	–0.128	0.040	0.344

Items details	df	Chi-square	Significance	Pearson correlation	Significance	Eta
124. Status, power and influence	20	56.25	0.000	0.18	0.003	0.221
125. Opportunities and more chances to serve people	18	143.18	0.000	–0.328	0.000	0.354
126. Opportunity, freedom to do original work	18	135.71	0.000	–0.203	0.001	0.226
127. Professional competence	18	57.32	0.000	–0.209	0.001	0.219
128. Less work, little responsibility, no risk	20	70.29	0.000	–0.087	0.16	0.227
129. Prestige and reputation in society	18	69.47	0.000	0.184	0.002	0.199
130. Best salary structure in government	18	98.75	0.000	0.031	0.34	0.344

Chi-square significance is on two-tailed analysis

5.9.1. Economic Security

Every individual while studying and growing invariably looks forward to future financial security in the job one intends to join. With the entry of multinational companies into the Indian market, the financial package has bloated beyond imagination. Individual officer's future economic needs continue to multiply and he finds it difficult to manage the domestic affairs within available pay packets. Children education in a coveted and reputed school, own house in the city of choice, preferably in the metropolitan city and other luxury items to meet the ever-increasing demand from a spouse. On the face of it, every All India Services Officer talks about morality and values. But in the core of their heart, economic security for self, family, and physical materialistic needs for them predominant every time. In due course of time, when the All India Services Officers find it difficult to fulfill financial needs, he resorts to unfair means to meet temptations. Individual officer sees that most of the retired and serving All India Services Officers enjoy a sound economic status in their daily life. Not all the comforts, the All India Services Officers are enjoying can be attained purely from the pay available to them. The All India Services Officers' financial security in real sense comes from immoral behavior. We have tried to study the individual officer's financial gratifications as a member of the All India Services.

The mean ranking value for the AIS is 4.52, which indicates that the All India Services Officers lay considerable importance to economic security. If we analyze data for respective services; the Indian Forest Service officers' mean value is 3.88 with maximum concern, followed by the Indian Administrative Service officers with a value of 4.81, and last the Indian Police Service officers indicate a value of 4.99. Standard deviations indicate that the Indian Administrative Service officers are most consistent in ranking economic security (1.73). Our null hypothesis and a common belief that the All India Services Officers are not worried about financial aspects are rejected and the alternate hypothesis that economic security influences the decision is accepted in Chi-square test, showing 0.000, significance level, also show a very good association of two variables.

30.0% of the Indian Administrative Service officers have ranked it sixth level, if we combine two lower ranks also, then 6th, 5th, and 4th rank combine make it 70%, i.e. 70% of the Indian Administrative Service officers consider financial security as an important motivator from 4th to 6th rank in priority. 24.7% is the highest score with 5th ranking assigned by the Indian Police Service officers, successive two ranks are the 19.6% and 12.4% as of 7th and 8th ranks. So, 56.7% of the Indian Police Service officers with 5th, 7th, and 8th rank consider economic security as important for motivation in the decision. 20.4% of the Indian Forest Service officers have ranked this item at first, two successive values 5.3% and 14.3% at 2nd and 3rd ranks. 50% of the Indian Forest Service officers feel with a rank of 1st to third that economic security is the motivator in the decision. The variation is the highest with the Indian Forest Service officers among three All India Services. The Indian Forest Service officers have distributed ranking among all the ranks except the 10th rank. This indicates deviation in opinion may be due to high uncertainty across the various cadres.

Exhibit Number 5.4: Chi-Square Test Results for Economic Security as Motivation in Variable Method of Recruitment

	Value	df	Asymp. Sig. (2-sided)
Pearson Chi-Square	35.241	9	0.000
Likelihood Ratio	35.243	9	0.000
Linear-by-Linear Association	6.212	1	0.013
N of Valid Cases	272		

Exhibit Number 5.5: Economic Security being Member of All India Services versus Method of Recruitment more Amenable to the Pressure

Motivation Factor			Method of recruitment more amenable to the political pressure		
			Direct recruit	Promotes	Total
Economic security being member of All India Services	First rank in priority	% of Total	5.10%	6.30%	11.4
	Second rank in priority	% of Total	4.80%	8.50%	13.3
	Third rank in priority	% of Total	7.00%	2.90%	9.9
	Rest of ranking	% of Total	14.70%	49.30%	65.4
% Total AISO		% of Total	31.60%	68.40%	100

Statistical analyses of motivation variable economic security versus biographic variable method of recruitment data show good associations and correlation. Results of this motivation variable in Exhibit 5.5 show 31.61% direct recruited and 68.4% promotes consider economic security as a motivating factor while taking a decision under political pressure. 33.0% of the AISO have given this in the first three ranking motivating variables in the decision. Exhibit 5.4 results for statistical analyses show highly significant values and demonstrate a good relationship of variables.

5.9.2. Retirement Benefits, Long-term Goals

Retirement's benefits are the long-term goals of All India Services and serve the safety need of these officers. If we look at this aspect, it works as a hygiene factor for the officers. The corporate sector and multinational companies float promise for hefty perks and post-retirements benefits. On the other hand, the government besides pension, gratuity, and limited leave encashment do not promise many more things. How the All India Services Officers look and visualize long-term benefits related to decision efficacy. The All India Services Officers in microscopic minority get gubernatorial assignments, which can be never be considered as part of such benefits to all the officers, but these things do affect the decision process while working in service.

The All India Services Officers have ranked it low with a mean value of 7.52; these mean values for the Indian Administrative Service officers, the Indian Police Service officers, and the Indian Forest Service officers are 7.4, 8.6, and 6.64 respectively. Results for the Indian Forest Service officers show a higher standard deviation of 3.1 and the Indian Police Service officers show the lowest standard deviation of 1.2. Results indicate that the Indian Forest Service officers give the highest considerations towards post-retirement benefits and the Indian Police Service officers are least concerned. Chi-square values indicate that alternate hypothesis is accepted stating that retirement's benefits available to the All India Services Officers motivate them to influence the decision, with 0.000 significance level and 18 degree of freedom with a very good association of two variables.

25.7% of the Indian Administrative Service officers ranked retirement benefits at 7th. Two successive ranks are 24.3% at 9th and 21.4% at 5th. These make 71.4% with an average rank of 7th, whereas the Indian Administrative Service officers feel that retirement benefits motivate them in the decision process. The Indian Police Service officers rank it lowest at 10th with a 39.8% score. If we combine two successive values of 22.7% (9th) and 17% (6th), it is 79.5% with an average rank of 8.3. The Indian Police Service officers do not get much motivated by retirement benefits in a decision. 21.1% of the Indian Forest Service officers with 9th rank and two successive ranks are 20.0% (8th) and 14.7% (6th). 55.8% of the Indian Forest Service officers feel with an average rank of 7.6-retirement benefits influence and motivate them in the decision. Among three All India Services, the Indian Forest Service officers show greater concern for the retirement benefits, however with a low ranking. This may be related to the sense of economic security and lesser chances to accumulate wealth, which provide them security while in service. Standard deviation is also highest for the Indian Forest Service officers, indicating the variable feelings across the cadres. This also indicates that the Indian Forest Service officers work under a high sense of insecurity in their job and decision. This is highly detrimental to the performance and efficacy of the decision.

Motivation variable retirement benefits available to the AIS relation with a biographic variable which level is more amenable to political pressure in decision statistical results for Chi-square are shown in Exhibit 5.6, this shows a good association of two variables with a significance level of 0.028.

Exhibit Number 5.6: Chi-Square Results for Retirement Benefits versus which Level is more Amenable to Political Pressure

		Value	df	Asymp. Sig. (2-sided)
AIS total	Pearson Chi-Square	31.124	18	0.028
	Likelihood Ratio	34.383	18	0.011

Statistical results placed at Exhibit 5.7 for the three All India Services showing motivation variable relation with the retirement benefits available to the All India Services. Their ranking with respect to the biographic variable to know which level of the AISO, is more amenable to pressure. Results show very low ranking to first option, rather last rank of 10th is 21.4%, 9th is 21%, 8th is 9.9%, 7th is 14.7%, a total of last ranks of 10th to 8th is 53.3% this variable show no priority in the decision. 63.20% top-level IAS, 56.40% top-level IPS, 57.90% top-level IFS, and 59.90% of the AISO show concern for political pressure keeping in mind retirement benefits. We may infer that the AISO near retirement may accept political pressure in the decision-making process keeping in mind retirement benefits available to them.

Exhibit Number 5.7: Retirement Benefits versus which Level is more Amenable to Pressure

Retirement Benefits Available to All India Services	Which Level Amenable to Pressure			Total
	Top level	Middle level	Lower level	
Indian Administrative Service	63.20%	24.80%	12.00%	100.00%
Indian Police Service	56.40%	25.60%	17.90%	100.00%
Indian Forest Service	57.90%	21.10%	21.10%	100.00%
Total AISO	59.90%	24.20%	15.90%	100.00%

5.9.3. Status and Power

The elitist concept of the Indian Administrative Service officers considers upcoming of other services to policy and power as a threat to their status and authority, which intensify insecurity and groupism among services. The prevalent opinion is that there is no equal power-sharing or means of combinations available among various services for that motivation. Such would be necessary for the present set up of public administration to give them temporary success to rebellion frustrations. Inferiority has arisen not from the reconciled work culture, but rather from the perceived status of other services vis-à-vis the Indian Administrative Service officers. Premonitions/portent of different combination reinforces the sense of insecurity among different services.

Relentless denunciation of other services by the Indian Administrative Service gives rise to a demand for thorough bureaucratic change. Frustrations and disdain are prevalent among officers of other services expressed in terms of their inability to adequately involving in the decision process. Failure to involve other services in policy and power at the top level, provide a cogent argument to maintain elite service hegemony. Equal involvement of all services will offer rationalization of elitist disdain. Elitist philosophy forces them to remain dominant over other services, in order to gain complete control and superimposing their ideas. Elitist concept flourishes in decision with the combination of insecurity, fear, ignorance, and disdain dimensions. This approach in long run is ruining any iota of innovative thinking that remained in the system. Elitists visualize any kind of social, political, and administrative change in the system as a threat to their own hegemony.

Five power bases influence the All India Services Officers' motivation in the decision. The All India Services Officers inculcate fear among subordinates due to their prominent location in the hierarchy. Under intoxication of power, the All India Services Officers intimidate others, so that everyone runs after them and respects them. This position of coercive power motivates the All India Services Officers to retain power. The All India Services Officers located at the top of the decision are in a position to distribute rewards, benefits, favors, promotions, or any other kind of benefits, which are valued by others. Here, if you sing songs in praise of the All India Services Officers, you will be rewarded, otherwise coaxed and coerced. Colonially created Indian bureaucracy has been structured and designed that all formal power goes with a position in the hierarchy in that department. That is why beliefs that install a fool in the chair you have to salute, chair command the power.

The Indian Police Service officers and the Indian Forest Service officers work with specialized knowledge and the Indian Administrative Service officers put themselves above all such expert knowledge. The Indian Administrative Service officers enjoy the power of pseudo-expert, even if they don't possess such skills, but they pose as if they are the only persons, who know everything on the earth and others are cipher in front of them. Bureaucratic system working is like that. If you admire your boss, you can progress otherwise you perish. The whole resources of the country are under the command of the All India Services Officers; others have no choice except bow in front of the All India Services Officers referent power.

The mean value for status, power, and influence among the All India Services Officers are 2.24, indicating individual officers are high status, power, and influence conscious and consider it most important in the acceptance of political pressure in the decision-making process. These values for the Indian Administrative Service officers, the Indian Police Service officers, and the Indian Forest Service officers are 1.71, 1.88, and 2.97 respectively. In comparison to the Indian Administrative Service officers and the Indian Police Service officers, status, power, and influence consciousness is the least among the Indian Forest Service officers. These lower values may be due to continuous powerlessness and frustration caused by the dominance of the Indian Administrative Service officers over them.

Very low standard deviation among the Indian Administrative Service officers and the Indian Police Service officers indicate pervasive power and status consciousness among them across the cadres. Comparative higher standard deviation among the Indian Forest Service officers indicates variation across the cadres in their feeling towards status and power, though the dominating percentage is status-conscious. Chi-square results (Exhibit 5.3) are highly significant at a significance value of 0.000 and show a very good association of two variables. Acceptance of alternate hypothesis that status, power, and feeling for influencing others affect the All India Services Officers towards acceptance of political pressure in the decision-making process. Spearman correlation and Pearson's correlation values are highly significant, showing 0.003, significance level.

68.6% of the Indian Administrative Service Officers ranked status and power at first, two successive ranks of 2nd at 11.4% and 3rd at 10%, add to make it 90%. This establishes beyond any doubt that the Indian Administrative Service Officers consciously accept political pressure in a decision to protect their status, power and to influence others. 61.5% of the Indian Police

Service officers gave the first rank to power, status and influence; whereas two subsequent ranks score is 17.7% (2nd) and 12.5% (5th), this cumulatively makes 91.7% with average rank slipping to 2nd. 48.5% of the Indian Forest Service officers gave the first rank to power and status, which is a very low percentage in comparison to the Indian Administrative Service officers and the Indian Police Service officers. Continuous dominance of the Indian Administrative Service officers over the Indian Forest Service officers has slowly but surely diminished and vitiated their status and power consciousness. Two subsequent values of 18.8% (2nd) and 5.9% (4th) constitute a comparatively low value of 73.2% only. Another disturbing factor observed is that 5.9% score has spilled from 4th to 7th rank, and rest of the values are scattered over all the ranks, whereas in case of other two All India Services, these are confined to first few ranks only.

However, our research results consistently corroborate that status, power, and desire to influence others is the most important factor, which forces All India Services Officers to accept political pressure in the decision-making process.

Exhibit Number 5.8: Chi-Square Test Status and Power in Motivation

Type of Service and Length of Service Versus Status and Power in Motivation		Value	df	Asymp. Sig. (2-sided)
Indian Administrative Service	Pearson Chi-Square	47.207	32	0.040
Indian Police Service	Pearson Chi-Square	32.299	32	0.040
Indian Forest Service	Pearson Chi-Square	58.531	28	0.000
Total	Pearson Chi-Square	78.815	40	0.000
	Likelihood Ratio	70.140	40	0.002

Exhibit Number 5.9: Ranking of Status, Power and Influence versus Length of Service

AIS Name	Rank	1 to 4	5 to 10	11 to 17	18 to 23	>24
IAS	1st ranking	17.00%	6.40%	12.80%	19.10%	44.70%
	2nd ranking	0.00%	37.50%	0.00%	12.50%	50.00%
IPS	1st ranking	5.40%	5.40%	14.30%	23.20%	51.80%
	2nd ranking	17.60%	5.90%	0.00%	5.90%	70.60%
IFS	1st ranking	8.90%	6.70%	24.40%	13.30%	46.70%
	2nd ranking	0.00%	5.30%	63.20%	0.00%	31.60%
Ranking results beyond 1st and 2nd are not produced in table to save space						
AIS	1st ranking	10.10%	6.10%	16.90%	18.90%	48.00%
	2nd ranking	6.80%	11.90%	27.30%	4.50%	50.10%

Exhibit 5.10 results for length of service of the AISO, their amenability towards acceptance of political pressure in decision relation with status, power, and influence are shown. Results indicate that 67.10% of IAS, 73.30% of IPS, and 53.60% of IFS officers with more than 18 years of service accept political pressure in the decision to maintain their status and power in their position. But

among IAS 32.90%, IPS 26.70%, and 46.30% IFS with less than 17 years' service show concern for status and power. 45.70% of AISO gets pressure in the decision. Exhibit 5.8 statistical results of Pearson Chi-square significance values show a good association of status, power, and influence variable with length of service of the AISO motivating them to accept pressure in the decision. Results placed at Exhibit 5.9 showing ranking within that service regarding status, power and influence motivating the AISO with different length of services indicate that 47.1% IAS with more than 24 years of service and 53.8% of IPS of that category and 35.1% of IFS at that stage of their career get influenced in a decision to maintain their status and power. Concern for status and power among the three services in the decision-making process increases with length of service results show this increase from 8.5% to 45.4% at the top level of services.

Exhibit Number 5.10: Status, Power and Influence versus Length of Service

Service % in Ranking within that Service Mentioned	Length of Service in Years (Figure in %)				
	1 to 4	5 to 10	11 to 17	18 to 23	>24
IAS	12.30%	11.00%	9.60%	19.20%	47.90%
IPS	10.00%	6.70%	10.00%	22.20%	51.10%
IFS	4.20%	11.60%	30.50%	14.70%	38.90%
% AIS	8.50%	9.70%	17.40%	18.60%	45.70%

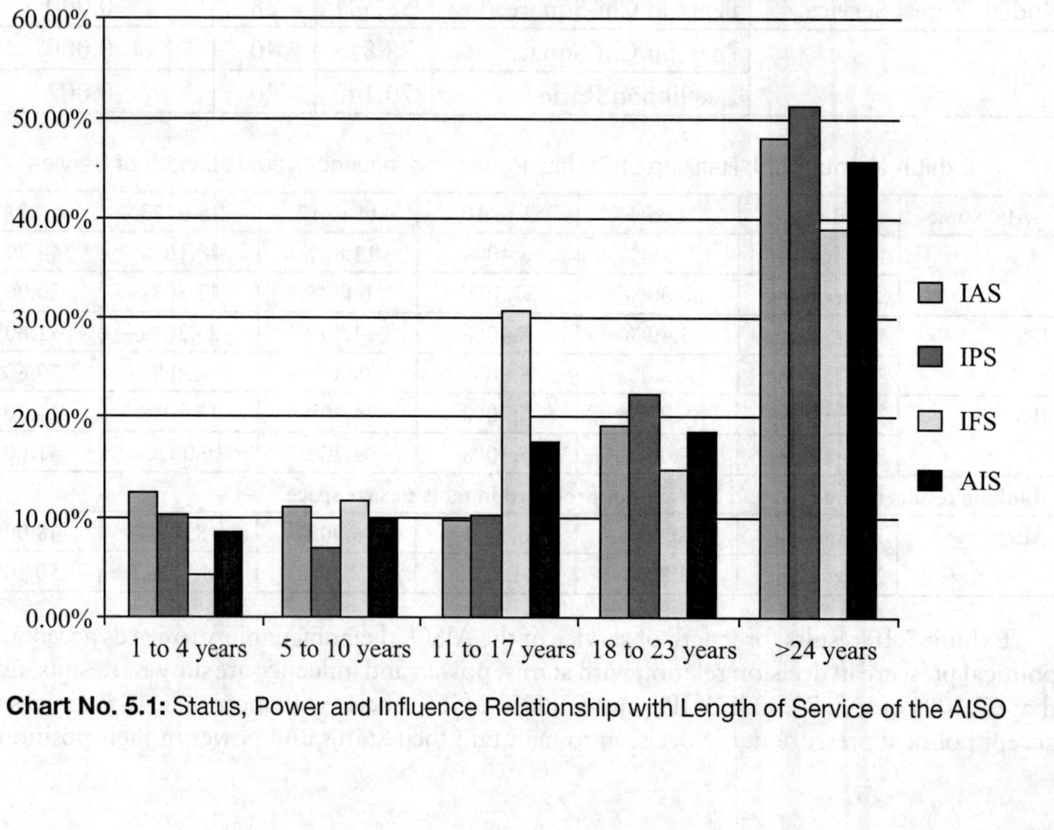

Chart No. 5.1: Status, Power and Influence Relationship with Length of Service of the AISO

5.9.4. Chances to Serve People

During UPSC interview many candidates were asked, why they want to join the AIS, the routine answer was the AIS provides higher opportunities and more chances to serve people. Do these All India Services Officers show great concern to serve people? Else for the sake of style, or they make clamor only. By virtue of the Constitutional obligation, the All India Services Officers are borne in their cadres to serve the public. However, all these obligations and duties got lost in the bureaucratic files only. Do the All India Services Officers think about people only to establish their claims for higher salaries and perks? All the facilities these super elites All India Services Officers enjoy in the name of the welfare of people, but in practice, they exploit them.

The Tribal's and villagers are saying that the All India Services Officers are recruited in the name of people-welfare, but in turn, these Bura Sahibs exploit poor and disadvantaged people in the most barbaric or uncivilized manner. The public fill coffers of government with their hard-earned money; in that process, the poorest of the poor are paying towards the All India Services Officers' expenses, perquisites, and facilities. These colonially created bureaucrats feel happy and enjoy, when the same public bow in front of them, touch their feet, beg their pardon, and address them as *Mai-Baap*. One's heart melts away, how continuously and mercilessly exploited people can repose their faith in these exploitative All India Services Officers. Tortures of subordinate employees, incidences of burning or killing, and public apathy have been reported on many occasions through media reports.[3] In the present-day set up, the All India Services Officers only work to serve their own, self-serving goals, which motivate them, rest is the throwing of dust in the eyes of the politicians and public.

Results indicate that the mean value of 6.49 (Exhibits 5.1 and 5.2), the All India Services Officers have very low priority for opportunities and higher chances to serve people. Among All India Services, the Indian Administrative Service officers show the lowest concern, with a mean value of 7.26, to serve people. The standard deviation for the Indian Administrative Service officers is 1.45, indicating that very low variability in their opinion. Higher chances and better opportunities to serve people have proved purely hollow, and do not affect much in acceptance of political pressure in the decision. The mean value for the Indian Police Service officers is 6.94, with a standard deviation of 1.28; indicates identical results as for the Indian Administrative Service officers. The Indian Forest Service officers with a mean value of 5.49, with a standard deviation of 2.83, indicating that they show higher concern to serve people among three All India Services, in spite of insurmountable problems. Comparatively high standard deviation indicates widespread feelings across the cadres and ranks prevalent among the Indian Forest Service officers. Pearson Chi-square values are highly significant showing 0.000, significance level, and good association of variables.

44.3% of the Indian Administrative Service officers ranked 7th service to people as motivation in the decision. Cumulative two successive percentages at 22.9% (8th) and 14.3% (9th) make average at 8th rank with 81.5% score. Very high percentage and very low ranking indicate that more opportunities with higher chances to serve people are not close to the heart of the Indian Administrative Service officers. Similar results are for the Indian Police Service officers with further increase in percentage at 49.5%, at 8th rank. The total of two successive percentages for the Indian

3. *The Times of India*, 20.12.1996. *The Tribune*, 20.12.1996. *The Times of India*, 17.10.1997.

Police Service officers is 94.9%, with an average rank of 7th. 17.8% of the Indian Forest Service officers ranked this issue at 6th, with a score of two successive scores of 14.9% with 8th rank and 12.9% with the first rank, make a total 45.6% with an average rank of 5th. The higher variation shows a widespread across the ranks for the rest of the values, including equally high values for top ranks. This indicates widespread feeling across the cadres and ranks of the Indian Forest Service officers that they are somewhat conscious and have concern for the service of people. Political pressure acceptance influences the chances and opportunities to serve the people.

Statistical results for Chi-square in Exhibit 5.11 for the motivation variable opportunities and more chances to serve people relationship with biographic variable officer regional background, show significance value of '0.010' indicating very good association of two variables and our research results are significant.

Motivation variable opportunities and more chances to serve people relationship with the demographic variable of officer regional background were analyzed results in Exhibit 5.12 show that the AISO from south India 28.35% and AISO from North India 24.60% indicate their choice to serve people as motivating in the decision under political pressure. Whereas in the ranking of variable the AISO gave very low ranking to this variable in a decision, total percentage and ranking seen together indicate that the AISO show very little concern to serve people while deciding on pressure.

Exhibit Number 5.11: Chi-Square Tests for Opportunities and more Chances to Serve People versus Officer Regional Background

	Value	df	Asymp. Sig. (2-sided)
Pearson Chi-Square	69.854	45	0.010
Likelihood Ratio	72.790	45	0.005
N of Valid Cases	272		

Exhibit Number 5.12: Opportunities and more Chances to Serve People versus Officer Regional Background

Ranking %	N-E part	Eastern	Western	Northern	Southern	Central	Total
Total	14%	15.80%	8.50%	24.60%	28.35%	8.80%	100%
Highest 8th	5.10%	7.00%	1.80%	6.30%	7.40%	1.50%	29.00%
1st rank	0	1.10%	0.40%	1.50%	1.10%	0.40%	4.40%
2nd rank	0.70%	0.00%	0.70%	0.70%	1.80%	1.50%	5.50%

5.9.5. Freedom to Do Original Work

The All India Services provide maximum freedom and opportunities to do original good work for the welfare of the nation. The AISO decisions and work have relevance and effect on every citizen of the nation. The All India Services Officers can make a tremendous contribution through their innovative decisions towards the development and progress of the nation. The All India Services Officers locations are persistent across the length and breadth of the nation and among most of the echelons of hierarchy in government administration. When they start their career from subdivision level, they are remotely located and in due course of time occupy the top positions as Chief Secretary/Cabinet Secretary, Director General of Police (HOP) and Principal Chief Conservator of Forests (HOF)/Director General of Forests in the decision-making process. Political pressure acceptance does affect the innovative original work spirits of these elites.

The mean value for opportunities and freedom to do original work is 6.11, with a standard deviation of 2.67, indicating low concern among the All India Services Officers. This value for the Indian Administrative Service officers is 6.7, with a standard deviation of 2.73. Values for the Indian Police Service officers are 6.49, with a standard deviation of 2.18, and for the Indian Forest Service officers 5.3, with a standard deviation of 2.85. These results indicate that the All India Services Officers are not conscious and worried about opportunities to do original innovative work. Pearson Chi-square value stands at 135.709; the degree of freedom is 18 and .000 level of significance showing a very good association of two variables. Our alternate hypothesis is accepted that political pressure acceptance is related to the performance to do original innovative work.

20% of the Indian Forest Service officers with 4th rank show concern for this item, which is a very low percentage by all means. Two successive scores are 16%, with 9th rank and 15% with 3rd rank, this makes 51% with average rank at 5th 35.7% of the Indian Administrative Service officers ranked it 8th; whereas two subsequent percentages are 24.3%, with 8th rank and 14.35 with 2nd rank. The total of subsequent scores is 74.3% with an average ranking of 6 among Indian Administrative Service officers. 42.7% of the Indian Police Service officers have assigned 7th rank; subsequent two scores are 19.8% with 9th rank and 13.5% with 2nd rank. 76% of the total of the three scores make an average ranking of 6th. Low average ranking with high percentages indicates that the All India Services Officers do not show too much desire and concern for doing innovative original work. However, the Indian Forest Service officers' scores showing great deviations across all the ranks indicate a lack of any firm opinion about the service as a whole; however, individual officers show different results.

Statistical results for Chi-square analyses of motivation variable opportunities and freedom to do original good work relationship with the demographic variable family economic background to know the type of service more amenable to political pressure (Cross tabulation) results placed at Exhibit 5.13 show a good association of two variables with '0.008' level of significance.

Exhibit Number 5.13: Chi-Square Freedom to Original Work versus Family Economic Background

Chi-Square	Value	df	Significance
Pearson Chi-Square	59.663[a]	36	0.008

The motivation variable of the opportunities and freedom to do original good work relationship with the family economic background to show which service is more amenable to accept political pressure in the decision-making process. Research analysis results placed in Exhibit 5.13A indicate that 34.9% of the AISO from a rich background and 24.1% from the upper-middle-class look for chances to show original work in the decision. Motivation results for this variable for within each service data indicate that 40.5% IAS (within service) from rich background and 38.0% IPS (within service) from a rich background, but in IFS 31.8% (within service) officer from middle class look for opportunities and freedom to look for original work in the decision-making process.

Exhibit Number 5.13A: Opportunities and Freedom to Do Original Good Work w.r.t. Family Economic Background

AIS Name	Family Economic Background				
	Rich	Upper Middle Class	Middle Class	Lower Middle Class	Poor
% within IAS	40.5%	19.8%	14.7%	15.5%	9.5%
% within IPS	38.0%	29.1%	12.7%	8.9%	11.4%
% within IFS	21.2%	25.8%	31.8%	18.2%	3.0%
% of AISO Total	34.9%	24.1%	18.4%	14.2%	8.4%

5.9.6. Professional Competence

Intellectual abilities and professional competency play a crucial role in information processing for decision-making. Professionally demanded abilities and capabilities enhance the process of decision. The All India Services Officers require strong verbal and mental processing abilities, quick reasoning, and balance interaction/communication skills. Positive attitudes and a high level of motivation to cope with inbuilt uncertainties in the decision. Higher professional competence may reduce officer job satisfaction and accumulation of frustration. Professional competencies have become a controversy in itself, due to the lack of objectivity and non-availability of reliable and uniform procedures for the evaluation procedures. "In developed societies, people are evaluated in terms of what they can do (achievement status) rather than in terms of what they are (ascribed status)", P. Singh et al. (1979). Non-performers are enjoying all the benefits at the cost of merit and performance in the system. When non-performers go ahead of performers, then efficient and performance-oriented officers are forced to think about the political pressure subjectivity. They realize that ultimately only political recommendation pays, performance is immaterial in career and posting decisions. Performance does not motivate them to take neutral and merit-based decisions.

The mean value for the All India Services is 6.19; this is 6.96 for the Indian Administrative Service officers, 6.39 for the Indian Police Service officers, and 5.41 for the Indian Forest Service officers with a standard deviation of 2.73, 2.71, and 2.80 for respective services. Pearson Chi-square value is 57.316, with 18 degrees of freedom and significance level is 0.000. Pearson Chi-square results are highly significant and demonstrate a very good association of variables. An alternate hypothesis is accepted that chances to demonstrate professional competence are not significant for the All India Services Officers. Higher mean values dominant among the All India Services Officers indicate lower concern for the professional competence and lack of will to perform most effectively. It is truly said that those who perform perish in government bureaucracy, non-performers; sycophants are rewarded and most liked.

22.9% of the Indian Administrative Service officers have ranked chances to show professional competence at lowest 10th rank. Subsequently, 21.4% with 9th rank and 15.7% with 2nd rank constitute 60.0% with average ranking for the service at 7th. Ranking down close to the lowest rank indicates that the majority of the Indian Administrative Service officers do not bother about competence and performance. They are the Indian Administrative Service officers and elite, so they have to be located at the top, performance, and competence are for others to establish or demonstrate. 27.1% of the Indian Police Service officers, ranked it 9th and 16.3% ranked it 2nd among Indian Forest Service officers. Subsequent scores are 16.7% with 6th rank and 12.5% with

4th rank, which comes out to be 56.3% with an overall average rank of 6th for the Indian Police Service officers. Subsequent scores are 15.3% with 5th rank and 13.3% with 6th rank, which comes out to be 44.9% with an overall average rank of 5th for the Indian Forest Service officers. Among the All India Services, the Indian Forest Service officers show greater concern for competence and performance; this may be due to prevalent powerlessness among them. Lesser security and low power consciousness motivate them to show competence and professional skills.

The AIS provides chances to show professional competence variable relation with the demographic variable of the educational background of the officer analysis results for Pearson Chi-square show value of 61.618 with df—36 and 0.005 significance value, which show a good association of two variables and study results is significant.

Exhibit Number 5.14: Chances to Show Professional Competence versus Educational Background of the Officer

Service Name	Educational Background of the Officer				
	B.A./B.Sc./ B.Com./Graduate	Engineer/B.Tech./ Technology	M.A./M.Sc./ M.Tech./Post Graduate	Management Diploma/ MBA/CA/CW	Ph.D.
% within IAS	28.7	22.6	33.9	7.8	7
% within IPS	32.9	20.3	24.1	17.7	5.1
% within IFS	18.8	17.2	46.9	9.4	7.8
% of AISO w.r.t. total	27.5	20.5	34.1	11.2	5.6

Research data analysis results concerning the All India Services Provide chances to show professional competence' relationship motivation variable with 'educational background of the officer' are placed in Exhibit 5.14. Results indicating which service is more amenable to accept political pressure in decision demonstrate that 34.1% M.A./M.Sc./M.Tech./Post Graduate and 27.5% of graduate look for showing professional competence in the decision under pressure, whereas it is lowest 5.6% in Ph.D. degree holders. Data for within that particular service show 33.9% of IAS and 46.9% of IFS postgraduates and in IPS 32.9% of graduates show concern for professional competence while deciding on political pressure.

5.9.7. Lower Responsibility

How people envisage responsibility in any job they perform? Whatsoever actions person is perforating, is he answerable for all types of implications? However, the practical implementer or the person, who executes that decision/work at the lowest level, is in a true sense held accountable for the failure of such decisions, law, and policy framed by the top officers. In circumstances, the All India Services Officers feel that any of their decision is likely to hit them back, generally, in such situations the All India Services Officers sacrifice lower functionaries on the altar of own incompetence. Most of the All India Services Officers look for little work, no responsibility, and no risky situations. Basic prevalent thinking is that grab the position with the least risk, little work, and maximum gains through perquisites and facilities. The Indian Administrative Service officers as Deputy Commissioner/District Magistrate only believe in coordination and control; any kind of success of any department, the credit will be taken by them, any problem or failure discredit will go to implementing department. Without well-defined accountability, any kind of control or coordination invariably hamper the work culture of other departments and develop parasitic thinking among the controllers.

The mean value for the responsibility of the All India Services is 8.33, these values for three services are, 8.36 for the Indian Administrative Service officers, 9.02 for the Indian Police Service officers, and 7.69 for the Indian Forest Service officers. Standard deviation values are 2.48 for the All India Services, 2.27 for the Indian Administrative Service officers, 1.41 for the Indian Police Service officers, and 3.17 for the Indian Forest Service officers. Among the All India Services, the Indian Police Service officers show the highest value, which may be due to prevalent discipline among the police forces, where actual physical responsibility for law enforcement is with the officers below them in the ranks. Pearson Chi-square results are highly significant with a significance value of 0.000 and indicate a very good association of variables under study. Our alternate hypothesis is accepted that higher responsibilities do not force them towards higher acceptance of political pressure.

51.4% of the Indian Administrative Service officers have assigned 10th rank to this item, with 14.3% each at 9th and 7th rank, which form 80% with an overall rank of 9 for the service. The Indian Administrative Service officers do not want to own any responsibility, they like to have little work and least risk at the workplace. Similarly, 44.6% of the Indian Police Service officers ranked it 10th, with an overall score of 86.9% (29.3% at 9th and 13% at 8th rank) with an average service rank of 9th. 50% of the Indian Forest Service officers gave it 10th rank, with a total of subsequent at 73.4% (13.8% at 9th and 9.6% at 7th rank) service members average ranking is 9th. Results are akin for all the All India Services Officers.

Exhibit 5.15 Chi-square results for the motivation variable less work, little responsibility, and no risk of the AISO relationship with the demographic variable of the place of birth of the officer and service are amenable to political pressure in the decision-making process. The significance value of 0.011 shows association of two variables is significant in our study.

Exhibit Number 5.15: Chi-Square Test-Less work, Little Responsibility and No Risk versus Place of Birth of the Officer

	Value	df	Asymp. Sig. (2-Sided)
Pearson Chi-square	37.15	20	0.011

Exhibit Number 5.16: Motivation in Less Work, Little Responsibility and No Risk versus Place of Birth of Officer

% Type of Service	Place of Birth of the Officer			
	Rural	Urban	Semi Urban	Total
% within IAS	21.8%	46.4%	31.8%	100%
% within IPS	17.1%	61.8%	21.1%	100%
% within IFS	41.3%	42.9%	15.9%	100%
% AIS	25.30%	50.20%	24.50%	100%

The AISO motivation variable for less work, little responsibility, and no risk while arriving at decision was studied to find out the relationship with the biographic variable place of birth of the officer and which service is amenable to accept political pressure. Data analysis placed at Exhibit 5.15 shows that the AISO 50.2% from urban background do not show interest in responsibilities and look for less work in the decision. In this variable, the AISO with urban background among three services also looked for less work, little responsibility, and no risk in the decision under political pressure. Data analysis results for within particular service show that 61.8% of IAS, 46.4% of IPS, and 42.9% of IFS show this type of motivation in decision.

5.9.8. Prestige and Reputation

The All India Services Officers savors distinctive prestige and reputation in the bureaucratic system, other services bureaucrats located in the system also like to have the benefit of the same. Elitists consider this as a direct challenge to their security, their power, their status, their reputation and prestige in society. "One of the most inclusive concepts of motivation embraces the desire to obtain certainty concerning the attainment of prestige and self-realization."[4] When a person prepares for the UPSC examination and joins the All India Services, they carry with them societal notions, what they have been seeing while growing. People motivate their children and relatives to join the All India Services for the sake of prestige and reputation enjoyed by them. After joining the All India Services, an individual officer may like to fulfill such long-cherished need of prestige and reputation from the service decisions. Any kind of harm, or decrease, or probability to induce a reduction in the prestige and reputation will motivate the All India Services Officers to accept political pressure in the decision-making process to enhance prestige through it.

The mean value for prestige and reputation among the All India Services is 3.03, this value for the Indian Administrative Service officers is 2.53, for the Indian Police Service officers 2.93, and for the Indian Forest Service officers is 3.52. Standard deviation values are 1.37, 1.24, and 2.34 for the respective services. Results indicate that the Indian Administrative Service officers and the Indian Police Service officers give high priority to prestige and reputation in society, whereas in the Indian Forest Service officers this feeling is comparatively low. The All India Services Officers show high concern for prestige and reputation in society, this motivates them to accept political pressure in the decision-making process. Chi-square results (Exhibits 5.1 to 5.3) indicate that findings are highly significant with a significance level of 0.000 and show a very good association of the variables. Spearman correlation and Pearson's correlation values are also significant at 0.002 significance level and show correlation with the acceptance of political pressure in the decision-making process.

35.7% of the Indian Administrative Service officers and 52.6% of the Indian Police Service officers rank it 2nd, whereas 21% of the Indian Forest Service officers have ranked it first. In a total of the successive score, 80% of the Indian Administrative Service officers have assigned an average of 2nd rank, with 22.9% with first rank and 21.4% with 4th rank. 89.7% of the Indian Police Service officers gave it an average of 3rd rank, 24.7% at 3rd rank, and 12.4% at 5th rank. 61% of the Indian Forest Service officers assigned it an average of 2nd rank, with 20% at 2nd and 3rd ranks. Results indicate that among the All India Services, the Indian Police Service officers are the highest conscious about the prestige and reputation in the society. This may be due to the

4. L.F. Shaffer and E.J. Shoben, *The Psychology of Adjustment.*

reason that common men do not have access to police officers, they have fear psychosis. Continuous denials of access to the masses make them more and more prestige and reputation conscious. Our results indicate that prestige and reputation consciousness prevalent and widespread among the All India Services Officers, motivate them to accept political pressure in the decision-making process.

Exhibit Number 5.17: Chi square-Prestige and Reputation in the Society Motivate with Place of Education after High School

	Value	df	Asymp. Sig. (2-Sided)
Pearson Chi-square	27.486	18	0.028

Chi-square analysis results placed at 5.17 for the variable prestige and reputation in the society motivate the AISO relation with a place of education of the officer after High School and service amenable to accept political pressure in a decision are significant with a significance value of 0.02 and association of variable is acceptable.

Exhibit Number 5.18: Prestige and Reputation in the Society Motivate with Place of Education after High School

% Type of service	Place of Education after High School		
	Rural	Urban	Semi Urban
% within IAS service	10.4%	61.7%	27.8%
% within IPS service	11.7%	62.3%	26.0%
% within IFS service	13.8%	66.2%	20.0%
% in the AIS	11.7%	63.0%	25.3%

Study of motivation variable prestige and reputation in the society motivate the AISO in respective services towards acceptance of political pressure in the decision and its relationship with the demographic variable place of education of the officer after High School data analysis results placed at Exhibit 5.18. Results indicate 63% of AISO from urban background look for prestige and reputation in the society while taking a decision under political pressure and rural background 11.7% AISO look for this variable. Results for within three respective services show 66.2% of IFS, 62.3% of IPS, and 61.7% of IAS from urban backgrounds look towards prestige and reputation in the social motivation while arriving at decision. Officers with urban backgrounds are more amenable to accept pressure in the decision in comparison to rural background officers in this variable.

5.9.9. Financial and Salary Structure

In the present bureaucratic setup, the All India Services Officers have a clear advantage over other services as far as salary structure is concerned. Available salary structure in a particular job provides satisfaction to biological needs and serves the extrinsic needs of the officer. Different pay scales for different group 'A' services have caused more harm than to serve any good purpose to the officers in India. Indian societal system is caste-ridden (Varna Ashram system) and persons grow with the sentiments of layering in their private life also. Structural layering in service pay-scales is the compulsive outcome of our caste-based societal layering system. Because the combination of the colonial outlook of decision makers and social differentiations upbringing motivate them to follow the same layering in the collaborator services in the bureaucracy.

Exacerbation of service alienation can be recognized in representations made in front of different pay commissions. Differential pay scales have increased the distance between the various services, such gaps must not be encouraged, and this is impairing the public administration in India. Anti-Indian Administrative Service, hostility is widely pervasive among various services in India. Prevalent opinions are that there is not enough power or means of combinations among other services; such would be necessary to give them satisfaction.

The mean value for the All India Services is 4.68 and the standard deviation of 2.28, indicating that the All India Services Officers have considered salary package as the fifth motivating factor in accepting the political pressure in the decision-making process. The mean value for the Indian Administrative Service officers is 5.20 with a standard deviation of 2.09; the same respective values for the Indian Forest Service officers are 5.12 and 2.49, indicate that they consider that the All India Services Officers enjoy the best salary structure in government. Whereas the Indian Police Service officers with a mean value of 3.74, indicating that they are not fully motivated by the present salary available to them. Pearson Chi-square results (Exhibits 5.1 to 5.3) are highly significant with a 0.000, significance level, and demonstrate a very good association of variables. The alternate hypothesis is accepted that the best salary structure does not motivate the All India Services Officers to reject the political pressure in the decision.

35.7% of the Indian Administrative Service officers have ranked its 4th level, if we combine two lower ranks also, then 4th, 5th, and 8th rank combine make it 80%, i.e. 80% of the Indian Administrative Service officers consider salary structure as a motivator with 6th rank in priority. 40.6% is the highest score with 4th ranking assigned by the Indian Police Service officers, successive two ranks are the 19.8% and 17.7% as of 3rd and 1st ranks. So, 78.1% of the Indian Police Service officers with 4th, 3rd, and 1st rank consider salary structure as motivation in the decision. 18.8% of the Indian Forest Service officers have ranked this item at fifth, two successive values 13.9% and 12.9% at 6th and 8th ranks. 45.6% of the Indian Forest Service officers feel with an average rank of 7th, that salary structure is the motivator in the decision. The variation is the highest with the Indian Forest Service officers among three All India Services. The Indian Forest Service officers have distributed ranking among all the ranks. This indicates deviation in opinion may be due to high uncertainty across the various cadre states.

Exhibit Number 5.19: Best Salary Structure Available in the Government versus Attitude of Family Members

	Value	df	Asymp. Sig. (2-Sided)
Pearson Chi-square	48.251	27	0.007

Statistical analysis for motivation variable best salary structure available to the AISO and its association with the biographic variable attitude of family members and type of service amenable to political pressure in decision show good correlation-ship, Exhibit 5.19 displayed significance level of 0.007 (two-tailed analysis). Research analyses are a significant and good association of two variables. Analysis for the AISO and within individual service results placed at Exhibit 5.20

show in 62.7% cases spouse attitude of the AISO influence in decision process under political pressure. Correlation of salary structure of the AISO and role of the spouse in the decision under pressure results show 64.9% of IAS, 60.8% of IPS and 60.5% of IFS feel the impact in the decision under pressure for these variables.

Exhibit Number 5.20: Best Salary Structure Available in the Government versus Attitude of Family Members

% Type of Service	Attitude of Family Members			
	Spouse	Children	Parents	Brother/Sister
% within IAS	64.9%	7.2%	18.0%	9.9%
% within IPS	60.8%	16.2%	18.9%	4.1%
% within IFS	60.5%	11.6%	20.9%	7.0%
% of the AIS	62.7%	11.0%	18.9%	7.5%

5.9.10. Career Progression

Every employee tries to look for growth and advancement of one's career as intrinsic values. Individual officer motivation is always related to career progression, stagnation kills the feeling of satisfaction. Stagnation slowly destroys the innovations in the decision. Risk-taking behavior and the capability to manage conflicts in the decision are invariably related to the growth in one's career. In case an individual officer is not going to get his promotion in time; any such denial will accumulate frustration. Among the All India Services Officers feeling of equity is dominant, individual officers compare promotion of one service with others in the same cadre and then to other cadres of the All India Services (Figure 5.3). Timely promotions and career progression infuse fresh blood in the dying system and individual officers wake up and start working with rejuvenated energy and a clean slate. Timely promotions provide new chances to show and demonstrate competence and professional skills. When non-performers go ahead of performers, then efficient and performance-oriented officers are forced to think that why they should not approach politicians for career advancement, which is bound to invite subjectivity in the decision. Pliable officers are enjoying all the benefits at the cost of merit, seniority, and efficiency in the system. They realize that ultimately only political recommendation pays, performance is immaterial in career advancement and service progressions. Performance at their own place and standing in a queue in the system does not motivate them to take neutral and merit-based decisions. In this race of self-aggrandizements, the All India Services Officers themselves are responsible for creating such frustration in the bureaucratic system.

Career progression mean value for the All India Services is 4.48; this is 4.0 for the Indian Administrative Service officers, 4.02 for the Indian Police Service officers, and 5.27 for the Indian Forest Service officers with a standard deviation of 1.65, 1.4, and 2.30 for respective services. Pearson Chi-square value is 104.248 with 18 degree of freedom and significance level is 0.000. Pearson Chi-square results are highly significant. The alternate hypothesis is accepted that timely promotions are significant for the All India Services Officers and any such denial or delay motivates the All India Services Officers to approach politicians to invite political pressure in the decision. Moderate mean values dominant among the All India Services Officers indicate concern for the career advancement and lack of will to avoid political pressure to perform most effectively in the decision-making process. It is believed that those promotions irrespective of merit and equity adversely affect the performance of government bureaucracy. Promotions provided to non-performers; sycophants as a reward for pliability; slowly destroy the innovations, merit, and objectivity from the decision-making process.

37.1% of the Indian Administrative Service officers have ranked timely promotions at 3rd rank. Subsequently, 32.9% with 6th rank and 10% with 2nd rank, constitute 80.0% with average ranking for the service at 3rd. Ranking higher up close to the highest rank indicates that the majority of the Indian Administrative Service officers show great concern for the promotions in their career. The Indian Administrative Service officers are elite, they are located at the top, and they get promotions in time irrespective of any kind of hurdle in the bureaucratic system. A complete bureaucratic system is at their command. Rules are applied, when cases for promotion come from other services. 40.2% of the Indian Police Service officers ranked it 3rd and 22% of the Indian Forest Service officers ranked it 7th. Subsequent scores are 20.6% with 4th rank and 19.6% with 5th rank, which comes out to be 80.4% with an overall average rank of 4th for the Indian Police Service officers. Subsequent scores are 14% with 4th rank and 13.0% with 5th rank, which comes out to be 49% with an overall average rank of 5th for the Indian Forest Service officers. Among the All India Services, the Indian Forest Service officers show pervasive frustration and lesser chances of promotions for them, which have induced prevalent powerlessness among them.

Statistical results for Pearson Chi-square with a value of 64.20, df 27, and 0.000 (Asymp. significance 2-sided) significance value show good correlation of timely promotions and career progression motivate with the profession of the spouse in respective All India Services. Exhibit 5.21 results indicate that 31.5% of entrepreneur spouse of the AISO demonstrate influence on the decision taken under political pressure. Data analysis for the three respective services, results for intra service show that how in particular service spouse profession of the officer has relation with a decision taken under political pressure. 39.7% of IAS and 41.9% of IPS entrepreneur spouse indicate impact in the decision, whereas in IFS it is 56% spouse influence decision, this may be due to reason that among IFS entrepreneur spouse number is lesser than that in comparison to IAS and IPS. Research results indicate spouse profession correlation with a timely promotion variable in the decision undertaken pressure.

Exhibit Number 5.21: Timely Promotions and Career Progression versus Profession of the Spouse

% Type of Service	Profession of Spouse			
	House Wife	Services	Entrepreneur	Business
% within IAS	16.4%	16.4%	39.7%	27.4%
% within IPS	15.1%	21.5%	41.9%	21.5%
% within IFS	56.0%	17.6%	14.3%	12.1%
% of total AIS	30.0%	18.7%	31.5%	19.8%

ANNEXURE 5.A: QUESTIONNAIRE ON THE AISO MOTIVATION UNDER PRESSURE

A.2. We have listed the most interesting features of the All India Services as 'a' to 'j'. Kindly, rank these ten items in terms of their priority in a job. Please mark 1 against the most important item, while deciding for a job and 2 against the second most important item, and so on mark up to the tenth rank.

(a) Economic security being a member of All India Services. ☐

(b) Retirement benefits are available to the All India Services. ☐

(c) Status, power, and influence through the All India Services. ☐

(d) Opportunities and more chances to serve people. ☐

(e) Opportunities and freedom to do original good work. ☐

(f) Provide chances to show professional competence. ☐

(g) Less work, little responsibility, and no risk. ☐

(h) Prestige and reputation in society. ☐

(i) Best salary structure available in the government. ☐

(j) Timely promotions and career progression. ☐

Unit 6

Lifestyle Orientation to Handle Pressure

"The mind is much wasted while one is engaged in worldly pursuits. And that loss can be made good only if one takes to life of renunciation or Sanyasa."—Shri Ramakrishna

"When environment changes, there must be a corresponding change in life."—Charles Lindbergh

"One should elevate oneself by one's own efforts and should not disgrace oneself; for one's own self is one's companion, and one's own self is one's adversary." *The Bhagavad Gita* 6.5

"The administration, whether it is small or large, it is, as a company or a state, it is with uniform or not. If the ignorant, immoral, loose-lips, uncultured and without etiquette, opportunistic, liar, mentality vain, dishonest and unfair people are there, I am just sure of it that the destination is the destruction, chaos, slavery, and hatred." —Ehsan Sehgal

- *Concept of the Lifestyle Orientation Process*
- *Centrifugal Centripetal Model*
- *Research Data Analyses Results*

The concept of lifestyle orientation with respect to All India Service has been described. The model of centripetal and centrifugal forces operating on the All India Service in public administration has been described. Research data analyses results for lifestyle orientation has been described for these elite bureaucrats.

6.1. Concept of Lifestyles Orientation Process

Alder (1930) suggested three styles of life as childhood, self-consistency, and constancy. Adler D. and Eckstein (1982) proposed instruments for assessing lifestyle. The All India Services Officers' mode of living and behavior pattern relate to service working condition realities, officer internal dispositions, and individual officer pattern of preferences, values, and beliefs. Everyone grows with a certain social-environmental set up within and around one's home. In the same way, every service has its own working environment, where officers grow. When the All India Services Officers are recruited by the UPSC, all officers come from the spatially similar and comparable social set up. Attitudes, values, perceptions, aspirations, and approach to life and their behavior are akin to that social setup. Their mental makes up or their behavior is similar irrespective of the service they are selected. Respective service peers and training institutes impart training to the All India Services Officers for grooming them for their orientation towards future needs of that service.

The young officer is malleable; we can call it second birth or reinventing oneself in a new role model identity. New behavior patterns and norms are re-imposed, boundaries for behavior are drawn, limits are fixed for society, the concept of new family and friends is codified, an entirely new world of mystery engulfs the personality of the officer. Officers are sacrificed on the sanctum sanctorum altar of word ***Elite***, for rest of their life, 'word' 'elite' eats them and devour them completely, but in the form of smallest particles. **'Elite'** becomes the molecular state of these officers. They are taught now you are above God, and God only created you, now onward you will create and control the whole society. So, the *Elite* God let loose one's rein of terror throughout their rest of life. Feeling of crushing anyone come in their way, they all will remain united and support any such whimsical act by any member of the *Elite* class. Grab as much you can, no rule is applicable to you. Rules are for fools; any way rules are framed for other than the *Elite* class.

If you do not fall in line with service expectations, it will become threatening for you. As officers grow in their service career, they continue to conduct an experiment with their service and own behavior. Most of the learning pertains to avoidance or prevention behavior, negative consequences are repeatedly told to them and avoidance behavior becomes an automatic lifetime habit. The All India Services Officers imbibe that in a bureaucratic system, circumstances are the dominant force, fear of disapproval response dominant and in case of any kind of pressure, the All India Services Officers first response to succumb under it. The bureaucratic system is such that it cultivates reactive responsive orientation among the All India Services Officers, which makes them selfish and goal-oriented. Training and grooming of the All India Services Officers have to be value and merit oriented. Continuous pressure from peers, seniors, politicians, and any other source forces the individual officer to recondition one's behavior with respect to time and place. Gradually, officers learn how to draw desired attention and full fill their own goals.

The All India Services Officers demonstrate their skills and knowledge in their respective services. Bureaucratic systems leave them alone or reward them as an outcome of their decisions. As officers grow in service, one's interests also grow and start relying more and more on self and interests group developed by him. In enlarging lifestyle officers shift away from service traditions and place more emphasis on adaptation of development of self. The All India Services Officers searches for the position of influence in his department and slowly their earlier relations with family and parents start weakening. Newfound position and power change the All India Services Officers values and he no longer enjoys the company of his college and university friends. The All India Services Officers' commitment to religion, social groups, and relatives become less meaningful.

Through experience, one learned that invariably top officers, seniors, or politicians are not helpful. In the world of service relations, fellow officers fail to extend desired help, and a crisis of faith develops in course of time. The All India Services Officers develop the opinion that power and authority are not necessarily always right. The All India Services Officers start exploring peers or person, who can really matter to him. Then officers break the hierarchical channels and start approaching politicians in power, which can mutually help each other in the attainment of self-goals. In due course of time, officer learns how persons in a high place can be unpredictable, unjust, selfish, petty, greedy, and dishonest. In services, today's friend is tomorrow foe and present-day foe can most reliably friend for time being in force. Inter-personal relationships in public administration are highly dynamic and amorous. Enfolding lifestyle officers cultivate and solidify their strength in their respective services.

The All India Services Officers develop a close attachment to a small circle of friends, who can extend help to him in time of need. The bureaucratic system reflects great variations in it, when you cooperate with your seniors, they may or may not like you, some times when you do not cooperate with them, they like you. The officers' experience with the system modifies his behavior appropriate to situations. Officer will repose faith somewhere in close family members or relatives with whom one will discuss all this. In case an officer has no such emotional pressure release arrangement, the officer may undergo a mental crisis and it has a serious adverse impact on the officers' personality. This is one of the reasons that as officers grow old, they show highly unpredictable and unstable behavior. Some of the officers find the system very dangerous, they learn to defend themselves to survive in the system, the methodology adopted may be right or wrong, and officers do not bother to adhere to departmental norms for their survival. Inbuilt frustrations in bureaucratic system force, even upright officers to accept political pressure or any other pressure exerted on them. The All India Services Officers find the present bureaucratic system unjust, unfair, biased, immoral, opportunist, self-seeking, bargaining, yielding, threatening, malice, distrust, and self-serving. The system motivates them to adopt pressure.

The All India Services Officers with responsive behavior respect the authority and conform to the prevalent bureaucratic system standards. Diverse conditions and situations of the bureaucratic system force them to respond in a sophisticated way, which ultimately binds an individual in their areas of consciousness. Pressure makes them decision conscious perhaps positive thinking for self and induce creativity for problem-solving. Situational behavior modifications occur towards stress reduction and consequence management.

The All India Services Officers with reactive orientation have faith in circumstances and they oppose any kind of pressure brought in the decision process. Officers with reactive behavior suspect their colleagues, subordinates, and seniors with the same perception they have faith. Crisis in them, due to internal fear imbibed in them. They do not subscribe to any kind of advice or consultations. In the bureaucratic process, people force such officers to defend their decisions and they become more reactive in due course of time. Such defensive reactive behaviors styles give rise to hostilities and create acrimony in the system. Hostilities and acrimonious behavior style make such officers week and they become more prone to acceptance of pressure in the decision process. "Even nice and responsive people build up resentment over time because of their chronic position of powerlessness. When they amass enough resentment, they turn into difficult, reactive people", Robert Fritz (1994).

Psychological tension and anxiety pervade the bureaucratic system, which makes officers more vulnerable to pressure. Stress, anxiety, and reactive behavior decrease individual officer performance, and efficiency and quality in the decision are lost in the process. Political pressure and bureaucratic system generate circumstantial stimuli in the All India Services Officers, which force individual officers to take a decision under fear or anger, or compulsion. Political power will invariably influence the All India Services Officers' actions and decisions; officers will attribute their failure and succumbing behavior to circumstances.

6.2. Model of Centripetal and Centrifugal Forces

In the present bureaucratic system, power has been usurped by privileged few officers in connivance with political authority, majority of other officers feel a chronic position of powerlessness, which generate frustration and resentment among them and force them to adopt reactive behavior. Development of reactive behavior has been highest among the Indian Forest Service officers due to chronic powerlessness and lower level among the Indian Administrative Service officers due to complete usurping of power by them. Even those Indian Forest Service officers in responsive reaction temporarily shift to the reactive mode and throughout their career continue to oscillate between reactive and responsiveness behavior. Chronic resentment, guilt, and powerlessness in disadvantaged officers built up conflict among the officers in service and inter-services. The Indian Forest Service officers and the Indian Police Service officers due to the arrogant behavior of the Indian Administrative Service officers at various stages, feel that real effective power exists outside them. Success accomplished by some of the Indian Forest Service officers and the Indian Police Service officers in their career, they feel to avoid failures and unable to change the feeling of powerlessness.

Powerlessness inculcates a feeling of unsatisfied and officers feel that they are incomplete and unsecured. As the Indian Administrative Service officers have usurped real effective power, officers of the Indian Police Service and the Indian Forest Service do not experience gratification, achievement, and sense of accomplishment. Process of decision forces them to realize that decisions taken by them are insignificant and they learn about the purpose or real meaning of their service and their position with respect to the Indian Administrative Service officers, who ride over their decisions. As officers grow with such experience this existential crisis continues to grow in them. The Indian Administrative Service officers have realized that if they usurp power by changing outer circumstances of the bureaucratic system, then the Indian Administrative Service officers' whole group and their individual officers will remain totally secure. They have assumed whole control over power and politician authority and they decide the destiny of all others as an external force for them. The Indian Administrative Service as a well-knit group inculcates fear among officers of other services. The Indian Administrative Service officers position themselves beyond the reach or control of any other service officers.

The All India Services Officers observe that it is beyond their control to influence the power of circumstances or a particular situation, which impel the outcome of the decision in the bureaucratic system; they are small fry in those situations. Officers are unable to take a decision of their choice embroiled in such situations; they perceive the need to react/respond to the process of decision. In reactive response situations, the All India Services Officers perceive that situations in the decision process are more powerful than them and their position in a hierarchy. The All India Services Officers' chronic worry is how to design a preemptive strategy to avoid conflict and negative consequences in process of decision.

The All India Services Officers show differential conduct in front of their own service members, other All India Services members, own subordinates, sister department subordinates, public with power, public without power, protector politicians, the politician in power and other politicians, etc. Individual All India Services Officers devise their own hypocritical ways and means to avoid pressure (avoiding behavior), avoiding from the decision process. Some pose themselves as highly assertive, sophisticated, knowledgeable, politically well connected, unfriendly, arrogant, not paying any attention to visitors, leave room in the garb of attending the meeting, pretend to be busy and not accessible for appointments/discussions, etc. Some officers criticize themselves in front of others, pose insecure and irresponsible, loose temper easily, provocative conversation, start discussions on religious sects, start describing selfless deeds, indulge in files, do not develop eye contact, look left or right and ignore the visitor, etc. used as a preemptive strike to avoid pressure.

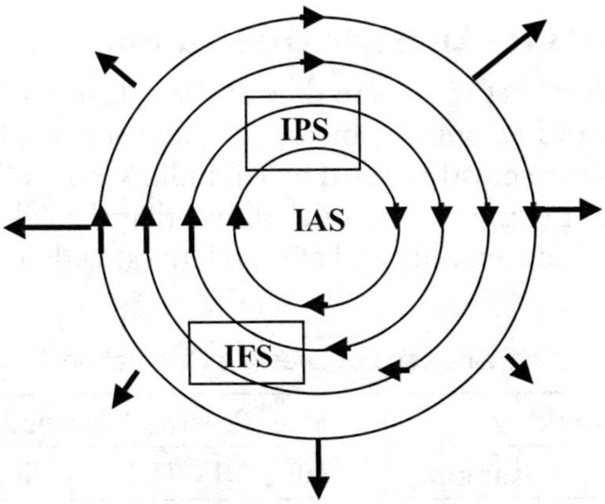

Centrifugal concept of AIS

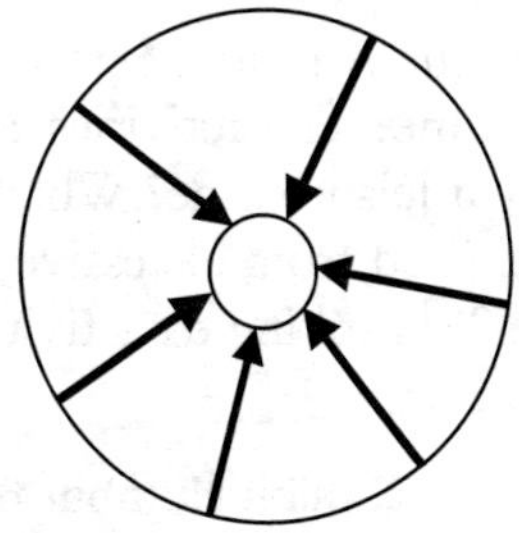

Centripetal forces

Figure No. 6.1: Rotational Model of Orientation

Officers in continuous defensive strategy design indicate their inner vulnerability and disapproval of pseudo security and in the process, they compromise for everything to achieve own goals. Such avoidance strategies slowly erode their sense of power and they shield more and more power around them, but in the end, they are reduced to powerless. Accumulation of power by the Indian Administrative Service officers will ultimately lead to a position of no power in due course of time.

According to the rotational model of orientation, as shown in Figure 6.1, other services are located on pseudo centrifugal force, whereas the Indian Administrative Service officers at the center of centripetal force, whereas by the movement of other services it gains momentum. The Indian Administrative Service officers at the center do not require any force of their own to propel it. Whereas services located in outer fringes cease to have momentum due to own force as well as by repulsive forces provided by the Indian Administrative Service officers and bureaucratic system (decrease in rotational motion through it out of path) also.

"If social justice is to be administrated, the District magistrate centric bureaucratic district administration, inherited from colonial rule, need to be replaced by people-centric democratic self-government functioning under the rule of law", K. Mathur (1991). The All India Services Officers seek trust, intimacy, interactions, and emotional friendship with the community, groups, and individuals. The All India Services Officers' desire for love, care, and esteem are fulfilled by such social support. Outside workplace individual All India Services Officer strives for mental support from family, relatives, and close friends, such support is essentially required for good health. Societal support works as a protective shield in the time crisis and uncertainty (Cobb, 1976). Social relations and affiliations provide strength to the All India Services Officers.

Enfolding lifestyle officers go for traditions, stability, and inward strength for personal and interpersonal satisfaction, a higher sense of humor. Enfolders' officers are people-oriented and impose norms on subordinates. **Enlarging lifestyle** officers devote time for goals and career growth, i.e. autonomy of self and others and more problem-centered, have a desire to help others.

6.3. Research Data Analyses Results for Lifestyle Orientation

Whenever the All India Services Officers get some free time at their disposal, how they like to spend that time? The activities are most often pursued by the All India Services Officers. How they spend their leisure time? Which areas are mostly chased by All India Services Officers in free moments and tired from excessive work pressure? Exhibit 6.1 shows that the All India Services Officers gave 2nd ranking to activities related to family and close relatives, with a mean value of 0.80.

Exhibit Number 6.1: Statistical Analyses of Lifestyle Orientation

All India Services, Mean and Ranking			Pearson Chi-square		
	Mean	Ranking	Value	Df	Significance
132. Family, close relatives	0.8	2	64	6	0.000
133. Occupational	0.79	3	163.8	6	0.000
134. Extra-professional	0.77	4	68.496	6	0.000
135. Religious	0.1	9	5.928	6	0.431
136. Self-improvement	0.51	7	26.674	6	0.000
137. Recreational	1.22	1	95.833	6	0.000
138. Friends, acquaintance	0.59	6	27.057	6	0.001
139. Reading, writing	0.41	8	39.519	6	0.000
140. Physical, spiritual	0.76	5	69.366	6	0.000

Df = degree of freedom

Recreational activities were ranked 1st with a mean value of 1.22 and 3rd ranking to activities related to the occupation (0.79). The All India Services Officers considered extra-professional social activities at 4th rank. This high rank to social activities may be somewhere related to activities connected with the mobilization of political pressure for self-goals. 2nd highest-ranking to family and relatives indicate that the All India Services Officers are highly self-goal conscious, and they can cross the departmental boundary lines for mobilization of political pressure to attain self-goals.

Exhibit Number 6.2: Lifestyle Orientation—Most Interesting Area

Activity Name	Ans not Rq.*		Ist** Choice		IInd *** Choice		IIIrd # Choice		Ranking (mean)
	Freq.	%	Freq.	%	Freq.	%	Freq.	%	
I.A.S.	##		##		##		##		
Family, close relatives	28	40%	36	51.4	6	8.6	0	0	0.73(1)
Occupational	38	54.3	3	4.3	1	1.4	28	40	1.32(4)
Extra-professional	34	48.6	5	7.1	26	37.1	5	7.1	1(3)
Religious	68	97.1	0	0	1	1.4	1	1.4	0(9)
Self-improvement	43	61.4	14	20	12	17.1	1	1.4	0.55(5)
Recreational	33	47.1	7	10	2	2.9	28	40	1.28(2)
Friends, acquaintance	46	65.7	1	1.4	16	22.9	7	10	0.73(6)
Reading, writing	65	92.9	4	5.7	0	0	1	1.4	0.15(7)
Physical, spiritual	65	92.9	1	1.4	4	5.7	0	0	0.16(5)
I.P.S.									
Family, close relatives	37	38.1	56	57.7	3	3.1	1	1	0.65(2)
Occupational	91	93.8	4	4.1	2	2.1	1	1	0(8)
Extra-professional	76	78.4	0	0	1	1	20	20.6	0.65(6)
Religious	95	97.9	1	1	0	0	1	1	0(9)
Self-improvement	75	77.3	20	20.6	1	1	1	1	0.26(5)
Recreational	22	22.7	0	0	43	44.3	32	33	1.9(1)
Friends, acquaintance	68	70.1	1	1	13	13.4	15	15.5	0.75(4)
Reading, writing	79	81.4	15	15.5	0	0	3	3.1	0.22(7)
Physical, spiritual	39	40.2	0	0	34	35.1	24	24.7	1.45(3)
I.F.S.									
Family, close relatives	44	44	17	17	28	28	9	9	1.02(2)
Occupational	25	25	51	51	13	13	9	9	1.07(1)
Extra-professional	71	71	5	5	3	3	19	19	0.67(5)
Religious	92	92	0	0	2	2	4	4	0.16(9)
Self-improvement	63	63	11	11	18	18	8	8	0.7(3)
Recreational	71	71	2	2	16	16	9	9	0.6(6)
Friends, acquaintance	85	85	3	3	3	3	9	9	0.35(8)

Activity Name	Ans not Rq.*		Ist** Choice		IInd *** Choice		IIIrd # Choice		Ranking (mean)
	Freq.	%	Freq.	%	Freq.	%	Freq.	%	
Reading, writing	63	63	10	10	9	9	16	16	0.77(4)
Physical, spiritual	78	78	0	0	8	8	14	14	0.57(7)

* Answer not required in ranking, as first three ranks have exhausted.
** First most interesting area for the life, where much time and energy is spent.
*** Second interesting area for the life, where time and energy is spent.
# Third interesting area for the life, where much time and energy is spent.
Frequency, i.e. number of respondents, who opted for that response (not ranked it).
% Percentage of respondents in that category.

Exhibit 6.2 results show very interesting facts and clearly depicting different lifestyle orientation for three services. Among the IAS high frequency in who have not included variable in first, three rankings are religious activities 97.1%, reading and writing 92.9%, improve physical and spiritual fitness 92.9% and moving out with friends 65.7%. This indicates that IAS Officers have very little interest in these activities. The IPS officer ranking is different and not shown interest in such as religious activities 97.9%, occupational activities 93.8%, reading and writing 81.4%, extra-professional activities 78.4%, course for self-improvement 71.3% and moving out with friends 70.1%. Research results show that these activities are not important for IPS Officers. The IFS Officers have not shown interest in 92% religious' activities, 85% moving out with friends, 78% to improve physical and spiritual fitness, and 71% each in recreational activities and extra-professional activities. This indicates that the IFS Officers have little interest in these activities. The AISO have not shown interest in religious activities. The IAS interest in occupational activities, extra-professional social activities, and self-improvement course, but the IPS interest is low in these activities rather shown interest in improving physical and spiritual activities. Data analysis results clearly show that the three services lifestyle orientation is different in respective areas; reasons for variation may be according to the demands of their profession and can be assumed this as an essence for their job.

Combination of all the first four activities indicates that the All India Services Officers at their own are motivated by their own needs, influenced by self-interests, and mobilize political pressure to meet self-goals. Except for interesting religious activities, Pearson Chi-square values are highly significant with '0.000' significance level; null hypotheses have been rejected in all these cases and alternate hypothesis is accepted. Our study results are highly significant and show a very good association of research variables.

6.3.1. Family and Close Relatives

Everyone is supposed to devote sufficient time and energy to look after one's family needs. The All India Services Officers have a very busy schedule; they do not find enough time to attend to the needs of family and close relatives. This has another aspect also, the higher the involvement in relatives and family affairs; the chances of acceptance of political pressure will also be higher in the decision-making process. On the other hand, support from family and relatives decreases job dissatisfaction and anxiety (Caplan, 1975). The All India Services Officers have to maintain a critical balance between family, relatives, and his official job. It is like walking on a tight rope. Any moment, any negligence, any casual attitude can cripple the decision-making process.

The All India Services Officers have ranked this activity at 2nd rank, with a mean value of 0.80. Pearson Chi-square results are highly significant, with a 0.000, significance level and demonstrating a very good association of variable. 51.4% of the Indian Administrative Service officers have assigned it first preference with the first rank, with a mean value of 0.73. Whereas the highest value among all the All India Services is 57.7% for the Indian Police Service officers. Among Indian Forest Service officers, 17% have assigned 2nd rank in first preference, and 28% as of 1st rank in second preference, with a high mean value of 1.02. So, among the All India Services, the Indian Police Service officers show the greatest concern for family and close relatives, and the Indian Forest Service officers show the least concern.

Statistical analysis for lifestyle variable activities related to family and relative's relation with the demographic variable of which level is more amenable to political pressure in the decision-making process. Statistical analyses result for Pearson Chi-square show value of 11.654, df 6, and significance value of '0.070' (asymptotic Sig. 2-sided) show good association and correlation of two variables.

Exhibit Number 6.3: Activities Related with Family and Relatives versus which Level is more Amenable to Pressure

% within service	Top	Middle	Lower
% within IAS	58.1%	23.0%	18.9%
% within IPS	51.0%	34.4%	14.6%
% within IFS	66.0%	17.0%	17.0%
% of AISO	58.5%	24.8%	16.7%

Data analysis results shown in Exhibit 6.3 indicate lifestyle orientation activities related to family, relatives, and its correlation with which level is amenable to political pressure acceptance in decision among the All India Services. Results show that top-level 58.5% and middle level 24.8% of the All India Services officer are more amenable to accept pressure in the decision. Results for three All India Services show that 66% of IFS, 58.1% of IAS, and 51% of IPS at the top level and individual service officer activities related to family and relatives influence the decision-making process under political pressure.

6.3.2. Occupational Activities

Every employee is supposed to maintain his knowledge steadily abreast and updated in his occupation. The All India Services Officers are also showing keen interest in activities related to their profession; they have ranked it third, with a mean value of 0.79. 40% of the Indian Administrative Service officers have assigned the third preference to professional activities with a mean value of 1.32. 91% of the Indian Police Service officers have considered occupational activities as immaterial with only 6 counts in all ranks. 51% of the Indian Forest Service officers have given it the first choice in first preference, with a mean value of 1.07. The Indian Forest Service officers have shown a good amount of interest in all the preferences, indicating that forest officers are highly conscious about their occupation. Among the All India Services, the Indian

Forest Service officers show the highest concern for occupational activities, and the Indian Police Service officers show the least concern towards occupational activities.

Statistical analysis shows a good association and good significance with Pearson Chi-square value of 25.94, df 9, and significance level 0.002 (asymp. significance 2-sided), good correlationship of occupational activities with an attitude of family members in three services towards amenability to accept political pressure in the decision. Exhibit 6.4 depicting analysis results for lifestyle orientation variable occupational activities related to the biographic variable attitude of family members among three services with respect to which service is amenable to political pressure. Results show spouse attitude of 65.2% of IAS, 61.3% of IPS, and 60.5% of IFS indicate relation with occupational activities of the AISO in the decision-making process. Other members of family percentage score are low indicating lesser interference in the All India Services officer decision-making process.

Exhibit Number 6.4: Occupational Activities versus Attitude of Family Members

% Type of Service Amenable to Pressure	Attitude of Family Members			
	Spouse	Children	Parents	Brother/Sister
% within IAS	65.20%	7.10%	17.90%	9.80%
% within IPS	61.30%	16.00%	18.70%	4.00%
% within IFS	60.50%	11.60%	20.90%	7.00%
% of AISO	63.00%	10.90%	18.70%	7.40%

6.3.3. Socialization

When the All India Services Officers have leisure time, they engage themselves in extra-professional social activities. Such activities are frequently used to develop and cultivate a relationship with persons other than related to their job. These outside relationships with the different social segments help them to propagate self-goals or political relations for self-advancement. Social support reduces excess workload tension and dissatisfaction, and work as a buffer (LaRocco and Jones, 1980).

The All India Services Officers have ranked it fourth with a mean value of 0.77. In the second interesting area, 37.1% of the Indian Administrative Service officers have ranked it at number one, with a mean value of 1.0. Results indicate that every third IAS officer likes to maintain social interactions. 78.4% of the Indian Police Service officers with a mean value of 0.65 have not shown interest in any such activities and ranked it 6th, showing that they like to keep a social distance; this may be due to IPS being a uniform service. 19% of the Indian Forest Service officers have considered it as the first option as the third interesting preference, with a mean value of 0.67, which indicates somewhat interest in social activities and different from the IPS.

Lifestyle orientation variable of extra-professional social activities of the AISO relation with biographic variable community background of the officer to assess the type of service amenable to political pressure in decision-making process analyses results show Pearson Chi-square value of 6.402 with df = 9 and asymptotic significance (2-sided) value 0.600. Results indicate that variable of extra professional social activities of the AISO relation with their community background showing reasonable association. Data analyses for the respective All India Services indicate that

46% of the IAS general category and 54% of IFS in general category pursue extra-professional activities, whereas 40.5% of the IPS among SC officers show a relation with extra-professional social activities. Exhibit 6.5 results show that 45.6% of the AISO general, 36.8% of SC category, and 14.0% of ST Officers show an inclination towards extra professional social activities in their lifestyle orientation.

Exhibit Number 6.5: Extra-Professional Social Activities and Community Background of the Officers

% Type of Service Amenable to Pressure	Community Background			
	General	Other Backward Classes	Scheduled Castes	Scheduled Tribes
% within IAS	46.00%	4.40%	36.30%	13.30%
% within IPS	37.80%	1.40%	40.50%	20.30%
% within IFS	54.00%	4.80%	33.30%	7.90%
% of AISO	45.60%	3.60%	36.80%	14.00%

6.3.4. Religion

Religion also plays important role in shaping the overall personality of a person. Values, ethics, and perceptions grow with a person's upbringing in the family environment. Joseph (1980), studied the support from religion provides to any person, he found that it helps the person to cope with adversaries. Some studies have observed that faith in religion is related to the level of education, security, and financial position of a person at any given time. Higher education and wealth tend to develop lesser reliance on religion. The All India Services Officers are well educated, enjoy secured careers, and generally financially well-off, which should reduce their reliance on religion.

The All India Services Officers' mean value for religion is 0.1, indicate, and establish their secular outlook. They devote a very insignificant time to religious activities. 97.1% of the Indian Administrative Service officers, 97.9% of the Indian Police Service officers, and 92.0% of the Indian Forest Service officers have not assigned any rank to religious activities. Most of the All India Services Officers do not consider it important to spend any time pertaining to religion. Most of the All India Services Officers are secular in outlook and beliefs or projected so.

Exhibit Number 6.6: Religious Activities and Method of Recruitment Amenability to the Pressure

% Type of Service Amenable to Political Pressure	Method of Recruitment more Amenable to the Pressure	
	Direct Recruit	Promotes
% within IAS	26.20%	73.80%
% within IPS	17.10%	82.90%
% within IFS	61.50%	38.50%
% in AISO	31.90%	68.10%

Pearson Chi-square value of 3.58 with df of 3 and asymptotic significance value of 0.310 (significance 2-sided) indicating a poor association of religious activities of the AISO with the method of recruitment in the AISO. Exhibit 6.6 shows data analysis results indicating 68.1% of promoting AISO show religious inclination in comparison to 31.9% of direct recruited AISO. Three AIS data analyses results show that 73.8% of IAS and 82.9% of IPS promote officers show religious inclination but in IFS 61.5% of direct recruit officers show religious inclination in lifestyle orientation in the decision-making process.

6.3.5. Self-Improvement

The frequent availability of flexible distance education system, online educational programs, the concept of learns while earning according to your needs. Numbers of different educational programs are available for self-improvement in today's borderless world. It is up to the individual All India Services Officer that how much interest one show in any course of self-improvement. The All India Services Officers overflowing with their floated ego and arrogance stay back as considering themselves as most learned persons in the country. Under the enfolding lifestyle, officers look for traditions, stability, and inward strength for personal and interpersonal satisfaction with a higher sense of humor. These enfolder officers are people-oriented and impose norms on their subordinates.

The mean value of 0.51 for the All India Services indicates that somewhat interest is being shown towards this activity. Pearson Chi-square results are highly significant with, 0.000, significance level. 20% of the Indian Administrative Service officers have shown 1st preference, with 1st rank to go for the course for self-improvement; 17.1% opted for second preference with 3rd rank, mean value of 0.55. Among the Indian Forest Service officers, 11% ranked 3rd, in first preference and 18% ranked it 2nd in third preference, with a mean value of 0.70. Among the Indian Police Service officers, 20.6% ranked it 2nd in first preference, with a mean value of 0.26. Results indicate that among the All India Services, the Indian Police Service officers show lower interest in any activity related to undertaking any kind of course for self-improvement. Perhaps regular departmental courses might have been clubbed with self-improvement contents or the police officers do not realize any need for self-improvement courses.

Data analysis is shown in Exhibit 6.7 demonstrate a course for self-improvement relation with the education of spouse among three services and which service is amenable to political pressure in the decision. 43.1% of the AISO spouse with postgraduate education indicates an impact on the decision for this variable. Data analysis results for within individual service show that 45.7% of IAS, 46.1% of IPS, and 34.9% of IFS spouses with postgraduate education show correlation with self-improvement courses among the AISO in lifestyle orientation. Exhibit 6.8 shows statistical results for Chi-square show very weak association of variables, rather we can infer both variables are independent to each other.

Exhibit Number 6.7: Course for Self-improvement versus Education of Spouse

% Type of Service Amenable to Political Pressure	Education of Spouse			
	Matriculate	Graduate	Post-Graduate	Ph.D.
% within IAS	12.90%	32.80%	45.70%	8.60%
% within IPS	13.20%	31.60%	46.10%	9.20%
% with in IFS	14.30%	31.70%	34.90%	19.00%
% of AISO	13.30%	32.20%	43.10%	11.40%

Exhibit Number 6.8: Statistical Results: Course for Self-improvement versus Education of Spouse

Type of Service Amenable to Political Pressure		Value	df	Asymp. Sig. (2-sided)
Total AISO	Pearson Chi-square	9.141	9	0.424

6.3.6. Recreation

After a continuous long spell of stressful work, everyone likes to relax mental nerves through the desired kind of recreations. Some of the All India Services Officers may be located at such places, where little or no facilities for recreation are available; on such locations, whenever they get the chance, they come out to metropolitans for such facilities. Technological innovations have created some room for consolation, where some reprieve has been made by the information sharing end. By any scale, levels of facilities available in remote districts are inferior to that of metropolitans or mega-poles or urban agglomerations. The All India Services Officers invariably get tempted for recreational activities under a feeling of starvation and unfulfilled desires.

The All India Services Officers have considered it 1st most important activity after family welfare, with a mean value of 1.22. Pearson Chi-square results are highly significant, with a 0.000, significance level. With a score of 10%, the Indian Administrative Service officers have ranked it third in first preference and 40% in first in third preference, with a mean value of 1.28. The Indian Police Service officers have assigned the overall first ranking among all activities; 44.3% of officers have given it first ranking in second preference and (33%) third preference, with a mean value of 1.9. In the case of the Indian Forest Service officers, 11.0% have ranked third in first preference and 18% ranked 2nd in third preference, with a mean value of 0.70. Among the All India Services, the Indian Police Service officers are the highest seeker of recreational activities. This may be related to a higher amount of monotony in the job.

Exhibit Number 6.9: Chi-Square Results: Recreational Activities versus which Level is more Amenable to Pressure

	Value	df	Asymp. Sig. (2-sided)
Pearson Chi-square	12.302	6	0.056

Exhibit Number 6.10: Recreational Activities versus which Level is more Amenable to Pressure

%Type of Service Amenable to Political Pressure	Which level is more Amenable to Political Pressure		
	Top level	Middle level	Lower level
% within IAS	61.10%	25.40%	13.50%
% within IPS	54.90%	28.00%	17.10%
% within IFS	60.00%	21.70%	18.30%
% of AISO	59.00%	25.40%	15.70%

Results shown in Exhibit 6.10 indicate recreational activities variable of lifestyle orientation relationship with the biographic variable of which level is more amenable to political pressure acceptance and type of service amenable to pressure in the decision. 59% of top-level AISO look for recreational activities in lifestyle orientation. Results analysis for within individual service show 61.1% of IAS, 60% of IFS, and 54.9% of IPS top-level is amenable to pressure in decision towards recreational activities in lifestyle orientation. Exhibit 6.9 shows Chi-square results demonstrating a good association of two variables with a significance value of 0.056.

6.3.7. Friends and Acquaintances

During leisure time, do the All India Services Officers look for the company of fellow colleagues and friends? Association with friends somewhere will be related to the inter-personal relations in the department. When an individual officer is scared of fellow friends, he is cautious to share any information under the inherent fear that such information can be misused against him in the future. Other aspects of perception regarding friends can be small group formation or interest groups in the All India Services or same service. High hesitation can be associated with inner frustration and depression also. Lack of initiative can be explained in different aspects of psychology.

The All India Services Officers mean value for this item is 0.59, with 6th rank; indicate that officers give low priority to move out with friends and acquaintance. Pearson Chi-square values are highly significant, with a 0.000, significance level. 22.9% of the Indian Administrative Service officers have ranked it the second interesting area with 2nd rank, mean value of 0.73, the high mean value indicates their interest in friends. Among the Indian Police Service officers, ranked it 1st, 44.3% in second preference and 33% in third preference, mean value of 1.90. Results for the Indian Forest Service officers indicate that 11% of them have ranked 3rd in first preference, 18% ranked 2nd in second preference with a mean value of 0.70. Among the All India Services, Indian Police Service officers move out with friends and acquaintances in maximum number. They show the strongest desire to peruse this activity.

Exhibit Number 6.11: Moving Out with Friends and Acquaintance versus Family Economic Background

% of Type of Service Amenable to Political Pressure	Family Economic Background				
	Rich	Upper middle class	Middle class	Lower middle class	Poor
% within IAS	40.70%	19.50%	14.40%	16.10%	9.30%
% within IPS	38.00%	29.10%	12.70%	8.90%	11.40%
% within IFS	21.50%	26.20%	30.80%	18.50%	3.10%
% of AISO	35.10%	24.00%	17.90%	14.50%	8.40%

Results for data analysis placed at Exhibit 6.11 indicate lifestyle variable moving out with friends and acquaintance correlation with the demographic variable family economic background to know which type of service is amenable to political pressure. Highest score of the AISO show 35.1% rich and 24% upper-middle-class economic background officers' inclination towards moving out with friends and acquaintance. Results within individual service show 40.70% of IAS and 38% of IPS rich and in second score 19.50% of IAS and 29.10%of IPS in upper-middle-class show interest in moving out with friends, but IFS score 30.80% from the middle class and 26.20%

percentage in upper-middle-class is different from IAS and IPS lifestyle orientation. Chi-square results in Exhibit 6.12 displaying a significance value of 0.02 indicate a good association of two variables and our results are significant.

Exhibit Number 6.12: Chi-Square: Moving Out with Friends and Acquaintance versus Family Economic Background

	Value	df	Asymp. Sig, 2-sided
Pearson Chi-square	24.076	12	0.02
Likelihood Ratio	26.376	12	0.009
N = 262			

6.3.8. Reading and Writing

Commonly believed and expected from the highest caliber of the All India Services Officers, that they must be devoting a lot of time to update their knowledge and skills. Reading and writing in the areas of interest have been assigned 8th rank by the All India Services Officers, which display very low interest in this activity. If we consider results for respective services, 92.9% of the Indian Administrative Service officers, 81.4% of the Indian Police Service officers, and 63% of the Indian Forest Service officers have not considered these activities in the first three ranks. Only the Indian Forest Service officers have shown little concern for reading, this may be due to the highly technical nature of their job. Technology is changing at a fast pace, without reading and writing habits, the All India Services Officers cannot survive, and for long in positions. People commonly say that after UPSC examinations, the All India Services Officers read-only departmental allocations and newspapers, nothing else. These words have been floating with somewhat truth for a long time in our social system.

Lifestyle orientation variable of reading and writing in areas of interest related to the demographic variable of the AISO length of service to find out which service is amenable to accept political pressure in the decision-making process. Chi-square analysis results placed at Exhibit 6.13 show good association and correlation of two variables with Chi-square significance value of '0.01'.

Exhibit Number 6.13: Chi-Square: Reading and Writing in Areas of Interest versus Length of Service

Pearson Chi-Square	26.086	12	0.01
Likelihood Ratio	26.114	12	0.01
Linear-by-Linear Association	3.187	1	0.074
N of Valid Cases	260		

Analysis results placed at Exhibit 6.14 regarding lifestyle orientation of variable reading and writing in areas of interest related with length of service to show 53.80% of IPS, 47.10% of IAS and 31.10% of IFS at the top level with more than 24 years of service goes with this variable. 45.40% of the AISO with more than 24 years of service go for the reading and writing variable.

Exhibit Number 6.14: Reading and Writing in Areas of Interest versus Length of Service

% of Type of Service Amenable to Political Pressure	Length of Service and AISO Amenable to Political Pressure				
	1 to 4 years of service	5 to 10 years of service	11 to 17 years of service	18 to 23 years of service	More than 24 years of service
% within IAS	6.70%	7.60%	17.60%	21.00%	47.10%
% within IPS	5.00%	7.50%	16.30%	17.50%	53.80%
% within IFS	16.40%	14.80%	21.30%	16.40%	31.10%
% of AISO	8.50%	9.20%	18.10%	18.80%	45.40%

6.3.9. Spiritual and Physical Fitness

Physical fitness programs provide deep relaxation to the body system, the impact of yoga and meditation are dramatic on the mind and consciousness of the officers. A sound mind lives in a sound body only. Success in decision demands stamina, physical and spiritual dexterity in management is ever demanding in a bureaucratic system. Physical and mental fitness is invariably related to the performance and efficiency of the decision. The All India Services Officers must possess high strength with the ability to expend energy to execute highly demanding works. Effective body co-ordination maintains a balance in thinking and shows the ability to maintain equilibrium under uncertainty. The All India Services Officers require stamina for prolonged and stretching working hours also. Physical fitness is the essential and first requirement for the efficacy and performance in the work execution. Up to what extent, the All India Services Officers are conscious about their health or only they look for wealth, which is considered as panaceas for all ailments.

The All India Services Officers have ranked fitness as 9th rank, which indicates that it is immaterial for them. 35.1% of the Indian Police Service officers have considered physical fitness as 2nd interesting area, 40.2% gave it 3rd rank in a first interesting area and 24.7% assigned 2nd rank in the third interesting area. The Indian Police Service officers being a uniformed service, they have shown genuine interest in keeping the physical and spiritually fit. Only 14% of the Indian Forest Service officers have shown little interest in third preference. 92.9% of the Indian Administrative Service officers have no interest in their physical and spiritual fitness.

ANNEXURE 6.A: QUESTIONNAIRE ON THE AISO LIFESTYLE ORIENTATION

Which areas of life are the most interesting? How much time and energy are spent on the activities listed below. Based on your general feeling, what is important? Please, **rank the three most important** responses as 1st, 2nd, and 3rd.

132. Activities are related to family and close relatives. ☐
133. Occupational activities. ☐
134. Extra-professional social activities. ☐
135. Religious activities. ☐
136. Self-improvement courses. ☐
137. Recreational activities. ☐
138. Moving out with friends and acquaintances. ☐
139. Reading and writing in areas of interest. ☐
140. To improve physical and spiritual fitness. ☐

The person thriving on the sense-objects perceptions develops attachment for them; from attachments, springs up craving, and from craving (unfulfilled) develop resentment. *The Bhagavad Gita* 2.62

"Persons with egoism, position-power-authority, arrogance, lust, and anger, etc. and denigrating others; such persons disregard the GOD dwelling in their own hearts, as in those of others." *The Bhagavad Gita* 16.18

Part–Three
Group Variables Impact on Decision under Political Pressure

"A man is a method, a progressive arrangement; a selecting principle, gathering his like to him; wherever he goes."—Ralph Waldo Emerson

"Individualities may form communities, but it is institutions alone that can create a nation."—Benjamin Disraeli

Unit 7

Behaviour Influences and Decision

Falsehood implies the making of a wrong statement by one who is overwhelmed by inner passions. Upasakadasanga Sutra

Therefore, go on efficiently doing your duty at all times without attachments. Doing work without attachment person attain the Supreme. *The Bhagavad Gita* 3.19

"Government is a trust and the officers of the government are trustees, and both the trust and the trustees are created for the benefit of the people."—Henry Clay

- *Concept of Individual Behavior*
- *Behavior Dynamics Concept*
- *Concept of Values and Preference in Behavior*
- *Perceptions in Behavior*
- *Attitude Role in Handling Pressure*
- *Factors Affecting Decision-making Behavior*
- *Research Data Analyses Results of All India Services Behavior*

This unit starts with the concept of individual behavior and interactions of various economic and social variables dynamics in the behavior of an individual officer. Role of values and preferences influence on decision behavior concept is given. How the process of perceptions, attitudes, and intensions interactions of individuals operate in the decision-making behavior of All India Services officers has been described. Various factors affecting decision-making behavior mentioned. Research data analyses results of different variables studied have been presented in this unit.

7.1. Concept of Individual All India Services Officer Behaviour

7.1.1. Variables Interactions

Large numbers of variables influence the behaviour of an individual All India Services Officers at any given point of time, place and situation. Some of the important variables, which invariably influence the decision-making process under political pressure have been analysed in proceeding text. An individual officer's expectations and desires for his own career and family life influence behaviour towards the fulfillment of such desires, which in turn make the officer more vulnerable to accept pressure in the decision. Individual officer beliefs grow and multiply according to past experience-imbedded layers of life, such beliefs make benchmarks in individual personality and individual handling of any kind of political pressure will be influenced by such beliefs. Based on individual experience in the management of different situations, certain assumptions are built-in, concerned officers handle political pressure in a decision based on such assumptions.

As an individual grows in **personal life and service** according to own experience within interactions of prevalent conditions. In given situations and service conditions, individual aspirations get modified and remolded, any political pressure in the decision-making process will be handled by the individual officer as directed by self-aspirations in that system. Individual officer service objectives and life objectives are dynamic and reshaped according to available space for the attainment of such objectives. Behaviour in political pressure handling will be influenced and directed according to the importance of such objectives. Individual officer thinking pattern, approach towards life, and control over emotions influence one's behaviour in the decision-making process under political pressure.

Emotions influence the needs and individual officer **needs** invariably regulate the behaviour in the decision under pressure. Quantum and extent of needs, attainment and non-attainment feelings instil fears inside the individual officer and accordingly determine the behaviour of an officer. Previous experience in the management of needs and fears encountered in the process gives rise to certain inhibitions, which shape the individual behaviour in the decision under pressure. Inhibitions in due course of time generate drives in an individual officer; feelings under such drives influence the decision behaviour. **Drives** in individual officer behaviour can be related and influenced by a number of variables. Individual officer develops certain instincts, which regulate individual behaviour in case of political pressure.

In due course of service and career growth, a certain amount of **name and fame** is built around individual actions and decisions. Once individual officers get fame in one's cadres, one tries to retain and enhance such positive fame, and accordingly, this fame comes in the way to decide about political pressure handling. In the process, some officer gets the celebrity status or get associated with some celebrity in their cadres, individual officer jealously tries to protect such image, political pressure handling behaviour get influenced by such external characters. Some of the individual officers are lucky, that perchance they refused the acceptance of political pressure form most crucial top source and nothing adverse happened to them, rather other officers appreciated such a decision, all of the sudden newfound fortune than regulate the behaviour of such officer in future.

Status is the biggest block in the behaviour of the All India Services Officers, most of the time individual remain busy in maintaining own status; individual officers accept political pressure and ultimately status consciousness invariably determine their behaviour in the decision. In due course of one's career, every individual officer develops some relations in and around work sphere, in case one derives satisfaction from such relations, then these satisfying relations determine the future behaviour of an officer.

Individual behaviour caries its influence on decision and in turn decision outcomes will have an impact on the individual officer's behaviour. Thus, the decision-making process and behaviour of an officer make a cycle in itself, continuously influencing each other. The individual location provides him with the power to make a decision and power have potential to influence attitude, values and thinking (covert behaviour) or behaviour and action in the group and individual both (overt), Raven 1993, Hersey and Blanchard 1982.

7.1.2. Economic Variables

Every officer is an economic identity. Different economic variables influence the behaviour of an All India Services Officers in the decision. Individual officer earnings from his own salary and other sources shape the internal desires and in turn income maximization process influence the behaviour of an officer. Consumption pattern and attitude towards materialism of an individual officer will influence the behaviour, thereupon. Mostly human behaviour is in pursuit of relentless economic benefits for self. An economic man will move as bargain hunter and he never pay more than he needs, he gets less than he could get at the price.

Every individual officer shows fully **ordered preferences** and collects perfect information while computing economic power. Individual economic preferences will be related to the service one belongs and social milieu one's lives in. Every individual officer tries to maximise his own utilities, and in pursuit of power and materialism, he chases economic goals at all costs. An individual officer desire for economic pursuits sacrifice attitudes, love for humankind, duty towards the nation and social responsibilities.

Continuous neglect of ethical foundations leads to the collapse of values. Unchecked competition for economic interests creates social tensions. Dominant market forces create a competitive economic environment in that service decision process. Decision outcomes are left to market forces, which determine the economic direction of a decision. This gives rise to a tendency to obtain results directly, rather than going through the proper process.

The All India Services Officers develop **'split orientation'**, under which officer develop a tendency to continue pursuit of self-economic pleasures in the midst of uncertain bureaucratic system climate. The living style of some of the money-oriented officers generate aspirations among other officers, in lust to maintain high economic standards, the officer tries to attain that without bothering for means. Unequal distribution of abilities among officers generates tendencies for adopting unfair means and immoral practices pertaining to economic variables. Economic needs motivate individual officer to accept political pressure in the decision-making process.

7.1.3. Social Relations

Individual officer social background and social environment in which one has been brought up influence the decision behaviour of that officer when he interacts with political pressure in it. Individual All India Services Officers behaviour in the decision is also related to the social sanctions prevalent in that system at that time. Different social groups in different cultural settings nourish different mode of behaviour, which they expect at different times according to the dominant socio-cultural setup. Eating non-vegetarian food is an anti-social for the Bishnoi's and in some parts of Haryana, whereas it is part of their routine life in northeastern and eastern India. Childhood social norms also direct future behaviour and influence the decisions one takes during one's life. Social ethics and values invariably carry its influence on decisions one arrives at.

7.2. Behaviour Dynamics Concept

Individual officer behaviour gets modifications and change under political pressure or due to continuous impending threats of pressure. Incidences of frequent political pressure in routine decisions induce a change in the thinking of the All India Services Officers. In due course of time, individual All India Services Officer becomes highly intolerant towards uncertainties. In course of time, the All India Services Officers do not attend pressure properly or develop a lack of interest in his work or such decisions. The All India Services Officers start behaving defensively, excessive defensiveness makes them no risk-taker. Go safe, decision or no decision, let the system go to hell.

Continuous political pressure makes officer insensitive towards public, department and official work. Such All India Services Officers show restlessness in working and get frequently irritated on small issues. Continuous pressure may lead to poor interpersonal relations and officers may adopt risky behaviour. A lot of officers have been seen resorting to heavy drinking or chain-smoking, rely on drugs and body language/gestures indicative of nervous stress due to continuous conflict and pressure on them. We have interacted with a number of officers with hypertension, depression, loss of appetite and anxiety due to heavy doses of pressure-generated conflict in the decision process.

The long-term stress was studied by Zung (1964), experiencing confusion, feeling of hopelessness, psychological agitation in the person, dissatisfaction from the profession, person show indecisiveness, emptiness, physiological disturbances, low self-esteem, etc. Uncertainties reduce the performance, efficiency and speed of work, Cohen (1980). Fatigue, emotional drain, feeling arousal to anger and aggression, loss of interest, suppression of environmentally directed activities; withdrawal behaviour is commonly observed in the officers.

An individual All India Services Officer reactions and interactions with political pressure in the decision process are related to the personality of the officer, which in turn related to the molecular structure of genes in chromosomes. Satisfaction with the outcome of the decision is related to personality in particular environmental and situational setup and personality traits of the officer.

Extroverts individual All India Services Officer, who is sociable, talkative and assertive, spend more time in enjoying political relationships and friendships with a large number of persons outside the sphere of their duty. This provides them with a sense of security in the job and makes them comfortable with unexpected pressure in the decision. Introverts solitude makes them uncomfortable towards pressure and more amenable towards acceptability of pressure. It is believed that co-operative, trusting and well-mannered individual All India Services Officer value harmony more than own needs, they try to manage pressure in a mutually acceptable form.

An individual All India Services Officers, who are opposite to this behaviour focus more on their own needs and goals, which force them to invite pressure for the decision process. An individual All India Services Officer, who are innovative, sensitive and imaginative inclined to be transparent and innovatively manage pressure and divert the pressure somewhere else, but those who score low on this use conventional methods to handle pressure and damage the system.

Responsible, dutiful, dependable, competent, perseverant, and accomplishment oriented individual All India Services Officers pursue fewer interests, and low goal orientation reduces amenability to pressure. An Individual All India Services Officer scoring low on this, tend to pursue many goals and interests, which force them to accept political pressure easily. The individual All India Services Officers with high emotional stability can cope with pressure in the most desired way.

Every All India Services Officer comprises individual needs and values. Individual officer abilities and capabilities provided him with different experiences through interactions in his service, related to his personality. Individual officer "consists of a number of subsystems, being hierarchically organised, with feedback loops to the supra system the brain, which monitors, controls and regulates the functioning of the entire system. There is dynamic equilibrium maintained within and among all the subsystems of the officer" (Asha Bhandarker, 1985).

Many officers have no desire to endanger their opportunities to rise to heights/pinnacles of name and fame. The consciousness of fear, perhaps this give rise to aberrant behaviour, evaporates initiatives. "The atmosphere of sycophancy has polluted the portals of administration", K. Seshadri (1994). The mechanism of service incentives guarantees co-operation among ranks of the All India Services. The codes of professional ethics are evaporating away. Political pressure does infest mechanism of negative incentives, animosities among groups, individuals, or services, which do not enthuse for the betterment of public administration.

The All India Services officers' energies are often depleted in petty and insignificant personal conflicts. This has made it impossible for them to unite behind a single concerted effort for the development of the country. Problem with this behaviour is that sometimes status feelings make them bitter enemies of each other. Width and breadth of India are strewn with boulders and rubbles of obstructive hostility among various services. Let us forget the Elliot-MacDonnell controversy of British India, even these hostilities stories are more pronounced towards top hierarchical levels in present-day also. Dislikes for successor/predecessor and concocted controversies for various groups/individuals are grinding the mill of different offices. These controversies are a tiny fraction of unlimited dimensions of individual officer animosity, possessiveness and hostility among the All India Services Officers.

Hardness, self-composure, coolness in face of pain and danger are the characters of the All India Services Officers behaviour. First few years' experiences of an individual officer during initial career plays a crucial role and decide the determinants of future behaviour of All India Services Officers. Political and social influence of the All India Services officers is across the spectrum of civilian opinion. Excessive insulation of these services has created the apprehensions and anti-All India Services feelings. Hostility towards these services is pervasive across the country. Tendencies of constant interference by the elitist services and continuous meddling by them in the policy related to the sphere of their incompetence generate frustration among other services. The elitist view is doubtlessly dominating and influencing the political authority at the top, which in turn reshape their behavior.

The All India Services create dilemma through manipulations and distortions in policies effect the winning and sustenance equations of political parties. The strategy of centralizing policy power with elite services creates euphemism for diversion of control for pertinent issues, which is reflected through the embarrassment of political leadership. The dominance of elitist view in policy generates opposition among bureaucracy and public, both. The policy of limited partnership provides steering for elitist manipulations and distortions. Distortions generate public animus against the policy, which thwart the good intentions of political leadership.

The Mahabharata lay down 36 principles for the public administrator (ruler) some of them were: never abandon kindness, observe duties without malice, never inflict punishment without careful enquiry, never cherish malice, and serve his seniors with sincerity.

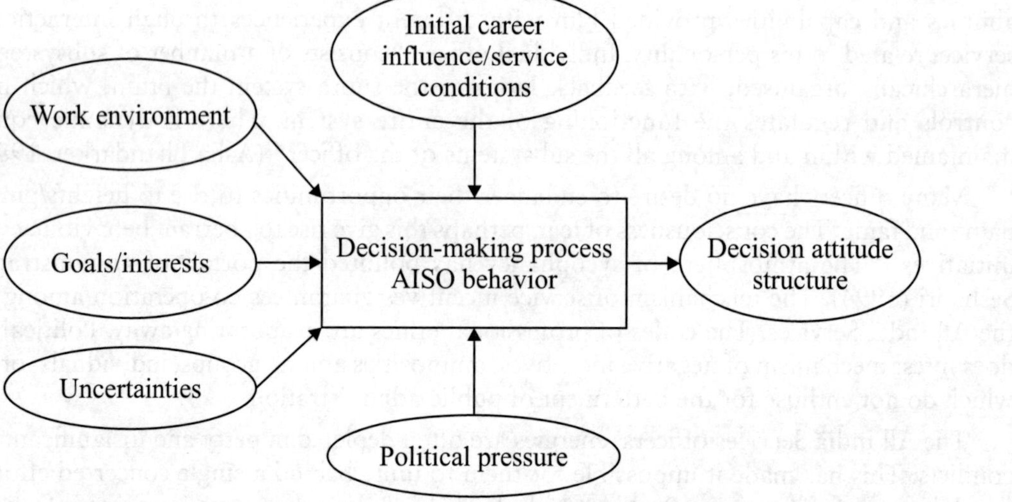

Figure No. 7.1: Development of Political Orientation in the AISO Decision Attitude

Based on research work, decision process behaviour of the All India Services Officers has been depicted in Figure 7.1. It has been observed that workplace environment (including socio-cultural aspects, Unit 16), individual goals/interests and uncertainties working on the individual officer influence and decide the attitude structure in decision behaviour. Political pressure, initial career impressions and service conditions play a crucial role in deciding decision behaviour of an All India Services Officer.

The Chanakya had described major variables for the behavior of public administrator. Some of them were intelligent like God, capable of seeing through the eyes of experienced persons, who love virtues, full of strength and valor, straightforwardness, the public must believe in his words, gratefulness, capable of achieving targets, purity of spirit, deep and profound knowledge, good memory and retention power, strong and quick in the decision, high caliber, capable of taking hard decisions, i.e. inflict punishment on wrongdoers and reward for ability, dignity, foresight, the capability to protect in unforeseen danger and uncertainties, responsive to responsibilities, the capability to humorous without any damage to dignity, free from any kind of bias (caste, money, greed, hatred, fickleness), good manners, sympathy and humane in nature, devotion to duty, polite in conduct and behavior with others and capable of leading his team (the *Arthsastra Book* vi. Cp. 1).

7.3. Values and Preferences in Behaviour Concept

The All India Services Officers values or functions of preferences their relationship towards interests, attitudes and sentiments are determined by what these officers want or think they expect from service. Individual All India Services Officer prediction dreams to use various ways and means to attain it. The individual officer makes assumptions about their decision in public administration they carry out. Individual All India Services Officers tinker the bureaucratic system, as a result of transactional processes bureaucratic system operate upon them. Existence and values are intimately related and interdependent. "Values are manifested in ideas, expressional symbols, and in the moral and aesthetic norms evident in behavioural regularities" (Kluckhohn et al., 1951).

Values for the All India Services Officers in the decision are related to the individual officer's desires, perceptions, conceptions, and selection elements of the process. An individual All India Services Officer use-value as a goal object, instead of goal maintains the own values. Every individual officer constructs meanings of values against his own characteristics and environmental culture. Values and beliefs are continuously shifted and re-interpreted to own configurations of an officer. Mode of conduct of an All India Services Officer in decision their personal existence, socially and publicly adopted preference (public preference) in the decision-making process under political pressure are complex and influence the behaviour of the officer.

When political pressure is exerted, individual All India Services Officer ideas, thinking about the desirability of the intensity of political pressure, mode of political pressure, and outcome of decision are ranked according to individual values. Individual All India Services Officer values influence the perceptions about the pressure in the decision. An individual officer values drive preferences towards objectivity and rationality in the decision-making process under political pressure. Values influence the attitude, perception, behaviour, and accordingly allocate performance and satisfaction in the decision under political pressure.

The All India Services Officers derive values from factors such as family background, community background, method of recruitment, location and position in the hierarchy, education of self and family, the attitude of members of the family, profession of the spouse, and domicile state of the officer and family, rural/urban background, type of training imparted, regional cultural background, service work culture, department work environment, personal orientation, inter-personal relations, career progression, transfer/posting policy, promotion policy, power and status available in the post. These factors can be ascribed to three categories such as the individual personality of the All India Services Officer, the bureaucratic system, and the social-political system. This has been presented through a triangular way in Figure 7.2. Previous research works indicate that 40% of variations in values can be explained by the genetics of a person.

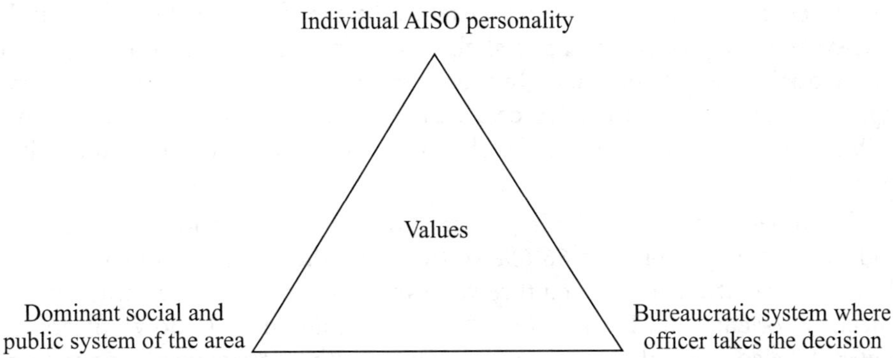

Figure No. 7.2: Values Triangle Model of the All India Services Officers

Family, self-financial requirements and financial security available in the All India Services also influence the values and preferences of an individual officer. Individual All India Services Officer finds out accomplishment in decision according to their own ideas and values. Particular officer and service achievement in life also influence the values of an officer. Every All India Services Officer has a frame of own goals and career goals expectation from his service. Achievement of goals during a service career determines the values preferences in behaviour. Respective services and individual officers possess a preference for the challenges in the decision; the meeting of such challenges has an impact on the values an officer cherishes. Inner conscious continues to remind individual officer what is the expectation from service, conscious satisfaction satisfies oneself and create coolness and calmness in the decision.

Biographical characters play a crucial role to explain variations in the values in decisions prevalent among the All India Services Officers. Regional and the Cadre State values continuously reinforce certain values over the length of time. Societal influences over values and beliefs in handling decision cannot be ignored in case of the All India Services Officers. Individual All India Services Officers workplace environment, service culture prevalent in that service, where the concerned officer has been groomed, accordingly cultivates the values in them. Achievement in the job, co-existence, peace, co-operation, sense of fearlessness, feeling for others, feeling for the group, feeling for family, and politics are the societal values.

When an individual joins the All India Services, he undergoes institutional training and on the job training, during that process, many values are altered and changed according to the new service environment and requirements. Concept of elite and supreme, alter and align values within service culture, and concerned officer slowly increases the distances from his past. During individual career progression, service environment endures those values towards political pressure handling. The concept of desirable and undesirable values is imbibed during service culture through workplace environment and outcomes of departmental politics and policies. The individual societal environment in which one grows endures different values towards authority, colleagues, and group culture. "Organisational culture, decision-making process, the process of managerial planning, co-ordination, control motivation, etc. are significantly influenced by managerial values" (P. Singh et al., 1979).

For our study, we can assume values up to eighties batches has higher belief in hard work, were more conservative, faith in the joint system of management, belief in hierarchy, loyal to bureaucratic system, more conformist and slight autonomy seekers. Later in the nineties, batches are more individual success-oriented, ambitious, hard work towards loyalty to career, autonomy demanding, and quality conscious. Officers of this twenty-first century (2000 onward) have higher flexibility in thinking, leisure time seeker, nuclear family-oriented, and loyalty to current relationships.

The All India Services Officers hailing from different states; regions with different cultural backgrounds and values; at present 66.6% of them are allotted cadre other than parent state. So, they have to face different work culture values than their childhood values at contradicting values in decision orientation. During our LBSNAA training days (fellow officers used to say); Haryanvi were labeled culturally simple and down to earth, more transparent and open-minded due to cultural milieu; whereas persons from the Gangetic plains don't open up their cards easily, and believe in saliently achieving their goals and coolly manipulate decisions. Persons from

Bengal showed very high value towards the proletariat psyche. Gujaratis were seen as high for co-operative values in the system and less competitive in goals. The All India Services Officers from Hindi speaking so-called cow belt and coastal India show power distance; readily accept the unequal power distribution in the bureaucratic system. An officer from North-Eastern India shows lower power distance (these assumptions were discussed verbally).

Culture of individualism has invaded the All India Services. Cut-throat competition is prevalent for such values among the All India Services Officers. Teamwork, collectivism, group feeling, and departmental values are on the decline among the All India Services Officers. Present-day some of the All India Services Officers assert themselves vehemently at the cost of other persons for own gains and goals. Individual All India Services Officers like to avoid stress, tension, anxiety to avoid any kind of uncertainty in the decision, which makes them vulnerable to politician and political pressure.

Independence in work and independence in decision motivate an officer to work and provide a sense of satisfaction, thus it influences the values of a person. Service culture and departmental working relations, senior/junior relations, and extending appropriate help to officers at the time of need reshape their values in the system, so getting desired help molds values. The Indian Administrative Service officers get their work done by other officers belonging from different departments, where they are working, this sharpens their acumen in handling the different persons, at the same time develop parasitical behaviour, getting the task done by others to change their value preferences. Individual officer satisfaction of needs in private life and job provide peace and satisfaction to self, this work as a motivating factor, this progress in life reshape the value and choices of officer behaviour. Continuity in service and place of posting change the values and preference of an officer and about the system working and decision process also.

Family attitude towards own utilities and goals, family values for the system invariably influence individual All India Services Officers values in the decision under pressure. The All India Services Officers family set up and background provides him strength and boosts the sagging morale of the officers in case of any crisis to manage the pressure, they do influence values pursued by the All India Services Officers in the decision. The All India Services Officers' frequent transfers got destabilized, feeling of uncertainty makes him highly unsecured, so the safety of tenure/posting does influence values. Continuity and assertiveness in a position provide job satisfaction and values towards pressure will be different in such All India Services Officers, others change their values and preference.

On job training programs and capsule courses for development improves the officer abilities, skill up-gradation programs has an impact on values in decision-making behaviour. Stagnation in the bureaucracy makes the mind rusty, close any chance of innovations, to remove deadwood, and rejuvenate the system through restructuring, which has an impact on values in decision-making behaviour. Specific training may be provided repeatedly to strengthen skills in how to handle and manage pressure successfully, so that, it carries a long-lasting impact on the decision-making behaviour of the All India Services Officers.

Present-day officers continuously work in the choked system, communication skill gets stereotyped, which need ever-changing attuning to meet the need of the hour, so that it has an impact on values in the decision-making behaviour of the All India Services Officers. The decision-making process is full of uncertainties and risk, it seriously lacks any kind of motivation except self-goals nourishment unofficially, a positive and good decision will have an impact on values in the decision-making behaviour of the All India Services Officers. Even if, some officers work with innovations, fight unnecessary political pressure, and save the merit and public interests, but such actions are never recognized and in no way help in career advancement. The good decision may be recognized and used for career advancement, which will influence the values in long run.

The All India Services Officers are greatest hypocrites in practice, they seek status while dealing with officers of other government departments, but prostrate in front of politicians and even low-level political workers, who has nuisance values. They see the loss of personal goals as a weakening of their status. Continuous relations with the politician and obliging them in decisions slowly induce weakening of status and sustained relation with politicians has a negative effect on the values of the All India Services Officers. Strong desires to maintain status motivate individual All India Services Officer to oblige politician continuously and endlessly. This very status generates stress and strain inside the individual officer. Which forces him to change values to seek status; compromise in the decision in search of status will create distances from the public and ultimately individual All India Services Officer lose fairness and merit. This formal and informal relationship web with a politician, cause modification of the behaviour of individual officer and also interpersonal relations in the bureaucratic system.

7.4. Perceptions in Behaviour

Recognition or attention perception will influence individual officers to accommodate the problem in the decision. Officer will correlate problem in the decision to self-knowledge base and own experience for handling pressure. Individual officer appreciates own needs and motivation from the decision-making process. The individual officer will draw a construction about the problem with his own actual experiences in past. Individual grouping of the problem will be according to own perceptions and stimuli from the outcome. Political pressure will give rise to a multitude of attention awareness based on individual officers' earlier experience indecision and accordingly will close the options in handling the pressure. Different gains by decision outcomes may encourage continuity in acceptance of pressure and future perceptions will set expectations from the pressure outcomes. The experience of an officer causes prejudices in the interpretation of political pressure. Individual officer attribution to pressure will be internally and externally both. Internal and external goals are in consensus, an officer will lose no time to accept pressure and behaviour perceptions will be accordingly. Perceptions will see mouldability (plasticity) and modifiability decision according to pressure demands.

Individual officer interprets pressure according to own attitudes and the individual motives, interests, and expectations from the decision outcomes influence it. Satisfied and unsatisfied motives stimulate individual officer in pressure perception accordingly. Perceptions motions, distinctiveness, vividness and perspective influence the behaviour. Individual perceptions are influenced by the service one belongs, when the majority of the officers accept the political pressure for self- benefits, individual officers follow service traits in their own behaviour also. Self-goals attainments in a particular All India Services cause a halo effect on the behaviour of an individual in the decision. Individual interpretation and social comparison by the All India Services Officers influence the individual perceptions and behaviour in the decision.

The All India Services Officer influences the perceptions along with the influence of the source of political pressure in the decision-making process as shown in Figure 7.3. The individual officer senses pressure inputs, the source is recognized and officer attention is drawn to it. The individual officer draws a framework for the pressure perception and pressure is represented and interpreted with respect to the outcomes. After weighing the pressure contents in relation to outcome utility, the concerned officer starts action inputs to get the desired outcome from the acceptance of the pressure in the decision.

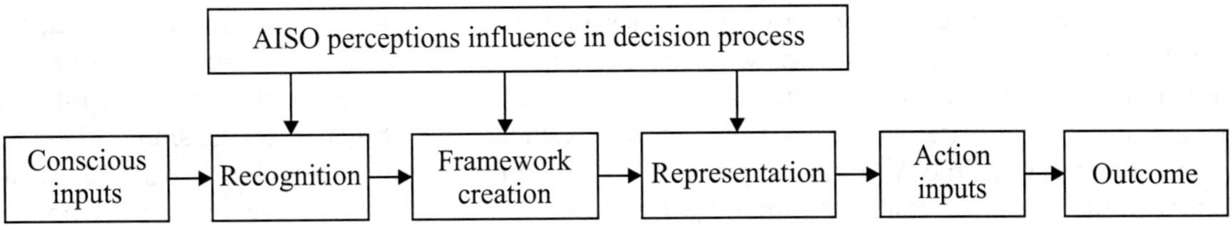

Figure No. 7.3: Process of Perception in All India Services Officers in Decision Process

Influences of the political pressure on the perception of the All India Services Officers in the decision-making process are described in Figure 7.4. Invariably, the All India Services Officers reactive inputs are directed by the outcomes. Bureaucratic system operations influence the kind of system inputs used by an officer in the decision. Individual officer computes these inputs according to self-goals. During the analysis stage individual officer explore the possibilities for achieving self-oriented outputs. Perceptional models of the decision-making process under political pressure is invariable with reactive inputs and directed outputs oriented.

The AISO organize and interpret impressions of political pressure in their individual mental framework. How they perceive political pressure may be different from the politician's objectives and reality. In most cases, there may be disagreement with the pressure.

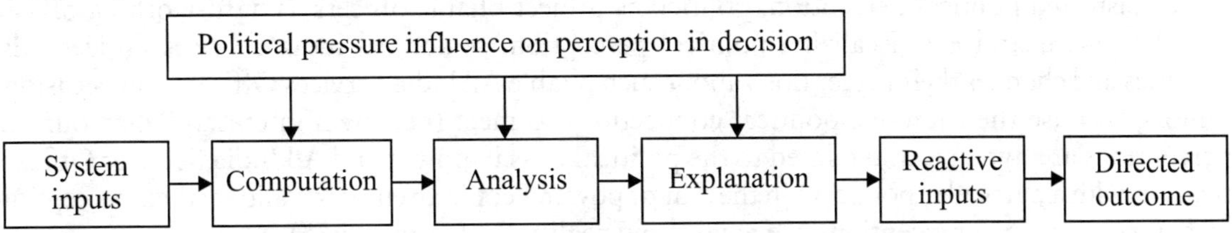

Figure No. 7.4: Political Pressure Influence on Perception in Decision

Due to self-goal achievement perception, the All India Services Officers perceive pressure as a means to attain their own goals. On the other hand, what politicians perceive about pressure on the All India Services Officers may be contrary to individual officer perception. Perceptions regarding pressure are related and affected by attitudes, interests, beliefs, motives, experience, and future expectations from it. One officer may enjoy the pressure and perceive it as means (motive) to develop a relationship with a politician to meet their own goals. Same pressure work as mind wrecking to another All India Services Officers, it fluctuates in time and space from individual to individual attitudes. The All India Services Officers with personal insecurity feel threatened, insecure, surprised and perceive pressure as subordinate's efforts to threaten his position.

Individuals' interests and past-experience in handling political pressure give different connotations to political pressure. In the present system, the AISO manipulates political pressure to use it to achieve future expectations, goals and interests, and targets. The All India Services Officers see political pressure as a mechanism to meet targets, then manipulate political pressure time, background, notion, quantum, and method to suit their own needs and perceptions. The All India Services Officers and politician to suit own needs manipulate situation setting, time of political pressure, social setting, and work setting.

When political pressure develops a balance between external and internal behaviour, the AISO move in the direction of achieving self-goals and accept political pressure as a source of personal gratifications. In case external factors in political pressure are clashing with internal behaviour, conflict arises in the All India Services Officers, which generates tension and stress. On many occasions, the All India Services Officers and politicians develop consensus about the extent of the pressure, which is mutually gainful to both parties consistently. Feedback from the public in the performance of decision is often distorted by the All India Services Officers before it reaches a politician. This provides an opportunity for public manipulators/touts/powerbrokers to serve their ends through political pressure in the outcome of the decision. Any kind of failure is passed on to the system or subordinates, whole credit for success is harvested by All India Services Officers in own favour.

The individual officer has a tendency to perceive political pressure selectively suitable to own needs, interests and goals, background, experience, and attitudes. Politicians judge the All India Services Officers only on the bases of pliability or fulfillment of his goals, other aspects of the officer as innovations, imagination, honesty, public relations, and dedication to the job are ignored or relegated. Merit becomes the causality due to self-interests halo effects. The politician tends to evaluate and compare the All India Services Officers based on amenability to own goals and interests. This has an everlasting impact on the behaviour of the All India Services Officers.

In distorted political perception, politicians project pliable officers as hard-working officers ahead of merit and law. Realizing political perception, senior All India Services Officers also modifies and changes their perceptions about such pliable All India Services Officers. On occasions, seniors also use their junior's political connections to meet their own interests. Behaviour and perceptions are dynamic and related to the political boss in power and All India Services Officers' relation with a particular politician in the seat of power. People attempt to validate their perceptions of reality; even such perceptions are away from reality (L. Jussim, 1986).

Performance appraisal by the politician depends on the perceptual process. Subjective appraisal shapes the foundation for career progression and behavior revolves around political pressure. In a public bureaucracy, subjective judgments are susceptible to perceptual distortions and political bias. Politician's perceptions about pliable All India Services Officers that they are loyal to them and their party is misconceived, pliable officers are loyal to self-interests only, nothing beyond that. In fact, such All India Services Officers are the real troublemaker or whistleblower among All India Services Officers for immoral behaviour.

7.5. Attitudes Role to Handle Pressure in Decision

The AISO attitude and intentions towards political pressure differ from individual to individual officer at a given time and place. When politician exerts pressure to seek manipulations in the decision, the outcome of the decision is related to the attitude and behaviour of individual All India Services Officer. When children grow with family and societal environment and acquire attitude from parents, teachers, friends, family, and peers in that societal system. Present-day television, audio, video, Internet, chatting, WhatsApp groups, Twitter handles and visual communication media also leave their imprints on individual attitudes.

In society, when people see All India Services Officers moving with flasher light on top of the car (now not so common) and bumping sound of a siren, gunmen tottering around them, that growing child will develop a negative attitude towards such officers or lust will accumulate and grow with his age. When they fail to attain those things as an adult and occupy the chair as political head, still have the inbuilt fear from the All India Services Officers position will occupy one's mind. While dealing with the All India Services Officers as Minister, politician attitudes get a jolt and get modified continuously. Politicians find the All India Services Officers as weak and submissive instead of the steel frame, he finds individual All India Services Officers most biased not neutral, observes them clamoring for pity gains and postings and completely ignoring the public welfare.

Again, when a politician is out of power, his attitudes start changing regarding the All India Services Officers by seeing their chameleon colours. In a similar way, individual All India Services Officer attitudes also continue to change as need demanded behaviour. The All India Services Officers cultivate different attitudes, some of such attitudes, we have tried to describe in sections about motivation, culture, workplace environment, and lifestyle orientations. Attitudes pertaining to innovations, risk, and conflict management have been dealt with elsewhere in another units/ chapters.

The All India Services Officers' attitude towards interference of political pressure in decision influence their working, professional satisfaction, their commitment to public administration and involvement in the welfare of the public at large. Individual All India Services Officer tries to reconcile divergent attitudes and align those in line with political pressure. The All India Services Officers conduct themselves in such a way and manner that their attitudes towards politicians appear rational, justified, merit-based, and consistent. Individual All India Services Officer hypocrite efforts to display consistency in one's attitudes, behaviour, and political pressure seriously distort the decision process. Contradictions generate inconsistency, which forces individual All India Services Officers to return to a consistent equilibrium state between attitudes and behaviour.

Bureaucratic processes influence the attitude change about political pressure. How they react with pressure and resolve it. The All India Services Officers on most occasions perceive that they don't have any control over the results from political pressure. They think inbuilt uncertainties are so large that they are not capable to exercise any control over the choices available to them. The All India Services Officers perceive limited chances in a change of outcome from the decision, so they voluntarily change their attitude towards pressure and behaviour with a politician. Individual All India Services Officer, then try to justify the acceptance of political pressure to subordinates and the public to rationalize the outcome most hypocritically.

Politicians generously shower rewards on such All India Services Officers, whose attitudes are favorable for them. Rewards as part of a multi-pronged strategy reduce the tension and inherent dissonance among the All India Services Officers. Stability of tenure, prized posting, career advancement, and attainment of self-goals reduce the stress and increase the consistency in accepting the political pressure by individual All India Services Officer. Political pressure generated tensions and strains is impaired by All India Services Officer perception that the politician, which bureaucratic system is unable to control at any hierarchy level, has forced uncertainty in decision. In such cases, individual All India Services Officers perceive inbuilt rewards in political pressure are crucial to neutralize the pressure generated stress and strains. When individual All India Services Officers at every level start enjoying and exploiting the rewards for self from a politician, no one critically analyzes the long-term impact of the political pressure in the decision. Slowly, whole bureaucracy hankers after rewards, and then influential persons from public and business houses follow it.

Inequality and favoritism in decisions get absorbed as part of individual All India Services Officer attitudes. Future implications of such continuously changing and modifying attitudes and behaviour are serious. Present-day, most of the decision outcomes from bureaucracy are compatible with politicians' feelings and desires. Politician increases the uncertainties in the decision-making process, modified behaviour of the All India Services Officers moderated by choices among rewards and goals. Attitudes modifications moderate the behaviour of an individual All India Services Officer towards political pressure in the decision.

Assured political supports for the All India Services Officers inculcate a sense of insulation from social constraints, among the All India Services Officers. The All India Services Officers slowly stop thinking about public welfare and relegate social issues to the advantage of manipulators or politicians or businesspersons. This slowly evaporates the fear of social pressure and feelings for the society in the decision. As All India Services Officers climb the ladders of career, past-experiences with political pressure and rewards, moderate the variables for behaviour in pressure. Attitudes layering fact after fact make political pressure and rewards precede guide actions on acceptance of pressure in the decision.

In public bureaucracy top management influence the behaviour of the members of individual services (AIS). Government policies, goals, approach of the political party in power, bureaucratic hierarchy, resource allocation power, invariably influence the power of various organized services and their behaviour in the decision-making process. Member of the Indian Administrative Service officers' cadres decides and determines the departmental hierarchy, empowerment of individual members in that hierarchy. The Indian Administrative Service as a group influences behaviour of formal relationships in any department. Formal rules, regulations, procedures, and laws for any service or department are ultimately in the control of the Indian Administrative Service, thus the Indian Administrative Service officers influence the behaviour and attitude of the other members of different services.

The Indian Administrative Service officers at the apex control all resource allocation at the center or state level. The allocation of men, material, machinery, and even technology is in the tight grip of the Indian Administrative Service officers. These powers of controls regulate the behaviour and attitude of officers from other services. Career progression in a particular service is controlled by the Indian Administrative Service officers as and when they determine on their whims, whom to promote when and where, and to put whom in what manner. The Chief Secretary/ Cabinet Secretary and as an Administrative Secretary (Additional Chief Secretary or Financial Commissioner and Secretary or with any other designation as designations are different in different states) in any department, the Indian Administrative Service officers exercise tight control over the key positions and locations, everywhere. This determines the behaviour and attitude of a member of other services at all levels.

The Indian Administrative Service officers at the top of the bureaucratic system finally decide the annual performance appraisal reports/ACR for individual officers and evaluation of departmental works also. The Indian Administrative Service officers project successfully absolute failure works as a grand success and absolute successful works as miserable failures. This supreme position of the Indian Administrative Service officers determines the behaviour of other services. The Indian Administrative Service officers at the top selectively confer rewards on great sycophants and frighten the real workers to crush a particular service or department. They poison the ears of the politician also against that targeted service of a department. The Indian Administrative Service officers ensure that always their own failures and partner failures are absolutely hidden from the politician's eyes.

To determine the work culture of any department or service is in the absolute grip of the Indian Administrative Service officers. They enforce own choices of work standards, regulate the definition of honesty and integrity, modify the values and ethics, thus the overall culture and work environment, which shape the behaviour of other services is in the exclusive hands of the Indian Administrative Service officers only. In case any service work is successful, they manipulate and change the work setting to ensure others are failures and only Indian Administrative Service officers survive at the end of the tunnel to see the light. This process continuously restructures the attitude and beliefs of an individual officer, politicians, and the public, this proportionately influences the decision-making process.

7.6. Factors Affecting Decision-Making Behavior

The most important individual factors affecting decision-making behavior are a type of service, method of recruitment, length of service, regional background, family economic background, education, culture, work environment, locus of control, individual officer behavior, lust for power and status, transfer and postings, promotions, flexibility in the law, sources of pressure, and modes of pressure, etc. Immoral behavior among the All India Services Officers is the product of all these or many more factors interacting in the decision-making process. Individual officer's service work environment and culture promote unethical activities and unregulated acceptance of pressure. Individual capacity to analyze what is ethically correct is related to the individual level of moral development, dependency on the system, location in service and department, dependency on societal system, the influence of peers, locus of control, place of posting, and location in the hierarchy.

The All India Services Officers with an external locus of control are less likely to own responsibility and consequences of their own behavior and more amenable to pressure acceptance. Officers with internal locus go by their own standards and accept political pressure in the decision to attain higher self-goals. Particular service culture to extend support to individuals in case of trouble, own service peers' role in transfer and postings, career advancement opportunities, and support in case of hard decision are crucially important for decision-making behavior. The reaction of hierarchy and location in the bureaucratic system mold the decision behavior. Availability of freedom and assertiveness of the top officer of a particular service determine and regulate decision behavior.

The Indian Police Service officers and the Indian Forest Service officers suffer due to the above-mentioned limitations, respective service heads are not allowed full freedom in the decision, so throughout their career, their behavior with the Indian Administrative Service officers remain that of secondary. Continuous dominance kills the initiative and skill development in these services. The ever-changing role of the Indian Administrative Service officers in government and their frequent movement across the services creates conflict in the All India Services Officers' behavior. Ever-changing roles and positions induce a change in attitude, perceptions, and behavior of the Indian Administrative Service officers towards the Indian Police Service officers and the Indian Forest Service officers. Indian Administrative Service officers get stimuli in suppressing them.

Continuous position and posting on dominance change the Indian Administrative Service officers' role expectation from the Indian Police Service officers and the Indian Forest Service officers. Ultimately, make the Indian Administrative Service officers more aggressive and enhance expectations from Indian Police Service officers and Indian Forest Service officers. Increased role expectancy among the Indian Administrative Service officers, create conflict and contradictions among Indian Administrative Service officer's behavior.

The Indian Police Service officers and the Indian Forest Service officers are staying continuously in a position of bargain, which cause a negative impact on their performance and job satisfaction behaviour. Divergent expectations in the bureaucratic system increase tension and frustration and have a negative impact on the behavior of the All India Services Officers. The Indian Forest Service officers predominantly have a feeling of powerlessness, which has caused a retarding impact on their behavior. Increasing control by the Indian Administrative Service officers endanger the Indian Police Service and Indian Forest Service cadre norms and influence the behavior in the decision process. After joining the All India Services continuous dominance of the Indian Administrative Service slowly replaces the equality norms, in-process powerful Indian Administrative Service officers are in a position to modify the individual Indian Police Service officer and Indian Forest Service officer abilities and behavior towards a decision.

The Indian Administrative Service officers in their dealing with the Indian Police Service officers and the Indian Forest Service officers frequently make explicit statements, which has a serious negative impact on the behavior of others. The Indian Administrative Service officers carry with them the arrogant behavior of colonial Deputy Commissioner/Collector/District Magistrate throughout their service up to administrative secretary level; past and future coalesce to negatively affect the behavior of the Indian Police Service officers and the Indian Forest Service officers. This negative impact of Indian Administrative Service officers generates service feeling among respective All India Services Officers. This encourages the formation of IAS, IPS, and IFS distinctive service groups; motivates members to express values to their respective associations.

Behavior towards conforming to expectations increases under enhanced pressure. Conformity demands from services associations, profession, family, political pressure, career generate tremendous conflict in behavior. Individual officers try to withstand political pressure; he is likely to feel tremendous pressure to align with the members of the service. The Indian Administrative Service officers' cadre strength also enhances individual efforts to accept more and more pressure in the decision. The Indian Administrative Service officers feel that other services may not eat away their dominance in power and governance, the individual officer is motivated service goals, the dominance of Indian Administrative Service officers for self-interests are not consistent with collective societal behavior.

The Indian Administrative Service officers are more pragmatic, maintain emotional distance, and believe that means can serve the ends, and maximize exploitation until it works. The Indian

Administrative Service officers manipulate more than desirable levels until they win the game, they rarely believe in persuasions. Ethical implications are ignored in their performance evaluation process. The Indian Administrative Service officers as a group show exceptionally high bargaining skills. The All India Services Officers believe that they possess high abilities to attain success. High self-esteem among the All India Services Officers motivates them to carry out unconventional and copes with risk uncertainty. Some officers with low self tend to accept political pressure and do not like to take an unpopular decision.

The All India Services Officers with a sense of self-evaluation are more sensitive towards external pressure desire for more promotions has created a conflict in their family life and public life. The All India Services Officers with high self-evaluation response are quick to changing circumstances. The All India Services Officers with aggressive thinking live under time pressure, stress obsessed with success, and number game. Political pressure works as both positive and negative reinforcement, behavior tends to weaken. Political pressures on the All India Services Officers manipulate, stimulate, and respond to achieve personal goals as response behavior outcome. "Its essence is the assumption that what is most important is a certain kind of behaviour, a behaviour which minimizes friction between equals and delicately impresses inferior with the conviction of their own crudity. Its imperfect assurance of its own rightness, and its belief that correct manners are more to be desired than intellect, or artistic creation, or a vital energy" (Mach, E., 1941).

Excessive dependence on the government resources induces scarcity of resources. Resources demand is higher than supply, which induces stiff competition for resource maximization to self-advantage. Increasing population increases the demand for resources and services. Public expenditure for infrastructure development and rural development programs got a very high increase in allocations, misappropriation on large scale by the bureaucracy (media reports). The public funds spending process is full of large-scale leakages. The Indian Administrative Service officers' dominance in top position and their expenditure orientation in target achievements influence the behaviour of politicians and individual officers.

Developmental funds have been indiscriminately allocated to generalists, who believed in self-maximization. They are not accountable for the decisions taken by them. Laxity in supervision, loose or poor monitoring of the decision process, and little responsibility. Unregulated and unrestricted growths of cadres for the All India Services motivate them for indiscriminate use of power. The rapid invasion of ever-changing technology raised the consumerism culture. Imperial services culture and outlook induced cynicism among the officers. All these aspects influence the decision-making process in the bureaucratic system.

Scraping of spiritualism on the altar of materialism created a total loss of Indian values and ethics. Our education system has failed to inculcate moral values from school to college level. Dominant Indian psychology of slavery induced social acceptance and tolerance for any kind of immorality of any extent, no pains for sins. Law of jungle prevailed with the colonial outlook of bureaucrats. Indian Administrative Service officers saved their own people and slowly fear of prosecution disappeared from other services also. The utter failure of reforms in services and socio-religious structures induced evaporation of the inspirations. The pollution of politics has percolated at all levels of the bureaucratic system. Indian society has a soft and highly tolerant public opinion. Excessive indulgences of authority in social affairs have influenced the decision-making behaviour of the All India Services Officers.

The absolute failure of the bureaucratic system has motivated large-scale acceptance of political pressure. Mega heavy administration to meet own service interests and cultivate individual service orientation of officers and subordinates. The bureaucratic methodology of slow and no action has killed the stimulations. Delaying decision tactics and lack of accountability for such delays in the bureaucratic system have an impact on the behaviour of the officers. Obnoxious and exclusively Indian Administrative Service officers oriented regulatory process and system has surrogated the decision behaviour.

The Indian Administrative Service officers got an excessive and undesirable concentration of power in their hands. The British imperialism oriented undesirable secrecy mainly to save the failures of the Indian Administrative Service officers and power holders exclusively. The bureaucratic system has provided undesirable control in the hands of inept and selfish officers. The elitist and separatist approach in administration, with a policy of exclusion and suppression of stakeholders, modifies the behaviour of officers. The unresponsive and irresponsible attitude of power holders in the bureaucratic system has increased the immoral behaviour in the decision. Imperial All India Services are status and diarchy believers. Structural layering in society and services has created space to accommodate political pressure in the decision.

Sustenance of politicians-businessmen-bureaucrats-criminals nexus enhances the immoral behaviour in the decision. Slender majority requirements for the survival in the power induce cheap survival tactics. Failures of leadership generate slowly brewing dissent against the political leadership. Caste, creed, region, and regionalism orientation in politics has eroded values and motivated pressure acceptance behaviour. Money and power orientation for running, surviving in the power of politics lead to the propagation of immoral behaviour. Discretionary allocation of government largesse to power holders and politicians generate immoral behaviour. Space for pressure groups manipulations in politics to install the persons of their choice in the chair sustains the immoral behaviour. The discretionary quota system in the bureaucratic system and excessive control of officers has helped in multiplying the vested interests in the decision. Out of turn allotments of government resources and space for discretionary decisions is equally harmful to the decision process. Newfound extraordinary reliance on NGOs has become the source, mechanism, and process of immoral behaviour.

7.7. Analyses of the AISO Behaviour: Research Results

In this study of the behavior of All India Services Officers, we have kept 12 items, which are considered important for interactions in the decision. It is very difficult to select any one item for study, after long study, analyzing various interacting parameters, and discussing with a large number of officers, we retained these items. The two lowest mean values are 3.93 for devotion to duty and 5.0 for honesty and integrity (Exhibit 7.1) expected from the All India Services Officers. The highest mean value of 10.27 for caste and/or religion/region, indicates that the All India Services Officers assign the lowest priority to caste and/or religion/region in the decision process. Devotion to duty, honesty, and integrity are the jewels, which every All India Services Officer is expected to adhere all the time. Results for different services indicate that 52.4% of the Indian Forest Service officers have assigned first priority to honesty and integrity among the All India Services Officers.

Exhibit Number 7.1: All India Services, Behaviour-Statistical Results

Behaviour Variable	Frequency		Chi-square			Cramer		Rho		M	SD
	Total	Valid	Value	df	Sigf	Value	Sigf	Value	Sigf		
Honesty and integrity	281	249	96.65	20	0.000	0.6	0.000	–0.4	0.000	5	3.7
Professional competence	281	271	113.42	20	0.000	0.46	0.000	–0.4	0.000	5.4	3.2
Good mannerism	281	265	42.01	22	0.006	0.28	0.006	–0.1	0.1	7	2.8
Caste/religion/region	281	249	87.69	22	0.000	0.42	0.000	–0.3	0.000	10.2	3.2
Sympathetic and humane	281	269	126.1	22	0.000	0.48	0.000	–0.5	0.000	6.9	2.9
Straightforwardness	281	266	87.03	22	0.000	0.4	0.000	–0.1	0.2	6.1	3.3
Helping attitude	281	267	53.7	20	0.000	0.32	0.000	–0.2	0.000	5.7	2.7
Political affiliation	281	252	114.3	22	0.000	0.48	0.000	0.4	0.000	8.2	2.9
Devotion to duty	281	268	88.45	20	0.000	0.4	0.000	0.2	0.001	3.9	2.9
Politeness	281	265	95.39	22	0.000	0.42	0.000	0.3	0.000	6.4	2.8
Conduct with others	281	269	99.69	22	0.000	0.43	0.000	0.3	0.000	5.2	2.8
Teamwork	281	270	81.65	22	0.000	0.39	0.000	0.2	0.001	5.3	2.8

M = Mean values. SD = Standard deviation values. Sigf = Significance level. df = Degree of freedom.

Chart 7.1 statistical analyses result for behavior variables for the AISO have been depicted on the chart, one easily compares how different variables are working among three services decision-making behavior. The honesty and integrity line is skewed and different for three services. Similarly, sympathetic and humane nature also shows differences between the three services. Some variables are clustering with a small difference.

Exhibit Number 7.2: Results for Behavior of All India Services Officers

Variable Name	I.A.S. N = 74			I.P.S. N = 95			I.F.S. N = 103			Total N = 272		
	rk	%	Rk	rk	%	Rk	rk	%	Rk	rk	%	Rk
167. Honesty and integrity	11	32.4	11	1	17.9	2	1	52.4	1	1	31.6	1
168. Professional competence	6	28.8	6	12	25.3	11	1	25.2	2	2	14.8	3
169. Good mannerism	10	24.3	10	5	14.7	6	9	20.8	10	10	15.5	10
170. Caste/religion/region	12	64.8	12	12	75.8	12	12	41.0	12	12	55.4	12
171. Sympathetic and humane	9	41.1	9	9	49.5	8	3	18.8	3	9	32.0	9
172. Straightforwardness	3	28.8	3	10	25.3	9	3	16.3	5	3	17.7	4
173. Helping attitude	8	31.1	8	10	25.3	10	4	22.4	6	8	16.9	8
174. Political affiliation	7	25.7	7	6	20.2	7	11	45.2	11	11	22.2	11
175. Devotion to duty	1	32.4	1	1	41.1	1	3	17.2	4	1	26.5	2
176. Politeness	5	33.8	5	3	26.3	3	8	22.9	8	5	19.6	7
177. Conduct with others	2	32.4	2	4	33.7	4	5	16.0	7	4	21.2	5
178. Teamwork	4	24.3	4	4	20.0	5	9	22.8	9	4	16.3	6

rk = Respondent ranking of that item. % = Highest percentage of that item. Rk = Ranking after analyses among all items.

Exhibit 7.2 indicates that 41.1% of the Indian Police Service officers and 32.4% of the Indian Administrative Service officers have assessed devotion to duty as being the first and foremost quality among the All India Services Officers. 31.6% of the All India Services Officers have desired that honesty be given first over ridding priority in the decision. Pearson Chi-square analysis shows a strong association of these behavior items with the decision-making process, with 0.000, level of significance. Cramer's value for V indicates a good relationship of items understudy for behavior and decision-making process with 0.000, level of significance. Except for two items, all other items establish strong relation with 0.000 significance of decision-making process and behavior of the All India Services Officers. Statistical analyses show our results are highly significant. Only good mannerism and straightforwardness reflect that there are 12% and 23% chances that All India Services Officers' behavior may be independent of the decision-making process.

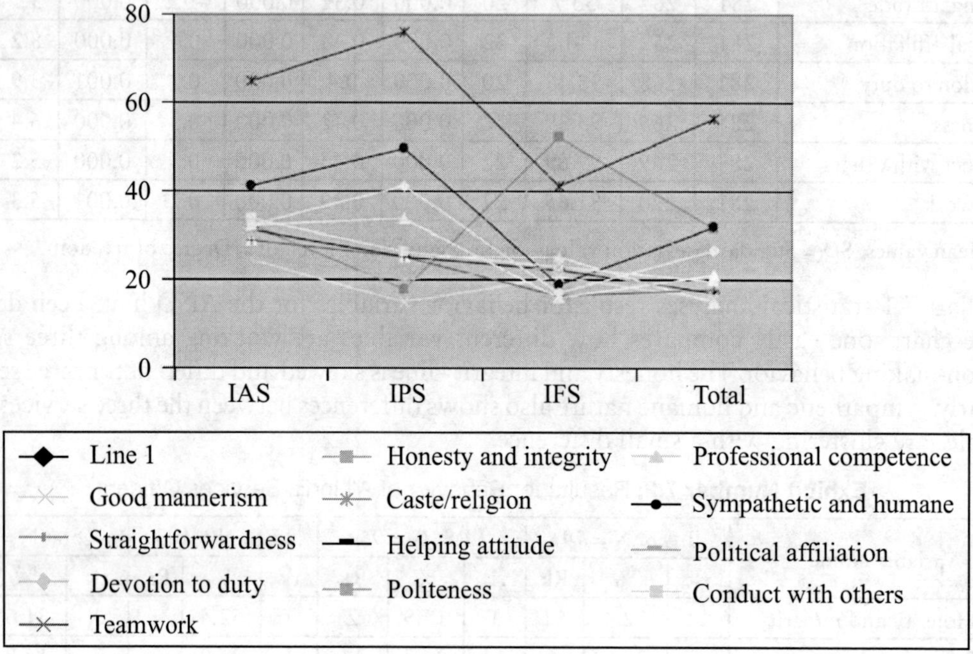

Chart No. 7.1: Behaviour Variables Depiction of the AISO

7.7.1. Honesty and Integrity

Honesty and integrity are the essential and compulsive requirements for the All India Services Officers so that they can arrive at decision free from any bias. Decisions taken by these officers have wide repercussions across the different social segments. Any kind of lust or temptation will force the decision taker to protect the interests of pressure inducers. Pearson Chi-square demonstrates a strong association of honesty and integrity with the decision, with 0.000, level of significance. An alternate hypothesis is accepted with strong relations with the decision. Cramer's and Rho values show a strong correlation with 0.000, level of significance.

32.4% of the Indian Administrative Service officers have ranked honesty at the last 11th rank, other values are scattered in different ranks. 17.9% of the Indian Police Service officers have assigned honesty 1st rank, which is closely chased by other traits of 16.8% of 11th and 6th ranks at same figures. 52.4% of the Indian Forest Service officers have assigned it first rank. 31.6% of the All India Services Officers consider honesty and integrity as the first priority. Our results indicate that the Indian Police Service officers show the least concern for honesty and Indian Forest Service officers show serious and maximum concern for honesty in the decision-making process.

Exhibit Number 7.3: Chi-Square: Honesty and Integrity versus which Level is more Amenable to Pressure

	Value	df	Asymp. Sig. (2-sided)
Pearson Chi-Square	25.59	20	0.18

Exhibit Number 7.4: Honesty and Integrity versus which Level is more Amenable to Pressure

Honesty and Integrity	Which level is more amenable to pressure			Total
	Top level	Middle level	Lower level	
First most important quality	19.00%	7.30%	4.40%	30.80%
Second most important quality	3.70%	0.40%	2.60%	6.60%
Third important quality	5.10%	2.20%	2.20%	9.50%
4th to 12th	30.40%	15.00%	7.60%	53.10%
% of Total	58.20%	24.90%	16.80%	100.00%

Analysis results placed in Exhibit 7.4 show the relationship of behavior variable honesty and integrity with a demographic variable which level is more amenable to political pressure. Results indicate 30.80% of the AISO considered honesty and integrity as the most important quality at first rank and in that top-level 19% of the AISO considered it on the first rank but middle and lower levels have not considered this variable as an important quality among the AISO. The largest 53.10% ranked honesty and integrity at lower ranks from 4th to 12th. Results for all ranks show 58.20% top-level AISO considered honesty and integrity variable from first to 12th rank and 24.90% middle level AISO considered it among all ranks. This indicates that honesty and integrity in the behavior of the AISO across different levels of bureaucracy is not an important variable while taking a decision under political pressure.

7.7.2. Professional Competence

The bureaucratic system has reposed great faith in the competence of the All India Services Officers. No one can afford to raise finger on their professional competence, undoubtedly, they are the best and better than others. Individual member's relevant intellectual abilities can predict the behaviour of the All India Services Officers. Among the All India Services Officers, it happens that behaviour of some average (comparison among the AISO only) officer due to determination, support from powerful politicians, seniors, favorable and conducive environment can produce wonderful results in the decision. Individual All India Services Officer competence and abilities influence the behaviour and performance of the whole group. In a time of crisis, the whole group may survive by projecting individual performance and influence the performance of the whole service. Behaviourally, individual All India Services Officer with high competence and abilities tends to involve himself more with the service activities. In case such talent is utilized effectively, they produce wonderful results for the service and the nation. But, generally, other members of the All India Services get jealous of such officer's works and career, with a fear to avoid him to attain leadership role. Such negative thinking is pervasive among All India Services Officers and influences the performance of the whole service in long run.

The mean value of 5.40 with a standard deviation of 3.21; indicate that the All India Services Officers show concern for professional competence. Chi-square results show a strong association of competence with the decision, with a significance value of 0.000. Cramer's correlation and Rho correlation results are highly significant with a 0.000 level of significance and demonstrate a strong relationship of professional competence with the decision-making process.

Exhibits 7.1 and 7.2 indicate 14.8% of the All India Services Officers (very low score) have ranked competence at 2nd rank. A close score of more than 10% is spread over four other ranks of 1st, 4th, 6th, and 12th indicate dominant confusion prevalent among the All India Services Officers regarding this item. 28.8% of the Indian Administrative Service officers have considered that competence at 6th rank and the rest of the score spilled over all the ranks indicate low priority for this item. 25.3% of the Indian Police Service officers have ranked it last, indicate no consideration for professional competence in the decision. 25.2% of the Indian Forest Service officers have assigned it 1st rank preference in their decision. The highest concern for professional competence by the Forest officers can be due to the technical nature of their job, without high skills they cannot convince their subordinates to implementation technical works. Very low concern by the Indian Police Service officers may be related to a high degree of obedience to the line of command.

Exhibit Number 7.5: Chi-Square: Professional Competence versus Length of Service

	Value	df	Asymp. Sig. (2-sided)
Pearson Chi-Square	48.208a	40	0.175
Likelihood Ratio	53.197	40	0.079

Exhibit Number 7.6: Professional Competence versus Length of Service

Professional Competence	Length of Service and AISO Amenable to Political Pressure					Total
	1 to 4 years of service	5 to 10 years of service	11 to 17 years of service	18 to 23 years of service	More than 24 years of service	
First most important quality	0.80%	1.10%	2.70%	1.50%	2.70%	8.80%
Second most important quality	0.00%	1.10%	3.10%	2.30%	8.40%	14.90%
Third most important quality	0.40%	1.10%	1.50%	1.90%	4.20%	9.20%
Rest of ranking	7.20%	7.00%	10.30%	13.10%	29.50%	58.30%
% of Total	8.40%	10.30%	17.60%	18.80%	44.80%	100.00%

Data analysis placed in Exhibit 7.6 regarding professional competence variable relation with the length of service variable and the AISO amenability to political pressure acceptance in the decision indicates that 44.80% of officers with more than 24 years of service considered this variable. Further results ranking show that 2.70% in 1st rank, 8.40% gave it 2nd rank, 4.20% considered it for 3rd rank, this clearly shows that professional competence is not considered important in making a decision under political pressure. If we look at the importance of professional competence ranking, only 8.80% of the AISO have considered it in 1st ranking and, 14.90% in 2nd ranking, make it amply clear that professional competence has lost its luster as behaviour ingredient among the AISO while taking a decision.

7.7.3. Good Mannerism

All India Services Officers have the highest degree of interaction with the masses. A high degree of public involvement demands that these officers must show commendable manners while dealing with people. As our research findings indicate, the All India Services Officers are highly status-conscious and their ego and arrogance force them to be harsh with people. The mean value of 7.09 with a standard deviation of 2.82 clearly demonstrates that the All India Services Officers give very low priority to good mannerism. Chi-square results at a significance level of 0.006 show association with the decision. Rho value of –0.1 for correlation with 0.12 significance, indicates that there are 12% chances that variables may be independent of each other.

Exhibits 7.1 and 7.2 highest-ranking show 15.5% of the All India Services Officers have ranked mannerism at 10th rank. 24.3% of the Indian Administrative Service officers have assigned it 10th rank. 14.7% of the Indian Police Service officers have put it 5th rank and 20.8% of the Indian Forest Service officers have given it 9th rank. The rest of the score is scattered over different ranks and lesser than the highest rank, with a negligible percentage in higher ranks. This clearly establishes that the All India Services Officers do not show much concern for good mannerism.

Exhibit Number 7.7: Chi-Square: Good Mannerism and Place of Birth of the Officer

	Value	df	Asymp. Sig. (2-sided)
Pearson Chi-Square	37.587	22	0.02

Exhibit Number 7.8: Good Mannerism and Place of Birth of the Officer

Good Mannerism	Place of Birth of the Officer			Total
	Rural	Urban	Semi Urban	
First most important quality	0.40%	2.40%	0.40%	3.20%
Second most important quality	3.60%	2.80%	0.80%	7.10%
10th the highest rank	1.60%	7.90%	5.60%	15.10%
2nd highest 9th rank	6.00%	4.40%	4.00%	14.30%
Rest of ranks	15.00%	32.10%	13.00%	60.30%
% of Total	26.60%	49.60%	23.80%	100.00%

Exhibit 7.7 shows Pearson Chi-square results with a significance value of 0.02 demonstrating a good association of two variables under study. Exhibit 7.8 shows results of correlation of variable good mannerism in the behaviour of the AISO with the place of birth of the officer, and 10.30% of the AISO consider it as good quality, this indicates that good mannerism has no importance

in the behaviour of the AISO. Good mannerism in the behaviour of the AISO relation with the place of birth has indicated urban background officer ranked this variable 49.60% in all ranks, though the very low percentage of 5.2% in first two ranks. Overall results show good mannerism in the behaviour of the AISO is not considered as essential for the officers in relation to the place of birth of the officer.

7.7.4. Caste/Religion/Region

We Indians are the product of a highly structured and layered societal system. Different layerings in society have created and reinforced layering in services also, any outcome from such a system is bound to be influenced by the caste, religion, and region. In a previous analysis, it has been demonstrated that the All India Services Officers have nominal or no concern for the religion. Chi-square analyses show a strong association of these items with the decision with 0.000, level of significance. The highest values of the mean of 10.27 with a standard deviation of 3.22 indicate that the All India Services Officers give the lowest ranking to caste/religion/region. Cramer's and Rho's values indicate a strong correlation ship of these factors with the decision-making process. Results are highly significant with a level of significance at 0.000.

Results in Exhibits 7.1 and 7.2 show 55.45% of the All India Services Officers have given it last rank of 12th to this variable. 75.8% of the Indian Police Service officers and 64.8% of the Indian Administrative Service officers have assigned it 12th rank. 41.0% of the Indian Forest Service officers have considered it at 11th place. If we study the percentage in 1st foremost ranks, there appear to be some problems in an item, small numbers of officers feel that problem does exist but it is insignificant.

Exhibit Number 7.9: Chi-Square: Caste and/or Religion/Region and Officer Regional Background

	Value	df	Asymp. Sig. (2-sided)
Pearson Chi-Square	73.987	55	0.045

Exhibit Number 7.10: Caste and/or Religion/Region and Officer Regional Background

Caste and/or Religion/ Region	Officer Regional Background						Total
	North eastern part	Eastern part	Western part	Northern part	Southern part	Central part	
1st most important quality	0.00%	2.00%	0.80%	0.40%	2.80%	0.00%	6.10%
2nd most important quality	0.40%	0.00%	0.00%	0.00%	0.40%	0.00%	0.80%
Highest 12th rank	9.70%	8.90%	5.70%	11.70%	15.00%	5.30%	56.30%
2nd highest rank 11th	1.60%	2.00%	0.80%	7.30%	8.10%	2.00%	21.90%
% of Total	13.40%	15.80%	8.10%	25.10%	30.00%	7.70%	100.00%

Statistical analysis Pearson Chi-square results at Exhibit 7.9 show with significance value 0.045 good association of two variables. Exhibit 7.10 show analysis results for correlation of two variables that caste and/or religion/region of the AISO and officer regional background, and only 6.90% of the AISO gave it first two ranks, this means officer regional background and caste or religion or region has no importance for the AISO behaviour in the decision taken under political pressure. Results in Exhibit 7.10 for all regions show a very low percentage in the first three ranks and in all twelve ranks, 30% of the officer from southern India have ranked it among twelve ranks as the highest percentage among all the AISO.

7.7.5. Sympathetic Nature

People expect that when they go to a government office for their works, the concerned person should be sympathetic and humane in approach. This is only possible when the officer-in-charge of that district is also sympathetic in his behaviour. Chi-square results indicate a good association between decision and sympathetic and humane nature of the All India Services Officers. The strength of such relationships with the decision is demonstrated by Rho and Cramer's values, which are highly significant and leave no scope for the chance factor. 6.95 mean values with standard deviation 2.93, indicate that the All India Services Officers do not consider sympathetic attitude requirement in the bureaucratic system.

Exhibits 7.1 and 7.2 statistical results show that 32.0% of the All India Services Officers have ranked sympathetic humane nature at 9th rank. So, these officers do not assign much importance to this item in their behaviour. 49.5% of the Indian Police Service officers and 41.1% of the Indian Administrative Service officers, who rule the system have not considered it relevant and gave it 9th rank. 18.8% of the Indian Forest Service officers ranked it at 1st rank saying that officers must behave most sympathetically. This may be due to the reason that they are not getting sympathetic treatment from arrogant Indian Administrative Service officers or their senior officers.

Exhibit Number 7.11: Chi-Square: Sympathetic and Humane Nature and Cadre of the Officer

	Value	df	Asymp. Sig. (2-sided)
Pearson Chi-Square	36.006	22	0.03
Likelihood Ratio	44.825	22	0.003

Exhibit Number 7.12: Sympathetic and Humane Nature and Cadre of the Officer

Sympathetic and Humane Nature	Cadre of the Officer			Total
	Home Cadre	Outside Cadre	From Neighbouring State	
9th rank highest	8.90%	15.00%	8.90%	32.80%
10th rank 2nd highest	2.80%	7.30%	2.40%	12.60%
8th rank	1.20%	5.30%	3.60%	10.10%
7th rank	3.20%	5.70%	1.20%	10.10%
% of Total	32.00%	47.40%	20.60%	100.00%

Exhibit 7.11 shows Pearson Chi-square and likelihood ratio results for variables sympathetic and humane nature of the AISO and cadre of the officer, significance level of 0.03 and 0.003 show good relationships of two variables. Data analysis results placed at Exhibit 7.12 show 47.40% of the AISO working in outside cadre consider the humane nature of the officer is important. Results for ranking show very low raking to this variable, highest rank in 9th with

32.80% indicate that the humane nature of the AISO and cadre of the officer are immaterial in the decision-making process.

7.7.6. Transparency and Straightforward

While carrying out the preliminary study, many persons expressed that the All India Services Officers have followed the politicians and, on that pattern, they never supply the correct information, due to this hypocritical behaviour, people suffer a lot. Whatsoever are the problems and expectations, the All India Services Officers must be straightforward in telling the truth. Straightforward behaviour of the All India Services Officers can help masses in a great way to save their money, time and energy. The Chi-square results show a strong association of this item with the decision. Cramer's value also indicates strong correlation with 0.000 level of significance. 6.12 mean values with a standard deviation of 3.34, indicating that the All India Services Officers have assigned reasonably good importance to transparency in the decision-making process.

Exhibit 7.2 shows the highest percentages of 17.7% of the All India Services Officers have given it 3rd important rank. Only the Indian Police Service officers do not consider it important, and 25.3% of them have ranked it 10th in priority. 28.8% of the Indian Administrative Service officers and 17.7% of the Indian Forest Service officers have ranked it 3rd important aspect in the decision. The need for transparency and straightforwardness adopted by the All India Services Officers will be a bonus for the decisions taken by them. Analyses results indicate that the All India Services Officers do not practice transparency and straightforwardness in their decision behaviour.

Exhibit Number 7.13: Statistical Results: Straightforwardness versus Place of Birth of Father

	Value	df	Asymp. Sig. (2-sided)
Pearson Chi-Square	38.308	22	0.017
Likelihood Ratio	40.029	22	0.011

Data analysis results in Exhibit 7.14 indicate that variable straightforwardness in behaviour relation with the place of birth of father shows only 6.60% of the AISO gave it 1st rank and the highest percentage in 3rd rank with 17.50 %. 3rd and 4th ranks combined together make 31.50%, only, we can infer to some extent that the place of birth of the father shows little relation with straightforwardness behaviour of the AISO. Statistical analysis results at Exhibit 7.13 show a 0.017 significance value in Pearson Chi-square, which shows good relation between two variables.

Exhibit Number 7.14: Straightforwardness versus Place of Birth of Father

Straightforwardness	Place of Birth of Father			Total
	Rural	Urban	Semi-Urban	
3rd rank 1st highest	5.40%	6.20%	5.80%	17.50%
4th rank 3rd highest	3.90%	7.80%	2.30%	14.00%
10th rank 2nd highest	5.40%	3.10%	6.20%	14.80%
1st rank is 6th	3.50%	1.90%	1.20%	6.60%
% of Total	35.00%	38.10%	26.80%	100.00%

7.7.7. Helping Attitude

The All India Services Officers occupy the position of prominence, from where they can extend great help to needy persons, so these officers must adopt helping attitude in their day-to-day work. Persons come from far-flung areas of the district or regional office or state; they come with great expectations that the officer at the helms of affairs at the district or regional or state capital will help them in solving their problems. They expect a fair, honest and unbiased decision from the All India Services Officers. Let us see, what these All India Services Officers feel about it. Chi-square analyses show god relationship between decision and helping attitude of the All India Services Officers. Strength of this relationship is highly significant with 0.000, level of significance, both through Cramer's and Rho values.

The All India Services Officers show the mean value of 5.75 with a standard deviation of 2.70; indicate that officers have good concern for this item and they feel that they must adopt a helping attitude in their behaviour (Exhibit 7.1). Results places at Exhibit 7.2 show 17% of the All India Services Officers have ranked it 8th. 31.1% of the Indian Administrative Service officers with a rank of 8th and 23.2% of the Indian Police Service officers with a higher rank of 5th have realized that a helping attitude facilitates the decision. 22.4% of the Indian Forest Service officers have assigned it a higher rank of 4$^{th.}$ The Indian Forest Service officers have given maximum importance to the behaviour of helping attitudes and the Indian Administrative Service officers have assigned the least importance to it.

Exhibit Number 7.15: Statistical Results: Helping Attitude and Spouse Place of Birth

	Value	df	Asymp. Sig. (2-sided)
Pearson Chi-Square	30.192	20	0.067

Statistical analysis for a variable helping attitude of the AISO relation with demographic variable spouse place of birth shows reasonable association indicating significance value of 0.067 shown in Exhibit 7.15. Chi-square analysis of data in Exhibit 7.16 indicates that helping attitude in the behaviour of the AISO relation with spouse place birth is not significant as the AISO ranked it 8th with 18% and 2nd highest rank with 13.30% in 5th rank. Exhibit 7.16 results show 54.50% of urban background spouses considered the helping attitude of the AISO in the decision-making behaviour of an officer.

Exhibit Number 7.16: Helping Attitude and Spouse Place of Birth

Helping Attitude	Spouse Place of Birth			Total
	Rural	Urban	Semi-Urban	
1st rank highest is 8th	4.70%	9.80%	3.50%	18.00%
2nd rank highest is 5th	1.60%	8.60%	3.10%	13.30%
2nd highest is 4th	3.10%	8.20%	2.00%	13.30%
3rd highest is 6th important	3.50%	7.80%	1.20%	12.50%
% of Total	21.20%	54.50%	24.30%	100.00%

7.7.8. Political Affiliation

The All India Services Officers may get disgusted from the frequent political pressure; they see that some officers have developed an affiliation with the politicians and then they enjoy the results of their choice (self-goal aggrandizement). Slowly, this motivates other All India Services Officers to cultivate political affiliation to meet self-goals. Such political affiliations creep inside the decision and take hold of it ultimately. The Chi-Square results indicate a good association between political affiliation and the decision-making process (Exhibit 7.1). Strength of such relationship is shown by the value of Rho and Cramer's correlations, results are highly significant. The All India Services Officers demonstrated a mean value of 8.27 and 2.90 standard deviation, this indicates that officers do not consider it important to develop political affiliations as part of their behaviour.

Exhibit 7.2 shows that 15.1% of the All India Services Officers have ranked this item at 7th. 25.7% of the Indian Administrative Service officers have given it 7th rank. 20.2% of the Indian Police Service officers consider it worth for 6th rank. 45.2% of the Indian Forest Service officers have ranked it at 11th rank. The Indian Forest Service officers have relegated political affiliation to the lowest rank, but at the same time, a high percentage indicates that these officers feel that politicians play a crucial role in their decision-making process. Protection by seniors and hierarchy play a leading role in the case of the Indian Administrative Service officers and the Indian Police Service officers, but the Indian Forest Service officers have powerlessness, which is indicated by looking towards politicians.

Exhibit Number 7.17: Statistical Results: Political Affiliation versus Family Economic Background

	Value	df	Asymp. Sig. (2-sided)
Pearson Chi-Square	69.351	40	0.003

Exhibit 7.17 showing statistical analyses results for behaviour variable political affiliation relation with demographic variable family economic background show very good association of two variables. Results are highly significant with a significance value of '0.003'. Political affiliation in the behaviour of the AISO and its relation with family economic background data analysis placed in Exhibit 7.18 indicates that the AISO has ranked its lowest rank of 11th with 21.60%. The highest score of 35.50% among rich economic family background among all ranks considered a political affiliation with only 5.30% in the highest score at 11th rank. Results indicate these variables are not of much importance in the decision-making process.

Exhibit Number 7.18: Political Affiliation versus Family Economic Background

Political Affiliation	Family Economic Background					Total
	Rich	Upper middle class	Middle class	Lower middle class	Poor	
11th ranking 1st importance	5.30%	5.30%	4.90%	4.90%	1.20%	21.60%
7th ranking 2nd importance	6.10%	6.10%	1.60%	1.20%	0.40%	15.50%
6th ranking 3rd importance	3.70%	2.90%	2.00%	1.60%	1.60%	11.80%
12th ranking 4th importance	5.70%	8.30%	22.70%	3.10%	18.20%	10.20%
% of Total	35.50%	24.50%	18.00%	13.10%	9.00%	100.00%

7.7.9. Devotion to Duty

People expect the highest level of devotion to duty from the All India Services Officers. These officers work day and night, with a highly flexible work schedule, sometimes without any rest or sleeping for days together. A lot of work has been carried out regarding individual devotion to work, attitudes towards own service group, and behaviour of such individuals. Higher devotion to work enhances service unity; improves the work relations and culture among members of that service. The All India Services Officers devoted to working tends to be independent on thinking, self-reliant in work, and more sociable in the bureaucratic system. At the same time, authoritarian attitude and behaviour of dominance adopted by the Indian Administrative Service officers, reduce the individual officer devotion to duty and decrease the involvement in the decision process, reduce individual interactions in service and lower the overall performance of the All India Services Officers. Behaviour towards devotion to duty is interrelated and dependent on the behaviour of seniors, the behaviour of the Indian Administrative Service officers located at the top, their relation with the concerned politician at the top, and the attitude of all of them towards the outcome of work in the decision.

The All India Services Officers mean value of 3.93 with a standard deviation of 2.96, indicating that these officers lay down high emphasis on devotion to their duty. Chi-square values (Exhibit 7.1) establish a strong association of devotion to duty with the decision. Strength of such correlation ships shown by Cramer's and Rho values are highly significant.

26.5% of the All India Services Officers have ranked (Exhibit 7.2) devotion to duty at 1st rank. 41.1% of the Indian Police Service officers and 32.4% of the Indian Administrative Service officers have given it 1st rank. 17.2% of the Indian Forest Service officers have ranked it 3rd important factor in the decision. The majority of scores for different values are spread over the first five ranks only, this indicates that the All India Services Officers consider devotion to duty as an important variable.

Exhibit Number 7.19: Statistical Results: Devotion to Duty versus Attitude of Family Members

	Value	df	Asymp. Sig. (2-sided)
Pearson Chi-Square	48.398	30	0.018
Likelihood Ratio	49.958	30	0.013

Exhibit Number 7.20: Devotion to Duty versus Attitude of Family Members

Devotion to Duty	Attitude of Family Members				Total
	Spouse	Children	Parents	Brother/Sister	
1st rank in 1st importance	16.30%	4.80%	7.50%	2.20%	30.80%
2nd rank in 5th importance	9.30%	0.40%	4.40%	0.90%	15.00%
3rd rank in 2nd importance	6.60%	2.60%	1.80%	2.20%	13.20%
% of Total	62.60%	11.00%	18.90%	7.50%	100.00%

Data analysis results placed at Exhibit 7.20 show relationships of variable devotion to duty of the behaviour among the AISO with a demographic variable attitude of family members;

and 30.80% of the AISO ranked it 1st and spouse influence 62.90% among all ranks. Statistical analyses placed at 7.19 in Pearson Chi-square with a significance value of 0.018 show a good association of two variables. Our results are significant.

7.7.10. Politeness

The All India Services Officers must be sober and polite in their behaviour, while dealing with people. People expect politeness from these officers and politeness improves communication for the efficacy of the decision. The mean value of 6.39 with a standard deviation of 2.85 indicates low reliance on politeness by these officers. Chi-square values show the association between politeness and decision. Cramer's values and Rho correction indicate a positive relationship between decision and politeness.

Exhibit Number 7.21: Chi-Square: Politeness versus Attitude of Family Members

	Value	df	Asymp. Sig. (2-sided)
Pearson Chi-Square	45.384	33	0.074

Exhibit 7.2 indicates 19.6% of the All India Services Officers ranked politeness at 5th. 33.8% of the Indian Administrative Service officers have assigned same 5th rank to this item. 26.3% of the Indian Police Service officers ranked it 3rd. But 22.9% of the Indian Forest Service officers have ranked it 8th. Results are surprising that police officers show the highest concern for politeness and forest officer with the least.

Statistical analysis results placed at Exhibits 7.21 and 7.22 show relation of variable politeness in the behaviour of the AISO with a demographic variable attitude of family members, lower association with '0.074' significance level. Very low percentage in ranking among first two levels show the AISO do not consider politeness in behaviour as important for them, only 21.20% of the AISO placed it at 5th ranking importance and spouse with 11.90% came in 1st rank and overall, among all ranks spouse got 62.40%, which indicate spouse attitude matters while taking a decision to some extent.

Exhibit Number 7.22: Politeness versus Attitude of Family Members

Politeness	Attitude of Family Members				Total
	Spouse	Children	Parents	Brother/Sister	
1st rank in 5th importance	11.90%	2.70%	4.90%	1.80%	21.20%
2nd rank in 3rd importance	8.00%	3.10%	4.90%	1.30%	17.30%
3rd rank in 9th importance	8.40%	0.40%	2.70%	0.90%	12.40%
% of Total	62.40%	11.10%	19.00%	7.50%	100.00%

7.7.11. Behaviour with Others

The All India Services Officer's behaviour with the formal departmental group shows deviation due to collusion with a politician. Under the self-goal influence, informal group bondages are bound to increase because such bondages are need-oriented. Such social contacts and acquaintances with politician help each other, so the All India Services Officers show most courteous behaviour. However, task group boundaries at the district level are mostly under strain. The Indian Administrative Service officers, the Indian Police Service officers, and the Indian Forest Service officers respectively like to perpetuate their own goals and needs with the politicians, so, mostly behave in a most secretive manner. But at times politicians, who develop equally good relations with all the three All India Services chiefs at the district level, help in decreasing tension among these officers. In such cases, they share their pleasures and sorrows to a limited extent and share common political pressure.

In case, all the three All India Services Officers in the district are under pressure from the same politician, then chances of sharing personal information/experience increases, under pressure opening up behaviour develop into friendship group also. Power status and self-esteem consciousness of the three service members are not likely to allow the development of strong affiliations. The behaviour of the All India Services Officers with politician pressure groups and the public are related to the existence of pressure in the decision. The All India Services Officers tend to be autocratic and status-oriented in case of weak political pressure or no political pressure. Higher intensity of pressure on the decision process behaviour of the All India Services Officers tends to be open to the public covered with layers of status and power. Strong political leadership tends to reduce the status and power consciousness among the All India Services Officers and develop cordial accessible behaviour with the public. In case of absence of political leadership or full collaboration with political leadership, the All India Services Officers decrease the access to other departmental employees and the public both. But in such situations, the All India Services Officers are more personal goal-oriented.

The mean value of 5.25 with a standard deviation of 2.82 indicates that the All India Services Officers put a good amount of emphasis towards their conduct and behaviour with others. Chi-square results are highly significant and show a good association between decision-making process and the All India Services Officers' behaviour with others. Cramer's and Rho values showing good correlation-ship establish the significance of strength of such relations.

Exhibit 7.2 shows 21.2% of the All India Services Officers have ranked it at 4th rank. Among the All India Services, 32.4% of the Indian Administrative Service officers have assigned the highest rank of 2nd. 33.7% of the Indian Police Service officers have given it at 4th rank. Surprisingly, only 16% of the Indian Forest Service officers have ranked it 5th. The Indian Administrative Service officers have the highest concern for their behaviour with others, while the Indian Forest Service officers have shown the lowest concern.

Exhibit Number 7.23: Chi-Square: Conduct and Behaviour with Others versus which Level is more Amenable to Pressure

	Value	df	Asymp. Sig. (2-sided)
Pearson Chi-Square	30.549	22	0.106

The statistical analysis shown in Exhibits 7.23 and 7.24 relating to two variables relationship of the AISO conduct and behaviour with others with respect to which level among the AISO is more amenable to political pressure acceptance in the decision. It demonstrates that 58.40% top level of the AISO among all ranks and 10% in the first rank at 4th importance considered conduct and behaviour are important in the decision-making process. Chi-square results in a significant value are more than 0.05 indicating independence of two variables.

Exhibit Number 7.24: Conduct and Behaviour with Others versus which Level is more Amenable to Pressure

Conduct and Behaviour	Which Level is more Amenable to Pressure			Total
	Top level	Middle level	Lower level	
1st rank in 4th importance	10.00%	8.90%	2.20%	21.20%
2nd rank in 2nd importance	12.60%	4.80%	3.30%	20.80%
3rd rank in 10th importance	8.20%	1.50%	1.50%	11.20%
% of Total	58.40%	24.50%	17.10%	100.00%

7.7.12. Teamwork

Team leadership has been considered as a universal remedy for solving problems and imperative for creating conducive work productivity in behavioral science. Team leader like to involve team members and share decision-making powers with the subordinates. But in the case of the All India Services Officers, it has a number of serious implications because most of the decisions are to be kept secret and hidden from the system. In public administration, any kind of leakage may cause great embarrassment to individual All India Services Officer and the government. The All India Services Officers have to conduct a raid, how he can share information with the team members? Results can be disastrous. At the same time, the All India Services Officers require inter-departmental consultation for many decisions. The number of departments takes many such decisions jointly, in such time importance of team increases.

Participation of other departments increases the commitment to the decision. The concerned All India Services Officer has to be selective, tactful, secretive, goal-oriented in team participation; the extent of participation will vary from the decision to decision and in the same decision situation to situation. All such momentary decisions have to take in the most intelligent way with optimum participation of the politician and team of officers. Team efforts are more than the sum of individual efforts put in solving and decision-making. Teamwork improves technical and interpersonal skills, which have an impact on behaviour. The All India Services Officers have to work under tremendous diversity; only good team leadership can contribute and improvise the decision. The team improves the integrity, openness, competence, consistency, and loyalty in the decision.

Teamwork is the greatest strength and essential ingredient for the All India Services Officers. 5.38 mean value with 2.84 standard deviations show that the All India Services Officers appreciate the feeling for teamwork. Chi-square results establish a strong association between decision and teamwork inferences that are highly significant. Their correlations demonstrated by Rho and Cramer's values are highly significant and with the significance of 0.000.

16.3% of the All India Services Officers have ranked it 4th. 24.3% of the Indian Administrative Service officers have given teamwork 4th important rank. 20.% of the Indian Police Service officers have ranked it 4th. 22.8% of the Indian Forest Service officers have considered it for 9th rank. The Indian Administrative Service officers have demonstrated the highest consideration for teamwork and the Indian Forest Service officers have shown the least concern for teamwork in the decision-making process. This also indicates a lack of faith and trust dominant among the Indian Forest Service officers.

Exhibit Number 7.25: Chi-Square: Teamwork versus Place of Education after High School

	Value	df	Asymp. Sig. (2-sided)
Pearson Chi-Square	29.317a	22	0.136

Teamwork behaviour variable of individual officer relationship with the place of education of the officer after High School analyses results are placed at Exhibit 7.26 and Pearson Chi-square significance value of 0.136 in Exhibit 7.25 indicate independence of two variables. Only 17.50% of the AISO ranked it in 1st rank with 4th importance level and 2nd rank of 14.40% with 1st importance level is a low percentage, indicate every seventh AISO consider the place of birth after high school in his teamwork in the decision-making process.

Exhibit Number 7.26: Teamwork versus Place of Education after High School

Teamwork	Place of Education after High School			Total
	Rural	Urban	Semi-Urban	
1st rank at 4th importance	2.70%	10.10%	4.70%	17.50%
2nd rank at 1st importance	1.20%	10.10%	3.10%	14.40%
3rd rank at 8th importance	0.80%	8.60%	4.30%	13.60%
% of Total	11.70%	63.00%	25.30%	100.00%

7.8. Conceptual Analysis of Political Pressure and System Decision Outcomes

Individual All India Services Officer encounters political pressure in the decision-making process to limited exposure to the realities of human beings. Every individual officer handles uncertainty according to their own characteristics, which influences individual behaviour in the decision. Different biographical characters, individual personality, individual perceptions, individual values, attitudes, individual officer capabilities, individual beliefs about politicians, and decision outcomes influence the behaviour in the decision-making process. When an individual joins the respective services, individual locus of control, individual level of motivation, individual generic behaviour, individual innovations, and creativity invariably influence the behaviour in the decision-making process under political pressure. Most of the individual behavioural characteristics remain intact in individuals, when officers handle the political pressure, throughout the career these variables retain their impact on behaviour, however, some changes take place through the passage of time (Figure 7.5).

Every individual officer's actions in the decision are according to their own ways, but in-group their behaviour is more than the sum total of individual actions. Individual All India Services Officer behaviour will be different, when in own service group and when he is alone. If a particular person could not have joined a particular All India Services, then that individual person behaviour could have been different. If the same person is made a member of other service group, slowly individual person behaviour will be influenced by that service behaviour. In this study different variables, which influence the group behaviour are discussed. These are sources of pressure, modes of pressure and areas of political pressure acting on different service groups. Reasons for accepting political pressure, conflict handling and risk-taking behaviour by a service are also related to a service group. The Indian Administrative Service officers as a group, in the name of coordination influence the communication of other services groups. Pressure handling by respective services groups is also related to the composition and overall structure of the All India Services and other services in that State. Members of respective services groups working as a head of departments in government hierarchy influence the decision behaviour of that service. Position of the Chief Secretary and Cabinet Secretary occupied by the Indian Administrative Service officers do influence the decision behaviour of their service group and other service groups.

Formal structures in a particular government hierarchy influence the individual and group behaviour of the All India Services. Government bureaucratic structure behaviour is more than the sum of group behaviour and individual behaviour. Dominant bureaucratic system culture, environment, different departmental structure, government policies, government practices, government hierarchical structure and divisions in the decision, etc. all have an impact on the dependent variables and influence the decision behaviour of the All India Services Officers. The ultimate outcome of a decision from a system and its acceptability, rationality, efficacy, uncertainties, and satisfaction in that system will be related to the bureaucratic system of that place working under political pressure and leadership in that system.

Figure 7.5: Analysis of Political Pressure in Conceptual Way (figure number narrative and names are shown in the diagram on p. 216)

1. Officer individual-level decision-making process variables.
2. Family and social background inputs during the decision-making process.
3. Individual officer cultural and community background.
4. Individual officer knowledge and beliefs in the decision-making process.
5. Individual officer competence, aptitude and capability.
6. Individual officer inclination, values, and attitudes in the decision.
7. Individual officer personality working under pressure in the decision.
8. Individual officer other biographical variables in the decision.
9. Individual officer environmental and societal setup indecision.
10. Individual officer innovations in the decision process.
11. Individual officer behaviour under pressure in the decision process.
12. Individual officer motivation in the decision process.
13. Individual officer perceptions about pressure in the decision.
14. Individual officer locus of control (internality and externality) indecision.

---

15. *Individual officer decision-making behaviour.*

---

16. I.A.S., I.P.S. and I.F.S. respective service as one group in cadre level.
17. Risk management under political pressure by a service in the decision.

18. Conflict in a service decision process under political pressure.
19. Reasons for accepting political pressure by a service in the decision.
20. Areas of political pressure for a service in the decision-making process.
21. Modes used by a politician to exert pressure in the decision on a service.
22. Sources of political pressure working on a service in the decision.
23. Power and politics played by service groups of the AIS in the decision.
24. IAS officers as a group, on the name of coordination, control communication in a department across the lines and services cadres.
25. Government structure, location of the AISO in it, and inter-service relationships.
26. As service group occupying positions in government departments influencing department working, IAS, IPS and IFS officers as the head of different departments and Secretary, etc.
27. The leadership provided by the Chief Secretary/Cabinet Secretary as service group heads and political leadership provided by Chief Minister/Prime Minister and their Cabinet colleagues as group heads.

---

28. Decision making by respective service groups.

---

29. System-level decisions in government bureaucracy.
30. The environment of the bureaucratic system and workplace.
31. The bureaucratic structure of various government departments.
32. Culture of bureaucratic system and department.
33. Government hierarchal structure and divisions in decision.
34. Government policy and practices in the bureaucratic system.

---

35. Decision outcome from system, acceptability, rejection, uncertainty, rationality, efficacy and satisfaction in system.

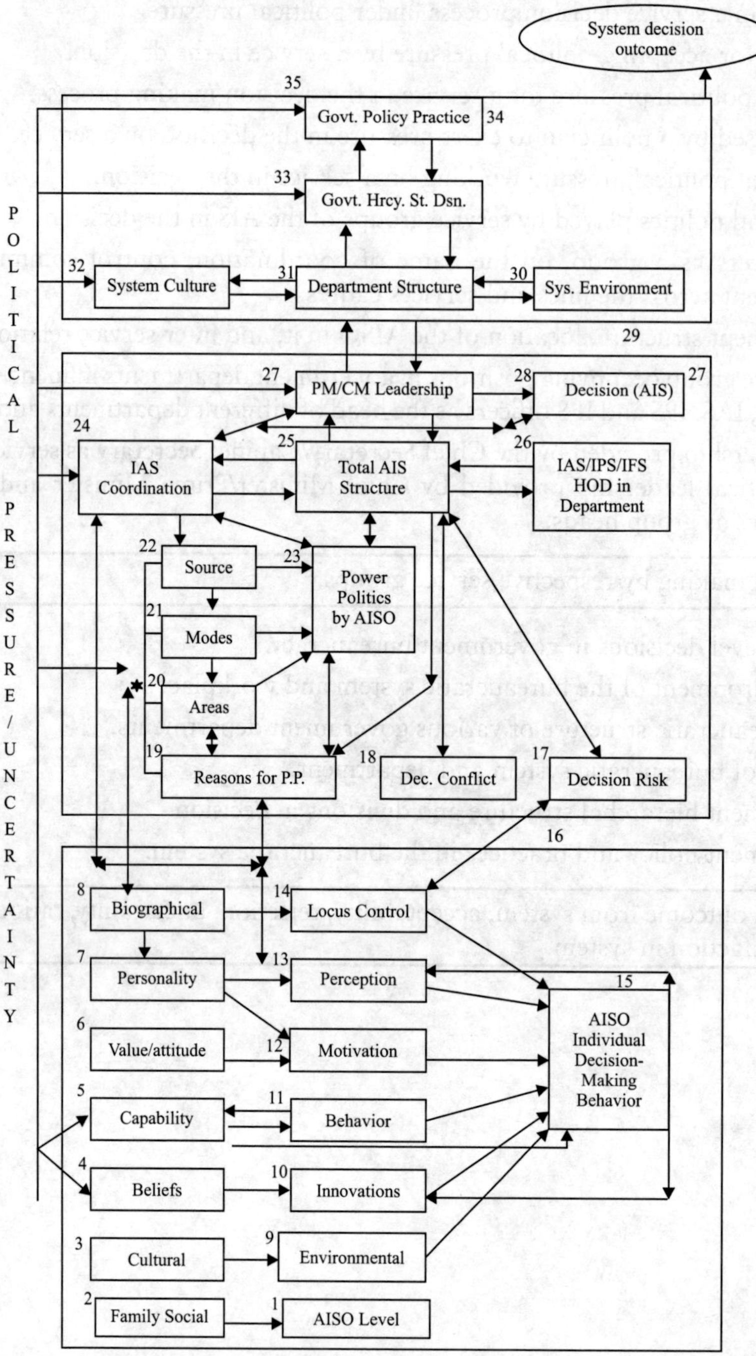

Figure No. 7.5: Analysis of Political Pressure in Conceptual Way System Decision Outcome

ANNEXURE 7.A: QUESTIONNAIRE ON AISO BEHAVIOUR STUDY

In your opinion, what qualities should be given maximum importance for an officer of the All India Services? Please, **rank** the below-mentioned qualities as 1 to 12. Most important quality may be marked as 1 and so on:

167. Honesty and integrity ☐
168. Professional competence ☐
169. Good mannerism ☐
170. Caste/religion/region ☐
171. Sympathetic and humane nature ☐
172. Straightforwardness ☐
173. Helping attitude ☐
174. Political affiliation ☐
175. Devotion to duty ☐
176. Politeness ☐
177. Conduct and behaviour with others ☐
178. Teamwork ☐

Unit 8

Risk Management in Decision

There are three characteristics of a hypocrite: when he speaks, he lies; when he makes a promise, he acts treacherously; and when he is trusted, he betrays. Hadith

"With the realization of the placidity of mind, all his grief's ceased; and the intelligence of such a person of calm mind quickly retreating itself from all sides, becomes steadfastly established in divinity." *The Bhagavad Gita* 2.65

- *Concept of All India Services Officers risk management*
- *Research analyses result: impact on decision*
- *Affiliation*
- *Control*
- *Expert influence*
- *Dependency*
- *Extension*
- *Achievement*

The public administration decision-making process invariably brims over with risk. The All India Services Officers explore various utilities in risk handling. How risk under political pressure is managed by the individual officer in any given circumstances has been described in this unit. Tricks of risk management are described here. Decisions outcome variations with space and time in prevalent conditions described.

8.1. Concept of AISO Risk Management

Risk in the decision-making process under political pressure involves a number of payoffs (utilities) from the outcomes, one utility for each possible state of nature. Individual officer decision criterion under risk will be based on all possible utilities for each strategy. Individual All India Services Officer may select one or more utility based on his experience with political pressure. Individual All India Services Officers, who can take a moderate risk or calculated risk, are found to have high internality. Wolk and DuCette (1984) studied persons with internality and found a moderate, significant, positive correlation between achievement motivation and preference for moderate risk.

Individual All India Services Officer perceived attributes reflect a way in which risk is handled in the decision process. Perceived attributes of the All India Services Officers are related to the service culture and departmental working conditions, where the officer is located. The All India Services Officers risk management approach can be discussed with different dimensions as power, growth, security, status, stress, conflicts, standards, conformity, warmth, support, decisions, rewards, communication, control, goals, and immoral behavior (15 major reasons for accepting political pressure has been described in Unit 14).

Individual All India Services Officer orientation for the pressure and his concern for the risks are important, how one can handle the risk in decision. Individual All India Services Officers with excellent interpersonal relationships with colleagues, seniors, and juniors are more successful in handling the risk in decision. The All India Services Officers' interpersonal relations provide them the strength to protect their own interests. Small groups are formed to extend help to each other in times of crisis.

Individual All India Services Officer's excellent relationships with the top hierarchy are the greatest morale booster for him to manage risk. Individual All India Services Officer with positive orientation visualizes risk as a challenge, elicits, and seeks views from hierarchy to handle it. The similar nature of pressure and risk is managed by different All India Services Officers in different ways and styles. How they visualize the problem in their own context? Service experience in annoyance and tolerance is the greatest teacher for All India Services Officers, through their mistakes and control in the previous handling of risk, they learn a lot. Individual All India Services Officers' assessment of the conflict in risk is significant in the management of the problem.

Individual All India Services Officer trust in bureaucratic decision process and belief in members of the hierarchy is crucial for risk handling. Individual All India Services Officer capability to extract desired information and selectivity in sharing information with concerned, invariably related to risk management. Individual All India Services Officer adopt different approaches in decision making to achieve results through risk management according to own capabilities. Innovative All India Services Officers manage risk and initiate change in the established system comfortably.

Politicians influence the All India Services Officer to achieve their goals and in this process values, attitudes, and behavior of individual officers are influenced. Political pressure has a serious impact on the problem-solving behavior of individual officers and limits the autonomy of individual officers. Influencing style of pressure can be discussed in functional and dysfunctional ego states of Harries (1969). Individual All India Services Officer in OK ego state of adult and parent can manage with the risk effectively. Individual All India Services Officers reactive child and adaptive child ego state will confront the pressure and will be resilient. An All India Services Officers in adult and parent ego state of not OK will be rule-abiding and seek support from senior, this has been shown in Figure 8.1. Best results for risk management are shown by the All India Services Officers when the politicians and concerned officer both are in OK ego state of mind.

		The Politicians	
		Not OK	OK
The AISO	Not OK	Avoidance	Insecure
	OK	Controlling	Confident Ableness Innovative Risk taking

Figure No. 8.1: Risk Management in Transactional Analysis

High risk-taking propensity under the political pressure of an individual officer forces him to demonstrate effective performance. How much information an All India Services Officers require for calculation of risk quantum in the decision is related to personality traits. Low-risk taker All India Services Officers tends to slow down the decision process and try to delay the decision or wait for transfer or change of leadership. The cultural milieu has relations with the risk-taking behavior of the AISO. The All India Services Officers believe that uncertainties are pre-ordained.

The All India Services Officers try to shift their position under aggression in the decision process. Political pressure influences and reflects the dominant decision-making norms in the process. The All India Services Officers in the process familiarized with system and political pressure, familiarization enhances the risk-taking willingness. Supports from seniors, peers also motivate individual All India Services Officers to face risk. Individuals having a high feeling for responsibility are induced towards a willingness to accept risk. In the All India Services, even if the decision fails chances of punishments are limited up to transfer, this also increases willingness for taking a risk in decision.

During the colonial period, decisions by the All India Services Officers were full of risks, to reduce this feeling of risk, dual control by the Viceroy of India and state was introduced. High cohesiveness between service members and feeling for fellow members also increases risk-taking behavior. The Indian Administrative Service indicates a high concern for fellow members, but this decreases as we move from Indian Police Service towards Indian Forest Service. As a service, IFS group risk propensity is different from the other two services; due to feeling of losing in risk, induces risk-taking behavior among them. Situations providing a high amount of uncertainty induce risk among the All India Services Officers.

Political pressure from such sources about which little or no information is available, involve high challenges cause risk among the All India Services Officers, reduce risk associations, decisions are delayed or passed on different levels to dilute the impact. Individual All India Services Officers, who manage risk without damage to self-career, are perceived as a positive image enhancer. Individual All India Services Officers, who are unable to withstand the consequences of risk, conform to the political pressure and decisive move in the direction of pressure. The All India Services Officers conscious about self-image gather higher information about sources of political pressure and try to develop an association with them to save the decision and self.

Individual All India Services Officer realizes risk and fear from the outcomes of pressure, such officers put various explanations to the politician, narrate different excuses to avoid the risk from the decisions. Where in conditions, an All India Services Officer visualizes the way out under pressure but wants to avoid facing consequences of risk, request politicians, and apologizing for inaction. When an individual All India Services Officer analyzes that source of pressure is manageable, an All India Services Officer mobilizes subordinates, gives the impression of perceivable, and indulge in flattery with the politician to avoid risk in the decision. Highly goal-oriented All India Services Officer has focused on the self-goals, enter into bargaining with the politician in lieu of risk undertaken in the decision. 'I shall extend favors to you; you kindly shower favors to me'. Some individuals All India Services Officers under risk like to avoid actions, and adhere to rules and regulations to save themselves. Depersonalization is the trick often used by the All India Services Officers to avoid risk; they explain that so and so a person will make a decision. It is not under his preview, or he is not competent to make a decision or different excuses to pass on the problem to somewhere else in the system.

Most of the All India Services Officers pass on problems down to juniors, who become scapegoats. The intelligent way used by the All India Services Officers to stretch the decision and pose as if they are occupied with the problem and decision may be taken during ensuing any time. They buy time; wait for a change of politician or transfer of self to go to another place. Many All India Services Officers openly support the pressure in front of a politician, but to avoid risk will not do anything. Keep papers pending under process, or ensure objections are got raised through juniors that decision gets lost in the papers and risk is averted.

The All India Services Officers indulge in rigorous documentation collection of information, pass time until politicians get changed or get lost in the ocean of information. Still smarter All India Services Officers sterilize risk by weighing the pros and cons of success. In case of success, they take credit from politicians. If chances of risk, send it to seniors for approval, '*sabko lapet lo*' (involve all), send it to experts for expert opinion, delay it as much as you can, until it was converted into the no-risk situation. Even the All India Services Officers take shelter under the misrepresentations, distortion, deception, obstruction, and present only selective information to the politician to avoid risk in the decision process. Do not bring any noting or paper, which may harm them in the future, only favorable things are placed in a file for a decision, they reduce risk by manipulations. Very few All India Services Officers like to take the risk, any risk may endanger career and may become a liability for the future.

Present-day, the All India Services Officers are highly self-goal oriented, defensive behavior is the only way to save their skin. The All India Services Officers do not like to lose the trust and support of the politicians or peers, which may be of some use for them in future. The All India Services Officers know that defensive behavior diminishes their image and fairness from the decision but reduces the risk. The All India Services Officers like to delay a decision to reduce risk, to reduce tension, sacrifice equity, and develop relations with the powerful persons at the cost of the public. Slowly, the All India Services Officers lose concern for the people and department both and remain busy in cultivating new relations, which are self-goal oriented. Political pressure has politicized the whole decision process in the direction of pressure.

8.2. Research Analyses Results of Risk Impact on Decision

The lowest mean value of 2.89, with a standard deviation of 1.55, indicates that the All India Services Officers show the highest reliance on their immediate seniors in case of any risk and demonstrate high dependency behavior in risk management. At the same time, the All India Services Officers show the lowest extension behavior in risk management. The mean value of 4.31, with a standard deviation of 1.58, indicates that the All India Services Officers show very low concern for their subordinate staff in case of any risk. In ranking also, the All India Services Officers have shown seeking support from seniors at first rank and it is seen practically also that in case of any risk, the first priority of the individual officer will be to seek help from service seniors. Our research results are significant as demonstrated by the Pearson Chi-square analyses, with a .000, level of significance.

Exhibit Number 8.1: Statistical Analysis of Risk Management

Item of Evaluation	Frequency = N			Mean	S.D.	Chi-square			Rank
	Total	Miss	Valid			Value	df	Sigf	
186. Affiliation	281	10	271	2.94	1.7	26.34	10	0.003	1
187. Control	281	11	270	3.57	1.67	61.17	10	0.000	4
188. Expert influence	281	12	269	3.31	1	21.26	10	0.019	6
189. Dependency	281	13	268	2.89	1.55	57.05	10	0.000	2
190. Extention	281	11	269	4.31	1.58	49.63	10	0.000	5
191. Achievement	281	15	266	4.01	2.1	39.83	10	0.000	3

S.D. = Standard deviation, df = degree of freedom, Sigf = significance value

8.2.1. Affiliation

Under affiliation motive in risk, the All India Services Officers develop and maintain close personal relations with seniors, friends, and colleagues. Under risk in such situations, the All India Services Officers like to express their views freely with friends and discuss pressure issues with them. The All India Services Officers explore help and support from such sources to manage the risk in the decision-making process. Sometimes such affiliation relations provide ways and means to manage the risk with the least harm to an individual officer.

27.3% of the All India Services Officers have ranked it as the first priority to seek support from seniors and a friend in case of any risk is involved in the decision. 33.7% of the Indian Police Service officers and 30.1% of the Indian Administrative Service officers have ranked it at 1st option to request their seniors and friends to extend help in the event of risk in the decision-making process under political pressure. 24.3% of the Indian Forest Service officers have assigned it 2nd rank to approach their friends and seniors in case of risk, the Indian Forest Service officers as a service reflect lower faith in their seniors. This lower dependence on seniors may be due to powerlessness because their seniors also do not enjoy full protection, so how they can protect their juniors. Another factor may be due to higher selfishness due to lesser opportunities and frequent fighting is for transfers and posting, etc. Pearson Chi-square results indicate a good association between variables of the decision-making process. The affiliation has been ranked at number one in the overall ranking in risk-taking behavior. This indicates that in case of any kind of risk in the decision-making process due to political pressure, the All India Services Officers first priority will be searching for help inside friend's circle and from seniors in the department or service.

Exhibit Number 8.2: Affiliation—Seek Support from Seniors and Friends

Items Name	Ranking of Preferred Approaches (%)						Total	Best rank
	1st	2nd	3rd	4th	5th	6th		
I.A.S.								
Frequency = N	22	15	6	5	18	7	73	1
% within service	30.1	20.5	8.2	6.8	24.7	9.6		
% of A.I.S. total	8.1	5.5	2.2	1.8	6.6	2.6	26.9	
I.P.S. = N	32	27	7	6	13	10	95	1
% within service	33.7	28.4	7.4	6.3	13.7	10.5		
% of A.I.S. total	11.8	10	2.6	2.2	4.8	3.7	35.1	
I.F.S. = N	20	25	19	20	12	7	103	2
% within service	19.4	24.3	18.4	19.4	11.7	6.8		
% of A.I.S. total	7.4	9.2	7	7.4	4.4	2.6	38	
N =	74	67	32	31	43	24	271	1
% of total	27.3	24.7	11.8	11.4	15.9	8.9	100	

8.2.2. Control

The All India Services Officers like to impress upon the bureaucratic system that they are the great follower of rules and regulations. They are the system abider; believe in adherence to rules and regulations. Officer exhibits high personal standards and power. In control situations, officers monitor the decision process closely and regularly. When individual All India Services Officers realize that politicians will not move away from the pressure area, and the politician in question is powerful, he can harm the interests of the officer; in such situations officer take shelter under the rules and regulations to save oneself from the onslaught of political pressure.

In case of danger from political pressure in the decision-making process, 23.3% of the All India Services Officers seek obedience to rules and orders at 5th rank, but only 13.7% give it first priority. 35.1% of the Indian Police Service officers and 26% of the Indian Administrative Service officers with 5th rank think that they seek help from the rules and orders in such situations. This indicates that for the Indian Administrative Service officers and the Indian Police Service officers, there are many other avenues, which they can use at the time of risk, so they have given low ranking to it. But the Indian Forest Service officers do not see many openings and 28.2% of them stick to rules and orders to save themselves from the onslaught from the powerful sources of pressure in the decision-making process. Pearson Chi-square values are highly significant with the level of significance at 0.000. This indicates a good association of variables with the political pressure in the decision-making process.

Exhibit Number 8.3: Control—Stick to Rules and Obedience to Orders

Items Name	Ranking of Preferred Approaches (%)						Total	Best Rank
	1st	2nd	3rd	4th	5th	6th		
I.A.S.								
Frequency = N	6	12	8	10	19	18	73	5
% within service	8.2	16.4	11	13.7	26	24.7		
% of A.I.S. total	2.2	4.4	3	3.7	7	6.7	27	
I.P.S. N =	2	11	21	10	33	17	94	5
% within service	2.1	11.7	22.3	10.6	35.1	18.1		
% of A.I.S. total	0.7	4.1	7.8	3.7	12.2	6.3	34.8	
I.F.S. N =	29	29	18	10	11	6	103	1
% within service	28.2	28.2	17.5	9.7	10.7	5.8		
% of A.I.S. total	10.7	10.7	6.7	3.7	4.1	2.2	38.1	
N =	37	52	47	30	63	41	270	5
% of total	13.7	19.3	17.4	11.1	23.3	15.2	100	

8.2.3. Expert Influence

The All India Services Officers think that expert advice can help them in mitigating the impact of risk adopted in the decision process. The All India Services Officers underlying feeling that he can convince other officers/seniors that decision taken by him is also supported by the experts on the given issue. The AISO brings expert support to bring justification to his actions, so that, he is safe. The All India Services Officers have an underlying urge to change the decision outcome and at the same time win the heart of departmental officers. Expert advice is used as a shield to protect oneself and ultimately it becomes a ploy to hide self-incompetence to handle the risk in the political pressure.

When the All India Services Officers visualize that political pressure acceptance will be risky, they use different ways and means to save themselves from any damage. 38.7% of the All India Services Officers have ranked expert advice at 4th rank. 50.5% of the Indian Police Service officers refer the matter for expert advice; we think legal help from an expert in the great saving device for the Indian Police Service officers, to save themselves from risk from political pressure in the decision-making process. 41.15% of the Indian Administrative Service officers and 36.9% of the Indian Forest Service officers with a rank of 3rd think that expert help can save them from the damage and risk of political pressure. The Indian Forest Service officers have indicated a lower percentage in seeking advice from the expert, this may be due to the technical nature of their job and they themselves are specialists in their sphere of work.

Exhibit Number 8.4: Expert Influence—Seek Advise of Expert

Items Name	Ranking of Preferred Approaches (%)						Total	Best Rank
	1st	2nd	3rd	4th	5th	6th		
I.A.S.								
Frequency = N	3	7	30	28	4	1	73	3
% within service	4.1	9.6	41.1	38.4	5.5	1.4		
% of A.I.S. total	1.1	2.6	11.2	10.4	1.54	0.4	27.1	
I.P.S. N =	1	12	31	47	2	0	93	4
% within service	1.1	12.9	38.3	50.5	2.2	0		
% of A.I.S. total	0.4	4.5	11.5	17.5	0.7	0	34.6	
I.F.S. N =	8	17	38	29	8	3	103	3
% within service	7.8	16.5	36.9	28.2	7.8	2.9		
% of A.I.S. total	3	6.3	14.1	10.8	3	1.1	38.3	
N = A.I.S.	12	36	99	104	14	4	269	3
% of total	4.5	13.4	36.8	38.7	5.2	1.5		

8.2.4. Dependency

Under dependency motive, individual All India Services Officer will approach his senior for help, so that he can protect his own interests in the decision-making process. The All India Services Officers propose new ideas and thoughts to his seniors and other concerned persons, who take a decision in the higher hierarchy. The All India Services Officers show a strong desire to maintain relations with senior persons. Dependency behavior in risky situations also indicates weak self among the All India Services, and at the same time, it can be interpreted for high discipline among these services. However, the dependency is used as a ploy to manage the risk in the decision-making process.

26.9% of the All India Services Officers with the rank of 2nd think that seniors can advise them such ways and means to save them from the risk of accepting political pressure. 39.7% of the Indian Administrative Service officers and 29.5% of the Indian Police Service officers repose their faith in their immediate seniors in case of risk in accepting political pressure in the decision-making process, with 1st rank. 31% of the Indian Forest Service Officers thought with 4th ranking that immediate seniors can extend some help in the event of a crisis. The Indian Administrative Service officers show the highest dependence and belief in their immediate seniors; it means that frequently immediate seniors are extending help to save them from the risks of accepting political pressure. But similar faith in immediate boss among the Indian Forest Service officers indicates the erosion of the power of seniors. This corroborates the sentiments of the few Indian Forest Service officers, who wrote on the questionnaire, "seniors are dicey and unreliable." Pearson Chi-square analyses show variables' good association with the political pressure in the decision-making process. Pearson Chi-square results are highly significant with a significance level of 0.000. The strength of the correlation is indicated by R and Rho values (0.4) with a significance level of 0.000.

Exhibit Number 8.5: Dependency—Approach Immediate Seniors

Items Name	Ranking of Preferred Approaches (%)						Total	Best Rank
	1st	2nd	3rd	4th	5th	6th		
I.A.S.								
Frequency = N	29	22	4	7	6	5	73	1
% within service	39.7	30.1	5.5	9.6	8.2	6.8		
% of A.I.S. total	10.8	8.2	1.5	2.6	2.2	1.9	27.2	
I.P.S. N =	28	28	15	9	15	0	95	1
% within service	29.5	29.5	15.8	9.5	15.8	0		
% of A.I.S. total	10.4	10.4	5.6	3.4	5.6	0	35.4	
I.F.S. N =	5	22	17	31	17	8	100	4
% within service	5	22	17	31	17	8		
% of A.I.S. total	1.9	8.2	6.3	11.6	6.3	3	37.3	
N = A.I.S.	62	72	36	47	38	13	268	2
% of total	23.1	26.9	13.4	17.5	14.2	4.9		

8.2.5. Extension

In situations of risk, some of the All India Services Officers display high concern for their subordinates and employees. The All India Services Officers like to win the confidence of staff and pose as well-wishers of the employees. The All India Services Officers convey a message to a politician that he could have helped him but the interests of employees are at stake. The All India Services Officers try to find out an employee for such projections, who may be well connected to the ruling party interests. The All India Services Officers try to convince a politician that acceptance of pressure will be against the departmental interests and against the norms of the bureaucratic system.

Many All India Services Officers change sides and all of a sudden start showing great concern for the welfare of their subordinate's staff to avoid political pressure. They present excuses to seek shelter in the incompetence or political connections of their staff and present stories regarding the acceptance of political pressure and consequences out of it. 28.3% of the All India Services Officers have ranked such situation at last rank of 6th. Only 10% of them seek to refuse in this extension motive. Among the All India Services, the Indian Administrative Service officers are the greatest relief seeker by this method, and 28.8% ranked it at 3rd. The Indian Forest Service officers are the least used of these tactics, and 47.5% of them ranked it at last rank of 6th. 30.5% of the Indian Police Service officers have ranked it at 5th. But in the first rank, the highest percentage is that of the Indian Police Service officers, with 13.7%. Pearson Chi-square results are highly significant with a significance level of 0.000. The great good association is indicated by the Chi-square analysis. Rho and R values of 0.3 and 0.2 show the good significance of relations with significance level at 0.000 and 0.004 respectively.

Exhibit Number 8.6: Extension—Change Sides and Show Concern for Staff

Items Name	Ranking of Preferred Approaches (%)						Total	Best Rank
	1st	2nd	3rd	4th	5th	6th		
I.A.S.								
Frequency = N	3	2	21	18	17	12	73	3
% within service	4.1	2.7	26.8	24.7	23.3	16.4		
% of A.I.S. total	1.1	0.7	7.8	6.7	6.3	4.5	27.1	
I.P.S. N =	13	7	14	16	29	16	95	5
% within service	13.7	7.4	14.7	16.8	30.5	16.8		
% of A.I.S. total	4.8	2.6	5.2	5.9	10.8	5.9	35.3	
I.F.S. N =	11	2	8	8	24	48	101	6
% within service	10.9	2	7.9	7.9	23.8	47.5		
% of A.I.S. total	4.1	0.7	3	3	8.9	17.8	37.5	
N = A.I.S.	27	11	43	42	70	76	269	6
% of total	10	4.1	16	15.6	26	28.3		

8.2.6. Achievement

Some of the All India Services Officers reflect concern for excellence in risk management. The All India Services Officers try to adhere to the departmental standard, set up outstanding examples, which are appreciated by the departmental hierarchy. Individual officers are aware of inherent problems of risk set up challenging goals for self to take calculated risk to manage in a most efficient manner. The officer is aware that risk management is full of obstacles. Officer put persistent efforts and use innovative means to handle risk. Officer predominant concerns for excellence help him to manage risk in a positive way.

It is not that all the times, the All India Services Officers try to evade the political pressure and seek this or that excuse. We thought that the All India Services Officers should have a very high achievement motive in risk management. But our beliefs are belied and far from reality. 40.2% of the All India Services Officers have ranked this approach at last and 6th rank. 53.8% of the Indian Police Service officers and 42.5% of the Indian Administrative Service officers also have ranked it 6th rank. This indicates a very low feeling towards achievement in case of risk. This infers that the Indian Police Service officers and the Indian Administrative Service officers do not take recourse to hard work and achievement in the decision. 37% of the Indian Forest Service officers have indicated the first preference for achievement in the time of risk. This infers that every third Indian Forest Service officers has faith in his competence and hard work in avoiding risk from political pressure in the decision-making process. Pearson Chi-square results are highly significant with a significance level of 0.000. This indicates a good association among the variables.

Exhibit Number 8.7: Achievement—Resolve Problem in Efficient Way

Items Name	Ranking of Preferred Approaches (%)						Total	Best Rank
	1st	2nd	3rd	4th	5th	6th		
I.A.S.								
Frequency = N	10	15	4	0	13	31	73	6
% within service	13.7	20.5	5.5	0	17.8	42.5		
% of A.I.S. total	3.8	5.6	1.5	0	4.9	11.7	27.4	
I.P.S. N =	13	8	8	1	13	50	93	6
% within service	14	8.6	8.6	1.1	14	53.8		
% of A.I.S. total	4.9	3	3	0.4	4.9	18.8	35	
I.F.S. N =	37	9	2	0	26	26	100	1
% within service	37	9	2	0	26	26		
% of A.I.S. total	13.9	3.4	0.8	0	9.8	9.8	37.6	
N =	60	32	14	1	52	107	266	6
% of total	22.6	12	5.3	0.4	19.5	40.2		

ANNEXURE 8.A: QUESTIONNAIRE ON THE AISO RISK MANAGEMENT

When an officer of All India Services (AISO) takes a decision under pressure, a certain amount of **risk** is involved. We have listed **six** such situations for risk-taking. Kindly, **rank 1, as most preferred to 6 as least preferred approach.**

186. When the risk is involved AISO seeks support from seniors and friends. ☐
187. When there is a risk, AISO sticks to rules and obedience to orders. ☐
188. Under risk, AISO may like to seek the advice of experts. ☐
189. In risk AISO approach to their immediate seniors. ☐
190. In risky situations, AISO change the side and show great concern for their staff. ☐
191. AISO do take the calculated risk to resolve the problem in an efficient way. ☐

Unit 9

Innovations to Change System

"Neither God determine the perpetrator/executor nor the actions of men, not even result of actions; but it is disposition alone that does all this." *The Bhagavad Gita* 5.14

No man should talk one way with his lips and think another way in his heart. Talmud, Baba Metzia 49

"Innovations distinguish between a leader and a follower."—Steve Jobs, Apple co-founder

- *Concept of Innovations in Handling Pressure*
- *Process of Innovations in Decisions*
- *Research Analyses Results of Innovations*
- *Expert Influence*
- *Custom Influence*
- *Imagination Influence*
- *Control Influence*
- *Dependency Influence*
- *Confidence Influence*
- *Achievement Influence*
- *Affiliation Influence*
- *Extension Influence*

Since the colonial era, innovations in public administration are rare and not appreciated by the bureaucratic system itself. Sharing team values, ideology, skill resource structure, and roles are described under this unit. Five stage process of innovation comprising knowledge, persuasion, decision, implementation, and confirmation stages has been described here as the process of innovation. The role of innovations in the bureaucratic system is described.

9.1. Concept of Innovations and Pressure Management

All the All India Services Officers have great innovation potential. They are the best and have maximum freedom to work in a given bureaucratic system. The use of innovations in a decision is related to the bureaucratic hierarchy, structure, environment, and behavior. Such potential remains covered under bureaucratic layers. Individual All India Services Officers differ in inherent innovations. C.G. Morris, 1996 found that less than 1% of people are exceptionally creative, 10% are highly creative, 60% are somewhat innovative. Space for freedom, independence, instructions from seniors, tends to increase innovations. Lateral growth in service and lateral thinking correct at every step and ideas relevant-visualize pressure in a new way.

Historically, many innovations are not expected from the All India Services Officers. "Not much creative initiative was expected or desired from District Magistrate."[1] During the colonial era also these officers were devoid of creativity. "The men who are most successful are those who are machines devoid of individuality, without original ideas or who humor the ignorance of their seniors."[2] Robert Carstairs believed that his fellow district officers were more worried about the opinions of their superiors than about the welfare of or status of the Indian masses, this is true for today working of the All India Services Officers also, and present-day officers are away from creativity.

The All India Services Officers justify their timidity and sycophancy through quoting examples, an officer who stepped out of line, invariably stayed at the bottom of the heap. Innovations in the bureaucratic system are labeled as eccentricities. Innovations had been continuing causality from British Raj. Lord Curzon rationalized the choice of C.H. Rivaz as Lieutenant Governor of Punjab in a similar fashion, "He (Rivaz) has neither the considerable ability nor great energy. On the other hand, he is sober-minded, level-headed, in no way a crank...."[3] Henry Beveridge and Sir William Wedderburn were buried under a heap of history files because they were innovative. The All India Services Officers have taken a cue from past civil servants and buried the innovations with the passage of time.

In rarest of rare innovative ideas come to the All India Services Officers, their dominant emphasis is on caution, especially in matters related to political pressures. Eventually, the All India Services Officers dictate the policy of minimum change and show maximum concern for the status quo. The All India Services Officers feel that innovations in policy discussions may have serious repercussions on their career advancement. Due to a lack of creative orientation among the All India Services Officers, they become a habitually negative thinker. Inner forces get weakened or left without inner force, so they move in direction of the dominant force either they like it or not.

A small number of officers, who are creative essentially report to self irrespective of prevailing circumstances in the system, a decision will be in direction of inner conscious. The All India Services Officers largely commit to bureaucratic process rather than the results; what the public can expect from them. The whole apparatus of the All India Services is operating in a manner, which discourages creativity among officers of different services and subordinates.

---

1. H.J.S. Cotton Chief Commissioner of Assam wrote to Curzon, on 5.5.1899.
2. Robert Carstairs, *The Bengal Civil Service*, p. 32.
3. Curzon to Hamilton, from camp on 30.10.1900.

The All India Services Officers have been unable to do anything to loosen the steel framework of obsequiousness. Any light of independent action or thought among different services or subordinates is blown off with full force. Hypocrisy between stakeholders/ruling elite is more insidious; they expose each other to garner power for their service. In the passage of time, the All India Services are proving to be a weak instrument, collective responsibility to hierarchy has been blurred, and their ultimate accountability to political authority is fading away.

Various aspects related to team innovations are sharing values, team ideology, skill, resources, structure, roles and rules, and leadership process. Any departmental decision outcomes influence the innovative capabilities building that system. Any decision is influenced by the factors spurring innovations, innovations facilitating structures; control to facilitate innovations, culture building for innovations, conflict resolution for innovation, and innovative success. Not all these factors are allowing innovations to grow in the bureaucratic system, where these All India Services Officers operate.

Further to assess the innovative sponsoring capabilities of the All India Services Officers. One has to emphasize various aspects such as: (a) productivity for social innovations, (b) environmental and political sensitivity, (c) challenge facing and stress tolerance, (d) problem-solving skills, (e) resource and support mobilization, (f) task accomplishment drive, (g) win drive, (h) confidence, (i) interpersonal sensitivity and skill.

In public administration, the All India Services Officers can handle innovations in numerous areas of administration. Some of them can be: short-term and long-term planning, target assignment, objective forecasting, impoverished budgeting, training, human resource development, costing, cost control, selection and promotion methodology, participative decision, team management, improvement and development in department, job enlargement, job enrichment, delivery of services and improvement in the hierarchy, etc. Innovations are directed towards bringing efficiency, control operations, enhance capability and capacity, improved understanding, motivating the staff, and line officials/officers, and achievement of objectives in the decision. Innovations used by the All India Services Officers will have a direct bearing on decision-making behavior and career progression of a large number of the personnel.

9.2. Process of Innovations in Decision

In the process of innovation, we develop creative ideas, form an attitude, adopt or reject to implement new ideas and to confirm this to a decision. "Technological adoption, innovation, and acceptance of new ideas are found to be correlated with attitudes and beliefs (Dubey, 1955; Sinha, 1972; Rajgopalan, 1971; P. Singh, 1979). Process of innovations comprises a number of actions and options over time through which individual officer and/or department evaluate such new ideas and decide regarding the incorporation of such thoughts into practice to reduce the uncertainties.

Innovations in the department are concerned with the processes through which improvement in efficiency takes place. There cannot any one best uniform approach for managing them, all innovations involve coping with uncertainty. Uncertainty requires an approach to get innovative activity to cope with it. The political dimension of innovations implies that those entrusted with innovation must have the capability to influence others and win support for innovations. Officer has to persuade those in favor of a new outcome, who will get an advantage form innovative decisions. Enlisting powerful support in favor of innovation is essential to implement innovation and eliminate resistance.

The process of innovations decision making mainly comprises seven stages as mentioned here.

- 9.2.1. **Knowledge:** The All India Services Officers gather knowledge about information seeking, develop learning skills, and enhance exposure and understanding about the information.
- 9.2.2. **Persuasion:** The All India Services Officers' persuasions, attitude formation, and information processing will influence the computation for innovations.
- 9.2.3. **Justification:** Options explorations, comparison of choices and preferences, and rationalization.
- 9.2.4. **Decision:** The All India Services Officers adopt or reject innovation choices in arriving at a decision.
- 9.2.5. **Implementation:** The All India Services Officers use innovations in practice, apply to a decision towards the implementation of it.
- 9.2.6. **Confirmation:** The All India Services Officers work for reinforcement of innovations. Conflicts in innovations are resolved. Innovations outcomes are confirmed and ratified.
- 9.2.7. **Action Motivation:** Research, evaluation, and motivation from past experiences.

9.2.1. Knowledge

Information seeking and learning by an individual officer about the existence and functions of innovation in the decision process operate in this stage. Communication and information flow generate awareness regarding operations and the existence of innovations. Individual officer attitudes, interests, and needs influence their behavior towards learning of communication ideas. Every officer has a tendency to accept and interpret messages, which are consistent with one's attitudes and beliefs. When an officer feels the need for innovations and thinks that such innovations can improve the decision process outcome, usually learn it. E.M. Rogers visualizes need as a state of dissatisfaction or frustration that occurs when desires outweigh one's actualities, when 'wants' outrun 'gets'. Political pressure generates new needs among the All India Services Officers when they indicate the existence of desirable new ideas or goals.

Lust for appeasement of new goals motivates them to the adoption of political pressure in the decision process. Individual officer demands for competing goals begin innovations decision process. Some officers are so creative and innovative that innovations create a need for them. Feelings of change agents in their inner self play the most distinctive and crucial role for incorporating innovations decision process. Keith (1968) studied variables and their correlation with knowledge. Information seeking innovation by an individual officer will be related to education level, community background, and type of service, and length of service of that officer.

9.2.2. Persuasion

Individual officers after learning about the information, process it for favorable and unfavorable impact on decision process mold his attitudes. Individual officer involves oneself in mind and soul with the innovations, search information, acquire messages, and compute information. Individual officer understanding of relative advantages and complexity of innovations in decision process determines the individual behavior. Anticipated future situations from innovations in the decision process will determine the officer's favorable and unfavorable attitude toward the innovations.

Degree of uncertainty due to decision outcomes for innovations in decision and senior's opinion, induce in individual officer to search the need for social and family reinforcement to mold attitude towards new ideas. To reduce the uncertainty of the expected consequences of innovations, officers get motivated to evaluate innovation information. Positive evaluation feedback from seniors and departmental peers motivate individual officer to pursue innovations. In case the All India Services Officers feel that there will not be any undesirable outcome from decision without use of innovations, he is not likely to pursue innovations. On the other hand, when officers see that one who used innovations achieved their goals and got recognition and acceptance from seniors, they explore innovations for the attainment of their interests.

9.2.3. Justification

The All India Services Officers, while perusing innovations in the decision-making process, explore the available options and seek justifications for each option. The individual officer tries to find out the rationality for one's proposed actions and compare the choices for innovations. Then the individual analyzes consequences for the adoption of innovations. Based on detailed point-to-point investigations, individual officer justifies about the preferences adopted for innovations, which can be used for the decision-making process.

9.2.4. Decision

After learning and processing of information, an individual officer involves in the process of elimination of choices for adoption or rejection of innovations. The All India Services Officers have reservations regarding the use of innovations due to inherent uncertainty overflowing with future consequences, as the public and politicians may perceive innovations in a different way. Inbuilt freedom in the decision process of public administration, provide enough leverage or safety cushion so that the All India Services Officers can try innovations on small scale to decrease their perceived uncertainty. Some colleagues demonstrate the use of innovations successfully, and then such incidents motivate and build up the confidence of individual All India Services Officers to adopt innovations on a larger scale.

In case seniors or peers have used innovations (which are rarest of rare) or are using innovations, juniors adopt more innovations in the decision process with higher confidence. Use of innovations is very low in the All India Services Officers, once they get into service, they feel satisfied, no need to put extra efforts. Innovations rejection rate is high among the All India Services Officers, then it is either active rejection or passive rejection. It is generally believed that the active rejection proportion may be higher due to political consequences; the All India Services Officers behave in a passive mode of behavior.

9.2.5. Implementation

Unless innovations in a decision are not applied in the public administration, it is like making castles in the air. Applications of innovations require modifications in behavior. Uncertainty and consequences of innovations in decision implementation have bearing on behavior. Operations of innovation in the technical environment of operation require multi-skill assistance. Government administration is complex for innovations due to large-scale hierarchical inconsistencies and a long line of command.

Officers in the hierarchy have their different political and peers' connections, they may put resistance to the implementation of innovations or may not implement it at all or delay implementation. Due to inter mediators' protection available in the system, innovation-decision has been implemented in due course of time, it loses its distinctive quality and freshness of ideas and considered as part of routine administration. Charters and Pellegrin (1972), who launched reinvention, observed that the innovations were shaped to a different degree in different organizations. Re-invention makes innovations in public administration more appropriate and responsive to new problems arising in the innovation-decision process. The process of modification is continuous every idea gets improved in its course of implementation as part of adopter behavior.

9.2.6. Confirmation

After the implementation of the decision, the All India Services Officers seek reinforcement and support or ratification for the innovations; he has incorporated in the decision process. The All India Services Officers get motivated by a favorable response to the decision and try to seek more information about the innovations. In this process, change agent (AISO) has to provide support to his subordinates, so that adopted messages are not discontinued at the same time the All India Services Officers expect support from peers and politicians also. Negative political pressure on innovations in the decision process motivates negative or rejection or disenchantment discontinuance of previously adopted innovations. Positive feedback from colleagues encourages replacement discontinuance.

"Human behavior change is motivated in part by a state of internal disequilibria or dissonance, an uncomfortable state of mind that the individual seeks to reduce or eliminate. When an individual feels dissonance, he or she will ordinarily be motivated to reduce this condition by changing his or her knowledge, attitude, or actions," E.M. Rodgers. Leuthold (1965), Silverman et al. (1965), and E.M. Rodgers observed that "later adopters are more likely to discontinue innovations than are earlier adopter." In the case of the All India Services Officers also individuals, who took initiative for introducing innovations in the decision process endeavored to continue the innovations, but late starters discontinue such efforts at an early stage or with a slight fear of political pressure.

9.2.7. Action Motivation

Innovations motivate individual All India Services Officers to adopt creativity in future decisions. When an individual officer after a lot of calculations decides to incorporate innovations in the decision-making process and persons in the department evaluate such actions and appreciate such an officer, then actions propensity propel desire to chase innovations. The past experience with innovations used in the decision-making process influences individual officers' future approach towards innovations. It has been observed that officer attitude; past experience; values and beliefs play a crucial role in the adoption of innovations and discontinuance of innovations decision process. Officer capability to open up communication channels and his communication methodology is related to the innovation's information gathering, information processing, and innovation-decision process. Length of service, their experience, and time required by individuals has relation with the period taken to adopt the innovation-decision process. Mass media and publicity have a positive relationship with innovation behavior, desire for publicity or positive publicity stimulate adopters of innovations, but those who are slow in innovations require strong doses of publicity stimulants.

9.3. Research Analyses of AISO Innovations Used in Decision

Research data analysis indicates that the All India Services Officers show the lowest mean value of 3.83, inferring that these officers before taking any decision they consult their immediate seniors. The All India Services Officers' low concern for the innovations is indicated by a mean value of 3.83 ± 2.41 (standard deviation of 2.41) showing ranking 2nd rank to 7th rank preferences. The highest mean value of 6.68 ± 2.15 standard deviation in the extension motive, indicates a very low ranking for innovations and the least concern for bringing out any change. Pearson Chi-square analyses show a good association between variables under study. Pearson Chi-square results are highly significant with a significance level of 0.000. This leaves no ground for the chance factor in an association. Factor analysis using the principal component method without rotation indicates a good correlation among the entire variables in one-tailed analysis significance.

Exhibit Number 9.1: Statistical Results for Innovations and Change in System

Item Name	Frequency		Mn	S.D.	Chi-square			Rk	Correlation value			
	Total	Valid			Value	df	sigf		R	sif	Rho	sif
192. Expert influence	281	264	4.91	2.73	44.7	16	0.000	2	0.3	0.000	0.3	0.000
193. Custom influence	281	269	5.13	2.34	47.7	16	0.000	6	−0.2	0.02	−0.2	0.01
194. Imagination	281	265	5.20	2.55	71	16	0.000	5	−0.3	0.000	−0.3	0.000
195. Control influence	281	268	4.0	2.59	45.7	16	0.000	1	0.3	0.000	0.3	0.000
196. Dependency influence	281	267	3.83	2.41	47.1	16	0.000	3	0.1	0.05	0.2	0.01
197. Confidence reliance	281	269	4.33	2.29	58.1	18	0.000	8	−0.1	0.11	−0.1	0.13
198. Achievement motive	281	265	5.05	2.62	43.8	16	0.000	4	−0.1	0.4	−0.1	0.4
199. Affiliation influence	281	263	5.79	2.47	40.8	16	0.001	7	−0.3	0.000	−0.2	0.000
200. Extension motive	281	265	6.68	2.15	40.8	16	0.003	9	−0.3	0.000	−0.2	0.000

Mn = Mean value, SD = standard deviation, sigf. or sif. = significance level, R = Pearson's correlation, Rho = Spearman correlation

The values of Rho and R for correlations are with a significance level of 0.000 in five items, lower than 0.05, significance level in two items, and 0.11 and 0.4 in two items also support the strength of association. Thus, only one item that innovations are ordered by a highly result-oriented person has 40% chances that the innovation may not have a relation with the decision under political pressure. Rest all the variables show a good correlation.

9.3.1. Expert Influence

All India Services Officers think that due to paucity of time, whenever there is a demand for innovations and change in the decision-making process, they like to refer the matter to an expert or specialist, and this can save them from any external interventions. 19.3% of the All India Services Officers have ranked this approach at 3rd rank with second-highest of 16.3% with first ranking. 31.9% of the Indian Administrative Service officers have ranked it 3rd most important approach and 15.3% with the first rank. Among Indian Police Service officers, 24.2% have shown 1st rank and 19% of 3rd rank, indicating high reliance on expert by them.

Exhibit Number 9.2: All India Services Officers has no Time, they Refer Matter to Experts/Specialist

Service Name	% In Service and Ranking for Innovation in this Item									Total	
	1	2	3	4	5	6	7	8	9	N	%
I.A.S.% within service	15.3	8.3	31.9	9.7	8.3	9.7	6.9	6.9	2.8	72	27.3
I.P.S.% within service	24.2	6.3	18.9	11.6	2.1	12.6	6.3	7.4	10.5	95	36
I.F.S.% within service	9.3	6.2	10.3	8.2	6.2	8.2	12.4	11.3	27.8	97	36.7
Total N =	43	18	51	26	14	27	23	23	39	264	
Total % of rank	16.3	6.8	19.3	9.8	5.3	10.2	8.7	8.7	14.8		100

27.8% of the Indian Forest Service officers have given it last and 9th rank, indicating the lowest reliance on experts by them. The Indian Forest Service officers being specialists themselves in their area do not realize any importance for the experts' innovations in the decision-making process under political pressure. Our results indicate that the Indian Forest Service officers do not rely on the expert advice and what so ever innovation they have, they use them. But the Indian Administrative Service officers and the Indian Police Service officers rely heavily on expert advice and this snatches away the opportunity for innovations. Due to excessive reliance by them on experts, overall ranking has been at number two. Pearson Chi-square results are highly significant and good association among variables, with a significance level of 0.000. The strength of such correlations is demonstrated by the Rho and R values with a good significance level (0.000).

9.3.2. Custom Influence

Exhibit Number 9.3: AISO Rely on Traditional and Conventional Solutions for Change

Service Name	% In Service and Ranking for Innovation in this Item									Total	
	1	2	3	4	5	6	7	8	9	N	%
I.A.S.% within service	4.1	4.1	6.8	15.1	35.6	9.6	6.8	6.8	11	73	27.1
I.P.S.% within service	2.1	12.6	5.3	6.3	29.5	10.5	5.3	14.7	13.7	95	35.3
I.F.S.% within service	14.9	11.9	10.9	15.8	10.9	5.9	10.9	15.8	3	101	37.5
Total N =	20	27	21	33	65	23	21	35	24	269	100
Total % of rank	7.4	10	7.8	12.3	24.2	8.6	7.8	13	8.9		100

The All India Services Officers indicate a very low preference for their reliance on traditional and conventional solutions to bring change or innovations in the decision-making process, which is supported by the 6th overall ranking to this approach. In 5th rank, 24.2% of the All India Services Officers have reposed their faiths. 35.65 of the Indian Administrative Service officers and 29.5% of the Indian Police Service officers have also ranked it 5th and shown moderate reliance on customary influence in innovations. 15.8% of the Indian Forest Service officers have assigned it 4th rank and 15% with the first rank and 11.9% and 10.9% in 2nd and 3rd ranks, indicate that majority of them rely on the customary approach to handle change.

Among the All India Services, the Indian Forest Service officers have shown a higher preference for innovations by using traditional ways and means. If we see the overall scene, the All India Services Officers show low concern for the innovations. The All India Services Officers spend most of their time in buttering the politicians and seniors, so no time is left for thinking about the innovations. Chi-square results are highly significant and show good associations among variables, with a significance level of 0.000. The strength of such correlations is demonstrated by the Rho and R values with a good significance level <0.05.

9.3.3. Imagination

Imagination in thinking is the hallmark for innovations in the decision-making process, there cannot be innovations without imagination. When given options for devising innovative original for complex problems, 19.6% of the All India Services Officers ranked it 6th and 14.3% with 1st rank and 7th rank each. This indicates that the All India Services Officers assign low to moderate importance in finding out original solutions for the problems faced in the decision.

Exhibit Number 9.4: AISO are Innovative and Devise Original Solutions to Complex Problems

Service Name	% In Service and Ranking for Innovation in this Item									Total	
	1	2	3	4	5	6	7	8	9	N	%
I.A.S.% within service	6.8	2.7	6.8	9.6	9.6	38.4	6.8	6.8	112.3	73	27.5
I.P.S.% within service	8.8	0	5.5	13.2	7.7	18.7	23.1	7.7	15.4	91	34.3
I.F.S.% within service	24.8	14.9	12.9	4	9.9	6.9	11.9	4	10.9	101	38.1
Total N =	38	17	23	23	24	52	38	16	34	265	
Total % of rank	14.3	6.4	8.7	8.7	9.1	19.6	14.3	6	12.8		100

38.4% of the Indian Administrative Service Officers have also ranked it at 6th rank. 23.1% of the Indian Police Service Officers have ranked 7th and 18.7% at 6th rank. So, both services show low ranking for any kind of effort to find out original solutions and innovations. 24.8% of the Indian Forest Service officers have ranked its first rank in thinking and devising original solutions. High concern by the Indian Forest Service officers for the innovations and original thinking may be due to excessive powerlessness prevalent among them or due to excessive pressure from top to work, find and manage problems on their own. Lack of support from the top and seniors forces them to devise original solutions to fend them with innovations. Pearson Chi-square results are highly significant with 16 degree of freedom and 0.000, level of significance. The strength of negative correlation-ships is indicated by Pearson's correlation and Spearman correlation value with a level of significance at 0.000.

9.3.4. Control Influence

The top orders innovations and changes and most powerful persons in the department, this indicates the influence of control mechanism, which is of typical and most significant in a government bureaucratic system. 24.35% of the All India Services Officers have ranked it at 1st rank. 32.9% of the Indian Administrative Service officers and 28.4% of the Indian Police Service officers have also ranked this at 1st rank, which is reflected in overall rank also. This indicates both these services are highly control-oriented, since officers from both of the services are occupying top positions in their respective areas, so they may consider themselves in that position or showing respect for their seniors to incorporate any kind of innovations. A high percentage located in subsequent ranks of 2nd, 3rd, and 4th consolidate such inferences.

Exhibit Number 9.5: Top and Most Powerful Persons in Department Order the Innovations and Changes

Service Name	% In Service and Ranking for Innovation in this Item									Total	
	1	2	3	4	5	6	7	8	9	N	%
I.A.S. % within service	32.9	21.9	13.7	1.4	2.7	21.9	2.7	1.4	1.4	73	27.2
I.P.S.% within service	28.4	18.9	11.6	1.1	0	25.3	5.3	8.4	1.1	95	35.4
I.F.S.% within service	14	14	6	5	12	21	10	11	7	100	37.3
Total N =	65	48	27	7	14	61	17	20	9	268	
Total % of rank	24.3	17.9	10.1	2.6	5.2	22.8	6.3	7.5	3.4		100

21% of the Indian Forest Service officers have assigned 6th rank and more than 50% lying in subsequent ranks indicate that these officers show low reliance on top and powerful officers for incorporating innovations. Only 28% score lay in the first two ranks indicating that only fourth Indian Forest Service officers show reliance on top officers for innovations, whereas more than 50% score lay in the first three ranks for the Indian Administrative Service officers and the Indian Police Service officers. The level of significance at 0.000 in Pearson Chi-square results indicates that association among variables is significant and important. The R and Rho values support the strength of the correlation, with a level of significance at 0.000. Due to the high dependence of the Indian Police Service officers and the Indian Administrative Service officers towards the top, this item has got overall 1st ranking.

9.3.5. Dependency Influence

Exhibit Number 9.6: All India Services Officers Consult their Seniors Before Thinking about Change

Service Name	% In Service and Ranking for Innovation in this Item									Total	
	1	2	3	4	5	6	7	8	9	N	%
I.A.S.% within service	20.5	32.9	13.7	0	0	13.7	12.3	0	6.8	73	27.3
I.P.S.% within service	17.9	29.5	14.7	7.4	0	10.5	13.7	0	6.3	95	35.6
I.F.S.% within service	10.1	18.2	15.2	13.1	12.1	14.1	7.1	4	6.1	99	37.1
Total N =	42	70	39	20	12	34	29	4	17	267	
Total % of rank	15.7	26.2	14.6	7.5	4.5	12.7	10.9	1.5	6.4		100

The All India Services Officers consult their immediate senior before thinking about any change or bringing about any kind of innovations. The All India Services Officers rely heavily on their immediate senior as supported by the results, which demonstrated by the 2nd rank assigned by three services unanimously. In the case of the Indian Administrative Service officers, 32.9% at 2nd rank, 20.5% at 1st rank, and 13.7% at 3rd rank indicate heavy reliance on their immediate boss. Among the Indian Police Service officers, 29.5% at 2nd rank, 17.9% at 1st rank, and 14.7% at 3rd rank also prove their dependence on immediate boss. These scores for the Indian Forest Service officers are of lower percentages, with 18.2% at 2nd rank, 15.2% at 3rd rank, and 10.15% at 1st rank show less than 50% score. As shown elsewhere also, the Indian Forest Service officers show low reliance on their immediate boss and seniors, which indicates a high degree of prevalent distrust among them. This infers that the Indian Forest Service officers do not get enough support from the system in the decision-making process. Pearson Chi-square results are highly significant at a level of significance of 0.000. Good association between innovation and decision is supported by R and Rho values.

9.3.6. Confidence Influence

Exhibit Number 9.7: AISO Use Trusted Ways, Methods and Means to Bring any Change

Service Name	% In Service and Ranking for Innovation in this Item									Total	
	1	2	3	4	5	6	7	8	9	N	%
I.A.S.% within service	1.4	23.3	1.4	42.5	6.8	2.7	2.7	5.5	13.7	73	27.1
I.P.S.% within service	0	24.2	11.6	31.6	13.7	0	2.1	6.3	10.5	95	35.3
I.F.S.% within service	8.9	19.8	17.8	17.8	8.9	10.9	7.9	3	5	101	37.5
Total N =	10	60	30	79	27	13	12	13	24	269	
Total % of rank	3.7	22.3	11.2	29.4	10	4.8	4.5	4.8	8.9		100

The All India Services Officers use trusted methods, ways, and means to bring any change, indicate their confidence level and reliance is on the system. With 4th rank, 29.4% of the All India Services Officers show moderate reliance on trusted methods in innovations. 42.5% of the Indian Administrative Service Officers and 31.6% of the Indian Police Service Officers support the overall rank of 4th. Officers from both of these services show 23.3% and 24.2% in 2nd rank, bringing moderate to high reliance on confidence. 19.8% of the Indian Forest Service Officers have ranked it at 2nd rank and 17.8% each at 3rd and 4th ranks indicating high to moderate reliance on confidence. If we analyze different ranks scores, the All India Services Officers show reliance on trusted ways, means, and methods for innovations and changes. Pearson Chi-square results show a good association at the level of significance at 0.000. Correlation results indicate 11% to 13% chances that innovations by trusted methods in the decision may not be related to the political pressure. Our results are highly significant.

9.3.7. Achievement Influence

Exhibit Number 9.8: Highly Result-Oriented Individuals only Initiate Changes and Innovations

Service Name	% In Service and Ranking for Innovation in this Item									Total	
	1	2	3	4	5	6	7	8	9	N	%
I.A.S. % within service	12.3	1.4	9.6	8.2	15.1	0	24.7	12.3	16.4	73	27.5
I.P.S. % within service	14.3	2.2	8.8	16.5	13.2	8.8	7.7	17.6	11	91	34.3
I.F.S. % within service	18.8	11.9	7.9	17.8	11.9	6.9	11.9	8.9	4	101	38.1
Total N =	41	15	23	39	35	15	37	34	26	265	
Total % of rank	15.5	5.7	8.7	14.7	13.2	5.7	14	12.8	9.8		100

Achievements influence the thinking that innovations in the decision-making process are initiated by highly result-oriented individuals only; a sense of achievement influence the innovations. In available options for devising innovative solutions, result-oriented officers devise original solutions for complex problems, 15.5% of the All India Services Officers ranked it 1st and 14.7% with 4th rank and 14% with 7th rank. This indicates that the All India Services Officers assign moderate to low importance in finding out solutions for the problems faced in the decision. 24.7% of the Indian Administrative Service officers have also ranked it at 7th rank. 17.6% of the Indian Police Service officers have ranked 8th and 16.5% at 4th rank. So, both services show low ranking for any kind of effort by result-oriented officers to find out solutions and innovations in the decision-making process.

18.8% of the Indian Forest Service officers have ranked its first rank in thinking and devising original solutions by result-oriented officers. High concern by the Indian Forest Service officers with low percentage for the innovations may be due to lack of support prevalent among them or due to excessive pressure from top to work, find and manage problems at their own efforts. Lack of support from the top and seniors forces them to fend for themselves. Pearson Chi-square results are highly significant with 16 degree of freedom and 0.000, level of significance. The strength of negative correlation-ships is indicated by Pearson's correlation and Spearman correlation value with a level of significance at 0.000.

9.3.8. Affiliation Influence

Exhibit Number 9.9: AISO do not Disturb Existing Set Up, Seldom Initiate Innovation and Change

Service Name	% In Service and Ranking for Innovation in this Item									Total	
	1	2	3	4	5	6	7	8	9	N	%
I.A.S.% within service	5.5	5.5	6.8	9.6	2.7	1.4	26	28.8	13.7	73	27.8
I.P.S.% within service	6.7	7.8	17.8	7.8	20	0	20	13.3	6.7	90	34.2
I.F.S.% within service	8	2	8	10	10	11	18	20	13	101	38
Total N =	18	13	29	24	30	12	55	53	29	263	
Total % of rank	6.8	4.9	11	9.1	11.4	4.6	20.9	20.2	11		100

Low ranking for the approach that the All India Services Officers do not like to disturb existing set up, they seldom initiate change innovations in the decision-making process. 20.9% of the All India Services Officers have ranked it at 7th place, indicating low concern. 28.8% of the Indian Administrative Service officers and 20% of the Indian Forest Service officers have shown 8th rank for not to disturb existing setup. 20% of the Indian Police Service officers have assigned 7th rank. The All India Services Officers do not believe in adopting the status-quo approach and this has been reflected in the results. Pearson Chi-square results show a good association with the level of significance at 0.000. Our results are significant as indicated by the significance value.

9.3.9. Extension Influence

The All India Services Officers extension motive is indicated by the concern they show for adverse effects from the innovations and they like to take consensus decision. The alternate hypothesis is accepted that the All India Services Officers do not show concern for others while incorporating any change. Pearson Chi-square results are highly significant with the level of significance at 0.000. 24.2% of the All India Services Officers have ranked it at 9th place indicating very low to lowest priority for this approach. 28.8% of the Indian Administrative Service officers and 20% of the Indian Forest Service Officers also ranked it low with 9th and 8th rank. 29.7% of the Indian Police Service officers assigned it 9th rank. These results indicate that the All India Services Officers do not bother to take consensus decisions and do not show concern for any kind of adverse effects of their decision on others.

Exhibit Number 9.10: AISO have Concern for Others, so Take Consensus Decisions

Service Name	% In Service and Ranking for Innovation in this Item									Total	
	1	2	3	4	5	6	7	8	9	N	%
I.A.S.% within service	1.4	0	2.7	5.5	19.2	2.7	11	28.8	28.8	73	27.5
I.P.S.% within service	0	0	1.1	6.6	16.5	9.9	14.3	22	29.7	91	34.3
I.F.S.% within service	6.9	5.9	7.9	5.9	18.8	10.9	7.9	19.8	15.8	101	38.1
Total N =	8	6	11	16	48	22	29	61	64	265	
Total % of rank	3	2.3	4.2	6	18.1	8.3	10.9	23	24.2		100

ANNEXURE 9.A: QUESTIONNAIRE FOR THE AISO INNOVATIONS IN DECISION

All India Services Officers (AISO) occupy pivotal positions in the public administration. By virtue of their location, they can incorporate **innovations and changes in the system.** We have listed situations (a) to (i) Kindly, **rank** 1 as the most commonly preferred situation to 9 as the least preferred approach.

(a) AISO has no time or do not bother much, they refer such matters to experts/specialists. ☐

(b) AISO rely on traditional and conventional solutions to bring any change. ☐

(c) AISO are innovative and devise original solutions to complex problems. ☐

(d) The top and most powerful persons in the department order innovations and changes. ☐

(e) Before thinking about any change AISO consult their immediate senior. ☐

(f) AISO use trusted ways, means, and methods to bring any change. ☐

(g) Highly result-oriented individual only initiates innovations or changes. ☐

(h) AISO do not like to disturb exiting set up, they seldom initiate change/innovations. ☐

(i) AISO has great concern for the adverse effect of the change on others they take consensus decisions. ☐

Unit 10

Conflict Management in Decision

"When your intellect bemused by conflicting versions, rest steadily in meditation on a supernatural being, you will attain union with the Supreme." *The Bhagavad Gita* 2.53

This is punishment of a liar: he is not believed, even when he speaks the truth. Babylonian Talmud

- *Sources of Conflict and Management Approach Concept*
- *Conflict Management Process in Decision*
- *All India Services Officer Conflict Handling*
- *Research Analyses Results*
- *Negotiation*
- *Withdrawal*
- *Resignation*
- *Confrontation*
- *Arbitration*
- *Compromise*
- *Appeasement*

How conflict management is the art of understanding the conflict itself has been explained. How negative pressure on the All India Services Officers creates dissonance with a self-image of the officer, under negative pressure, individual officer tends to show defensive behavior is mentioned. Political systems and power structures in public administration generate conflicts in the process of decision. The government bureaucratic system is full of internal and external uncertainties that generate uncertainty over the behavior of individual officers. How individual officers react to such uncertainties and outcomes of that are explained in this unit. Research analyses result along with how conflict is being handled is explained.

10.1. Conflict Management Approach: Concept and Style

Conflict happens in every organization and occasionally it infuses efficiency and innovations in the decision. Controversies are also healthy as disagreements; arguments share their thinking, and solutions for better interpreting different aspects of intellection, mental synthesis, formulation, conceptualization, cognition, perceptions, and target achievement. Conflicts can produce innovative outcomes by individual officers in the bureaucratic decision-making process.

The All India Services Officers frequently have to make decisions under a state of conflict, where rational opponents are involved. Opposition carefully considers the various means and ends involved in the decision process. Taking a decision under conflict is like playing a game in other court. Any gains for one group are the losses for the other group. In competing goals, the All India Services Officers have to decide in a win-win position for all the stakeholders.

Conflict management is the art of understanding the conflict itself. Negative pressure on the All India Services Officers creates dissonance with the self-image of the officer, maybe threatening to one's ego. When an officer receives negative pressure, an individual officer tends to be defensive and defensive behavior is used to deal with such pressure. Such a defensive behavior will create the delusion that he has dealt with the pressure. Through training and other means, we try to modify the behavior of the All India Services Officers without changing the underlying behavior pattern, which causes that behavior to incorporate change in behavior of individual All India Services Officers. We have to change the cognitive contents, which determine the behavior of an officer. Underlying self-goals and interests generate fluctuations in the makeup of psychological structure and oscillations due to differential tension in each part of the structure of structural conflict prevalent in tension resolution systems. Desires and beliefs individual All India Services Officer want to accomplice generate disagreements in the system. Any change of structure produces emotional change, a lot of the All India Services Officers fail to cope up with emotional pressure. They try to minimize the prevailing conflict and stay in an area of contradictions, which they can tolerate. The system continues to produce changes but individual officer feels he can manage the conflict in process of decision.

Every All India Services Officer oscillates between defensive and confronting behavior in the decision under conflicting situations created by political pressure, some of these traits are mentioned in Exhibit 10.1.

An individual officer has a different degree of tolerance and can tolerate conflict up to a point (elasticity or elastic limit of tolerance). When conflict crosses that point one shift in the direction, which determines the outer limit of tolerance for conflict. Even slight pressure beyond this limit, the officer will feel uncomfortable. The best approach to manage conflict in public administration is to minimize the aspirations level, goals, or interests of individual All India Services Officer. Time tested Upanishad's philosophy to minimize individual aspirations and needs has been directed towards reducing conflicts in one's daily life.

The All India Services Officers' approach of continuously adopting a defensive approach (Exhibit 10.1) may result in a conflicted self of these officers. When these officers continuously use defensive behavior, it may reduce their relationship of trust and openness among themselves. Any officer who continuously uses defensive behavior will be less effective in his dealing with the pressure in the decision process. Individual All India Service Officer, who is not open may receive more pressure from others or different quarters. First, such an officer will try to manipulate the pressure, and then the officer will be unavailable, which will have an adverse impact on the decision process and conflict management. Individual officer, who is conscious of others feelings, will express his interactions in the outcome of the decision process in a positive manner. Some officers, who are conscious of their limitations, will not like to take any risks in conflict management in the decision process. Such All India Services Officers, who do not open to express the pressure in the decision process, internally will be conscious about the outcome of the pressure.

Exhibit Number 10.1: Defensive and Confronting Behavior in Conflict

Defensive Behavior Traits	Confronting Behavior Traits
Denial	Owning
Rationalization	Self-Analysis
Projection	Empathy
Displacement	Exploration
Quick Acceptance	Data Collection
Withdrawal	Expressing Feeling
Aggression	Help Seeking
Humor	Concern
Competition with Authority	Listening
Cynicism	Positive Critical Attitude
Intellectualization	Sharing Concern
Generalization	Experimenting
Pairing	Relating to Group
Resulting in a Conflicted Self	Resulting in an Integrated Self

Conflicts are inevitable for every department and agreement is not possible on all occasions. Likert and Likert supported these views with shreds of evidence that a participatory style of management improves conflict management. Conflicts in the decision process are generated due to external pressures, the bureaucratic system itself, political pressure, internal factors due to inconsistency in service, and individual behavior (Figure 10.1). In conflict-avoidance behavior, individual All India Services Officers give unilateral small concessions to the politicians with a message that no pressure will be conceded in the future. The All India Services Officers mutually exchange concessions with politicians to soften the conflict.

The political system and power structure in public administration generate conflicts in the process of decision. The government bureaucratic system is full of uncertainties, internal, and external uncertainties of the bureaucratic system produce uncertainty over the behavior of individual officers also, which is shown in Figure 10.1.

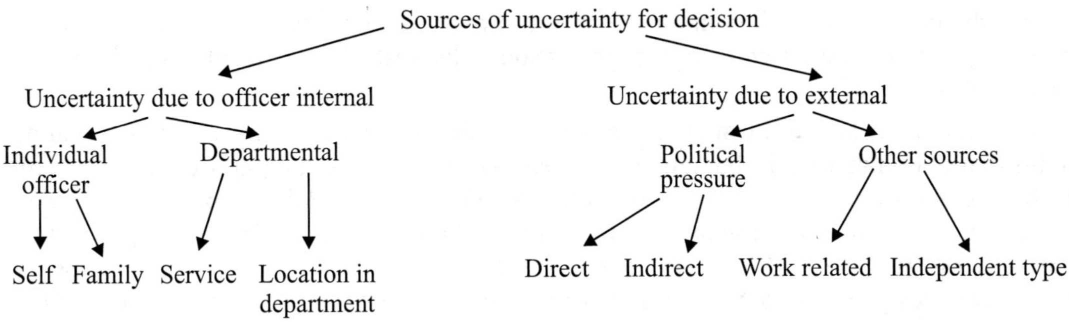

I. Understanding	I. System for Self-goals	I. Departmental Employees
II. Concerns	II. Department Goals	II. Bureaucratic Expectations
III. Family	III. Obligations	III. Programmes Related
IV. Motivations	IV. Power/Authority	IV. Work Environment
V. Values & Attitudes	V. Seniors Attitude	V. Political Expectations

Figure No. 10.1: Sources of Uncertainties and the All India Services Officers

The All India Services Officers foresee adversaries in conflict, show a willingness to appease politicians, and give concessions in the process. Assessing conflict in the decision-making process, an individual All India Services Officer arranges an informal meeting with a politician and discuss freely and frankly regarding negotiations and compromise in conflict. The cost of such negotiations and compromise is extracted from the system. When the All India Services Officers fall short of political connections or negotiations, they approach and use an intermediary. In such situations, intermediaries extract concessions from both sides and increase more conflict in the decision.

On many occasions conflict in the process itself work as pressure, many All India Services Officers take decisions, only when there is pressure on them, in situations conflict motivate them to take the decision to reduce pressure. Some senior officers as a strategy intensify conflict in the decision process, which reflect unwanted consequences for not making a decision, under this pressure officer will take an early decision. Under any kind of pressure conflict, individual All India Services Officers arrive at a decision to reduce the pressure and conflict. Outcomes of such decisions may not be of their choice or desired direction. Conflict structures dominate the behavior of the All India Services Officers when they like to manage conflict. Negative consequences of the conflict dominate individual officer mind outside the area of tolerable conflict. Conflict reduces group performance (Liddel et al., 1976), reduces confidence, and induces poor performance (Schuler, 1980).

Political pressure continues to increase and accrue conflict among the All India Services Officers. Individual officers experience conflict to a critical limit (elasticity), beyond which, an officer is unable to manage the conflict in the decision process. Then officer is forced to make a decision in direction of least resistance, which is invariably controlled and directed by the pressure. The outcome may be short-termed but it releases the accumulated tension in the individual officer and the officer feels relieved irrespective of the consequences of the decision. How long individual officers can manage to cope with this situation of conflict in the decision process? In due course of their career, officers feel powerlessness in front of pressure. They try different approaches to manage the pressure, but all without any result in their desired direction. Positive correlations have been found between conflict and professional dissatisfaction and job-related tension by Oliver and Brief (1978).

Political situations confirm that the All India Services Officers are a pawn in hands of circumstances dominating the bureaucratic system. They achieve nothing; consequential situations motivate them for goal displacement or shift towards self-goals. Political power and authority manipulate the pressure to raise the emotions of the All India Services Officers and play with it to achieve self-goals. The All India Services Officers may be chronically worried under continuous pressure, or show concern for the decision process (self or public), or react emotionally to pressure to make a decision. Continuously playing with manipulation of conflict in the decision process for years, the All India Services Officers feel less and less powerful and their capability to take action in conflict drastically goes down.

Our research has affirmed that seniors at the top with growing experience are more amenable to pressure. We cannot build any service stronger based on conflict, because this continuous conflict in the decision process of the All India Services Officers destroys creativity and innovations. Continuous pressure accumulates conflict among the All India Services Officers, slowly it will override natural instinct and an individual officer will behave in a counter instinctive manner to lose a sense of reality, constantly alienation will occur concomitantly in the individual officer behavior.

Prevalent system of political pressure and ingrained conflict in the decision-making process of public administration. The All India Services Officers have been attuned to external conflicts in the decision. If political pressure is reduced, many officers will not like to take any decision. In which manner, can we manipulate the intensity of conflict in our bureaucratic system? Will conflict reduction lead to improved operations? Can conflict manipulation produce improved performance? Strategies to manage conflict have to be such that the system gets conditioned responses in the decision. But these kinds of conflict manipulations reduce the individual growth; chances of change and officers do not grow. Any effort to bring any change by the Indian Administrative Service officers, feelings of powerlessness will reinforce powerlessness and erosion among the Indian Police Service officers and the Indian Forest Service officers. For conflict manipulation in the decision process of the All India Services Officers, we have to inculcate a positive attitude, positive thinking, positive reinforcement, and strong inspiration.

The All India Services Officers with strong willpower try to come over the inbuilt conflict, their own firmness, and resolution push the decision in direction of their own desires. For a while, they feel they have manipulated the conflict, in due course of time different kinds of new pressures corrode their confidence and they feel exhausted of energy and stamina, and frustration of failure creep inside them. Ultimately, they realize powerlessness and follow the path of least resistance in the decision. This frustrating experience, they go through their entire career, then individual officer lives under constant tension, start feeling that the bureaucratic system is like that.

When the All India Services Officers see the persons, who have moved with political pressure have acquired and gained all comforts of service and progressive and cozy career. Accumulated inner frustrations and powerlessness reinforce them to accept pressure without a fuss. Due to conflict officers select the options in the decision process, which they do not desire, they confirm avoidance behavior to reduce tension. In normal routine cases, an individual officer could have selected desired outcome options in the decision process. Structural conflicts in the All India

Services Officers behavior force them to resolve un-resolvable conflicts in the direction of least resistance. In a life of constant conflicts and belief of powerlessness, the All India Services Officers experience emotional comfort, when they decide the direction of pressure to reduce their fear and worries generated inside them.

Demands from public administration generate inevitable conflict. The All India Services Officers got pressurized in a situation of no solution and helplessness, which motivate them to the power struggle. In such situations of conflict, each service member looks after first individual interests and then the interests of their own service group. Location and position of the Indian Administrative Service cadres ensure maximization of gains for them, so conflict ensure their survival on top by adopting approach-based orientation. Inbuilt system fears among the Indian Forest Service officers force them to adopt avoidance orientation in conflict management. The Indian Forest Service officers try to find out solutions by individual efforts or try to rationalize or deny or avoid the problem.

When individual All India Services Officers find that compliance with political pressure in a decision is complicated and difficult, contradictory expectations from decisions generate conflict. The All India Services Officers will seek stability and show higher concern towards expectations of spouse and children. The public administration process expects and requires concern for the public, these differential expectations create total chaotic condition inside the All India Services Officers, which one to choose. Such diversity of outcome from decision generates serious tension and accumulates frustration and diverse behavioral responses engage in the officer. The All India Services Officers resort to rules, regulations, and procedures to resolve such conflicts, or withdraw from the political pressure.

Conflict is perceived in the decision-making process under political pressure when the All India Services Officers feel that they themselves or another party is adversely affected by protecting the interests of the source of pressure. Conflict is natural and inevitable over the outcome of any decision. Even if, the All India Services Officers perform absolutely and necessarily with the utmost fairness, then also conflict will remain associated with the decision. It is not proper to visualize conflict as a dysfunctional outcome.

To avoid conflict, causes of conflict have to be addressed. The prevalent notion that conflict has eaten away the performance and equity is not well-founded. Conflict and situations responsible for such conflict have to be evaluated in a most systematic manner. It cannot be denied that excessive conflicts ruin decision quality. Conflict within permissible limits can be tolerated and may sustain the productivity of the decision. The All India Services Officers have to learn to live with the conflict. In public administration, it is the responsibility of policymakers to maintain the functional conflict below desirable limits to keep decision creativity. How individual All India Services Officers perceive conflict to influence the decision according to such perceptions, attitudes, and beliefs and make conflict functional and dysfunctional.

10.2. Conflict Management Process in Decision

We can describe the conflict management process among the All India Services Officers according to the seven stages concept as described below in Figure 10.2.

Stage 1. Potential opposition or incompatibility dealing officer personal variables.

Stage 2. Cognition and personalization of conflict by the individual officer.

Stage 3. The All India Services officer intensions to handle conflict.

Stage 4. Political parties and other party behavior in conflict.

Stage 5. Outcomes of public administration decision taken under conflict.

Stage 6. Conflict resolutions by the All India Services officer.

Stage 7. Conflict evaluation and follows up the outcome of conflict by the officer and system.

Stage I	**Stage II**	**Stage III**	**Stage IV**	**Stage V**
Potential Opposition or Incompatibility	Cognition and Personalization	Intentions	Behavior	Outcomes

Stage VI Conflict Resolution and

Stage VII Conflict Evaluation follow after outcome of conflict

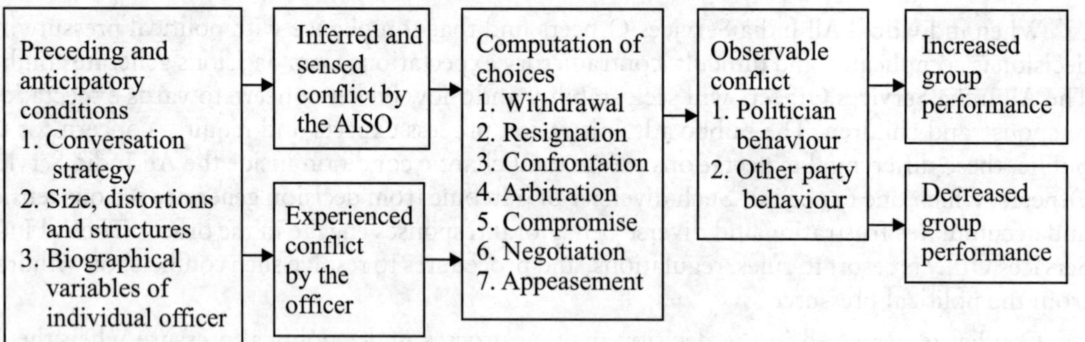

Figure No. 10.2: The Conflict Process in the All India Services[1]

10.2.1. Stage I. Pre-Conflict Position

The sources and modes of political pressure give rise to conflicts in the decision process. The prevalent belief is that in process of pressure management, the All India Services Officers do not communicate with the politicians properly, timely, and in an effective manner. Appropriate communication strategy/modes of conversations can help the All India Services Officers and politicians both, towards a better and proper understanding of the problem from the right perspectives. The All India Services Officers orientation of status, power, fear, and apprehensions induce poor communication, which creates misunderstanding with the public and politician both. An increase in the level of communication will reduce the barriers and improves the inter-personal relations, in such improved relations politicians without any hesitation will exert pressure on the All India Services Officers.

In case politicians do not know the individual, All India Services Officers and do not have any working personal relations with All India Services Officer, politicians can explain his inability to the public regarding asserting pressure on such officers. Little or no inter-personal relations with the politicians, sometimes work as blessings in disguise for an individual All India Services

1. Adapted and Modified from *Organizational Behavior*, Stephen P. Robins (1998), p. 437.

Officer. In the case of the All India Services Officers and politician conflict is coming out from the goal's directions, gain to one individual is a loss to other interests. No communication with politicians also helps in reducing the pressure in a number of instances.

The extent of political pressure, size, structure, and degree of distortions in the decision process, extent and jurisdiction of political pressure, goal compatibility with pressure, degree of dependence of public, systems of benefits, and individual style of work are related to the structure of conflict process. Research indicates that the size of service and technical specialization in that service act as forces to stimulate conflict. Tenure of a post and conflict has been found inversely related. Young officers perceive conflict higher than elderly officers. The higher the uncertainty in the decision outcomes, the more the conflict accumulates in the decision process.

The Indian Administrative Service officers fight for the retention of control over resources of other services. The All India Services Officers pursue different goals to meet diverse ends, also increases chances of conflict in the bureaucratic system. The people participation approach promotes differences in expectations for rewards, which causes conflict in the decision. The Indian Police Service officers and the Indian Forest Service officers depend on the Indian Administrative Service officers' cadres for major decisions, in such interdependence every one like to grow at the cost/expense of other services, this increase the conflict.

Biographic variables of All India Services Officers do influence the outcome of decision and conflict associated with it. Individual All India Services Officers' approach, personality, attitudes, perceptions, behavior towards political pressure and politician, and conflict influence the outcome of the conflict. Biographical characters are related the conflict management. Some of the All India Services Officers develop expertise in the management of the greatest quantum of political pressure without much conflict in the process. Some All India Services Officers get scared in the name of political pressure and they break down and start yielding before such pressure is exerted. The All India Services Officers cultural background, value system contributes towards conflict management.

10.2.2. Stage II. Perception of Conflict

Under political pressure in a decision, the All India Services Officers realize that one or more parties will be affected by the outcome of their decision, create awareness about conflict. Interested parties (politicians and the public) contest the outcome of the decision and their anxiety and hostility involve them emotionally with the outcomes. In this stage, the individual officer perceptions about conflict may delineate the possible settlements. Negative interpretations by any party reduce the trust and positive relationship bound to increase the relationship and produce more innovative solutions (Robins, 1998). The All India Services Officers accept pressure and enhance the relationship with the politician for future use or manipulations. In this stage, the All India Services Officer's emotional level is crucial and plays the foremost role regarding perceptions and delineations of pressure in the decision.

10.2.3. Stage III. Computation of Choices

The All India Services Officers' intentions work between the politicians thinking and emotional behavior of the All India Services Officers towards political pressure. Individual All India Services Officers infer how to reply or act with political pressure. Inappropriate intentions can cause tremendous conflict in the All India Services Officers psyche. Intensions about the decision and behavior of the All India Services Officers cause conflict in the self of the officer. The All India

Services Officers compute choices either to co-operate with the political pressure or protect the bureaucratic system expectations. At this stage officers' cognitive feelings, attitudes, beliefs cause serious concern and conflict in three directions. Individual officer computations will oscillate among seven choices; negotiation, withdrawal, resignation, confrontation, arbitration, compromise, and appeasement or any other choice to manage the conflict in the decision.

The All India Services Officers attempt to satisfy different concerns or conflicting goals from the decision. The All India Services Officers attempt to explain to self about his intentions relations with the outcomes of the decision. Deep in the mind of the All India Services Officers show concern about the outcomes of the decision and the consequences associated with it. The All India Services Officers re-conceptualize and change intensions, emotional reactions to behavior. The All India Services Officers adopt the avoidance style of conflict management and show resignation, withdrawal, and appeasement modes. In case someone adopts an approach style of management, one follows confrontation, compromise, arbitration, and negotiation modes. Different officers adopt different preferences determined by their personality characteristics, capabilities, and biographical variables. The All India Services Officers' intentions to handle conflict will be controlled by personality, nature of pressure, and its ramifications to individual future life-goals.

10.2.4. Stage IV. Actions and Reactions

This stage comprises the actions and reactions behavior of the All India Services Officers towards conflict and conflicting parties and their behavior. The All India Services Officers attempt to include and accommodate the intentions of all parties. When an officer is working on the decision process then his behavior deviates from calculated intensions. Such deviations are also affected by internal stimuli and wrong calculations if any. The All India Services Officer thinks about politicians' physical or aggressive approach, threats and ultimatums generated through politicians or other parties, questioning and challenges arising from public or interested parties, disagreements and misapprehensions creeping in the bureaucratic system and political parties and public. The All India Services Officers try and test various conflict management techniques at this stage to arrive at decision.

10.2.5. Stage V. Decision Results

"The action reactions interplay between conflicting groups results in consequences.... These outcomes may be functional in conflict results in an improvement in the group's performance or dysfunctional in that hinders group performance" (Robins, 1998). Political pressures beget conflicts and that forces All India Services Officers to take decisions. At times politicians adopt the aggressive posture and force reluctant All India Services Officers to take a decision, but for the pressure, the All India Services Officers could have postponed or relegated the decision to die down in files. Conflict indirectly plays a constructive role to enhance the performance of idle and dying to stagnate bureaucracy. Many All India Services Officers will not agree to the concept constructive. As political pressure rarely infuses innovations and improve the quality of the decision. The All India Services Officer experience that political pressure enhances conflict in the decision, but at the same time problem is solved, and accumulating tension in the All India Services Officers' mind is released.

Any decision is better than no decision. The All India Services Officers active role is better than the passive and withdrawing role. Due to political pressure, the All India Services Officers are forced to change their style and evaluate themselves in the light of a prevalent scenario. At the same time, decision outcomes under pressure neglect the welfare of the minorities and other stakeholders in this process. Political pressure has forced the All India Services Officers to think and reposition themselves with time and space. But for the political pressure, the All India Services Officers could have adopted the pure autocratic behavior and purely for their own interests' maximization. Which is the case when the All India Services Officers develop a close relation with politicians or politician is week.

The All India Services Officers under pressure relegate the considerations for the system; try to explore different alternatives and work to change the prevailing position. We may think within different rational parameters, we may criticize political pressure to any extent. But the reality is that pressure infuses new ideas in the decision. It enhances the possibilities to create and bring forth new solutions appropriate to changing scenarios. The All India Services Officers' sycophancy and inertness to change do not allow restructuring in functional outcomes in positive directions. The pressure generated conflict improves the performance of respective services and enhances the strength of these services.

Excessive and uncontrolled political pressures generate frustration and weaken the relationship among the service members. Excessive pressure reduces communication with the public and politicians. Individual All India Services Officer starts fighting among the services, which reduces the service unity and threatens the survival of service goals. Excessive conflict increases the tension levels and affects the nervous system to create stress, depression, and hypertension among the All India Services Officers. Slowly, All India Services Officers develop inertness and start developing distance from the pressure. The job of the top bureaucrats is to reduce dysfunctional conflict and allow functional conflict only. Excessive conflicts turn All India Services Officers into yes man and indulge in sycophancy. Politicians at the top and senior bureaucrats have to re-assess the extent of political pressure to maintain the functioning of the decision system.

10.2.6. Stage VI. Conflict Resolution

How to convert dominant political pressure into a productive way and keep it at a functional level is the main question. Bureaucracy can use some of the time-tested methods practiced elsewhere in different places for this process. Greatest conflicts start with the resource distribution or resource allocation by politicians through the All India Services Officers. While working in bureaucratic systems, the All India Services Officers develop their own feelings and attachments about scarce resource allocation in the system. Resource scarcity in time and space with expanding goals requires expansion of resource control. Conflict resolution comprises the continuous redefining of the goals, realigning the service members, and reducing the interdependence on resources. Continuously updating the rules, regulations, procedures, law, and policy along with the restructuring of the All India Services and delivery system also help in conflict resolution.

Politicians at the top should think about bringing outsider experts, who are neutral to resources. This helps in analyzing the All India Services Officers' perceptions, values, attitudes about resource attachment, and use. Infuse critical arguments against the majority power holders. Improve communication with threatened power holders. Threatening messages do increase the conflict level in the bureaucratic system. Politicians must learn to use their authority and command irrespective of concern for three services advice. Mostly, All India Services Officers manipulate conflict to own service advantage, which has seriously damaged the system beyond irreparable limits. Politicians have to wake up and start thinking independently as an institution without any feedback from any member of any service. This will help in changing service variables working in the decision. Independent thinking by a politician will change the behavior of officers of these services.

The sense of monopoly has to be reduced to a minimum to zero for any service, which creates conflict for the rest of the services. It is imperative that political leadership must wake up to change governmental hierarchical variables in the decision. Excessive co-ordination at different levels has created more conflicts than any solutions for the decision. The politician has to restart co-ordination work and take in their hands or create a democratic system for co-ordination. Assigning a co-ordination job to bureaucratic positions inflates the conflict and tension among decision-makers. Political leadership has to work hard to reduce the differences among the All India Services Officers and has to create common interests for all the services. Present conflicting service interests; inflate dissent, which has to be zeroed down. Eventually, suppression of the public and all other members of the bureaucracy by few elites All India Services Officers have to be removed and reduced to zero.

The system cannot suppress the conflict forever. How long bureaucratic system will continue to avoid the disease/infection in the system? No system can function without the cooperation of all conflicting parties. Political leadership must create shared goals for all officers, services working in the system. Political leadership has to discuss the problem face to face with all the parties to resolve the conflict. All the conflicting parties must participate in resolving the conflict from the public point of view. The bureaucratic system will fully generate conflict in the decision and beauty is that invariably the power holders reward contradictions and the All India Services Officers, those who reduce conflict are punished. Sycophants and yes men, who cause the conflict, are the first persons to approach and inform their bosses about conflict and in turn, bosses feel obliged and reward them with different plum postings, promotions for pseudo confidentiality, which will slowly destroy the image of that boss along with inefficiency in the system.

10.2.7. Stage VII. Evaluation and Recurrence

Conflict resolution by any individual All India Services Officer and politicians' outlook towards such management will influence the future recurrences of the conflict in the decision-making process of the bureaucratic system. Individual officer evaluates past conflict handling according to their own capabilities and personality. Political leadership may develop different perceptions about conflict management by the bureaucracy and political evaluation remains independent of the consequences of past incidences to any individual officer. Politicians' future generation of conflict through political pressure in the decision-making process derives its strength from past success rate. For effective and better management of conflict, it is imperative that the All India Services Officers and politicians must sit together for evaluation to avoid future recurrences of undesirable conflict in the decision-making process. Conflict continues to accrue due to the negligence of this stage in the process of conflict management.

10.3. The AISO Conflict Handling in Decision: Research Analyses

Our analysis (Exhibit 10.2) with the lowest mean value of 3.33 indicates that most of the All India Services Officers think that in due course of time conflicting issues will be resolved automatically. It clearly infers that the public and politician both never assert their position and are casual in their approach. They tend to forget the issues slowly and the All India Services Officers relegate such matters in the files to die down natural death. The All India Services Officers who were supposed to deliver the decision in odd situations are over-whelmed and overpowered by the ideas of resignation in conflicting situations. Why did the public continue to have expectations from such a dying system?

Exhibit Number 10.2: Statistical Analysis for Conflict in Decision-making Process

Item Name	Frequency			M	SD	Chi-square		
	Total	Miss	Valid			Value	df	sigf
179. Succumb under pressure	281	13	268	4.09	2.32	87.13	12	0.000
180. Withdraw, do nothing	281	15	266	4.04	1.63	52.68	12	0.000
181. Resolved, course of time	281	11	270	3.33	1.82	40.16	12	0.000
182. Fight to implement it	281	10	271	4.46	2.31	63.12	14	0.000
183. Help of seniors/friends	281	14	267	3.75	2.07	57.23	12	0.000
184. Mutually acceptable	281	13	268	3.41	1.64	28.45	12	0.005
185. Concession to politician	281	14	267	4.47	1.96	79.43	16	0.000

M = Mean value, SD = Standard deviation, df = degree of freedom, sigf = significance

The second most common approach adopted by the All India Services Officers to manage conflict in the decision-making process is that they resort to mutually acceptable solutions with politicians. This is the reason that for every work public approach politician. Some of the All India Services Officers are unable to confront, have lost initiatives, and only deliver tailor-made decisions when politicians pressurize them. Invariably decision is taken under pressure as desired by the politicians.

The interesting part of this analysis is that feeling of fighting out for the right things or merit in the decision has been assigned the lowest rank. It clearly indicates that the All India Services Officers scarcely will fight out or adopt confrontation with the politicians. The public image that the All India Services Officers may take a stand and try hard to implement the right decisions is the legendary only. Pearson Chi-square results are highly significant and establish good relations with the decision. '0.000' significance values establish a very good association of variables.

Exhibit 10.3 conflict management relation with the length of service indicates that the All India Services Officers' highest preference for conflict management shows that they allow a situation to be resolved automatically in due course of time. The highest percentage of 24.6% of the All India Services Officers have given 1st rank to that conflict will be resolved in due course of time. The second-best approach with 1st rank is that 24% of All India Services Officers like to succumb under political pressure in the decision-making process in resolving conflict. In Exhibit 10.3, conflict management has been studied with relation to the level of the All India Services Officers in the hierarchy. Our results indicate that top-level adopt the path of least resistance in conflict management in the decision-making process.

Exhibit Number 10.3: Conflict Management with Length of Service

Name of Approach	Length of Service	Rank of the Approach Adopted for Conflict Handling							Total
		1st	2nd	3rd	4th	5th	6th	7th	
Succumb under pressure	Top	12.4	6	6	7.5	3.4	10.9	12	58.1
	Middle	8.6	2.2	0.7	4.5	2.2	1.1	5.6	25.1
	Lower	3	1.9	2.6	1.1	0.7	1.9	5.6	16.9
	Total	24	10.1	9.4	13.1	6.4	13.9	23.2	100
Withdraw do nothing	Top	3	9	15	6	16.1	3.7	5.6	58.4
	Middle	1.9	4.5	4.1	4.5	6.7	1.9	1.9	25.5
	Lower	0.7	1.1	3	3.4	4.5	2.6	0.7	16.1
	Total	5.6	14.6	22.1	13.9	27.3	8.2	8.2	
Issue will be resolved in due course of time	Top	18.4	5.1	10.7	4	7.4	1.8	10.7	58.1
	Middle	3.3	2.6	4.4	2.6	4.8	0.4	7	25.1
	Lower	2.9	2.4	2.9	2.2	2.2	0.4	6.1	16.9
	Total	24.6	10.7	18	8.8	14.3	2.6		
Fight out to implement it	Top	12.9	2.2	3.7	8.8	4.8	9.2	16.5	58.2
	Middle	4.8	1.5	1.5	3.3	2.2	3.7	8.1	24
	Lower	3.3	1.1	1.1	2.9	1.1	3.7	3.7	17.2
	Total	21	4.8	6.3	15.1	8.1	16.5	38.3	
Take help from friends/ seniors to solve it	Top	5.6	19	6.7	9	2.2	7.1	8.6	58.2
	Middle	3	4.5	4.9	1.9	0.4	4.9	5	24.6
	Lower	3	4.9	2.6	1.9	1.5	0.7	2.6	17.2
	Total	11.6	28.4	14.2	12.7	4.1	12.7	16.2	
Mutually acceptable solution with politicians	Top	7.4	9.7	14.5	12.3	9.3	4.5	0.7	58.4
	Middle	4.1	4.5	4.5	3	3.3	3.3	1.9	24.5
	Lower	3	2.2	3.7	4.1	2.2	1.9	0	17.1
	Total	14.5	16.4	22.7	19.3	14.9	9.7	2.6	
Give concession to politicians	Top	3.4	6	4.1	9	12.4	4.8	13.5	58.3
	Middle	4.1	4.9	3	3.8	3.8	3.4	1.9	24.8
	Lower	1.9	1.9	1.5	1.5	3.8	3	3.4	16.9
	Total	9.4	12.8	8.6	14.3	19.8	16.2	18.8	

10.3.1. Negotiation

When politicians and the All India Services Officer both are mature and seasoned, both sides sit together to find out a mutually acceptable solution for the problem. Conflict in the decision is resolved in an amicable way. Politicians and the All India Services Officers on both sides share the gains and achieve their goals. It is the sharing of public resources in a mutually acceptable manner at the cost of the public ultimately. Such a relationship will continue for long period, the All India Services Officers, and the politicians share and try to maintain family relations for future use. The outcome of this type of relations is that the All India Services Officers cultivate them throughout their career. Politicians feel comfortable; even if one is out of power then also such relations are handy for them to meet their self-goals. Shepard and Mouton (1964) and Likert and Likert (1976) termed this as a problem-solving approach.

The All India Services Officers assess the conflict then politicians and the All India Services Officers identify mutually attainable goals. Then they share views on various possibilities to resolve conflict. The All India Services Officers and politicians both identify means for the achievement of goals. Sometimes All India Services Officers keep their goals covered under administrative procedure or express at a later appropriate time so that politicians do not realize it. In the negotiations process, complete bureaucratic systems down to bottom share the benefits so, there are minimum outcries or complaints. Negotiation involves a sacrifice of values, ethics, and norms for the attainment of own goals and task.

Exhibit Number 10.4: All India Services Officers Succumb under Political Pressure

Name of Service	Rank of the Approach Adopted to Manage Conflict							Total
	1st	2nd	3rd	4th	5th	6th	7th	
Indian Admn. Service								
Frequency N	18	14	6	9	5	10	10	72
% within rank	26.5	51.9	24	29	29.4	25.6	16.4	
% in the service	25	19.4	8.3	12.5	6.9	13.9	13.9	
% of total A.I.S.	6.7	5.2	2.2	3.4	1.9	3.7	3.7	26.9
Indian Police Service								
Frequency N	39	9	15	13	8	1	9	94
% within rank	57.4	33.3	60	41.9	47.8	2.6	14.8	
% in the service	41.5	9.6	16	13.8	8.5	1.1	9.6	
% of total A.I.S.	14.6	3.4	5.6	4.9	3	0.4	3.4	35.1
Indian Forest Service								
Frequency N	11	4	4	9	4	28	42	102
% within rank	16.2	14.8	16	29	23.5	71.8	68.9	
% in the service	10.8	3.9	3.9	8.8	3.9	27.5	41.2	
% of total A.I.S.	4.1	1.5	1.5	3.4	1.5	10.4	15.7	38.1
Total N	68	27	25	31	17	39	61	268
% of Total	25.4	10.1	9.3	11.6	6.3	14.6	22.8	

25.45% of the All India Services Officers like to yield under political pressure to manage it and consider it the best approach. 41.5% of the Indian Police Service officers have chosen to succumb under political pressure as the best approach to manage the conflict as 1st rank. 25% of the Indian Administrative Service officers have ranked it at 1st priority in conflict management to oblige politicians, whenever there is political pressure in the decision-making process. 41.2% of the Indian Forest Service officers have ranked it at 7th priority to oblige politicians in the decision-making process. Among the All India Services, the Indian Forest Service officers have shown the lowest priority for the politician in case of conflicting situations, and the Indian Police Service officers have shown the highest concern.

10.3.2. Withdrawal

The All India Services Officers may nurture a desire to withdraw and ignore the conflict. Officers think that in case they avoid potential pressure conflict best approach is to disappear in oblivion. Out of sight is out of mind. The All India Services Officers may avoid the pressure conflict but they may be willing to discuss it with the politicians. Such withdrawals they use as situational in case pressure conflict repercussions seriously affect the career, the All India Services Officers snap relations with the politicians. Transfer and postings are the widely used tools for withdrawing from pressure conflict.

Exhibit Number 10.5: All India Services Officers Withdraw from Situation and Do Nothing

Name of Service	Rank of the Approach Adopted to Manage Conflict							Total
	1st	2nd	3rd	4th	5th	6th	7th	
Indian Admn. Service								
Frequency N	1	8	21	12	22	3	5	72
% within rank	6.7	20.5	35.6	33.3	28.9	15	23.8	
% in the service	1.4	11.1	29.2	16.7	30.6	4.2	6.9	
% of total A.I.S.	0.4	3	7.9	4.5	8.3	1.1	1.9	27.1
Indian Police Service								
Frequency N	11	18	27	15	11	2	9	93
% within rank	73.3	46.2	45.8	41.7	14.5	10	42.9	
% in the service	11.8	19.4	29	16.1	11.8	2.2	9.7	
% of total A.I.S.	4.1	6.8	10.2	5.6	4.1	0.8	3.4	35
Indian Forest Service								
Frequency N	3	13	11	9	43	15	7	101
% within rank	20	33.3	18.6	25	56.6	75	33.3	
% in the service	3	12.9	10.9	8.9	42.6	14.9	6.9	
% of total A.I.S.	1.1	4.9	4.1	3.4	16.2	5.6	2.6	38
Total N	15	39	59	36	76	20	21	266
% of Total	5.6	14.7	22.2	13.5	28.6	7.5	7.9	100

These analyses show that 28.6% of the All India Services Officers have ranked running from the scene as 5th rank. 42.6% of the Indian Forest Service officers and 30.6% of the Indian Administrative Service officers like to disappear from the situation in case of conflict and assigned it 5th rank. 29% of the Indian Police Service officers have assigned it 3rd rank and in case of conflict withdraw from the situation. Pearson Chi-square results are highly significant with 0.000, level of significance and strength of correlations is supported by Rho values.

10.3.3. Resignation

Officers like to avoid conflict as they find themselves in a helpless situation. They find that political pressure is unreasonable to accept. On occasions the All India Services Officers turn hostile to political pressure; service group rarely extend them desired help. Some offices feel it is more comfortable to ignore the mounting pressure. Officers think that in due course of time pressure problems will be solved or he will be transferred out, the next incumbent will solve the problem.

24.4% of the All India Services Officers have ranked at 1st rank that problem gets resolved in due course of time, they need to do nothing. 44.4% of the Indian Administrative Service officers do not like to intervene in the conflicting situation and believe that issue will be resolved in due course of time. Time is the best healer; the Indian Administrative Service officers leave things at the mercy of time. 25.3% of the Indian Police Service officers have ranked it at 3rd and think that in due course of time problems will be solved. 28.2% of the Indian Forest Service officers have ranked it 4th rank. Among the All India Services, Indian Administrative Service officers are the highest believer in expecting solutions at the mercy of time and system. They do not like to take any kind of tension by trying to find out a solution for the conflict in the decision-making process, whenever there is political pressure. Pearson Chi-square analysis good relationships and results are highly significant.

Exhibit Number 10.6: AISO Think in Due Course of Time Issue will be Resolved

Name of Service	Rank of the Approach Adopted to Manage Conflict							Total
	1st	2nd	3rd	4th	5th	6th	7th	
Indian Admn. Service								
Frequency N	32	4	8	10	5	13	0	72
% in the service	44.4	5.6	11.1	13.9	6.9	18.1	0	
% of total A.I.S.	11.9	1.5	3	3.7	1.9	4.8	0	26.7
Indian Police Service								
Frequency N	16	14	24	13	6	18	4	95
% in the service	16.8	14.7	25.3	13.7	6.3	18.9	4.2	
% of total A.I.S.	5.9	5.2	8.9	4.8	2.2	6.7	1.5	35.2
Indian Forest Service								
Frequency N	18	10	24	29	11	8	3	103
% in the service	17.5	9.7	23.3	28.2	10.7	7.8	2.9	
% of total A.I.S.	6.7	3.7	8.9	10.7	4.1	3	1.1	38.1
Total N	66	28	56	52	22	39	7	270
% AIS Total	24.4	10.4	20.7	19.3	8.1	14.4	2.6	100

10.3.4. Confrontation

The All India Services Officers try to satisfy their own goals/interests regardless of the politicians' goals. The All India Services Officers like to obey rules, regulations, and law; politicians want to meet their goals and targets suitable for their needs. In such situations, both parties perceive the other side as unreasonable, both sides like to see decisions in their favor, this gives rise to confrontation. The All India Services Officers and politicians attack each other and protect and enhance their own position. In a confrontation, situation politicians use coercion from high-ranking politicians or chief ministers or mobilize public pressure on the All India Services Officers. In such situations, the All India Services Officers and politicians keep a close watch on each other to harass each other in fault finding a way to get the upper hand or commanding position. The All India Services Officers and politicians feel fail to maintain power, which may lead to hostilities. Confrontations bring higher role clarity with improved problem-solving skills. Confrontation improves the All India Services Officers willingness to deal with difficult situations and problem creating employees. The All India Services Officers provide better team leadership in such conflict situations.

Exhibit Number 10.7: All India Services Officers Fight their Way out to Implement it

Name of Service	Rank of the Approach Adopted to Manage Conflict							Total
	1st	2nd	3rd	4th	5th	6th	7th	
Indian Admn. Service								
Frequency N	7	2	1	9	5	19	30	73
% in the service	9.6	2.7	1.4	12.3	6.8	26	41.1	
% of total A.I.S.	2.6	0.7	0.4	3.3	1.8	7	11.1	26.9
Indian Police Service								
Frequency N	14	2	5	10	10	18	36	95
% in the service	14.7	2.1	5.3	10.5	10.5	18.9	37.9	
% of total A.I.S.	5.2	0.7	1.8	3.7	3.7	6.6	13.3	35.1
Indian Forest Service								
Frequency N	33	9	14	20	6	8	13	103
% in the service	32	8.7	13.6	19.4	5.8	7.8	12.6	
% of total A.I.S.	12.2	3.3	5.2	7.4	2.2	3	4.8	38
Total N	54	13	20	39	21	45	79	271
% AIS Total	19.9	4.8	7.4	14.4	7.7	16.6	29.1	100

29.1% of the All India Services Officers have assigned will to fight out with political pressure in case of conflict at 7th and last rank. 41.1% of the Indian Administrative Service officers and 37.9% of the Indian Police Service officers have ranked this at 7th and last rank, so they do not like to fight out with the politician in case of any conflict. However, 32% of the Indian Forest Service officers have expressed their will at 1st rank to fight out with politicians in case of conflict in the decision. Among the All India Services, the Indian Forest Service officers have shown the highest determination to fight out in case of conflict and the Indian Administrative Service officers show the lowest concern to put any resistance to politicians. Our analyses regarding adopting the confrontation approach, in case of conflict are highly significant under Pearson Chi-square results. There is a good correlation and results are highly significant with a 0.000 level of significance. Rho and R (0.4) values establish the strength of correlation with 0.000, level of significance.

10.3.5. Arbitration

Exhibit Number 10.8: AISO may Take Help from Friends/Seniors to Solve it

Name of Service	Rank of the Approach Adopted to Manage Conflict							Total
	1st	2nd	3rd	4th	5th	6th	7th	
Indian Admn. Service								
Frequency N	2	20	10	9	0	15	17	73
% in the service	2.7	27.4	13.7	12.3	0	20.5	23.3	
% of total A.I.S.	0.7	7.5	3.7	3.4	0	5.6	6.4	27.3
Indian Police Service								
Frequency N	6	15	12	15	7	15	22	92
% in the service	6.5	16.3	13	16.3	7.6	16.3	23.9	
% of total A.I.S.	2.2	5.6	4.5	5.6	2.6	5.6	8.2	34.5
Indian Forest Service								
Frequency N	23	40	16	9	4	5	5	102
% in the service	22.5	39.2	15.7	8.8	3.9	4.9	4.9	
% of total A.I.S.	8.6	15	6	3.4	1.5	1.9	1.9	38.2
Total N	31	75	38	33	11	35	44	267
% AIS Total	11.6	28.1	14.2	12.4	4.1	13.1	16.5	100

Political pressure is such that the All India Services Officers are unable to meet it. In some cases, politicians adopt a harsh approach and mobilize full pressure to get things done in their favor. The All India Services Officers feel that they are unable to do that, in such situations third party steps in for arbitration for a solution acceptable to both groups. Third party should consider a positive attitude for open disagreement, feelings of both sides and maintain a balance of power. Third party use excellent communication skills, continuous follow-up, and build confidence on the sound previous record of accomplishment. In most of the cases, the All India Services Officers have to pay the price of arbitration. Future inquiries and harassment are endless throughout one's career in lieu of such arbitration.

28.1% of the All India Services Officers have ranked it 2nd to take help from seniors and friends in event of conflicting situations in the decision. 39.2% of the Indian Forest Service officers and 27.4% of the Indian Administrative Service officers have ranked it 2nd and like taking help from seniors and friends under conflict. But 23.9% of the Indian Police Service officers have ranked it 7th and last rank; they give last preference to seek help from outside. Pearson Chi-square results show good relationships with 0.000, level of significance. R and Rho values (0.4) at 0.000, level of significance have established the strength of these correlations.

10.3.6. Compromise

In a compromise, the All India Services Officers satisfy concern for all parties; each side is willing to give up. This is a mutually beneficial, win-win situation. In certain situations, politicians are sober and sophisticated they behave reasonably. Then the All India Services Officers feel that compromise is the better option. When a politician is powerful, the All India Services Officers feel that by sharing gains, both will stand benefited. Politicians and the All India Services Officers compromise and bargain over benefits for mutual gains. Decision conflict remained unresolved in such situations.

Exhibit Number 10.9: All India Services Officers may Find Mutually Acceptable Solution with Politician

Name of Service	Rank of the Approach Adopted to Manage Conflict							Total
	1st	2nd	3rd	4th	5th	6th	7th	
Indian Admn. Service								
Frequency N	9	13	18	19	10	4	0	73
% in the service	12.3	17.8	24.7	26	13.7	5.5	0	
% of total A.I.S.	3.4	4.9	6.7	7.1	3.7	1.5	0	27.2
Indian Police Service								
Frequency N	13	13	12	18	16	13	7	92
% in the service	14.1	14.1	13	19.6	17.4	14.1	7.6	
% of total A.I.S.	4.9	4.9	4.5	6.7	6	4.9	2.6	34.3
Indian Forest Service								
Frequency N	18	19	28	15	14	9	0	103
% in the service	17.5	18.4	27.2	14.6	13.6	8.7	0	
% of total A.I.S.	6.7	7.1	10.4	5.6	5.2	3.4	0	38.4
Total N	40	45	58	52	40	26	7	268
% AIS Total	14.9	16.8	21.6	19.4	14.9	9.7	2.6	100

21.6% of the All India Services Officers have ranked it 3rd in management approach. 27.2% of the Indian Forest Service officers have ranked it 3rd. 26% of the Indian Administrative Service officers and 19.6% of the Indian Police Service officers have ranked mutually acceptable solutions at 4th rank. This indicates that the All India Services Officers do not assign high importance to compromise; either they deliver decision as desired by a politician or according to own whims and fancies.

10.3.7. Appeasement

The All India Services Officers consider that politicians' interests are above their own and system interests, in this bargaining process officers, they sacrifice their own interests. The All India

Services Officers find political pressure in a decision is embarrassing and highly disturbing, and then they look for temporary relief measures. They give a small concession to arrange temporary peace with the politicians. When they think, they can postpone conflicts by giving small concessions to political pressure. In practical situations, it rarely happens that politicians get satisfied, rather politicians think that the All India Services Officers are week and they will continue to submit under their will. The process of appeasement takes the shape of never-ending demands.

19.9% of the All India Services Officers have ranked appeasement approach to 5th rank in conflict management. 39% of the Indian Forest Service officers have ranked 7th and last approach to give concessions to politicians in the decision-making process under conflict. 31.5% of the Indian Administrative Service officers ranked giving concessions to politicians at 5th rank. 19.6% of the Indian Police Service officers think it worth 4th rank, with close ranks of 18.5% at 2nd rank. Dispersion of data indicates that the Indian Police Service officers believe in giving concessions to politicians in case of conflict. Pearson Chi-square results are highly significant with a significance level of 0.000. Correlation values for R and Rho also indicate good correlation ships with the decision-making process.

Exhibit Number 10.10: All India Services Officers may Give Concession to the Politician

Name of Service	Rank of the Approach Adopted to Manage Conflict							Total
	1st	2nd	3rd	4th	5th	6th	7th	
Indian Admn. Service								
Frequency N	4	12	11	8	23	5	10	73
% in the service	5.5	16.4	15.1	11	31.5	6.8	13.7	
% of total A.I.S.	1.5	4.5	4.1	3	8.6	1.9	3.7	27.3
Indian Police Service								
Frequency N	17	16	6	18	17	14	4	92
% in the service	18.5	17.4	6.5	19.6	18.5	15.2	4.3	
% of total A.I.S.	6.4	6	2.2	6.7	6.4	5.2	1.5	34.5
Indian Forest Service								
Frequency N	4	6	5	11	13	24	39	102
% in the service	3.9	5.9	4.9	10.8	12.7	23.5	38	
% of total A.I.S.	1.5	2.2	1.8	4.1	4.9	9	14.9	38.2
Total N	25	34	20	37	53	43	51	267
% AIS Total	9.4	12.7	8.2	13.9	19.9	16.1	19	100

ANNEXURE 10.A: QUESTIONNAIRE ON AISO CONFLICT MANAGEMENT

Political pressure exerted on the decision-making process generates conflicts in the bureaucratic system. All India Services Officers may adopt a situational approach for conflict management. Please, **rank** below mentioned **seven** approaches in terms of preferences in conflict management. Kindly, rank 1 as the best approach and 7 as the last approach.

(a) Officers may succumb under pressure. ☐
(b) Officers may withdraw from the situation & do nothing. ☐
(c) Officers think, in due course of time issue will be resolved. ☐
(d) Officers may fight out their way out to implement it. ☐
(e) Officers may take the help of friends/seniors to solve it. ☐
(f) Officer may find a mutually acceptable solution with a politician. ☐
(g) Officers may give concessions to the politician. ☐

The knower, knowledge, and object of knowledge—these three motivate actions. Even so, the doer, the organs, and activity—these are three ingredients of action. *The Bhagavad Gita* 18.18

The world will not be destroyed by those who do evil, but by those who watch them without doing anything.—Albert Einstein

What people fail to appreciate is that the currency of corruption in elective office is, not money, but votes.—James L. Buckley

Part–Four System-Related Variables: Dynamics of Political Pressure in Decision

In this part, various dimensions, forms, modes, areas, sources of political pressure, cultural and work environment have been studied with reference to the decision-making process by the All India Services Officers. Why the All India Services Officers accept the political pressure? Reasons or causes for acceptance of political pressure in the decision-making process by the All India Services Officers have been studied.

Unit 11

Major Sources of Political Pressure in Decision

"He who sees inaction in action, and action in inaction, he is wise among men, who have performed all actions." *The Bhagavad Gita* 4.18

"Political leadership has behaved in an irresponsible manner having no other act except garner all sorts of votes by hook or crook." K. Seshadri (1994)

"Government is a trust and the officers of the government are trustees, and both the trust and the trustees are created for the benefit of the people."—Henry Clay

- *Sources of Pressure and Impact on Decision*
- *Factors Influencing Sources of Pressure*
- *Political Pressure Management*
- *The Methodology Adopted for Handling Pressure*
- *Types of Political Pressure Management*
- *Process of Pressure Management*
- *Research Analyses Result for Pressure Sources*
- *CMs, Ministers, MP, MLA, District-level Politicians*
- *Block-level Politicians, Village-level Workers*
- *Power Brokers, Communication media*
- *Hidden Financiers*

The politician's apex positions invariably influence the decision process and behavior of the All India Services Officers to serve political goals. Starting from village level to Prime Minister level, different sources of pressure and their impact on decisions have been studied in this unit. Various factors related to an individual politician, related to the individual officer, and related to the bureaucratic system affecting decision have been explained. Political pressure management techniques and approaches have been explained here. Process of pressure management has been explained with diagrams in this unit.

11.1. Sources of Pressure and Impact on Decision

Groups are accepted as an integral part of public administration. Different factors enhance and accelerate the process of fusion of self-interests, such as government policy, a political party in power, administration approach, rules and regulations, hierarchy in government, ambiguity in procedures, lack of transparency, biased selection procedure, subjective rewards system operating in public administration in India. Politicians at the top, performance evaluation, people misconceived perceptions, flexible norms, status inequalities, individual task or goal-oriented approach, the cohesiveness of the All India Services influences the expectations from the decision. The All India Services Officers convert their power into action; politicians use their political acumen, skills, and abilities to use powerbases effectively to their own advantage.

The politicians occupy the position from where he can influence the decision process and behavior of the All India Services Officers to serve their own political goals. By location and constitutional authority, politicians continue efforts to influence the distribution of rewards, advantages, and disadvantages according to their own needs in public administration. The All India Services Officers behavior is own goals oriented, politician is aware of this fact and maximizes political efforts to influence the goals, criteria, rules, procedures, and process of decision-making.

The politicians' location is supreme in public administration. Politicians have connections and rapport with the masses at the lowest level and control over bureaucrats from the top, which is a unique power in itself. The politician has access to confidential information, which he can use for spreading rumors against the individual All India Services Officer, particularly while in opposition, the same politician indulges in whistleblowing and approach media to misguide the public. While in power same politician busy exchanging favors, maximization of personal benefits, lobbying for alternative decisions to own advantage, and misuse of position and power for personal gains. Make hay while sunshine's, mudslinging, when out of power is commonly adopted approach.

The All India Services Officers experience that for politicians, everything is legitimate and his words carry weight. Politicians can resort to any method to exert pressure and intensify it until targets are achieved. Politicians engage in false complaints to the top bosses, form coalition with top bosses, develop syndicate with a group of politician or ministers, bypass chain of command, obstruct departmental policies, inaction in law, delay in the decision, excessive adherence to a particular rule/law, use different jugglery tricks to mobilize pressure to get things done. The illegitimate behavior of the politician is the real risk for public administration. However, the politician is the constitutional head and the executive is to implement policy/law for public administration under them.

The politicians and bureaucrats have to co-exist with each other in prevailing circumstances. If politicians are essentially required nuisance, then the All India Services Officers are the compulsive exploiters for the system (parasitic behavior). Resources are limited, everyone desires to maximize resources for self-gains, and this generates conflict for self-goals. Such perception of self-goals fulfillment intensifies competition for scarce resources, which improve in the direction of dominant pressure (Figure 11.1). Various sources of pressure on policy framework at various levels and influence allocation, delivery vehicle, and distribution of resources from government administration.

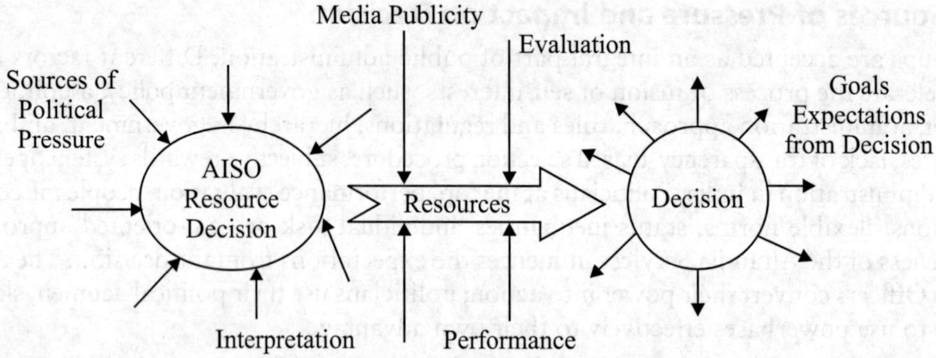

Figure No. 11.1: Resources and the AISO in Decision Process

Vested groups try to gain a position in allocation, delivery, distribution, performance, evaluation, assessment, and publicity work. Association or access to information in public administration is misinterpreted, misused, misdirected to maximize own goals by every individual in the process. This accumulates and compiles an unaccountable amount of pressure on the decision. Political sources play a crucial role in influencing the outcomes of any decision taken by the All India Services Officers. Numerous sources and factors are operating on the bureaucratic system at any given time. Those trying to influence the process of exertion and acceptance of political pressure by the All India Services Officers. These factors related to system and individuals can be classified into the following groups.

11.2. Factors Influencing the Sources of Pressure

11.2.1. Factors Pertaining to Individual Politician

11.2.1.1. High Power Orientation: The politician with a high power orientation will mobilize all his sources and intensify pressure with the highest intensity to get things done in the decision-making process, according to own interests.

11.2.1.2. Leadership Approach: An outlook of the political party in power, composition of ruling party, and approach of its top leadership towards pressure and decision-making process influence the intensity and extent of exertion of political pressure from various sources. The well-seasoned leader with a sound political base will behave in a sober way; political pressure exerted by them can be managed with the right kind of acumen. Highly organized political parties with disciplined cadres do not allow every source to exert pressure at every level. In case of top leadership support workers then they indulge in misbehavior.

11.2.1.3. Political Party Recurrence of Power: Ruling political party perception about power, party power occupancy time and recurrence of power by that party influence the exertion of political pressure through various sources in the decision-making process. Any political party coming to power the first time or party with two-thirds majorities and for short time with uncertainty will exert a higher and crude type of political pressure. Make hay while the sun shines ("*Loot Sako utna loot lo*"), ranks, and files (different sources) will exert political pressure independently in the decision-making process to get maximum out of it.

11.2.1.4. Politician Position in Party: Politicians exerting political pressure will intensify efforts for acceptance of pressure according to their political background, relations with the top leadership, and position in the political party hierarchy. The All India Services Officers have to assess the pressure source position and stature with respect to the ruling party.

11.2.1.5. Politician Relations with the Public: Any source of political pressure exerting pressure on the All India Services Officers, intensity and extent of pressure mobilized will be related to the politician relations with the public and their expectations from him. A politician with lesser relations with the public will mobilize lesser pressure on the decision-making process. The closeness of the politicians with the public increases their expectations and the public force politicians to mobilize pressure with higher intensity.

11.2.1.6. Expectation for Success: When politicians expect higher chances of success from the All India Services Officers, chances, and frequency of political pressure will be higher on such officers. Chances of success motivate to exert pressure and scope for failures reduces the chances of political pressure in the decision-making process.

11.2.1.7. High Self-Esteem: Politicians with high self-esteem exert political pressure in a calculated manner and calculated places only. Politicians with low self-esteem can approach any level of bureaucracy at any time irrespective of chances of success. Politicians with high self-esteem like to avoid unknown officers and places for exerting political pressure.

11.2.1.8. Personality Traits: Individual politician personality regulates the extent and method of pressure exertion on the All India Services Officers. Personality traits will influence individual politician behavior the way he will cope with public demand and analyze the rationality of every issue in the decision-making process. Some remotely located politicians do not care much about the public.

11.2.1.9. Locus of Control: Politicians with high internality locus of control will exert higher political pressure in a more rational manner. Politicians with a locus of control for externality for others will not exert political pressure with high intensity. Politicians with externality for luck will like to watch things happen.

11.2.1.10. Biographical Characters: Political pressure exerted by any politician or any other source will be regulated by one's biographical characters as a level of education, family background, personal experience in a political party, area/region politician representing and extent of his constituency, etc. Individual biographical characters invariably influence the extent and type of pressure.

11.2.1.11. Politician Knowledge Level: Politician's extent of exposure regarding the working of the bureaucratic system, operational rules and regulations, and procedure will also determine the pressure behavior of the politicians.

11.2.1.12. Politician Financial Status: Some of the rich politicians do not bother much about public demands and remain busy in the maximization of their own resources. Issues related to their wealth maximization they exert maximum pressure and get lesser time for the public and keep a safe distance (self aura) from masses. Bureaucrats expect lesser pressure from such highly arrogant politicians.

11.2.1.13. Politician Social Background: Politicians' social background and vis-à-vis voter social composition in the area are invariably related to the pressure behavior of the leader. On occasions, politicians try to get a posting of the AISO of the dominant social groups of voters or own social background. Politicians of high immorality will try to officer with immoral behavior, so that; both can be in a win-win situation.

11.2.1.14. Capacity to Understand Bureaucratic System: Experienced politicians or those politicians who understand the bureaucratic system know which level of bureaucracy, or who are the bureaucrats, who will readily accept the pressure. Politicians collect full information regarding the concerned officer, and then only decide regarding the extent of pressure to be exerted. Such politicians get things done with lesser efforts. They do not waste their energy with officers who are known for their adherence to rules.

11.2.1.15. Time and Location of Politicians: Politicians work very intelligently, gather full information from the public, assess their own location and position, and select the best time or target for their works to be done. In case a politician is very close to the top brasses of the political party they use top brasses of a party to exert pressure for getting their things done.

11.2.1.16. Politicians Relation and Equation with Bureaucracy: Some politicians cultivate excellent relations with bureaucrats and use such relations for getting things done in their favor. Both sides help each other, win-win situation for both politicians and bureaucrats. Politicians' equations with bureaucrats determine pressure extent, style, and pressure areas.

11.2.1.17. Standards of Politician Lifestyle: What standards are maintained by the politician in his daily life, that also determine one's influence over bureaucracy and in turn the extent of pressure one can exert in the decision. Moreover, its expectancy level of acceptance by bureaucrats.

11.2.1.18. Self-Discipline of the Politicians: Self-discipline maintained by the politicians cultivate some aura around that leader in the area, and that aura feedback reaches to bureaucrats and public both, which in turn decide the extent and level of pressure to be exerted and accepted by the officers.

11.2.1.19. Conduct of Politicians: How are the conduct of the politician with the bureaucracy and public both that will invariably decide the extent and outcome of pressure used by any politicians?

11.2.2. Factors Related to Individual All India Services Officer

Different sources of political pressure and its endeavor are related to the individual All India Services Officer decision-making process. In case it is evidently recognized that such and such AISO will not accept or will not appreciate the pressure, most sources of pressure will not try to approach such officer. Any officer who is easily amenable to political pressure will invite political pressure from any source at any location with any extent and any time. Sources of political pressure exerting on the individual officer will be in proportion to diverse behavioral factors operating on an individual officer at any given time.

11.2.2.1. High Achievement of Goals: The All India Services Officers with high self-goal orientation will show more chances towards acceptance of political pressure. Accordingly, sources of pressure will mobilize political pressure on him. The All India Services Officers with lesser or no self-goals will discourage different sources to exert political pressure on him.

11.2.2.2. High Power Need: The All India Services Officers with high power needs will invite a higher extent of political pressure to maintain their position in power. Politicians aware of this power need of individual officers will exert frequent and unpredictable pressure on such officers. Individual officers with lower power needs can ignore the pressure and various sources are discouraged to approach him.

11.2.2.3. Locus of Control: Individual officers with high internality are high achievers and show higher self-confidence to handle political pressure. The feelings of achievement take such officers to different sources of pressure and likely to accept political pressure under the feeling of goal achievement. But such officers are selective in approach. Individual officers with high externality accept political pressure easily and different sources of pressure will exert more pressure on such officers.

11.2.2.4. Perceived Decision Alternatives: In the decision-making process, individual All India Services Officers perceive different decision alternatives according to personal background, such perceptions about the outcomes lead to acceptance of political pressure from various sources. Perceptions about the source of political pressure and its relation with decision outcome also motivate for recognizing such sources validity and acceptance.

11.2.2.5. Career Advancement: Individual All India Services Officer desires for career advancement induce him towards recognizing the utility of the type of pressure sources for his own career advancement. When an individual officer finds the personal utility of such a source, he readily accepts the political pressure in the decision-making process.

11.2.2.6. Self-Monitors: Inside every person, self-monitors continuously monitor and evaluate the decision options. Such self-monitors in individual officers recognize pressure sources and reflect fairness in acceptance of it according to relation with an individual approach, outlook, and thinking pattern. Values, beliefs, and ethos of an individual influence self-monitor.

11.2.2.7. Self-Serving Interests: Individual officer self-serving interests and goals dominate in analyzing the source of political pressure in the decision-making process. If such sources of pressure serve self-interests, the individual officer will accept the political pressure.

11.2.2.8. Resource Control Power: Individual All India Services Officers are highly control power-oriented, everyone likes to enjoy control over the government resources. Resource control is a great power enhancer, feeling for power motivates them to accept the various sources of political pressure in the decision-making process.

11.2.2.9. Resource Allocation and Use: Resource allocation powers enhance the status of an individual officer. In a bureaucratic system stiff competition for resource allocation and its use, such resource attachment leads individual officers to accept sources of political pressure in the decision-making process.

11.2.2.10. Demographical Characters: Individual All India Services Officers will recognize the different sources of political pressure in the decision-making process according to individual demographical characters. Variety of such characters described in Unit 3, influence the reorganization of sources of political pressure.

11.2.2.11. Individual Political Connections: Individual AISO political awareness and connections invariably influence and determine the extent and nature of pressure acceptance in the decision process. Officers with close relations with politicians will invite recurrent pressure from politicians in day-to-day affairs.

11.2.2.12. Attitudes and Perceptions: Psychological disposition and ingrained personality determine the extent and level of acceptance of pressure in the decision-making process. Officers with strong honesty perceptions, beliefs in values, and ethics invariably avoid acceptance of political pressure.

11.2.2.13. Self-Controls/Regulations: Individual discipline and adherence to rules and regulation orientation influence the pressure acceptance or preferences in the assessment of pressure in the decision process. Highly disciplined and persons with high self-control orientation tends to avoid or reject pressure in the decision.

11.2.2.14. Self-Esteem: Persons with high self-esteem demonstrate a lesser inclination towards acceptance of pressure. Self-esteem encompasses beliefs about oneself or emotional states, such officers try not to accept pressure.

11.2.2.15. Post and Position Hold: Position and post held by any AISO invariably determine the extent and quantum of pressure acceptance. In the bureaucracy, some positions are such that where chances of pressure are minimal and some positions with high public dealings invite the highest level of public pressure. For the AISO pressure is directly related to the position and post held by the individual officer.

11.2.2.16. Personality Traits: Personality traits like introversion/extroversion, openness, conscientiousness, agreeableness, social intelligence, and neuroticism invariably determine the approach towards pressure handling in any decision.

11.2.2.17. Interpersonal Relationships in Hierarchy: Interpersonal relationships of any officer in the hierarchy are directly related to any officer's pressure handling behavior. The officer with close and direct relation with higher levels of hierarchy feels comfortable in handling pressure in the decision, whereas officers not having good relation with high up in hierarchy will hesitate to handle pressure and invariably see pressure with doubts.

11.2.2.18. Need Orientation: Time tested message of the Upanishads to remove need orientation for peaceful living. Any officer having high needs and need orientation is bound to accept pressure irrespective of its illegality or legality status. Need orientation is the basic and fundamental in pressure acceptability behavior and make officers vulnerable to external temptations.

11.2.2.19. Status Consciousness: Status consciousness is a fundamental and essential part of these elite services. Status consciousness works in both ways to repel or invite pressure, depending on the extent of such consciousness and other ingredients of the personality of any individual officer. Officers' aspiration to maintain status may repel pressure and in some cases, officers accept pressure to maintain status also.

11.2.3. Bureaucratic System-Related Factors

Not only politicians and political parties, but the bureaucratic system itself is also the greatest attracter of the sources of pressure to invite pressure in the decision-making process. Individuals come and go; it is a bureaucratic system, which sustains the survival of the decision. The capability and capacity of any source to exert pressure is invariably related to the system, from permeable bureaucratic system boundaries they like to extract benefits.

11.2.3.1. Departmental Culture: Prevalent culture of any government department influences the attitudes and approach of pressure sources and pressure accepter. The extent of political pressure exerted and the type of pressure source approaching the All India Services Officers will be according to the dominant departmental culture of that workplace.

11.2.3.2. Powers to Allocate Resources: In bureaucratic system, persons with the highest powers in resource allocation will invite the highest political pressure and types of sources of pressure will be related to the location of resource allocators' in the hierarchy. Resource demands motivate different sources to mobilize pressure to maximize resource allocation for self.

11.2.3.3. Control over Promotions, Punishment, and Rewards: In a bureaucratic system, person who controls the promotions, punishments, and rewards distributions will get higher political pressure. The type of sources exerting pressure will be according to the controller located in the hierarchy.

11.2.3.4. Transfer, Posting, and Recruitment: In a bureaucratic system, officers according to one's position enjoy powers for transfer, posting, and recruitment. Different sources of political pressure approach appropriate level officers for such works. The higher the flexibility in such aspects, the more sources will exert higher political pressure in the decision-making process.

11.2.3.5. Policy, Rules, Regulations, and Law-Framing: The All India Services Officers exercise control over policy, rules, regulations, and law formulation process, accordingly different sources of pressure exert political pressure to protect their own interests in this process. The extent of pressure exerted and the type of source approaching the All India Services Officers will be related to an officer position in this procedure.

11.2.3.6. Control over Performance Review: In a bureaucratic system, whosoever exercises control over the performance review, will get pressure and enjoy the position of prominence. The All India Services Officers will listen to such a control mechanism.

11.2.3.7. Grievance Redressing Mechanism: The process of delivery of services is full of ifs and buts. Any process of delivery is bound to cause grievances; in a bureaucratic system, politicians have such power to redress the grievances of the public and affected party. The All India Services Officers are liable to listen to such authority in that system to save themselves from the onslaught of the grievances. Accordingly, various sources exert political pressure in the decision-making process.

11.2.3.8. Supremacy in System: Whomsoever exercise control and enjoy the supremacy in the bureaucratic system will have the power to influence the decision outcomes. Politicians' supremacy position in the bureaucratic system provides him power and authority to exert political pressure in the decision-making process.

11.2.3.9. Low Trust: Prevalent low trust among the All India Services Officers in the bureaucratic system, provide opportunities to different sources of pressure to exert political pressure in the decision-making process. Higher trust in fairness, justice, and equity from the bureaucratic system will reduce the chances of pressure. Everyone can hope to get ones due in course of time, why to run here and there. It is low trust in the bureaucratic system, which increases the chances for pressure in the decision-making process.

11.2.3.10. Self-Monitoring Powers: Politicians with a strong desire for power engage their self-monitoring desires; exert higher political pressure in the decision-making process. The All India Services Officers' locus of control to enjoy more power accept that political pressure easily with a high internal locus of control, desire for maintaining power motivate them to accept political pressure. Among All India Services, the Indian Administrative Service officers show a higher level of sensitivity to social control desire to manipulate situations in their favor compel them to approach political pressure, invite it to fulfill the desire for power and self-interest. The All India Services Officers perceive investment in political pressure as a mechanism to fulfill goals, expectations, and an alternative to success in career.

11.2.3.11. Bureaucratic System Expectations: Higher-level All India Services Officers have higher expectations from the public administration; higher is the acceptability to pressure by them. Increases in service or individual benefit in the future motivate the All India Services Officers to invite political pressure. Under the cover of self-interests, the All India Services Officers find unable to differentiate between what is legitimate and illegitimate political pressure. Continuous handlings of political pressure polish the skills of the All India Services Officers in how to exploit political pressure to own advantage under camouflage.

11.2.3.12. System Demands: Bureaucratic system itself promotes cultivate sustenance of political pressure. Increasing the population enhances the public demand for the decision-making process, this induces stiff competition and decrease the opportunities for attaining the goals and fulfilling needs. High demands reduce the trust among resource providers and resource users. At the same time, the All India Services Officers frequent dislocation, reduction in prize postings, uncontrolled and unregulated growth of the All India Services induce competition for rewards.

11.2.3.13. Ambiguity: Prevalent ambiguity in the decision-making process or role ambiguities induce officers to accept pressure. The All India Services Officers are not clear about their role, mistrust among colleagues, ambiguity in the decision process, flexible performance review system, long distribution of decision-making process, lack of accountability, lack of transparency, only financial achievements, no system of systematic evaluation of decision, flexible and ever-changing parameter, self-serving seniors, high political pressure on decision, pubic demand, huge chain of command dilution of the responsibility, no parameter for the decision, a threat to position, fear of losing power, status consciousness, high level of ego/arrogance, lack of devotion to duty and prevalent immoral behavior induce individual All India Services Officers to accept political pressure.

11.2.3.14. Decreasing Trust: Increasing politicizing of the bureaucracy has stimulated conflict and uncertainty in the system. Limited opportunities for career advancement and promotion are highly prevalent among the Indian Forest Service, which positively influence the decision-making process in favor of political pressure. Decreasing trust among the All India Services and among individuals of that service has inhibited the illegitimate actions for the political pressure. The All India Services members want to grab maximum positions for them.

11.2.3.15. Lateral Movement: Lateral movement has harmed the Indian bureaucracy to the greatest extent. This has blocked all the chances of advancement to technocrats and other officers, which accumulate frustration and powerlessness. Among the All India Services, the Indian Police Service and the Indian Forest Service officers feel that they also should get lateral positions. So, every service member runs after politicians to grab more chances/postings for self-service. The bureaucratic performance review system is subjective and encourages individuals engaged in flattery and submissiveness to power. Monopolization of whole power by the Indian Administrative Service has induced a stiff race for political favors to retain power.

11.2.3.16. Service Exclusiveness: Continuously, other service officers are losing faith in the Indian Administrative Service is the top boss and approach politicians for redressing their problems, which initiate political pressure. The bureaucratic system has surrogated inputs from groups lateral services, subordinated in the decision. Unilateral decision practice has damaged the system heavily, eroded the faith from the bureaucratic system, and shifted faith in the individual. Powerful officers meet the self-servicing goals by explaining political serving behavior at the cost of public welfare. Those who are located in a position of power can explain and convince the top politician that unfair and unjust goals are fair and just in the interests of the public. The All India Services Officers with immoral behavior can justify and articulate their unethical practices most successfully. A strong power base serves as a covering shield to corrupt and change the direction of investigation and doubts towards powerless and innocent officers.

11.2.3.17. Devoid of Transparency: Lack of transparency in the bureaucratic system decision-making process creates space for ambiguity. Excessive secrecy in the system creates distance from the public and clarity in the outcome of the decision. The system itself is responsible for inviting pressure in the decision.

11.2.3.18. Negligence of Equity and Objectivity: Bureaucratic system is devoid of equity and objectivity, which in turn creates space for political pressure. No one is held responsible for any lapses in the bureaucratic system which sustains and supports invasive political pressure in the decision.

11.2.3.19. Hierarchical Structures: Hierarchical structures or different layers in the bureaucratic system make it difficult for held any one level accountable for any decision taken by the system. From the state secretariat at the top level down to the subdivision level, no one knows who is responsible for failures. No one is responsible for anything in hierarchical levels.

11.3. Political Pressure Management

Political pressure from various sources is being exerted on the lowest, village-level government functionaries to the highest level at Chief Secretary/Cabinet Secretary. Government functionaries at all levels bargaining with the political pressure are related to the individual and system factors. A multi-pronged process of bargaining may be laterally and vertically within the department, across the departmental channels with the public, and with the known/unknown third-party interventions. Political pressure management is the process, where two or more parties attempt to trades the interests of self or group to agree upon some trading benefits for the one or more parties.

Under political pressure, it is not necessary that political pressure sources carry out trading for self, it may be for the third party or may be chain of benefits delivery system at various levels. Prime Minister/Chief Minister/Minister may direct Cabinet Secretary/Chief Secretary for a particular benefit delivery down to the hierarchy of Secretary to departmental head than to functional heads may ultimately affect grassroot level public immediately or in long run. Such pressures perceived at the top level and conceived as top-level pressure spread its manifestations and tentacles like a virus in the bureaucratic system. On occasions, the Cabinet Secretary/Chief Secretary may not perceive it as pressure, as their own interests are not immediately affected, but in a real sense, a chain of so-called small decisions have long-term deleterious impact and implications on the whole social system and country. When we think about ramifications at the national level, officers/officials in different levels of hierarchy may not realize that by accepting particular political pressure for self-goals, they are transferring its adverse impact on many other places. But according to the law of nature, the slightest advantage to any individual will be a disadvantage to someone else in the bureaucratic system.

During discussions, some of the All India Services Officers boasted that they hardly obey politicians and rarely execute few percent transfers under political pressure. Such officers also claim that they faithfully and honestly ensure that person transfer does not cause any problem and hardship to any third person. On the other side of the fence, some of our colleagues justified the acceptance of pressure without any harm to the bureaucratic system.

No, it is not a true picture; common people, who have approached politicians for helping themselves indicates in the first place that the bureaucratic system has violated merit and objectivity in the decision. Secondly, that a common person has lost faith in the hierarchy of the government. Thirdly, All India Services Officers have failed to deliver goods up to commoner expectations and system parameters; otherwise, that person could have approached immediate seniors in that bureaucratic system. When such officers go to the next place in the bureaucratic system, they will work to protect the interests of that politician, who has helped them. His colleagues and other employees are bound to be affected by such abnormal behavior. In due course slowly, others will also lose faith in the seniors and bureaucratic system. Ultimately, discipline, rules, regulations, and procedures are sacrificed.

This will slowly give rise to self-interest protections and goal maximization. This initiates the formation of pressure groups and political groups and so on a long chain involving lowest employee to highest and village level political worker to Prime Minister/Chief Minister levels, engrossed deep in the business of political pressure inducement. What the All India Services Officers do, while sitting in air-conditioned rooms, they only justify their own inactions and own goals from day one, when they join service to the day they retire or die, even after retirement heart and soul of most the officers swarm in government offices. The web of self-goals, interests, and needs only to survive in the end. 'I appreciate your goals and you appreciate my goals', in this process of bargaining every power holder maximizes own goals. Bureaucrats and politicians spend their whole career in mutual interchanging and exchanging goods and services for self-maximization. The process of bargaining is influenced by the individual personality, values, beliefs, attitudes, and socio-cultural background of the parties involved in it.

11.4. Handling of Pressure Sources

11.4.1. Methodology and Approaches Adopted

There are several areas on which political pressures are being exerted on the All India Services Officers. We have selected fifteen major areas for the pressure in seventy-six pressure points related to such areas (Unit 12—Areas/Points of Pressure). In the present study, the All India Services Officers behavior, personality traits, attitudes, beliefs, and perceptions about sources of pressure in the decision-making process have been covered. Political leadership (sources) assess the All India Services Officers' behavior through feedback from subordinates, seniors, and the public. Different pressure groups are aware that these highly aggressive All India Services Officers will allow them limited advantages in the decision. In such situations, pressure groups also explore to find out individual officer goals, their weakness, and temptations toward high yielding from the bargaining process.

Politicians may enter into integrative bargaining to sort out mutual goals/interests, where the All India Services Officers and politicians both enjoy a win-win situation. The All India Services Officers also visualize and realize the importance of long-term relationships with politicians, which help these officers to facilitate joint working to attain future mutual goals. In such conditions, the politicians and All India Services Officers will maintain flexibility and show sensitivity and concern for each other needs. Gender doesn't make a significant difference to political pressure management, where the All India Services Officers are situated in similar power bases. Interpersonal relationships of the All India Services Officers within the department, with the political party in power and across of the social setup play a crucial role in pressure source management.

How much the All India Services Officers rely on facts and think logically? Individual officer perceptions and past-experience in political concessions provided by him and outcomes received by such officer in return are crucial for political pressure source management. Emotional attachment and emotional quotient of the All India Services Officers determine spontaneity of interaction with sources of political pressure. Feelings for the masses, public, subordinates, and seniors determine the approach to cope up with pressure sources. Background status and position, relations of a politician with the top politicians/Chief Minister/Prime Minister also influence techniques adopted for the pressure management by individual All India Services Officers. The All India Services Officers views, ideals, thinking about political pressure sources decide the extent of acceptance of the political pressure in the decision-making process.

Section of the All India Services Officers feels that any acceptance of political pressure will be indicative of an officer's weakness, whereas other section sees pliability as part of progressive thinking. Some of the All India Services Officers think that political pressure in the bureaucratic system fades away in due course of time, so they take a very long time in responding to any source of the political pressure. Many All India Services Officers perceive negotiation with political pressure source as a never-ending process, so they do not like to open a plethora box of problems for them, say good-bye to pressure on the first instance. Such officers convey to politicians that he never accepts the political pressure, so is in this case also. Kindly, excusing me.

The All India Services Officers also think that they are committed to working for the politicians. Politicians occupy the apex position, so officers are committed to accept political pressure and mix such commitment with the work culture. The All India Services Officers with strong impatience and high desires for developing a relationship with politicians, delay acceptable political pressure acceptance to the level that politicians show proper respect towards that individual officer and develop relations of liking for each other. The All India Services Officers with distributive bargaining approach manage pressure with a view that we gain at your expense and vice-versa. Come and share the booty. The All India Services Officers and source of pressure both engross own targets, goals in the aspiration range of other parties. Both attempt to feel generous towards each other and accept demands at a settlement point acceptable to both.

When the All India Services Officers are unable to resolve the stalemate of political pressure or other party or both parties may approach a third party in the system or out of the system or sympathizer to resolve the pressure. Either parties or one-party search third neutral party, who can facilitate the solution by bargaining or persuasion or suggesting viable reasons or alternatives find out a solution for the problem. But commonly such pressure is contested. In case of urgent, need higher authorities such as Prime Minister/Chief Minister/Minister/senior bureaucrat work as an arbitrator. Such authority can use compulsory force or power to find the solution. On many occasions, transfer and postings are commonly used as forcing force for acceptance of pressure. Such inducement of force can be physical, monetary, or harming career or anything with the sky as the limit. Such authorities are the power holders and power holders use their power without any rationale or justification. Such arbitrators can be an authority within a hierarchy or outside hierarchy, which can force the All India Services Officers to show concern for arbitration.

Rarely, but it happens in public administration that conciliator provides informal communication and works as an intimidator. Such conciliator may be the person from social groups, cultural group, caste group, region or religion group or some time well-wishers in same department or friends in other departments but known to both parties, and work as a conduit for communication for both parties. In policy-related case, in some projects, government-owned corporations; dissent between political pressure and bureaucrats is solved with the help of expert consultants also. However, this is a recent and new phenomenon limited to selective places in public administration only.

11.4.2. Types of Political Pressure Management

Different types adopted for political pressure source management can be grouped into three categories:

11.4.2.1. Pull Type: This type is used to diminish and destroy the pressure.

11.4.2.2. Push Type: Persuade pressure to put forward to be assertive.

11.4.2.3. Avoid Type: Avoid pressure, withdraw, or resign from the scene.

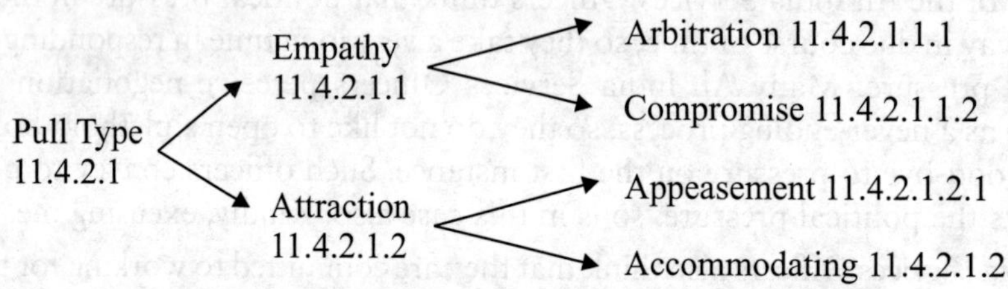

Figure No. 11.2: Pull Type Pressure Management

11.4.2.1. Pull to Destroy/Diminish the Pressure:

(i) Haul up the pressure with void impact.

(ii) Drag pressure, enhance friction and wait until it dies down.

(iii) Reduce (break) pressure into parts accept relevant parts only.

(iv) A scuffle with pressure to divert and destroy it.

(v) Raid and destroy at first encounter, ensure peace for the future.

(vi) Strike hard to bowl pressure out.

(vii) Demolish the bastion of pressure to derive out the decision.

Pull out pressure:

(i) Move out pressure, when serving no interest for self.

(ii) Sweat others under pressure watch it.

(iii) Retard influence of pressure to decide.
(iv) Wrench pressure under counter pressure.

11.4.2.1.1. Empathy:

(i) Drag pressure and get back to your own advantage.
(ii) Influence pressure towards self-goals.
(iii) Precede your efforts with pressure to attain goals.
(iv) Print pressures on the system to achieve goals under its shadow.
(v) Rein the pressure, control the direction, and keep it under control.
(vi) Assume sanctity of pressure compromise with it.
(vii) Recover self-interests/needs from pressure.
(viii) Harmony with pressure to reduce damages.

11.4.2.1.1.1. Arbitration: Arbitrate with pressure sources; must be free from bias, show consistency, and transparency. The AISO arbitrates to its own advantage.

11.4.2.1.1.2. Compromise: Compromise with the pressure sources. The AISO facilitator may be an immediate senior or someone reliable for both sides and compromise may be beneficial to both sides. Respect pressure, achieve self-goals and buy future peace for self.

11.4.2.1.2. Attraction:

(i) Attract (invite) pressure for goal attainment.
(ii) Separate pressure points, sources, and modes to attain goals.
(iii) Suck pressure (suck it) to merge with your own goals.
(iv) Pluck pressure (like a flower) and adore it for future gains.
(v) Move pressure in the direction of self-needs.

11.4.2.1.2.1. Appeasement: Avoids conflict between both sources of pressure and the AISO. Appeasement in the decision is frequently discredited as a weakness of the AISO and officers convert it into recognition. Circumstances intended for and the AISO may successfully attain its own goals in that.

11.4.2.1.2.2. Accommodating: Decision discrete choices, decision factors, hierarchical factors are considered by the AISO, and the decision will follow the careful analysis of all prevailing factors to accommodate pressure in the decision to meet self-goals and take credit for fulfilling self-needs.

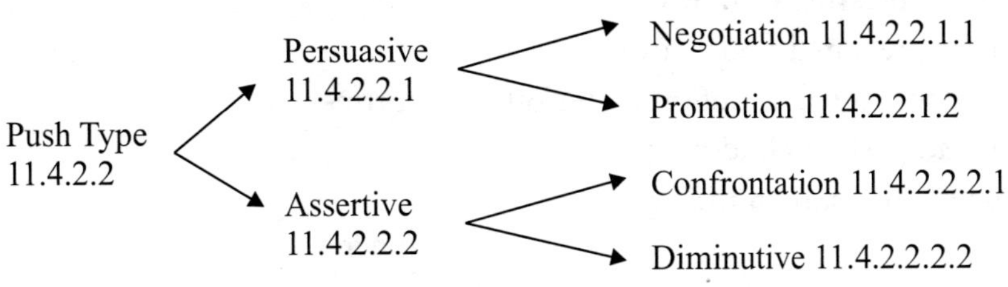

Figure No. 11.3: Push Type Pressure Management

*11.4.2.2.1. **Persuasive Push***

11.4.2.2.1.1. Negotiation:

(i) Move pressure to influence your own advancement.
(ii) Increase weight on the pressure to push away.
(iii) Persuade and propel pressure under their own propulsion (thrust).
(iv) Bring inducement decision to induce pressure push away.
(v) Reserve pressure for future events.
(vi) Sell pressure top politicians and subordinates to push for self-goal.

11.4.2.2.1.2. Promotion:

(i) Promote pressure to another place.
(ii) Advance pressure for self-advancement.
(iii) Promote pressure in the bureaucratic system to meet own needs.
(iv) Contest pressure to gain in future for later on adoption.
(v) Advertise pressure for future use.

*11.4.2.2.2. **Assertive Push:***

(i) Force pressure away from your decision.
(ii) Exert self over pressure your position to move away.
(iii) Assert pressure over political pressure to cancel it.
(iv) Assert self with pressure to meet own goals, suppress others.
(v) Attack pressure with full force to push away.

11.4.2.2.2.1. Confrontation:

(i) Confrontation type management harm the AISO.
(ii) Forcefully push away pressure for compliance with rules and regulations.
(iii) The AISO manipulate oneself firmly to resist pressure.
(iv) The AISO remain status and reputation conscious during the assertion process.

11.4.2.2.2.2. Diminution:

(i) Pushing (shove) like a billiard ball, do not strike it, no noise.
(ii) Blow out pressure to keep self-clean.
(iii) Driveaway pressure instantly.
(iv) Strain the pressure to push away.
(v) Shift pressure towards subordinates/other departments.
(vi) Ignore and push as child play.
(vii) Discuss the pressure in the first place.

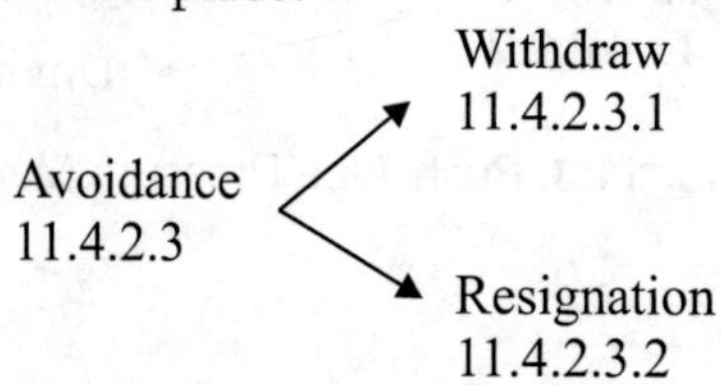

Figure No. 11.4: Avoidance Type Pressure Management

11.4.2.3. Avoidance:

(i) Move out slowly from the decision.
(ii) Shun yourself from pressure.
(iii) Escape pressure keeps running.
(iv) Evade pressure wait up to the appropriate time.
(v) Defeat pressures resign from the decision.
(vi) Elude pressure, it continuously chases you in the hope to enchase never available.
(vii) Withdraw from the decision.
(viii) Quash preemptive strike to avoid pressure.

11.4.2.3.1. Withdraw:

(i) The AISO buy time and delay decision outcomes.
(ii) The AISO have a feeling of weakness and compute consequences.
(iii) Results outcome may force the AISO to turn away from the decision.
(iv) To explore security run from pillars to posts for protection shield.
(v) Escape decision in search of a suitable time.
(vi) Invalidate or repeal pressure in the decision.

11.4.2.3.2. Resignation:

(i) Explore all possibilities and quit the decision.
(ii) Evade not recognizing the source of pressure.
(iii) Spread that the AISO not available for decision.
(iv) Seek transfer or change of place.
(v) Walkout from the decision to save yourself.

11.5. Process of Political Pressure Management

Political pressure management in the decision-making process is very complex and situational to any individual All India Services Officer w.r.t. time, space, and place. It is difficult to confine such situational unlimited and non-measurable pressure to any process models. After our research, we have tried to simplify the process of political pressure management in seven steps.

11.5.1. Individual Officer and Politician Behavior under Attack

Political goals motivate politicians to commence political pressure. The All India Services Officers' goals and needs to create chaos in the behavior of individual officers. Politician behavior towards pressure is related to the public/voter/friend's expectations from the decision under his influence. Politicians come under pressure from various parties or stakeholders in the democratic election process. Manipulations, distributions, or aberrations in the election process are directly related to causes of political pressure. The All India Services Officers are the product of the same social system; social contradictions, manipulations, and expectations have a serious impact on the All India Services Officers' personality and behavior. The whole web of external forces acts on the bureaucratic system to generate aberration and distortion to manipulated need-oriented decisions. The All India Services Officers also develop different perceptions and attitudes towards pressure. Politicians and stakeholders in a democracy are under a change in attitude towards the All India Services Officers and politicians. Web of self-interests attempt to generate pressure on each other to make pressure in circular path motion under the pressure of self-interests of public, politicians and the All India Services Officers, and ultimately went out of control of everyone in the process. As shown in Figure 11.5, three points linear forces get converted into circular motion force and which never stops and three stakeholders merge in one motion and forever moving wheel of self-goals.

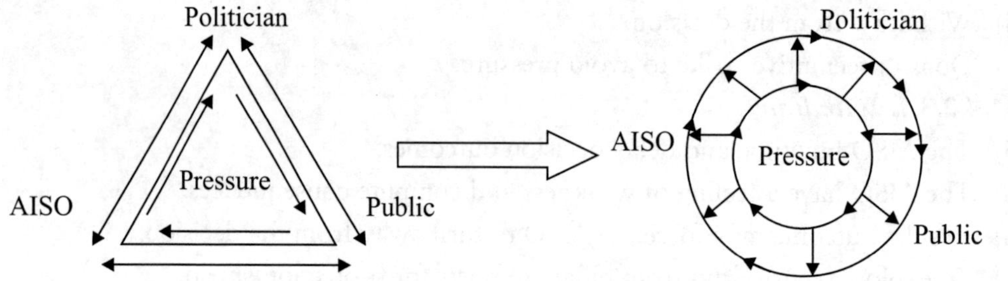

Figure No. 11.5: Web of Interests, Pressure Model

11.5.2. Calculation, Intention, and Plotting of Pressure in Democracy

Stakeholders in government administration evolve their own perceptions and beliefs about the decision-making process. Such perceptions develop their intentions and carry out computation and calculation for attainments of such intensions. Then they plot their own needs, goals in the domain of public administration. Different group's goals and interests force them to formulate issues, which may be possibly accepted by the bureaucratic system. The vested group carries out an assessment of the system vis-à-vis fulfillment of its own issues. Tangible, intangible, direct, or hidden interests and benefits force various stakeholders to develop different strategies for achieving goals. The blueprint for responding to politicians or bureaucrats in case of denial or resistance is formulated. Stakeholders, politicians, and decision-makers develop and determine the lowest values acceptable to them. The All India Services Officers devise the best alternatives available with reference to own personality. Stakeholders also in this stage develop clearer ideas about different alternatives, which serve or maximize their goals.

11.5.3. Drawing Boundaries/Operational Strategy

Stakeholders formulate a strategy for how to present pressure. The vested party thinks about future obstacles the All India Services Officers may bring inside it. They try to gather information about government rules, regulations, procedures, and laws from different sources. The interested party decides who will approach at what level with help of a politician or source of pressure at what time. Place and mode of communication, i.e. WhatsApp type, Internet (remote access), telephone call or personal meeting or written communications, all such aspects are decided at this stage. Either issue will be told to the All India Services Officers by the source of pressure or third party close to power holders. At this stage, stakeholders discuss the sources of pressure to finalize the modalities of pressure. Power holder may depute someone else assessing the importance of the issue. Proportionate to the issue pressure source also finalize mode of pressure, method of pressure, time of pressure, pace for pressure, and exigency plan if any.

11.5.4. Presentation and Justification Stage

Keeping in mind the issues in question, sources of pressure according to areas of pressure approach the All India Services Officers at different locations and positions. Source of pressure explain own position, clarify the demands, and in case need amplify the public feeling associated with the issue or other consequences. Up to this stage invariably there is no confrontation with the All India Services Officers and sources of pressure. All parties try to exploit this stage to inform each other point of view and educate about the individual and bureaucratic system constraints and problems. Immature or arrogant persons at the stage of justification enter into ulterior transactions, which indicate a low emotional quotient. The All India Services Officers should remain cool and calm at this stage.

11.5.5. Goal Conflict in Problem Solving

All India Services Officers are aware of the political pressure; try to rationalize the political pressure in the context of government rules, regulations, procedure, and law operational at that point in time. Source of political pressure bargain hard to get accepted his demand. This stage is full of conflicts. In problem-solving every party wants to maximize their own goals. Self-goals perused by the All India Services Officers force him to enter into collaboration with the sources of political pressure. To protect their own actions the All India Services Officers bargain with a source of political pressure for individual officer protection and goal maximization. The AISO indulges in the assessment of future repercussions and implications.

11.5.6. Decision about Pressure

In this stage, the All India Services Officers arrive at decision, up to what extent pressure will be accepted. How that decision will be implemented by appropriate levels in public administration? This stage is full of tension. The All India Services Officers repeatedly discuss with seniors and juniors to take his subordinates into confidence for implementation of the decision. On scores of occasions, hundreds of decisions are never implemented in public administration. The All India Services Officers wait for new lease of life for a change of politician or political party in power. Stakeholders continue to flock around the source of pressure. They are also aware that in government decision implementation is difficult. So, reinforcement of political pressure repeatedly until a decision is implemented.

11.5.7. After Effects, Monitoring, and Status Quotient

Most of the decisions in government bureaucracy have recoiling effects. When public or opposition parties come to know about the decision, they revolt, raise a banner of protest, go to courts for contesting such decisions. The All India Services Officers and political source of pressure have to be vigilant about after-effects and the need arises again to enter into a bargaining process to neutralize the after-effects. In the case of a contest, they defend the legal process. Then regular monitoring, which is rarely carried out in government administration. Even the decision has been implemented, after many years some decisions are modified, changed, or reversed by the next power holder. So, the stakeholder is never sure about to enjoy the comforts of their efforts and the pressure they have mobilized. So, they continue to maintain pressure for the status quo in the decision and future issues.

11.6. Analyses of Sources of Political Pressure

After analyzing a large number of sources of pressure, the ten best possible sources of direct political pressure have been selected, which are commonly exerted on the All India Services Officers in the decision-making process. The intensity of pressure exerted by each source has been studied. Statistically, all the sources of political pressure show good association with the decision-making process, as indicated by the Pearson Chi-square analysis. Our all results are significant, mostly with a level of significance at 0.000 or less than 0.05. The strength of the relationship of various sources of political pressure with the decision-making process is demonstrated by the significant values of Pearson's correlation and Spearman correlation. These values have been shown in Exhibit 11.1 and our research analysis results are highly significant.

Mean values vary from 2.43 to 3.63, and standard deviation values from 0.97 to 1.43. This indicates that most of these sources of political pressure exert pressure frequently on the All India Services Officers. Our results show that MLA/MLC (1st in ranking) exerts the highest or maximum political pressure on the decision-making process of the All India Services Officers. Member Legislative Council/Member Legislative Assembly, District Level Politician/Zila Parishad Members (2nd in ranking), and Center or State Ministers (3rd in ranking) are the sources, which exert political pressure most frequently and with the greatest intensity. These sources of pressure are interacting and interface with the masses and public approach to them for their things to be done in an ethical or unethical manner. Self-goals oriented public also does not lay emphasis on rules, regulations, and law or justice.

Exhibit Number 11.1: Sources of Political Pressure—Statistical Analysis

Sources	Freq. N = 281		Chi-square			Pearson's R		Spearman Rho		Mean	s.d.	Rk.
	Miss	Valid	Value	d.f.	sif.	Value	sif.	Value	sif.			
366. P.M./C.M.	30	251	71.411	8	0.000	0.282	0.000	0.35	0.000	3.63	1.16	10
367. Ministers	17	264	71.644	8	0.000	0.386	0.000	0.393	0.000	2.79	1.33	3
368. M.P.	19	262	51.736	8	0.000	0.207	0.001	0.238	0.000	3.33	0.97	9
369. M.L.A.	18	263	53.234	8	0.000	0.386	0.000	0.394	0.000	2.43	1.2	1
370. D.L.P.	18	263	20.597	8	0.008	0.191	0.002	0.201	0.001	2.73	1.35	2
371. B.L.P.	30	251	28.955	8	0.000	0.193	0.002	0.187	0.003	2.74	1.2	4
372. V.L.W.	31	250	27.949	8	0.000	0.168	0.008	0.179	0.004	3.04	1.34	7
373. P.B.	24	257	45.321	8	0.000	0.351	0.000	0.358	0.000	2.97	1.43	6
374. Media	32	249	43.01	8	0.000	0.163	0.010	0.181	0.004	3.12	1.27	8
375. H.F.	32	249	127.6	8	0.000	0.593	0.000	0.592	0.000	3.3	1.36	5

mis = missing frequencies. s.d. = standard deviation. Rk = rank. sif. = significance level

If we look at the respective services and sources of pressure, results are different for different services. This is due to the reason that the nature of the job performed by them are different, so the extent of political pressure and sources of pressure has to be accordingly different. If we look at Indian Administrative Service officers, the three most common sources of political pressure are from (a) Member Legislative Council/Member Legislative Assembly, (b) Center or State Minister, and (c) Hidden Financiers.

In the case of the Indian Police Service officers, these are (a) District-Level Politician/Zila Parishad Members, (b) Member Legislative Council/Member Legislative Assembly, and (c) Communication Media. The Indian Forest Service officers show some variation in getting political pressure as (a) District-Level Politician/Zila Parishad Members, (b) Member Legislative Council/Member Legislative Assembly, and (c) Village Heads/Village-Level Workers. Our results indicate that Member Legislative Council/Member Legislative Assembly are the greatest source of political pressure and they are frequently exerting political pressure on All India Services Officers.

Our results for factor analysis in (Exhibit 11.2) correlation matrix, upper half results show Pearson's correlation coefficient between all the pairs of sources of the political pressure. The lower half of Exhibit 11.2, indicate the one-tailed significance of this coefficient. All the ten sources of direct political pressure correlate fairly well with all others and show a good relationship among them. Our correlation values are large, the highest value is 0.668 and the lowest value is 0.097. All the values for the significance are less than the acceptable level of 0.05. For our data determinant value is 7.306E-03 (which is greater than the necessary value of 0.00001) indicates that multi-co-linearity is not a problem for our data.

Kaiser-Meyer-Olkin (KMO) measure of sampling adequacy value is 0.815; it is great, we are confident that factor analysis is appropriate for these sources of pressure. Our value is greater than 0.5, it indicates that our sample was adequate. Bartlett's test of Sphericity measure the null hypothesis, our analysis significance value is 0.000 (less than 0.05), indicate that our correlation matrix is not the identity matrix; therefore, a significant relationship between the variables is shown. Bartlett's test is highly significant; hence, factor analysis is appropriate for study.

We have calculated Eigen values of our correlation matrix, which in turn help us to know about the number of components (eigenvectors) in this R-matrix. The magnitudes of associated Eigen values determine the importance of component and two components have been retained with values more than 1 (Kaiser Criterion), our SPSS analyses have shown Eigen values before extraction, after extraction, and after rotation. SPSS has identified 10 components within the data set; Eigen values associated with each factor explain the variance of that component. The percentage of variance has been shown in the next column, component one shows 48% of the total variance, and component 2 shows 12.85 of the total variance. SPSS has discarded the values less than 1, in extraction sums of squared loadings; only two components have been retained. In the final part, SPSS has retained the values for rotation sums of squared loadings. The rotation has optimized the factor structure and equalized two factors with a 30% variance.

The proportion of common variance with in variance is communalities. Principle component analysis works on assumption that all variance is common initially as 1. Extraction values from 0.388 to 0.803, reflect common variance. 70.4% of the variance is associated with the Chief Minister/Prime Minister source of political pressure is common and shared and lowest of (0.388) 38.8% of shared variance related with the hidden financiers source of political pressure. In communalities amount of variance in each source of political pressure is explained by all the sources after extraction.

SPSS have extracted two factors by Kaiser's criterion. In the rotated component matrix, we have used the Varimax rotation method with Kaiser 'normalization' in principle component analysis as the extraction method. Component matrix results show that most factors were loaded onto the first factors. Rotated Matrix shows that four variables are highly loaded onto the same factor. And two show significant loading. These variables are Center or State Minister, Chief Minister/Prime Minister, Member Parliament, and Member Legislative Council/Member Legislative Assembly. These all are elected through the Election Commission, Government of India. We can label this factor as a *Legislatures' factor* elected through the Government of India. Loading of variables in the second factor are District-Level Politician/Zila Parishad Members, Block-Level Politician/ Block Samiti, Village Heads/Village-Level Workers and Power Brokers/touts/musclemen, form one group of politicians, who work below the Legislature category. We can label them *localized politicians' factor*. Media and hidden financiers show loading with the factor one, can be clubbed with this factor. As the hidden financiers and communication media relation with higher politicians is more than localized politicians. Our six sources will be clubbed in one group and another four variables into the second category.

The component transformation matrix provides information about the degree to which factors were rotated. Results show a symmetrical matrix, with the diagonal value of 0.705 and 0.709. Component score coefficient matrix used for calculation of covariance matrix of factor scores. The component score coefficient matrix provides us information about the relationship between factor scores.

Exhibit Number 11.2: Factor Analysis—Correlation Matrix

Variable	Code	366	367	368	369	370	371	372	373	374	375
Correlation	366	1.000									
	367	0.640	1.000								
	368	0.502	0.595	1.000							
	369	0.584	0.516	0.358	1.000						
	370	0.425	0.350	0.305	0.463	1.000					
	371	0.377	0.435	0.368	0.537	0.513	1.000				
	372	0.268	0.097	0.225	0.360	0.538	0.59*3	1.000			
	373	0.436	0.335	0.319	0.668	0.318	0.636	0.461	1.000		
	374	0.577	0.474	0.265	0.425	0.372	0.400	0.389	0.384	1.000	
	375	0.387	0.432	0.411	0.320	0.270	0.432	0.313	0.479	0.288	1.000
Significance	366	0.000									
(1-tailed)	367	0.000									
	368	0.000	0.000								
	369	0.000	0.000	0.000							
	370	0.000	0.000	0.000	0.000						
	371	0.000	0.000	0.000	0.000	0.000					
	372	0.000	0.095	0.001	0.000	0.000	0.000				

Variable	Code	366	367	368	369	370	371	372	373	374	375
	373	0.000	0.000	0.000	0.000	0.000	0.000	0.000			
	374	0.000	0.000	0.000	0.000	0.000	0.000	0.000	0.000		
	375	0.000	0.000	0.000	0.000	0.000	0.000	0.000	0.000	0.000	

KMO and Bartlett's Test—Kaiser-Meyer = Olkin Measure of Sampling Adequacy .815

Bartlett's Test of Sphericity; Apx. Chi-square = 879.693, d.f. = 45, Significance = 0.000

Communalities (Extraction method: Principal Component Analysis)

Variable No.	366	367	368	369	370	371	372	373	374	375	
Initial	1.000	1.000	1.000	1.000	1.000	1.000	1.000	1.000	1.000	1.000	
Extraction	.704	.803	.570	.596	.508	.707	.762	.604	.440		

Total Variance Explained

Component	Initial Eigenvalues			Extraction Sums of Square Loadings			Rotation Sums of Squared Loadings				
	Total	var.%	cum.%	Total	var.%	cum.%	Total	var.%	cum.%		
	4.803	48.035	48	4.8	48	48	3.05	30.5	30.5		
	1.278	12.78	60.8	1.278	12.8	60.8	3.03	30.3	60.8		
	.872	8.7	69.5								
	.764	7.6	77.17								
	.647	6.5	83.647								
	.485	4.8	88.5								
	.430	4.3	92.8								
	.280	2.8	95.6								
	.254	2.5	98.1								
	.186	1.85	100								

Component Matrix (Principal component analysis as extraction method)

Component	369	371	366	373	367	374	370	368	375	372	
1	0.772	0.770	0.759	0.738	0.710	0.661	0.653	0.621	0.616	0.601	
2	1.9E	0.337	–0.358	0.244	–0.547	5.8E	0.285	0.43	–9.0E	0.633	

Rotated Component Matrix (Principal component analysis, Varimax Rotation Method)

Component	367	366	368	374	375	372	371	373	370	369	
1	0.889	0.79	0.74	0.51	0.51	1.9E	0.31	0.35	0.26	0.53	
2	0.113	0.28	0.33	0.43	0.37	0.87	0.78	0.69	0.66	0.557	

We have shown frequently frequency results through a pie chart (Chart 11.1.). Further, we have analyzed results for the method of recruitment and its relationship with the different sources of political pressure in the decision-making process. Results in Exhibit 11.3 indicate that invariably political pressure acceptance is higher among promoted officers than directly recruited officers.

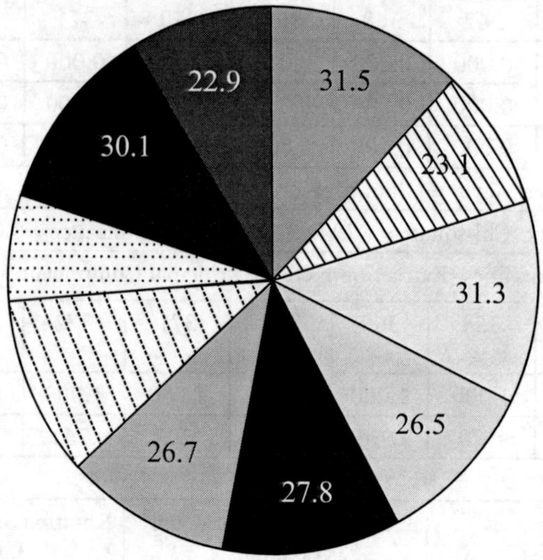

Chart No. 11.1: Frequently Pressure and Frequency of Sources

Exhibit Number 11.3: Method of Recruitment and Sources of Political Pressure

Sources of PP	Recruitment Method	Intensity of Political Pressure					Total
		Always	Usually	Frequently	Sometimes	Never	
PM/CM	Direct	0.4	2	7.6	8	12.4	30.3
	Promotee	4.8	4.8	23.9	19.1	17.1	69.7
	Total	5.2	6.8	31.5	27.1	29.5	100
Minister Center/State	Direct	5.3	5.3	6.4	10.6	3.8	31.3
	Promotee	18.1	15.8	17	12.5	5.3	68.7
	Total	23.4	21.1	23.4	23	9.1	100
MP	Direct	1.1	4.6	8.7	10.6	5.7	30.8
	Promotee	4.2	14.8	22.4	24	3.8	69.2
	Total	5.3	19.4	31.2	34.6	9.5	100
MLA/MLC	Direct	9.1	5.3	9.8	3.8	3.4	31.4
	Promotee	22.7	16.7	15.9	11	2.3	68.6
	Total	31.8	22	25.8	14.8	5.7	100
DLP	Direct	8.3	4.9	11	2.3	5.3	31.8
	Promotee	21.2	16.3	13.3	12.5	4.9	68.2
	Total	29.5	21.2	24.2	14.8	10.2	100

Sources of PP	Recruitment Method	Intensity of Political Pressure					Total
		Always	Usually	Frequently	Sometimes	Never	
BLP	Direct	6	7.5	7.5	4.8	6.7	31.7
	Promotee	9.5	23.4	19.8	10.3	5.2	68.7
	Total	15.5	31	27.4	15	11	100
VLW	Direct	3.6	5.2	8.4	6.8	8	31.9
	Promotee	9.2	14.7	20.7	16.7	6.8	68.1
	Total	12.7	19.9	29.1	23.5	14.7	100
PB	Direct	4.7	7.4	5.8	6.6	6.2	30.7
	Promotee	14.8	17.5	12.1	15.6	9.3	69.3
	Total	19.5	24.9	17.9	22.2	15.6	100
Media	Direct	2.8	4	9.6	7.2	7.6	31.3
	Promotee	8.8	14.5	20.9	14.1	10.4	68.7
	Total	11.6	18.5	30.5	21.3	18.1	100
HF	Direct	4	6.8	6.4	4.8	10.4	31.7
	Promotee	10	14.5	16.9	12.4	14.5	68.3
	Total	14.1	20.5	23.3	17.3	24.9	100

11.6.1. Chief Minister/Prime Minister

Chief Minister and Prime Minister mostly influence the high-level party decisions and administrative decisions, which can influence the party prospectus. This source of political pressure is used for policy decisions, framing law and acts, change of rules, regulations and procedures, resource allocation, transfer and postings, and recruitment related areas. This source of political pressure mostly interacts with the top-level All India Services Officers. Generally, political pressure is exerted through the concerned minister, head of the department, Cabinet Secretary/Chief Secretary, Administrative Secretary, and senior officers; so it works as indirect political pressure for the field functionaries and direct political pressure for the top-level All India Services Officers. On occasions, field functionaries are unable to identify such political pressure, because, for them, it comes as a policy directive, rule, order, law, and directive from their respective senior officers. It is most difficult to measure this source of political pressure, due to many reasons prevalent in the bureaucratic system.

When a Prime Minister/Chief Minister ask his minister to do a certain thing, the bureaucratic system will consider that pressure coming from that minister or politician. When a Prime Minister/ Chief Minister ask his Cabinet Secretary/Chief Secretary to influence certain issues, concerned officers down below might consider it pressure from the top bureaucracy. "Have we ever heard of a Prime Minister is democratically elected government being a Prime Minister for certain parts of the nation or only of certain communities which strongly supported him in elections?" And author further elaborates, "He is the Prime Minister of India and of all the Hindus, Muslims,

Sikhs, Christian, and other communities who live within the boundaries of India. A Prime Minister who feels that he is only obliged to a certain section of the citizenry and must do everything in their support, right or wrong, would fail and he condemned as being unworthy of the office he holds," Yogendra Narain, 2013.

Exhibit Number 11.4: Direct Sources of Pressure Exerted on the All India Services Officers—An Analysis

Direct Sources	Name of Service	Intensity of Political Pressure					Total	Rank
		Always	Usually	Frequently	Sometimes	Never		
PM/CM	I.A.S.	4.4	10.3	50	19.1	16.2	27.1	10
	I.P.S.	1.1	8	48.3	20.7	21.8	34.7	10
	I.F.S.	9.4	3.1	3.1	37.5	46.9	38.2	8
	AIS	5.2	6.8	31.5	26.7	29.9	100	9
Ministers State/ Center	I.A.S.	45.8	16.7	16.7	18.1	2.8	27.3	2
	I.P.S.	19.8	36.5	26	8.3	9.4	36.4	5
	I.F.S.	10.4	9.4	25	41.7	13.5	36.4	5
	AIS	23.5	21.2	23.1	23.1	9.1	100	3
MP	I.A.S.	0	26.3	50	14.5	9.2	29	9
	I.P.S.	13.3	18.9	24.4	40	3.3	37.4	8
	I.F.S.	2.1	14.6	22.9	44.8	15.6	36.6	9
	AIS	5.3	19.5	31.3	34.4	9.5	100	9
MLA	I.A.S.	62	21.1	15.5	0	1.4	27	1
	I.P.S.	25	22.9	28.1	15.6	8.3	36.5	2
	I.F.S.	16.7	21.9	30.2	25	6.3	36.5	2
	AIS	31.9	22.1	26.5	14.8	5.7	100	1
DLP	I.A.S.	42.1	21.1	18.4	9.2	9.2	28.9	4
	I.P.S.	29.2	19.1	32.6	9	10.1	33.8	1
	I.F.S.	20.4	21.4	22.4	24.5	11.2	37.3	1
	AIS	29.7	20.5	24.7	14.8	10.3	100	2
BLP	I.A.S.	19.4	29.2	27.8	13.9	9.7	28.7	6
	I.P.S.	17.9	36.9	34.5	8.3	2.4	33.5	6
	I.F.S.	10.5	26.3	18.9	22.1	22.1	37.8	4
	AIS	15.5	30.7	26.7	15.1	12	100	4
VLW	I.A.S.	11.9	25.4	35.8	13.4	13.4	26.8	7
	I.P.S.	14.4	24.4	23.3	32.2	5.6	36	7
	I.F.S.	11.8	10.8	29	21.5	26.9	37.2	3
	AIS	12.8	19.6	28.8	23.2	15.6	100	7

Direct Sources	Name of Service	Intensity of Political Pressure					Total	Rank
		Always	Usually	Frequently	Sometimes	Never		
PB	I.A.S.	36	22.7	18.7	12	10.7	29.2	5
	I.P.S.	20.5	35.2	15.9	15.9	12.5	34.2	4
	I.F.S.	5.3	17	18.1	36.2	23.4	36.6	6
	AIS	19.5	24.9	17.5	22.2	16	100	6
Media	I.A.S.	5.9	22.1	33.8	23.5	14.7	27.3	8
	I.P.S.	23	20.7	37.9	5.7	12.6	34.9	3
	I.F.S.	5.3	14.9	20.2	31.9	27.7	37.8	7
	AIS	11.6	18.9	30.1	20.5	18.9	100	8
HF	I.A.S.	43.1	21.5	20	9.2	6.2	26.1	3
	I.P.S.	7.3	35.4	30.2	8.3	18.8	38.6	9
	I.F.S.	0	3.4	17	34.1	45.6	35.3	10
	AIS	14.1	20.5	22.9	17.7	24.9	100	5
Highest % in	score	45.8	36.5	48.3	44.8	46.9	38.6	36.5
	service	IAS	IPS	IPS	IFS	IFS	IFS	IPS IFS
	source	Minister	Minister	CM	MP	CM	HF	MLA

When Prime Minister/Chief Minister discusses any issue in a meeting or other official forum, such pressure will be covered under the wrap of the bureaucratic system. When this source interacts with the head of department or concerned secretary, the pressure becomes the executive order for the department and Prime Minister/Chief Minister remains nowhere in the picture. This source is enumerated as pressure when a Prime Minister/Chief Minister issues a direct directive to the concerned the All India Services Officers for implementation of his directives. Such instances are very rare.

However, the author has come across direct political pressure from the Prime Minister and Chief Minister on a number of occasions and both of them intervened in-person to victimize the author. This source of political pressure is exerted in lesser frequency, but impact over the All India Services Officers is the highest. Political pressure from this source has a serious impact on the mind, personality, and career of the concerned All India Services Officers. Even with lesser intensity, it has wider ramifications in the decision-making process.

Our results indicate that 69.15 of the Indian Administrative Service officers and 69% of the Indian Police Service officers get political pressure for this source 'frequently' to 'sometimes'. 37.54% of the Indian Forest Service officers get political pressure 'sometimes' from Prime Minister/Chief Minister and 46.9% of them 'never' get political pressure from this source. 31.5% of the All India Services Officers get 'frequent' political pressure from this source and 29.9% of them 'never' get political pressure. Our results clearly indicate that the Indian Administrative Service officers get the maximum political pressure from the Prime Minister/Chief Minister because they are located close to this power center. But an interesting score is that of 'always' intensity, where the Indian Forest Service officers score is highest with 9.4%. This is more than twice the pressure perception by the Indian Administrative Service officers in the same category.

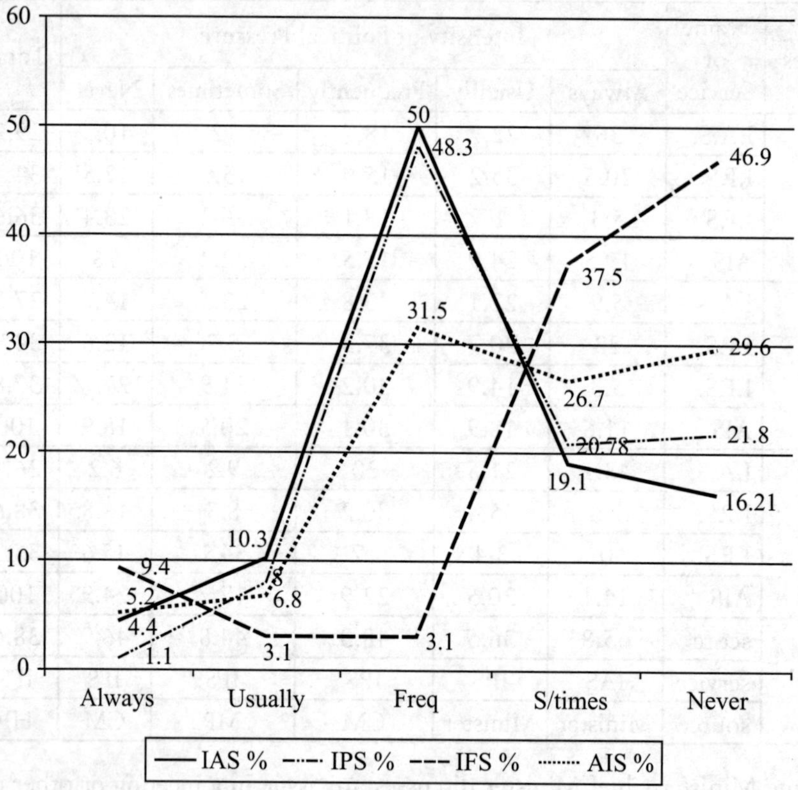

Chart No. 11.2: Pressure from CM/PM

Exhibit Number 11.5: Prime Minister/Chief Minister and Hierarchy Level more Amenable to Pressure

Source	Frequency of Pressure		Level Amenable to P.P.			Total
			Top	Middle	Lower	
Prime Minister/ Chief Minister	"Always" as frequency of political pressure	Count	12	1		13
		% of Total	4.8	0.4		5.2
	"mostly" as frequency of political pressure	Count	11	4	2	17
		% of Total	4.4	1.6	0.8	6.8
	"frequently" as frequency of political pressure	Count	41	27	11	79
		% of Total	16.5	10.8	4.4	31.7
	"sometimes" as frequency of political pressure	Count	41	13	10	64
		% of Total	16.5	5.2	4	25.7
	"never" as frequency of political pressure	Count	41	18	17	76
		% of Total	16.4	7.2	6.8	30.5
Total		Count	146	63	40	249
		% of Total	58.6	25.3	16.1	100

This may be due to the reason that the Indian Administrative Service officers have absorbed pressure as part of their duty and they do not consider routine political pressure as the pressure exerted on them. The Indian Forest Service officers consider any deviation from rules and procedures as the pressure exerted on them. Most of the instances for relaxation of rules go to the Government of India for approval, so sources of pressure are exposed and known to the Indian Forest Service officers. In the case of the Indian Administrative Service officers and the Indian Police Service officers, revenue, law, and order are the State subjects; the pressure exerted on officers gets rectified in the State only. Administrative Service officers consider it 10th, Police Service officers think it at 10th and Forest Service officers rank it at 8th level of source of political pressure in the decision-making process.

Exhibit Number 11.6: Prime Minister/Chief Minister and Family Economic Background Relationship

Source	Frequency of Pressure		Family Economic Background					Total
			Rich	UC	MC	LMC	Poor	
Prime Minister/ Chief Minister	"Always" as frequency of political pressure	Count	6	3		1	3	13
		% of Total	2.51	1.26		0.42	1.26	5.439
	"mostly" as frequency of political pressure	Count	8	2	2	1	4	17
		% of Total	3.35	0.84	0.84	0.42	1.67	7.113
	"frequently" as frequency of political pressure	Count	36	25	5	4	6	76
		% of Total	15.1	10.5	2.09	1.67	2.51	31.8
	"sometimes" as frequency of political pressure	Count	18	15	14	13	2	62
		% of Total	7.53	6.28	5.86	5.44	0.84	25.94
	"never" as frequency of political pressure	Count	13	16	21	16	5	71
		% of Total	5.44	6.69	8.79	6.69	2.09	29.71
Total		Count	81	61	42	35	20	239
		% of Total	33.9	25.5	17.6	14.6	8.37	100

Exhibit Number 11.7: Chi-Square Tests PM/CM versus Economic Background

	Value	df	Asymp. Sig. (2-sided)
Pearson Chi-Square	49.54202669	16	0.000
Likelihood Ratio	52.28219929	16	0.000
Linear-by-Linear Association	6.551002165	1	0.001
N of Valid Cases	239		

Exhibit Number 11.8: PM/CM and Lust to Grab Power as Reason to Accept Pressure

Source	Frequency of Political Pressure		Lust to Grab Power					Total
			Most Import	Very Import	Important	Least Import	Not Import	
Prime Minister/ Chief Minister	"Always" as frequency of political pressure	Count	9	3				12
		% of Total	3.81	1.27				5.085
	"mostly" as frequency of political pressure	Count	9	4	3	1		17
		% of Total	3.81	1.69	1.27	0.42		7.203
	"frequently" as frequency of political pressure	Count	38	23	14	2		77
		% of Total	16.1	9.75	5.93	0.85		32.63
	"sometimes" as frequency of political pressure	Count	22	15	10	4	10	61
		% of Total	9.32	6.36	4.24	1.39	4.24	25.85
	"never" as frequency of political pressure	Count	20	11	9	15	14	69
		% of Total	8.47	4.66	3.81	6.36	5.93	29.24
Total		Count	98	56	36	22	24	236
		% of Total	41.5	23.7	15.3	9.32	10.2	100

Data analysis for level in the hierarchy (Exhibit 11.5) and CM/PM as a source of political pressure indicate that top level (16.5%) frequently accept pressure in the decision-making process. Total frequency indicates that 58.6% of top level, 25.3% of middle level, and 16% of lower level accept the political pressure. The relationship of CM/PM as a source of political pressure and its relationship with the economic background of the All India Services Officers (Exhibit 11.6) indicate that 59.4% of officers from the rich and upper class accept political pressure in the decision-making process. These relationships are highly significant at a 0.000, level of significance (Exhibit 11.7). Relationship of lust to grab power by All India Services Officers (Exhibit 11.8) and CM/PM as a source of political pressure was also studied; results indicate that 32.6% of them frequently accept pressure to grab power.

Exhibit Number 11.9: Chi-Square Tests: PM/CM versus Lust to Grab Power

	Value	df	Asymp. Sig. (2-sided)
Pearson Chi-Square	50.60722104	16	0.000
Likelihood Ratio	60.56196044	16	0.000
Linear-by-Linear Association	33.39078701	1	0.000
N of Valid Cases	236		

11.6.2. Ministers

Center or State Ministers are located on the top of the bureaucratic system. Center or State Minister enjoys the discretionary powers and authority in the decision-making process of the department under their control. Most of the files pertaining to crucial decisions are routed through them. Center or State Ministers enjoy tremendous powers and exercise full administrative control over bureaucrats under their control. This administrative control makes their position super powerful, in a situation, where the majority of officers are without any backbone to stand up on their legs. "Rampant and mounting corruption, especially among the political class, i.e. Ministers and MPs, who exercise real power in a democracy," U.C. Agarwal, 2013.

Members of the bureaucratic system are highly self-goal motivated, high self-goal orientation and lack of values and ethics in the bureaucratic system make them vulnerable in front of the in-charge Minister. Center or State Minister has great powerbase in the bureaucratic system and regulate the decision-making process according to self-interests. The All India Services Officers and Ministers are motivated by the self-goal's achievement, self-interests maximization makes them dependent on each other. Bureaucrat and politician nexus is steered by the selfish individual officers at the cost of government treasuries. This nexus sustains the growth of immoral behavior and flourish the corruption in the bureaucratic system. One thing is sure that ministers alone cannot sustain the immoral practices in the system. It is the willful and active participation of the All India Services Officers, who propagate and continue immoral practices for supporting their own interests.

The Indian Administrative Service officers consider it 2nd, the Indian Police Service officers think it at 5th and the Indian Forest Service officers rank it at 5th level of source of political pressure. 62.5% of the Indian Administrative Service officers get political pressure from Center or State Ministers 'always' to 'mostly' in the decision-making process. 62.5% of the Indian Police Service officers get political pressure 'mostly' in the decision. 66.7% of the Indian Forest Service officers come across political pressure from Center or State Minister 'sometimes' to 'frequently' in the decision. The All India Services Officers total score is spilled over 'always' to 'sometimes' from 21.2% to 23.5%, and the highest score of 23.5% in 'always' category. 90.9% of the All India Services Officers get political pressure from Center or State Ministers 'always' to 'sometimes'.

This indicates that ministers exert pressure on the All India Services Officers for most of the decisions taken by them. The Indian Administrative Service officers get the highest political pressure from the ministers and the Indian Forest Service officers get the least political pressure from this source. Results show that ministers exert the greatest extent of highly effective and result-oriented political pressure in the bureaucratic system. There is no escape from the political pressure exerted by the minister of the concerned department, he is located on your head to review and follow it up regularly, till the goal is fulfilled or goods are delivered up to the minister's satisfaction. This source of political pressure is a highly result-oriented and surest way to work. This source of political pressure has been ranked as the third most important source of pressure working on the All India Services Officers.

Exhibit Number 11.10: Center/State Minister and Length of Service of Officer

Source	Frequency of Pressure		Length of Service of Officer in Years					Total
			1 to 4 years of service	5 to 10 years of service	11-17 years of service	18- 23 years of service	>24 years	
Center or State Minister	"always" as frequency of political pressure	Count	6	5	6	12	32	61
		% of Total	2.37	1.976	2.371	4.743	12.64	24.11
	"mostly" as frequency of political pressure	Count	2	7	4	10	31	54
		% of Total	0.79	2.766	1.581	3.952	12.25	21.34
	"frequently" as frequency of political pressure	Count	7	3	14	10	24	58
		% of Total	2.76	1.185	5.533	3.952	9.486	22.92
	"sometimes" as frequency of political pressure	Count	4	9	15	11	18	57
		% of Total	1.58	3.55	5.928	4.347	7.114	22.52
	"never" as frequency of political pressure	Count	3	2	5	5	8	23
		% of Total	1.18	0.790	1.976	1.976	3.162	9.10
Total		Count	22	26	44	48	113	253
		% of Total	8.69	10.27	17.39	18.97	44.66	100

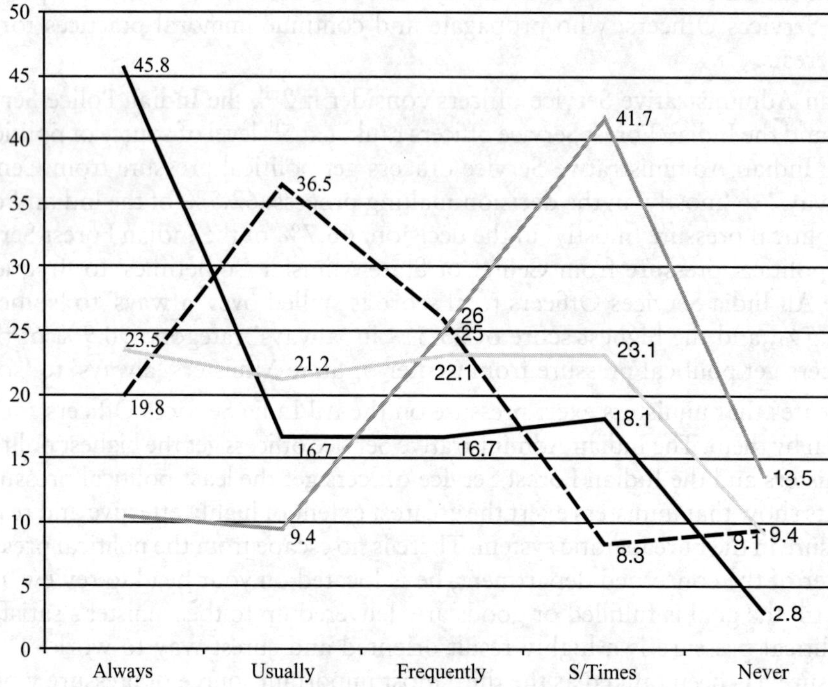

Chart No. 11.3: Source of Pressure from Minister

Exhibit Number 11.11: Center or State Minister and Place of Birth of the Officer

Source	Frequency of Pressure		Officer Birthplace			Total
			Rural	Urban	S/Urban	
Center or State Minister	"always" as frequency of political pressure	Count	5	36	17	58
		% of Total	2.008	14.46	6.827	23.29
	"mostly" as frequency of political pressure	Count	17	25	11	53
		% of Total	6.827	10.04	4.418	21.29
	"frequently" as frequency of political pressure	Count	20	26	14	60
		% of Total	8.032	10.44	5.622	24.1
	"sometimes" as frequency of political pressure	Count	17	25	12	54
		% of Total	6.827	10.04	4.819	21.69
	"never" as frequency of political pressure	Count	7	12	5	24
		% of Total	2.811	4.819	2.008	9.639
Total		Count	66	124	59	249
		% of Total	26.51	49.8	23.69	100

Political pressure exerted by Centre or State Ministers on decision-making process of All India Services Officers and its relationship with the length of service of the officer (Exhibit 11.10), officer rural/urban background (Exhibit 11.11), family member attitudes (Exhibit 11.12), status consciousness (Exhibit 11.13) and transfer as area (Exhibit 11.15) have been studied and results are shown from Exhibits 11.10 to 11.16. Pearson Chi-square results are significant with a 0.000, level of significance, which demonstrates very good strength of such relationships. All India Services Officers with >24 years of service show the highest-pressure acceptance in all these frequencies. All India Services Officers from urban backgrounds indicate the highest acceptance of political pressure from the Centre or State Ministers. Pressure source from Centre/State Minister frequency has been shown in Chart 11.3 for respective services and Chart 11.4 pressure frequency intensity.

In family members attitude, 62.95% of All India Services Officers indicate that spouse influences them maximum to accept political pressure from the Center or State Ministers. 53.5% of All India Services Officers accept political pressure from Center or State Ministers for enhancement of their status and 87.2% of them ranked it more than important frequency. Pearson Chi-square results are significant with a 0.000, level of significance, which demonstrates good strength of such relationships. 43.85% of All India Services Officers 'always' get political pressure in transfers from Center or State Ministers. Pearson Chi-square results for transfer are significant with 0.000, level of significance, which demonstrates the strength of relationships of transfer and political pressure from Center or State Ministers.

Exhibit Number 11.12: Center or State Minister and Family Members Attitude

Source	Frequency of Pressure		Attitude of Family Members				Total
			Spouse	Children	Parents	Brother/ Sister	
Center or State Minister	"always" as frequency of political pressure	Count	36	9	11	4	60
		% of Total	16.07	4.1	4.9	1.8	26.8
	"mostly" as frequency of political pressure	Count	29	8	10	5	52
		% of Total	12.95	3.5	4.5	2.3	23.2
	"frequently" as frequency of political pressure	Count	29	5	11	7	52
		% of Total	12.95	2.2	4.9	3.1	23.21
	"sometimes" as frequency of political pressure	Count	35		7	1	43
		% of Total	15.63		3.1	0.5	19.2
	"never" as frequency of political pressure	Count	12	2	3		17
		% of Total	5.6	0.9	1.3		7.6
Total		Count	141	24	42	17	224
		% of Total	62.95	10.7	18.75	7.8	100

Exhibit Number 11.13: Center/State Minister Source versus Enhancement of Status

Source	Frequency of Pressure		Enhancement of Status					Total
			Most I.	Very I.	Imp.	Least I.	Not I.	
Center or State Minister	"always" as frequency of Political Pressure	Count	45	9	4		1	59
		% of Total	18.52	3.704	1.65		0.41	24.28
	"mostly" as frequency of political pressure	Count	32	15	6	1		54
		% of Total	13.17	6.173	2.47	0.41		22.22
	"frequently" as frequency of political pressure	Count	29	12	6	6	3	56
		% of Total	11.93	4.938	2.47	2.469	1.23	23.05
	"sometimes" as frequency of political pressure	Count	17	9	13	13	5	57
		% of Total	6.996	3.704	5.35	5.35	2.06	23.46
	"never" as frequency of political pressure	Count	7	7	1	2		17
		% of Total	2.881	2.881	0.41	0.823		6.996
Total		Count	130	52	30	22	9	243
		% of Total	53.5	21.4	12.3	9.053	3.7	100

Exhibit Number 11.14: Chi-Square Tests, Minister Source of Pressure versus Status Enhancement

	Value	df	Asymp. Sig. (2-sided)
Pearson Chi-Square	54.140	16	'0.000'
Likelihood Ratio	58.409	0.16	'0.000'
N of Valid Cases	243		

Exhibit Number 11.15: Center or State Minister and Transfers Relationship

Source	Frequency of Pressure		Transfers					Total
			Rarely	Sometimes	Frequently	Most oftenly	Always	
Center or State Minister	"always" as frequency of political pressure	Count			11	15	28	54
		% of Total			5.89	8.021	14.97	28.9
	"mostly" as frequency of political pressure	Count		1	10	11	17	39
		% of Total		0.53	5.35	5.882	9.090	20.9
	"frequently" as frequency of political pressure	Count	2		5	13	17	37
		% of Total	1.07		2.68	6.951	9.090	19.8
	"sometimes" as frequency of political pressure	Count		3	8	13	16	40
		% of Total		1.6	4.28	6.951	8.556	21.4
	"never" as frequency of political pressure	Count	4	1	1	7	4	17
		% of Total	2.14	0.5	0.54	3.743	2.140	9.09
Total		Count	6	5	35	59	82	187
		% of Total	3.21	2.6	18.71	31.55	43.85	100

Exhibit Number 11.16: Chi-Square Tests: Center or State Minister and Transfers Relationship

	Value	df	Asymp. Sig. (2-sided)
Pearson Chi-Square	40.02671713	16	0.001
N of Valid Cases	187		

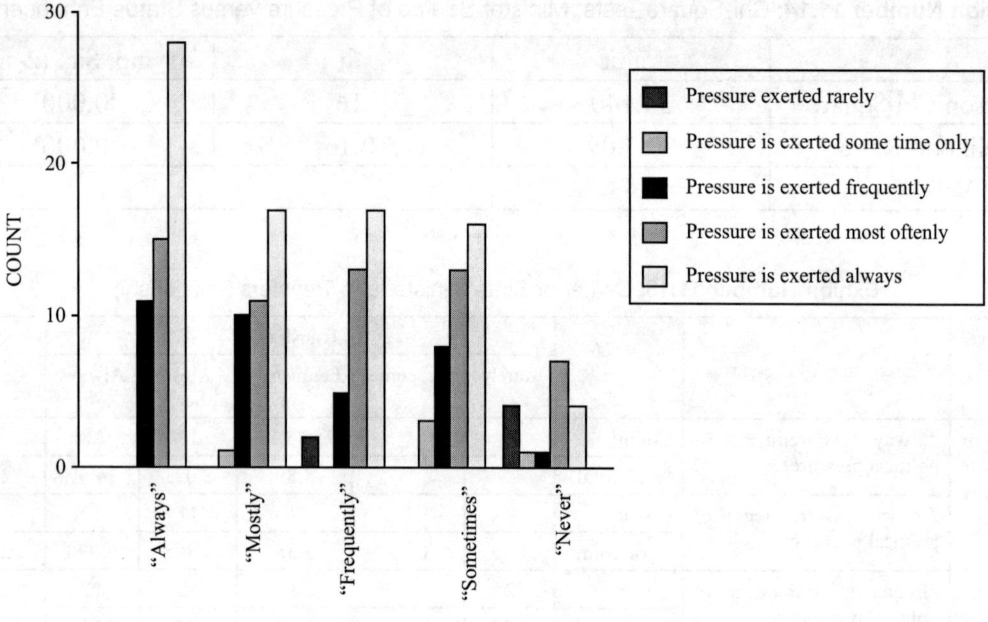

Chart No. 11.4: Centre/State Minister and Pressure Frequency for Transfers

11.6.3. Member of Parliament

Member of Parliament exertion of political pressure is related to their equation in the party and relations with the top politicians in the ruling party. When some member of Parliament has an excellent working relationship with the Prime Minister/Chief Minister or a particular Center or State Minister, they exert pressure on such places, where they think desired things will be done. When they do not have an excellent working relationship with powerful politicians, the intensity of political pressure gets reduced in proportion to their stake in power. When the All India Services Officers do not move in their direction of pressure or the individual officer does not do their job, members of Parliament do not possess any mechanism by which, they can pressurize officers to do the things. The All India Services Officers are also intelligent enough to assess the situation and invariably oblige politicians according to their powerbase for harming officer's interests. In such situations, members of Parliament try to develop friendly relations with the concerned officer or approach officers through known bureaucrats or friends, so that, the concerned officer can accept pressure as a personal obligation to some extent.

Exhibit Number 11.17: Member of Parliament and Transfers Crosstabulation

Source	Frequency of Pressure Source		Transfers as Pressure Area					Total
			Rarely	Sometimes	Frequently	Most oftenly	Always	
Member of Parliament	"always" as frequency of political pressure	Count			5	6	2	13
		% of Total			2.645	3.174	1.058	6.88
	"mostly" as frequency of political pressure	Count	1		13	10	20	44
		% of Total	0.53		6.878	5.291	10.58	23.3
	"frequently" as frequency of pressure	Count		1	4	13	31	49
		% of Total		0.5291	2.116	6.878	16.40	25.9
	"sometimes" as frequency of pressure	Count	2	2	6	24	28	62
		% of Total	1.06	1.0582	3.174	12.698	14.81	32.8
	"never" as frequency of political pressure	Count	3	2	5	5	6	21
		% of Total	1.59	1.0582	2.645	2.645	3.174	11.1
Total		Count	6	5	33	58	87	189
		% of Total	3.17	2.6455	17.46	30.687	46.03	100

Exhibit Number 11.18: Chi-Square Tests MP Source of Pressure in Transfers

	Value	df	Asymp. Sig. (2-sided)
Pearson Chi-Square	38.723	16	0.001
N of Valid Cases	189		

76.3% of the Indian Administrative Service officers get political pressure from Member of Parliament 'mostly' to 'frequently.' 69.2% of the Indian Forest Service officers and 64.9% of the Indian Police Service officers come across political pressure 'sometimes' to 'frequently' from the Member of Parliament. 65.7% of the All India Services Officers also get 'sometimes' to 'frequent' political pressure from the Member of Parliament. The intensity of political pressure is highest on the Indian Administrative Service officers, as they are located in places that are more important and oblige easily to politicians. The score of political pressure exerted is distributed mainly in the three frequencies, 'mostly' to 'sometimes', indicate moderate to the high intensity of political pressure used by the Member of Parliament. This source of political pressure has been ranked as the 9th source of pressure working on the All India Services Officers. Administrative Service officers consider it 9th, the Indian Police Service officers think it at 8th and the Indian Forest Service officers rank it at 9th level of source of political pressure.

Exhibit Number 11.19: Member of Parliament and Officer Regional Background Crosstabulation

Source	Frequency of Pressure Source		Officer Regional Background						Total
			N/E	East	West	North	South	Central	
Member of Parliament	"always" as frequency of political pressure	Count	1	4		4	4	1	14
		% of Total	0.39	1.54		1.54	1.54	0.39	5.41
	"mostly" as frequency of political pressure	Count	10	6	6	7	19	3	51
		% of Total	3.86	2.32	2.32	2.7	7.34	1.16	19.7
	"frequently" as frequency of political pressure	Count	13	13	6	15	23	10	80
		% of Total	5.02	5.02	2.32	5.79	8.88	3.86	30.9
	"sometimes" as frequency of political pressure	Count	9	16	8	29	21	7	90
		% of Total	3.47	6.18	3.09	11.2	8.11	2.7	34.8
	"never" as frequency of political pressure	Count	5	2	2	8	5	2	24
		% of Total	1.93	0.77	0.77	3.09	1.93	0.77	9.27
Total		Count	38	41	22	63	72	23	259
		% of Total	14.7	15.8	8.49	24.3	27.8	8.88	100

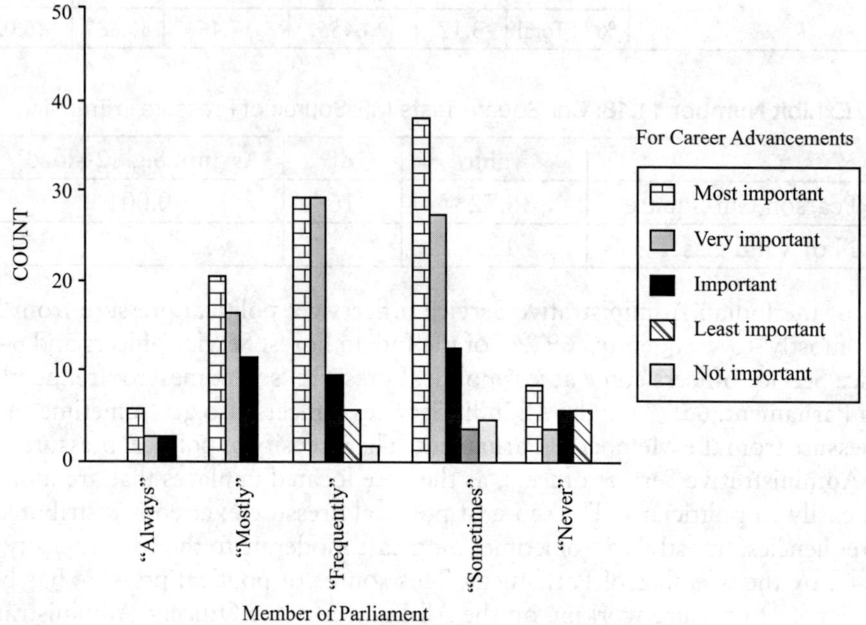

Chart No. 11.5: Career Advancement and Pressure from M.P.

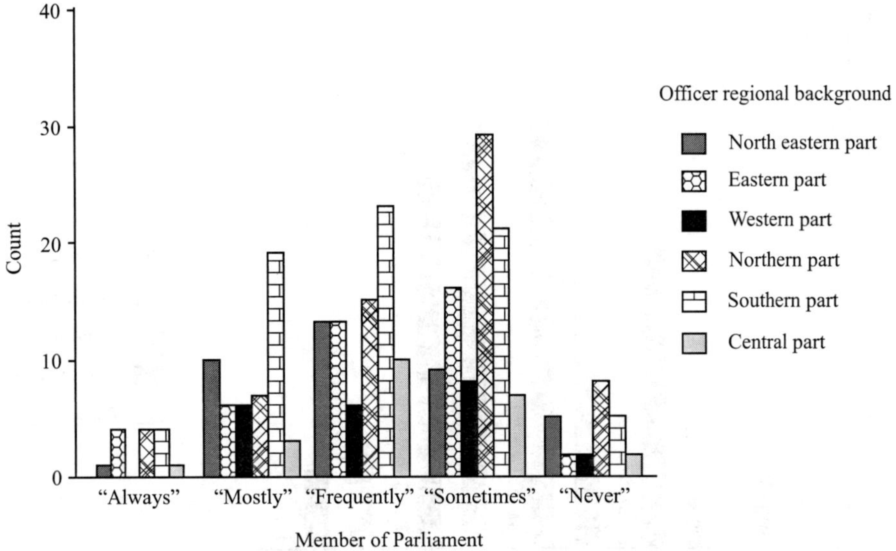

Chart No. 11.6: Regional Background and Pressure from M.P.

Exhibit Number 11.20: Member of Parliament and Education of the Parents Relationship

Pressure Source	Frequency of Pressure		Education of the Parents				Total
			Matriculate	Graduate	P.G.	Ph.D.	
Member of Parliament	"always" as frequency of political pressure	Count	1	4	6	1	12
		% of Total	0.41	1.65	2.49	0.415	4.979
	"mostly" as frequency of political pressure	Count	5	11	23	10	49
		% of Total	2.07	4.56	9.54	4.149	20.33
	"frequently" as frequency of political pressure	Count	14	20	32	10	76
		% of Total	5.81	8.29	13.28	4.149	31.53
	"sometimes" as frequency of political pressure	Count	32	17	28	5	82
		% of Total	13.3	7.053	11.62	2.074	34.02
	"never" as frequency of political pressure	Count	8	7	6	1	22
		% of Total	3.32	2.904	2.49	0.414	9.128
Total		Count	60	59	95	27	241
		% of Total	24.9	24.48	39.42	11.2	100

Exhibit Number 11.21: Chi-Square Results: Member of Parliament versus Education of Parents

	Chi-Square Tests		Asymp. Sig. (2-sided)
	Value	df	
Pearson Chi-Square	25.529	12	0.013
N of Valid Cases	241		

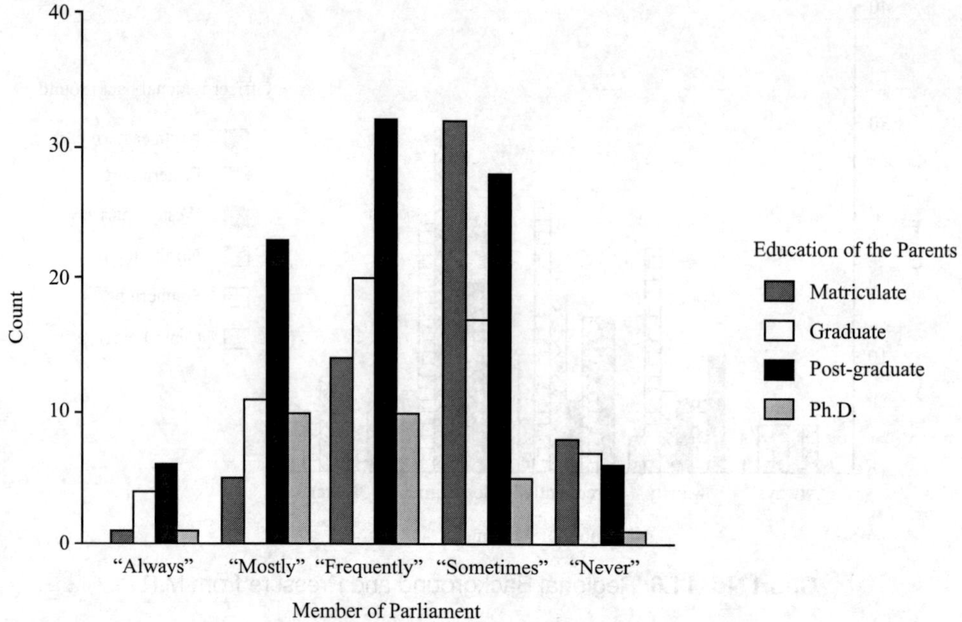

Chart No. 11.7: Education of Parents and Pressure Source as M.P.

The relationship of political pressure from the Members of Parliament and different variables of the All India Services Officers were studied and results have been indicated in Exhibits 11.17 to 11.21 and in Charts from 11.5 to 11.7. Political pressure from Members of Parliament and its relationship with the regional background of the officer indicates that 56% of them accept pressure 'frequently' to 'always', in this 27.8% from southern India show the highest acceptance of pressure. 46.3% of All India Services Officers 'always' get political pressure from Members of Parliament and Pearson Chi-square results are significant with a 0.001, level of significance, which demonstrates the reliability of strength in such relationships. Concerning reasons for acceptance of political pressure from Members of Parliament, results indicate that career advancement is the most important variable in acceptance of pressure in decision-making process. 39.42% of postgraduate parents influence their offspring has to accept political pressure from the Members of Parliament and Pearson Chi-square results are significant with 0.013, level of significance, which demonstrates the strength of such relationships.

11.6.4. Member Legislative Council/Member Legislative Assembly

Member Legislative Council/Member Legislative Assembly use their influence and position to the highest extent to extract benefits from the bureaucratic system. This source of political pressure has been ranked at 1st most important source of pressure being exerted on the All India Services Officers in the decision-making process. M.L.A. develop a strong working relationship with prominent persons of his constituency for his own political survival and sustenance. For this level of politicians, political activities are confined to a smaller area in close coordination with the people. Since, at this level politician has to continue and cultivate personal relations with voters, in turn, voters exert a high amount of frequent pressure on the M.L.A. to get things done for them. M.L.A. has no option, except to approach concerned individual officers for getting things done for his interested parties and their wishful interests. Contact with the masses is the highest at this level of politicians, so as the pressure exerted by them is also highest by the M.L.A. This can be inferred as the political pressure exerted by politicians on the All India Services Officers is directly related to the politician's contact and behavior with the people.

Exhibit Number 11.22: MLA/MLC Source versus Attitude of Family Members

Source	Frequency of Pressure		Family Members Attitude				Total
			Spouse	Children	Parents	Brother/Sister	
Member of Legislative Assembly/ Council	"always" as frequency of political pressure	Count	45	8	22	3	78
		% of Total	20	3.56	9.78	1.34	34.67
	"mostly" as frequency of political pressure	Count	31	7	8	6	52
		% of Total	13.78	3.12	3.55	2.67	23.11
	"frequently" as frequency of political pressure	Count	34	7	6	6	53
		% of Total	15.12	3.12	2.66	2.67	23.56
	"sometimes" as frequency of pressure	Count	23	1	4	1	29
		% of Total	10.23	0.45	1.78	0.44	12.89
	"never" as frequency of political pressure	Count	8	2	2	1	13
		% of Total	3.56	0.89	0.89	0.44	5.78
Total		Count	141	25	42	17	225
		% of Total	62.67	11.12	18.7	7.56	100

83.1% of the Indian Administrative Service officers get political pressure 'always' to 'mostly' from the Member Legislative Council/Member Legislative Assembly in the decision-making process. 76% of the Indian Police Service officers and 79.5% of the All India Services Officers get the political pressure 'frequently' to 'always' from Member Legislative Council/Member Legislative Assembly in the decision. 77.1% of the Indian Forest Service officers get political pressure from Member Legislative Council/Member Legislative Assembly 'frequently', 'sometimes', and 'mostly' in the decision. The Indian Administrative Service officers get the highest political pressure from this source. A very low score in the 'never' category indicates that invariably political pressure is exerted by the Member Legislative Council/Member Legislative Assembly on the bureaucratic system to things done according to political desires.

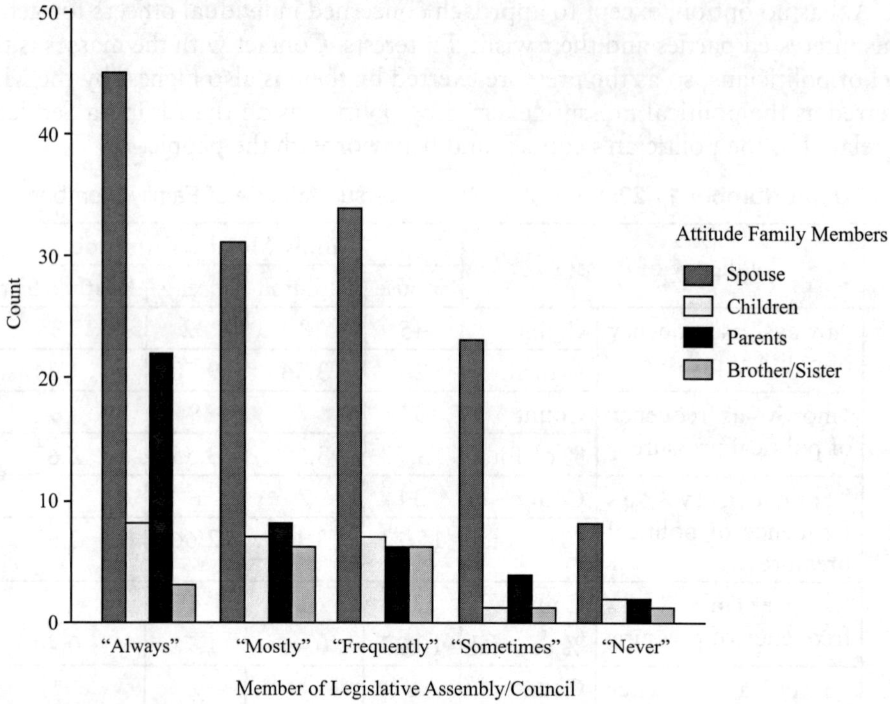

Chart No. 11.8: Family Member Attitude and M.L.A., Source of Pressure

The Indian Administrative Service officers consider it 1st, the Indian Police Service officers think it at 2nd and the Indian Forest Service officers rank it at 2nd level of source of political pressure. This source of political pressure is hazardous for the bureaucrats; politicians at this level can use any methodology to any extent to pressurize the individual officers. Most of the misbehavior incidents are experienced at this level. The depth of political pressure exerted by the Member Legislative Council/Member Legislative Assembly is severe and it starts from the lowest level to the highest level of administration. We can say that political pressure from the Member Legislative Council/Member Legislative Assembly is pervasive across all the levels of the hierarchy and all the locations in all the public offices.

Political pressure exerted by Member of Legislative Assembly/Council on decision-making process and its relation with the different variables in our study show a good relationship of acceptance of political pressure with them. Relation with pursuing goals for self and family (Exhibit 11.26) as reasons for acceptance of political pressure indicates that 27.7% of All India Services Officers consider it 'most important' to accept political pressure from Member of Legislative Assembly/Council. 49.4% of All India Services Officers from urban background after high school accept (Exhibit 11.25) political pressure 'frequently' to 'always' from Member of Legislative Assembly/Council.

Exhibit Number 11.23: Chi-Square Tests Results for Cadre of the Officer versus M.L.A./M.L.C.

	N	Value	df	Asymp. Sig. (2-sided)
Pearson Chi-Square	240	21.382	8	0.006

Exhibit Number 11.24: M.L.A./M.L.C. and Cadre of the Officer

Source of Pressure	Frequency of Pressure		Cadre of the officer: Home cadre	Outside cadre	Neighbour state	Total
Member of Legislative Assembly/ Council	"always" as frequency of political pressure	Count	9	44	19	72
		% of Total	3.75	18.333	7.917	30
	"mostly" as frequency of political pressure	Count	20	23	11	54
		% of Total	8.333	9.583	4.583	22.5
	"frequently" as frequency of political pressure	Count	19	31	13	63
		% of Total	7.916	12.916	5.417	26.25
	"sometimes" as frequency of political pressure	Count	17	14	6	37
		% of Total	7.083	5.833	2.5	15.41
	"never" as frequency of political pressure	Count	8	5	1	14
		% of Total	3.333	2.083	0.417	5.83
Total		Count	73	117	50	240
		% of Total	30.42	48.75	20.83	100

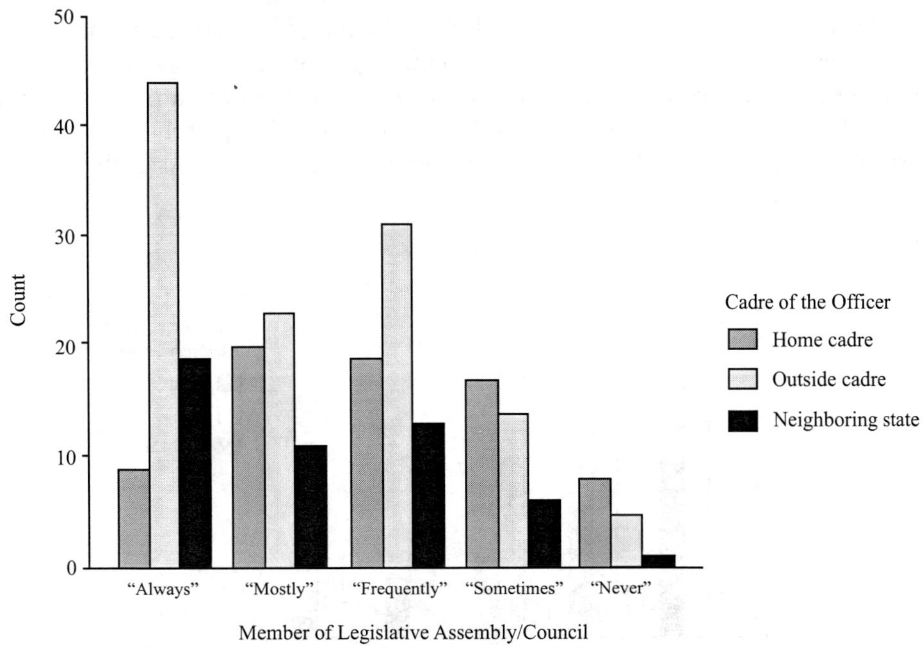

Chart No. 11.9: The Cadre of the Officer and Pressure from M.L.A./M.L.C.

Exhibit Number 11.25: M.L.A./M.L.C. and Place of Education after High School

Source of Pressure	Frequency of Pressure		Education after High School			Total
			Rural	Urban	Semi-Urban	
Member of Legislative Assembly/ Council	"always" as frequency of political pressure	Count	14	43	24	81
		% of Total	5.65	17.34	9.678	32.66
	"mostly" as frequency of political pressure	Count	7	29	18	54
		% of Total	2.82	11.69	7.259	21.77
	"frequently" as frequency of political pressure	Count	7	48	11	66
		% of Total	2.82	19.35	4.436	26.61
	"sometimes" as frequency of pressure	Count	2	23	8	33
		% of Total	0.81	9.274	3.226	13.31
	"never" as frequency of political pressure	Count		11	3	14
		% of Total		4.435	1.21	5.645
Total		Count	30	154	64	248
		% of Total	12.1	62.1	25.81	100

Relation with the cadre (Exhibit 11.24) of the officer and political pressure from Member of Legislative Assembly/Council indicate that 58.7% of All India Services Officers outsiders in cadre accept pressure from Member of Legislative Assembly/Council 'frequently' to 'always'. Pearson Chi-square results are significant with a 0.006, level of significance, which demonstrates reliability in the strength of such relationships. In the family member attitude (Exhibit 11.22) category 48.9% of All India Services Officers think that spouse 'frequently' to 'always' category influence them to accept political pressure from Member of Legislative Assembly/Council.

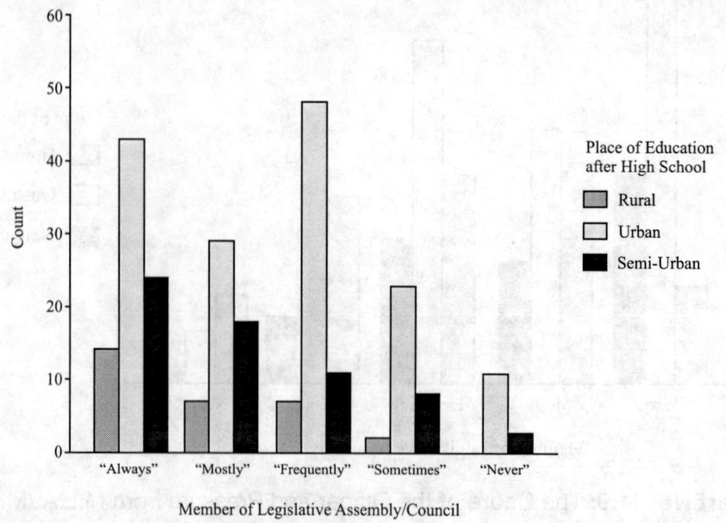

Chart No. 11.10: Place of Education after High School versus Pressure from M.L.A./M.L.C.

Exhibit Number 11.26: Acceptance of Pressure from M.L.A./M.L.C. versus Pursue Goals for Self and Family

Source	Frequency of Pressure		Pursue Goals for Self and Family					Total
			Most Imp.	Very Imp.	Important	Least Imp.	Not Imp.	
Member of Legislative Assembly/ Council	"always" as frequency of political pressure	Count	37	16	14	13	3	83
		% of Total	14.45	6.25	5.47	5.08	1.17	32.4
	"mostly" as frequency of political pressure	Count	14	12	9	14	5	54
		% of Total	5.47	4.69	3.56	5.47	1.96	21.1
	"frequently" as frequency of political pressure	Count	10	17	18	13	9	67
		% of Total	3.91	6.65	7.04	5.08	3.52	26.2
	"sometimes" as frequency of pressure	Count	5	7	9	13	5	39
		% of Total	1.95	2.74	3.52	5.08	1.95	15.2
	"never" as frequency of political pressure	Count	5	1	4	1	2	13
		% of Total	1.95	0.39	1.57	0.39	0.78	5.08
Total		Count	71	53	54	54	24	256
		% of Total	27.7	20.7	21.09	21.09	9.38	100

Exhibit Number 11.27: Pursue Goals for Self versus Member Legislative Assembly Pressure

	N	Chi-Square Tests		Asymp. Sig. (2-sided)
		Value	df	
Pearson Chi-Square	256	33.07	16	0.007

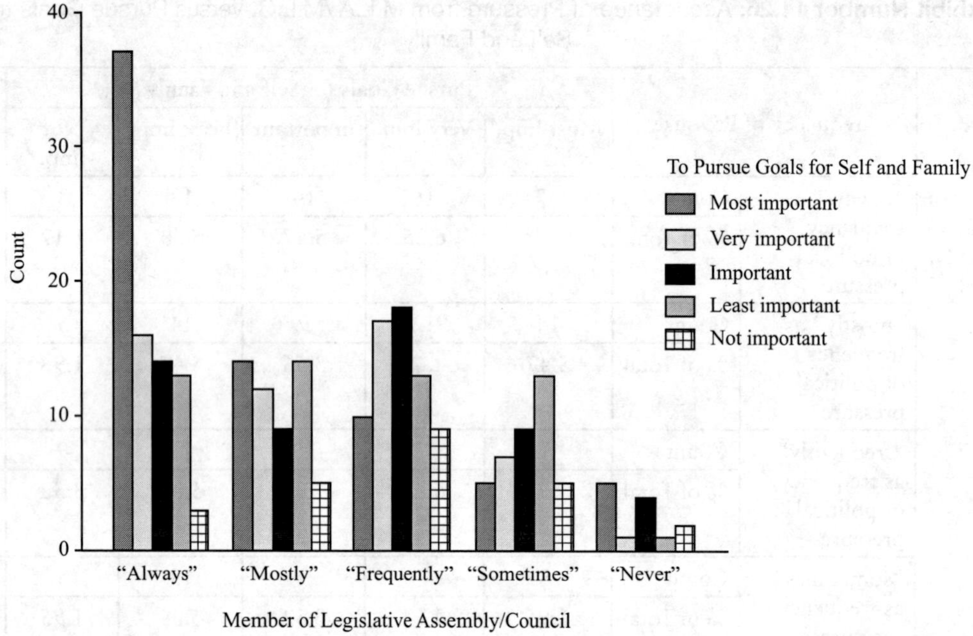

Chart No. 11.11: Pursue Goals for Self and for Family versus M.L.A./M.L.C. Pressure

11.6.5. District-Level Politician/Zila Parishad Members

The All India Services Officers get maximum political pressure in the decision-making process at the district-level. Most of the field implementation decisions are taken at this level or under their jurisdiction. Colonially created bureaucratic system has invested most of the powers under different laws, acts, rules, regulations, and procedures to district-level officers. Our social system has accepted it as the norm of their life and psychologically people consider district heads as virtual kings in the area. People have experienced that even if they get orders from the top persons in the bureaucratic hierarchy, district level officers take shelter under different rules and regulations to deny their inherent rights. In case, district level officers are not happy, decisions are never implemented and orders from the top remain confined to files under the wrap of never-ending objections.

The delivery mechanism in our bureaucratic system is such that people are forced to move around district-level officers. District-level politicians/Zila Parishad Members are aware of this hard fact to get things done for people. District-level politicians cultivate a good relationship with the district officers. Since these politicians are located at the district headquarters or nearby and can afford to visit district level officers frequently. District-level politicians try to develop a strong relationship with district-level individual All India Services Officers, these officers also need support from these politicians, and in the process, both groups serve each other interests. These mutual dependence relationships help both groups to maximize the achievement of individual goals. Own goals achievements sustain and enhance such relationships, which in turn turned out into immoral behavior. These district-level politicians/Zila Parishad Members enhance their financial bargaining power from a close relationship with the All India Services Officers, in turn, individual officers get political patronage and protection from these district politicians. In case of transfer or any other problem, these district-level politician/Zila Parishad Members mobilize political support to retain these officers posted in their districts. As an outcome of the process of mutual bargains, both groups exploit government treasuries to own advantage and ultimately in the long run people are the sufferer. Equity and equality get lost or relegated.

Exhibit Number 11.28: Zila Parishad/District-Level Politicians versus Security and Stability in Job/ Least Disturbances Reason to Accept Pressure

Source of Pressure	Frequency of Pressure		Security/Stability in Job/Least Disturbances					Total
			Most Imp.	Very Imp.	Important	Least Imp.	Not Imp.	
Zila Parishad/ District-level Politicians	"always" as frequency of political pressure	Count	32	29	9	2		72
		% of Total	12.96	11.7	3.643	0.809		29.1
	"mostly" frequency of political pressure	Count	17	17	10	5	4	53
		% of Total	6.883	6.88	4.048	2.024	1.62	21.5
	"frequently" frequency of political pressure	Count	22	23	5	9	7	66
		% of Total	8.907	9.31	2.024	3.643	2.83	26.7
	"sometimes" frequency of political pressure	Count	13	12	3	1	2	31
		% of Total	5.263	4.86	1.214	0.404	0.81	12.6
	"never" frequency of political pressure	Count	10	3	7	3	2	25
		% of Total	4.049	1.21	2.834	1.214	0.81	10.1
Total		Count	94	84	34	20	15	247
		% of Total	38.06	34	13.765	8.1	6.07	100

Exhibit Number 11.29: Chi-Square Tests for Security and Stability in Job versus DLP Pressure

	N	Value	df	Asymp. Sig. (2-sided)
Pearson Chi-Square	247	32.919	16	0.010
Likelihood Ratio		32.076	16	0.010

Exhibit Number 11.30: DLP Pressure versus Method of Recruitment more Amenable to the Pressure

Source of Pressure	Frequency of Pressure		Method of Recruitment		Total
			Direct recruit	Promotes	
Zila Parishad/ District-level Politicians	"always" political pressure	% of Total	8.33	21.21	29.54
	"mostly" political pressure	% of Total	4.92	16.29	21.21
	"frequently" political pressure	% of Total	10.98	13.26	24.24
	"sometimes" political pressure	% of Total	2.27	12.5	14.77
	"never" political pressure	% of Total	5.3	4.92	10.23
Total		% of Total	31.82	68.18	100

Exhibit Number 11.31: Chi-Square Tests: Method of Recruitment versus DLP Pressure

	N	Value	df	Asymp. Sig. (2-sided)
Pearson Chi-Square	264	17.602	4	0.001

The All India Services Officers have ranked political pressure from district-level politician/Zila Parishad Members as 2nd most important source of pressure in the decision-making process. 74.9% of the All India Services Officers, 81.6% of the Indian Administrative Service officers, and 80.9% of the Indian Police Service officers get political pressure 'always' category to 'frequently' category from the district-level politician/Zila Parishad Members. 68.3% of the Indian Forest Service officers get political pressure 'mostly' to 'sometimes' from district-level politician/Zila Parishad Members.

The Indian Administrative Service officers get the highest political pressure from this source and they mostly develop excellent rapport with them for their own goals maximizations. This source of political pressure causes the greatest damage to the bureaucratic system and also harms the people and government to the greatest extent. This source of politicians also exploits, pilfer, embezzle, and illegally grab the highest amount of government resources in connivance with district-level All India Services Officers. Maximum government funds are spent at this level, and maximum hanky-panky is made at this level. The Administrative Service officers consider it 4th, the Indian Police Service officers think it at 1st and the Indian Forest Service officers rank it at 1st level of source of political pressure.

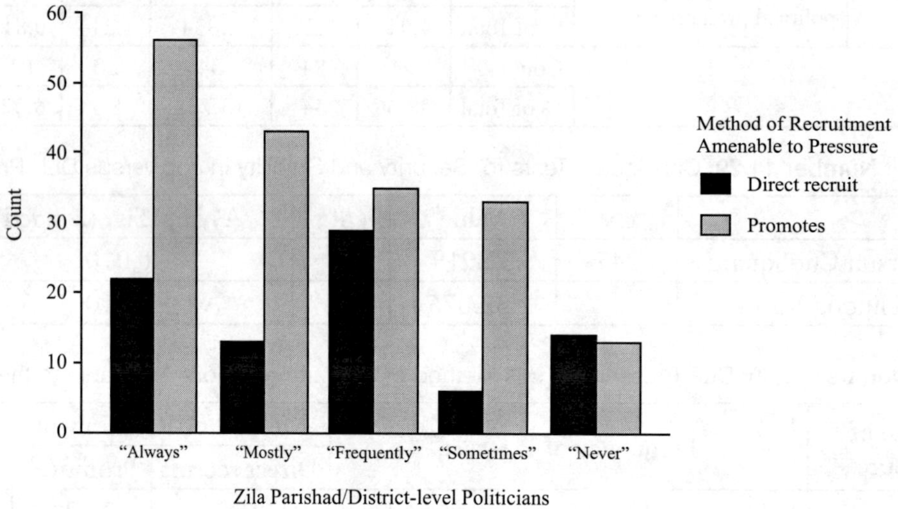

Chart No. 11.12: Method of Recruitment versus Pressure from DLP/ZLP

Exhibit Number 11.32: Zila Parishad/District-Level Politicians versus Community Background of Officer

Pressure Source	Pressure Frequency		Community Background				Total
			General	OBC	SC	ST	
Zila Parishad/ District-level Politicians	"always" as frequency of political pressure	Count	33	3	23	14	73
		% of Total	13.692	1.24	9.54	5.81	30.29
	"mostly" frequency of political pressure	Count	24	3	21	5	53
		% of Total	9.958	1.24	8.71	2.07	21.99
	"frequently" frequency of political pressure	Count	25	1	22	11	59
		% of Total	10.373	0.41	9.12	4.56	24.48
	"sometimes" frequency of political pressure	Count	16	2	10	4	32
		% of Total	6.639	0.82	4.14	1.65	13.27
	"never" frequency of political pressure	Count	10		13	1	24
		% of Total	4.149		5.39	0.41	9.959
Total		Count	108	9	89	35	241
		% of Total	44.813	3.73	36.9	14.5	100

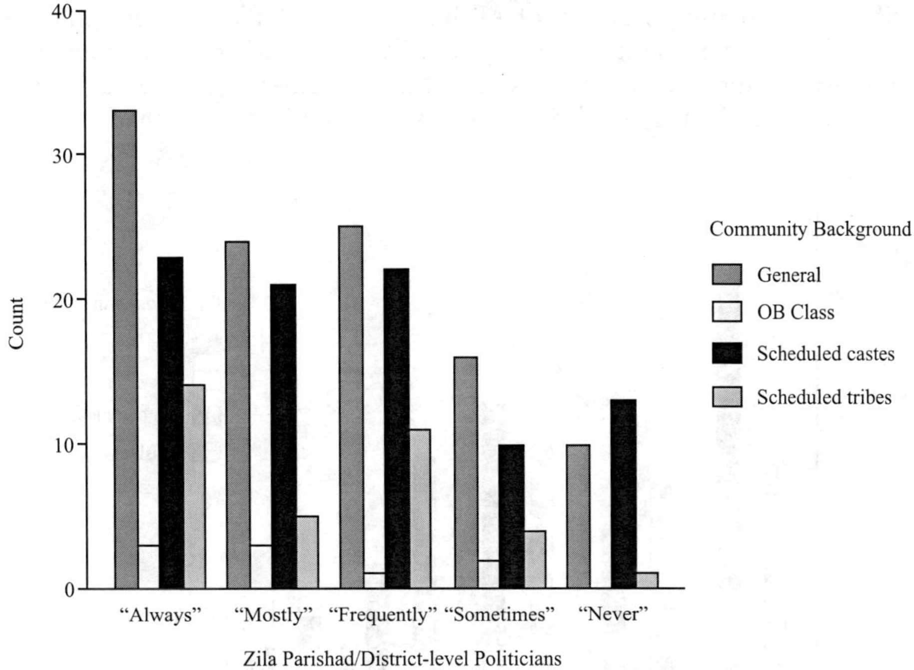

Chart No. 11.13: Community Background versus Pressure from DLP/ZLP

Exhibit Number 11.33: District-Level Politicians versus Profession of the Spouse

Source	Frequency of Pressure Source		Profession of the Spouse				Total
			Housekeep	Services	Entrepreneur	Business	
Zila Parishad/ District-level Politicians	"always" frequency of political pressure	Count	18	12	31	14	75
		% of Total	7.1	4.8	12.3	5.6	29.76
	"mostly" frequency of political pressure	Count	16	12	13	13	54
		% of Total	6.3	4.8	5.1	5.1	21.42
	"frequently" frequency of pressure	Count	20	11	22	9	62
		% of Total	7.9	4.4	8.7	3.6	24.61
	"sometimes" frequency of pressure	Count	18	4	10	4	36
		% of Total	7.2	1.6	3.9	1.6	14.28
	"never" frequency of political pressure	Count	6	9	4	6	25
		% of Total	2.4	3.6	1.6	2.3	9.92
Total		Count	78	48	80	46	252
		% of Total	30.9	19.1	31.7	18.253	100

The AISO acceptance of political pressure from district-level politicians/Zila Parishad Members has been studied in relation to different variables; results are shown in Exhibits 11.28 to 11.34 showing different relationships. 38.7% of All India Services Officers accept political pressure 'frequently' to 'always' from district-level politicians/Zila Parishad Members to protect their security and stability or least disturbances in a job (Exhibit 11.28). Pearson Chi-square results are significant with a 0.010, level of significance, which demonstrates reliability in the strength of such relationships.

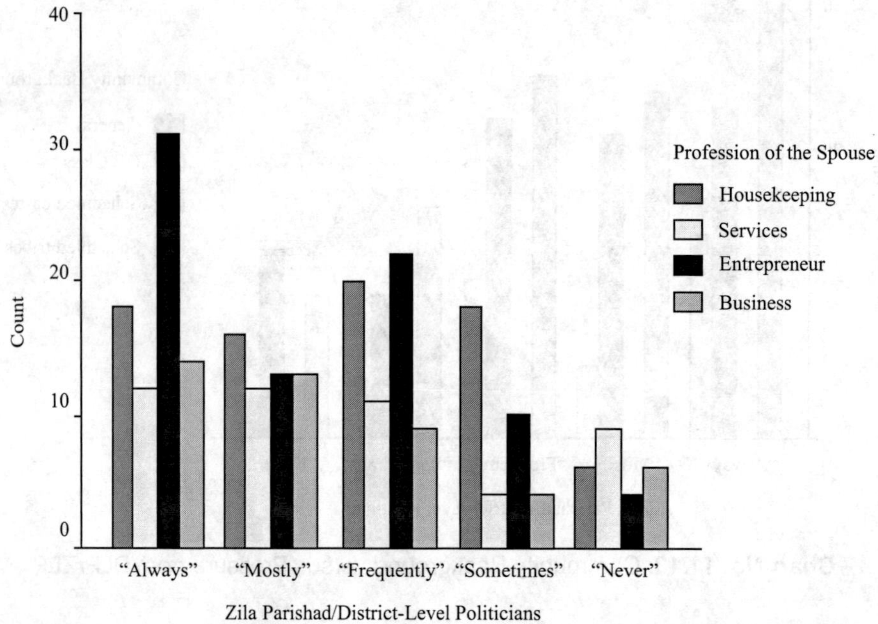

Chart No. 11.14: The Profession of the Spouse and Pressure from DLP/ZPM

Exhibit Number 11.34: District Level Politicians and Developmental Work-related Issues

Pressure Source	Pressure Frequency		Developmental Work-related Issues					Total
			Rarely	Sometimes	Frequently	Most Oftenly	Always	
Zila Parishad/ District-level Politicians	"always" as frequency of political pressure	Count	6	16	14	11	6	53
		% of Total	3.896	10.4	9.09	7.14	3.89	34.41
	"mostly" frequency of political pressure	Count	2	15	7	6	3	33
		% of Total	1.298	9.74	4.54	3.89	1.94	21.42
	"frequently" frequency of political pressure	Count	3	9	10	6	2	30
		% of Total	1.948	5.84	6.49	3.89	1.3	19.48
	"sometimes" frequency of political pressure	Count	4	9	6	5		24
		% of Total	2.597	5.84	3.89	3.24		15.58
	"never" frequency of political pressure	Count	1	5	7		1	14
		% of Total	0.649	3.24	4.54		0.65	9.09
Total		Count	16	54	44	28	12	154
		% of Total	10.38	35.06	28.57	18.18	7.79	100

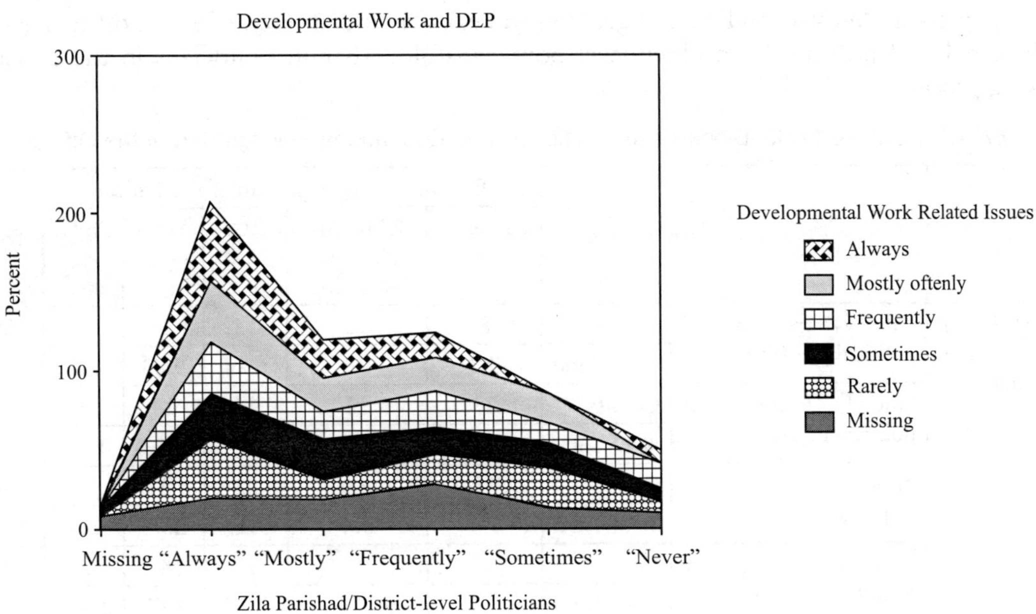

Chart No. 11.15: Development-related Works and Pressure from DLP/ZPM

Results for the method of recruitment (Exhibit 11.30) indicate that 50.8% of promoted officers accept political pressure 'frequently' to 'always'. Relationship of community background

(Exhibit 11.32) and district-level politicians/Zila Parishad Members source of political pressure indicate that 40.6% of SC+ST and 34% of general category officers 'frequently' to 'always' accept political pressure in decision-making process. In the profession of spouse (Exhibit 11.33) and district-level politicians/Zila Parishad Members, relationship indicate that 26.1% entrepreneur spouse influence All India Services Officers to accept pressure 'frequently' to 'always'. 34.4% of All India Services Officers always accept pressure.

11.6.6. Block-Level Politicians/Block Samiti

The frequency of political pressure at the block level may be very high. Block-level politicians are having the strongest affiliation with the public at the grass-root level and they develop a family relationship among prominent persons/families in villages of that block. Block-level politicians most of the time come for small issues, such as transfer of lower-level functionaries, allocation of resources for villages, and development funds for their villages. In most of the cases, villages of that block remain the unit for their activities. While visiting district officers, persons at this level move along with the Center or State Minister or Member Legislative Council/Member Legislative Assembly, political pressure from this source invariably is not independent. Block-level politicians/Block Samiti politicians mobilize higher-level politicians' support to get their things done.

Administrative Service officers consider it 6th, the Indian Police Service officers think it at 6th and the Indian Forest Service officers rank it at 4th level of source of political pressure. 57.4% of the All India Services Officers, 70.4% of the Indian Police Service officers and 57% of the Indian Administrative Service officers get 'mostly' to 'frequently' political pressure from block-level politicians/Block Samiti. In the case of the Indian Forest Service officers, 26.3% of them get political pressure 'mostly' and 22.1% get 'sometimes'. The Indian Police Service officers get the highest political pressure from block-level politicians/Block Samiti politicians in the decision-making process.

Exhibit Number 11.35: Block-Level Politicians and Educational Background of the Officer

Source	Frequency of Pressure Source		Educational Background of the Officer					Total
			Graduate	Engineer/ B.Tech./ Technology	P.G.	MBA	Ph.D.	
Block Samiti/ Block-Level Politicians	"always" frequency of political pressure	Count	8	13	15	2	1	39
		% of Total	3.3	5.4	6.25	0.83	0.417	16.25
	"mostly" frequency of political pressure	Count	23	11	24	14	1	73
		% of Total	9.6	4.6	10	5.83	0.417	30.41
	"frequently" frequency of pressure	Count	18	13	22	5	6	64
		% of Total	7.5	5.4	9.17	2.08	2.5	26.66
	"sometimes" frequency of political pressure	Count	13	6	10	4	5	38
		% of Total	5.4	2.5	4.17	1.67	2.083	15.83
	"never" frequency of political pressure	Count	6	8	7	1	4	26
		% of Total	2.5	3.3	2.92	0.42	1.67	10.83
Total		Count	68	51	78	26	17	240
		% of Total	28.3	21.25	32.5	10.8	7.083	100

Exhibit Number 11.36: Block-Level Politicians versus Securing Political Patronage as Reason for Accepting Pressure

Source	Frequency of Pressure Source		To Secure Political Patronage					Total
			Most Imp.	Very Imp.	Important	Least Imp.	Not Imp.	
Block Samiti/ Block-Level Politicians	"always" frequency of political pressure	Count	21	4	2	5	7	39
		% of Total	8.71	1.659	0.82	2.074	2.904	16.18
	"mostly" frequency of political pressure	Count	41	8	20	5	2	76
		% of Total	17.01	3.319	8.3	2.074	0.829	31.53
	"frequently" frequency of political pressure	Count	27	5	11	15	9	67
		% of Total	11.21	2.074	4.6	6.224	3.734	27.81
	"sometimes" frequency of political pressure	Count	7	9	12	1	2	31
		% of Total	2.9	3.734	4.9	0.414	0.829	12.86
	"never" frequency of political pressure	Count	6	6	7	7	2	28
		% of Total	2.49	2.489	2.9	2.904	0.829	11.61
Total		Count	102	32	52	33	22	241
		% of Total	42.33	13.27	21.6	13.69	9.128	100

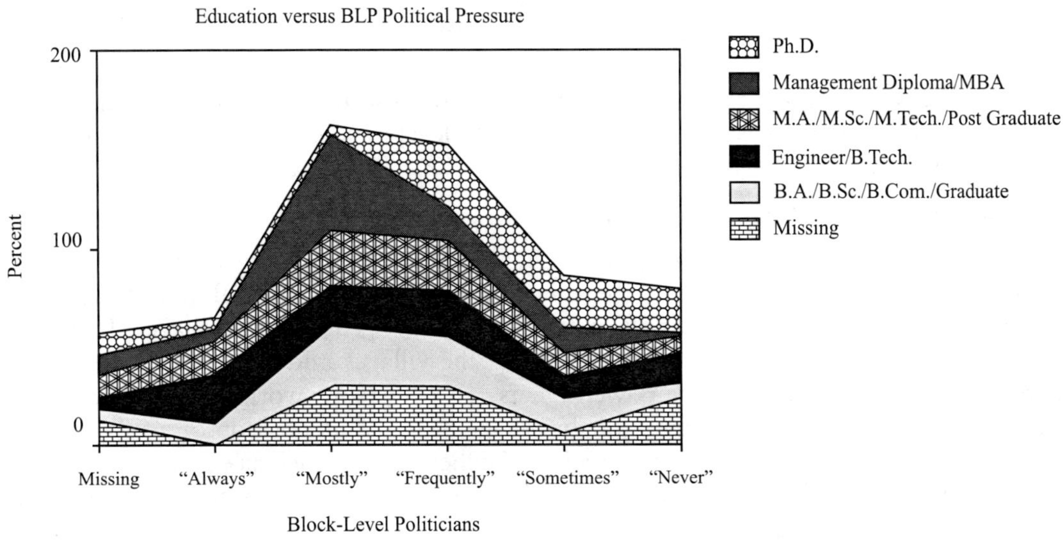

Chart No. 11.16: Education of the AISO and BLP Pressure

Exhibit Number 11.37: Chi-Square Test: Securing Political Patronage versus BLP Pressure

	Value	df	Asymp. Sig. (2-sided)
Pearson Chi-Square	50.125	16	0.000

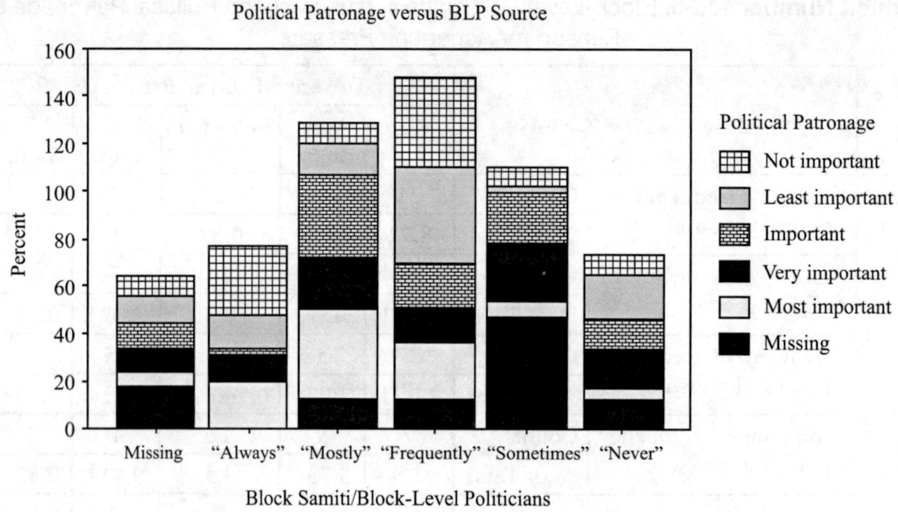

Chart No. 11.17: Political Patronage and Block-Level Politician as a Source of Pressure

Data analysis results indicate that 25.4% of the All India Services Officers with postgraduate qualifications (Exhibit 11.35) accept political pressure 'frequently' to 'always'. The total of this category in accepting political pressure from block-level politicians/Block Samiti Members show 73.3% of All India Services Officers are in 'always' to 'frequently' frequency. To find out the relationship with the reason (Exhibit 11.36) for accepting political pressure, 75.5% of All India Services Officers 'frequently' to 'always' accept pressure to secure political patronage. Pearson Chi-square results are highly significant with a 0.000, level of significance, which demonstrates reliability in the strength of such relationships.

11.6.7. Village Heads/ Village-Level Workers

In our democratic system, the village is the smallest unit of the administration. Village Head, Sarpanch, or *Mukhiya* is the person in the village, who enjoys the political influence. However, where development has been faster, multi-power centers have grown in the villages. These power centers contest the power of dominant persons in the villages and try to enhance their own reputation as political agents or the power agents. These persons work as power brokers and openly challenge the traditional power of the village heads. This position of growth of multi-power centers is highly suitable to the politicians. Higher-level politicians encourage such power agents and do their work over the priority of village heads. This process enhances the status of village-level political workers. In turn, these village-level political workers mobilize gatherings for political rallies and other purposes. This process of mutual interests of politicians and village-level worker proved strength to these lowest functionaries. Under the influence of acquired political power, these grassroots level workers approach the individual officers to get things done for others and self to enhance their own stature in the village and meet own goals/interests. Administrative Service officers consider it 7th, the Indian Police Service officers think it at 7th and the Indian Forest Service officers rank it at 3rd level of source of political pressure.

Exhibit Number 11.38: Villages Heads/Grass Root Workers versus Recruitment

Source	Frequency of Source		Recruitment					Total
			Always	M. Oftenly	Frequently	S/Times	Rarely	
Villages Heads/ Grassroot workers	"always" frequency of political pressure	Count	6	2	7			15
		% of Total	4.28	1.428	5			10.71
	"mostly" frequency of political pressure	Count	14	13	6		1	34
		% of Total	10	9.285	4.285		0.71	24.28
	"frequently" frequency of political pressure	Count	14	22	10	3		49
		% of Total	10	15.71	7.142	2.142		35
	"sometimes" frequency of political pressure	Count	7	14	12			33
		% of Total	5	10	8.571			23.57
	"never" frequency of political pressure	Count	1	4	3	1		9
		% of Total	0.71	2.857	2.142	0.714		6.428
Total		Count	42	55	38	4	1	140
		% of Total	30	39.28	27.14	2.857	0.71	100

Exhibit Number 11.39: Village Heads/Grass Root Workers versus Earn Money/Property and Enhance Resources

Source	Frequency of Source		Earn Money/Enhance Resources					Total
			Most Imp.	Very Imp.	Important	Least Imp.	Not Imp.	
Village Heads/ Grass root workers	"always" frequency of political pressure	Count	10	3	14		5	32
		% of Total	4.166	1.25	5.83		2.08	13.33
	"mostly" frequency of political pressure	Count	12	7	19	6	5	49
		% of Total	5	2.91	7.91	2.5	2.08	20.41
	"frequently" frequency of political pressure	Count	25	15	14	11	5	70
		% of Total	10.41	6.25	5.83	4.58	2.08	29.16
	"sometimes" frequency of political pressure	Count	12	9	11	11	9	52
		% of Total	5	3.75	4.58	4.58	3.75	21.66
	"never" frequency of political pressure	Count	12	8	6	5	6	37
		% of Total	5	3.33	2.5	2.09	2.5	15.41
Total		Count	71	42	64	33	30	240
		% of Total	29.58	17.5	26.66	13.75	12.5	100

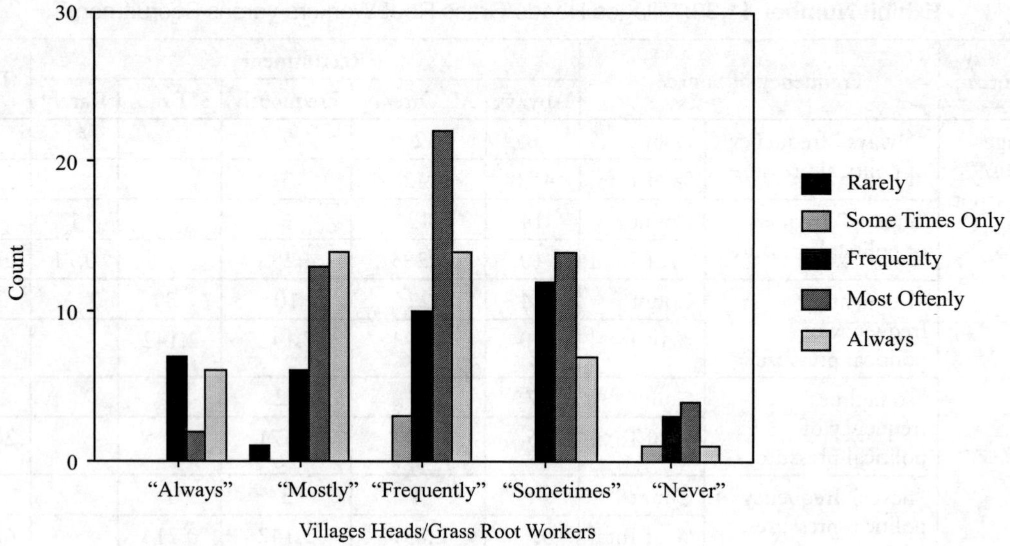

Chart No. 11.18: Recruitment versus Village Heads Pressure

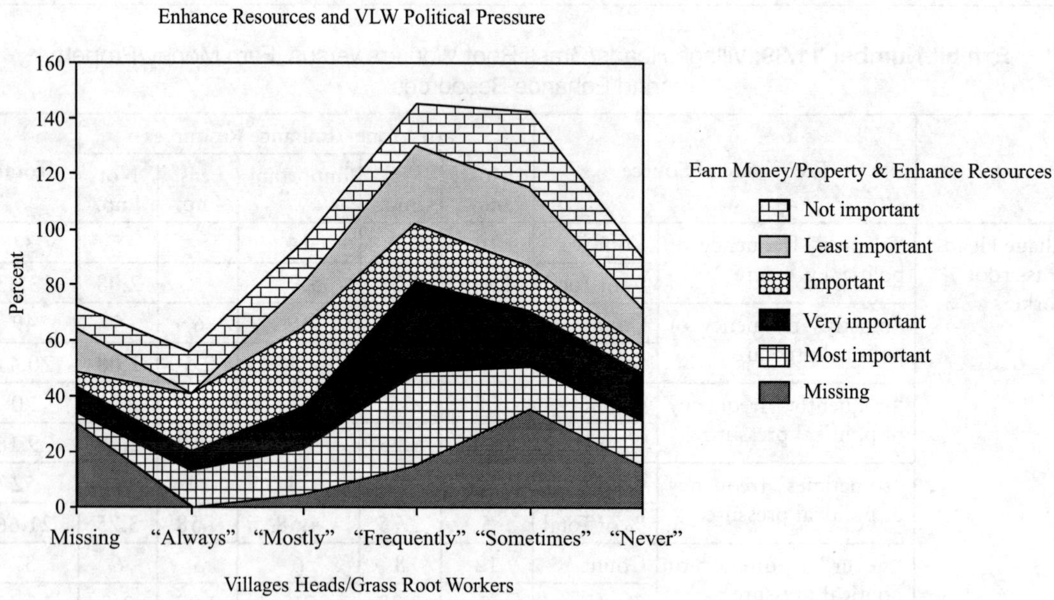

Chart No. 11.19: Earn Money/Property and Enhance Resources versus VLW Pressure

70% of All India Services Officers 'frequently' to 'always' category get political pressure from village-level workers/village heads in the recruitment area as shown in Exhibit 11.38. To find out the relationship between the earning of money/property and enhancement of resources is 'most important' for 19.6% of All India Services Officers in accepting pressure from village-level workers/village heads as shown in Exhibit 11.39.

11.6.8. Power Brokers/Touts/Musclemen

Power brokers/touts/musclemen are working at all levels and they develop their connections according to their need and suitability. This type of source of political pressure is pervasive all over across global barriers. The nature of these agents is that they work across the social barriers and money is their god. Power brokers/touts/musclemen major target is to mint money, either legal or illegal, fair means or unfair means, lower level or highest level, politicians or bureaucrats, and businessmen or public, etc. methods are immaterial for them. These persons remain busy in expanding their network on professional lines, they use all types of latest gadgets/techniques, and in some cases their generations after generations are involved in this type of work. Money minting remains their sole criteria.

Colonially created the bureaucratic system in India by its origin has carried and supported the system of power brokers/touts/musclemen for its own convenience. British officers required them as conduits to interact with Indians citizens, convey their feelings to spoilers, sustain the exploitation, and overrule the Indian masses. The present bureaucratic system also cultivates these power brokers/touts/musclemen to nurture self-interest, goals for own benefit maximization. Individual officers also utilize them as conduits for accepting and collect money on their behalf, so that they can escape the inquiries and departmental disciplinary actions.

These power brokers/touts/musclemen collect the huge money for the power holder All India Services Officers. As the All India Services Officers move higher on the ladders of hierarchy to occupy higher positions, more they become dependent on such agents for money collections. It is not necessary that always such agents be from the public. On many occasions, lower-level subordinates work as such agents for politicians and bureaucrats both. Instances are there when the All India Services Officers themselves work as an agent for the powerful political leader or minister or Chief Minister or Prime Minister. This provides a safety valve to these powerful politicians. There are instances that politicians themselves work as such agents and amass huge wealth in turn, which he can use for political purposes.

Businesspersons working as power brokers/touts/agents are common and they consider it as part of the business. Rather this is one of the best and sure ways to mint money in the shortest time. Many businesspersons invest huge amounts in the All India Services Officers and politicians for this purpose only. Initially, massive parties are organized in their honor and such parties are used as a source to develop a connection and to impress upon prospective clientele that they enjoy the access to power nerves to get things done. Many people consider these parties as a way to move their files and pay heavily to these agents. These shops for an agency are available to those persons, who are well connected to the power-holders. This is the oldest way to get things done; it has variations according to the needs of the region and culture of the different areas. This methodology changes with time and space as demanded by the clients and facility providers.

The Indian Administrative Service officers consider it 5th, the Indian Police Service officers think it at 4th and the Indian Forest Service officers rank it at 6th level of source of political pressure. This source has been ranked as the 6th 'most important' source of political pressure. 77.4% of the Indian Administrative Service officers, 71.6% of the Indian Police Service officers, and 61.9% of the All India Services Officers get political pressure 'always' category to 'frequently' from the power brokers/touts/musclemen. 54.3% of the Indian Forest Service officers get 'mostly' to 'frequent' intensity political pressure from this source and 23.4% of them 'never' gets political pressure from power brokers/touts/musclemen. Indian Administrative Service officers get the highest amount of political pressure from power brokers/touts/musclemen.

Exhibit Number 11.40: Power Brokers/Touts/Musclemen versus Freedom in Goal Achievement/Funds Misuse

Source	Frequency of Source		Freedom in Goal Achievement/Funds Misuse					Total
			Most Imp.	Very Imp.	Important	Least Imp.	Not Imp.	
Power brokers/ touts/muscle men	"always" frequency of political pressure	Count	18	4	4	9	9	44
		% of Total	8.145	1.81	1.81	4.07	4.07	19.91
	"mostly" frequency of political pressure	Count	18	16	10	6	9	59
		% of Total	8.145	7.23	4.52	2.71	4.07	26.69
	"frequently" frequency of political pressure	Count	12	6	7	8	4	37
		% of Total	5.43	2.71	3.16	3.61	1.809	16.74
	"sometimes" frequency of political pressure	Count	5	8	8	7	17	45
		% of Total	2.263	3.62	3.61	3.16	7.692	20.36
	"never" frequency of political pressure	Count	4	13	3	9	7	36
		% of Total	1.81	5.88	1.35	4.07	3.167	16.28
Total		Count	57	47	32	39	46	221
		% of Total	25.79	21.3	14.47	17.64	20.81	100

Exhibit Number 11.41: Chi-Square Tests: Power Brokers versus Freedom in Self Goal Achievement

	Value	df	Asymp. Sig. (2-sided)
Pearson Chi-Square	35.692	16	0.003

The relationship of political pressure from power brokers/touts/musclemen and other variables have been studied and results are shown in Exhibit 11.40 to 11.43. In variable to get freedom in (Exhibit 11.40) goal achievement/funds misuse, 21.6% of All India Services Officers get 'frequently' to 'always' political pressure from the power brokers/touts/musclemen. Pearson Chi-square results are significant with a 0.003, level of significance. 82.5% of All India Services Officers get 'frequently' to 'always' political pressure from the power brokers/touts/musclemen to get postings (Exhibit 11.42) in postings related matters.

Exhibit Number 11.42: Power Brokers/Touts/Musclemen versus Postings

Source	Frequency of Source		Postings					Total
			Rarely	Sometimes	Frequent	Most oftenly	Always	
Power brokers/ touts/ musclemen	"always" frequency of political pressure	Count	3	5	11	7	7	33
		% of Total	1.86	3.11	6.83	4.34	4.34	20.49
	"mostly" frequency of political pressure	Count	1	6	15	9	15	46
		% of Total	0.62	3.72	9.31	5.59	9.31	28.57
	"frequently" frequency of political pressure	Count	7	1	8	10	12	38
		% of Total	4.34	0.62	4.96	6.21	7.45	23.60
	"sometimes" frequency of political pressure	Count			5	14	8	27
		% of Total			3.11	8.69	4.96	16.77
	"never" frequency of political pressure	Count		5	3	7	2	17
		% of Total		3.11	1.86	4.34	1.24	10.55
Total		Count	11	17	42	47	44	161
		% of Total	6.83	10.55	26.08	29.19	27.32	100

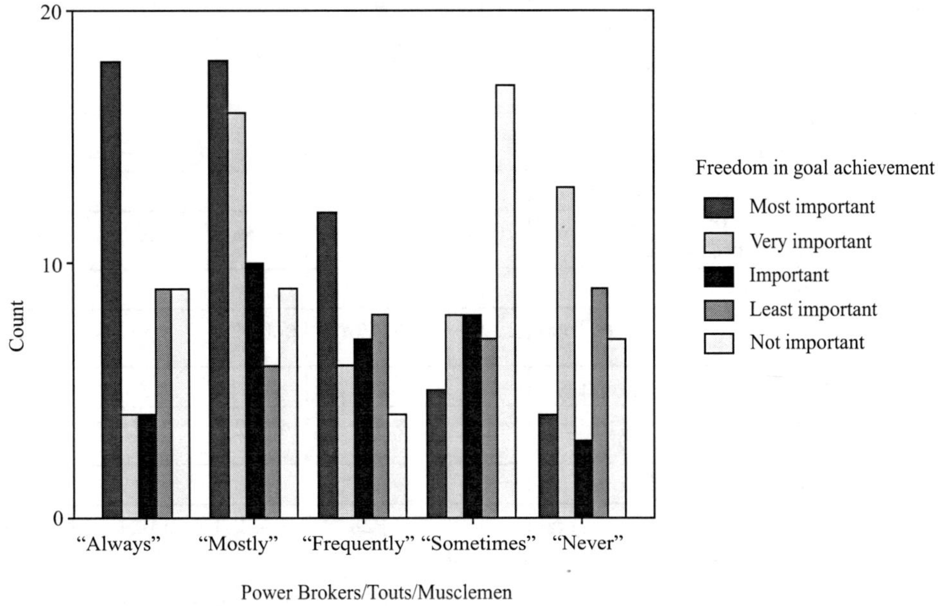

Chart No. 11.20: Freedom in Goal Achievement versus Power Broker Pressure

11.6.9. Communication Media

Communication media is mostly power-oriented and highly pervasive all over the world. With the unregulated growth of the media, its dimensions and yellow journalism has grown out of proportions in India. Right from the owners of these newspapers to down below to the lowest level of stringers/hawkers/agents, a large number of them remained preoccupied with wealth maximization. When we discussed the problem at the lowest level, they explained that newspaper owners do not provide them enough for their survival. When we discussed the problem at the top, the top management said that they cannot afford to pay so much to lowest level stringers, as costs incurred are enormous and beyond their resources to meet with that.

When no one is getting enough, where all of them will go, and what they will do? Naturally, they approach politicians and the All India Services Officers for getting so many things done illegally and use the pressure of the press to meet their self-goals. The All India Services Officers also use this opportunity to secure their own position and by obliging the press, individual officers ensure their own safety that nothing against them comes out in media. Both parties remain happy and nexus works to sustain each other goals for the sustenance of the system. Communication media persons are located from the lowest level to the highest and extract benefits according to their own needs and capabilities. Quantum of benefits harvested by communication media is directly related to the bargaining power of the individual person or organization. Communication media persons exert pressure on all the areas as mentioned in Unit 12, starting from collection on the name of the subscription to allotment of land or number of resources.

Exhibit Number 11.43: Communication Media versus Family Economic Background

Source of Pressure	Frequency of Pressure		Family Economic Background					Total
			Rich	Upper Middle Class	Middle Class	Lower Middle Class	Poor	
Communication Media	"always" frequency of political pressure	Count	11	7	3	3	2	26
		% of Total	4.61	2.928	1.255	1.255	0.836	10.87
	"mostly" frequency of political pressure	Count	26	7	2	7	4	46
		% of Total	10.88	2.928	0.836	2.928	1.673	19.24
	"frequently" frequency of political pressure	Count	31	15	12	8	7	73
		% of Total	12.98	6.276	5.021	3.347	2.928	30.54
	"sometimes" frequency of pressure	Count	11	18	11	7	6	53
		% of Total	4.61	7.531	4.602	2.928	2.511	22.17
	"never" frequency of political pressure	Count	8	7	13	12	1	41
		% of Total	3.35	2.928	5.439	5.021	0.418	17.15
Total		Count	87	54	41	37	20	239
		% of Total	36.41	22.59	17.15	15.48	8.368	100

69.5% of the All India Services Officers and 79.4% of the Indian Administrative Service officers get pressure from communication media 'mostly' to 'sometimes'. 81.6% of the Indian Police Service officers get pressure from communication media 'always' to 'frequently' in the decision-making process. 67% of the Indian Forest Service officers get pressure from communication media 'mostly' to 'sometimes' and 27.7% of them 'never' get pressure from the press. The Indian Police Service officers get the highest pressure from the media and the Indian Forest Service officers get the lowest pressure from this source. Police officers getting the highest pressure indicate that communication media influence the decisions pertaining to law and order maintenance. The Administrative Service officers consider it 8th, the Indian Police Service officers think it at 3rd and the Indian Forest Service officers rank it at 7th level of source of political pressure. Analyses of variable economic background show, 28.5% of All India Services Officers from the rich family background (Exhibit 11.43) 'frequently' to 'always' accept political pressure from communication media in the decision-making process.

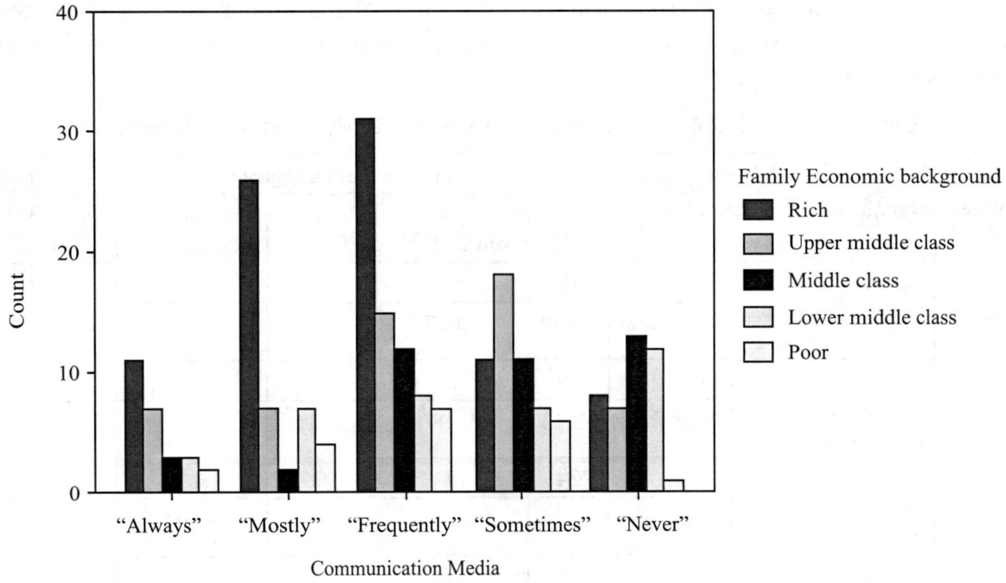

Chart No. 11.21: Family Economic Background versus Communication Media Pressure

11.6.10. Hidden Financier

The concept of hidden financiers is akin to power brokers/touts/musclemen. However, we have studied this as a separate source of pressure. Such financiers are invariably for short time period operations and after certain objectives are met, they disappear or stop visiting politicians or the All India Services Officers. These persons like to operate from oblivion or behind the screen. In some cases, they never meet the concerned officers or politicians. These persons may be a part-time operator or region-specific operators. They pay money to politicians, finance their elections, or finance some of the political rally or activity or a specific job for the All India Services Officers. They invest money under pressure or without pressure according to reason specific, but they like to recover their money from the success of this or that action, so they pressure politicians to exert political pressure on the All India Services Officers for doing a specific accomplishment or decision. These persons may not be visible on the surface, but on occasions exert tremendous political pressure to get the decision-making process distorted in their favor.

Most of the time, these hidden financiers exert pressure on the policy, the Laws and Acts, rules, regulations, and procedures. On occasions, these financiers have access to the highest level in political circles and even the ministers do not get air about them. Top bureaucrats just work under the directive of the Chief Minister/Prime Minister and real pressure remains hidden. Same way, some of such sources develop a connection with the highest officers in the bureaucratic system, and their subordinate or concerned Center or State Minister remain unaware of it, and different levels oblige the source unknowingly. Politicians also use this hidden source, when they are out of power. Knowingly or unknowingly, all the power holders use such sources according to their convenience.

57.5% of the All India Services Officers and 84.6% of the Indian Administrative Service officers get pressure 'always' intensity to 'frequently' intensity from hidden financiers in the decision-making process.

Exhibit Number 11.44: Hidden Financiers versus Family Economic Background

Source	Frequency of Pressure Source		Family Economic Background					Total
			Rich	Upper Middle Class	Middle Class	Lower Middle Class	Poor	
Hidden Financiers	"always" frequency of political pressure	Count	13	14	4	1	2	34
		% of Total	5.439	5.857	1.673	0.418	0.836	14.22
	"usually" frequency of political pressure	Count	29	8	6	5	3	51
		% of Total	12.13	3.347	2.511	2.092	1.255	21.33
	"frequently" frequency of political pressure	Count	24	9	6	11	6	56
		% of Total	10.04	3.765	2.511	4.602	2.511	23.43
	"sometimes" frequency of political pressure	Count	9	10	11	6	4	40
		% of Total	3.765	4.184	4.602	2.511	1.673	16.73
	"never" frequency of political pressure	Count	11	16	14	14	3	58
		% of Total	4.602	6.694	5.857	5.857	1.255	24.26
Total		Count	86	57	41	37	18	239
		% of Total	35.98	23.84	17.15	15.48	7.531	100

Exhibit Number 11.45: Chi-Square Results: Hidden Financier versus Economic Background

	N	Value	df	Asymp. Sig. (2-sided)
Pearson Chi-Square	239	38.844	16	0.001

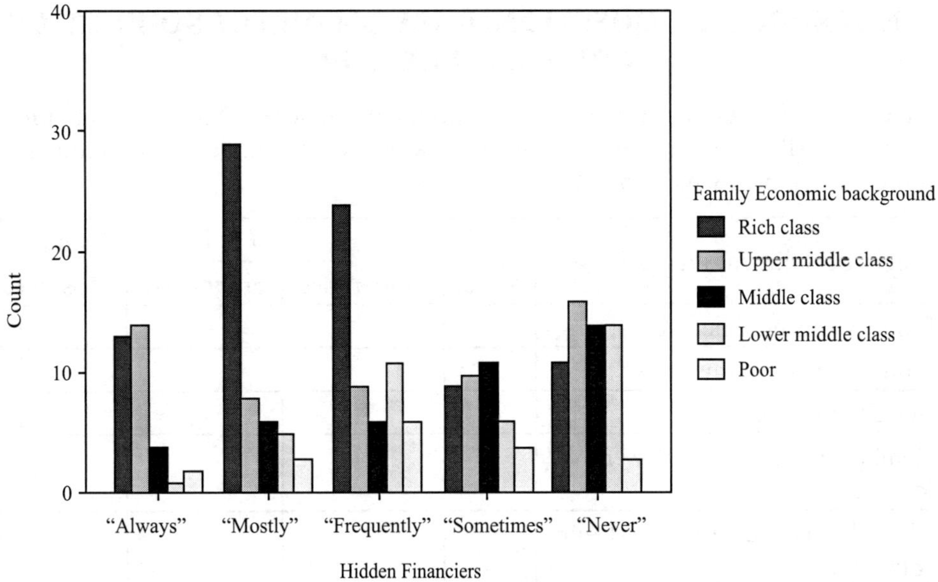

Chart No. 11.22: Family Economic Background versus Hidden Financier Pressure

65.6% of the Indian Police Service officers get 'mostly' intensity to 'frequently' intensity political pressure from this source. 51.1% of the Indian Forest Service officers get political pressure 'frequently' to 'sometimes' intensity and 45.5% of them 'never' get pressure from the hidden financiers in the decision. The Indian Administrative Service officers get the highest pressure and the Indian Forest Service officers to get the least pressure from this source, this may be related to their locations in the bureaucratic system and positions occupied by them. This source has been ranked 5th most important source of political pressure. The Indian Administrative Service officers consider it 3rd, the Indian Police Service officers think it at 9th and the Indian Forest Service officers rank it at 10th level of source of political pressure. 40.4% of All India Services Officers from rich and upper rich class background 'frequently' intensity to 'always' intensity accept political pressure in the decision-making process from hidden financiers.

ANNEXURE 11.A: QUESTIONNAIRE ON DIRECT SOURCES OF POLITICAL PRESSURE

We have listed 10 possible sources of direct political pressure, which are sometimes exerted on the officers of All India Services in decision making. Kindly, indicate the frequency of each source of pressure in below mentioned five point scale.

Sources of Political Pressure	Frequency of Political Pressure				
	Never	Sometimes	Frequently	Mostly	Always
(366) Prime Minister/Chief Minister					
(367) Center or State Minister					
(368) Member of Parliament					
(369) Member of Legislative Assembly/ Council					
(370) Zila Parishad/District-Level Politicians					
(371) Block Samiti/Block-Level Politicians					
(372) Village Heads/Grass Root Workers					
(373) Power Brokers/Touts/Musclemen					
(374) Communication Media					
(375) Hidden Financiers					

Unit 12

Types of Pressure on Different Pressure Points/Areas in Bureaucracy

"If something can corrupt you, you are corrupted already."—Bob Marley

"It is always easier to fight for one's principles than to live up to them."—Alfred Adler

Corruption is Authority plus Monopoly minus Transparency.

"He who apparently preventing the organs of perception and action sits psychologically cognizing on the objects of senses, that man of deceived intelligence is called hypocrite."
The Bhagavad Gita 3.6

- *Bureaucratic framework and areas*
- *Points of pressure in decision*
- *Research analyses result for pressure areas*
- *Transfer, Postings, Recruitment*
- *Resource allocation, Rewards, Punishments*
- *Promotions. Rules & Regulations*
- *Policy issues, Change of law*
- *Demure in the decision, Development works*
- *Crime, Training & tours and Social issues*

This unit is the longest; 76 variables related to various pressure points or areas or types, where invariably political pressure is being exerted and that have serious repercussions in decision outcomes are studied. In this research analysis, results of the intensity of pressure exerted by ten important sources of pressure (Unit 11, The Prime Minister to village level) on decisions with respect to respective 76 pressure points have been described. Political pressure measurement analysis results are rare and very interesting as presented in exhibits.

12.1. Bureaucratic Framework and Areas/Points of Political Pressure in Decision

Political pressure has been seen as a catalytic function to influence the decision-making process. The powers of the politicians may be in proportion to one's abilities to dispossess the department decision process. Withdrawal of controlling functions of the All India Services Officers, in turn, works as a power enhancer for the politicians. The use of discretion in the decision process is the real power enhancer to the power holders. Among the All India Services Officers, only the Indian Administrative Service officers have full access and control over these areas. They use these enhancers for their competence building. Government hierarchy, the management system in public administration, spatial distances, and self-governing All India Services Officers diminish the development of expert power of politicians at various levels. Fifteen areas or pressure points, which are most commonly used by politicians as power enhancers, have been discussed in this study.

Politicians occupy the top position in the hierarchy of government administration, followed by the Indian Administrative Service officers, who have positioned themselves next to the politician in importance. In the name of coordination, the Indian Administrative Service officers create interdependence of other services on them. In case of interdepartmental working under threat from another source, the Indian Police Service, the Indian Forest Service, and the Indian Administrative Service groups pool their propelling powers to attain self-goals and objectives through the process of public administration. In case of reporting progress of different departments, which are mostly headed by the Administrative Secretary at the top, they make it sequential interdependent. This interdependence of services and with politicians and the IAS at the top has created the greatest uncertainty in the decision, which has customized response of the All India Services Officers infrequently accepting the pressure. The existence of continuous pressure deviates the goals orientation of the All India Services Officers and vis-à-vis politicians also. Politicians make use of this to exert pressure on the decision-making process through different 15 areas.

"*Divide et impera* or divide and rule policy would in long run recoil upon our own heads."[1] This is bound to resurface again as the entire bureaucratic system has been divided into class layers and service groups. This structural layering has led to the mobilization of political pressure. "These appointments are among the most troublesome bits of my life. Frequent transfers and promotions desired by civil servants are disruptive of administrative continuity and efficiency."[2] This pusillanimous behavior of the All India Services Officers indicates pervasive insecurity among them and concern for self-goals. Efficiency in public administration has been eaten away by the virus of political pressure and contradictions prevailing among the services. "Weakness on part of the administration created a belief in the public that though the government is committed to removing corruption yet the corrupt persons are not taken to task due to sort of political influence which gives protection to the culprits and corrupt individuals," R.K. Bhardwaj (1978).

These colonially created All India Services were assigned job overseeing the routine revenue collection and maintenance of law and order. They were inevitably engaged in political work with local collaborators and others, nursing support structures and moving for advantage in fluid situations, while never oozing sight of imperial aims and requirements (D.C. Potter). "Reserving strategic posts for the All India Services, imperial power had a profound influence over the entire structure of the imperial state," which has become redundant now and deserves to be

1. Dufferin wrote to Lord Cross on 4.1.1887.
2. Lord Elgin wrote to Lord Harris on 14.5.1894.

discontinued. "There is widespread cynicism and disillusionment with government and functioning of Institutions," Former President, Pranab Mukherjee (Independence Day speech 2013).

D.C. Potter, explained some issues, "Political support for structures, behavior patterns and norms and values of the traditions. The process of political support for an administrative tradition is complex.... One is the agency of power exercised by administrators with in-state working actively to retain their tradition in the face of opposition. The other is the broad structure of state and class power in which bureaucracy is located. The second process is obtaining similar successors on a continuing basis. This involves the steady replacement of retiring administrators by younger recruits similar in educational and class background and at least familiar with the principles norms and values of traditions.... Shaping successor is deliberate attempts by experienced administrators to mold new recruits to behavior patterns of traditions." The present system and training process adopted for imparting training to the All India Services Officers has become the surest way to continue and propagate colonial imperialistic services at the top.

The All India Services Officers are fully aware that as long as political support is available for present services, structure, and composition, they will continue to produce a similar successor to uphold the traditions of imperialism in India. Determination of bureaucracy is evinced by the fact that the bureaucratic system continues to produce new power-holders even during stiffest political opposition from 1920 to 1947 and later on also.

Bureaucratic system structure, rules, regulations, procedures, norms, and values had not changed through time to replace the system. How we can expect change from a system, which cherishes the traditions and norms from the colonial past. If we carefully analyze different features with a free mind at a particular time, appropriate to the realistic needs of the country. We can visualize the urgency for change. The All India Services Officers, whose number is minuscule with respect to population, discretely organize the campaign to retain their position. The All India Services' traditional control over bureaucracy motivates them to retain overriding control over other services in the system and tends to develop nexus with political leadership.

External political pressure and political forces are thought to be less decisive to regulate the performance of the decision. We cannot imagine a wholly independent powerful bureaucracy in democratic sovereign states. Autonomous civil society also cannot be ruled with mere proletariat slogans. Excessive autonomy tends to shift dependence on the economic base. Increased relations of the politician and bureaucracy is the manifestation of the self-goals attainment.

"The whole team is of such a low caliber—with of course few exceptions-that one cannot really see the outlines of bold thrashing confident leadership.... Men of straw now aspire to become men of power."[3] The All India Services Officers consider themselves authoritative, most of the decisions are political, and they behave as if they are the politicians. Most of them are involved in pursuing partisan objectives by mobilizing groups in society to support those objectives and oppose different political orientations. In the name of law and order, they serve the interests of the ruling party and crush the opposition party. During the imperial Raj, they maintained 'Pax Britannica' now they only maintain law order for power. During the imperial Raj favors were showered on the loyal persons and shivering crushing to patriotic persons disloyal to the British Raj.

3. *Administration, Politics and Development in India* by C.N. Bhalerao.

If you are loyal to the elite Indian Administrative Service officers, you can enjoy all the favors, any feeling of disloyalty to the IAS, all the problems are stored for you; even politicians cannot save you from the wrath of the Indian Administrative Service officers. British legacy of harassment by Collector to opponents, continue with full vigor, and their senior officers support whole heartily any such repression as valor and brave person. The exploitation of their own honest persons has become synonymous with bravery and valor. If any officer other than the Indian Administrative Service officer complains against the Collector, such officer is heavily scolded and victimized, if Collector writes a letter against any district officer, such officer is transferred or penalized by that department through the IAS Administrative Secretary of that department. Legacies of Imperial Raj have different variants and are used by new Indian egoist rulers from the middle class. If any department is not liked by the Indian Administrative Service officers, then take it granted that slowly different budgetary allocations will dry up for that department in the name of resource crunch under the cover of planning or other budgetary controls. If any department regularly shares leakages with the Indian Administrative Service bureaucracy that department is bound to get higher funds allocations on the name of this or that scheme.

This reminds us of the Humes (1930), words as Collecter Rourkee, "I whispered the names of one or two (Congress Dictators) in Captain Billy Gough's ear and hinted that they might advantageously be interviewed by few Gurkhas. Billy took and acted on the hint to the full.... (Indians were) found in canal bathing, (their body) was white washed and paraded about nude." In a desire to maintain their own hegemony, these officers try every opportunity to maintain own position, by reward, thwart, harass, support and moving or destroying such departments. The All India Services Officers enjoyed trust, autonomy, and discretion to act appropriately in the British Raj, and reached the top in India; this distinctive feature of colonial rule was not true of service class in Britain.

"Within-class distinctions of this kind have always been difficult to make. Renner suggests that such distinctions within the service class, although difficult, are in principle possible on the dimensions of more or less trust reposed in a section. Those who have secured and well-rewarded career structures within the service class may have a distinct identity as compared to those who are less secure and less well rewarded. On this dimension, as it happens, ICS identity within the state was very distinct: they were members of one of the Secretary of State's services, exceptionally secured and well rewarded. There were only four other such services between the wars. None of the others had this special identity. This arrangement, peculiar to imperial rule, tended to set up a conflict of interest between the ICS, who wanted to retain their special identity and other services within the state", D.C. Potter, 1986. "It is everybody's duty to live in consonance with *Dharma*. It represents man's basic nature and governs our actions and lives", Yogendra Narain, 2013.

Continuous assured success to the Indian Administrative Service officers, develop the feeling and frame of mind that only they are superior and successful, others are to be ruled, ultimately superiority complex cripple the decision. Officers from other services develop the mind frame of unsuccessful in the long run and lead to the slow destruction of motivation and innovations. This destroys the self-respect among the people and gives rise to class superiority to a particular group of officers, ultimately develop pathological contempt for disadvantaged groups and cultivate a desire to make them suffer. This strong feeling of superiority gives rise to social and cultural aloofness generates service arrogance, and this arrogance fuel the perception and drives them to seek reprieve from such suppression. This forces the masses to approach politicians.

Bureaucratic system feature of reserving all the top posts and controls for elite political administrator moving frequently in government, generalist overruling specialist, excluding and ignoring the specialist and experts, lead to slow discontentment against the decision and create a place for political interventions. Imperial culture is still in the mental framework of these All India Services Officers and provides normative support to them, this creates distance from reality and masses. As the colonial/imperial All India Services Officers used to feel British, act British, talk British, think British, eat British way, live British way, so colonial arrogance has permeated deep inside the system and its culture.

The IAS is basically responsible for such pressure on most of these areas, in the process of bargain Indian Administrative Service officers carry out to save their position in the eyes of politicians. Some officers have raised the issue that areas of political pressure cannot be generalized by visualizing the vastness of the country and cultural differences. After interaction for a number of years with different officers, it was agreed that not all the 76 points or areas might be relevant to every area of pressure; major areas on which political pressure is exerted are mostly among these points only.

The All India Services Officers are given a lead role in the states and at the center, their behavior and norms must be supportive and public equity-oriented. Feelings of 'elite' and 'supreme' should not have any place in the training or the behavior of these officers. Courtesy, consideration, politeness, personal relations, discipline, commitment to equity, humbleness, honesty, team mover, and sympathizer should be an essential ingredient for these officers. The All India Services Officers should be like a realized saint; people must have faith in their impartiality.

The Indian Administrative Service Officers' relations with the politicians were seen as "step on each other's toes constantly". Politicians blame the IAS for being snob, the IAS underestimate the politicians' intelligence and overestimate their own. So, a compromise is necessary, they think. The politician is rendered ineffectual without the administrator and the administrator lost without the politician; hence, it is best in the interest of both that they meet halfway. The attitude towards local politicians should not be that their only job is interference. When a politician approaches you (IAS) as the collector for an odd job like a license for a fair price shop, or an arms license, land allotment, postponement of the date of recovery of a government loan, postponement of the sale of property for recovery of a government loan, a plea on behalf of some persons to protect them from *goonda* elements, etc. It is essential to examine the pros and cons frankly, with politeness and tact. If you cannot oblige a politician, state clearly the reasons, why. Also, even when politicians come with a complaint, they are serving a useful function (as alternate information); an administrator who relies on only his subordinates develops a jaundiced view," Davis, C.P. 1986.

The All India Services Officers themselves are responsible for the situations for the exertion of political pressure due to lack of strong discipline among them. An IAS probationer, Mr. V.K. Singh and P.S. Appu episode is well known, how political influence is mobilized from the day these officers join the service. Similarly, an IAS officer who was said to have murdered his own members of the family and went scot free, because he was IAS, another IAS officer reported having burnt his class IV employee and serving merrily in the state with full arrogance.[4] Therefore, a new crop

4. *The Tribune*, 20.12.1996. *The Times of India*, 20.12.1996 and 17.10.1997.

of these elite bureaucrats does not hesitate to commit any heinous crime with full impunity. How they will behave with the public and fellow officers with any sense of responsibility. If a politician is not in the picture, there are chances that the situation will be worse than the imperial atrocities.

Nexus between immoral heinous organized crime committer and some All India Services Officers have become pervasive across the cadres with the passage of time. Public have no access to these arrogant elites. The urgent need of the hour is that India does not need the elite at any cost. We need a common person who is like others, who can appreciate people's problems, who can share their poverty for development. We need a kind humanitarian person with a compassionate heart, not elite All India Services Officers with a rod with the spirits of arrogant imperialistic *Bura Sahibs*, who consistently want look-alike the English *Bura-Sahib*. The All India Services Officers behaves with different styles and approaches in different states. It is said that the nastiest type of arrogance is prevalent in UP, Uttarakhand, Bihar, Jharkhand, Orissa, Haryana, and MP, i.e. so-called cow belt is under the bad type of exploitation and subjugation. How a single person can affect the system, Rajasthan cadre people say the credit goes to late B. Mehta, who emphasized good inter-personal relations.

Public enterprise companies' growth enticed the All India Services Officers and postings in these enterprises have grown rapidly over time. This mobility indicates the All India Services power and pervasiveness within the government bureaucracy. They already occupy the top positions in the States and Centre and with the grabbing of the public sector their presence became omnipresent at all top places. This shows as if in India others are born to serve as subordinates and All India Services Officers are born to command and enjoy top positions. This has enhanced the chances for a higher level of political pressure acceptance in decisions everywhere. Among these, All India Services, Indian Administrative Service officers are pervasive, omnipresent, and omnipotent to grab every opportunity. Besides this all-major decision pertaining to public enterprises regarding budget allocation, major appointments, expansion, production, and big contracts are finalized by the Indian bureaucratic system headed by mostly All India Services officers.

"Modern Indian Administrative Service officers dealing with political forces also behaved in certain detailed ways rather differently from the detailed ways of their ICS predecessors. There were, however, some exaggerated notions on this score principally that IAS officers overall tended to bend more when coping with pressure and that levels of corruption had increased. Increased corruption may be characteristic of the Indian bureaucracy", D.C. Potter, further explained it. "Any successful political administrator must bend to some extent when dealing with politicians, must be resilient, and accommodating while holding firmly to law and basic principles, and there are instances of Indian Administrative Service officers who may have been given way too much."

Excessive reservation of higher posts for the Indian Administrative Service officers evaporate the hope for reaching the desired place and as a consequence of it develop extraordinary distance between the services at different levels; for awesome people in those strategic posts who made rules to govern the whole of India. This creates a subterranean feeling of hostility among civil servants, this hostility and dispute go to politicians for reprisal and provide opportunities to politicians to mobilize political pressure in the decision-making process. The process of retention of power among different services activates the process of a bargain for own advantage and self-goals. Every service tries to win the politician with a promise to provide them loyal services in lieu of their own benefits. This starts the political interference in the decision-making process.

12.2. Political Pressure on the AISO on Decision Points/Areas—Research Analyses

While evaluating the questionnaire, it has been observed that the All India Services Officers have ignored or skipped the general area of pressure in most of the cases that is why there are large missing values in those scores. The highest total score for transfers and postings indicates that maximum numbers of the All India Services Officers have responded and political pressure pertaining to transfer and postings is exerted to the greatest extent. The highest modal value (Exhibit 12.1) as a group is in the crime-related issues; this indicates invariably political pressure is exerted in issues related to the crime. The total score is also second-highest for the crime-related issues, this indicates that expansion of crime in the social system is the outcome of politician-bureaucratic-criminal nexus. Any offenses committed by the ordinary person, willfully or unwillingly, or by ignorance were institutionalized in the bureaucratic system under the political-bureaucratic protection. The intensity of political pressure is the highest on the transfer, postings, and crime-related issues.

12.2.1. Political Pressure Regarding Transfers

Old memoirs are full of stories about transfers under pressure, the average tenure of field postings have been around a year from 1920 to 1945, however, they enjoyed more than one stint of three years tenures also. Though the tenure system worked, exigency caused due to leave, illness, accidents, promotions, administrative reasons, and certainly off late political disliking affected frequent transfers. Especially 1937 onwards, political interferences in transfers have been recorded in records. The All India Services carried out lobbying for plumb postings, causing early transfers. "Transfers causing him more annoyance and tribulation of spirit than any part of my work."[5]

During 1980, when Congress came in power at the Centre and in many States, Indian Administrative Service officers loyal to the Congress were reinstated in plumb postings, and those who have done well under Janta Party were shunted out. The Indian Administrative Service officers imbibed political loyalty more important than service ethics for career advancement and retention of plumb postings. Till politicians keep these Indian Administrative Service officers happy, they will be all around as most sycophants and singing songs for the politicians. The moment any politician denies or curb any Indian Administrative Service officers wrongdoing, the whole Indian Administrative Service officers lobby start criticizing that politician and use all means to defame him. Any denial to Indian Administrative Service officers means that politicians labeled as corrupt and overnight become highly inefficient.

Any moment bureaucracy observes that minister is weak, "Then begin to emerge within the civil service persons who 'curry favor' with ministers, anticipate their views, and make recommendations to please them. They get promotions and increasingly fill coveted posts, while others who give correct and factual advice are pushed aside or penalized by being transferred from post to post. All this has a deleterious effect on the morale of the whole administration," D.C. Potter 1986.

Now, these days there is no specific season or time for the transfers, the All India Services Officers are transferred year the round like a village fair merry go round and politicians and bureaucracy enjoy it. Whenever a transfer proposal is initiated, invariably some officer will be working behind the scene in camouflage to meet his own interests, but the whole blame is passed on to politicians ceremoniously. Times and again three years tenure has been discussed again

5. Viceroy Curzon wrote to Hamilton on 9.4.1902.

and again like planetary orbital motion, is of no use. The All India Services Officers themselves make rules and they violate for self-interests. One thing must be made clear, how an Indian Administrative Service officer is affected when he is shifted to other department in the secretariat; he is going to get the same salary. Then, why these officers indulge in sycophancy and mobilize political pressure to grab the prize postings. How politicians know that who will like which post, only bureaucrats educate politicians on how to sideline a particular officer and whom to sideline at what time. Politicians frequently get changed and bureaucrats remain there in the system to misguide the public and spread rumors to save themselves.

Exhibit Number 12.1: Results of Statistical Analyses Pressure Areas/Points

Variable	N		Mean	Median	Mode	Std. Deviation	Variance	Sum
	Valid	Missing						
Transfers	194	87	4.13	4.00	5	1.004	1.008	802
On the basis of financial considerations	255	26	3.29	3.00	3	1.182	1.397	840
Pressure of frequent dislocation to serve clientele needs	260	21	3.00	3.00	3	1.232	1.517	781
To meet the individual goals/ needs	259	22	3.16	3.00	3	1.290	1.664	819
Serve public interests for improvement of system & services	255	26	2.14	2.00	1	1.237	1.531	546
To please the large social groups to serve their social needs	255	26	2.22	2.00	1	1.243	1.544	567
Postings	172	109	3.62	4.00	4	1.191	1.418	623
To provide wet/plumb postings who serve political goals	243	38	4.12	4.00	5	1.045	1.092	1002
To deny/delaypostings who resist political pressure	263	18	3.56	4.00	4	1.174	1.377	936
To provide posting on the basis of financial considerations	236	45	3.45	3.00	3	1.053	1.108	814
To ensure continuity of tenure on the basis of pliability	242	39	3.92	4.00	5	1.109	1.230	948
Cater the need of caste/religion/ region or individual interests	246	35	3.39	4.00	4	1.216	1.480	834
Recruitment	156	125	3.90	4.00	4	0.878	0.771	609
Creation of posts for recruitment to get services in future	258	23	3.38	3.00	3a	1.217	1.482	872
Violation/distortion of recruitment procedure	240	41	2.82	3.00	3	1.142	1.305	676
Ignoring merit or relaxation in rules for physical standards	269	12	3.20	3.00	4	1.266	1.604	862
Selection on the basis of financial consideration	252	29	3.28	3.00	4	1.192	1.421	826

Variable	N		Mean	Median	Mode	Std. Deviation	Variance	Sum
	Valid	Missing						
Selection on basis of caste/region/religion/considerations	253	28	3.69	4.00	4	1.098	1.206	934
Recruitment on humanitarian grounds or death cases	232	49	2.28	2.00	1	1.300	1.690	528
Resource Allocation	139	142	2.67	2.00	2	1.253	1.571	371
Related with land allotment, requisition and distribution	240	41	2.76	3.00	1	1.455	2.117	662
Human resource allocation to get popularity in the area	258	23	3.08	3.00	4	1.245	1.550	794
Budgetary allocation for new/maintenance/ongoing works	237	44	2.95	3.00	2	1.403	1.967	698
Allocate/increase/decrease supply of goods and material	249	32	2.69	3.00	2	1.187	1.410	669
Allocation/deployment of Govt. vehicles & machinery	241	40	2.82	3.00	3	1.080	1.167	679
Rewards	170	111	2.61	3.00	3	1.039	1.079	444
Help in advancement of career progression or desired ACR	232	49	2.58	2.00	2	1.137	1.292	599
Appointment on special posts, board and corporations	240	41	3.61	4.00	3	1.000	1.000	867
Granting special pay/advance increments/honorarium	223	58	2.43	2.00	2	1.239	1.535	543
Allotment of government houses, vehicles and resources	246	35	2.62	2.00	2	1.073	1.150	645
Public praise/issue appreciation letters for future benefits	261	20	2.58	3.00	3	1.102	1.213	674
Punishment	160	121	2.49	3	3	0.876	0.767	399
Frequent dislocations/withdraw vehicle and house	226	55	2.46	2	2	1.251	1.565	555
Blockage of career progression/suspension/punishment	253	28	2.43	2	2	1.091	1.191	615
False complaints, vigilance inquiry and public criticism	265	16	3.49	4	4	1.056	1.114	924
Adverse ACR/spoiling the records	237	44	2.55	3	3	1.133	1.283	604
Dis-allowing/reducing the punishment	247	34	2.6	3	3	1.096	1.2	642
Promotions	193	88	3.22	3	3	1.073	1.15	621
Out of turn promotions to serve individual needs	242	39	3.37	3	4	1.146	1.313	816

Variable	N		Mean	Median	Mode	Std. Deviation	Variance	Sum
	Valid	Missing						
Ignoring/violation of merit to promote individuals	253	28	3.13	3	3	1.105	1.22	793
Promotion on the basis of considerations	228	53	2.96	3	3	1.078	1.161	674
Seniority violations to extend future financial benefits, pension, etc.	230	51	2.32	2	3	1.094	1.196	533
Creation of new posts to avoid stagnation and frustration in cadres	232	49	2.02	2	1	1.077	1.16	468
Rules, Regulations & Procedure	179	102	2.36	2	2	1.032	1.064	423
Ignore/circumvent rules to serve individual interests/goals	263	18	3.12	3	3	1.104	1.219	820
To simplify rules, regulations and procedures to avoid ambiguity	238	43	2.55	3	3	1.171	1.371	606
Frame new rules and regulations to meet political goals	254	27	3.12	3	3	1.088	1.183	793
Clientele-oriented enforcement and maintenance of rules	264	17	3.09	3	3	1.137	1.292	816
Amend/change rules for disadvantageous persons/ windows/orphans	251	30	1.89	1	1	1.198	1.436	474
Policy-Related Issues	156	125	2.61	3.00	3	1.026	1.053	407
Implement policy is such way to serve individual goal	261	20	3.17	3.00	3	1.181	1.395	827
To amend policy to serve changing social needs and interests	247	34	2.66	3.00	1	1.408	1.981	657
Policy for conservation and preservation of local resources/ culture	221	60	2.27	2.00	1	1.274	1.624	501
To frame policy to serve individual/regional future needs	249	32	2.66	3.00	3	1.187	1.410	663
Ignore/circumvent policy to meet political party goals/interests	231	50	3.26	3.00	3	1.163	1.352	754
Change of Law/Acts	188	93	2.62	2.00	2	0.885	0.783	492
New legislation for preservation/ conservation of culture/resources	258	23	2.25	2.00	2	1.070	1.144	580
Law to meet changing social needs/extend benefits to large groups	256	25	2.28	2.00	2	1.119	1.252	583

Variable	N		Mean	Median	Mode	Std. Deviation	Variance	Sum
	Valid	Missing						
Implementation of law to serve clientele needs	254	27	3.31	3.00	4	1.153	1.330	841
Amend/ignore/circumvent law to meet political interests and goals	250	31	3.36	3.00	3a	1.199	1.437	841
Frame new law to safeguard political interests for political gains	237	44	3.32	3.00	3	1.295	1.676	787
Demur in Decision Process	158	123	3.39	3.00	3	1.082	1.170	536
Election-related matters at various levels (schedule/ eligibility/nomination/results/ recounting, etc.)	234	47	3.52	3.50	3	1.194	1.427	824
Tenders or execution of work to avoid displeasure of masses	261	20	2.93	3.00	3	1.334	1.780	765
Land allotment/distribution and other land-related matters	229	52	2.79	3.00	1	1.385	1.918	640
Issues related with services matter/ employees to encash delays	236	45	2.55	3.00	3	1.138	1.296	601
Issues-related crime to avoid certain groups of people	253	28	3.27	3.00	4	1.253	1.570	827
Developmental Work-Related Issues	156	125	2.77	3.00	2	1.100	1.211	432
Sanction/reject/accept request for loans/subsidy/grants/aids	225	56	2.98	3.00	2	1.425	2.031	670
Include/exclude certain areas for applicability of project/schemes	251	30	3.08	3.00	3	1.187	1.410	773
Sanction new programmes and projects for their areas	265	16	3.20	3.00	3	1.220	1.489	849
Upgrade existing infrastructure/ institutions/facilities	258	23	3.01	3.00	2	1.287	1.658	776
Open/start new institutions/ schools/building/roads/canals	236	45	3.05	3.00	2	1.328	1.764	719
Crime-Related Issues	187	94	3.68	4.00	4	1.211	1.461	688
Manipulate arrest/release of persons of their interest	240	41	3.72	4.00	5	1.385	1.919	892
Detention/extension of individuals in custody for considerations	247	34	3.59	4.00	3	1.182	1.398	886
Settling score/disputes with the help of government machinery	255	26	3.56	4.00	5	1.256	1.577	909

Variable	N		Mean	Median	Mode	Std. Deviation	Variance	Sum
	Valid	Missing						
Registration/cancellation of FIR to misuse the ambiguity of law	249	32	3.65	4.00	5	1.275	1.625	908
Grabbing public property to serve political/individual goals	241	40	3.70	4.00	5	1.465	2.145	891
Training/Tours Related	155	126	2.49	2.00	1	1.439	2.070	386
Include/exclude names for foreign tours/training/visits	214	67	2.47	2.00	1	1.362	1.856	528
Start, open and upgrade institutions for training	244	37	2.16	2.00	1	1.084	1.175	528
Manipulate training results to serve the clientele needs	249	32	2.19	2.00	2	1.067	1.138	545
Allow/disallow, delay/expedite, keep pending proposal for training	240	41	2.39	2.00	2	1.216	1.478	574
Select/reject the training courses/ programmes/schedules	219	62	2.17	2.00	1	1.222	1.493	476
Social Issues	165	116	2.50	2.00	2	1.069	1.142	413
To generate employment opportunities in the constituency	237	44	2.86	3.00	1	1.425	2.030	677
Relaxation of govt. norms/ conditions to serve political goals	244	37	2.95	3.00	2	1.272	1.619	720
Misuse of govt. machinery to meet need of social groups	252	29	2.61	2.00	2	1.191	1.418	658
Auction of govt. property/land, etc.	243	38	2.54	2.00	2	1.150	1.324	618
Punitive action against the political opponents/groups	256	25	3.50	4.00	4	1.155	1.333	895

The basic and mute question is that any changes in political leadership, transfers are affected in wholesale. It is commonly said politician has brought officers of own choice and transfers reflect political interests. But the reality is that it is bureaucrats, who start mobilizing political pressure even they get an air of change and start meeting politicians to present their case and criticizing the officer currently in position. These officers sell dreams and promise to the politicians, politicians get moved by such words and initiate the process of transfers. Can we think for a minute that, if all the officers in the bureaucratic system work according to law, then who is left behind to oblige the politicians for doing wrong things and ultimately politicians will be forced to work on the basis of merit only.

"There is much truth to the idea that elected officials regularly abuse their executive authority to arbitrarily transfer civil servants and that this presents a serious obstacle to efficient bureaucratic functioning," *The Hindustan Times*, September 22, 2016. It is baseless to blame exclusively politicians for exerting pressure; the pressure phenomenon is both way and mutually inclusive for each other. Political interference with every change of government is not the political compulsion, but it is the bureaucratic lust manipulated by the politicians. Why on new government formation, politicians transfer first of all to Indian Administrative Service officers than others, because these are the officers, who are willing to oblige politicians to the greatest extent. They consider it their primary duty to manipulate the politicians regarding the transfers. If there are no transfers, why people will come and salute them? It is not the politician alone, but it is the IAS bureaucracy, who likes to create new opportunities and business through transfers industry for encashment for themselves. When these officers are posted at the State Secretariat level if resolve to provide correct advice to the politicians, how they will be adversely affected. Most of the time, they continue in the same town and same government residential house, and then what is the meaning of change for them? It is the change of lust and self-goals only. It is misleading to blame merely politicians for the transfers, they may be interested in a particular work for which a particular officer approaches them and promise to do it for them. In fact, it is bureaucracy, who has converted transfer into business for them.

Exhibit Number 12.2: Intensity/Frequency of Political Pressure in Transfers

Item Name	Service Name	Intensity of Pressure					Chi-square			R		Rho		Ranking
		5 Always	4 Most Oftenly	3 Frequently	2 Sometimes	1 Rarely	Value	df	Signif.	Value	Signif.	Value	Signif.	
Transfers in general	I.A.S.	70.1	17.9	10.4	1.5	0								
	I.P.S.	25.8	43.5	29	0	1.6								
	I.F.S.	40.6	29.7	15.6	6.3	7.8								
	AIS	46.1	30.1	18.1	2.6	3.1	40.2	8	0.000	–0.3	0.000	0.3	0.000	
On the basis of financial considerations	I.A.S.	19.7	38	32.4	4.2	5.6								1
	I.P.S.	17.1	19.5	46.3	8.5	8.5								2
	I.F.S.	14.4	32	18.6	19.6	15.5								2
	AIS	16.8	29.6	31.6	11.6	10.4	29.8	8	0.000	–.2	0.006	–0.2	0.01	2
Pressure of frequent transfers to serve clientele needs	I.A.S.	17.3	20	26.7	13.3	22.7								3
	I.P.S.	12.9	21.2	42.4	14.1	9.4								3
	I.F.S.	10.4	22.9	30.2	21.9	14.6								3
	AIS	13.3	21.5	33.2	16.8	15.2	12.1	8	0.14	*	*	*	*	3
To meet individual needs/goals	I.A.S.	18.7	21.3	18.7	26.7	14.7								2
	I.P.S.	21	34.6	24.7	9.9	9.9								1
	I.F.S.	16.3	17.3	34.7	16.3	15.3								1
	AIS	18.5	24	26.8	17.3	13.4	18.1	8	0.02	*	*	*	*	1
Serve public interests improvement of system & services	I.A.S.	15.5	11.3	22.5	23.9	28.8								4
	I.P.S.	0	0	2.6	44.9	52.6								5
	I.F.S.	5.98	17.8	14.9	21.8	39.6								5
	V	6.8	10.4	13.2	29.8	40	53.6	8	0.000	*	*	*	*	4
Please the large social groups to serve social needs	I.A.S.	3	13.6	13.6	28.8	40.9								5
	I.P.S.	2.2	2.2	25.3	19.8	50.5								4
	I.F.S.	8.6	22.6	23.7	18.3	26.9								4
	AIS	4.8	12.8	21.6	21.6	39.2	35.9	10	0.000	0.2	0.001	0.2	0.001	5

Some officers are of a different opinion and think, "They face a lot of interference from the politicians to change certain decisions to favor a particular employee or to cancel the transfer order of a subordinate employee and refrain from taking disciplinary action against his subordinates. If he remains firm to keep the morale of the administration, he soon finds himself in trouble. His actions are modified, altered, and totally quashed by the ministers and deputy ministers on the advice of their political friends. The individual officer loses faith in the bureaucratic system, existing laws, and the fair deal, which he had learnt to respect. He then become skeptic, flexible, keeps himself ready to act according to the wishes of the politicians and influential persons of the locality, irrespective of the dictates of the conscience. He loses interest in the work, never goes deep into the matter, and always passes files for order to his superiors," B. Panda (1978).

Mean value of 4.13, with a median of 4 and modal value of 5, with a standard deviation of 1.0 (Exhibit 12.1); indicate that political pressure is exerted 'always' to 'most often' for transfers. 70.1% of the Indian Administrative Service officers, 40.6% of the Indian Forest Service officers and 46.1% of total All India Services Officers encounter political pressure 'always' in the transfers. 43.5% of the Indian Police Service officers 'most often' encounter with political pressure in transfers. The strong association of transfer with the political pressure in the decision is shown by the Pearson Chi-square results with a significance level of 0.000. Pearson's correlation and Spearman correlation values are highly significant with 0.000, level of significance indicates good relation of transfer with the decision-making process.

The All India Services Officers frequently think that politicians pressurize them <u>due to financial considerations</u>, 31.6% of them feel that political pressure is exerted on them 'frequently' due to financial considerations. 38% of the Indian Administrative Service officers and 32% of the Indian Forest Service officers 'most often' come across political pressure for transfers and 46.3% of the Indian Police Service officers think that 'frequently' political pressure is exerted on them for transfers because of financial considerations. Results are highly significant with a 0.000, level of significance in Pearson Chi-square analysis. Financial considerations in transfers have a strong relation with the decision-making process, whereas the values of Pearson's correlation and Spearman correlation are significant at 0.006 and 0.01, level of significance.

Those All India Services Officers, who do not oblige politicians, are frequently transferred so that <u>due to fear of frequent dislocations</u>, such officers also oblige politicians for transfers. Analysis indicates that 33.2% of the All India Services Officers think that 'frequently' political pressure is exerted on them under the garb of dislocation. 42.4% of the Indian Police Service officers, 30.2% of the Indian Forest Service officers, and 26.7% of the Indian Administrative Service officers 'frequently' get pressure from a politician for serving their clientele.

The individual person under the <u>temptation to meet their own goals and needs</u> approach politician to get posted such officers so that they meet their goals. 34.6% of the Indian Police Service officers 'most often' come across political pressure for such transfers. The Association of this area of political pressure with the decision is significant as shown by the Chi-square results. 34.7% of the Indian Forest Service officers and 26.8% of the All India Services Officers think that they 'frequently' get political pressure subservient to goals. 26.7% of the Indian Administrative Service officers feel that 'sometimes' they get political pressure for transfer with a motive to serve goals.

Most often it is argued that transfers are carried out in public interest to serve the public for improvement of the system and for the sake of toning up a particular service. Lengthy letters are written and sermons are delivered for improvement of administration, to weed out undesirable elements transfer is a commonly used tool. 40% of the All India Services Officers are unanimous that very 'rarely' politicians exert pressure for transfers for improvement of the system. 52.6% of the Indian Police Service officers, 39.6% of the Indian Forest Service officers, and 26.8% of the Indian Administrative Service officers think that politicians 'rarely' exert pressure in the interest of the bureaucratic system and towards the improvement of service conditions. Pearson Chi-square results show a good association with 0.000, level of significance. Our research results clearly indicate that no one bothers for the improvement of the bureaucratic system and in the name of improvement very rarely politicians exert political pressure on the All India Services Officers.

Exhibit Number 12.3: Transfers versus Level more Amenable to Pressure

Area of Pressure	Frequency of Pressure on Area		Amenable Level			Total
			Top Level	Middle Level	Lower Level	
Transfers	Pressure is exerted 'rarely'	Count	2	4		6
		% of Total	1.0471	2.0942		3.1413
	Pressure is exerted 'some times' only	Count	4	1		5
		% of Total	2.0942	0.5235		2.6178
	Pressure is exerted 'frequently'	Count	25	6	4	35
		% of Total	13.089	3.1413	2.0942	18.324
	Pressure is exerted 'most oftenly'	Count	28	16	14	58
		% of Total	14.659	8.3769	7.3298	30.366
	Pressure is exerted 'always'	Count	53	20	14	87
		% of Total	27.748	10.471	7.3298	45.549
Total		Count	112	47	32	191
		% of Total	58.638	24.607	16.753	100

Politicians exert political pressure to please large social groups to serve their social needs. This type of political pressure is used for the furtherance of political interest and increasing the vote bank by appeasing dominant social groups. To study how politicians are looking after societal groups to serve their purpose, 39.2% of the All India Services Officers feel that 'rarely' politicians exert political pressure for appeasement of social groups. 50.5% of the Indian Police Service officers, 40.9% of the Indian Administrative Service officers, and 26.9% of the Indian Forest Service officers think that politicians 'rarely' exert pressure to look after the interests of large social groups. Our research results indicate that politicians give low priority to large social groups; most of the political pressure is exerted to meet the individual needs. Our results are significant at 0.000, level of significance under Pearson Chi-square analysis. Strong association and relationship are indicated by Pearson's correlation and Spearman correlation, which are significant at 0.001, level of significance.

Exhibit Number 12.4: Ranking of Different Sources of Pressure Working on Transfers Areas

Pressure Sources	Rank Priority	IAS	IPS	IFS	AIS
PM/CM	1st	6.40%	9.00%	12.50%	8.50%
	2nd	2.90%	2.60%	0.00%	2.30%
	3rd	6.00%	2.60%	0.00%	3.70%
	Total	15.30%	14.20%	12.50%	14.50%
Centre/State Minister	1st	54.10%	55.10%	45.80%	52.70%
	2nd	7.80%	2.60%	17.50%	7.70%
	3rd	7.00%	1.30%	5.30%	4.70%
	Total	68.90%	59.00%	68.60%	65.10%
Member Parliament	1st	1.80%	0.00%	0.00%	0.90%
	2nd	9.70%	1.30%	0.00%	5.00%
	3rd	9.00%	7.90%	5.30%	7.90%
	Total	20.50%	9.20%	5.30%	13.80%
MLA/MLC	1st	27.50%	15.40%	22.90%	22.60%
	2nd	44.70%	51.90%	42.50%	46.80%
	3rd	7.00%	3.90%	15.80%	7.50%
	Total	79.20%	71.20%	81.20%	76.90%
Zila Parishad/District-level Politicians	1st	2.80%	10.30%	4.20%	5.50%
	2nd	13.60%	11.70%	12.50%	12.70%
	3rd	14.00%	9.20%	10.50%	11.70%
	Total	30.40%	31.20%	27.20%	29.90%
Block Samiti/Block-level Politicians	1st	0.00%	0.00%	0.00%	0.00%
	2nd	2.90%	10.40%	2.50%	5.50%
	3rd	9.00%	7.90%	2.60%	7.50%
	Total	11.90%	18.30%	5.10%	13.00%
Village Heads/Grassroot level worker	1st	0.00%	0.00%	0.00%	0.00%
	2nd	0.00%	0.00%	0.00%	0.00%
	3rd	3.00%	10.50%	5.30%	6.10%
	Total	3.00%	10.50%	5.30%	6.10%
Power Brokers/Touts	1st	0.90%	0.00%	0.00%	0.40%
	2nd	6.80%	10.40%	17.50%	10.00%
	3rd	13.60%	10.70%	4.70%	29.00%
	Total	21.30%	21.10%	22.20%	39.40%

Pressure Sources	Rank Priority	IAS	IPS	IFS	AIS
Communication Media	1st	2.80%	6.40%	6.30%	4.70%
	2nd	6.80%	2.60%	5.00%	5.00%
	3rd	4.00%	3.90%	10.50%	5.10%
	Total	13.60%	12.90%	21.80%	9.70%
Hidden Financiers	1st	3.70%	3.80%	8.30%	4.70%
	2nd	4.90%	6.50%	2.50%	5.00%
	3rd	12.00%	22.40%	18.40%	16.80%
	Total	20.60%	32.70%	29.20%	26.50%

Exhibit 12.4 shows results for the intensity of political pressure exerted from different sources for transfers. Exhibit 12.4 indicates that Member Parliament pressure intensity regarding transfer goes on increasing from 1st priority to 3rd priority onward, e.g. 0.9% in 1st priority, 5% and 7.9% subsequently, whereas in case of Minister and MLA/MLC quantum of pressure go on decreasing from 1st priority to 3rd priority. This indicates that the AISO give 1st priority to the Minister, MLA/MLC, and CM/PM pressure for transfers, as most of their demand is met within a first priority, then for the remaining part they consider other sources of pressure. Similarly, pressure intensity from the district-level politicians are also the highest level of acceptance in 3rd priority as pressure on the IAS in three categories varies from 2.8%, 13.6%, and 14%. Among the three services, the highest pressure intensity was observed on the IAS 30.4%, on the IPS 31.2%, on the AIS 29.9%, and the IFS 27.2%. Respondents' number (frequency) in three priorities is not the same, because every respondent has not mentioned all three priorities (1st, 2nd, and 3rd) in their ranking, due to this, there is variability. We added together three priorities (based on answered numbers).

68.9% on the IAS, 68.6% on the IFS, 59% on the IPS, and 65.1% on the AIS pressure is exerted from Centre/State Minister for the transfers. Data for the respective sources of pressure intensity indicate that PM/CM pressure 12.5% on the IFS (may be due to Forest Conservation Act, 1980, diversion cases), 9% on the IPS, and 6.4% on the IAS in first priority is away from expected thinking. Perhaps the IAS has considered pressure as routine, in case of the addition of three priorities the IAS gets the highest pressure of 15.30%, followed by 14.2% for the IPS, 14.5% on the AIS, and 12.5% for the IFS. Among all the sources of pressure, this level of PM/CM is 3rd in importance. The highest pressure regarding transfers is exerted by the Centre/State Ministers on the AISO and followed by the MLA/MLC as shown in Exhibit 12.4.

Amenability to accept pressure by different levels of bureaucracy is shown in Chart 12.11, where top-level bureaucrats get maximum pressure in 'always' intensity for the transfers. A very interesting part of the results in Exhibit 12.4 indicates that power brokers/touts/musclemen, communication media and hidden financiers pressure acceptance for transfers is higher than block level politicians, village-level workers. This indicates that for transfer-related issues the power brokers/touts/musclemen play a great role followed by the hidden financiers and then communication media. Newsmakers also influence transfers in bureaucracy. Power brokers may be milking the transfer industry and hidden financiers get their things done through transfer related issue. This also indicates a syndicate of powerful companies whose projects are related to the government. They manage the transfer of pliable bureaucrats so that their files are cleared according to their desires. Hidden financiers' highest aggregate score is 32.7% for the IPS, followed by the IFS 29.2% and the IAS 20.6%. This can be considered an unfair hindrance in government working by the hidden financiers.

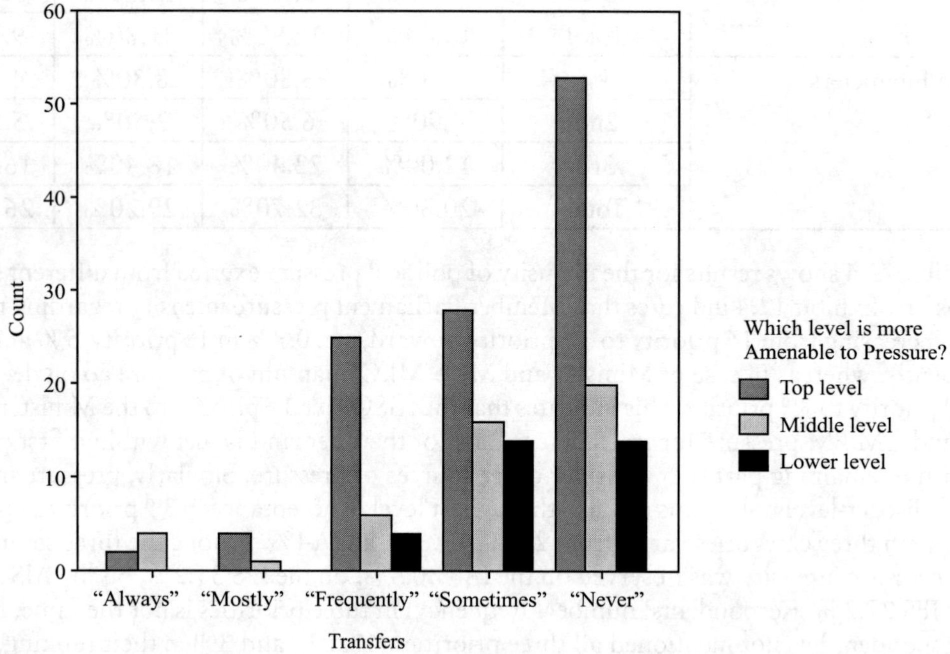

Chart No. 12.1: Level more Amenable to Pressure in Transfers

12.2.2. Political Pressure for Postings

On occasions, officers remain on the same headquarter (town) but they are posted out to different positions (change of duty), we have taken a change of duties without change of headquarters in this category of posting also. Postings are related to positions held by an officer. The transfer involves the element of change of place or movement (commonly but not strictly). However, every transfer necessarily involves an element of postings in it, and that has been discussed under the heading transfer (12.2.1). It is commonly felt that the All India Services Officers without influence or excellent political connections are commonly posted to uncomfortable stations and posts. Postings are necessarily related to the position in the hierarchy at a particular position, level, and place having relation with the duties discharged in that particular position or post. In the same place, there may be some posts, which carry aura and maybe another post without work or public dealing or any powers. Postings are seen with powers and prestige associated with a particular post.

The posting process has been grossly misused historically. "Although Viceroys had the prerogative to appoint whomever they wanted to the highest positions, they wisely spared neither time nor pains in their anxious efforts to appease all the possible claimants to a vacancy."[6] Some senior officers preferred to remain as Collectors to the end as their salaries were top of ICS scales. Longer than three years tenure was considered dangerous and an officer has the risk to put down roots, get personally involved in local issues.

"Yet the Indian Administrative Service officers still held control posts in districts and secretariats. Although changes in the range of posts held by IAS and nature of their work reflected the changed orientation of the Indian state, their location and activities followed broadly the pattern set by ICS in the 1920 and 1930s", D.C. Potter, 1986. "There is no *Brahmastra* or magic wands to end corruption at one go," U.C. Agarwal, 2011. The clout of the IAS is well known. "Such is the clout of the EO and Cabinet Secretary that Ministers and Chief Ministers need to send their emissary to the lowly EO to try to influence his decisions. This clearly shows that where power lies in India. Our elected politicians have no real powers to deliver their election commitments. Our democracy is thus being choked from within—by the unaccountable and ultra-powerful IAS," *The Times of India*, June 1, 2019.

Immediate after a change of government, political interferences in transfers and postings are invariably influenced by the selfish officers to fulfill self-goals under the cover of political color. In the name of shifting of incompetent officers, own officers are rewarded by promotions, but in this process, most incompetent officers grow and mobilize the greatest amount of political support. Therefore, postings in the disguise of improving competence have no relevance in the present system. Now officers start scheming for postings right from the probation period and individual officers mobilize political pressure from the first day they join the service. Then, how we can blame only politicians for these postings?

What is the definition of wet or plumb postings? It is immaterial for politicians. It is All India Services Officers, who create such definitions in the garb of children education, urban location, housing facility, even officers have heard of saying straight trunk dialing telephone facilities (during the nineties) and what not, list expand according to time and nature of politician. Politician participation in administration is inherent in a democratic setup. Why top officers do not make norms and ensure adherence by these officers, instead of blaming politicians. Powers for postings regarding subordinate employees at the district are with the All India Services Officers posted in the district; this provides an opportunity to both politician and individual officer to enter into bargaining for mutual benefits maximization.

Postings, in general, have a mean value of 3.62 with a standard deviation of 1.19; indicate that political pressure is exerted 'most often' to 'always' in the matter related to the postings. Mean and modal value of 4, clearly indicates that most often political pressure is encountered in postings. 29.2% of the All India Services Officers, 37.9% of the Indian Police Service officers, and 25.4% of the Indian Administrative Service officers 'most often' come across political pressure in postings. 31% of the Indian Forest Service officers 'always' encounter political pressure in postings.

6. D.M. Wallace wrote to D. Fitzpatrick, Chief Commissioner, CP, Calcutta on 11.2.1887.

Exhibit Number 12.5: Intensity of Political Pressure Exerted for the Postings

Service	Intensity	281 Posting	282 Plumb/wet	283 Deny/delay	284 Financial	285 Pliability	286 Reg/caste
I.A.S.	'always'	20.6	45.2	25.8	29	37.1	31.8
	'mostly'	25.4	29	36.4	21	33.9	36.4
	'frequently'	19	12.9	27.3	35.5	24.2	21.2
	'sometimes'	20.6	11.3	7.6	14.5	1.6	1.5
	'rarely'	14.3	1.6	3	0	3.2	9.1
I.P.S.	'always'	34.8	51.3	26.1	11.3	60.5	21.8
	'mostly'	37.9	39.7	26.1	28.2	27.6	34.6
	'frequently'	27.3	9	34.8	52.1	11.8	37.2
	'sometimes'	0	0	6.5	2.8	0	0
	'rarely'	0	0	6.5	5.6	0	6.4
I.F.S.	'always'	31	42.9	23.8	17.3	22.2	7.2
	'mostly'	21.4	33.7	30.7	31.6	36.4	33
	'frequently'	31	11.2	25.7	38.8	20.2	25.6
	'sometimes'	11.9	5.1	7.9	4.1	13.1	17.5
	'rarely'	4.8	7.1	11.9	8.2	8.1	16.5
TOTAL	'always'	28.7	46.2	25.1	18.6	38.4	18.7
	'mostly'	29.2	34.5	30.5	27.7	32.9	34.4
	'frequently'	25.1	10.9	29.3	42	18.6	28.2
	'sometimes'	10.5	5	7.3	6.5	5.9	7.5
	'rarely'	6.4	3.4	7.7	5.2	4.2	11.2
Ranking			1	3	5	2	4
All figures are in %							

If we combine all scores above 'frequently' intensity, we see that 100% of the Indian Police Service officers, 74.3% of the Indian Forest Service officers, and 65% of the Indian Administrative Service officers feel that political pressure is rampant in decisions about posting. Low score by the Indian Administrative Service officers may be due to the factor that in case of their own postings, the Chief Secretary plays a major role, and being a member of their service, he can manipulate postings for them. Pearson Chi-square value of 30.5, with 8 degree of freedom, 0.000, level of significance; show that our results are highly significant. Strength of relationship indicated by Pearson's correlation value of 0.2, with 0.01, level of significance, and Spearman correlation value of 0.2, with 0.02, level of significance.

We have studied postings with five variables or five factors in different situations, whereas politicians and the All India Services Officers manipulate it. The All India Services Officers, who serve political goals, are provided with wet and plumb postings, where politicians and officers both serve their self-interest. Modal value of 5 and the median value of 4 indicate that political pressure is used 'most often' to 'always' intensity for getting wet and plumb postings. 80.7% of the All India Services Officers are of the view that posting is managed to serve political goals. Results for the respective All India Services indicate that 91% of the Indian Police Service officers, 76.6% of the Indian Forest Service officers, and 74.2% of the Indian Administrative Service officers consider that 'most often' to 'always' political pressure intensity is exerted to serve political goals. Political goals in postings and decision-making process have a good association, as indicated by the Pearson Chi-square results, with a value of 22.8, with 8 degree of freedom, and a level of significance with 0.004. The Indian Police Service officers serve a comparatively higher number of political goals than the other two services to get plumb postings.

Those All India Services Officers, who resist political pressure in postings, may be denied postings on good places/positions. In case the politician finds that departmental head has submitted a proposal for postings, which carry the names of such officers, who may not attune in their scheme of actions, politicians delay such proposals till concerned officer come to him for showing his obedience. The mean value of 3.52, median and modal value of 4, indicate that 'most often' such tactics are used by the politicians. 55.6% of the All India Services Officers realize that 'most often' to 'always' political pressure is used to deny and delay postings to such officers, who resist it. The score for respective services also indicates the same thing, 62.2% of the Indian Administrative Service officers, 54.5% of the Indian Forest Service officers, and 52.2% of the Indian Police Service officers are of the same view. This clearly establishes the fact that politicians 'most often' misuse their position to deny postings to such officers, whom they think that person will not oblige them.

It is a common belief that politicians provide posting based on financial considerations, even if they do not get direct money, future considerations or financial expectations from the decision taken by the All India Services Officers may be in mind. The mean value of 3.45 and modal value of 3; indicate that 'frequently' financial considerations work in the postings. 42% of the All India Services Officers, 52.1% of the Indian Police Service officers, 38.8% of the Indian Forest Service officers, and 35.5% of the Indian Administrative Service officers think that 'frequently' financial considerations influence the postings. If we combine the score from 'frequently' intensity to 'always', results indicate that 91.6% of the Indian Police Service officers, 87.7% of the Indian Forest Service officers, and 85.5% of the Indian Administrative Service officers are of the view that political pressure is exerted based on financial considerations. 23.4 value of Pearson Chi-square with 8 degree of freedom show 0.003, level of significance. This shows that there is a good association of financial considerations in postings with the decision-making process.

Those who resist political pressure are denied posting, then those All India Services Officers, who are pliable and like to work in hands in gloves with the politicians, can ensure their longer tenure on the wet postings. Our results show the mean value of 3.92 with a standard deviation of 1.11, a median of 4, and a modal value of 5, clearly indicate that pliability is 'always' considered and used for ensuring continuity in the posting of choice. Pliability is both ways compromise behavior and here All India Services Officers feel that they are in a win-win situation, whereas public and decision process is the sufferer. 71.4% of the All India Services Officers consider pliability 'most often' to 'always' accustom to ensure continuity in the desired post. 88.1% of the Indian Police Service officers, 71% of the Indian Administrative Service officers, and 58.6% of the Indian Forest

Service officers think that they continue in a plumb posting by adopting pliability. So, for the All India Services Officers, distortion in the decision-making process has not much importance, just to ensure their postings on good places and positions, they deliver highly pliable decisions as desired by the politicians irrespective of merit. This indicates that how a lust for postings can kill the decision-making process. Pearson Chi-square value is 42.6, with 8 degree of freedom and 0.000, level of significance. Pearson's correlation and Spearman's negative correlation value of –0.22 are significant with a level of significance at 0.001.

Exhibit Number 12.6: Postings versus Length of Service and AISO Amenable to Political Pressure

Postings		Length of Service Amenability to Political Pressure					Total
		1 to 4 years of service	5 to 10 years of service	11 to 17 years of service	18 to 23 years of service	>24 years of service	
'Rarely' pressure is exerted	Count	1		2	3	5	11
	% of Total	0.613		1.226	1.84	3.067	6.748
'Sometimes' only pressure is exerted	Count	2	2	1	3	10	18
	% of Total	1.226	1.226	0.613	1.84	6.134	11.042
'Frequently' pressure is exerted	Count	3	3	8	7	21	42
	% of Total	1.84	1.84	4.9	4.294	12.883	25.766
'Most oftenly' pressure is exerted	Count	4	4	4	7	27	46
	% of Total	2.453	2.453	2.453	4.294	16.564	28.22
'Always' pressure is exerted	Count	4	3	9	9	21	46
	% of Total	2.453	1.84	5.521	5.521	12.883	28.22
Total	Count	14	12	24	29	84	163
	% of Total	8.588	7.361	14.723	17.791	51.533	100

Politicians are often accused that they take decisions regarding postings based on caste, region, and religion to cater to the needs of individuals on such a basis. It is alleged that in the highly structured society of India, caste, region, and religion play a major role in the decision-making process for postings. Our results show that mean value of 3.39 with a standard deviation of 1.22, also the median value of 4 and modal value of 4, all these indicate that 'most often' posting decision are taken on the considerations based on caste, region, and religion. 53.1% of the All India Services Officers think that caste and region play their role 'most often' in postings. 68.2% of the Indian Administrative Service officers, 56.4% of the Indian Police Service officers, and 40.2% of the Indian Forest Service officers feel that 'most often' posting decisions are caste and region-based to cater to the needs of individuals. Chi-square value of 43.4, with 8 degree of freedom with 0.000, level of significance, results establish the association of the caste consideration in postings with the decision-making process. The strength of this relationship is shown by Pearson's correlation and Spearman correlation values of 0.3, with a 0.000, level of significance.

Posting relationship with the length of service variable of the All India Services results placed at Exhibit 12.6 and Chart 12.2 show that 51.5% of All India Services officer with more than 24 years of service and 17.8% with 18 to 23 years of service get pressure for postings. Amenability towards acceptance of political pressure increases with the length of services among three All India Services.

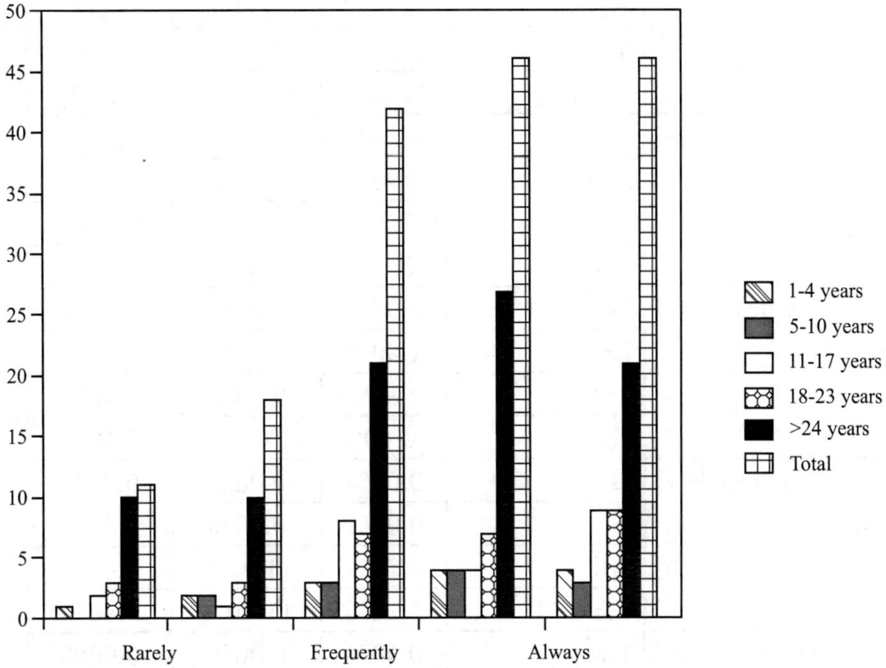

Chart No. 12.2: Length of Service and Amenability to Pressure in Postings

Exhibit Number 12.7: Priority Ranking of Different Sources of Pressure on Posting as Pressure Point

Pressure Sources	Rank Priority	IAS	IPS	IFS	AIS
PM/CM	1st	13.40%	12.80%	15.20%	13.60%
	2nd	3.60%	3.80%	0.00%	3.00%
	3rd	6.50%	4.50%	0.00%	4.60%
	Total	23.50%	21.10%	15.20%	21.20%
Centre/State Minister	1st	48.20%	44.90%	41.30%	45.80%
	2nd	25.90%	14.10%	28.60%	22.40%
	3rd	5.40%	3.00%	0.00%	3.60%
	Total	79.50%	62.00%	69.90%	68.20%
Member Parliament	1st	0.00%	0.00%	2.20%	0.40%
	2nd	4.50%	1.30%	2.40%	3.00%
	3rd	15.10%	4.50%	10.80%	10.70%
	Total	19.60%	5.80%	15.40%	14.10%

Pressure Sources	Rank Priority	IAS	IPS	IFS	AIS
MLA/MLC	1st	26.80%	17.90%	19.60%	22.50%
	2nd	38.40%	43.60%	33.30%	39.20%
	3rd	6.50%	4.50%	16.20%	7.60%
	Total	71.70%	61.50%	69.10%	69.30%
Zila Parishad/District-level Politicians	1st	4.50%	14.10%	6.50%	8.10%
	2nd	8.90%	7.70%	9.50%	8.60%
	3rd	17.20%	11.90%	16.20%	15.20%
	Total	30.60%	33.70%	32.20%	31.90%
Block Samiti/Block-level Politicians	1st	0.00%	0.00%	0.00%	0.00%
	2nd	1.80%	10.30%	2.40%	4.70%
	3rd	8.60%	9.00%	2.70%	7.60%
	Total	10.40%	19.30%	5.10%	12.30%
Village Heads/Grassroot level worker	1st	0.00%	0.00%	0.00%	0.00%
	2nd	0.00%	0.00%	0.00%	0.00%
	3rd	2.20%	11.90%	5.40%	6.10%
	Total	2.20%	11.90%	5.40%	6.10%
Power Brokers/Touts	1st	0.90%	0.00%	0.00%	0.40%
	2nd	6.30%	10.30%	16.70%	9.50%
	3rd	20.40%	20.90%	18.90%	20.30%
	Total	27.60%	31.20%	35.60%	30.20%
Communication Media	1st	2.70%	6.40%	6.50%	4.70%
	2nd	6.30%	2.60%	4.80%	4.70%
	3rd	4.30%	4.50%	10.80%	5.60%
	Total	13.30%	13.50%	22.10%	15.00%
Hidden Financiers	1st	3.60%	3.80%	8.70%	4.70%
	2nd	4.50%	6.40%	2.40%	4.70%
	3rd	14.00%	25.40%	18.90%	18.80%
	Total	22.10%	35.60%	11.10%	9.40%

Statistical analyses of research data placed at Exhibit 12.7 regarding priority ranking of different sources of pressure on posting point/areas on the AISO. During the research, the AISO were asked to rank 1st, 2nd, and 3rd priority while dealing with political pressure for postings points. In 1st priority Centre/State Minster 48.2% of the IAS, 44.90% of the IPS, 41.3% of the IFS, and 45.8% of the AISO ranked posting in 1st priority pressure intensity. Respondents' number (frequency) in three priorities is not the same, because every respondent has not mentioned all three priority (1st, 2nd, and 3rd) ranking, due to this variability, we added together three priorities (based on answered numbers). The three priorities total indicate 79.5% of the IAS, 69.9% of the IFS. 62% of the IPS and 68.2% of the AISO indicated the occurrence of political pressure for postings areas. In 1st priority, 2nd most pressure exerting source is MLA/MLC and 22.5% of the AISO, 26.8% of the IAS, 19.6% of the IFS, and 17.9% of the IPS realize pressure in the decision-making process for the postings from this source.

The PM/CM as a source of political pressure for postings areas in the decision-making process came 3rd in the first priority of ranking. 13.6% of the AISO, 15.2% of the IFS, 13.4% of the IAS, and 12.8% of the IPS feel the pressure from this source. Whereas the total score for three priorities is 23.0 % for the IAS, 21.1% for the IPS, 15.2% for the IFS, and 21.2% for the AISO. The AISO have shown pressure from Member Parliament 0.4% to 14.1% and district-level politicians 8.1% to 15.2% increasing from 1st priority towards 3rd priority, this indicates that after considering the Minister, MLA/MLC and Prime Minister/CM pressure, the Officers listen to the MPs and DLPs.

Another interesting feature indicates that hidden financiers, power brokers/touts play important role in postings areas/points, this also indicates the role of money in postings. In these two sources of pressure the intensity increases from 1st priority towards 3rd priority indicating that after the Ministers, MLA/MLC third important pressure source is power brokers/touts followed by hidden financiers. It may not be out of context that results show how postings are used as an industry in bureaucracy. When such sources of pressure interfere in postings decisions, then the AISO is bound to work under their influence on many related decisions in the bureaucracy. According to the common perception that block-level politicians and village-level workers could have got importance after MLA/MLC, who manage votes and work for the politicians and political parties, but these two sources of pressure have been relegated to last with a very low percentage score.

12.2.3. Political Pressure Related to Recruitment

The recruitment process invites the greatest amount of political pressure and it is difficult to carry out any kind of recruitment without the intervention of political pressure. Politicians adopt different ways and means to exert political pressure in the recruitment process. In the present system, the All India Services Officers as district head enjoy lots of powers for recruitment in case of group IV and some group III employees (the AISO are heads of department for some employees). These inherent powers motivate politicians and individual officers to enter into a bargaining process for mutual benefits. With frequent interventions of the courts and frequent interpretation of ever-changing local law and rules is another reason, which motivates officers and politicians to form a syndicate to meet their own interests. "Recruitment must be made solely on the basis of merit preferably by an independent agency...if a...political leader interferes with the selection of policemen (as usually happens), the plan for improvement of police is doomed," Dr. R. Prasher (1986).

"Colonially created All India Services by imperialist power required big number of soldiers and administrators to govern the Indian subcontinent of size of Europe, few were recruited by imperial power in London, rests were found cheaply in India. They were the trusted agents of imperial power to look after the economic strategic interest of the British Government' (D.C. Potter). He has further elucidated on elite attitude as "for one thing, recruiting a few young men each year to separate service, and then giving them, and only them, a clear run to top, commanding handsome salaries most of the way, is the height of elitist administration. This meant that other administrators who did not, or could not get into service were forever denied access to top positions, however able they might subsequently become." Highly stratified imperial bureaucracy excluded all other services from reaching any important position, which reduced the dynamism amongst those services.

During the last two decades, maximum numbers of recruitment-related cases are going to the courts and large-scale litigation itself proves that a high degree of political intervention in recruitment and acceptance of pressure by the AISO. Different courts (local level to the Supreme Court) have quashed or observed violations in recruitments process by different State Governments or PSUs establishes that political interference in recruitment and many politicians and bureaucrats are in jails due to violations of recruitment procedure/rules.

The All India Services Officers get political pressure whenever and wherever they try to carry out the recruitment at whatsoever level or position. Procedure for recruitment is also used as a mode of pressure to mobilize support and get many other things done by the bureaucracy. Mean value of 3.90, a median of 4, and modal value of 4, with a standard deviation of 0.88, indicating that in the area of recruitment intensity of political pressure is high and 'most often' political pressure is exerted for the recruitment. The highest values indicate that 38.7% of the All India Services Officers, 56.8% of the Indian Forest Service officers, and 35.7% of the Indian Administrative Service officers 'most often' come across political pressure in recruitment. 35.5% of the Indian Police Service officers 'frequently' come across political pressure in recruitment. Comparatively lower political pressure on the Indian Police Service officers may be due to the specialized nature of recruitment made by them. In some States recruitment of constables in the police is observed with very high political pressure. 'Most often' and 'always' combined score shows that, 70.3% of the Indian Forest Service officers, 67.8% of the Indian Administrative Service officers, and 64.5% of the Indian Police Service officers come across political pressure in recruitment in 'most often' cases. Pearson Chi-square analysis results with a value of 18.7, show significant association with the decision-making process with a significance level of 0.01.

On many occasions, when politicians are in power, they use their position to create new posts, which can be used for recruitment, with the intention that, such newly recruited persons will be helpful for them in the future. They expect that those persons recruited under their influence will provide services to serve their future goals. The mean value of 3.38 with a standard deviation of 1.22 and median and modal value of 3 also indicate that politicians for getting services in the future exert 'frequently' political pressure in the process of recruitment. 40.6% of the Indian Administrative Service officers and 30.3% of the All India Services Officers get 'frequent' political pressure in recruitment for future services. 33% of the Indian Forest Service officers and 27.8% of the Indian Police Service officers think that 'most often' they get political pressure in recruitment to get benefits in the future.

When politicians find that recruitment procedure itself is obstructive for the recruitment of their persons, they try to change such procedure, in case change is not possible, they pressurize the All India Services Officers for distortions, and violations of such procedure for own advantage. The moderate mean value of 2.82 with a median and modal value of 3; indicate 'frequent' exertion of political pressure for violation of procedures in recruitment. 37.4% of the All India Services Officers, 43.4% of the Indian Police Service officers, and 40.6% of the Indian Administrative Service officers realize that politicians ask them 'frequently' for violation or distortion of recruitment procedures. 31.6% of the Indian Forest Service officers get 'most often' political pressure for violation of recruitment procedure as the highest score. Politicians' demand for violation of recruitment procedures has a good association with the decision-making process, as demonstrated by Pearson Chi-square value of 33.9, with 8 degree of freedom and 0.000, level of significance.

Exhibit Number 12.8: Intensity of Political Pressure in Recruitment Variables

Service Name	Intensity of Pressure	287 Recruitment	288 Creation of Posts	289 Procedure Violation	290 Ignoring Merit	291 Financial Demands	292 Region/ Caste	293 Ex-gratia
I.A.S.	'always'	32.1	17.2	14.1	9.6	14.9	28.1	15.5
	'mostly'	35.7	29.7	28.1	27.4	26.9	32.8	17.2
	'frequently'	25	40.6	40.6	30.1	13.4	28.1	20.7
	'sometimes'	5.4	4.7	10.9	20.5	23.9	9.4	20.7
	'rarely'	1.8	7.8	6.3	12.3	20.9	1.6	25.9
I.P.S.	'always'	33.9	26.7	1.3	30.5	13.3	40.7	0
	'mostly'	30.6	27.8	7.9	34.7	41	37.2	0
	'frequently'	35.5	25.6	43.4	18.9	43.4	19.8	4.1
	'sometimes'	0	13.3	22.4	8.4	2.4	0	23
	'rarely'	0	6.7	25	7.4	0	2.3	73
I.F.S.	'always'	13.5	16	4.2	8.3	17.5	13.3	12.6
	'mostly'	56.8	33	31.6	26	29.9	33.7	12.6
	'frequently'	21.6	28	30.5	29.2	25.8	36.7	28.4
	'sometimes'	8.1	8	17.9	18.8	16.5	5.1	28.4
	'rarely'	0	15	15.8	17.7	10.3	11.2	17.9
AIS	'always'	28.4	20.1	6	16.7	15.4	26.6	9.3
	'mostly'	38.7	30.3	23	29.5	32.8	34.7	9.7
	'frequently'	28.4	30.3	37.4	25.8	28.3	28.6	18.5
	'sometimes'	3.9	9.1	17.4	15.5	13.8	4.4	24.7
Total	rarely	0.6	10.2	16.2	12.5	9.7	5.6	37.9
Variable Ranking			2	6	3	4	1	5

Politicians come across the problem that the people in whom they are interested in recruitment do not fulfill the necessary requirements of the prescribed physical standards. Concerned persons assert pressure on politicians to pass on political pressure on the All India Services Officers to relax the physical standards for such persons (police and forests recruitment physical standards are important). Such political pressure is most common for the Indian Police Service officers and the Indian Forest Service officers. 34.7% of the Indian Police Service officers and 29.5% of the All India Services Officers get political pressure 'most often' for relaxation of physical standards. 30.1% of the Indian Administrative Service officers and 29.2% of the Indian Forest Service officers get political pressure 'frequently' for violation of procedures in recruitment. A mean value of 3.2 with a standard deviation of 1.27 indicates 'frequent' exertion of political pressure for violation of recruitment procedures. Pearson Chi-square results indicate a good association of such violation of procedures in recruitment with the decision-making process; a value of 30.2 with 8 degree of freedom and 0.000, level of significance indicates that our results are significant.

The All India Services Officers frequently whisper about selections and recruitment because of financial considerations. In such financial considerations' politician and individual officer both are involved in many cases. It may be possible that only politicians are influenced by the financial considerations; in turn, exert political pressure on the All India Services Officers for recruitment. The mean value of 3.28, with a median of 3 and modal value of 4; indicates that 'frequently' to 'most often' political pressure is exerted on the basis of financial consideration in the process of recruitment. 61.1% of the All India Services Officers, 84.4% of the Indian Police Service officers, 55.7% of the Indian Forest Service officers, and 40.3% of the Indian Administrative Service officers are 'most often' to 'frequently' intensity influenced by the politician financial considerations in the process of recruitment. Pearson Chi-square value of 45.3 with 8 degree of freedom and a level of significance at 0.000, indicates a good association of financial considerations with the decision-making process.

Exhibit Number 12.9: Recruitment versus Cadre of the Officer Crosstabulation

Variable	Pressure Intensity		Cadre of the Officer			Total
			Home Cadre	Outside Cadre	Neighbouring State	
Recruitment	'rarely' pressure is exerted	Count	1			1
		% of Total	0.709			0.709
	'sometimes' only pressure is exerted	Count	3	1	2	6
		% of Total	2.127	0.709	1.418	4.255
	'frequent' pressure is exerted	Count	11	20	9	40
		% of Total	7.801	14.184	6.382	28.368
	'most oftenly 'pressure is exerted	Count	15	22	16	53
		% of Total	10.638	15.602	11.347	37.588
	'always' pressure is exerted	Count	8	23	10	41
		% of Total	5.673	16.312	7.092	29.078
Total		Count	38	66	37	141
		% of Total	26.95	46.808	26.241	100

Politicians exert pressure for recruitment because of caste, region, and religion of the individual person in question. While exerting such pressure, the politician is influenced by the own goals and interests to be achieved in long run. The mean value of 3.69, with mode and a median value of 4, indicates that 'most often' political pressure exerted is because of the individual caste and region considerations. 32.8% of the Indian Administrative Service officers and 34.7% of the All

India Services Officers get 'most often' pressure in recruitment due to individual caste and region. 41.7% of the Indian Police Service officers get 'always' intensity political pressure in recruitment based on consideration as caste and region, whereas 36.7% of the Indian Forest Service officers get 'frequent' political pressure based on such considerations. Pearson Chi-square value of 34.3, with 8 degree of freedom and 0.000, level of significance indicates good association. The relationship of such an association is indicated by Pearson's correlation and Spearman correlation value of 0.2, with 0.002, level of significance.

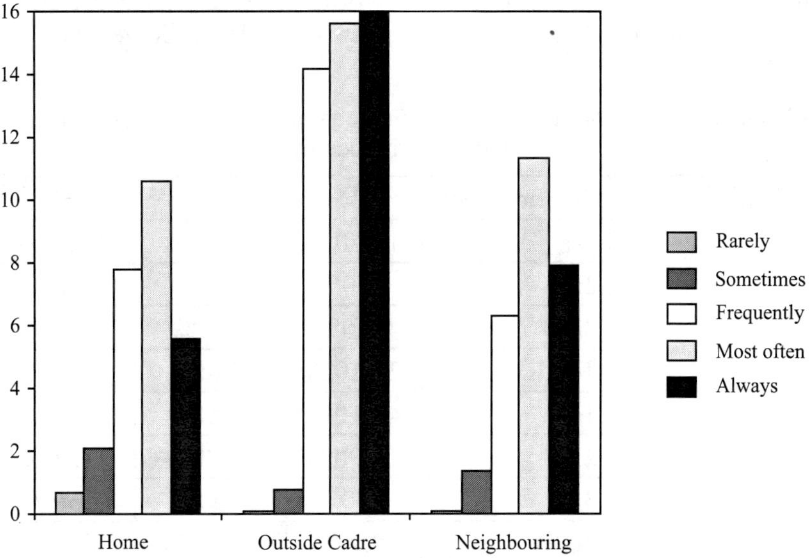

Chart No. 12.3: Recruitment versus Cadre of the Officer Pressure Acceptance

After the death of an employee, most of the governments provide employment on the humanitarian ground to next of kin as ex-gratia employment. In the case concerned person belongs to politician political groups, then politicians exert out of way pressure for such recruitment/ appointments. Mean value of 2.28 with a modal value of 1 indicate that politician exerts pressure 'rarely' to 'sometimes' only for recruitment on humanitarian grounds. 73% of the Indian Police Service officers, 25.9% of the Indian Administrative Service officers, and 37.9% of the All India Services Officers 'rarely' get any political pressure for ex-gratia recruitment. 28.4% of the Indian Forest Service officers 'sometimes' get political pressure for humanitarian ground recruitment. Pearson Chi-square value of 72.7, with 8 degree of freedom and 0.000, level of significance indicates that there is a good association of this variable with the decision. These results indicate that the All India Services Officers and politicians both have very low interest in genuine needy cases of recruitment, but they show high interest in issues related to their own goals and interests.

Exhibit 12.9 and Chart 12.3 indicate the relation of the recruitment variable with the cadre of the AISO. Results show 48.81% of the AISO in outside of home state cadre, 26.95% working in the home state and 26.2% officers working in neighboring states are amenable to accept political pressure in the recruitment process of decision making.

Statistical data analysis placed at Exhibit 12.10 shows very interesting results towards priorities ranking of different sources of pressure on recruitment areas/points. Exhibits 12.4 and 12.7 show priority ranking for transfer and postings, where the intensity of pressure from PM/CM level was comparatively very low in comparison to Ministers and MLAs, here in case of recruitment the PM/CM level pressure is on the higher side though first level pressure is from Ministers level. Centre/State Ministers' sources of pressure in 1st priority indicate the intensity of pressure is on 40.7% of the AISO. This intensity is 47.4% on the IPS (highest among three services), 43.1% on the IAS, and 22.8% on the IFS officers. 2nd priority for recruitment pressure from the PM/CM level show 17.3% for the AISO, 20.5% highest on the IFS followed by 16.7% on the IPS and 16.5% on the IAS.

Exhibit Number 12.10: Priority Ranking of Sources of Pressure on Recruitment Points/ Type in Bureaucracy

Pressure Sources	Priority Rank	IAS	IPS	IFS	AIS
PM/CM	1st	16.50%	16.70%	20.50%	17.30%
	2nd	4.60%	1.30%	0.00%	2.70%
	3rd	0.00%	2.60%	0.00%	0.90%
	Total	21.10%	20.60%	20.50%	20.90%
Centre/State Minister	1st	43.10%	47.40%	22.80%	40.70%
	2nd	11.90%	18.00%	21.10%	15.50%
	3rd	4.70%	0.00%	2.50%	2.70%
	Total	59.70%	65.40%	46.40%	58.90%
Member Parliament	1st	0.00%	1.30%	6.80%	1.70%
	2nd	6.40%	1.30%	0.00%	3.60%
	3rd	10.40%	7.80%	12.50%	9.90%
	Total	16.80%	10.40%	19.30%	15.20%
MLA/MLC	1st	11.90%	6.40%	15.90%	10.80%
	2nd	43.10%	47.40%	28.90%	42.20%
	3rd	16.00%	19.50%	15.00%	17.00%
	Total	71.00%	73.30%	44.80%	70.00%
Zila Parishad/District-level Politicians	1st	13.80%	15.40%	13.60%	14.30%
	2nd	5.50%	5.10%	10.50%	6.20%
	3rd	6.60%	3.90%	5.00%	5.40%
	Total	25.90%	24.40%	29.10%	25.90%

Pressure Sources	Priority Rank	IAS	IPS	IFS	AIS
Block Samiti/Block-level Politicians	1st	0.00%	1.30%	2.30%	0.90%
	2nd	6.40%	5.10%	5.30%	5.80%
	3rd	7.50%	3.90%	7.50%	6.30%
	Total	13.90%	10.30%	15.10%	13.00%
Village Heads/Grassroot level worker	1st	0.00%	0.00%	0.00%	0.00%
	2nd	4.60%	6.40%	2.60%	4.90%
	3rd	6.60%	5.20%	7.50%	6.30%
	Total	11.20%	11.60%	10.10%	11.20%
Power Brokers/Touts	1st	0.00%	0.00%	0.00%	0.00%
	2nd	10.10%	5.10%	15.80%	9.30%
	3rd	25.50%	26.00%	25.00%	25.60%
	Total	35.60%	31.10%	40.80%	34.90%
Communication Media	1st	8.30%	10.30%	11.40%	9.50%
	2nd	4.60%	3.80%	7.90%	4.90%
	3rd	6.60%	1.30%	5.00%	4.50%
	Total	19.50%	15.40%	24.30%	18.90%
Hidden Financiers	1st	6.40%	1.30%	6.80%	4.80%
	2nd	2.80%	6.40%	7.90%	4.90%
	3rd	16.00%	29.90%	20.00%	21.50%
	Total	25.20%	37.60%	34.70%	31.20%

Respondents' number (frequency) in three priorities is not the same, because every respondent has not mentioned all three priorities (1st, 2nd, and 3rd) while ranking, we added together three priorities (based on answered numbers). Results show MLA/MLC exert the highest intensity of pressure on 70% of the AISO, break up for three services indicate 73.30% on the IPS (highest among the AIS), 71% on the IAS, and 44.88% on the IFS. In this additive category, the second position goes to Centre/State Ministers with 58.9% for the AISO, 65.4% for the IPS (highest among the AIS), 59.7% for the IAS, and 46.4% for the IFS, this is different from 1st priority ranking.

The most revealing part of data analysis results shows high-pressure intensity on recruitment from the power brokers/touts and hidden financiers. Pressure from these two sources is higher than the Members Parliaments, district-level politicians, communication media, and village-level workers; this is an indirect indication of the recruitment process influenced by the role of external influence/money in it. The PM/CM, Centre/State Ministers, district-level politicians and communication media show a decreasing trend of pressure, highest from 1st priority to lower in 2nd priority and lowest in 3rd priority, this indicates that the AISO give due to importance or first priority to these sources of pressure and others are relegated by the AISO in lower priorities. In case of pressure from Members Parliament, block-level politicians and communication media priorities intensity go on increasing from 1st to 3rd priority, this indicates lesser importance of these sources of pressure in recruitment decision making.

Results at Exhibit 12.10 show power broker/touts pressure intensity for recruitment on the IFS 40.5%, on the IAS 35.6%, on the IPS 31.1%, and the AISO 34.9%. In the case of hidden financiers, this pressure intensity is 37.6% on the IPS, 34.7% on the IFS, 25.2% on the IAS, and 31.2% on the AISO. In these two sources of pressure on the recruitment area is higher on the IFS and the IPS respectively, this indicates the relation of officers of these services with the hidden financiers and power brokers and touts. The intensity of pressure from communication media is also unexpectedly on the higher side towards recruitment areas. This indicates that communication media also uses its relation with the AISO for self-goals gratifications. Analysis results indicate least pressure on recruitment is accepted from village-level workers or political workers, which is worrisome.

12.2.4. Pressure for Resource Allocation

The concept of pooling the resources at the disposal of the Deputy Commissioner has created a chaotic situation and forced all the politicians to approach this single power center for allocation of a different resource. This concept is bound to recoil in the form of failures and misappropriation of huge funds. The Deputy Commissioner who lacks technical expertise (in many cases) allocates resources guided by self-bias keeping in mind their own goals. Any district officers, who are honest and expert in one's work do not get proper funds till one promises to share leakages or obligations with the Deputy Commissioner or agree with the chair in doing things as desired by the power holder. Invariably own self-goals and motives in any allocation of resources, guides many Deputy Commissioners. The very institution of the imperial district head will continue to generate dishonesty until this will continue to remain in this form. The moment the institution of the Deputy Commissioner will be changed the single greatest pressure point will be diluted or removed, and politicians will not be blamed for every wrong, pliable and illogical decision taken by these All India Services Officers.

In many States' colonial reminiscence of the Deputy Commissioner/Collector has overriding powers over many departments, such as food and supplies, prohibitions, etc. Politicians are fully aware of these powers and approach the weakest target for the fulfillment of self-goals. This colonial control over other departments makes the Deputy Commissioner/Collector highly vulnerable to political pressure (power and status consciousness). With high self-goals orientation, the Deputy Commissioner/Collector feels himself on very weak ground and readily accepts any kind of political pressure to retain his power and accomplishment of his own goals. The system of licenses and excessive control of the Deputy Commissioner/Collector in the bureaucratic system invites political pressure for them on many unwanted and undesirable areas also.

The All India Services Officers, who are supposed to be neutral while allocating resources, now have become a passive arbitrator and left with an allocation of scarce resources in the desired direction of the politician, taken the role of promoter or sponsor for the ruling party in power. Now it has become the bygone era that the All India Services Officers will implement the works and distribute the resources based on merit and objectivity to provide justice to the public and win their hearts and support. Politicians' motive is to win the votes and the All India Services Officers allocate resources only on the recommendation of the politicians. We have seen a Deputy

Commissioner/Collector, who used to carry huge cash in his car along with the Chief Minister in violation of all rules/norms, so that worthy Chief Minister can distribute cash on the site on the name of developmental schemes and win the support for coming elections. Now command over resources has become a way and mechanism to serve own-goals and oblige political ends irrespective of development orientation. Going by the present trend, disadvantaged people are bound to be pushed to the corner and political power mobilizers' will only get whole resources at their will. Resources allocations have become purely a means to serve their own ends. "Civil service is not a spoils system.... This unfortunate perception is best captured in the quote of Malcolm Forbes who said 'Once in a civil service job, one needs only to live to rise'," Pulok Chatterji, *The India Today*, August 14, 2012.

Exhibit Number 12.11: Intensity of Political Pressure for Resource Allocation

Service Name	Pressure Intensity	294	295	296	297	298	299
		Resource Allocation	Land Allotment	Human Resources	Budget Allocation	Goods & Material	Machinery Deployment
I.A.S.	'always'	16.3	21.7	30.1	41.5	24.6	13.8
	'mostly'	16.3	38.3	38.4	23.1	20	37.9
	'frequently'	4.1	20	16.4	15.4	35.4	29.3
	'sometimes'	32.7	10	9.6	18.5	16.9	13.8
	'rarely'	30.6	10	5.5	1.5	3.1	5.2
I.P.S.	'always'	2.3	2.5	1.2	2.9	1.2	1.2
	'mostly'	4.7	2.5	3.6	4.3	2.4	1.2
	'frequently'	14	2.5	21.7	0	15.7	43.4
	'sometimes'	79.1	32.9	49.4	49.3	47	44.6
	'rarely'	0	59.5	24.1	43.5	33.7	9.6
I.F.S.	'always'	13	27.1	14.4	15.3	4.2	11.5
	'mostly'	34.8	15.6	36.1	29.6	26	13.5
	'frequently'	19.6	31.3	29.9	27.6	34.4	36.5
	'sometimes'	17.4	12.5	15.5	14.3	21.9	26
	'rarely'	15.2	13.5	4.1	13.3	13.5	12.5
AIS	'always'	10.9	17.4	14.6	19	8.6	8.4
	'mostly'	18.8	17	26.1	20.3	16.4	15.2
	'frequently'	12.3	18.7	23.3	15.9	28.3	37.1
	'sometimes'	42	18.7	24.9	25.9	29.1	29.5
Total	rarely	15.9	28.1	11.1	19	17.6	9.7
Ranking			2	3	1	4	5

In present times of resource scarcity, there is stiff competition for distribution, deployment, and management of resources. Every individual likes to usher self-goals from the resources to meet their own interests. Resource control is a big power; politicians at the top of the hierarchy also influence the All India Services Officers for the allocation of resources to their own advantage. Mode (2), median (2) and mean values (2.67) indicate the low intensity of political pressure, which is exerted 'sometimes' in general for allocation of the resources. 57.9% of the All India Services Officers feel that political pressure is exerted 'rarely' to 'sometimes' for resource allocation. 79.1% of the Indian Police Service officers, 63.3% of the Indian Administrative Service officers, and 32.6% of the Indian Forest Service officers come across political pressure 'rarely' to 'sometimes' in resource allocation. However, in the case of the Indian Forest Service officer's highest choice score of 34.8% of them 'most often' get political pressure in resource allocation. Value of 53.4, with 8 degree of freedom, and 0.000, level of significance in Chi-square results indicate a good association with the decision. The strength of the relationship is indicated by the Spearman correlation value of 0.217, with a level of significance of 0.011.

The land is the most common resource, which is valued very highly by politicians and voters. Public approach politicians for allotment, requisition, distribution, and management of land have become an important issue for the exertion of the political pressure in resource allocation.

The mean value of 2.76 with a standard deviation of 1.46 and a median value of 3; indicates that political pressure is exerted 'sometimes' category to 'frequently' in the land resource allocation. In general, the low concern of politician towards land resource allocation, it means that the All India Services Officers have got a lot of freedom to allocate land according to administrative demands. The highest priority score indicates that 38.3% of the Indian Administrative Service officers 'most often' get political pressure for requisition, allotment, and distribution of land resources. Only the Indian Administrative Service officers get the highest pressure pertaining to land resources among the All India Services. 31.3% of the Indian Forest Service officers get political pressure 'frequently' related to issues pertains to a land allotment. Since the Indian Police Service officers do not deal with much of the issues pertain to land allotment, 92.4% of them get political pressure 'rarely' to 'sometimes' only on this variable. Chi-square value of 115.7 with 8 degree of freedom and 0.000, level of significance, show a good association of land relates resources with the decision-making process.

Politicians exert pressure for the deployment of the choicest personnel's in various departments, as part of human resource allocation. Politicians carry out manipulations for getting personnel in excess of or less than sanctioned cadre strength for the regions of their interests. The mean value of 3.08, a standard deviation of 1.25, and a modal value of 4 indicate that political pressure is exerted 'frequently' to 'most often' in human resource allocation. The two highest scores show that 73.5% of the Indian Police Service officers get 'sometimes' to 'rarely' pressure in the allocation of human resources. 68.5% of the Indian Administrative Service officers get 'always' to 'most often' political pressure in the deployment of human resources. 66% of the Indian Forest Service officers get political pressure 'most often' intensity to 'frequently' in human resource allocation. The Indian Administrative Service officers get maximum political pressure in this variable; this may due to their location on the top of every department. The lowest political pressure on the Indian Police Service officers may be due to the highly specialized nature of their job. Chi-square value of 98.967 with 8 degree of freedom and 0.000, level of significance, indicates a good association of human resource allocation with the decision-making process. Our results are significant. Political pressure exerted for human resource allocation is different for all the All India Services.

Politicians exert pressure on the All India Services Officers for allocation of budget for new works; maintenance of old works and speedy completion of ongoing works. The mean value of 2.95 and a median value of 3, with a standard deviation of 1.40; indicate that political pressure is exerted 'frequently' on the All India Services Officers for budgetary allocations. 64.6% of the Indian Administrative Service officers get political pressure 'always' to 'most often' in budget allocation for different sectors. 57.2% of the Indian Forest Service officers get political pressure 'most often' intensity to 'frequently' for allocation of budget for various areas. 92.8% of the Indian Police Service officers get political pressure 'sometimes' intensity to 'rarely' for budget allocations. The lowest political pressure on police officers may be due to fact that they do not execute any development work, whatsoever political demands may be related to the maintenance of constabulary in different areas. Chi-square value of 114.957, with 8 degree of freedom and 0.000, level of significance, indicating that political pressure on budgetary allocation is associated with the decision-making process. Pearson's correlation value of –0.127 is significant with a 0.05, level of significance.

In government administration, different goods and materials are allocated to different areas from the State capital. Such goods and material have a direct bearing on the politicians' popularity in his area. This ensures the availability of goods and material to his voters at subsidized prices or a higher quota of items in short supply, etc. Particularly in the licensing era and high dependence on the public distribution system, political pressure for higher allocation is crucial and politicians compete for that. The mean value of 2.69 and a median value of 3; indicate 'frequent' exertion of political pressure for increasing, decreasing, and allocation of goods and material. 29.1% of the All India Services Officers get political pressure 'sometimes' for allocation of material and goods resources. 80% of the Indian Administrative Service officers and 64.6% of the Indian Forest Service officers get political pressure 'frequently' intensity to 'always' for goods and material allocation. Results indicate that the Indian Administrative Service officers get maximum political pressure for this variable because they are the persons located as head of many State Departments and even as the Deputy Commissioner/Collector they enjoy vast powers in the district. Chi-square value of 84.9, with 8 degree of freedom, and 0.000, level of significance, indicating that our results are significant, goods and material allocation and the decision-making process are associated. Relationships of the resource allocation with the decision are indicated by Pearson's correlation value of –0.148, with a level of significance at 0.020.

For executing development works in any area, a lot of machinery and vehicles are required. Up to now, we have discussed the requirement of men, money, and material, here the fourth important aspect of machinery will be discussed. 37.1% of the All India Services Officers and 36.5% of the Indian Forest Service officers get political pressure 'frequently' in deployment and allocation of machinery. 37.9% of the Indian Administrative Service officers get 'most often' political pressure in the allocation of machinery and vehicles. The Indian Police Service officers get low political pressure of 44.6% of them 'sometimes' only. Low political pressure on police officers may be due to fact that they do not occupy positions across the departments. Chi-square values of 54.2, with 8 degree of freedom, and 0.000, level of significance, indicate a good association of political pressure in the decision-making process with the machinery allocation. Pearson's correlation value of –0.158, with a level of significance at 0.01, indicates the relationship is significant.

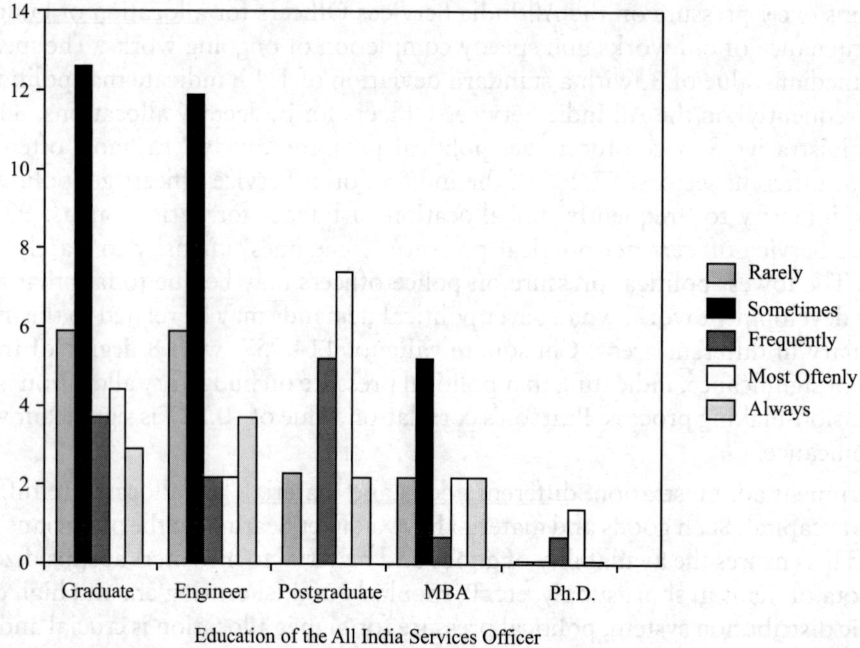

Chart No. 12.4: Educational Qualifications versus Pressure in Resource Allocation

Exhibit No. 12.12: Resource Allocation versus Educational Background of the Officer

Variable	Intensity		Educational background of the officer					Total
			Graduate	Engineer/ B.Tech./ Technology	Post Graduate	MBA/ CA/CW	Ph.D.	
Resource Allocation	'Rarely' pressure is exerted	Count	8	8	3	3		22
		% of Total	5.970	5.971	2.238	2.238		16.41
	'Sometimes' only pressure is exerted	Count	17	16	16	7		56
		% of Total	12.68	11.94	11.94	5.223		41.79
	'Frequently' pressure is exerted	Count	5	3	7	1	1	17
		% of Total	3.731	2.238	5.223	0.746	0.746	12.68
	'Most oftenly' pressure is exerted	Count	6	3	10	3	2	24
		% of Total	4.477	2.238	7.462	2.238	1.492	17.91
	'Always' pressure is exerted	Count	4	5	3	3		15
		% of Total	2.985	3.731	2.238	2.238		11.19
Total		Count	40	35	39	17	3	134
		% of Total	29.85	26.11	29.11	12.68	2.238	100

Chart 12.4 and Exhibit 12.12 show resource allocation pressure points relationship with the demographic variable of the educational background of the All India Services Officer. 29.85% of the All India Services Officer with graduate educational background and 29.10% with postgraduate qualifications realize pressure intensity in resource allocation areas and officers with Ph.D. qualifications get the least pressure of 2.2% in this variable. Political pressure of 'sometimes' intensity 41.79% is exerted maximum on resource allocation point. 29% cases pressure is exerted in 'always' plus 'most often' intensity on the All India Services officer for resource allocation.

Statistical data analyses result for the measurement of the intensity of different sources of political pressure exerted on resource allocation area of the decision-making process are placed in Exhibit 12.13. The All India Services Officer measured intensity of pressure on resource allocation in 1st priority gets the highest pressure from the Centre/State Ministers 33.5%, we can infer that for every third resource allocation decision pressure come from this source. Among the three services pressure varies as 34.9% on the IAS, 34.2% on the IPS, and 29.2% on the IFS. Second ranking of political pressure comes from Member Legislative Assembly/MLC source and 25.7% of the All India Services Officer get pressure from this source at second in 1st priority; three service data show 29.2% of the IFS, 25% of the IPS and 24.5% of the IAS get this intensity of pressure for resource allocation. In 1st priority other sources of pressure on the All India Services Officer in the ranking are 10.4% from district-level politicians at third place, 8.3% from block-level politicians at the fourth rank, 7.4% from PM/CM level at the fifth rank, and 4.8% from Members Parliament at sixth rank in decisions related to resource allocations.

Respondents' number (frequency) in three priorities is not same, because not every respondent has mentioned all three priority (1st, 2nd, and 3rd) ranking, due to this variability additive total of three priorities may be little skewed, we added together three priorities (based on answered numbers). When three priorities are added together results show different ranking and Member Legislative Assembly/MLC exert the highest pressure with 82.6% on the All India Services Officer, 81.6% on the IPS, 80.5% on the IFS, and 64.70% on the IAS. And second in exerting pressure is the district-level politicians; 77.9% on the All India Services Officer, 84.4% on the IPS, 76.1% on the IAS, and 71.8% on the IFS. Results show that resource allocation pressure from power brokers, communication media, and hidden financiers is almost low to negligible.

Exhibit Number 12.13: Ranking of Priority of Sources of Pressure on Resource Allocation Point of Pressure

Pressure Sources	Priority Rank	IAS	IPS	IFS	AIS
PM/CM	1st	7.50%	7.90%	6.30%	7.40%
	2nd	0.00%	1.40%	5.40%	1.40%
	3rd	1.00%	1.40%	2.70%	1.40%
	Total	7.50%	10.70%	14.40%	10.20%
Centre/State Minister	1st	34.90%	34.20%	29.20%	33.50%
	2nd	11.80%	9.90%	13.50%	11.40%
	3rd	5.00%	2.90%	0.00%	3.40%
	Total	51.70%	47.00%	42.70%	48.30%

Pressure Sources	Priority Rank	IAS	IPS	IFS	AIS
Member Parliament	1st	7.50%	1.30%	4.20%	4.80%
	2nd	20.60%	11.30%	21.60%	17.60%
	3rd	6.00%	5.70%	10.80%	6.80%
	Total	34.10%	18.30%	36.60%	29.20%
MLA/MLC	1st	24.50%	25.00%	29.20%	25.70%
	2nd	40.20%	43.70%	29.70%	39.50%
	3rd	19.00%	12.90%	21.60%	17.40%
	Total	64.70%	81.60%	80.50%	82.60%
Zila Parishad/District-level Politicians	1st	10.40%	14.50%	4.20%	10.40%
	2nd	12.70%	9.90%	16.20%	12.40%
	3rd	53.00%	60.00%	51.40%	55.10%
	Total	76.10%	84.40%	71.80%	77.90%
Block Samiti/Block-level Politicians	1st	7.50%	6.60%	12.50%	8.30%
	2nd	11.80%	23.90%	13.50%	16.20%
	3rd	2.00%	2.90%	0.00%	1.90%
	Total	21.30%	33.40%	26.00%	26.40%
Village Heads/Grassroot-level Worker	1st	4.70%	3.90%	6.30%	4.80%
	2nd	2.00%	0.00%	0.00%	1.00%
	3rd	11.00%	12.90%	10.80%	11.60%
	Total	17.70%	16.80%	17.10%	17.40%
Power Brokers/Touts	1st	2.80%	6.60%	6.30%	4.80%
	2nd	0.00%	0.00%	0.00%	0.00%
	3rd	1.00%	1.40%	0.00%	1.00%
	Total	3.80%	8.00%	6.30%	5.80%
Communication Media	1st	0.00%	0.00%	0.00%	0.00%
	2nd	0.00%	0.00%	0.00%	0.00%
	3rd	0.00%	0.00%	0.00%	0.00%
	Total				
Hidden Financiers	1st	0.00%	0.00%	2.10%	0.40%
	2nd	1.00%	0.00%	0.00%	0.50%
	3rd	2.00%	0.00%	2.70%	1.40%
	Total	3.00%	0.00%	4.80%	2.30%

12.2.5. Pressure for Awarding Rewards

The All India Services Officers and politicians use rewards as a motivator and use them frequently for bartering in the process of achieving of own goals. The All India Services Officers consider career progression and enhancement in a career as a reward for them. The All India Services Officers mobilize political pressure to get an appointment on lucrative posts in desired boards and corporations. The All India Services Officers keep their political bosses in good spirits to get out of turn desired government houses in good locations, to get control over resource allotment, and many times to get vehicles for status enhancement and misuse. We have observed that many All India Services Officers mobilize political support, so that, politicians appreciate them publicly and they can misuse such goodwill for future benefits. On some occasions, individual officers garner political goodwill to get monetary benefits in the form of perks, special pay, and honorarium.

Exhibit Number 12.14: Intensity of Political Pressure in Rewards Distribution

Service Name	Intensity of Pressure	300	301	302	303	304	305
		Rewards	Career Advancement	Special Posts	Special Increment	House Allotment	Praise Letters
I.A.S.	'always'	6.7	9.6	25.4	28.1	19.7	8.5
	'mostly'	31.1	19.2	25.4	19.3	6.6	19.7
	'frequently'	37.8	34.6	44.1	17.5	19.7	46.5
	'sometimes'	20	28.6	5.1	26.3	49.2	19.7
	'rarely'	4.4	7.7	0	8.8	4.9	5.6
I.P.S.	'always'	0	0	16.9	0	1.2	1.1
	'mostly'	0	1.3	48.1	1.5	0	6.8
	'frequently'	50.6	23.4	26	7.6	24.7	27.3
	'sometimes'	25.3	48.1	7.8	57.6	56.8	43.2
	'rarely'	24.1	27.3	1.3	33.3	17.3	24.6
I.F.S.	'always'	9.1	11.2	25.3	5.3	9.1	10.3
	'mostly'	11.4	22.4	22.2	14.7	17.2	9.3
	'frequently'	36.4	24.5	36.4	21.1	36.4	32
	'sometimes'	25	29.6	14.1	34.7	30.3	27.8
	'rarely'	18.2	12.2	2	24.2	7.1	20.6
Total A.I.S.	'always'	4.2	7	22.6	9.6	9.1	6.6
	'mostly'	11.3	14.5	31.5	11.9	8.7	11.3
	'frequently'	43.5	26.4	34.9	16.1	28.2	34.4
	'sometimes'	23.8	35.7	9.8	39.4	44	30.9
	'rarely'	17.3	16.3	1.3	22.9	10	16.6
Ranking			4	1	2	3	5
All Figures are in %							

Rewards of any kind in the bureaucratic system enhance the status of the officers. In a situation, when career progression is a chance to exceed their expectations, a person experiences greater satisfaction in his job (Arthur et al., 1965). The absence of a reward system has a negative impact on a person's expectations and abilities. Control and power of rewards distribution in public administration invariably multiply the power of distributors as power enhancers. Rewards allocation powers develop power and inculcate initiative and creativity. Uniform or no reward for performance prevalent in public administration begets demoralization or virtual non-performance in the government decision process. Officers, who want to excel or high performers feel helpless in due course of time, stop performing, and only work to get routine treatments/packages. Lust for rewards in the form of meeting self-goals, motivate the All India Services Officers to develop loyalty towards the politicians. "Loyalty to party in power became part of their reward structure which had not been true before. Those who were loyal were now much more likely to get promotion and desirable postings," D.C. Potter, 1986. Retied IAS views politicians: "They are true representatives of the people. We should not fall into the mindset of looking on them as antagonists," Pulok Chatterji, *The India Today*, August 14, 2012.

67.3% of the All India Services Officers get political pressure for <u>rewards</u> 'frequently' to 'sometimes' in the decision-making process. 75.9% of the Indian Police Service officers and 61.4% of the Indian Forest Service officers encounter 'frequent' to 'sometimes' intensity of political pressure in the process of reward distribution. 68.9% of the Indian Administrative Service officers come across political pressure 'most often' to 'frequently' intensity in rewards allocation. Among the All India Services, the intensity of political pressure is higher on the Indian Administrative Service officers; this may be due to their location in the important positions of power. Pearson Chi-square value of 39.6, with 8 degree of freedom and level of significance with 0.000, indicating that our results are highly significant. The strength of this negative association of rewards with the decision-making process is indicated by the Spearman correlation value of –0.2, with a level of significance at 0.01. The mean value of 2.61 with a standard deviation of 1.04, and median and modal value of 3, indicates that All India Services Officers get 'frequent' political pressure for rewards.

The All India Services Officers seek political help for their <u>career advancement</u> and getting desired annual confidential reports. Mean value of 2.58, with a standard deviation of 1.14, for career advancement as rewards, and median and modal value of 2, indicate that political pressure is exerted 'sometimes' to 'frequently' intensity. 62.1% of the All India Services Officers get political pressure 'frequently' to 'sometimes' intensity for rewards pertaining to career progression and desired annual confidential reports. 64.4% of the Indian Administrative Service officers and 54.1% of the Indian Forest Service officers are getting political pressure 'frequently' to 'sometimes' for rewards allocations. 75.4% of the Indian Police Service officers get political pressure 'sometimes' to 'rarely' category in rewards distribution for career progression. Rewards demand for career advancement is maximum with the Indian Administrative Service officers and least with the Indian Police Service Officers, this may be due to the high discipline in police forces that lesser number of persons approaches for political influence. Pearson Chi-square value of 38.4, with 8 degree of freedom, and level of significance at 0.000, indicate a good association of rewards in career advancement with the decision-making process. An alternate hypothesis is accepted that individual officers mobilize political pressure for career advancement.

The All India Services Officers mobilize strong political support for self and also get most often political pressure for appointment on lucrative positions in government boards and corporations. The mean value of 3.61, with a standard deviation of 1.0, along with the mode of 3, and a median value of 4, indicates that the All India Services Officers 'most often' get political pressure in appointments for good posts in government boards and corporations. In the highest score, 34.9% of the All India Services Officers, 44.1% of the Indian Administrative Service officers, and 36.4% of the Indian Forest Service officers get the 'frequent' intensity of political pressure in appointments for boards and corporations. 69.5% of the Indian Administrative Service officers, 74.1% of the Indian Police Service officers, and 66.4% of the All India Services Officers get 'most often' to 'frequent' intensity political pressure in appointment in government boards and corporations. 61.7% of the Indian Forest Service officers feel that 'always' to 'frequently' frequency political pressure is exercised to get postings on the good corporations and boards. 19.7 value of Pearson Chi-square, with 8 degree of freedom along with 0.011, level of significance, indicating that our results are significant and there is a good association between the managing political pressure for appointments on good positions of corporations and decision-making process.

Political pressure is exercised for getting special pay, honorarium, and special increments in the service at different levels. We have considered this as an influence for getting rewards. 90.9% of the Indian Police Service officers, 58.9% of the Indian Forest Service officers, and 62.3% of the All India Services Officers think that 'sometimes' to 'rarely' they get political pressure for grant of special pay, advance increments, and honorarium. But in the case of the Indian Administrative Service officers, 28.1% of them get 'always' intensity political pressure, and 26.3% get political pressure 'sometimes' in granting special pay an honorarium, etc. The Indian Administrative Service officers get the highest political pressure for requests for releasing special pay or honorarium and the Indian Police Service officers get the least political pressure for these issues. 58.8 value of Pearson Chi-square, with 0.000, level of significance indicate that our results are significant. Association of the decision-making process and political pressure for the release of special benefits are strongly related to each other. This strength is indicated by Pearson's correlation negative value of –0.239, with a level of significance 0.000. The modal and median value of 2, also corroborates our findings that 'sometimes' political pressure is exerted for this variable.

The All India Services Officers and their subordinate employees show a high preference for getting houses in desired locations and good vehicles, which can enhance their status. Control over resources is the crucial question and always there is stiff competition for retaining such control to own advantage. The mean value of 2.62, with a standard deviation of 1.07; indicates that 'sometimes' to 'frequently' intensity political pressure is exerted for this issue. Median and modal value of 2, indicate only 'sometimes' political pressure is exerted for house and vehicle allotments. 44% of the All India Services Officers get political pressure 'sometimes' for house allotment. 56.8% of the Indian Police Service officers and 49.2% of the Indian Administrative Service officers get political pressure 'sometimes' only. 36.4% of the Indian Forest Service officers get 'frequent' political pressure for allotment of houses and vehicles. The highest pressure is exerted on the Indian Administrative Service officers, as indicated by the 19.7% score in 'always' category, and least political pressure is received by the Indian Police Service officers, may be related to the location in the hierarchy. Pearson Chi-square value of 47.1 indicates high significance with a level of significance at 0.000. Good association of political pressure and decision-making process is indicated by the Spearman correlation level of significance at 0.03, which is less than that of an acceptable level of significance of 0.05.

Individual officers influence politician for issuing statements in public for the appreciation of their own work, some of them manage appreciation letters so that such manipulations can be used in the future for garnering undue benefits. This can be seen in most of the districts, Deputy Commissioner/Collector issuance of appreciation letter and certificate to self and own group of people through politicians on special occasions as Independence Day or Republic Day or special functions. Here, the Indian Administrative Service officers are the distributor and they themselves are the gainer wonderful way to manipulate the whole system to own advantage. Distributions of rewards have become the mockery of the bureaucratic system. The mean value of 2.58, with a standard deviation of 1.10, the median value of 3, indicates that political pressure is used 'frequently' for issuance of appreciation letters. 70.5% of the Indian Police Service officers, 66.2% of the Indian Administrative Service officers, 65.3% of total All India Services Officers, and 59.8% of the Indian Forest Service Officers come across 'frequent' to 'sometimes' intensity of political pressure while issuing appreciation letters. Pearson Chi-square value of 31.953, with 8 degree of freedom, and along with 0.000, level of significance indicates relations. Good association of political pressure with the decision-making process is indicated by the Spearman correlation with the level of significance at 0.01.

Exhibit Number 12.15: Rewards Distribution and Officer Regional Background, Crosstabulation

Variable	Pressure Intensity		Officer Regional Background						Total
			North eastern part	Eastern part	Western part	Northern part	Southern part	Central part	
Rewards	'Rarely' pressure is exerted	Count	8	5	2	5	9		29
		% of Total	4.733	2.958	1.183	2.958	5.325		17.15
	'Sometimes' only pressure is exerted	Count	2	7	5	13	10	3	40
		% of Total	1.183	4.142	2.958	7.692	5.917	1.7752	23.66
	'Frequently' pressure is exerted	Count	13	9	8	13	24	6	73
		% of Total	7.692	5.325	4.733	7.692	14.21	3.551	43.19
	'Most oftenly' pressure is exerted	Count	3	5	1	5	4	2	20
		% of Total	1.775	2.958	0.591	2.958	2.366	1.183	11.83
	'Always' pressure is exerted	Count	2	1			4		7
		% of Total	1.183	0.591			2.366		4.142
Total		Count	28	27	16	36	51	11	169
		% of Total	16.56	15.97	9.467	21.31	30.17	6.509	100

Exhibit 12.15 shows variable rewards distribution relationship with officer regional background in acceptance political pressure. Statistical analysis results show 30.2% of the All India Services Officer from southern India are amenable to pressure and in second-ranking 16.57% of the All India Services Officer from the north eastern part accept pressure in this variable. Chart 12.5 also displays these results on the chart.

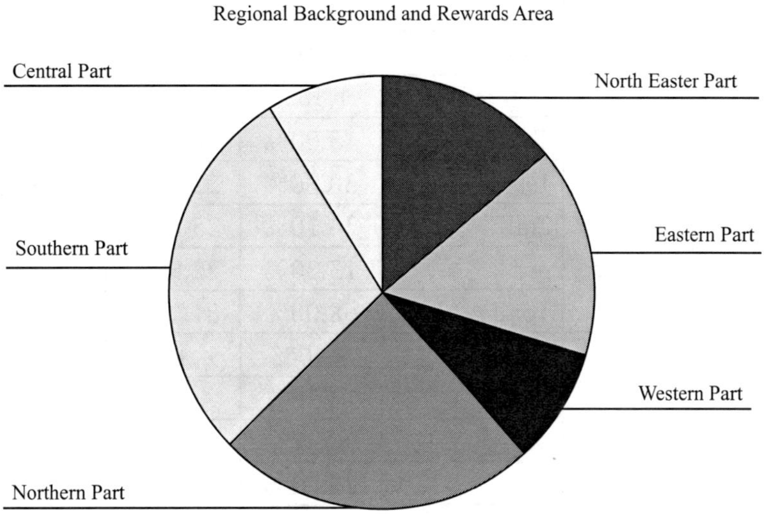

Chart No. 12.5: Regional Background and Rewards Distribution

Statistical data analyses result for political pressure intensity measurement being exerted from different sources of pressure are placed at Exhibit 12.16. Results display how the All India Services officers have ranked these sources of pressure while taking decision for award/reward distribution. The Centre/State Minister source shows the highest intensity of pressure in rewards distribution in 1st priority with 30.8% on the AISO, 32.4% on the IPS, 30.6% on the IAS, and 28.6% on the IFS. In 1st priority, the MLA/MLC source of pressure is at second position with an intensity of pressure of 40.5% on the IFS, 30.5% on the IAS, 29.4% on the AISO, and 21.6% on the IPS. The other sources of the pressure on the All India Services officers ranking are the PM/CM at third position 11.8%, the block-level politicians at fourth position 7.6%, the Members of Parliament at fifth position with 7.1%, and the district-level politicians at sixth position with a score of 6.6%, other sources show low score.

Decreasing and increasing percentage in priority rankings of different sources of pressure indicates handling of such pressure, in what manner the All India Services officers consider, or treat the pressure from the PM/CM level to the last hidden financiers. Respondents' number (frequency) in three priorities is not same, because not every respondent has mentioned all three priorities (1st, 2nd, and 3rd) ranking, due to this variability additive total of three priorities may be little skewed, we added together three priorities (based on answered numbers). An aggregate total of three priorities also reveals a different story. The MLA/MLC show the highest aggregate of 92% on the AISO, 95.1% on the IPS, 94.1% on the IFS, and 87.8% on the IAS. Pressure intensity from the power brokers is unexpected and not desirable in rewards distribution and seen as harmful to the bureaucratic system.

Exhibit Number 12.16: Priority Ranking of Sources of Pressure on Reward Type Pressure

Pressure Sources	Priority Rank	IAS	IPS	IFS	AIS
PM/CM	1st	10.50%	16.20%	7.10%	11.80%
	2nd	1.20%	0.00%	5.90%	1.60%
	3rd	1.30%	1.60%	3.00%	1.80%
	Total	13.00%	16.20%	16.00%	15.20%
Centre/State Minister	1st	30.60%	32.40%	28.60%	30.80%
	2nd	24.10%	25.80%	20.60%	24.00%
	3rd	13.30%	22.90%	15.20%	17.20%
	Total	68.00%	81.10%	64.40%	72.00%
Member of Parliament	1st	8.40%	4.10%	9.50%	7.10%
	2nd	13.30%	4.50%	2.90%	8.20%
	3rd	8.00%	6.60%	15.20%	8.90%
	Total	29.70%	15.20%	27.60%	24.20%
MLA/MLC	1st	30.50%	21.60%	40.50%	29.40%
	2nd	25.30%	36.40%	32.40%	30.60%
	3rd	32.00%	37.70%	21.20%	32.00%
	Total	87.80%	95.70%	94.10%	92.00%
Zila Parishad/District-level Politicians	1st	4.20%	10.80%	4.80%	6.60%
	2nd	25.30%	30.30%	32.40%	28.40%
	3rd	20.00%	16.40%	18.20%	18.30%
	Total	49.50%	57.50%	55.40%	53.30%
Block Samiti/ Block-level Politicians	1st	6.30%	12.20%	2.40%	7.60%
	2nd	1.20%	1.50%	0.00%	1.10%
	3rd	10.70%	6.60%	12.10%	9.50%
	Total	18.20%	20.30%	14.50%	18.20%
Village Heads/Grassroot-level Worker	1st	1.10%	0.00%	0.00%	0.50%
	2nd	0.00%	0.00%	0.00%	0.00%
	3rd	0.00%	1.60%	3.00%	1.20%
	Total	1.10%	1.60%	3.00%	1.70%

Pressure Sources	Priority Rank	IAS	IPS	IFS	AIS
Power Brokers/Touts	1st	0.00%	1.40%	0.00%	0.50%
	2nd	9.60%	1.50%	5.90%	6.00%
	3rd	4.00%	4.90%	6.10%	4.70%
	Total	13.60%	7.80%	12.00%	11.20%
Communication Media	1st	0.00%	0.00%	0.00%	0.00%
	2nd	0.00%	0.00%	0.00%	0.00%
	3rd	9.30%	1.60%	6.10%	5.90%
	Total	9.30%	1.60%	6.10%	5.90%
Hidden Financiers	1st	8.40%	1.40%	7.10%	5.70%
	2nd	0.00%	0.00%	0.00%	0.00%
	3rd	1.30%	0.00%	0.00%	0.60%
	Total	9.70%	1.40%	7.10%	6.30%

12.2.6. Pressure for Punishment to Inculcate Fear

Punishment is not only a punitive action for wrong or unlawful activities but also more commonly used as inculcating fear for consequences in case of defiance of politicians or power holders' illegal orders. Punishments have great deterrent power, an officer may not be having the impact of punishment, but the fear from future implications of any kind punishment, force them to easily accept the whims of politician and power holder in any given situation. Punishment is not confined to imposing penalties for wrongdoings, without any fault of the All India Services Officers and any disciplinary proceedings, officers can be harmed and scared more than the real penalties.

When politicians exercise their authority in connivance with top bureaucrats, they can award such punishments, for which there cannot be any appeal to any place. Such decisions are not covered under the definition of punishments. The All India Services Officers may be dislocated frequently on the name of administrative exigencies; officers can be posted on such place and position, where there is no vehicle and without any facility of housing or forced to execute a work, which cannot be done without the help of specific officials. This is a slow and sure way to kill and destroy the motivation and innovations from the All India Services Officers. Motivated by political goals, career progression can be blocked through different means and ways.

Politicians may engage in false criticism in public and spread false propaganda against some officer, who do not oblige them, in such situations, some selfish individual officers connive with politicians to serve own goals out of such victimizations and continue to misguide the politicians. Politicians initiate false inquiries against the individual officer, motivate the public to file false complaints against a particular officer, and then indulge in public criticism. Politicians occupy the top position in the hierarchy, he can spoil the records of the officer, and even they can record adverse entries in the annual appraisal/confidential report. When the All India Services Officers impose some punishment on the subordinates for wrongdoings, politicians in an appeal set aside such orders or reduce punishments to such a low level that it has no meaning. This will ensure the insubordination in the jurisdiction of such officer and initiate the process of causing failure to him.

Punishment in general along with five different situations, we have studied here. Mean value of 2.49, a median of 3, and modal value of 3; indicate that 'frequent' intensity political pressure is exerted in the different areas of punishment. Pearson Chi-square value of 23.428 is significant with a level of significance of 0.003. This indicates the association of political pressure in the decision-making process with punishment as an area of pressure. 85.5% of the Indian Police Service officers, 76.6% of the All India Services officers, 72.7% of the Indian Administrative Service officers, and 68.3% of the Indian Forest Service officers come across political pressure 'frequently' to 'sometimes' intensity in the matters related to punishments. The highest score of the All India Services Officers is in the intensity of 'frequently'. A high score for punishment for police indicates that police people impart punishments more often and the award of such punishments invites political pressure, which is exerted highest on them in comparison to other All India Services. The Indian Forest Service officers get the least amount of political pressure in the matter related to punishments. It may be due to the factor that forest people are less connected to politicians than the other two services persons.

Politicians pressurize for frequent dislocations of particular person and assert their position for withdrawal of vehicle and house from targeted individual persons. Reduction in facilities or withdrawal of perquisites is the most common way of pressurizing the All India Services Officers. But low mean value with 2 modal values indicates that political pressure is exerted 'sometimes' for dislocation of persons. 95.4% of the Indian Police Service officers and 57.9% of the All India Services officers feel that 'sometimes' to 'rarely' intensity political pressure is exerted for frequent dislocations of persons. 66.7% of the Indian Administrative Service officers and 46.8% of the Indian Forest Service officers get 'most often' to 'frequent' intensity political pressure to dislocate persons or withdrawal of house and vehicles. Association of political pressure for dislocation and decision-making process is indicated by the Pearson Chi-square analysis, value of 66.528, with 8 degree of freedom and level of significance of 0.000.

Politicians also pressurize for the blockage of career progression of certain persons, sometimes pressurize for suspension without any fault, as punishment to a particular person. Median, mode and mean values indicate that political pressure is exerted 'sometimes' for suspension of a particular person to terrorize him for getting their work done from such officer. 37.7% of the Indian Administrative Service officers get 'frequent' political pressure for career blockage of certain persons. 45.5% of the Indian Police Service officers, 38.4% of the Indian Forest Service officers, and 39.1% of the All India Services officers 'sometimes' get political pressure to victimize some persons for political gains. Pearson Chi-square value of 48.789, with a level of significance of 0.000, indicates a good association of punishment political pressure with the decision-making process. Pearson's correlation significance is satisfactory, and the results are significant.

Politicians engage in false criticism, initiate fake complaints, and start inquiries on false grounds to pressurize individual officers to get things done from him. Median, mode and mean values are indicative of the 'most often' intensity of political pressure on this area. 69.35 of the Indian Police Service officers, 65.3% of the All India Services Officers, 65.1% of the Indian Administrative Service officers, and 61.75 of the Indian Forest Service officers think that 'most often' to 'frequently' intensity of political pressure is exerted on them in connection with the matter, which is false and vigilance inquiry is initiated on fake issues. Pearson Chi-square value of 31.418, with 8 degree of freedom and 0.000, level of significance, indicates a good association of this variable with the decision-making process.

Exhibit Number 12.17: Intensity of Political Pressure through Punishment

Service Name	Pressure Intensity	306 Punishment	307 Frequent Dislocation	308 Career Blockage	309 False Complaints	310 Appraisal Report	311 Reducing Punishment
I.A.S.	'always'	1.8	10	3.3	12.1	11.5	8.1
	'mostly'	12.7	15	14.8	34.8	19.7	14.5
	'frequently'	54.5	40	37.7	30.3	36.1	43.5
	'sometimes'	18.2	26.7	31.1	21.2	29.5	24.2
	'rarely'	12.7	8.3	13.1	1.5	3.3	9.7
I.P.S.	'always'	0	1.5	0	27.4	0	0
	'mostly'	1.6	1.5	1.1	41.1	0	0
	'frequently'	321.3	1.5	19.3	28.4	24.3	50
	'sometimes'	53.2	44.6	45.5	2.1	40.5	22
	'rarely'	12.9	50.8	34.1	1.1	35.1	28
I.F.S.	'always'	0	13.5	11.1	14.1	9.3	8.1
	'mostly'	17.1	18.8	20.2	26.3	14.4	19.2
	'frequently'	39	20.8	19.2	35.4	38.1	32.3
	'sometimes'	29.3	26	38.4	16.2	20.6	20.2
	'rarely'	14.6	20.8	11.1	8.1	17.5	20.2
Total A.I.S.	'always'	0.6	9	5.2	18.5	6.9	5.3
	'mostly'	9.5	12.7	12.1	33.8	11.2	11.5
	'frequently'	41.8	20.4	23.8	31.5	33.2	41.2
	'sometimes'	34.8	31.7	39.1	12.3	29.3	21.8
	'rarely'	13.3	26.2	19.8	3.8	19.4	20.2
Ranking			2	5	1	3	4
All Figures are in %							

Instances of spoiling annual appraisal/confidential report and other service records of such officers who do not fall in line with a desired political direction, such instances are common happenings. We have studied the extent and frequency of such pressure on the All India Services Officers. Median, mode, and mean values indicate that the intensity of political pressure through control over annual confidential report is 'frequent'. Politicians use fear of annual appraisal/confidential reports to get their things done. The intensity of such pressure is observed lowest among the Indian Police Service officers, 75.6% of them feel the intensity of pressure is 'sometimes' to 'rarely'. 65.6% of the Indian Administrative Service officers, 58.7% of the Indian Forest Service officers, and 62.5% of total All India Services Officers think that 'frequently' to 'sometimes' intensity of political pressure is exerted for making adverse entries in their annual confidential report. Pearson Chi-square value of 46.952 with 8 degree of freedom is significant, with the level of significance of 0.000. Fear of annual confidential reports is related to the acceptance of political pressure in the decision-making process.

Exhibit Number 12.18: Punishment and Educational Background of the Officer

Variable Name	Pressure Intensity		Educational Background of the Officer					Total
			Graduate	Engineer/ B.Tech./ Technology	Post Graduate	MBA/ CA/CW	Ph.D.	
Punishment	'Rarely' pressure is exerted	Count	11	3	4	3	1	22
		% of Total	7.189	1.961	2.614	1.961	0.653	14.37
	'Sometimes' only pressure is exerted	Count	12	14	19	8	1	54
		% of Total	7.843	9.151	12.41	5.228	0.653	35.29
	'Frequently' pressure is exerted	Count	15	16	16	11	4	62
		% of Total	9.803	10.45	10.45	7.189	2.614	40.52
	'Most oftenly' pressure is exerted	Count	5	2	5	2		14
		% of Total	3.267	1.3071	3.267	1.307		9.151
	'Always' pressure is exerted	Count	1					1
		% of Total	0.653					0.653
Total		Count	44	35	44	24	6	153
		% of Total	28.75	22.87	28.75	15.68	3.921	100
Figures in %								

The All India Services Officers in the exercise of day-to-day administration enjoy various powers for an award of punishments. In the process of bureaucratic administration, while discharging their duties, punishments are also awarded. Politician use his position in allowing and disallowing or reducing such punishments and exercise control over the All India Services Officers. 50% of the Indian Police Service officers, 43.5% of the Indian Administrative Service officers, and 32.3% of the Indian Forest Service officers think that politicians 'frequently' regulate punishment mechanism in their own favor through appellant powers available to them. 41.2% of the All India Services Officers 'frequently' come across political misuse of appellant power by the politicians. The value of 31.316 of Pearson Chi-square is significant, with a level of significance of 0.000. The association of the decision-making process and political appellant powers is good.

Exhibit 12.18 and Chart 12.6 show the relation of the punishment variable with the demographic variable of the educational background of the officer. Results indicate 28.75% of graduate and 28.75% of postgraduate educational qualification officers are amenable to accept political pressure in the punishment variable. The lowest score of 2.39% is indicated with Ph.D. qualification, which may be lesser amenable to pressure acceptance.

Priority ranking of the intensity for different sources of pressure exerted on the variable punishment in the decision-making process and related statistical data analyses results are placed in Exhibit 12.19. First priority from different sources of pressure influencing decision related to punishment and results indicate that highest priority is given to the MLA/MLC with 42.9% for the All India Services Officer, 50% on the IAS, 45% on the IFS, and 32.4% on the IPS in punishment variable decision process. Second priority pressure intensity ranked is from the Centre/State Ministers with a score of 27.4% on the All India Services Officer, 32.4% on the IPS, 25% on the IAS and IFS each. In 1st priority, other sources of pressure on the All India Services Officer are ranked as the district-level politicians at third place with 11.2% score, the block-level politicians at fourth place with 8.7% score, and the PM/CM at fifth place with 2% score.

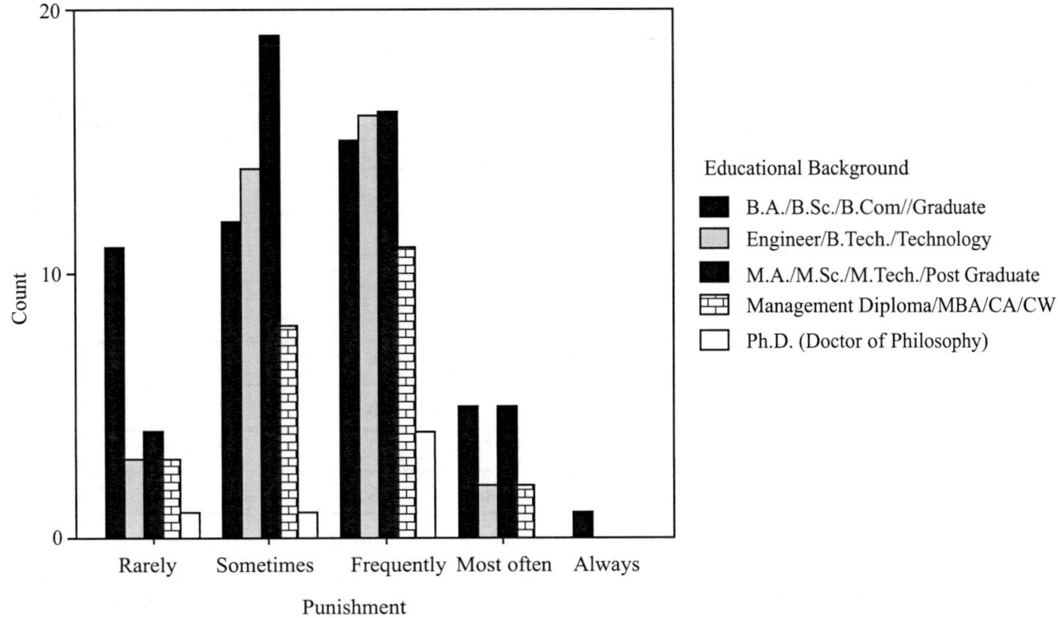

Chart No. 12.6: Educational Background and Pressure in Punishments

Respondents' number (frequency) in three priorities is not the same, because every respondent has not mentioned all three priority (1st, 2nd, and 3rd) ranking. Due to this variability additive total of three priorities may be a little skewed (Exhibit 12.19), we added together three priorities (based on answered numbers), ranked by the All India Services Officer for the different sources of political pressure in punishment areas of the decision-making process. Data analysis results show 94.5% of the AISO, 96.5% of the IPS, 93.6% of the IFS, and 92.2% of the IAS feel pressure from the MLA/MLC in the first place. The Centre/State Ministers exert pressure on punishment variable at 2nd place in aggregate of three priorities and score show 65.5% on the AISO, 52.9% on the IPS, 48.7% on the IFS and 48.2% on the IAS officer get pressure from these sources in the decision process for punishment variable. The district-level politicians exert pressure at the third position in cumulative priorities with a score of 61.5% on the AISO, 67.6% on the IPS, 60.8% on the IAS, and 50.7% on the IFS officers while deciding for punishment variable.

Exhibit Number 12.19: Priority Ranking of Sources of Pressure for Punishments Types

Pressure Sources	Priority Rank	IAS	IPS	IFS	AIS
PM/CM	1st	0.00%	2.90%	5.00%	2.00%
	2nd	7.60%	7.60%	13.30%	8.60%
	3rd	0.00%	0.00%	0.00%	0.00%
	Total	7.60%	10.50%	18.30%	10.60%
Centre/State Minister	1st	25.00%	32.40%	25.00%	27.40%
	2nd	11.40%	10.60%	20.00%	12.60%
	3rd	11.80%	9.90%	3.70%	25.50%
	Total	48.20%	52.90%	48.70%	65.50%
Member of Parliament	1st	0.00%	0.00%	2.50%	0.50%
	2nd	3.80%	0.00%	3.30%	2.30%
	3rd	12.50%	6.60%	10.70%	9.90%
	Total	3.80%	6.60%	16.50%	12.70%
MLA/MLC	1st	50.00%	32.40%	45.00%	42.90%
	2nd	24.10%	37.90%	20.00%	28.60%
	3rd	18.10%	26.20%	28.60%	23.00%
	Total	92.20%	96.50%	93.60%	94.50%
Zila Parishad/District-level Politicians	1st	10.20%	13.20%	10.00%	11.20%
	2nd	36.70%	36.40%	30.00%	35.40%
	3rd	13.90%	18.00%	10.70%	14.90%
	Total	60.80%	67.60%	50.70%	61.50%
Block Samiti/Block-level Politicians	1st	6.80%	13.20%	5.00%	8.70%
	2nd	6.30%	3.00%	0.00%	4.00%
	3rd	20.80%	14.80%	21.40%	18.60%
	Total	33.90%	31.00%	26.40%	31.30%
Village Heads/Grassroot-level Worker	1st	1.10%	0.00%	0.00%	0.50%
	2nd	8.90%	4.50%	13.30%	8.00%
	3rd	2.80%	1.60%	0.00%	1.90%
	Total	12.80%	6.10%	13.30%	10.40%
Power Brokers/Touts	1st	0.00%	1.50%	0.00%	0.50%
	2nd				
	3rd	4.20%	4.90%	3.60%	4.30%
	Total	4.20%	6.40%	3.60%	4.80%

Pressure Sources	Priority Rank	IAS	IPS	IFS	AIS
Communication Media	1st	6.80%	4.40%	7.50%	6.10%
	2nd				
	3rd	1.40%	0.00%	0.00%	0.60%
	Total	8.20%	4.40%	7.50%	6.70%
Hidden Financiers	1st				
	2nd	1.30%	0.00%	0.00%	0.60%
	3rd	0.00%	0.00%	3.60%	0.60%
	Total	1.30%	0.00%	3.60%	1.20%

12.2.7. Pressure for Promotions-related Issues

Every All India Services Officers join these services with an expectation that sufficient and good chances of promotion will be available in these services. Individual officers get out of turn promotions and one out of turn promotion under political pressure may influence many more to approach politicians to get such benefits in the future. Politicians' influence can help in creating new posts (ex-cadre mainly and cadre both types), politicians may influence based on considerations or other political interests. The Indian Administrative Service officers are close to power, the influence exercised by them and their associates have overriding importance in the process of decision regarding promotions. Such factors proved more significant than the seniority or year of allotment or merit or suitability of the officer for the post. "As more may be learned about the criteria for promotion from those who failed to achieve success as from the careers of leading officials. Men at the bottom (i.e. those remaining in the dull, dusty work of the districts throughout their official careers) were consistently men devoid of connections."[7] "As promotions and status dominated the motivations of men at the top of the hierarchy, so deference and caution characterized their actions throughout much of their careers. They were tragically paradoxical figures in the sense that their obsequious mentality had resulted from deference to an aristocracy, who then turned on them over and over again, most notably Curzon had condemned them for lack of initiative, backbone, creativity, and character."[8]

Exhibit 12.21 shows that 66% of the All India Services Officers think that 'most often' to 'frequently' intensity of political pressure is exerted for promotions. Mean (3.22), mode (3) and median (3) values indicate that 'frequently' political pressure is exerted for the promotions. 69.7% of the Indian Police Service officers, 64.3% of the Indian Administrative Service officers, and 62% of the Indian Forest Service officers get 'most often' to 'frequent' intensity of political pressure in the process of promotions. The Indian Police Service officers get maximum pressure in the promotions and the Indian Forest Service officers get the least pressure. High political pressure in police promotions is not conducive to the efficiency of any police force. Our results for Pearson Chi-square are significant and with a 0.03, level of significance. The association of political pressure in promotions with the decision-making process is good. Negative relations shown by Pearson's correlation value of –0.216 is significant with a 0.003, level of significance.

7. *British Bureaucracy in India* by B. Spangenberg, p. 161.
8. *Ibid.*, p. 256.

Politicians may pressurize the All India Services Officers for out-of-turn promotions to serve individual person needs. Mode value of 4, the median value of 3, and the mean value of 3.37 with a standard deviation of 1.15 indicate that political pressure is exerted 'frequently' to 'most often' for the promotions. 70.7% of the Indian Administrative Service officers get political pressure 'always' to 'most often' in the promotions. 68.7% of the Indian Police Service officers, 54.1% of the Indian Forest Service officers, and 61.2% of the All India Services Officers get 'most often' to 'frequent' category political pressure for promotions. The highest intensity of political pressure is on the Indian Administrative Service officers; this high pressure may be due to their location on the top of so many departments and easy amenability to political pressure. Pearson Chi-square value of 51.847 is with 8 degree of freedom and show level of significance at 0.000. Association of political pressure for out of turn promotion and decision-making process is indicated by Pearson's negative correlation value of –0.345 and Spearman correlation value of –0.316, both with 0.000, level of significance. This indicates that our results are highly significant.

People approach politicians for their promotion, many individuals want that merit may be violated so that individual can get undue favor in their promotion, politicians are kind-hearted and get moved under individual person pressure to exert pressure for such promotions. Median (3), mode (3) and mean values (3.13) indicate that 'frequent' political pressure is exerted on the All India Services Officers for out of turn promotions in violation of merit to promote certain individuals. 68.5% of the All India Services Officers get 'most often' to 'frequent' political pressure for out of turn promotions. 69.5% of the Indian Police Service officers and 67.3% of the Indian Forest Service officers come across political pressure 'most often' to 'frequently' in the matters pertaining to promotions, with demand for violation of merit to extending benefits to individuals. 72.7% of the Indian Administrative Service officers get 'always' to 'most often' intensity of political pressure for out of turn promotions. The highest political pressure is exerted on the Indian Administrative Service officers. The most important aspect of the results is the indication that employees themselves are self-oriented and believer in favoritism, so they approach politicians for illegal and wrong orders in violation of merit. A high score on this variable indicates that the majority of partners in the bureaucratic system are biased and self-centered. How a system based on self-goals perpetuation can deliver justice to the public. It is never possible until such a selfish environment continues to persist and flourish under political patronage. Association of violation of merit for individual benefits and decision-making process is established by the Pearson Chi-square analysis. The value of Pearson Chi-square is 38.707, and with a 0.000, level of significance. Results for the strength of correlations are significant with 0.000, level of significance of Pearson's correlation and Spearman correlation (R = –0.263 and Rho = –0.262).

In our research, we have studied different mode of political pressure and different sources of political pressure, these modes and sources of political pressure exert pressure on different areas, on many occasions such pressure is motivated by the considerations also. While exerting political pressure politician work under the pressure of beneficiaries due to considerations and obligations which politician has enjoyed from the beneficiaries. Mean (2.96), mode (3) and median (3) values indicate that 'frequently' political pressure is exerted based on considerations. 38.6% of the All India Services Officers, 50% of the Indian Forest Service officers, and 35.5% of the Indian Police Service officers think that political pressure they get from a politician is exerted 'frequently' for promotions based on considerations. 43.5% of the Indian Administrative Service officers get political pressure based on consideration with 'most often' intensity. Pearson Chi-square value of 41.287, with 8 degree of freedom and 0.000, level of significance, indicates a good association of such considerations in the promotion and decision-making process. The strength of this negative relationship is indicated by Pearson's correlation value of –0.239 and Spearman's correlation value of –0.234, both with a level of significance at 0.000.

Exhibit Number 12.20: Intensity of Political Pressure in Promotions

Service Name	Intensity of Pressure	Promotions 312	Out of Turn Promotion 313	Ignoring Merit 314	On Basis of Consideration 315	Financial Benefits 316	Creation of Posts 317
I.A.S.	'always'	23.2	34.5	23.6	17	9.6	1.9
	'mostly'	28.6	36.2	49.1	45.3	28.8	9.6
	'frequently'	35.7	25.9	20	22.6	26.9	21.2
	'sometimes'	12.5	1.7	3.6	11.3	19.2	36.5
	'rarely'	0	1.7	3.6	3.8	15.4	30.8
I.P.S.	'always'	8.2	15.7	4.2	0	0	0
	'mostly'	21.2	25.3	23.2	23.7	1.2	2.4
	'frequently'	48.2	43.4	46.3	35.5	27.4	3.6
	'sometimes'	15.3	15.7	12.6	25	26.2	48.2
	'rarely'	7.1	0	13.7	15.8	45.2	45.8
I.F.S.	'always'	12	9.4	6.1	6.4	1.1	5.4
	'mostly'	18	33.3	25.5	13.8	11	16.1
	'frequently'	44	20.8	41.8	50	37.4	18.3
	'sometimes'	12	19.8	14.3	17	27.5	23.7
	'rarely'	14	16.7	12.2	12.8	23.1	36.6
Total	'always'	13.6	17.7	9.3	6.7	2.6	2.6
AISO	'mostly'	22.5	31.2	29.8	24.7	11.5	9.6
	'frequently'	43.5	30	38.7	38.6	31.3	13..6
	'sometimes'	13.6	13.9	11.3	18.4	25.1	35.5
	'rarely'	6.8	7.2	10.9	11.7	29.5	38.6
Ranking			1	3	2	4	5
All Figures are in %							

On occasions, politicians work under pressure regarding violation of seniority to extend future financial and pension benefits to some individuals. 31.3% of the All India Services Officers and 37.4% of the Indian Forest Service officers come across political pressure 'frequently' for seniority violations to extend future financial benefits. 45.2% of the Indian Police Service officers get such political pressure 'rarely', whereas 28.8% of the Indian Administrative Service officers get 'most often' political pressure for such considerations and violations in seniority. Political pressure for violation of seniority to extend financial benefits in the future is exerted maximum on the Indian Administrative Service officers and least on the Indian Police Service officers. Our results are highly significant with a 0.000, level of significance on Pearson Chi-square analysis, with a value of 48.669, with 8 degrees of freedom. The relationship of seniority violations for future benefits and the decision-making process is significant with a level of significance of 0.030, in Pearson's correlation.

On occasions, the bureaucratic system gets choked and persons approach politicians to remove stagnations from the cadres by creating new posts in the department. The mean value of 2.6, the modal value of 1, and a median of 2, indicate that political pressure is exerted 'rarely' to 'sometimes' for the welfare of the cadres. 38.6% of the All India Services Officers and 36.6% of the Indian Forest Service officers get 'rarely' political pressure for removing stagnations. 48.2% of the Indian Police Service officers and 36.5% of the Indian Administrative Service officers come across political pressure 'sometimes' for removing stagnations from the cadres. This indicates that for the welfare of the service or whole cadres, people are least worried. This infers the high individualistic orientation among service people and lack of feelings for others among them. The decision-making process and political pressure towards removing stagnation from the cadres have a good association, as indicated by the Pearson Chi-square value of 32.756, and level of significance at 0.000.

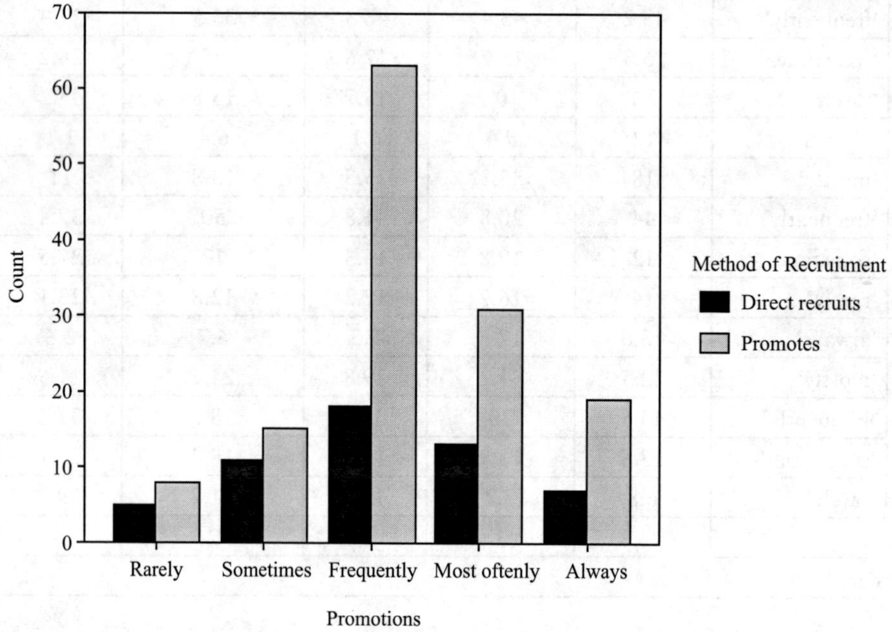

Chart No. 12.7: Method of Recruitment and Pressure for Promotions

Exhibit Number 12.21: Promotions and Method of Recruitment more Amenable to the Pressure

Variable Name	Intensity of Pressure		Method of Recruitment more Amenable to the Political Pressure		Total
			Direct Recruit	Promotes	
Promotions	'Rarely' pressure is exerted	Count	5	8	13
		% of Total	2.631	4.211	6.842
	'Sometimes' only pressure is exerted	Count	11	15	26
		% of Total	5.789	7.894	13.68
	'Frequently' pressure is exerted	Count	18	63	81
		% of Total	9.473	33.15	42.63
	'Most oftenly' pressure is exerted	Count	13	31	44
		% of Total	6.842	16.31	23.15
	'Always' pressure is exerted	Count	7	19	26
		% of Total	3.684	10	13.68
Total		Count	54	136	190
		% of Total	28.42	71.57	100

Exhibit 12.21 shows the relation of variable promotions with the demographic variable method of recruitment in the All India Services and chart 12.7 shows results on the chart; analysis results show 71.57% promote officers and 28.42% direct recruited All India Services officer accept political pressure in promotion-related decisions.

Exhibit Number 12.22: Priority Ranking of Sources of Pressure for Promotions Types

Pressure Sources	Priority Rank	IAS	IPS	IFS	AIS
PM/CM	1st	14.20%	7.70%	9.10%	11.00%
	2nd	6.40%	11.10%	14.70%	9.50%
	3rd	2.30%	0.00%	3.10%	1.60%
	Total	22.90%	18.80%	26.90%	22.10%
Centre/State Minister	1st	44.30%	52.60%	47.70%	47.90%
	2nd	12.80%	6.90%	11.80%	10.50%
	3rd	18.60%	10.40%	9.40%	14.10%
	Total	75.70%	69.90%	68.90%	72.50%
Member of Parliament	1st	5.70%	5.10%	9.10%	6.10%
	2nd	11.70%	0.00%	5.90%	6.50%
	3rd	17.40%	14.90%	18.80%	16.80%
	Total	34.80%	20.00%	33.80%	29.40%

Pressure Sources	Priority Rank	IAS	IPS	IFS	AIS
MLA/MLC	1st	18.90%	6.40%	22.70%	15.40%
	2nd	47.90%	54.20%	50.00%	50.50%
	3rd	19.80%	38.80%	25.00%	27.60%
	Total	86.60%	99.40%	97.70%	93.50%
Zila Parishad/District-level Politicians	1st	5.70%	9.00%	2.30%	6.10%
	2nd	20.20%	27.80%	14.70%	22.00%
	3rd	19.80%	19.40%	21.90%	20.00%
	Total	45.70%	56.20%	38.90%	48.10%
Block Samiti/Block-level Politicians	1st	8.50%	19.20%	6.80%	11.80%
	2nd				
	3rd	18.60%	9.00%	12.50%	14.10%
	Total	27.10%	28.20%	19.30%	25.90%
Village Heads/Grassroot-level Worker	1st	2.80%	0.00%	0.00%	1.30%
	2nd				
	3rd	1.20%	0.00%	3.10%	1.00%
	Total	4.00%	0.00%	3.10%	2.30%
Power Brokers/Touts	1st				
	2nd	1.10%	0.00%	0.00%	0.50%
	3rd	1.20%	3.00%	3.10%	2.20%
	Total	2.30%	3.00%	3.10%	2.70%
Communication Media	1st				
	2nd	0.00%	0.00%	2.90%	0.50%
	3rd	0.00%			
	Total			2.90%	0.50%
Hidden Financiers	1st	0.00%	0.00%	2.30%	0.40%
	2nd	0.00%	0.00%	0.00%	0.00%
	3rd	1.20%	4.50%	3.10%	2.70%
	Total	1.20%	4.50%	5.40%	3.10%

Statistical data analyses result for the AISO pressure intensity priority ranking of different sources of pressure in promotion variable of decision process show very interesting results placed at Exhibit 12.22. The Centre/State Ministers source of pressure has been ranked at 1st priority with a score as; 47.9% on the AIS, 52.6% on the IPS, 47.7% on the IFS, and 44.30% on the IAS. In 2nd priority of ranking pressure from the MLA/MLC has been ranked and the intensity percentage of pressure for the AIS is 15.4%, among services highest is 22.7% on the IFS, 18.9% on the

IAS, and 6.4% on the IPS. Other sources of pressure in 1st priority are ranked as the block-level politicians 11.8% at third position, the PM/CM 11% at fourth position, the Members Parliament 6.1% at fifth positions and district-level politicians 6.1% at sixth position.

Respondents' number (frequency) in three priorities is not same, because not every respondent has marked all three priority (1st, 2nd, and 3rd) ranking, due to this variability in an additive total of three priorities may be little skewed, we added together three priorities (based on answered numbers). Cumulative addition of three priorities for different sources of pressure indicates that the MLA/MLC sources score is the highest in an additive score of pressure intensity with 93.5% on the AIS, 99.4% on the IPS, 97.7% on the IFS, and 86.6% on the IAS. In this category of the additive score of different sources of pressure on the AIS indicate that the Centre/State Ministers influence 72.5% at second place, the district-level politicians 48.1% at third place, the block-level politicians 25.9% at fourth position, and the PM/CM 22.1% at fifth position in exerting political pressure on promotions related decisions in a bureaucratic system.

12.2.8. Enhance Own Power Exerting Pressure for Rules Regulations and Procedures

Excessive rules and regulations orientation provide power to the All India Services Officers, the element of such formalization reduce the need for politician attention. Politicians' sense of increasing their own power encourages the pressure and uses this as a power enhancer. Obedience to rules, lack of initiative, and hiding in the rules and procedures are the continuation of the Viceroy's era. Excessive reference to rules and procedure, in a hierarchy from an assistant/LDC to Cabinet Secretary/Chief Secretary is a continuation of inheritance from the British Raj. The decision process is the logical conclusion of contradiction between performance and claims made by the All India Service Officers under the shadow of rules. "Outmoded rules and controls stifled initiatives reducing the country to obsolescence, uncertainty, and decay in functioning. Vested interests developed in delaying and prevaricating, since it creates a fertile ground for corruption", K. Seshadri (1994).

Political leadership and elite power holders most commonly use manipulations of rules, regulations, and inter-service relationships among three All India Services. Such manipulations help in controlling the extent of amenability under political pressure. Standardized operational procedures reduce the chances of manipulations at will by the power holders and politicians. Transparency and clarity in rules can help All India Services Officers to resist pressure. Role clarity in rules can define who will do what, who will enjoy what powers. But bureaucratic system invariably coalesces and fuses rules and maintains a high degree of ambiguity to maximize interdependence to control inter-services activities.

Uncertainty is built in the rules. At any time and any moment, seniors can misuse the inherent powers of the juniors. So slowly, seniors always try to create instability in the rules, so that to exploit position for bargaining with the politicians in case of need. Government hierarchy is invariably misused in the name of regulating rules. The Indian Administrative Service officers surpass all other services in accepting political pressure. To please other politicians and attain political interests, the politician will put the IAS for coordination. In the name of coordination, IAS increases its own demands and thus leaves no time for the decision process. The Indian Administrative Service officers have made coordination as a game plan for usurping powers of other departments to own advantage.

The common saying in bureaucratic circles that show me face, we shall show you the rules. A bureaucratic system bounded by rules, regulations, and procedures is invariably full of distortions and manipulations to serve the individual goals. Mean (2.36), mode (2) and median (2) values indicate that in general rules, regulations and procedures are 'sometimes' under political pressure. 87.1% of the All India Services Officers, 99.2% of the Indian Police Service officers, and 83% of the Indian Administrative Service officers get political pressure 'frequent' to 'rarely' intensity in the manipulation of rules, regulations, and procedures. 84.3% of the Indian Forest Service officers get political pressure 'most often' to the 'sometimes' category to influence rules and regulations. The Pearson Chi-square indicates a good association of the decision-making process with rules, regulations, and procedures (35.856, with 0.000, level of significance). The strength of this relationship indicated by the Spearman correlation value of 0.2, with a level of significance at 0.01, also indicates that our results are significant.

Politicians exert political pressure on the All India Services Officers to circumvent rules to serve particular individual goals and interests. Mean (3.12), mode (3), and median values (3) indicate that 'frequently' political pressure is exerted to circumvent the rules to extend benefits to an individual person. 62.4% of the All India Services Officers, 71.4% of the Indian Administrative Service officers, and 62% of the Indian Forest Service officers get 'most often' to 'frequent' intensity of political pressure for ignoring or circumventing rules to serve individual personal goals.

71.6% of the Indian Police Service officers get political pressure 'frequently' to 'sometimes' for ignoring rules. Our results indicate that the Indian Administrative Service officers get the highest amount of political pressure in circumventing rules to provide benefits to individuals. Pearson Chi-square value is 31.156, with 8 degree of freedom and a 0.000, level of significance. This indicates a good relation of ignoring rules with the decision-making process. The negative relationship of this variable with the decision is shown by Pearson's correlation; the value is significant with a level of significance at 0.030.

Exhibit Number 12.23: Intensity of Political Pressure by Rules, Regulations and Procedures

Service	Intensity	Rules Regulations	Ignore Rules	Simplify Rules	New Rules	Clientele Oriented	Change Rules
		318	319	320	321	322	323
I.A.S.	'always'	4.3	19	8.5	16.4	20	8.8
	'mostly'	12.8	3.3	23.7	18.2	387.5	15.8
	'frequently'	31.9	38.1	42.4	45.5	35.4	24.6
	'sometimes'	23.4	7.9	22	18.2	3.1	12.3
	'rarely'	27.7	1.6	3.4	1.8	3.1	38.6
I.P.S.	'always'	1.3	9.5	0	9.6	7.4	0
	'mostly'	0	8.4	5.3	29.8	20	0
	'frequently'	21.3	48.4	21.1	35.1	40	0
	'sometimes'	51.3	23.2	25	16	18.9	15.1
	'rarely'	26.3	10.5	48.7	9.6	13.7	84.9

Service	Intensity	Rules Regulations 318	Ignore Rules 319	Simplify Rules 320	New Rules 321	Clientele Oriented 322	Change Rules 323
I.F.S.	'always'	5.9	12	9.1	9.9	11	7.2
	'mostly'	21.6	26	18.2	21.8	16	9.3
	'frequently'	39.2	36	30.3	41.6	42	24.7
	'sometimes'	23.5	15	26.3	15.8	16	21.6
	'rarely'	9.8	11	16.2	10.9	15	37.1
AISO	'always'	3.4	12.8	6	11.2	11.9	4.9
	'mostly'	9.6	21.3	15.4	24	23.1	7.3
	'frequently'	29.2	41.1	30.3	40	39.6	15.4
Total	'sometimes'	36	16.3	24.8	16.4	13.8	17
	'rarely'	21.9	8.5	23.5	8.4	11.5	55.5
Ranking			1	4	3	2	5
All Figures Except Ranking are in %							

Sometimes service representatives meet politicians and request simplifying rules, regulations, and procedures to remove the ambiguity from it to provide effective service to the people. Mean (2.55), mode (3) and median (3) values indicate that political pressure is exerted 'frequently' for simplifying rules and procedures. 55.1% of the All India Services Officers and 56.6% of the Indian Forest Service officers get 'frequent' to 'sometimes' intensity of political pressure for simplifying rules. 73.7% of the Indian Police Service officers get political pressure 'rarely' to 'sometimes' for avoiding ambiguity from the rules. 66.1% of the Indian Administrative Service officers get political pressure 'most often' category to 'frequently' for simplifying the rules and procedures to avoid ambiguity. The Indian Administrative Service officers get the highest political pressure among the All India Services Officers for simplifying rules and police officers get the least political pressure for this. Good association of amending and simplifying rules to avoid ambiguity and decision is shown by the Pearson Chi-square analysis. Pearson Chi-square value is 53.165, at 8 degree of freedom and 0.000, level of significance.

When politicians feel that present rules are a stumbling block in achieving the self-goals and interests, in such condition's rules are changed and new rules are framed to serve political and self-goals. Mean (3.12), median (3) and modal (3) values indicate that political pressure is exerted 'frequently' to frame new rules to serve political goals. Our results indicate that 64% of the All India Services Officers, 64.9% of the Indian Police Service officers, 63.7% of the Indian Administrative Service officers, and 63.4% of the Indian Forest Service officers get political pressure 'most often' to 'frequently' intensity for framing new rules to meet political goals. In this, all three services are of the same view and with identical scores. This confirms that political pressure is exerted to get new rules framed when politicians feel that old rules are obstructing the achievement of their goals.

In a democratic setup, politicians are in a serious problem, one person wants the rule to be interpreted in his favor, next time another person wants the different meaning of the same rule from the same officer. It becomes contradicting and cause serious conflict in the minds of the All India Services Officers, what to do, to serve clientele-oriented enforcement of rules as demanded by the politicians. 93.9% of the Indian Administrative Service officers get 'always' to 'frequently' political pressure for clientele-oriented enforcement of rules. 78.9% of the Indian Police Service officers, 74% of the Indian Forest Service officers, and 76.5% of the All India Services Officers get political pressure 'most often' to 'sometimes' for clientele-oriented maintenance of rules. The Indian Administrative Service officers get the highest political pressure for goal-oriented interpretation of rules. Our results are significant with a level of significance of 0.000, in Pearson Chi-square analysis, with a value of 27.964 and 8 degrees of freedom. The strength of the relationship of the decision-making process with the clientele-oriented enforcement of rules is shown by the Spearman correlation and Pearson's correlation with a value of –0.243 and level of significance of 0.000. This negative relationship shows that our results are significant.

Political groups and the interested public exert pressure on politicians to amend and change rules, so that, disadvantaged persons, widows, and orphans can get rehabilitation for their survival. This variable was studied; our results indicate that politicians 'rarely' exert political pressure for such a novel cause of action. 55.5% of the All India Services Officers, 84.9% of the Indian Police Service officers, 38.6% of the Indian Administrative Service officers, and 37.1% of the Indian Forest Service officers 'rarely' get political pressure for the rehabilitation of orphans, widows, and disadvantaged persons. Mean (1.89), median (1), modal (1) values indicate 'rarely' pressure is exerted for this welfare variable of the people. Pearson Chi-square value is 68.907, with 8 degree of freedom and 0.000, level of significance. This indicates that the association of political pressure with the decision is significant.

Exhibit Number 12.24: Rules, Regulations and Procedure Types of Pressure and Family Economic Background

Variable	Pressure Intensity		Family Economic Background					Total
			Rich	Upper middle class	Middle class	Lower middle class	Poor	
Rules, Regulations & Procedure	'Rarely' pressure is exerted	Count	17	13	3	2	3	38
		% of Total	10	7.647	1.764	1.176	1.764	22.35
	'Sometimes' only pressure is exerted	Count	30	14	5	5	6	60
		% of Total	17.64	8.235	2.941	2.941	3.529	35.29
	'Frequently' pressure is exerted	Count	21	9	4	11	4	49
		% of Total	12.35	5.294	2.352	6.471	2.352	28.82
	'Most oftenly' pressure is exerted	Count	2	4	7	1	3	17
		% of Total	1.176	2.352	4.117	0.588	1.764	10
	'Always' pressure is exerted	Count		1	3	2		6
		% of Total		0.588	1.765	1.176		3.529
Total		Count	70	41	22	21	16	170
		% of Total	41.17	24.11	12.94	12.35	9.411	100

Exhibit 12.24 and Chart 12.8 show the relation of the demographic variable family economic background of the All India Services Officer with acceptance of political pressure in implementation decision regarding rules, regulations, and procedures in the bureaucratic system. 41.18% of the All India Service with rich family economic background and 24.11% with upper-middle-class economic family economic background, total of two categories 65.29% officers from affluent economic background accept political pressure in implementation of rules, regulations and procedures. Political pressure acceptance for this variable is very low 9.41% among the AIS with poor family economic background.

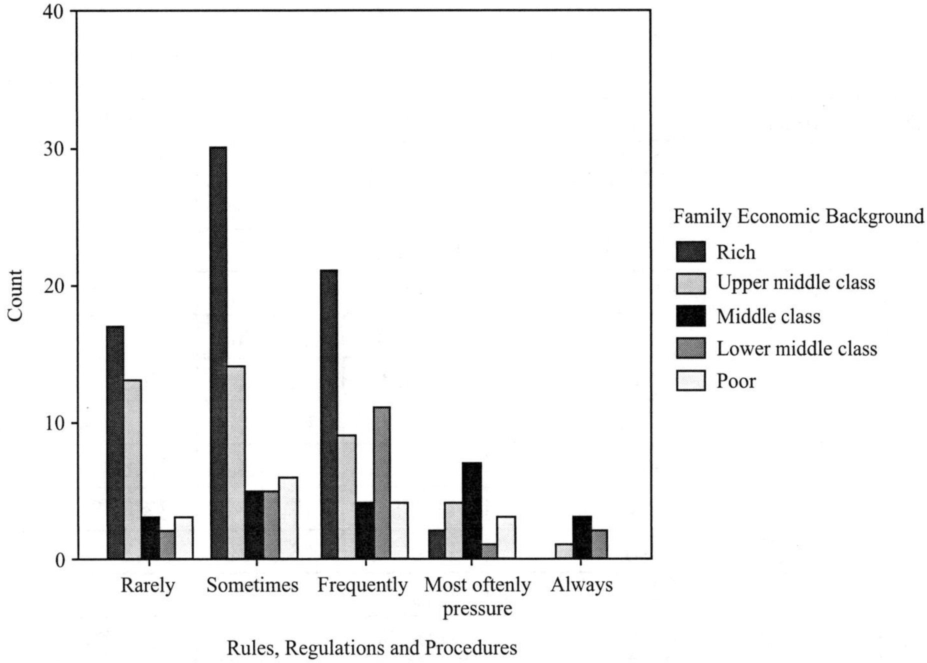

Chart No. 12.8: Family Economic Background and Pressure in Rules, Regulations and Procedures

Statistical data analyses results placed at Exhibit 12.25 are indicating very interesting phenomena, in what manner different sources of pressure exert political pressure (with its ranking) in implementation of rules, regulations, and procedure in the decision making the process of the All India Services and how these super elites consider that pressure. The Centre/State Ministers are ranked at 1st priority with 60% and the PM/CM at the second position in 1st priority with 21% intensity of pressure. The PM/CM pressure is accepted in 1st priority and it gets reduced at 7% during 2nd priority and further decline to 0.5% at 3rd priority and similarly pressure from the Centre/State Ministers also decline in respective priorities; 24.5% in 2nd priority and reduced to 2.7% at 3rd priority, whereas, such pressure intensity increases in lesser powerful political sources.

Data indicate that 1st priority source of pressure declines according to its importance and power of pressure sources in that variable. The MLA/MLC with 9.8% at 3rd position, the village-level politicians 6.4% at 4th position, and the block-level politicians with 1.5% at 5th position. If further priorities are considered then results show a different trend. We have shown the cumulative addition of all three priorities, where pressure decline from the most powerful source, political pressure increases in lower priorities for the less powerful politicians as shown by district-level politicians, the block-level politicians, and the Members Parliament.

Exhibit Number 12.25: Priority Ranking of Sources of Pressure for Rules and Regulations Types

Pressure Source	Priority Rank	IAS	IPS	IFS	AIS
PM/CM	1st	17.90%	27.80%	15.80%	21%
	2nd	5.30%	8.30%	9.10%	7.00%
	3rd	1.10%	0.00%	0.00%	0.50%
	Total	24.30%	36.10%	24.90%	28.50%
Centre/State Minister	1st	61.10%	63.90%	50.00%	60.00%
	2nd	22.10%	29.20%	21.20%	24.50%
	3rd	4.50%	0.00%	3.40%	2.70%
	Total	87.70%	93.10%	74.60%	87.20%
Member of Parliament	1st	0.00%	0.00%	2.60%	0.50%
	2nd	14.70%	8.30%	18.20%	13.00%
	3rd	14.80%	9.00%	13.80%	12.50%
	Total	29.50%	17.30%	34.60%	26.00%
MLA/MLC	1st	11.60%	4.20%	15.80%	9.80%
	2nd	41.10%	47.20%	33.30%	42.00%
	3rd	38.60%	43.30%	50.20%	41.80%
	Total	91.30%	94.70%	99.30%	93.60%
Zila Parishad/District-level Politicians	1st	0.00%	0.00%	2.60%	0.50%
	2nd	7.40%	2.80%	6.10%	5.50%
	3rd	25.00%	37.30%	13.80%	27.60%
	Total	32.40%	40.10%	22.50%	33.60%
Block Samiti/Block-level Politicians	1st	2.10%	0.00%	2.60%	1.50%
	2nd	6.30%	4.20%	9.10%	6.00%
	3rd	11.40%	3.00%	6.90%	7.60%
	Total	19.80%	7.20%	18.60%	15.10%
Village Heads/Grassroot-level Worker	1st	7.40%	4.20%	7.90%	6.40%
	2nd	1.10%	0.00%	0.00%	0.50%
	3rd	2.30%	1.50%	10.30%	3.30%
	Total	10.80%	5.70%	18.20%	10.20%

Pressure Source	Priority Rank	IAS	IPS	IFS	AIS
Power Brokers/Touts	1st	0.00%	0.00%	0.00%	0.00%
	2nd	1.10%	0.00%	3.00%	1.00%
	3rd	1.10%	3.00%	0.00%	1.60%
	Total	2.20%	3.00%	3.00%	2.60%
Communication Media	1st	0.00%	0.00%	2.60%	0.50%
	2nd	0.00%	0.00%	0.00%	0.00%
	3rd	0.00%	0.00%	0.00%	0.00%
	Total	0.00%	0.00%	2.60%	0.50%
Hidden Financiers	1st	0.00%	0.00%	0.00%	0.00%
	2nd	1.10%	0.00%	0.00%	0.50%
	3rd	1.10%	3.00%	3.40%	2.20%
	Total	2.20%	3.00%	3.40%	2.70%

Respondents' number (frequency) in three priorities is not same, because not every respondent has mentioned all three priority (1st, 2nd, and 3rd) ranking, due to this variability in a cumulative total of three priorities may be little skewed, we added together three priorities (based on answered numbers). The MLA/MLC sources of pressure with 93.6% cumulative aggregate show pressure intensity of 99.3% on the IFS, 94.7% on the IPS and 91.3% on the IAS at first place and 87.2% for the AIS, 93.5% on the IPS, and 74% on the IFS officer for this variable from the Centre/State Ministers. Results for the AIS show that the District Level Politicians intensity of 33.6% at 3rd position, the Members of Parliament scores with 26% at 5th position, the PM/Chief Minister score with 28.5% at 4th position and 15.1% the Block Samiti Politicians at 6th position.

12.2.9. Pressure for Clientele-Oriented Policy-Related Issues

Select elites have hijacked the policy formulation process in the bureaucratic system. Politicians' roles have been relegated to that of a spokesperson of these elites. Politicians are highly articulate and can represent the multi-ethnic interests of unorganized clientele in the policy. Politicians could have used the public podium for policy feedback, policy improvement, and political publicity. Politicians' broad base interactions with the public can bring innovative issues in the policy. Politicians are more considerate about the ideals and passion of all the parties in the policy. But policy procedural and administrative difficulties offer feelings of negligence/prejudice to politicians in the process. Frequent refusal due to bureaucratic system defects, prejudice, disinclination, and rules irritate politicians to keep a distance and aloofness from the policy process. Politicians this type of expected behavior suits to needs of the powerholders' bureaucrats, who get freedom and space in a decision for manipulations in policy at their free will. Politicians have feelings to move more aggressively and less objectively for the future in the policy.

The All India Services Officers spread the canards of neutrality, which they do not emerge. The All India Services Officers impress upon power holders that politicians do not like our neutrality. The policy process has become the nexus for mutuality's for benefits based on self-interests for the officers and voters for the politicians. The policy process is fully used for the promotion of self-interests by the power holders. Ultimately, policy carries the instinctive impression and perceptions of the interest-oriented elements. The All India Services Officers keep a thin line between policy determination and implementation. In the process, the policy serves the overlapping and complicated objectives/goals of the manipulators. In bureaucratic systems, policy distribution functions depend on the power potentials of each service and individual beneficiary. Administrative delays are in built-in policy to keep away politicians' expectations. In case politicians try to influence the policy, economic problems are incorporated in the policy, which will work as an excuse to deny access to politicians. Power elites try to incorporate group conflicts, law and order issues to keep politicians away from it so that elites can pursue particularistic goals through policy.

The policy has been continuously and historically used as an instrument for self-interest propagations. "That maintenance and stability of British Rule in India should form the basis of British policy; and that, in this view, a large proportion of British officers must be retained in more important posts."[9] Continuous elitist autocratic control over the policy has hindered liberal thinking and bureaucratic development. "Role of top management as policy formulator, strategic thinker, planner, and visionary has been reduced to that of a mere implementer of policy directed by bureaucrat and politician...They worship their political and bureaucratic deities by running from pillar to post in ministerial temples of New Delhi," P. Singh and Asha Bhandarker (1990). "New policies need to be carried out by the administration without tearing the socio-cultural fabric", V. Bhaskara Rao (1994) of the country.

The policy process has become a political process. The Indian Administrative Service officers exercise complete control over policy in the secretariat has ceased the relevance of democratic norms. They have hijacked it and taken to politicians, so that, politicians realize that the Indian Administrative Service officers are the most obedient servants and only they can serve a political purpose. The Indian Administrative Service officers mobilize politician support to retain the fullest grip and control over the policy in state and center. After independence policy process has been completely centralized instead of decentralizing. The Indian Administrative Service officers and politicians both find it convenient to manipulate in the way they desire and reduce specialists to cipher and in long run whole policy has been distorted in favor of the Indian Administrative Service officers only. We are lost to nowhere situation, where no one is answerable and accountable for the failure and lapses.

"A minister who conflicts with his secretary is liable to forfeit his office. Only those ministers have been successful who know the knack of carrying on with civil servants. The bureaucrats rule India; they know the politician can do nothing without them." S. Maheshwari, 1976. Politicians make a very limited contribution in the contents of the policy, it provides a framework for goals only, I.M. Dayal, 1979. In India, the political system is unrepresentative in the policy-making process and involved only in a general way. Political leadership provided a little way of policy inputs. "Occasionally powerful and resourceful minister would take charge to push hard to clear the policy and I.A.S. secretary will present one difficulty after another and continuously watch at their watches". "Ministers are underplayed in the files". Many sound proposals come from technocrats below but senior secretaries move their own proposals in the policy. "Various stratagems had been developed to this end. Senior secretaries, he said, may have little in the way

9. Secretary of the State, 22.10.1872.

of clear objectives or plans, but the ICS tradition had elevated them to the prime position in the middle of the policy process between political leadership on one side and people with the expertise on other" (D.C. Potter, 1986).

Exhibit Number 12.26: Intensity of Political Pressure by Manipulations in Policy-related Issues

Service Name	Pressure Intensity	Policy Issuers 324	Serve Self Goals 325	Social Needs 326	Resource Conservation 327	Future Needs 328	Political Goals 329
I.A.S.	'always'	2.1	20.6	10	1.7	15.5	31.1
	'mostly'	14.9	30.2	26.7	0	10.3	14.8
	'frequently'	31.9	36.5	25	22	15.5	34.4
	'sometimes'	17	11.1	18.3	27.1	15.5	11.5
	'rarely'	34	1.6	20	49.2	43.1	8.2
I.P.S.	'always'	0	15.1	25.3	19.4	7.9	11.8
	'mostly'	11.5	16.1	0	1.6	7.9	11.8
	'frequently'	39.3	36.6	4.8	3.2	34.8	54.4
	'sometimes'	37.7	24.7	19.3	27.4	404	20.6
	'rarely'	11.5	7.5	50.6	48.4	9	1.5
I.F.S.	'always'	6.4	16.8	7	6.3	8.2	23.5
	'mostly'	27.7	20.8	26	16.7	16.3	15.3
	'frequently'	27.7	23.8	29	36.5	39.8	30.6
	'sometimes'	36.2	28.7	20	17.7	23.5	25.5
	'rarely'	2.1	9.9	18	22.9	12.2	5.1
AISO	'always'	2.6	17.1	14	8.8	9.8	22
	'mostly'	17.4	21.4	17.3	7.8	11.8	14.1
	'frequently'	33.5	31.5	19.6	23	32.2	38.8
Total	'sometimes'	31	23	19.3	23	27.8	20.3
	'rarely'	15.5	7	29.6	37.3	18.4	4.8
Ranking			2	3	5	4	1
All Figures, Except Ranking are in %							

Politicians exert pressure on the All India Services Officers in a matter related to policy, so that it serves individual personal interests and goals, such individual may be self or political workers or vested groups. Politicians get the policy changed or amended to suit self needs and goals, policy may be clientele oriented or simplified to meet the needs.

Politicians influence the policy, in general, to churn the benefits out of it. Mean (2.61), mode (3) and median (3) values indicate that political pressure is exerted 'frequently' on the policy process to get undue mileage out of it. 64.5% of the All India Services are of the view that political pressure is exerted 'frequently' to 'sometimes' on policy matters. 77% of the Indian Police Service officers and 63.9% of the Indian Forest Service officers come across political pressure 'frequently' to 'sometimes' intensity in the policy. 65.9% of the Indian Administrative Service officers get political pressure in the policy 'frequently' and 'rarely' category. The intensity of political pressure on policy is moderate to low, it indicates that politician is not much bothered about policy and extent of political interference is limited to own interests only. Pearson Chi-square results indicate a very good association of political pressure in policy with the decision-making process. Pearson Chi-square shows a value of 30.377, and it is significant with a level of significance of 0.000. Pearson's correlation of political pressure in policy with the decision is significant with a 0.002, level of significance.

Politicians influence policy implementation in such a way, that it <u>serves individual interests and goals</u>. Mean (3.17), mode (3) and median (3) values indicate that 'frequently' political pressure is exerted on policy implementation and manipulation to serve individual goals. 54.5% of the All India Services Officers get 'frequent' to 'sometimes' intensity of political pressure on policy implementation to serve individual goals. The highest political pressure is exerted on the Indian Administrative Service officers and 66.7% of them get political pressure 'most often' category to 'frequently' in policy implementation to meet individual goals. 61.3% of the Indian Police Service officers and 52.5% of the Indian Forest Service officers get 'frequent' to 'sometimes' category of political pressure in policy implementation. Pearson Chi-square results are significant with a level of significance at 0.03. Association of political pressure on policy implementation with a decision is significant and Pearson's correlation negative relationship is valid with a level of significance at 0.012.

Politicians influence <u>policy amendment to serve to change social needs, and social interests</u> on a larger scale. Median (3) and mean (2.66) values indicate 'frequent' political pressure for policy amendments to serve voters' needs. Only the Indian Administrative Service officers get political pressure for policy amendment, and 51.7% of them get pressure 'most often' to 'frequently' intensity. The Indian Police Service officers get the least political pressure for policy amendments, most of them are located away from the policy formulations; 50.6% of them 'rarely' get political pressure in policy amendment. 55% of the Indian Forest Service officers get 'most often' to 'frequent' political pressure in policy to incorporate the change to serve social interests. 66.916 value of Pearson Chi-square is significant, with 8 degree of freedom, and 0.000, level of significance indicates very good association.

People approach politicians for <u>conservation and preservation of local resources and traditional culture</u>; they require politicians to influence towards the formulation of policy in such a way that it can help them. But politicians have a very low preference for such general matters. The highest score is lying in the 'rarely' category indicate that no one bothers with such issues. Modal value of 1, go in this direction of 'rarely' political pressure category. 76.3% of the Indian Administrative Service officers, 75.8% of the Indian Police Service officers, and 60.3% of the All India Services get political pressure 'rarely' to 'sometimes' for the conservation of culture and resources. 36.5% of the Indian Forest Service officers get 'frequent' political pressure and in the second score, 22.9% of them get 'rarely' pressure for conservation and preservation of resources and culture of local areas. Our results are significant as indicated by the Pearson Chi-square value of 59.049, with a level of significance of 0.000. Strength of association of decision and policy for conservation is good. Pearson's correlation value of 0.287 and Spearman's correlation value of 0.311 are significant with a 0.000, level of significance.

People exert pressure on politicians to frame policy in such a way that it serves future individuals/regional needs. Individual influential persons desire policy framing to serve their own future needs. Mean (2.66), mode (3) and median (3) values indicate 'frequent' use of political pressure for this variable. 32.2% of the All India Services Officers and 39.8% of the Indian Forest Service officers come across 'frequent' political pressure for the formulation of policy to serve the future needs of the region. 40.4% of the Indian Police Service officers get political pressure 'sometimes' and 43.1% of the Indian Administrative Service officers get 'rarely' political pressure for policy framing to serve the future needs of the region or the individuals. Framing policy to serving future goals and decision has a good association as indicated by the Pearson Chi-square analysis. 46.987 value of Pearson Chi-square is significant with 0.000, level of significance. The strength of the relationship is indicated by the Spearman correlation and is significant with a 0.006, level of significance.

Political party in power influence the All India Services Officers to ignore, circumvent policy directive in such a way that it serves the goals and interests of the political party in power. Mean (3.26), mode (3) and median (3) values are indicating that political pressure is exerted 'frequently' for ignoring and circumventing policy for part interests. 38.8% of the All India Services Officers, 54.4% of the Indian Police Service officers, 34.4% of the Indian Administrative Service officers, and 30.6% of the Indian Forest Service officers assess that they get political pressure 'frequently' for ignoring and circumventing the policy directives to serve the ruling party interests. The Indian Police Service officers get the highest political pressure for ignoring and bending the policy to serve the political party in power and the Indian Forest Service officers get the least pressure. Ignoring the policy for political interests and decision has a good association. This is indicated by the Pearson Chi-square results, which are significant with a 0.01, level of significance.

Exhibit Number 12.27: Policy-Related Issues Pressure Types and Community Background

Variable	Pressure Intensity		Community background				Total
			Gen.	OBC	SC	ST	
Policy-Related Issues	'Rarely' pressure is exerted	% of Total	8.511		3.546	3.546	15.61
	'Sometimes' only pressure is exerted	% of Total	13.47		12.05	4.964	30.49
	'Frequently' pressure is exerted	% of Total	12.05	4.255	12.05	4.255	32.62
	'Most oftenly' pressure is exerted	% of Total	9.929		7.801	0.709	18.43
	'Always' pressure is exerted	% of Total	2.127		0.709		2.836
Total		% of Total	46.09	4.255	36.17	13.47	100

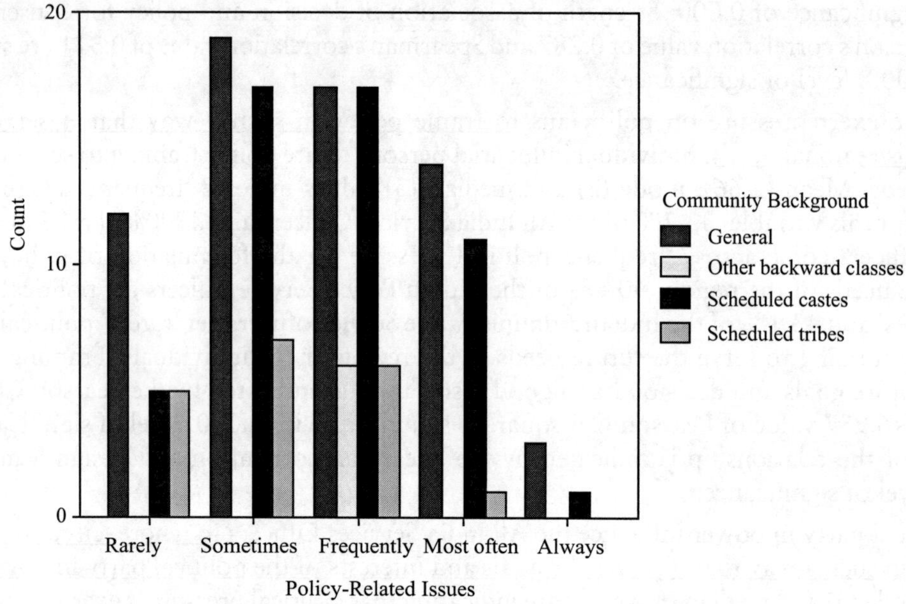

Chart No. 12.9: Community Background and Policy-Related Issues

Chart 12.9 and Exhibit 12.27 indicate the relationship of variable policy-related issues with the demographic variable of community background of the All India Services. Results indicate that 46.1% of the All India Services members belonging to the general category accept pressure in policy-related issues and 36.2% of the All India Services officers belonging to Scheduled Castes accept pressure. In policy-related issues, general category officers are more amenable to accept pressure in the decision.

Data statistical analyses result placed at Exhibit 12.28 for the AISO political pressure intensity priority ranking in policy-related decisions. The AISO ranked the Centre/State Ministers at 1st priority with 66.7% intensity of pressure and the PM/CM with 11.7% in the second position in 1st ranking and the Members of Parliament 11.3% intensity at fourth position in 1st priority.

The AISO priority ranking shows a decreasing intensity trend from 1st to 3rd priority in powerful sources as the PM/CM, the Centre/State Ministers but an increasing trend with the Members of Parliament, the MLA/MLC, the district-level politicians and the block-level politicians. Respondents' number (frequency) in three priorities is not the same, because every respondent has not mentioned all three priority (1st, 2nd, and 3rd) ranking. Due to this variability in a cumulative total of three priorities may be a little skewed, we added together three priorities (based on answered numbers), and results show the intensity of political pressure on the AIS from the Centre/State Minister is 89.2% (the IAS 89.1%, the IPS 94.1% and IFS 80.7%) at the first position and the MLA/MLC 88.7% on the AIS (91.3% on IFS, 89.1% on IAS and 86.4% on IPS) at the second position. In this category, further positions for cumulative intensity are the Members Parliament 47.8%, the district-level politicians 36.3%, and the PM/CM 18.7% intensity of pressure from these sources of pressure.

Exhibit Number 12.28: Priority Ranking of Sources of Pressure for Policy Matters Areas

Pressure Source	Priority Rank	IAS	IPS	IFS	AIS
PM/CM	1st	11.10%	9.20%	18.60%	11.70%
	2nd	5.40%	7.90%	7.70%	6.60%
	3rd	2.20%	0.00%	0.00%	1.00%
	Total	18.70%	17.10%	26.30%	19.30%
Centre/State Minister	1st	66.10%	77.60%	48.80%	66.70%
	2nd	14.30%	11.80%	20.50%	14.60%
	3rd	8.70%	4.70%	11.40%	7.90%
	Total	89.10%	94.10%	80.70%	89.20%
Member of Parliament	1st	13.40%	5.30%	16.30%	11.30%
	2nd	16.10%	11.80%	17.90%	15.00%
	3rd	22.80%	14.10%	31.40%	21.50%
	Total	52.30%	31.20%	65.60%	47.80%
MLA/MLC	1st	9.80%	5.30%	14.00%	9.10%
	2nd	55.40%	59.20%	48.70%	55.50%
	3rd	23.90%	21.90%	28.60%	24.10%
	Total	89.10%	86.40%	91.30%	88.70%
Zila Parishad/District-level Politicians	1st	0.90%	0.00%	0.00%	0.40%
	2nd	1.80%	0.00%	2.60%	1.30%
	3rd	29.30%	51.60%	17.10%	34.60%
	Total	32.00%	51.60%	19.70%	36.30%
Block Samiti/Block-level Politicians	1st	0.00%	1.30%	2.30%	0.90%
	2nd	0.90%	0.00%	0.00%	0.40%
	3rd	8.70%	3.10%	5.70%	6.30%
	Total	9.60%	4.40%	8.00%	7.60%
Village Heads/Grassroot-level Worker	1st	0.00%	0.00%	0.00%	0.00%
	2nd	0.00%	2.60%	0.00%	0.80%
	3rd	2.20%	0.00%	2.90%	1.60%
	Total	2.20%	2.60%	2.90%	2.40%
Power Brokers/Touts	1st	0.00%	0.00%	0.00%	0.00%
	2nd	0.00%	0.00%	0.00%	0.00%
	3rd	1.10%	3.10%	2.90%	2.10%
	Total	1.10%	3.10%	2.90%	2.10%

Pressure Source	Priority Rank	IAS	IPS	IFS	AIS
Communication Media	1st	0.00%	0.00%	0.00%	0.00%
	2nd	0.00%	0.00%	0.00%	0.00%
	3rd	0.00%	1.60%	0.00%	0.50%
	Total	0.00%	1.60%	0.00%	0.50%
Hidden Financiers	1st	0.00%	0.00%	0.00%	0.00%
	2nd	6.30%	6.60%	2.60%	5.70%
	3rd	1.10%	0.00%	0.00%	0.50%
	Total	7.40%	6.60%	2.60%	6.20%

12.2.10. Pressure to Change of Statuary Law/Acts

In India, district has been the unit of administration and the collector has been given hundreds of enumerated powers under different laws and rules. These excessive and unmanageable, unbelievable powers of the collector make him prime target for the political pressure. During colonial rule, it was suitable for them, as imperial power wants to control all the officers from one point. Now it is irreverent and has become a major cause of absolute rampant corruption. Not only the present incumbent with heavy doses of arrogance are unsuitable for such powers, which make them inhumane and demigod to enslave whole technocrats and specialists about which these collectors have no practical knowledge and experience.

Imperial power does not want to give any power to Indian politicians, but now it is high time to give powers to elected head in the districts. How long we can enslave our own people through arrogant collectors. Now, these days officers openly assign these autocrat collectors worse than British exploiters. These collectors use every available law to abuse other district officers who refuse to become a party to immoral behavior or hand in glove with the collector to loot the public exchequers. What is the law and how it is used are two opposite poles. Excessive power provided in numerous acts and laws to the Deputy Commissioner/Collector makes it inevitable for a politician to approach him because the subordinate officials misuse the powers of the Deputy Commissioner/Collector without his consent or take it granted that the Deputy Commissioner/ Collector being busy or prone to frequent misguidance subordinates behave in the way they like, which become a major source of corruption and anguish for the politicians and public.

Colonial centralization of legal powers is the greatest area and source of creating political pressure on the law. Massive collapse of the revenue administration down to village level, commonly low concern and pervasive immoral behavior for such matters at the middle level. The control of the Deputy Commissioner/Collector in an allotment, eviction, of land and house sites, make it imperative for a politician to approach district level officers for redressing and action in legal matters and it becomes a big area for political pressure. Sweeping powers of the Deputy Commissioner/Collector to drop action against the land grabbers, mafias, smugglers in essential commodities Act, food grains movements (some states), hoarders, black marketers, Panchayat Act, common lands, and government properties make him the first target for pressure mobilization. These district-level politicians and businesspersons are the fundraiser for the politicians and district-level officers.

With changing time and frequent militancy, changing attitude towards law and order, increased attempts to contain various activities and conflicting groups claims, justice itself becomes the benefit that different government must allocate to competing claimants. The delivery of justice has become the greatest area for political pressure because it has become rare and unattainable without pressure due to total loss of faith from the bureaucracy. The All India Services Officers have grossly failed to deliver the justice to masses for whom they were supposed to work, not to talk of common people even other officers of the same government are denied justice without bribing or strenuous efforts. In such a scenario, common people have no option except to request a politician for delivery of justice.

Legislation formulation is the prerogative of the politicians, but the involvement of the bureaucratic system is pervasive across the depth and breadth of the law. Ruling political party commonly uses the bureaucratic system towards formulation and change of law and Acts to meet their own future and present needs. Mean (2.62), median (2) and modal (2) values indicate that political pressure is exerted 'sometimes' for change of Law and Acts. 94.5% of the Indian Police Service officers, 83.9% of the Indian Administrative Service officers, 65.4% of the Indian Forest Service officers, and 82.7% of the All India Services Officers get 'sometimes' to 'frequent' intensity of political pressure for a change of Law and Acts. Our results are significant, with a Pearson Chi-square value of 63.188 showings 0.000, level of significance. Spearman's negative correlation value of –0.304 is significant with a 0.000, level of significance. This indicates that there is a good relationship between decision and political pressure for a change of Law and Acts.

People exert pressure on their political leaders regarding framing a law so that local resources and local culture can be preserved and conserved from depredation by external forces. Median (2), mode (2), and mean (2.25) values indicate that only 'sometimes' political pressure is exerted for the formulation of a new law for the conservation of resources and culture. 63% of the All India Services Officers, 75.3% of the Indian Police Service officers, 57% of the Indian Forest Service officers, and 54.1% of the Indian Administrative Service officers get 'sometimes' to 'rarely' intensity of political pressure for the formulation of new legislation towards conservation and preservation of local resources and culture. Research results indicate that neither politicians nor bureaucrats bother towards conservation of resources and culture of local areas. Association of pressure for making law towards conservation of resources and decision is shown by the Pearson Chi-square analysis. Our results are significant with a 0.002, level of significance.

Exhibit Number 12.29: Intensity of Political Pressure by Change of Law and Acts

Service Name	Pressure Intensity	Law/Acts	New Law for Culture	Social Needs	Clientele Needs	Political Goals	Safeguard Interest
		330	331	332	333	334	335
I.A.S.	'always'	4.8	1.6	3.4	18.5	38.1	32.7
	'mostly'	11.3	11.5	8.6	29.2	28.6	20
	'frequently'	61.3	32.8	17.2	21.5	27	36.4
	'sometimes'	22.6	34.4	44.8	29.2	4.8	9.1
	'rarely'	0	19.7	25.9	1.5	1.6	1.8

Service Name	Pressure Intensity	Law/Acts	New Law for Culture	Social Needs	Clientele Needs	Political Goals	Safeguard Interest
		330	331	332	333	334	335
I.P.S.	'always'	4.1	0	0	26.4	13.3	31.3
	'mostly'	1.4	3.2	1.1	35.6	26..5	15
	'frequently'	23.3	21.5	18.3	17.2	26.5	25
	'sometimes'	71.2	38.7	34.4	17.2	24.1	17.5
	'rarely'	0	36.6	46.2	3.4	3.3	11.3
I.F.S.	'always'	5.8	8	6.9	9.2	16	13.3
	'mostly'	13.5	13	26.7	23.5	28	31.6
	'frequently'	19.2	22	23.8	40.8	28	21.4
	'sometimes'	46.2	32	27.7	16.3	18	17.3
	'rarely'	15.4	25	14.9	10.2	10	16.3
AISO	'always'	4.8	3.5	3.6	17.6	20.7	24
	'mostly'	8	9.1	13.1	29.2	27.6	23.2
	'frequently'	34.8	24.4	20.2	27.6	27.2	26.2
Total	'sometimes'	48.1	35	34.1	20	16.7	15.5
	'rarely'	4.3	28	29	5.6	7.7	11.2
Ranking			5	4	3	2	1
All Figures Except Ranking are in %							

The socio-economic development process demands change in the law to meet the needs and demands of large social groups. People may pressurize politicians to frame a law to protect the interests of dominant group interests. Mean (2.28), median (2) and modal (2) values indicate that 'sometimes' political pressure is exerted for incorporating law to meet changing needs to extend benefits to large social groups. 63.1% of the All India Services Officers, 80.6% of the Indian Police Service officers, and 70.7% of the Indian Administrative Service officers feel that political pressure is exerted 'sometimes' to 'rarely' category for formulating a law to meet changing social needs. 61.5% of the Indian Forest Service officers come across 'sometimes' to 'frequent' political pressure for the law relating to meet changing social needs. Pearson Chi-square value of 52.937 with the degree of freedom at 8, and level of significance of 0.000, indicating that law to meet changing social needs and decision-making process has a good association. This association strength is indicated by the Pearson's correlation and Spearman correlation value of 0.3, with a 0.000, level of significance.

Politicians get pressure from the public and interested groups to exert political pressure on the All India Services Officers to implement the law in such a manner that it serves their clientele needs/interests. The mean value of 3.31 and modal value of 4; indicate that 'most often' political pressure is exerted for implementing the law to serve clientele needs. 56.8% of the All India

Services Officers and 64.3% of the Indian Forest Service officers get political pressure 'most often' to 'frequently' intensity to implement the law to serve the interests of the beneficiaries. 62% of the Indian Police Service officers come across political pressure 'always' to 'most often' category to implement law according to meet the clientele needs. Police officers' maximum political pressure for clientele-oriented maintenance of law. 50.7% of the Indian Administrative Service officers get political pressure 'most often' to 'frequent' intensity, but the second-highest score of 29.2% is also located in 'sometimes' intensity, this indicates that for clientele-oriented political pressure in implementation of the law, these officers get the least pressure. Our results are significant with a Pearson Chi-square value of 30.721 and a level of significance at 0.000. Spearman correlation shows a negative value with a 0.04, level of significance.

The political party in power pressurize the All India Services Officers for amending, ignoring, and circumventing the law, when they find it difficult; they initiate amendment in the law to serve political goals. Mean (3.36), mode (3) and median (3) values indicate that political pressure is exerted 'frequently' for ignoring the law to meet political goals. 54.8% of the All India Services Officers, 56% of the Indian Forest Service officers, and 53% of the Indian Police Service officers get 'most often' to 'frequent' political pressure for circumventing the law to serve the goals of the political party in power. 66.7% of the Indian Administrative Service officers come across political pressure 'always' to 'most often' category for amendment of the law to serve interests of the party in power. Pearson Chi-square value of 26.718 with a level of significance of 0.001, indicates a good association of decision with the political pressure for ignoring and changing the law to serve party goals. This relationship strength is indicated by Pearson's correlation value of –0.223, with a 0.000, level of significance. Our results are significant and show that political pressure in the implementation of the law for political interests will affect the quality of the decision delivered by the All India Services Officers.

When politicians realize that existing law is not enough to serve their political interests, in another situation, existing law may cause the problem to them in the future; they frame new legislation to derive mileage out of that and ensure the protection of political interests by new laws. 31.3% of the Indian Police Service officers get political pressure 'always' for framing new legislation to safeguard political interests. 31.6% of the Indian Forest Service officers 'most often' get political pressure for framing a new law to extract political mileage from it. 89.1% of the Indian Administrative Service officers get political pressure 'always' to 'frequently' intensity for framing a new law to safeguard political interests. The Indian Administrative Service officers get the highest political pressure in connection with the formulation of new legislation to meet the political goals and interests. Mean 3.32, mode 3, median 3 values indicate 'frequently' this variable is used for self gains by the politicians in bureaucracy. Political interests in law and the decision-making process have a good association, this is indicated by the Pearson Chi-square value of 28.092, which is significant with a 0.000, level of significance. Pearson's negative correlation is significant with a 0.003, level of significance.

Research data analyses placed at Exhibit 12.30 indicate the intensity of political pressure of different sources being exerted on Law and Acts implementation decisions by the AISO and its ranking. The intensity of pressure in 1st priority indicates the Centre/State Minister score of 49.4% on the AISO, 66.3% on the IPS, 48% on the IAS, and 23.8% on the IFS are at the first position. In the second position, pressure intensity in 1st priority comes from the PM/CM level for law and acts and the intensity measured is 23.4% on the AISO, 33.3% on the IFS, 21.6%

on the IPS, and 20.6% on the IAS. Results clearly indicate the interferences of politicians in the formulation and implementation of Laws and Acts for political gains. Pressure decrease in 2nd and 3rd priority from the PM/CM and the Ministers level but from other sources it increases in 2nd and 3rd priority.

Respondents' number (frequency) in three priorities is not the same, because every respondent has not mentioned all three priority (1st, 2nd, and 3rd) ranking. Due to this variability in cumulative/ additive total of three priorities may be a little skewed, we added together three priorities (based on answered numbers) and intensity of pressure in three priorities from different sources of pressure indicates different story. The Centre/State Ministers additive score indicates 85% on the AISO, 94% on the IPS, 84.6% on the IAS, and 71.7% on the IFS at the first position. The second position in this additive category pressure source from the MLA/MLC and intensity measured 65.3% on the AISO, 72.3% on the IPS, 63.6% on the IFS, and 60.5% on the IAS on a decision relating to areas of Law and Act issues. Other sources of pressure on the AISO are ranked as the district-level politicians 52% at third position, the PM/CM 27.4% at fourth position, the Member of Parliament 26.4% at fifth position.

Exhibit Number 12.30: Priority Ranking of Sources of Pressure for Laws and Acts Areas

Pressure Source	Priority Rank	IAS	IPS	IFS	AIS
PM/CM	1st	20.60%	21.60%	33.30%	23.40%
	2nd	1.00%	4.10%	0.00%	1.90%
	3rd	0.00%	3.10%	5.60%	2.10%
	Total	21.60%	28.80%	38.90%	27.40%
Centre/State Minister	1st	48.00%	66.30%	23.80%	49.40%
	2nd	26.50%	23.00%	36.80%	27.10%
	3rd	10.10%	4.70%	11.10%	8.50%
	Total	84.60%	94.00%	71.70%	85.00%
Member of Parliament	1st	2.00%	0.00%	0.00%	0.90%
	2nd	10.80%	10.80%	10.50%	10.70%
	3rd	20.20%	7.80%	13.90%	14.80%
	Total	33.00%	18.60%	24.40%	26.40%
MLA/MLC	1st	9.80%	2.70%	11.90%	7.80%
	2nd	29.40%	44.60%	21.10%	33.20%
	3rd	21.30%	25.00%	30.60%	24.30%
	Total	60.50%	72.30%	63.60%	65.30%
Zila Parishad/District-level Politicians	1st	13.70%	5.40%	21.40%	12.40%
	2nd	11.80%	4.10%	10.50%	8.90%
	3rd	27.00%	46.90%	11.10%	30.70%
	Total	52.50%	56.40%	43.00%	52.00%

Pressure Source	Priority Rank	IAS	IPS	IFS	AIS
Block Samiti/Block-level Politicians	1st				
	2nd	13.70%	6.80%	15.80%	11.70%
	3rd	1.10%	0.00%	0.00%	0.50%
	Total	14.80%	6.80%	15.80%	12.20%
Village Heads/Grassroot-level Worker	1st	0.00%	0.00%	0.00%	0.00%
	2nd	0.00%	0.00%	0.00%	0.00%
	3rd	15.70%	7.80%	27.80%	15.40%
	Total	15.70%	7.80%	27.80%	15.40%
Power Brokers/Touts	1st				
	2nd	0.00%	0.00%	2.60%	0.50%
	3rd	1.10%	3.10%	0.00%	1.60%
	Total	1.10%	3.10%	2.60%	2.10%
Communication Media	1st	5.90%	4.10%	7.10%	5.50%
	2nd	1.00%	0.00%	0.00%	0.50%
	3rd	1.10%	1.60%	0.00%	1.10%
	Total	8.00%	5.70%	7.10%	7.10%
Hidden Financiers	1st	0.00%	0.00%	2.40%	0.50%
	2nd	5.90%	6.80%	2.60%	5.60%
	3rd	2.20%	0.00%	0.00%	1.10%
	Total	8.10%	6.80%	5.00%	7.20%

12.2.11. Pressure to Demure in Decision Process for Own Advantage

Politicians pressurize the All India Services Officers to take a favorable decision or unfavorable decision to a particular party or delay the announcement of any decision. Postponement of the desirable or undesirable decision can serve politician goals in many ways and purposes. Politicians get time for manipulations and increase the value and stakes from the outcome of such decisions. In case an opposition party is going to get an advantage from the decision, the politician pressurizes to delay such decisions so that the affected party can extract minimum benefit from the decision. On many occasions, the ruling party go in appeal or mobilize support and pressure to negate such decisions, which they expect will benefit the opponents. Demur in the decision process is of vital importance to politicians, it has tremendous financial potential to enhance stakes, and extract self-benefits.

Elitist scheme of delay and diversion of decisions have proven more successful in wrecking the progress of development works than surreptitious collusion with political leadership. On the pretext of obliging political power, bureaucrats delay the decision for infinity to their self-advantage. The process of delay is used as an engine for the attainment and promotion of ulterior political designs and motives. Delay decision for something to extract out of it, delay for not doing something, delay to get something else done, delay to maintain goodwill with other party, connotations of delay vary from position to place correlated with time and space.

Multi-accountability to non-accountability in the All India Services is the obstacle to bold and innovative decisions. Politicians exercise its influence to delay decisions at subdivision level and district level to divert benefits to own people or to mobilize support instead of such decisions. Politicians try to encashment every decision in his favor. On many occasions, a routine administrative decision is delayed to the extent that the politician himself comes to announce such a decision and impress upon the public as if, this decision has been got done by him. Any negative decision is got delayed to avoid its impact during a particular time of election or people's support. Politicians get delayed many decisions at Regional Commissioner, Head of Department and Secretary levels, such policy decisions are again delayed to get both positive and negative mileage out of such decisions, as demanded by the situations.

Chief Secretary and Cabinet Secretary levels manipulations and delay in a decision are of wider repercussions and long-term ramifications. Any policy decision, which may not be beneficial at a particular point in time, may be delayed in an announcement. Before elections, all such negative decision is deferred until a post-election time and announced slowly. Some decisions are delayed and announced just before the elections so that politicians can impress upon the public to get higher support and vote in lieu of such routine administrative decisions. Physical and financial allocation decisions are often manipulated by the politicians and only announced according to political suitability to extract maximum benefit out of it. Target allocation and achievement of such targets is mostly politicized and the politicians according to political suitability announce all such routine administrative works. The bureaucratic system has become a pawn in the hands of politicians, individual officers at their own approach to the political leadership to win the confidence of politicians and misguide them for self-goals.

Politicians pressurized the All India Services Officers for taking a favorable or unfavorable decision, postponing or keeping decisions pending pertaining to different matters of their interest. Mean 3.39, mode 3, and median 3 values indicate that political pressure is exerted 'frequently' for demur in the decision process. Demur in the decision process has a good association with the decision-making process. This is shown by the Pearson Chi-square results, which are significant at a significance level of 0.000, and the value of 32.988. Pearson's negative correlation is significant, and the relationship is good with the decision. The highest score indicates that 37.4% of the All India Services Officers, 51.2% of the Indian Police Service officers, and 33.3% of the Indian Forest Service officers get political pressure 'frequently' to delay the announcement of the decision. 45.8% of the Indian Administrative Service officers come across political pressure 'most often' for delaying the decisions.

Politicians pressurize the All India Services Officers to delay different issues relating to elections; as fixing the election schedule and date, deciding the eligibility conditions for various elections, fixing the place and process of nomination for election, declaration of results for the elections, the decision relating to recounting and many more issues related with the elections. The mean value of 3.52 and median of 3.5; indicate that 'most often' political pressure is exerted for the issues related to the elections. 59.6% of the Indian Administrative Service officers 'always' to 'most often' category get political pressure in the process of election and different issues related to them. 62.1% of the Indian Police Service officers, 58.1% of the Indian Forest Service officers get 'most often' to 'frequent' intensity of political pressure during the election and work-related with them. The score for the All India Services Officers shows that 35.2% of them get 'frequent' political pressure and 26.1% of them get political pressure 'always' in a subject related to elections. Our results indicate that political pressure is exerted 'most often' in the decisions related to the elections.

Exhibit Number 12.31: Intensity of Political Pressure by Demur in Decision Process

Service Name	Pressure Intensity	Demure Decision	Election Related	Tenders Related	Land Allotment	Services Matters	Crime Related
		336	337	338	339	340	341
I.A.S.	'always'	20.8	29.8	25.8	26.2	13.1	10
	'mostly'	45.8	29.8	24.2	26.2	27.9	20
	'frequently'	31.3	28.1	33.3	31.1	29.5	48.3
	'sometimes'	2.1	7	4.5	4.9	21.3	10
	'rarely'	0	5.3	12.1	11.5	8.2	11.7
I.P.S.	'always'	14.6	28.7	7.5	1.5	0	30.1
	'mostly'	2.4	23	2.2	0	2.7	44.1
	'frequently'	51.2	39.1	26.9	9	20.3	8.6
	'sometimes'	29.3	1.1	33.3	31.3	33.8	7.5
	'rarely'	2.4	8	30.1	58.2	43.2	9.7
I.F.S.	'always'	21.2	20.9	18.4	147.4	4.1	11.3
	'mostly'	24.2	22.1	28.6	32	17.5	22.7
	'frequently'	33.3	36	26.5	23.7	37.1	29.9
	'sometimes'	16.7	11.6	12.2	17.5	26.8	20.6
	'rarely'	4.5	9.3	14.3	12.4	14.4	15.5
AISO	'always'	19.4	26.1	16.3	13.8	5.2	18
	'mostly'	25.2	24.3	17.9	20.9	15.5	30
	'frequently'	37.4	35.2	28.4	21.3	29.7	26.4
Total	'sometimes'	15.5	6.5	17.9	18.2	27.6	13.2
	'rarely'	2.6	7.8	19.5	25.8	22	12.4
Ranking			1	3	4	5	2
All Figures Except Ranking are in %							

The government bureaucratic system executes various developmental works through tenders, decisions at different stages towards execution of such works is delayed to get pleasure and appreciation from the public or to avoid the displeasure of the people. Mean 2.93, mode 3, and median 3 values indicate that political pressure is exerted 'frequently' to delay the execution of works. 46.3% of the All India Services Officers get 'frequent' to 'most often' intensity of political pressure to delay the tender for the execution of works. 57.5% of the Indian Administrative Service officers and 56.1% of the Indian Forest Service officers come across 'most often' to 'frequent' category political pressure in the execution of work to avoid public wrath. The Indian Police Service officers get the least political pressure in this variable, 63.4% of them get 'sometimes' to 'rarely' intensity of political pressure for delay of execution of works. This may be due to the low involvement of police officers in development works. Our results are significant, with a Pearson Chi-square value of 58.915, and 0.000, level of significance.

Government revenue land and village *Panchayat* land are under the direct or indirect supervision of the Deputy Commissioner/Collector of the concerned district. Politicians exert pressure for allotment and distribution of land-related aspects on the All India Services Officers, 25.8% of them get 'rarely' political pressure, and 42.2% of them get 'most often' to 'frequent' intensity of pressure. 55.7% of the Indian Forest Service officers and 57.3% of the Indian Administrative Service officers get the 'most often' to 'frequent' category of political pressure for the land-related aspects. 58.2% of the Indian Police Service officers get 'rarely' political pressure related to the allotment and distribution of the land. The lowest political pressure on the police officer may be due to fact that they are lesser involved in the process of land allotment. Only disputes and wrangling related land come to them. Pearson Chi-square value is 93.799, with a level of significance of 0.000. This indicates a good association between delay in land allotment matters and the decision-making process.

Day-to-day administration decisions are taken by the All India Services Officers, politicians are under pressure to extract benefits out of decisions for different issues related to the services and employees. On many occasions, delays help them to convert decisions into monetary terms. Mean 2.55, mode 3, and median 3 values indicate that political pressure is exerted 'frequently' to extract monetary benefits by delaying decisions relating to service matters. 57.4% of the Indian Administrative Service officers get 'most often' to 'frequent' intensity of political pressure to delay service decisions, so that politician can en-cash those decisions. 63.9% of the Indian Forest Service officers and 57.3% of the All India Services Officers get 'frequent' to 'sometimes' intensity of political pressure for delaying the administrative decisions so that politicians can get monetary benefits. But police officers get the least political pressure, 77% of them get it 'rarely' to 'sometimes' category only. The Indian Administrative Service officers get the highest political pressure and they are the most helpful to the politicians for encashment of delay in decisions. This delay shows a good association with the decision process; and Pearson Chi-square results are significant with a 0.000, level of significance. Pearson's correlation and Spearman's correlation show a negative relationship with the decision.

Whenever some crime is committed by any person, the first thing they do is to mobilize a group of influential persons, who can pressurize politicians, in turn, politicians pass political pressure on the All India Services Officers to save such persons under pressure from such groups. Mean 3.27, median 3 and modal 4 values indicate that political pressure is exerted 'frequently' to 'most often' to save a certain group of people. The Indian Police Service officers get the highest political pressure for the crime-related issues, 74.2% of them get 'most often' to 'always' intensity of political pressure to save the group of persons in crime-related aspects. 68.3% of the Indian Administrative Service officers, 52.6% of the Indian Forest Service officers, and 56.4% of the All India Services Officers get political pressure 'frequent' to the 'most often' category to save certain persons in the crime. Pearson Chi-square value of 52.616, with 8 degree of freedom, and

0.000, level of significance indicate that our results are significant. The pressure to save a group of persons have a good relationship with the decision-making process.

Exhibit Number 12.32: Priority Ranking of Sources of Pressure for Demure in Decision Areas

Pressure Source	Priority Rank	IAS	IPS	IFS	AIS
PM/CM	1st	4.30%	8.30%	9.80%	6.80%
	2nd	0.00%	3.10%	10.00%	2.80%
	3rd	11.40%	7.40%	11.50%	10.00%
	Total	15.70%	18.80%	31.30%	19.60%
Centre/State Minister	1st	54.80%	45.80%	43.90%	49.50%
	2nd	8.50%	7.80%	3.30%	7.40%
	3rd	18.60%	32.40%	11.50%	22.70%
	Total	81.90%	86.00%	58.70%	79.60%
Member Parliament	1st	0.00%	0.00%	7.30%	1.50%
	2nd	17.10%	9.40%	13.30%	13.60%
	3rd	4.30%	9.30%	11.50%	7.30%
	Total	21.40%	18.70%	32.10%	22.40%
MLA/MLC	1st	19.40%	11.10%	24.40%	17.50%
	2nd	48.80%	60.90%	43.30%	52.30%
	3rd	31.40%	29.60%	34.60%	31.30%
	Total	99.60%	101.60%	102.30%	101.10%
Zila Parishad/District-level Politicians	1st	12.90%	25.00%	4.90%	15.50%
	2nd	24.40%	17.20%	26.70%	22.20%
	3rd	11.40%	7.40%	11.50%	10.00%
	Total	48.70%	49.60%	43.10%	47.70%
Block Samiti/Block-level Politicians	1st	8.60%	9.70%	7.30%	8.70%
	2nd	1.20%	1.60%	0.00%	1.20%
	3rd	22.90%	11.10%	19.20%	18.00%
	Total	32.70%	22.40%	26.50%	27.90%
Village Heads/Grassroot-level Worker	1st	0.00%	0.00%	0.00%	0.00%
	2nd	0.00%	0.00%	0.00%	0.00%
	3rd	0.00%	1.90%	3.80%	1.30%
	Total	0.00%	1.90%	3.80%	1.30%

Pressure Source	Priority Rank	IAS	IPS	IFS	AIS
Power Brokers/Touts	1st	0.00%	0.00%	0.00%	0.00%
	2nd	0.00%	0.00%	3.30%	0.60%
	3rd	1.40%	0.00%	0.00%	0.70%
	Total	1.40%	0.00%	3.30%	1.30%
Communication Media	1st				
	2nd				
	3rd				
	Total				
Hidden Financiers	1st	0.00%	0.00%	2.40%	0.50%
	2nd	0.00%	0.00%	0.00%	0.00%
	3rd	1.40%	3.70%	0.00%	2.00%
	Total	1.40%	3.70%	2.40%	2.50%

Our results relating to political pressure exerted on All India Services Officers in crime-related issues show that it is a common phenomenon. Nexus or syndicate has been developed among the bureaucrats, politicians, and crime-related issues.

Research data analyses results paced at Exhibit 12.32 indicates that the Centre/State Ministers exert the highest intensity of political pressure on demure in decision process-related issues and the AISO have ranked this intensity 49.5% on the AISO, 54.8% on the IAS, 45.8% on the IPS and 43.9% on the IFS. The MLA/MLC intensity of pressure on demure in decision process-related issues in 1st priority results show 17.5% on the AISO, 24.4% on the IFS, 19.4% on the IAS, and 11.1% on the IPS. Third and fourth position in 1st priority goes to the district-level politicians and the PM/CM level pressure for demure in decision process-related issues.

Respondents' number (frequency) in three priorities is not the same, because every respondent has not mentioned all three priority (1st, 2nd, and 3rd) ranking. Due to this variability in a cumulative total of three priorities may be a little skewed. We added together three priorities (based on answered numbers), this cumulative addition of three priorities expressed by the AISO indicates that the highest pressure the MLA/MLC in 2nd priority and 3rd priority and IFS and IPS get the very high intensity of pressure for demure in decision-related issues. In order of positions of different sources of pressure; the Centre/State Ministers at second, the district-level politicians at third, the block-level politicians at fourth, and the Members of Parliaments at fifth position in exerting pressure on the AISO decisions related to delay in decision-related issues. The higher intensity of political pressure on the IPS may be due to delay in decisions related to legal and crime related issues. Political pressure on the IFS indicates how perilous the conservation of forests, wildlife, and our environment is. Perhaps diversion of forest land for non-forestry purposes may be a major reason for the high intensity of political pressure on the forests department.

12.2.12. Pressure on Development Works to Take Political Advantage

"Although many rural administrators seemed to able enough and dedicated to the goals of development plans, they appeared also to be heavily constrained, and sometimes virtually immobilized, by red tape; all public bureaucracies are necessarily bound by rules, of course, procedural control within which these administrators had to work seemed exceptionally stultifying.... The head of the district administration appeared to preside over these people from a great height, on very occasionally appearing amongst them in villages; he seemed to be concerned to ensure the maintenance of the rules yet he appeared not bound by them himself. He seemed to hold the key to the whole structure," D.C. Potter, 1986.

In the recent past, a large number of programs and schemes were formulated for development, which requires high inputs from a specialist and needs expert technical knowledge. The Indian Administrative Service officers have diverted those schemes implementation through them only, which have created antipathy among specialist. The bureaucratic system ensured the failure of most of such programs. At the district level, most of the technical officers have been discontented regarding their supervision and control passed on to the arrogant, Indian Administrative Service officers, who were not familiar with technical aspects for implementation of such schemes. We have heard a large number of stories, whereas Deputy Commissioner behaved in an illogical and irrelevant manner regarding the execution of technical works, irrespective of technical specifications and parameters.

How power holders change millions of years old law of nature just in few minutes on papers, in a review meeting in Government of India, once Deputy Commissioners were requested to send projects for Watershed Development along with clearly delineate proposed Watersheds in their states. Without knowing and understanding the scientific parameters of a watershed, one Deputy Commissioner said, "He has formed the 10 watersheds (writing 10 names of towns on a piece of paper", whereas the whole proposed area was a part of one watershed only in his districts and requested funds for that. Mockery of the system is that persons, who do not know even the definition of technical aspects, are the heading or made in charge of the department, and funds are put at their disposal. This ensures the surrogating of the specialists, failures of development work, and complete collapse of technicalities in the process.

The Indian Administrative Service as "Institution fit was poor when viewed more broadly in governance. As it has been suggested, the ICS (IAS) as an institution within a democratic federal constitution committed to the development, set up contradictions that had unfortunate administrative consequences more generally-preoccupation with the political demoralization amongst technical specialists in the civil service denied access to the top posts. And so on. Despite tensions, the IAS was still firmly in position," D.C. Potter, 1986.

Story of an Indian Administrative Service officer, who was head of DRDA, full of arrogance, rebuked an engineer and threatened to charge sheet him. Saying, why this R.C.C. pipe is costlier than C.C. pipes, when both are made of cement, to inflate the price you have added one 'R' to it.... That Indian Administrative Service officer does not know the difference between Cement Concrete and Reinforcement Cement Concrete pipe, but he was competent to incur expenditure for crores of rupees for this purpose. In another story, one Indian Administrative Service officers were boasting, "He reduced the cost of a drinking water supply project by 30%". After some time, the concerned engineer told his successor that people are not getting water even after the completion of the project. Because your predecessor reduced the size of the supply pipe to such a low level that because of the it—installed pipe is not sufficient to meet the water need of the town. Another new project has to be approved with a three-time hike in the cost and people remained without water and suffered for years in this process. Generalist hegemony is destroying social fabrics, delaying progress, and creating room for immoral behavior.

"The whole posture of the ICS traditions resulted in celebrations of amateur generalists in control at each level, thereby defining specialist expertise and innovation as somewhat peripheral and less rewarding. Any parliamentary democracy requires both generalist and specialist civil servants at tap equally for the political leadership of the day. As for receptiveness to local demands, rapid movements from one type of control posts to another, utterly appropriate for gentlemanly amateurs, tended both to produce administrative fragmentation between mobile officers and more stationery civil servants at lower levels and to incline the IAS to identify primarily the center, not the loyalty," David C.

Exhibit Number 12.33: Intensity of Political Pressure through Development Work-Related Issues

Service Name	Pressure Intensity	Development Related	Loans Subsidies	New Projects	Sanction Programms	Upgrade Infrastructure	Open New Things
		342	343	344	345	346	347
I.A.S.	'always'	19.2	32.8	22.7	23.9	28.8	32.3
	'mostly'	28.8	31	36.4	31.3	31.8	32.3
	'frequently'	28.8	19	21.2	25.4	12.1	6.5
	'sometimes'	21.2	10.3	13.6	16.4	25.8	29
	'rarely'	1.9	6.9	6.1	3	1.5	0
I.P.S.	'always'	0	18.5	9.8	8.6	8	1.4
	'mostly'	2	3.1	7.3	14	10.3	2.8
	'frequently'	19.6	9	41.5	29	16.1	16.7
	'sometimes'	66.7	43.1	29.3	29	39.1	54.2
	'rarely'	11.8	26.2	12.2	19.4	26.4	2522.2
I.F.S.	'always'	3.8	17.3	9.1	24	13	32.3
	'mostly'	21.2	17.3	31.3	25	31	21.2
	'frequently'	36.5	24.5	30.3	33	27	15.2
	'sometimes'	21.2	19.4	147.1	14	21	9.2
	'rarely'	17.3	21.4	15.2	4	8	18.5
AISO	'always'	7.7	21.7	13	18.5	15.4	23.2
	'mostly'	17.4	16.7	24.7	22.7	24.1	15.9
	'frequently'	28.4	18.6	31.6	29.6	19.4	30.9
Total	'sometimes'	36.1	24	19	20	28.5	11
	'rarely'	10.3	19	11.7	9.2	12.6	6
Ranking			2	5	3	4	1
All Figures Except Ranking are in %							

Politicians get a tremendous amount of pressure from the public of their constituency to get projects sanctioned for different development works for their voters. If such projects are sanctioned in the opponents' area, the public pressurizes politicians to get such works canceled also. Public approach politicians for getting new institutions in their area and request for up-gradation of existing facilities are also common. This indicates that for every work people approach politicians, this is the outcome of the absolute failure of the bureaucratic system. If the bureaucratic system and bureaucrats have been working impartially and with honesty, then the public could have entrusted faith in them and their decision. Total loss of faith from the bureaucratic system has forced masses to go to politicians for every kind of work, small or big, routine or special, or any kind of decision.

Mean (2.77) and median (3) values indicate that for development works political pressure is exerted 'frequently' on the All India Services Officers. 64.5% of the All India Services Officers and 86.3% of the Indian Police Service officers get political pressure 'sometimes' to 'frequently' category for development works. 57.7% of the Indian Forest Service officers and 57.6% of the Indian Administrative Service officers get 'most often' to 'frequent' intensity of political pressure towards development works. The Indian Administrative Service officers get marginal more political pressure than the Indian Forest Service officers for the issues pertaining to development in their jurisdiction. Pearson Chi-square value is 53.484 and is significant with a level of significance of 0.000. Political pressure for development work shows good association with the decision-making process. This relation is good and significant as shown by Pearson's correlation value of –0.259, with a 0.001, level of significance.

The government distributes and sanctions a lot of loans, grants, subsidies, and aids for different developmental works. For different areas and some activities, the government provides handsome subsidies, which are lucrative and in the form of easy money. Sanctioning, accepting, and rejecting such financial activities are full of political manipulations and mostly are sanctioned due to political pressure only. Median (3) and mean (2.98) values show that political pressure is exerted 'frequently' on the All India Services Officers towards sanctioning, accepting, or rejecting the request for loans, subsidies, aids, and grants.

Exhibit 12.33 shows that 63.8% of the Indian Administrative Service officers get political pressure 'always' to 'most often' intensity for sanctioning the loans and grants. The Indian Administrative Service officers get the highest political pressure in this variable. 69.3% of the Indian Police Service officers get political pressure 'sometimes' to 'rarely' category; least pressure is exerted on them, as they are not located in such positions where such loans are sanctioned. 43.9% of the Indian Forest Service officers and 43% of the All India Services Officers get political pressure 'frequently' to 'sometimes' intensity only. Pearson Chi-square value of 45.463, with 8 degree of freedom and 0.000, level of significance indicates that political pressure on sanctioning of loans and grants have good relation with the decision-making process. The strength of this relationship is shown by Pearson's negative correlation; our results are significant with a 0.003, level of significance.

Government formulates schemes/projects for developmental activities. People approach politicians for inclusion/exclusion of some areas for the applicability in such schemes/projects. When politicians come to know about such activities, they themselves approach the All India Services Officers for inclusion/exclusion of areas in the projects/schemes, so that benefits can reach desired areas and undesired areas are removed from the applicability zone of projects. Mean (3.08), median (3) and modal (3) values indicate that political pressure is exerted 'frequently' on the All India Services Officers for inclusion/exclusion of areas from the developmental activities. 70.8% of Indian Police Service officers get political pressure 'frequently' to 'sometimes', whereas 55.3% of the All India Services Officers get 'most often' to 'frequent' category of political pressure for applicability of schemes in specified areas. 59.1% of the Indian Administrative Service officers get political pressure 'always' to 'most often' intensity for inclusion/exclusion of areas in the schemes. 61.6% of the Indian Forest Service officers get political pressure 'most often' to the 'frequent' category. The Indian Administrative Service officers get the highest pressure for extension/removal of areas from the developmental activities list. This indicates that most of the developmental activities are carried out according to the whims and fancies of the politicians. The concepts of balanced development have been relegated to darkness and the bureaucratic system has failed to execute the developmental work based on the merit of the area. The All India Services Officers have completely surrendered in front of the politicians and they have replaced their duty with sycophancy and flattery. Our results are significant with a level of significance of 0.000, and a Pearson Chi-square value of 36.488. Association of political pressure for inclusion/exclusion of areas for development with the decision-making process is established by the Chi-square and the relationship is significant as shown by Pearson's correlation with the level of significance of 0.02.

Political pressure is exerted 'frequently' for <u>sanctioning the new programs and projects</u> as indicated by the mean (3.2), mode (3) and median (3) values. Politicians approach the All India Services Officers so that they get new programs and projects are sanctioned for the development of their areas. 52.3% of the All India Services Officers, 58% of the Indian Forest Service officers, and 56.7% of the Indian Administrative Service officers get political pressure 'most often' to 'frequent' intensity while sanctioning new projects and programs. The Indian Police Service officers get the least political pressure, as they are least related to such activities. Pearson Chi-square results are significant with 0.000, level of significance at 36.130 values. Political pressure in sanctioning new projects has a good association with the decision-making process.

Slowly, people have realized that the bureaucratic system has failed to deliver goods in time and based on merit, so they approach politicians for <u>up-gradation of existing infrastructure, facilities, and institutions</u>. However, the bureaucratic system could have routinely looked after this aspect and concerned departments must do upkeep and maintenance as a matter of routine administration. The All India Services Officers have failed to deliver the goods, so the public goes to politicians for uncommon and undesired issues pertaining to development. Median (3) and mean (3.01) values show that political pressure is required 'frequently' for up-gradation of existing infrastructure. 50.6% of the Indian Administrative Service officers get political pressure 'always' to 'most often' category for upgrading the existing facilities. Since the Indian Police Service officers are not located in places related to such decisions, so 65.5% of them get political pressure 'rarely' to 'sometimes' only. 58% of the Indian Forest Service officers get political pressure 'most often' to 'frequently' intensity for up-gradation of existing facilities and infrastructure. Pearson Chi-square value of 53.638, with 8 as a degree of freedom, shows a '0.000' level of significance. This indicates a good association of politician demand for up-gradation of existing institutions with the decision-making process.

Public approach senior officers in a bureaucratic system, when getting disappointed from these officers, they approach politicians for starting new institutions (mini-banks, dispensary, veterinary hospital, *Mahila Mandal,* etc.), opening a new school, construction of a new building in the village for public utilities (*Chopals*, religious place, cremation ground, cattle shade, etc.), construction of new road and canals for their area. The bureaucratic system has miserably failed to carry out its duties and fully surrendered in front of politicians to keep them happy to serve self-goals. Mean (3.05) and median (3) values show that political pressure is exerted 'frequently' for carrying out any new activity. 64.6% of the Indian Administrative Service officers and 55.5% of the Indian Forest Service officers get political pressure 'always' to 'most often' for the opening of new institutions, schools, new roads, and canals. The Indian Police Service officers are not located close to developmental activities, so they get the least political pressure, 69.2% of them get political pressure rarely to sometimes only. Our results are significant with a Pearson Chi-square value of 82.026, with 8 degree of freedom, and a 0.000, level of significance. This shows that political pressure for the opening of new institutions is related to the decision-making process.

Exhibit Number 12.34: Priority Ranking of Sources of Pressure for Developmental Works Areas

Pressure Source	Priority Rank	IAS	IPS	IFS	AIS
PM/CM	1st	1.80%	3.00%	0.00%	2.10%
	2nd	0.00%	1.30%	7.50%	1.70%
	3rd	4.80%	8.30%	7.90%	6.50%
	Total	6.60%	12.60%	15.40%	10.30%
Centre/State Minister	1st	31.90%	36.40%	39.10%	34.70%
	2nd	8.00%	6.50%	2.50%	6.50%
	3rd	19.20%	19.50%	13.20%	18.30%
	Total	59.10%	62.40%	54.80%	59.50%
Member Parliament	1st	15.00%	5.20%	13.00%	11.40%
	2nd	17.70%	10.40%	17.50%	15.20%
	3rd	5.80%	4.20%	7.90%	5.60%
	Total	38.50%	19.80%	38.40%	32.20%
MLA/MLC	1st	31.90%	36.40%	39.10%	34.70%
	2nd	45.10%	47.10%	47.00%	46.20%
	3rd	12.50%	16.00%	11.40%	13.80%
	Total	89.50%	99.50%	97.50%	94.70%
Zila Parishad/District-level Politicians	1st	9.70%	14.30%	10.90%	11.40%
	2nd	26.50%	33.80%	22.50%	28.30%
	3rd	32.70%	20.80%	28.90%	28.00%
	Total	68.90%	68.90%	62.30%	67.70%

Pressure Source	Priority Rank	IAS	IPS	IFS	AIS
Block Samiti/Block-level Politicians	1st	8.00%	20.80%	6.50%	11.90%
	2nd	2.70%	0.00%	0.00%	1.30%
	3rd	22.10%	15.30%	21.10%	19.60%
	Total	32.80%	36.10%	27.60%	32.80%
Village Heads/Grassroot-level Worker	1st	7.20%	5.20%	4.30%	5.90%
	2nd				
	3rd	1.00%	4.20%	2.60%	2.30%
	Total	8.20%	9.40%	6.90%	8.20%
Power Brokers/Touts	1st	0.00%	0.00%	2.20%	0.40%
	2nd				
	3rd	1.00%	2.80%	0.00%	1.40%
	Total	1.00%	2.80%	2.20%	1.80%
Communication Media	1st				
	2nd				
	3rd				
	Total				
Hidden Financiers	1st				
	2nd	0.00%	0.00%	2.50%	0.40%
	3rd	1.00%	0.00%	0.00%	0.50%
	Total	1.00%	0.00%	2.50%	0.90%

Statistical data analyses result for measuring the intensity of political pressure exerted by different sources of pressure on the developmental work-related issues are placed at Exhibit 12.34. The All India Services Officer measured the intensity of political pressure and observed that the highest pressure in 1st priority comes from the Centre/State Ministers and the MLA/MLC for the developmental-related issues and pressure intensity 34.7% on the AIS, 39.1% on the IFS, 36.4% on the IPS and 31.9% on the IAS. Data show in 1st priority ranking that political pressure from the block-level politicians at second position with an intensity of 11.9% on the AIS. Priority ranking patterns show increasing and decreasing trends with different sources of pressure. Developmental-related works are carried out in field areas. Where the district-level, the block-level, and the village/grassroot level persons are more concerned regarding these works. And our research results also show that the district-level politicians intensity of pressure on the AIS is (67.7%), the MLA/MLC pressure extent is 94.7% and the block-level politicians exert pressure 32.8% in variable trend as reflected in Exhibit 12.34. Respondents' number (frequency) in three priorities is not same, because not every respondent has mentioned all three priority (1st, 2nd, and 3rd) ranking, due to this variability in a cumulative total of three priorities may be little skewed, we added together three priorities (based on answered numbers).

12.2.13. Pressure on Crime-Related Issues for Political Advantage

Law and order is the major job of police people, but the other two services (IAS and IFS) are also related to the handling of crime in the discharge of their duties in their respective spheres. Of course, District Magistrate enjoys a lot of powers and exercises control in most of the issues relating to the law and order in the district. Subordinates of respective three All India Services are entrusted with powers of arrest and investigations under different Acts and Laws. Concerned officials have the powers to the detention individual up to a specified time. But the police of that area plays a major role in crime-related issues. "The police officer may levy a fee or receive a present for every duty he performs. The complainant has to often pay a fee for having his complaint recorded. He has to give the investigating officer a present to secure his prompt and earnest attention to the case," Police Commission Report, 1902-03, old observations are applicable on today also.

Exhibit Number 12.35: Intensity of Political Pressure on Crime-Related Issues

Service Name	Pressure Intensity	Crime Issues	Manipulate Arrest	Detention	Settling Score	FIR as Misuse	Grab Property
		348	349	350	351	352	353
I.A.S.	'always'	24.1	25	12.9	18	20.4	36.7
	'mostly'	31	25	29	31.1	24.1	18.4
	'frequently'	25.9	32.1	38.7	41	35.2	8.2
	'sometimes'	17.2	8.9	12.9	8.2	14.8	20.4
	'rarely'	1.7	8.9	6.5	1.6	5.6	16.3
I.P.S.	'always'	48.1	63.7	56.1	55.4	60.9	70.7
	'mostly'	27.3	12.1	24.4	13	21.7	7.6
	'frequently'	7.8	7.7	18.3	15.2	10.9	7.6
	'sometimes'	7.8	7.7	0	7.6	6.5	7.6
	'rarely'	9.1	8.8	1.2	8.7	0	6.5
I.F.S.	'always'	14	30.3	17.2	17.3	20.4	28.9
	'mostly'	38	25.8	20.2	26.5	23.5	20.6
	'frequently'	26	22.5	39.4	24.5	23.5	21.6
	'sometimes'	16	3.4	13.1	24.5	20.4	13.4
	'rarely'	6	18	10.1	7.1	12.2	15.5
AISO Total	'always'	31.4	41.9	29.2	31.5	35.7	46.6
	'mostly'	31.4	20.3	23.9	22.7	23	15.1
	'frequently'	18.4	19.1	32.1	25.1	21.3	13.4
	'sometimes'	13	6.4	8.6	14.3	13.9	12.6
	'rarely'	5.9	12.3	6.2	6.4	6.1	12.2
Ranking			2	5	4	3	1
All Figures Except Ranking are in %							

"To secure bias investigations, they like to shift blame from favored to the opposition party, distortion in a recording of statement to draw advantage out of it, cook up the case against innocent opponents, spoil evidence to save their party of interest, inbuilt procedural lacuna to lose evidence in favor of their interest to save them from prosecution, refuse to bail out accused in bailable cases or provide bail in non-bailable cases, not to take action in the lottery, prohibition, gambling, prostitution, traffic offences, the nexus between the police and the criminal has become open secret," K. Seshdri (1994).

We have discussed in previous units that how the strong nexus proliferates and spreads crime in the various areas. If every concerned official performs one's job honestly, incidences of crime will bound to be reduced to a great extent. But the crime has become business for the bureaucratic system. The business serves the self-goals only, so ultimately crime has become an instrument to serve the power holders in the bureaucratic system. Statistical results (Exhibit 12.35) show mean (3.68), median (4), and modal (4) values; which indicate that 'most often' political pressure is exerted on the issues related to the crime. 62.8% of the All India Services Officers, 75.4% of the Indian Police Service officers, and 55.1% of the Indian Administrative Service officers get political pressure 'always' to 'most often' intensity in crime-related issues. 64% of the Indian Forest Service officers get political pressure 'most often' to 'frequently' category in crime handling. Police officers get the highest political pressure in the handling of crime in their areas. The intensity of political pressure is very high in crime-related aspects, which in turn facilitate the spread of crime and these excessive political interferences adversely affect Police Officers to control crime-related issues. Pearson Chi-square value of 29.553, with 8 degree of freedom, and level of significance is '0.000'. This indicates a good association of political pressure in crime handling with the decision-making process.

People approach politicians for the arrest/release of particular person/s of their interests. Mean (3.72), median (4) and modal (5) values indicate that 'always' political pressure is exerted for the arrest/release of persons. 75.8% of the Indian Police Service officers get political pressure 'always' to 'most often' intensity for arrest and release of persons, in which politicians have interests. 56.1% of Indian Forest Service officers and 62.2% of the All India Services Officers get political pressure 'always' to 'most often' intensity for arrest and release of persons. 57.1% of the Indian Administrative Service officers get political pressure 'most often' intensity to 'frequently' in connection with release or arrest of persons. Pearson Chi-square values indicate a good association of political pressure for arrest and release with the decision-making process. Pearson Chi-square gives the value of 39.551, with 8 degree of freedom, and 0.000, level of significance.

It is often said that politicians exert political pressure based on considerations for detention/extension of individuals in custody; such considerations are open for wide interpretations and everlasting serious repercussions in the public and bureaucratic system. Mean (3.59), median (4) and modal (3) values indicate that political pressure is exerted 'frequently' for the individual based on considerations. 80.5% of the Indian Police Service officers think that they get political pressure 'always' to 'most often' intensity based on considerations. 67.7% of the Indian Administrative Service officers and 59.6% of the Indian Forest Service officers feel that political pressure exerted 'most often' to 'frequently' is based on the considerations. The All India Services Officers score indicates that 32.1% of them 'frequently' and 29.2% of them 'always' get political pressure based on considerations. Such considerations in political pressure have a good association with the decision-making process. Pearson Chi-square value of 55.896 is significant with a 0.000, level of significance.

It is commonly accused that government machinery is misused by the ruling party to settle scores and disputes to their own advantage. 67.4% of the Indian Police Service officers feel that 'always' to 'most often' government machinery is used for settling scores. 72.1% of the Indian Administrative Service officers and 51% of the Indian Forest Service officers get political pressure 'most often' to 'frequently' intensity to settle scores by using the government machinery. 31.5% of the All India Services Officers in highest score feel that politicians to settle their own scores with the opponents use 'always' government machinery. Mean (3.56), median (4) and modal (5) values indicate intensity of political pressure is exerted for this variable 'always' to 'most oftenly'. Pearson Chi-square value of 57.115, and 0.000, level of significance indicates a good association of politician use of official machinery with the decision-making process. Negative values of Pearson's correlation and Spearman correlation show a significant relationship with a 0.02, level of significance.

Whenever wheresoever crime is committed, a report has to be lodged in the nearest police station, so that, police can investigate the offense, and file a case for prosecution in the court of law based on the first investigation report (FIR). Politicians know how to misuse the ambiguity of law; people pressurize politicians to exert political pressure on the All India Services Officers for cancellation or registration of F.I.R. against persons of their choice. 58.7% of the All India Services Officers get political pressure 'always' to 'most often' intensity for cancellation or registration of F.I.R. 82.6% of the Indian Police Service officers get political pressure 'always' to 'most often' intensity for registration/cancellation of crime reports according to political whims. 59.3% of the Indian Administrative Service officers and 57% of the Indian Forest Service officers get political pressure 'frequent' to the 'most often' category pertaining to cancellation/registration of FIR pertaining to forest offenses. Police officers get the highest political pressure and the intensity of this pressure is very high to extent that it certainly hampers the proper and effective investigation in criminal cases. Mean (3.65), median (4) and modal (5) values indicate that political pressure intensity used is very high for this variable. Pearson Chi-square value of 54.449 is significant with a level of significance of 0.000. Political pressure relating to FIR cancellation/registration has a good association with the decision-making process. The strength of the relationship is shown by the Spearman negative correlation; results are significant with a 0.01, level of significance. Median, mean, and modal values indicate that always the intensity of political pressure is exerted for issues related to the F.I.R.

When a political party comes into power after elections, politicians and their workers start grabbing public property to achieve individual goals of self-benefits maximization or political goals. Modal value of 5, the median value of 4 and mean value of 3.70 ± 1.46 standard deviation, indicating that political pressure is exerted 'always' to 'most often' for grabbing government property to serve individual goals. The highest score indicates that political pressure is exerted 'always' on the officers of three services for grabbing public property to serve individual goals. 61.7% of the All India Services Officers, 70.7% of the Indian Police Service officers, 36.7% of the Indian Administrative Service officers, and 28.9% of the Indian Forest Service officers 'always' get political pressure for grabbing public property to meet individual interests. The Indian Police Service officers being in charge of police get the highest political pressure, this indicates that politicians and their workers grab the public property with the help of government machinery. Law enforcers act as a pawn in the hands of politicians and help in grabbing public property to serve individual goals. Pearson Chi-square results show a good association of political pressure for grabbing property to serve individual goals and the decision-making process. Pearson Chi-square analyses show a value of 41.096, with 8 degree of freedom and 0.000, level of significance.

Exhibit Number 12.36: Crime-Related Issues Pressure Types and Attitude of Family Members

Variable	Pressure Intensity		Attitude Family Members				Total
			Spouse	Children	Parents	Brother/ Sister	
Crime-Related Issues	'Rarely' pressure is exerted	Count	7	1	2	1	11
		% of Total	4.321	0.617	1.234	0.617	6.791
	'Sometimes' only pressure is exerted	Count	12	3	5	3	23
		% of Total	7.407	1.851	3.086	1.851	14.19
	'Frequently' pressure is exerted	Count	18	3	5		26
		% of Total	11.11	1.851	3.086		16.04
	'Most oftenly' pressure is exerted	Count	29	6	11	4	50
		% of Total	17.91	3.703	6.791	2.469	30.86
	'Always' pressure is exerted	Count	30	6	9	7	52
		% of Total	18.51	3.703	5.555	4.321	32.09
Total		Count	96	19	32	15	162
		% of Total	59.25	11.72	19.75	9.259	100

Statistical analyses result placed at Exhibit 12.36 and Chart 12.10 are related to crime-related issues variable and its relation to the All India Services officer family member's attitude role in the crime-related decision-making process. The All India Services officer receives maximum pressure from one's own spouse 59.29% and in second category parents, 19.75% exert pressure intensity, whereas pressure from brothers/sisters is minimal 9.2% only.

Research data statistical analyses placed at Exhibit 12.37 for the priority ranking of different sources of political pressure intensity measurement on the crime-related issues. Most of the crime-related issues happen in rural and undeveloped areas, intensity of pressure in 1st priority ranking also comes from the block-level politicians, 32.26% on the AISO, 4.1.4% on the IPS and IAS, and 17.1% on the IFS. In the second position, pressure comes from the Centre/State Ministers 22.1% on the AISO. Then in decreasing order pressure sources on the AISO are the MLA/MLC with 21.6% at third position, the district-level politicians with 15.4% at fourth position, and the PM/CM with 4.8% at fifth position in 1st priority.

Respondents' number (frequency) in three priorities is not the same, because every respondent has not mentioned all three priority (1st, 2nd, and 3rd) ranking. Due to this variability in a cumulative total of three priorities may be a little skewed, we added together three priorities (based on answered numbers), the cumulative aggregate of the intensity of pressure by adding three priorities. First position pressure comes from the MLA/MLC with 68% on the AISO, 72.9%

on the IPS, 88.3% on the IFS, and 87.1% on the IAS. In the second position, the pressure is being exerted from the district-level politicians; pressure intensity is 68% on the AISO, 72.9% on the IPS, 66.7% on the IAS, and 62.7% on the IFS officer for the crime-related issues. The block-level politicians exert pressure at the third position in this category with 49.66% on the AISO. Three AISO deals with crime-related issues but law and order is the major arena for the IPS Officers and maximum pressure is being exerted on them with high intensity, which is not good for control of crime-related issues and deserves detailed research in this area.

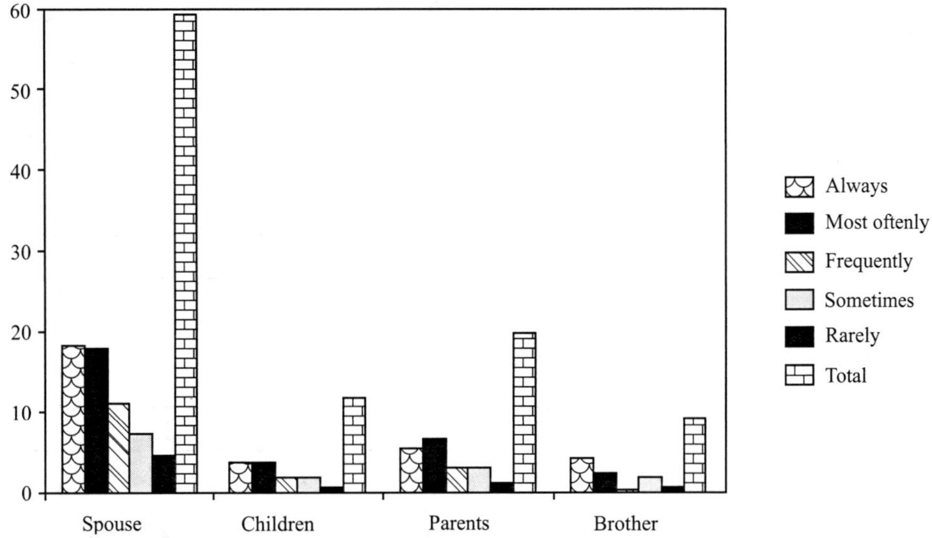

Chart No. 12.10: The Attitude of Family Members and Crime-Related Issues in Pressure

Exhibit Number 12.37: Priority Ranking of Sources of Pressure for Crime-Related Areas

Pressure Source	Priority Rank	IAS	IPS	IFS	AIS
PM/CM	1st	7.20%	1.40%	4.90%	4.80%
	2nd	5.60%	11.60%	10.80%	8.70%
	3rd	1.20%	1.60%	6.50%	2.30%
	Total	14.00%	14.60%	22.20%	15.80%
Centre/State Minister	1st	25.80%	21.40%	14.60%	22.10%
	2nd	10.10%	11.60%	27.00%	13.80%
	3rd	11.00%	15.60%	3.20%	11.30%
	Total	46.90%	48.60%	44.80%	47.20%
Member of Parliament	1st				
	2nd	7.90%	1.40%	0.00%	4.10%
	3rd	9.80%	4.70%	12.90%	8.50%
	Total	17.70%	6.10%	12.90%	12.60%

Pressure Source	Priority Rank	IAS	IPS	IFS	AIS
MLA/MLC	1st	19.60%	12.90%	41.50%	21.60%
	2nd	23.60%	20.30%	8.10%	19.50%
	3rd	43.90%	50.00%	38.70%	45.20%
	Total	87.10%	83.20%	88.30%	86.30%
Zila Parishad/District-level Politicians	1st	14.40%	20.00%	9.80%	15.40%
	2nd	43.80%	43.50%	43.20%	43.60%
	3rd	8.50%	9.40%	9.70%	9.00%
	Total	66.70%	72.90%	62.70%	68.00%
Block Samiti/Block-level Politicians	1st	41.40%	41.40%	17.10%	32.26%
	2nd	5.60%	7.20%	8.10%	6.70%
	3rd	15.90%	3.10%	12.90%	10.70%
	Total	62.90%	51.70%	38.10%	49.66%
Village Heads/Grassroot-level Worker	1st				
	2nd				
	3rd	6.10%	7.80%	12.90%	7.90%
	Total	6.10%	7.80%	12.90%	7.90%
Power Brokers/Touts	1st	2.10%	1.40%	0.00%	1.40%
	2nd	0.00%	2.90%	2.70%	1.50%
	3rd	2.40%	3.10%	0.00%	2.30%
	Total	4.50%	7.40%	2.70%	5.20%
Communication Media	1st	1.00%	0.00%	0.00%	0.50%
	2nd	0.00%	1.40%	0.00%	0.50%
	3rd	0.00%	0.00%	0.00%	0.00%
	Total	1.00%	1.40%	0.00%	1.00%
Hidden Financiers	1st				
	2nd	3.40%	0.00%	0.00%	1.50%
	3rd	1.20%	4.70%	3.20%	2.80%
	Total	4.60%	4.70%	3.20%	4.30%

12.2.14. Pressure on Training/Tours Issues

The imperial framework of the All India Services has not changed with changing times. Imperial culture is being consolidated during their training at LBSNAA (Mussoorie), Sardar Vallabhbhai Patel National Police Academy (Hyderabad), and I.G.N. Forest Academy (Dehradun) respectively. From the first day they join service, these officers are trained to be elite, which help in reconstructing, sustaining, and continuing their exploitive origin. Initial orientation training systems have a pronounced influence on the All India Services Officers' subsequent behavior during the service. Probationers, while undergoing on-job training in the field and their respective academies continuously imbibe imperial norms and values in the structure of the behavior of the individual All India Services Officer.

"Tendency for the Academy to puff up too high their sense of confidence and status, which hindered effective communication later with other civil servants in the district with whom they had to work. The exaggerated importance of IAS is taught at the Academy by ICS tyrants, making us 'demigods,'" Potter DC. The All India Services Officers are frequently sent on training in India and abroad. During such training, the All India Services Officers learn, imbibe, and upgrade their skills by participation, listening, and writing.

Exhibit Number 12.38: Intensity of Political Pressure through Training and Tours-Related Issues

Service Name	Pressure Intensity	Training Tours	Foreign Tours	Open New Institution	Clientele Needs	Allow Disallow	Training Courses
		354	355	356	357	358	359
I.A.S.	'always'	40.4	12.2	3.2	3.3	1.7	0
	'mostly'	9.6	6.1	14.3	14.8	20.7	17
	'frequently'	23.1	20.4	36.5	31.1	31	30.2
	'sometimes'	13.5	36.7	33.3	42.6	37.9	35.8
	'rarely'	13.5	24.5	12.7	8.2	8.6	17
I.P.S.	'always'	0	3.1	0	1.2	8.6	0
	'mostly'	2	1.5	2.5	1.2	1.2	1.5
	'frequently'	4.1	12.3	12.3	8.1	12.3	1.5
	'sometimes'	22.4	26.2	17.3	30.2	22.2	20.9
	'rarely'	71.4	56.9	67.9	59.3	55.6	76.1
I.F.S.	'always'	5.7	18.8	2.1	5.1	11.3	13.5
	'mostly'	15.1	20.8	17.7	10.2	12.4	13.5
	'frequently'	28.3	22.9	25	32.7	24.7	18.8
	'sometimes'	28.3	19.8	32.3	32.7	37.1	30.2
	'rarely'	22.6	17.7	22.9	19.4	14.4	24
AISO	'always'	15.6	12.4	1.7	3.3	8.1	6
	'mostly'	9.1	11.4	11.7	8.2	10.6	10.6
	'frequently'	18.8	19	23.8	23.7	22	16.2
Total	'sometimes'	21.4	25.7	27.5	34.3	32.2	28.7
	'rarely'	35.1	31.4	35.4	30.6	27.1	38.4
Ranking			1	5	4	2	3
All Figures Except Ranking are in %							

Politicians and power holders use training and short tours abroad as a double-edged weapon. Some training courses particularly abroad are well sought after, same way tour to a foreign country and other States in India. In certain courses, no one likes to go; various reasons can be assigned for such issues. Politicians and power holders reward pliable officers of their choice by sending/recommending their names for the choicest place and time period. Whereas on occasions, they desire to get rid of inconvenient officers, they send such officers on undesirable, strenuous training programs, long or short depending upon the nature of goals to be achieved during such absence. It serves two purposes, they convey the message that we have penalized you for not obeying us, and secondly, we have rewarded pliable officers, who have obeyed the political pressure. Training and ours need to be used for making bureaucrats more innovative so that they incorporate innovations in public administration. "A natural extension of this is to innovate the bureaucracy that implements those policies and have labs that focus on innovation in the structures of the public administration," Daniel Rogger, 2019.

Training is the part and parcel of regular human resource management practices. But these training programs in government bureaucratic system are used as a double-edged weapon. Any training, which helps in career advancement and where courses are limited, for such courses stiff political pressure decides the names of the trainees. Foreign pieces of training and tours are invariably in high demand, political pressure decides the fate of the trainee for such pieces of training and tours. Officers with strong support in the bureaucratic system are selected and sent for good and comfortable training programs. Any program, which is difficult and located at an inconvenient place, is used for penalizing the upright officers. When politicians find that a particular post has to be vacated for a person of his choice, they send an incumbent officer for long training and post the person of their choice for self-goals maximization.

Mean (2.49), median (2) and modal (1) values indicate that political pressure is exerted 'sometimes' to 'rarely' for training and tours. 40.4% of the Indian Administrative Service officers get the 'always' category political pressure for recommending names of persons of political choice for tours and training. 56.6% of the Indian Forest Service officers get political pressure 'frequent' to 'sometimes' intensity for training and tours. 56.5% of the All India Services Officers and 93.8% of the Indian Police Service officers get political pressure 'rarely' to 'sometimes' category only in issues related to training and tours. The Indian Administrative Service officers are located in crucial positions, so they get the highest political pressure for this variable. Our results are significant with a Pearson Chi-square value of 75.541, and a significance level at 0.000. Association of training and tours with the decision-making process is good and considerable relationship shown by Pearson's negative correlation values, with the 0.001, level of significance.

Foreign training, tours, and visits are highly in the demand among government employees. People are excited about going abroad. Somehow, this negative trend is very high among government employees; first and foremost, part of the cake goes to the Indian Administrative Service officers. If something is left over, then other services officers can approach politicians for the inclusion of their names for tours abroad. The mean value of 2.47 indicates that political pressure is exerted 'frequently', but the modal (1) value shows 'rare' incidences of political pressure. 57.1% of the All India Services Officers, 82.1% of the Indian Police Service officers, and 61.2% of the Indian Administrative Service officers get political pressure 'sometimes' to 'rarely' intensity for inclusion/exclusion of names from tours to abroad. 43.7% of the Indian Forest Service officers get 'most often' to 'frequent' political pressure for going on training abroad. The Indian Forest Service officers' work being of technical in nature, show a high desire for going abroad, and the highest political pressure is used for such training and tours. Pearson Chi-square value is 47.815, with 8 degree of freedom and 0.000, level of significance. This indicates a good association of the decision-making process with the political pressure used for the tours to go abroad. Pearson's correlation value of 0.239 and Spearman's correlation value of 0.266 are significant with a 0.000, level of significance. Present variable relations with the decision are good and reliable.

On occasions, people approach politicians to start new training institutions in their areas. Political pressure is used 'rarely' to 'sometimes' category only as indicated by the mean (2.16), median (2), and modal (1) values. 69.8% of the Indian Administrative Service officers get political pressure 'frequent' to 'sometimes' intensity and 57.3% of the Indian Forest Service officers get sometimes' to 'frequent' intensity of political pressure for starting new training institutes in their areas. '87.2% of the Indian Police Service officers and 62.9% of the All India Services Officers get political pressure 'rarely' to 'sometimes' only. The very low intensity of political pressure indicates low interests of the public and politicians in the opening of new training institutes in their areas. The Association of political pressure for the opening of new institutions and the decision-making process is good as shown by the Pearson Chi-square results. Pearson Chi-square value of 62.579 is significant with a level of significance of 0.000.

Speaking on the importance of training while addressing IAS probationers, Hon'ble Prime Minister Narender Modi said, "You need to take the bureaucracy out of this image. Instead of 'hard power' make 'soft power' your identity. Implement a simple system right from giving appointment till hearing," *The Times of India* (31.10.2019). The All India Services have their independent training institutions for imparting training to different subordinate cadres. Some training programs for subordinates are compulsory in nature and are related to career progression. Training results are important for some programs; people mobilize political pressure to get a certificate for successful completion of such programs or getting a distinction in these training programs so that it can help them in their career advancement. Mean (2.19), modal (2) and median (2) values indicate that 'sometimes' category political pressure is exerted for manipulation of results. 64.9% of the All India Services Officers and 89.5% of the Indian Police Service officers get political pressure 'rarely' to 'sometimes' to manipulate the results of the training to serve the individual needs. 73.7% of the Indian Administrative Service officers and 65.4% of the Indian Forest Service officers get political pressure 'sometimes' to 'frequently' for carrying out manipulations as a result of the training to serve the individual needs. The Indian Administrative Service officers get the highest pressure, but the intensity of political pressure is moderate only. Political pressure for results manipulations is associated with the decision-making process. This is shown by the Pearson Chi-square value of 63.524 and the results are significant with a level of significance at 0.000.

Politicians are located at the top of the bureaucratic system; people approach them for allowing/disallowing and expediting/delaying the proposals for the training. Mean (2.39), median (2) and modal (2) values indicate that political pressure is used 'sometimes' for processing the proposal for training. 59.3% of the All India Services Officers and 77.8% of the Indian Police Service officers get political pressure 'rarely' to 'sometimes' intensity for processing the proposal for training. 68.9% of the Indian Administrative Service officers and 61.8% of the Indian Forest Service officers get political pressure 'sometimes' to 'rarely' intensity for allowing/disallowing and expediting/delaying the proposals for the training. Pearson Chi-square has a value of 63.747, with 8 degree of freedom and 0.000, level of significance. Our analyses show a good association between pressure for training and the decision-making process.

Exhibit Number 12.39: Priority Ranking of Sources of Pressure for Training and Tours Areas

Pressure Source	Priority Rank	IAS	IPS	IFS	AIS
PM/CM	1st	31.50%	40.00%	27.90%	33.70%
	2nd	4.40%	10.00%	13.20%	8.00%
	3rd	7.00%	3.40%	6.50%	5.60%
	Total	42.90%	53.40%	47.60%	47.30%
Centre/State Minister	1st	48.90%	52.90%	46.50%	49.80%
	2nd	27.50%	34.30%	31.60%	30.70%
	3rd	15.50%	5.20%	9.70%	10.60%
	Total	91.90%	92.40%	87.80%	91.10%
Member of Parliament	1st	0.00%	1.40%	0.00%	0.50%
	2nd	24.20%	20.00%	21.10%	22.10%
	3rd	15.50%	10.30%	12.90%	13.10%
	Total	39.70%	31.70%	34.00%	35.70%
MLA/MLC	1st	10.90%	0.00%	16.30%	8.30%
	2nd	31.90%	27.10%	21.10%	28.10%
	3rd	42.30%	63.80%	58.10%	53.10%
	Total	85.10%	90.90%	95.50%	89.50%
Zila Parishad/District-level Politicians	1st	2.20%	1.40%	2.30%	2.00%
	2nd	1.10%	0.00%	2.60%	1.00%
	3rd	14.10%	12.10%	6.50%	11.90%
	Total	17.40%	13.50%	11.40%	14.90%
Block Samiti/Block-level Politicians	1st				
	2nd	7.70%	4.30%	10.50%	7.00%
	3rd	1.40%	0.00%	0.00%	0.60%
	Total	9.10%	4.30%	10.50%	7.60%
Village Heads/Grassroot-level Worker	1st	6.50%	4.30%	7.00%	5.90%
	2nd	1.10%	1.40%	0.00%	1.00%
	3rd	1.40%	0.00%	3.20%	1.30%
	Total	9.00%	5.70%	10.20%	8.20%

Pressure Source	Priority Rank	IAS	IPS	IFS	AIS
Power Brokers/Touts	1st				
	2nd	2.20%	0.00%	0.00%	1.00%
	3rd	1.40%	3.40%	3.20%	2.50%
	Total	3.60%	3.40%	3.20%	3.50%
Communication Media	1st				
	2nd				
	3rd	1.40%	1.70%	0.00%	1.30%
	Total	1.40%	1.70%	0.00%	1.30%
Hidden Financiers	1st				
	2nd	0.00%	2.90%	0.00%	1.00%
	3rd				
	Total	0.00%	2.90%	0.00%	1.00%

People approach politicians for rescheduling the training programs, which are not convenient to them. Political pressure is exerted on the All India Services Officers for approving or rejecting a particular training course on a particular time schedule. Mean (2.17), median (2) and modal (1) values indicate that political pressure is exerted 'sometimes' for approval of training schedules. 66% of the Indian Administrative Service officers get 'frequent' to 'sometimes' intensity of political pressure for such rescheduling the training programs. 97% of the Indian Police Service officers, 54.2% of the Indian Forest Service officers and 67.1% of the All India Services Officers get 'rarely' to 'sometimes' category political pressure for a change of training schedule programs. Our results show that Indian Administrative Service officers get moderate political pressure for the selection/rejection of the training programs. Pearson Chi-square value of 78.792 is significant with a level of significance of 0.000. This shows a good association of political pressure relating to training with the decision-making process.

Research data analyses result placed at Exhibit 12.39 for measurement of the intensity of political pressure exerted by different sources of pressure on the training and tour-related issues and priority ranking done by the All India Services officers. The Centre/State Ministers 49.8% pressure exertion intensity on the All India Services officers falls in 1st priority at first place and the PM/CM with a score of 33.7% at second place in 1st priority. Respondents' number (frequency) in three priorities is not same, because not every respondent has mentioned all three priority (1st, 2nd, and 3rd) ranking, due to this variability in a cumulative total of three priorities may be little skewed, we added together three priorities (based on answered numbers). Three priorities added together as cumulative pressure measurement indicate that 91.1% on the AIS, 92.4% on the IPS, 91.9% on the IAS, and 87.8% on the IFS get pressure from the Centre/State Ministers at the first position in the decision. Pressure from the MLA/MLC comes at the second position and the PM/CM at the third position.

The most interesting aspect is that pressure from other sources is very low or negligible for this variable. 1st priority ranking indicates a very low score of intensity also indicates that this variable is not very important to the politicians. Human resources development through training is a very crucial and important tool for multi-skilling and skill up-gradation, but unfortunately, this area is neglected. This is a very important area, where bureaucracy must devote time and resources for efficient management and effective delivery system.

12.2.15. Pressure on Social Issues

We have discussed most of the areas of political pressure, which are related to the individual cause of action. Politicians provide leadership for the whole society. How they influence the All India Services Officers for carrying out works for social causes. Some of the issues we have tried to discuss here are pertaining to a common cause or social cause. Earlier we have seen that very low to negligible political pressure is used for the common cause or the welfare of the social system. For social cause, we have kept employment generation for the masses and relaxation of norms of the bureaucratic system for the sake of social welfare. How many politicians are involved in the auction of public property for public welfare? Politician uses one's office for punitive actions based on the social groups and political affiliations or not?

"Initially officials who made money misusing their positions, alone knew the tricks of the trade, as they were conversant with the loopholes in the rules and regulations, more than the rules itself. But slowly unholy partnerships become more and more strong, as officials needed political protection to safeguard themselves against the penalties provided under the code of conduct. Gradually politicians become more and more conversant with the extraction tactics," Shalini Rajneesh, 2013. Then society suffers and social issues remain relegated to least importance, politicians focus on extracting benefits from the bureaucratic system.

Social issues, in general, are related to public welfare. Any political pressure exerted under this variable will be for a positive cause of action. It could have been a positive aspect or positive political pressure used for the welfare of the public. Mean (2.50), median (2) and modal (2) values indicate that only 'sometimes' political pressure is exerted on the All India Services Officers for social causes. 65.7% of the All India Services Officers, 74.5% of the Indian Administrative Service officers, and 51% of the Indian Forest Service officers get political pressure 'sometimes' to 'frequently' intensity for social issues. 73.2% of the Indian Police Service officers get political pressure 'sometimes' intensity to rarely for social issues. The Indian Administrative Service officers get moderate political pressure and police officers get the least pressure for social issues. Our results are significant with a Pearson Chi-square value of 41.256, with 8 degree of freedom and 0.000, level of significance. This shows a good association of social issues with the decision-making process. Pearson's correlation shows the strength of this relationship with a level of significance of 0.02.

Employment generation is the greatest and most common demand for almost every area in India. Whole society revolves around the opening of employment opportunities in different sectors. People must be pressurizing political leadership all the time for the creation of more and more opportunities for getting employment. Mean (2.86) and median (3) values indicate 'frequent' use of political pressure towards the generation of employment opportunities. 55.1% of the All India Services Officers and 88.4% of the Indian Police Service officers get political pressure 'rarely' to 'sometimes' intensity for creation of employment opportunities. 61.1% of the Indian Administrative Service officers get 'frequent' to 'sometimes' intensity of political pressure for the generation of employment for the society. 60% of the Indian Forest Service officers get political pressure 'always' to the 'most often' category for a generation of employment for masses. The Indian Forest Service officers get the highest political pressure among All India Services; this may be due to fact that locations of work sites are spread over the rural areas only. The nature of forestry works is such that most of their work is employment-oriented, and huge numbers of people are getting benefit out of such employment. Forest officers are the biggest employment provider among the All India Services. Our results are significant on Pearson Chi-square analysis and show a good association with the decision-making process. Pearson Chi-square value of 127.719, with 8 degree of freedom and 0.000, level of significance, are significant. Pearson's correlation value of 0.307 and Spearman's correlation value of 0.358 are significant with a level of significance at 0.000. Political pressure for employment generation in his constituency by a politician is strongly related to the decision process.

Exhibit Number 12.40: Intensity of Political Pressure on Social Issues

Service Name	Pressure Intensity	Social Issues	Generate Employment	Relaxing Norms	Misuse of Machinery	Auction Land	Punitive Action
		360	361	362	363	364	365
I.A.S.	'always'	0	12.8	21.3	13	9.4	27.1
	'mostly'	12.8	19.1	24.6	13	24.5	32.2
	'frequently'	44.7	40.4	24.6	37	26.4	25.4
	'sometimes'	29.8	21.3	21.3	29.6	22.6	15.3
	'rarely'	12.8	6.4	8.2	7.4	17	0
I.P.S.	'always'	1.5	2.3	1.2	1.1	3.4	21.5
	'mostly'	0	1.2	17.3	0	3.4	60.2
	'frequently'	25.4	8.1	12.3	11.8	24.1	8.6
	'sometimes'	44.8	33.7	38.3	62.4	52.9	3.2
	'rarely'	28.4	54.7	30.9	24.7	16.1	6.5
I.F.S.	'always'	12.2	34	19.4	17.8	8.1	13
	'mostly'	26.5	26	26.5	19.8	17.2	25
	'frequently'	24.5	24	28.6	26.7	28.3	28
	'sometimes'	26.5	11	20.4	21.8	22.2	22
	'rarely'	10.2	5	5.1	13.9	24.2	12
AISO	'always'	4.3	18	13.8	10.5	6.7	19.4
	'mostly'	11.7	15.5	22.9	10.9	13.8	39.7
	'frequently'	30.7	21.5	22.1	23.4	26.4	20.2
Total	'sometimes'	35	21.5	26.7	38.7	33.5	13.5
	'rarely'	18.4	23.6	14.6	16.5	19.7	7.1
Ranking			2	3	4	5	1
All Figures Except Ranking are in %							

People approach politicians for relaxation of bureaucratic norms and conditions to serve larger political interests. Mean (2.95) and median (3) values show that political pressure is exerted 'frequently' for relaxation of government norms and conditions to serve political goals. 48.8% of the All India Services Officers get political pressure 'frequently' to 'sometimes' category for relaxations of conditions. 69.2% of the Indian Police Service officers get 'sometimes' to 'rarely' intensity of political pressure for relaxation in government norms to serve political goals. 55.1% of the Indian Forest Service officers and 49.2% of the Indian Administrative Service officers get 'frequent' to 'most often' political pressure towards relaxation of norms and conditions to serve political goals. Our results show the association of this political pressure with the decision-making process. Our results are significant with a Pearson Chi-square value of 49.959, with 8 degree of freedom and 0.000, level of significance.

People pressurize political leadership for misuse of government machinery, so that social needs and requirements are met for social welfare. Mean (2.61), median (2) and modal (2) values indicate that political pressure is exerted 'sometimes' for misuse of government machinery for social causes. 62.1% of the All India Services Officers, 66.6% of the Indian Administrative Service officers, and 48.5% of the Indian Forest Service officers get political pressure 'frequently' to 'sometimes' category for relaxation of government norms and conditions to serve social goals. 87.1% of the Indian Police Service officers get political pressure 'sometimes' to the 'rarely' category. The Indian Administrative Service officers get the moderate political pressure and highest among All India Services, for social causes and police officers get the least pressure. Our results are significant and show a good association with the decision-making process. Pearson Chi-square value is 70.175, with 8 degree of freedom and show 0.000, level of significance. Relationship as shown by Spearman correlation is significant with 0.02, level of significance.

It is commonly said that political pressure is exerted while auctioning the government property and land, and decisions follow the political will and desires. Mean (2.54), modal (2) and median (2) values indicate that political pressure is exerted 'sometimes' for the auction of government property according to political wishes. 59.9% of the All India Services Officers, 77% of the Indian Police Service officers, and 50.5% of Indian Forest Service officers get political pressure 'sometimes' to 'frequently' intensity while disposing of government property and land. The Indian Administrative Service officers get the highest political pressure, 50.9% of them get 'most often' to 'frequent' intensity of political pressure while conducting an auction of government property and land. Our results are significant as shown by the Pearson Chi-square value of 31.732, and the level of significance is 0.000. Our variable understudy has a good association with the decision process.

Some of the social groups, who do not vote and support a particular political party, and that party, come in power. Under the influence of power, politicians initiate punitive action against such social groups through the All India Services Officers. Mean (3.5), modal (4) and median (4) values indicate that political pressure is exerted 'most often' to take punitive action against the political opponents. This indicates that the All India Services Officers have lost their path of justice to all. The All India Services Officers have just become the political tool in the hands of the ruling party. Continuous sycophancy and political opportunism among All India Services Officers have made them a burden on the bureaucratic system. Masses have lost total faith in the decisions taken by the All India Services Officers. 81.7% of the Indian Police Service officers and 59.3% of the Indian Administrative Service officers get political pressure 'always' to 'most often' category for taking punitive action against such social groups, who have not supported the ruling political party. 59.5% of the All India Services and 53% of the Indian Forest Service officers get political pressure 'most often' to 'frequently' intensity to victimize the political opponent social groups. Our results are significant as shown by the Pearson Chi-square value of 50.598, with 8 degree of freedom and 0.000, level of significance. This also indicates that the decision process and political pressure for punitive action against opponents have a good association.

The All India Services officer carried out priority ranking of different sources of political pressure for the social issues-related decisions, results are placed at Exhibit 12.41 the Centre/state Ministers intensity of pressure is highest in 1st ranking with an intensity of 26.8% on the AIS, 32.90 on the IPS and 27.5% on the IAS, and 15.2% on the IFS. Higher pressure on the IPS for social issues is something surprising and need explanations. It is quite possible that respondents have considered this type of pressure mixing with pressure related to crime and law implementation issues. Respondents' number (frequency) in three priorities is not the same, because every respondent has not mentioned all three priority (1st, 2nd, and 3rd) while ranking, due to this variability in a cumulative total of three priorities may be a little skewed, we added together three priorities (based on answered numbers).

Exhibit Number 12.41: Priority Ranking of Sources of Pressure for Social Issues Areas

Pressure Source	Priority Rank	IAS	IPS	IFS	AIS
PM/CM	1st	15.60%	21.10%	15.20%	17.30%
	2nd	0.00%	1.30%	0.00%	0.40%
	3rd	0.00%	2.80%	7.90%	2.30%
	Total	15.60%	25.20%	23.10%	20.00%
Centre/State Minister	1st	27.50%	32.90%	15.20%	26.80%
	2nd	11.70%	19.70%	19.50%	15.80%
	3rd	11.50%	15.50%	13.20%	13.10%
	Total	50.70%	68.10%	47.90%	55.70%
Member of Parliament	1st	0.00%	0.00%	2.20%	0.40%
	2nd	11.70%	10.50%	9.80%	11.00%
	3rd	10.60%	7.00%	15.80%	10.30%
	Total	22.30%	17.50%	27.80%	21.70%
MLA/MLC	1st	18.30%	17.10%	32.60%	20.80%
	2nd	31.50%	35.50%	22.00%	31.10%
	3rd	21.20%	29.60%	21.10%	23.90%
	Total	71.00%	82.20%	75.70%	75.80%
Zila Parishad/District-level Politicians	1st	7.30%	1.30%	6.50%	5.20%
	2nd	25.20%	26.30%	26.80%	25.90%
	3rd	25.00%	32.40%	15.80%	25.80%
	Total	57.50%	60.00%	49.10%	56.90%

Pressure Source	Priority Rank	IAS	IPS	IFS	AIS
Block Samiti/Block-level Politicians	1st	15.60%	22.40%	13.00%	17.40%
	2nd	3.60%	1.30%	4.90%	3.10%
	3rd	8.70%	2.80%	5.30%	6.10%
	Total	27.90%	26.50%	23.20%	26.60%
Village Heads/Grassroot-level Worker	1st	14.70%	5.30%	15.20%	11.70%
	2nd	2.70%	0.00%	0.00%	1.30%
	3rd	2.90%	1.40%	2.60%	2.30%
	Total	20.30%	6.70%	17.80%	15.30%
Power Brokers/Touts	1st				
	2nd	12.60%	5.30%	14.60%	10.50%
	3rd	1.00%	2.80%	2.60%	1.90%
	Total	13.60%	8.10%	17.20%	12.40%
Communication Media	1st				
	2nd	0.90%	0.00%	0.00%	0.40%
	3rd	18.30%	5.60%	15.80%	13.60%
	Total	19.20%	5.60%	15.80%	14.00%
Hidden Financiers	1st				
	2nd	0.00%	0.00%	2.40%	0.40%
	3rd	1.00%	0.00%	0.00%	0.50%
	Total	1.00%	0.00%	2.40%	0.90%

The cumulative aggregate of three priorities intensity is highest from the MLA/MLC with a score of 75.8% on the AIS, 82.2% on the IPS, 75.7% on the IFS, and 71% on the IAS at the first position. The district-level politicians at the second position and the Centre/State Ministers at the third position follow this. Pressure from the power brokers, the communication media, and the hidden financiers for social issues is surprising, though it is low and falls under 3rd priority. Results also indicate that politicians have a very low priority for social issues and relegate social issues to nowhere.

ANNEXURE 12.A: QUESTIONNAIRE ON AREAS OF POLITICAL PRESSURE ON PRESSURE POINTS/AREAS

All India Services Officers are located at pivotal/commanding position in the decision-making process. When they arrive decision related with the 15 kind of issues listed below, they may experience political pressure in this process. Kindly indicate the intensity/frequency of political pressure on five point scale.

Tick 5 in case pressure is exerted always. Tick 4 in case pressure is exerted most oftenly. Tick 3 in case pressure is exerted frequently. Tick 2 in case pressure is exerted sometimes only. Tick 1 in case pressure is exerted rarely.

Area of Political Pressure (Pressure Points)	Scale				
275. TRANSFERS	5	4	3	2	1
276. On the basis of financial considerations	5	4	3	2	1
277. Pressure of frequent dislocations to serve clientele needs	5	4	3	2	1
278. To meet the individual goals/needs	5	4	3	2	1
279. Serve public interests for improvement of system & services	5	4	3	2	1
280. To please the large social groups to serve their social needs	5	4	3	2	1
281. POSTINGS	5	4	3	2	1
282. To provide wet/plumb postings who serve political goals	5	4	3	2	1
283. To deny/delay postings to those who resist political pressure	5	4	3	2	1
284. To provide posting on the basis of financial considerations	5	4	3	2	1
285. To ensure tenure continuity on basis of pliability	5	4	3	2	1
286. Cater the need of caste/religion/region or individual interests	5	4	3	2	1
287. RECRUITMENT	5	4	3	2	1
288. Creation of posts for recruitment to get services in future	5	4	3	2	1
289. Violation/distortion of recruitment procedure	5	4	3	2	1
290. Ignoring merit or relaxation in rules for physical standards	5	4	3	2	1
291. Selection on the basis of financial consideration	5	4	3	2	1

Area of Political Pressure (Pressure Points)	Scale				
292. Selection on basis of caste/region/religion/ considerations	5	4	3	2	1
293. Recruitment on humanitarian grounds or death cases	5	4	3	2	1
294. RESOURCE ALLOCATION: Distribution, deployment and management to meet political goals	5	4	3	2	1
295. Related with land allotment, requisition and distribution	5	4	3	2	1
296. Human resource allocation to get popularity in area	5	4	3	2	1
297. Budgetary allocation for new/maintenance/ongoing works	5	4	3	2	1
298. Allocate/increase/decrease supply of goods and material	5	4	3	2	1
299. Allocation/deployment of govt. vehicles and machinery	5	4	3	2	1
300. REWARDS	5	4	3	2	1
301. Help in advancement of career progression or desired ACR	5	4	3	2	1
302. Appointment on special posts, boards and corporations	5	4	3	2	1
303. Granting special pay/advance increments/honorarium	5	4	3	2	1
304. Allotment of government houses, vehicles and resources	5	4	3	2	1
305. Public praise, issue appreciation letters for future benefits	5	4	3	2	1
306. PUNISHMENT	5	4	3	2	1
307. Frequent dislocations/withdraw vehicle and house	5	4	3	2	1
308. Blockage of career progression/suspension/punishment	5	4	3	2	1
309. False complaints, vigilance inquiry and public criticism	5	4	3	2	1
310. Adverse ACR/spoiling the records	5	4	3	2	1
311. Dis-allowing/reducing the punishment	5	4	3	2	1
312. PROMOTIONS	5	4	3	2	1
313. Out of turn promotions to serve individual needs	5	4	3	2	1
314. Ignoring/violation of merit to promote individuals	5	4	3	2	1
315. Promotion on the basis of considerations	5	4	3	2	1
316. Seniority violations to extend future financial benefits, pension, etc.	5	4	3	2	1
317. Creation of new posts to avoid stagnation and frustration in cadres	5	4	3	2	1

Area of Political Pressure (Pressure Points)	Scale				
318. RULES, REGULATIONS & PROCEDURE	5	4	3	2	1
319. Ignore/circumvent rules to serve individual interests/ goals	5	4	3	2	1
320. To simplify rules, regulations and procedures to avoid ambiguity	5	4	3	2	1
321. Frame new rules and regulations to meet political goals	5	4	3	2	1
322. Clientele oriented enforcement and maintenance of rules	5	4	3	2	1
323. Amend/change rules for disadvantageous persons/ windows/orphans	5	4	3	2	1
324. POLICY-RELATED ISSUES	5	4	3	2	1
325. Implement policy in such way to serve individual goal	5	4	3	2	1
326. To amend policy to serve changing social needs and interests	5	4	3	2	1
327. Policy for conservation and preservation of local resources/culture	5	4	3	2	1
328. To frame policy to serve individual/regional future needs	5	4	3	2	1
329. Ignore/circumvent policy to meet political party goals/ interest	5	4	3	2	1
330. CHANGE OF LOW/ACTS	5	4	3	2	1
331. New legislation for preservation/conservation of culture/resources	5	4	3	2	1
332. Law to meet changing social needs/extend benefits to large groups	5	4	3	2	1
333. Implementation of law to serve clientele needs	5	4	3	2	1
334. Amend/ignore/circumvent law to meet political interest and goals	5	4	3	2	1
335. Frame new law to safeguard political interests for political gains	5	4	3	2	1
336. DEMUR IN DECISION PROCESS: Taking favourable/ unfavourable, desirable decisions, postponing or pending the decision related with	5	4	3	2	1
337. Election-related matters at various levels schedule/ eligibility/nomination/results/recounting, etc.	5	4	3	2	1
338. Tenders or execution of work to avoid displeasure of masses	5	4	3	2	1

Area of Political Pressure (Pressure Points)	Scale				
339. Land allotment/distribution and other land-related matters	5	4	3	2	1
340. Issues related with services matter/employees to encash delays	5	4	3	2	1
341. Issue-related crime to avoid certain groups of people	5	4	3	2	1
342. DEVELOPMENT WORK-RELATED ISSUES	5	4	3	2	1
343. Sanction/reject/accept request for loans/subsidy/grants/aids	5	4	3	2	1
344. Include/exclude certain areas for applicability of project/schemes	5	4	3	2	1
345. Sanction new programmes and projects for their areas	5	4	3	2	1
346. Upgrade existing infrastructure/institutions/facilities	5	4	3	2	1
347. Open/start new institutions/schools/building/roads/canals	5	4	3	2	1
348. CRIME-RELATED ISSUES	5	4	3	2	1
349. Manipulate arrest/release of persons of their interest	5	4	3	2	1
350. Detention/extension of individuals in custody for considerations	5	4	3	2	1
351. Settling score/disputes with the help of government machinery	5	4	3	2	1
352. Registration/cancellation of FIR to misuse the ambiguity of law	5	4	3	2	1
353. Grabbing public property to serve political/individual goals	5	4	3	2	1
354. TRAINING/TOURS RELATED	5	4	3	2	1
355. Include/exclude names for foreign tours/training/visits	5	4	3	2	1
356. Start, open and upgrade institutions for training	5	4	3	2	1
357. Manipulate training results to serve the clientele needs	5	4	3	2	1
358. Allow/disallow, delay, expedite, keep pending proposal for training	5	4	3	2	1
359. Select/reject the training course/programmes/schedules	5	4	3	2	1
360. SOCIAL ISSUES	5	4	3	2	1
361. To generate employment opportunities in the constituency	5	4	3	2	1
362. Relaxation of govt. norms/conditions to serve political goals	5	4	3	2	1

Area of Political Pressure (Pressure Points)	Scale				
363. Misuse of govt. machinery to meet need of social groups	5	4	3	2	1
364. Auction of govt. property/land, etc.	5	4	3	2	1
365. Punitive action against the political opponents/groups	5	4	3	2	1

ANNEXURE 12.B. QUESTIONNAIRE ON RELATION OF SOURCES OF POLITICAL PRESSURE AND PRESSURE AREAS

In decision-making process direct political pressure from different sources (in columns) may be exerted in the 15 areas listed below. Kindly, tick 3 most important sources of political pressure in each row as 1st, 2nd, and 3rd priorities respectively.

Area of Pressure	Sources of Political Pressure									
	PM/CM	Mins.	MP	MLA/MLC	Dt. Lv.	Block	Village	Pow.	Media	Hid. Fin.
Transfer										
Posting										
Recruitment										
Resource allocation										
Rewards										
Punishment										
Promotions										
Rules and Regulations										
Policy matters										
Law/Acts										
Demur in decision process										
Development works										
Crime related										
Trg./Tours related										
Social issues										

Unit 13

Modes and Forms of Political Pressure

"Person whose conscious is free from feeling of doership, and whose perception is not affected by worldly aspirations/ambitions and activities, does not really damage, even causing damage, any sin doesn't accrue to that selfless person". *The Bhagaawad Gita* 18.17

"Government is a trust and the officers of the government are trustees, and both the trust and the trustees are created for the benefit of the people."—Henry Clay

"Individualities may form communities, but it is institutions alone that can create a nation."—Benjamin Disraeli

- *The framework of pressure groups in decision*
- *Analyses of modes & forms of pressure*
- *Bureaucratic system 9 modes of pressure*
- *Public & social power groups 5 modes*
- *Political parties 5 modes of pressure*
- *Power brokers 3 modes of pressure*

In any social system, people tend to organize themselves in small groups to get things done in their way of thinking. Such a process of collective bargaining induces drive to meet group needs and people willingly participate in such bargaining for self-interest fulfillment. In public administration impact of such modes of pressure has been studied. Data analysis results for such modes impact on the decision have been mentioned in this unit. Such pressure groups desire to exercise control over resources penetrate deep inside the bureaucratic system in India.

13.1. Framework of Pressure Groups in the AISO Decision

Since time immemorial, different pressure groups had been working in different forms and modes to influence the outcomes of the decisions in desired directions. In our daily life, we come across different types of pressure groups operating in different areas. In bureaucracy also, various interest groups perpetually operate to aggrandize their own self-ends. Organized interest groups wield considerable influence and manipulate outcomes in public administration. Such pressure on policy and governance generates new alignments, which has short-term and long-term impact on the process of decision.

Inbuilt imbalances in decision delivery mechanism inculcate consciousness among stakeholders. Over a period of time, people organize themselves in small groups to get things done in their favor. The process of collective bargaining induces a drive to meet group needs and people participate in such bargaining for a sense of fulfillment. Power supported vested interest groups perpetuate their desires to meet their self-goals at the cost of others and they join together for its fulfillment. Such pressure groups desire to exercise control over resources penetrate deep inside the bureaucratic system. The All India Services Officers are considered as protector and custodian of public cultural resources. In a bureaucratic system, public causes have been relegated to the backyard for the aggrandizement of their self-goals.

"Power is exercised at high levels by the political elites who have, in order to be able to exercise that power, have to get elected," T.N. Dhar, 2011. Our political system survives on power, influence, and corruption. "There is no group without its interest. An interest is equivalent of a group," A.F. Bentley (1949). According to him, wealth is responsible for social divisions. He further elaborated that interest is responsible for the existence of the group, or no interest can be considered to exist unless it manifested itself in-group actions. Individual initiative is not shared for the benefit of the group. Individual officer uses one's influence to achieve their own benefits and goals. Bureaucracy has been working to balance the various services, pressure groups. Different services represent their demands and justify them towards the satisfaction of their goals and needs. Such needs are reflected in political pressure.

D.B. Truman in his Disturbance Theory (1962) mentioned that political interest group is the outcome of disturbances in changing society. Different services groups disrupt the established pattern of behavior, as a consequence of it major changes are attained in status and rewards for own service. Such disproportionate gains alter the attitude and perceptions of the officers required for the cohesiveness of the services. Every service groups push vigorous claims for their benefits through politicians.

The success of one service group to stabilize relations with the politicians, create an inevitable problem for other services. This generates an inevitable need for modification of intra-service relationships. Such a need is bound to bring changes and alterations in the All India Services. According to group dynamics theory, the group will be divided according to loyalties for the aggrandizement of individual needs and goals. The IAS has emerged as the most powerful service. Moreover, provides resistance to the interests of the other two All India Services. This results in the inducement of organized political pressure among the All India Services.

According to J.C. Calhoun (1953), doctrine of the concurrent majority, interests of majority and minority were to be fairly balanced. Group in a dominant position is self-centered and selfish;

it can be tyrannical and oppressive. "By giving to each interest, or portion, the power of self-protection all strife and struggle between them for ascendancy is prevented, and thereby, not only every feeling calculated to weaken the attachment to the whole is suppressed, but the individual and social feelings are made to unite in one common devotion to country," Calhoun (1953). For smooth and effective working, each service group must be given constitutional powers to stop the acts of other elite services. If we look through it, the entire group 'A' services should be given equal powers for the welfare of the country.

"If the benefits fail, or are inadequate to warrant the cost of membership or the leaders get an inadequate return, the group collapses," Robert Salisbury. Different services members individually develop interpersonal relationships, so that they can extract something in exchange from each other. When one service individual is aware that he will not meet the desired goals, he will not enter into interpersonal relationships with them. This is happening in the field postings. When IAS officers feel that they can meet their needs and goals without help from IPS and IFS, they do not develop a working relationship with them. According to group theory, such a leader (IAS) tends to misuse the powers vested in him, and this generates corruption and immoral behavior.

The theory of collective action propounded by M. Olson (1968) on pressure groups revolves around the aggrandizement of individual monetary benefits and self-interests. Since time immemorial individual interests have been the human weakness, every person likes to satisfy self-goals on first priority. Interests of the group are the by-product of the process of aggrandizement of individual goals, to achieve group goals participation is a must otherwise dormant members will take advantage by colluding.

The IAS as the leading group exclusively seeks higher status and power for them by restricting access of other service groups to the nerve center. When other service groups exert pressure through political authority, IAS as a group behaves inclusively by relaxing the terms of governance. This signifies the T. Parsons and Smelser theory performance in a system is related to the rewards and sanctions. The All India Services as groups perpetuate their self-interests in the form of rewards and inclusive behavior under political sanctions. The IAS at the top enjoys the selective incentives in form of their monopoly over the power center. Their location and proximity to the power provide them the capability and enhance their capacity to mobilize the power in their favor.

Monopolizing the authority instills an incentive to maintain power. They become coercive and this influences individuals in latent IAS groups. The IAS group carries out vigorous lobbying for retaining supremacy among All India Services and other services groups. Any individual officer will not work for their service group without special incentives available to him. In the process of bargaining for a group, the IAS ensures benefits for self by virtue of their monopolistic control over the power positions, so they continue and perpetuate collective bargaining. These service groups are united and actuated by some common impulses of passion, or interest, adverse to the right of the citizen (other services) or the permanent aggregate interests of the community (Madison and Theodore, 1978). Every service group nourishes its own ambitions against the selfish tendencies of other service groups, which generate factionalism in the services.

In sheer disrespect for the public administration, various service groups approach political pressure groups to perpetuate their own expectations, which reveal their disrespect for the public welfare and administration in general. These various services groupism and their relations with the political pressure groups nourish their concern for the sphere of their own service jurisdiction rather than justice for the public. This open bargaining by service groups through political pressure groups impairs the process of decision, which demoralizes the entire bureaucratic system. Process of decision is the balance of conflicting forces prevalent among the All India Services Officers; a decision is the product of the degree of their consensus.

"Our attitude to pressure groups exemplifies an unwholesome admixture of frosted and affected prudery and a passive and escapist permissiveness", L.M. Singhvi. Different services use politicians' intervention to meet their own goals rather than the bureaucratic system. "The collective goal emerges either as a result of voluntary trading and contracting between individuals who have different personal goals. As in the case of social contract (Buchanan and Tullock, 1965), or because of conflict in which one of the personal goals is imposed upon rest. Goals will then change as individuals see scope for improving their collective benefits by means of a goal change, or if the dominant goal is toppled in the power struggle," P.M. Jackson (1983). Political groups visualize individual service trading to their own advantage. "Every act is in the interest of some group, which is capable of pooling their votes for a leader who goes out of way to mangle law and justice or to some powerful individual," K. Seshadri (1994).

13.2. Analysis of Modes and Forms of Political Pressure in Decision

Initially, a large number of modes and forms of political pressure were considered and after consultation with a select group, we finally selected 22 modes and forms of political pressure influencing the decision-making process for research work. These 22 modes or forms of political pressure are exerting pressure on 15 major areas and 76 pressure points (explained in Unit 12) in the decision, which provide power bases to the politicians. One-time politicians use one's position in the bureaucratic system and another time clamor with individual officers to get things done in one's favor. These modes or forms of political pressure can be classified into the bureaucratic system related (9), public and social power related (5), political parties related (5) and power brokers related (3) classes for sake of our study and analyses results are grouped accordingly.

Exhibit Number 13.1: Modes and Forms of Political Pressure—Statistical Analysis

Modes of Pressure	Frequency Mean Value for AIS					Mean	S.D.	Rk
	Total	Valid	I.A.S.	I.P.S.	I.F.S.			
208. Power to correct mistakes	281	253	0.09	0.01	0.07	0.06	0.45	18
209. Power brokers	281	253	1.42	1.5	1.48	1.47	2.5	4
210. Political groups/activists	281	254	1.4	1.8	1.57	1.58	2.27	5
211. Known/friendly bureaucrats	281	254	1.62	1.23	1.46	1.45	2.21	7
212. Bureaucratic system	281	254	3.15	2.37	3.07	2.87	2.42	3
213. Friends/relatives/colleagues	281	253	1.55	1.64	1.31	1.53	2.17	10
214. Communication media	281	253	0.82	0.32	1	0.7	1.71	11
215. Organised public	281	253	0.61	0.79	0.54	0.65	1.79	17
216. Member of citizenary	281	253	0.13	0	0.17	0.94	0.69	22
217. Muslemen and underworld	281	253	1.15	1.01	1.83	1.03	2.21	16
218. Open/hidden financier	281	253	1.59	1.63	0.81	1.46	2.17	11

Modes of Pressure	Frequency Mean Value for AIS					Mean	S.D.	Rk
	Total	Valid	I.A.S.	I.P.S.	I.F.S.			
219. Changing service rules	281	253	0.86	0.78	1.09	0.92	2.05	15
220. Abuse of authority/position	281	253	3.29	3.85	3.06	3.41	2.52	2
221. Grievance redressel	281	253	1.37	1.4	1.43	1.36	2.37	9
222. Performance review tool	281	253	1.88	2.1	1.98	1.96	2.58	13
223. Protecting individual rights	281	253	0.08	0.07	0.37	0.14	0.82	20
224. Open and accountable Govt.	281	255	0.15	0.15	0.22	0.13	0.78	19
225. Politician supremacy	281	255	2.18	2.27	1.98	2.14	2.3	6
226. Politician control over sys.	281	253	1.45	1.91	1.66	1.68	2.04	1
227. Appointment/promotions	281	253	1.4	1.1.6	1.28	1.28	2.05	8
228. Descretionary authority	281	254	1.23	1.12	1.89	1.35	2.17	12
229. Tours/training/fellowship	281	253	0.48	0.6	0.52	0.53	1.79	21
S.D. = Standard Deviation, Rk = Ranking done by Respondents								

Results: Politicians' control over public servants has been ranked as the first rank and abuse of position and authority by the politicians is ranked second most important mode of pressure in the decision-making process. Political pressure through member citizenry is ranked the last mode of pressure. Each variable ranking, mean values, and standard deviation for total All India Services have been shown in Exhibit 13.1. Frequency (N) of respondents responded and analyses results for mean value for each variable for the respective three services have been indicated in the above-mentioned exhibit.

Summary statistics (Exhibit 13.2) for the method of recruitment in All India Services for direct recruited and promoted officers' conditions in handling the various modes of political pressure in the decision-making process, we see that frequency of respondents have been 78 to 80 for direct recruited and 176 to 177 for promoted officers.

Exhibit 13.2 shows mean values for acceptance of different modes of political pressure in the decision-making process for directly recruited officers have been 0.28 to 3.68 with a range of standard deviation of 0.79 to 2.53; these values for promoted officers have been 0.11 to 9.09 with a standard deviation of 0.54 to 2.58 respectively. Our independent t-test results (Exhibit 7.2) are presented in two rows, one for equal variance assumed and the other for equal variance not assumed. Our assumption was that variance in both groups will be roughly equal, but some adjustments are needed where the variance is not equal, such assumptions can be deciphered through our results. Variances in standard deviation are the subject matter of interest for studies.

Our Levene's test for equality of variances, where significance values are less than 0.05 indicates that the null hypothesis is rejected, variances are significantly different, and the assumption of homogeneity of variance is violated. Where values are more than 0.05, we accept the null hypothesis, the difference between variance is zero, variances are roughly equal and the assumption is tenable. For significance values more than 0.05, Levene's test is non-significant and we have considered test statistics in the row labeled equal variance assumed, in case of such cases, where significance values are less than 0.05, in such cases, Levene's test is significant and values from row marked equal variance not assumed are considered for analysis.

After analyzing the homogeneity of variance, we have studied the t-test values. The mean difference and error of the difference is low in most items. T-values provided in (Exhibit 13.2) can be assessed against the values from t-tables with a given degree of freedom. In our results for t-test values, where the value of significance is greater than 0.05, we conclude that there was no significant difference between means of direct recruited and promoted officers' perceptions about modes of pressure. We can infer that both groups are amenable to political pressure in the decision-making process. Where significance is less than 0.05, we can infer that there was a difference between direct recruited and promoted officers' perception about modes of pressure, and amenability towards political pressure in the decision-making process was differential.

Exhibit Number 13.2: Independent Samples t-Test—Method of Recruitment in Modes of Political Pressure

		Levene's Test for Equality of Variances		t-test for Equality of Means						
		F	Sig.	t	df	Sig. (2-tailed)	Mean Difference	Std. Error Difference	95% Confidence Interval of the Mean	
									Lower	Upper
208	Equal variances assumed	9.307	0.003	–1.502	253	0.134	–9.09E-02	6.05E-02	–0.21	2.83E-02
	Equal variances not assumed			–2.244	175.000	0.026	–9.09E-02	4.05E-02	–0.17	–1.10E-02
209	Equal variances assumed	0.398	0.529	–0.425	253	0.671	–0.14	0.34	–0.81	0.52
	Equal variances not assumed			–0.431	154.576	0.667	–0.14	0.34	–0.81	0.52
210	Equal variances assumed	0.250	0.618	–0.472	254	0.637	–0.14	0.31	–0.75	0.46
	Equal variances not assumed			–0.474	153.746	0.636	–0.14	0.30	–0.75	0.46
211	Equal variances assumed	0.157	0.692	–0.565	254	0.573	–0.17	0.30	–0.75	0.42
	Equal variances not assumed			–0.556	147.163	0.579	–0.17	0.30	–0.77	0.43
212	Equal variances assumed	0.087	0.768	–0.840	254	0.402	–0.27	0.33	–0.92	0.37
	Equal variances not assumed			–0.830	148.260	0.408	–0.27	0.33	–0.93	0.38
213	Equal variances assumed	9.552	0.002	–2.312	253	0.022	–0.67	0.29	–1.25	–9.99E-02
	Equal variances not assumed			–2.455	174.194	0.015	–0.67	0.27	–1.22	–0.13
214	Equal variances assumed	10.989	0.001	1.681	253	0.094	0.39	0.23	–6.67E-02	0.84
	Equal variances not assumed			1.507	118.629	0.134	0.39	0.26	–0.12	0.90

		Levene's Test for Equality of Variances		t-test for Equality of Means						
		F	Sig.	t	df	Sig. (2-tailed)	Mean Difference	Std. Error Difference	95% Confidence Interval of the Mean	
									Lower	Upper
215	Equal variances assumed	3.211	0.074	1.053	253	0.293	0.25	0.24	−0.22	0.73
	Equal variances not assumed			1.023	140.461	0.308	0.25	0.25	−0.24	0.75
216	Equal variances assumed	3.126	0.078	0.900	253	0.369	8.37E-02	9.30E-02	−9.95E-02	0.27
	Equal variances not assumed			0.832	126.020	0.407	8.37E-02	0.10	−0.12	0.28
217	Equal variances assumed	8.235	0.004	−1.364	253	0.174	−0.41	0.30	−0.99	0.18
	Equal variances not assumed			−1.475	182.419	0.142	−0.41	0.28	−0.95	0.14
218	Equal variances assumed	8.578	0.004	−2.388	253	0.018	−0.70	0.29	−1.27	−0.12
	Equal variances not assumed			−2.661	196.760	0.008	−0.70	0.26	−1.21	−0.18
219	Equal variances assumed	2.888	0.090	1.091	253	0.276	0.30	0.28	−0.24	0.85
	Equal variances not assumed			1.050	137.514	0.296	0.30	0.29	−0.27	0.87
220	Equal variances assumed	0.005	0.942	1.238	253	0.217	0.42	0.34	−0.25	1.09
	Equal variances not assumed			1.235	149.404	0.219	0.42	0.34	−0.25	1.10
221	Equal variances assumed	1.855	0.174	0.846	253	0.399	0.27	0.32	−0.36	0.91
	Equal variances not assumed			0.832	144.693	0.407	0.27	0.33	−0.38	0.93
222	Equal variances assumed	0.130	0.719	1.074	253	0.284	0.37	0.35	−0.31	1.06
	Equal variances not assumed			1.077	151.334	0.283	0.37	0.35	−0.31	1.06
223	Equal variances assumed	13.689	0.000	1.809	253	0.072	0.20	0.11	−1.76E-02	0.42
	Equal variances not assumed			1.391	91.992	0.168	0.20	0.14	−8.51E-02	0.48
224	Equal variances assumed	10.218	0.002	1.552	255	0.122	0.18	0.12	−4.85E-02	0.41
	Equal variances not assumed			1.207	94.559	0.230	0.18	0.15	−0.12	0.48

		Levene's Test for Equality of Variances		t-test for Equality of Means						
		F	Sig.	t	df	Sig. (2-tailed)	Mean Difference	Std. Error Difference	95% Confidence Interval of the Mean	
									Lower	Upper
225	Equal variances assumed	0.943	0.332	–0.228	255	0.820	–7.07E-02	0.31	–0.68	0.54
	Equal variances not assumed			–0.223	145.287	0.824	–7.07E-02	0.32	–0.70	0.55
226	Equal variances assumed	1.271	0.261	–0.930	253	0.353	–0.26	0.28	–0.80	0.29
	Equal variances not assumed			–0.977	165.732	0.330	–0.26	0.26	–0.78	0.26
227	Equal variances assumed	2.941	0.088	–0.323	253	0.747	–9.03E-02	0.28	–0.64	0.46
	Equal variances not assumed			–0.341	170.942	0.734	–9.03E-02	0.27	–0.61	0.43
228	Equal variances assumed	6.053	0.015	2.065	254	0.040	0.61	0.29	2.81E-02	1.18
	Equal variances not assumed			1.965	133.974	0.051	0.61	0.31	–3.81E-03	1.21
229	Equal variances assumed	0.001	0.974	0.037	253	0.971	8.92E-03	0.24	–0.47	0.49
	Equal variances not assumed			0.037	151.257	0.971	8.92E-03	0.24	–0.47	0.49

13.2.1. Bureaucratic System-Related Modes

Bureaucratic system-oriented modes are: (i) politicians powers to correct mistakes in process of administration, (ii) through known and friendly bureaucrats, (iii) seniors in the bureaucratic system, (iv) by service rules and conditions, (v) abuse of official position and authority, (vi) politician powers in grievance redressing system, (vii) politicians powers in appointments and promotions, and (viii) politicians control over foreign tours, training and fellowships.

13.2.1.1. Power to Correct Mistakes in Process of Administration: Politicians occupy the top position in the democratic set up in the Union of India and the States. If politician perception is correct in approach and behavior towards the decision-making process, then it makes it very difficult for the bureaucratic system operators to retain subjectivity in their day-to-day work. Even if some of the All India Services Officers try to resort to manipulations, those can be shown the way out or checked. Politicians enjoy tremendous powers to correct mistakes in the process of administration. But the decision-making process has slipped out of politicians' hands, due to their negligence, casual attitude, and non-assertive leadership provided by them. Officers are intelligent; they entice the politicians with small temptations and they just share a bite of cake with the politicians and then slowly, coolly, calmly, and systematically carry the cake with them and enjoy it in a way they like.

Exhibit Number 13.3: Political Pressure by Power to Correct Mistakes in Process of Administration

Services Name		No Response		Ranking of the Mode/Form of Political Pressure						
		Freq.	%	1st	2nd	3rd	4th	5th	6th	7th
I.A.S.		74	100	0	0	0	0	0	0	0
I.P.S.		89	92.7	2.5	0	0	1.7	0	0	0
I.F.S.		83	100	0	0	0	1	0	0	0
Total	N	246		4	0	0		0	0	0
Total	%	97.2	97.2	1.6	0	0	1.2	0	0	0

Weaknesses of the politicians demonstrated through these results indicating 100% of the Indian Administrative Service officers and the Indian Forest Service officers and 92.7% of Indian Police Service officers think that politicians have failed to use their power to correct mistakes in the decision-making process. Pearson Chi-square value is 13.89, with 4, degree of freedom and with a level of significance at 0.008. This item has been ranked at 18th rank of importance among 22 items under study, indicating very low interference in decision.

13.2.1.2. Known/Friendly Bureaucrats: When politicians are out of power or they feel that a particular officer will not listen to them or they do not like to disclose their identity, in such cases politicians approach known bureaucrats and friendly officers, who in turn exert pressure on the concerned officer to get things done. Thus, indirect political pressure is exerted frequently and sometimes concerned officer even does not come to know about that, he has taken the decision under political pressure. This mode of pressure has been ranked 7th in the overall ranking of all the modes. Pearson Chi-square results show a good association of present mode of political pressure with the decision-making process, the value of 41.321, with 14 degree of freedom, level of significance at 0.000. The strength of the relationship is shown by Pearson's correlation value of 0.13 with a 0.03, level of significance.

60.2% of the All India Services Officers do not consider it an important mode of political pressure and 7.5% of them assigned it 1st rank. If we look into other ranks where priority is spread over all the ranks, this is a very important mode of political pressure used by the politicians. 46.4% of the Indian Forest Service officers, 40.5% of the Indian Administrative Service officers, and 33.3% of the Indian Police Service officers have considered this as an important mode of political pressure used by a politician in the decision-making process.

Exhibit Number 13.4: Political Pressure through Known Friends and Bureaucrats

Services Name		No Response		Ranking of the Mode/Form of Political Pressure						
		Freq.	%	1st	2nd	3rd	4th	5th	6th	7th
I.A.S.		54	59.5	10.8	12.2	0	6.8	0	10.8	0
I.P.S.		64	56.7	7.3	7.3	0	10.4	0	8.3	0
I.F.S.		45	53.6	4.8	8.9	3.6	8.3	6	4.8	10.7
Total	N	153		19	23	3	22	5	20	9
Total	%		50.2	7.5	9.1	1.2	8.7	2	7.9	3.5

Political pressure mode through known friends/relatives/colleagues' relationship with variable the All India Services officer regional buckhound results are placed at Exhibit 13.5. All India Services Officers from south Indian regional background accept political pressure in the maximum frequency of 27.7% through their relatives/friends. North region officers are 2nd with 24.1% and officers from the central region accept at least 9.64% pressure in the decision. Chart 13.1 displays the ranking of various ranks the pressure accepted by this mode by three All India Services. The IAS acceptance of pressure from this mode is ranked as highest among the three services. Perhaps this may be related to close association and maintenance of political relations even after a politician is out of power keeping in mind future utility.

Exhibit Number 13.5: Pressure through Friends/Relatives versus Officer Regional Background

Mode of Pressure	Ranking of the Mode		Officer Regional Background						Total
			North eastern part	Eastern part	Western part	Northern part	Southern part	Central part	
Political pressure through friends/ relatives/ colleagues	Answer not required	% of Total	7.63	10	4.82	16.5	17.3	6.43	63.1
	2nd important mode of p.p.	% of Total	0.8	0.4	0.4	2.01	1.61	0.4	5.62
	3rd important mode of p.p.	% of Total	0.4	2	0.8	1.2	2.01	0.8	7.22
	4th important mode of p.p.	% of Total	3.21	2.8	0.8	0.8	4.02	1.2	12.8
	5th important mode of p.p.	% of Total		0.4		0.8	0.8		2.01
	6th important mode of p.p.	% of Total	0.4	1.2	0.4	2.81	2.01	0.8	7.61
	7th important mode of p.p.	% of Total	1.2		0.4				1.61
Total		% of Total	13.7	17	7.63	24.1	27.7	9.64	100

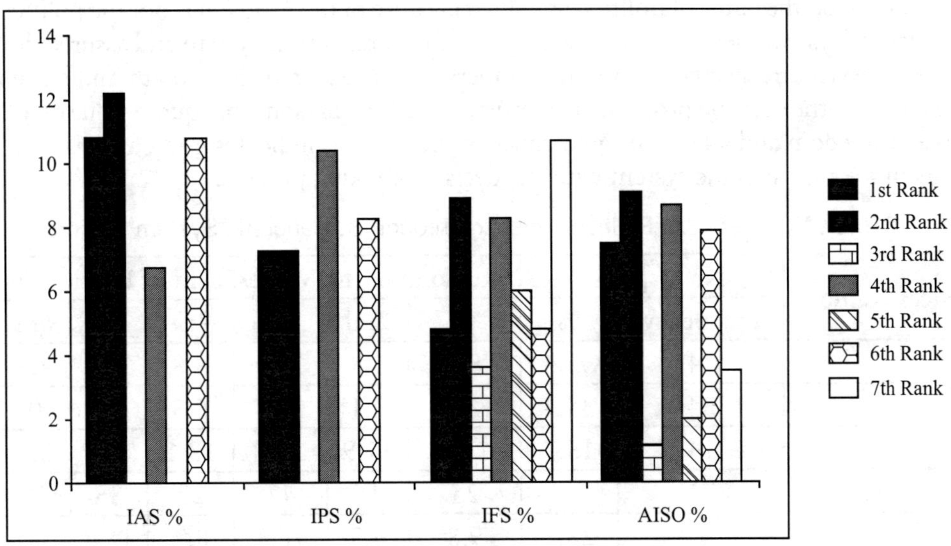

Chart No. 13.1: Pressure through Friends/Relatives/Colleagues in AIS

13.2.1.3. Bureaucratic System/Seniors: A bureaucratic system by its nature and inherent properties is full of pressure, and the beauty of this system is that it cannot be reflected or it remains hidden in the layers of the hierarchy by hiding behavior. Senior officers occupying higher positions, frequently and most deliberately use pressure tactics to coerce and victimize such officers, who raise any kind of resistance to yield under their unlawful temptations. It is commonly whispered that they deny politicians for wrong things but their own seniors never like to listen to anything from their juniors, as if juniors are their inherited slaves.

"Power holders may choose to behave in ways which further their own or others, interests. They may frame the matter for decision in a way, which suits their own, ends, or blocks the objectives of others. They push for preferred alternatives, whether or not these will lead to decisions, which are of organizational benefit. They manipulate information, withhold it, and ignore some or all of it. They negotiate for support and suppress opposition. This applies not only to those who are directly engaged in the process, but also to those who, although only indirectly involved, still have the power to influence the process in some way such as by having access to those who are more closely involved, or by providing information for the process. Since all interest groups may be engaging in similar behavior the process may be characterized by various forms of bargaining, negotiation, and compromise that may lead to outcomes which are less than optimum for all parties," S.J. Miller, D.J. Hickson and D.C. Willson (1996).

This is one of the crucial and very important modes of pressure used in the bureaucratic system; this mode has been ranked 3rd most important mode among all the modes analyzed in the research. 71.7% of the All India Services Officers consider it an important mode of political pressure and 9.8% of them have assigned it 1st rank. 83.3% of the Indian Forest Service officers, 67.6% of the Indian Administrative Service officers, and 64.6% of the Indian Police Service officers think that on maximum occasions political pressure is exerted through the bureaucratic system and their seniors. This indicates that the real problem lies inside the public administration system and the majority of members of the government system are part of it to meet individual goals and interests. These officers exploit the system to their advantage and when visualize any problem passing their failure and exploitation on the name of politicians. The real cause of the problem is not the politicians; it is the bureaucratic system itself, imperialistic origin of the bureaucratic system and assured dominance by the same service irrespective of political leadership has ensured the growth and sustenance of pressure tactics in the decision process. Our results provide a Pearson Chi-square value of 43.56 with 14 degree of freedom and a level of significance at 0.000. This indicates good association pressure by seniors in the bureaucratic system with the decision-making process.

Exhibit Number 13.6: Political Pressure through Bureaucratic System/Seniors

Services Name	No response		Ranking of the Mode/Form of Political Pressure						
	Frequency	%	1st	2nd	3rd	4th	5th	6th	7th
I.A.S.	24	32.4	8.1	5.4	18.9	6.8	16.2	4.1	8.1
I.P.S.	34	35.4	7.3	2.1	17.7	6.3	24	0	7.3
I.F.S.	14	16.7	14.3	11.9	13.1	13.1	4.8	8.3	17.9
All India Services	72		25	16	42	22	39	10	28
Total %		28.3	9.8	6.3	16.5	8.7	15.4	3.9	11

Exhibit Number 13.7: Pressure through Bureaucratic System versus Family Economic Background

Mode of Pressure	Ranking of Mode of Pressure		Family Economic Background					Total
			Rich Class	Upper Middle Class	Middle Class	Lower Middle Class	Poor Class	
Political pressure through bureaucratic system/seniors	Answer not required	Count	29	19	6	9	5	68
		% of Total	11.8	7.75	2.44	3.67	2.04	27.7
	First most important mode of political pressure	Count	6	7	6	2	1	22
		% of Total	2.44	2.85	2.44	0.81	0.40	8.97
	Second important mode of political pressure	Count		4	5	5	1	15
		% of Total		1.63	2.04	2.04	0.40	6.12
	Third important mode of political pressure	Count	17	10	8	3	4	42
		% of Total	6.93	4.08	3.26	1.22	1.63	17.1
	Fourth important mode of political pressure	Count	8	2	3	6	3	22
		% of Total	3.26	0.81	1.22	2.44	1.22	8.97
	Fifth important mode of political pressure	Count	20	8	8	2	1	39
		% of Total	8.16	3.26	3.26	0.81	0.41	15.9
	Sixth important mode of political pressure	Count	1	3	2	4	1	11
		% of Total	0.41	1.22	0.81	1.63	0.41	4.48
	Seventh in order of importance mode of political pressure	Count	9	4	5	4	4	26
		% of Total	3.67	1.63	2.04	1.63	1.63	10.6
Total		Count	90	57	43	35	20	245
		% of Total	36.7	23.2	17.5	14.2	8.16	100

Research data analysis results placed in Exhibit 13.7 show the intensity of political pressure exercised through the bureaucratic system/seniors and its relation with the demographic variable family economic background of the AISO. Results indicate 36.7% of the AISO with rich family economic background and 23.27% from the upper-middle-class family economic background (59.97% of both) are amenable to accept pressure from the bureaucratic system and seniors in the decision-making process. 11.8% of the AISO from rich family economic background have evaded answering this variable, so the total will be 71.77% in this category for acceptance of political pressure in the decision. These results are shown in Chart 13.2.

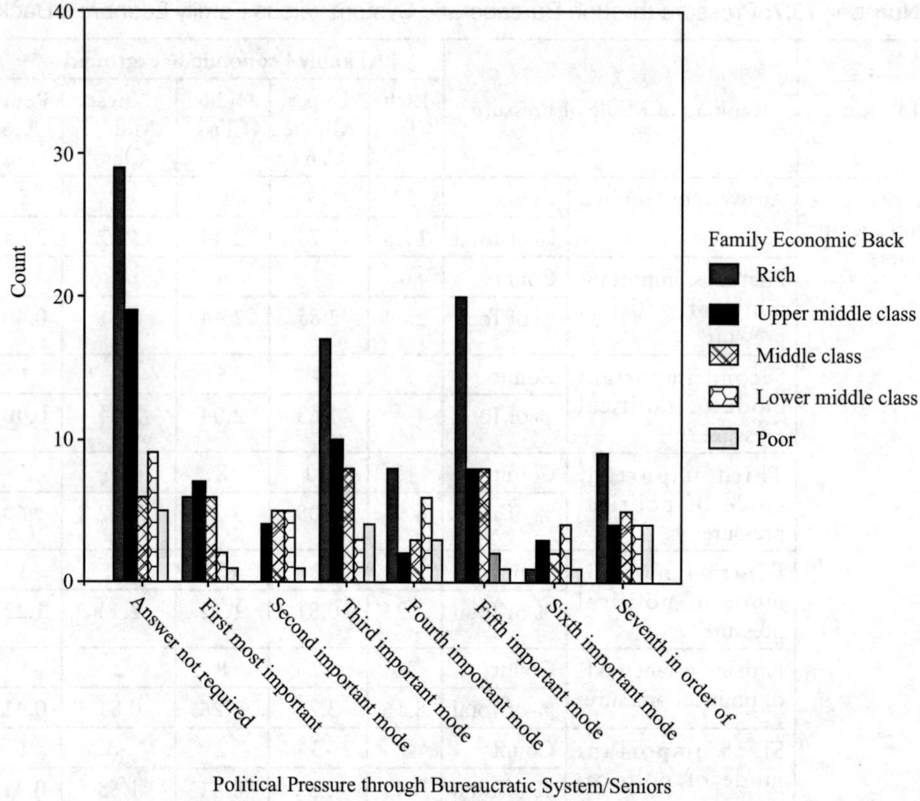

Chart No. 13.2: Family Economic Background versus Pressure through Bureaucratic System

13.2.1.4. Changing Service Conditions: It is frequently quoted that rules and service conditions are changed to accommodate a particular issue or extract advantage from the bureaucratic system. It whispered, "Show me face, I shall show you the rules". This type of pressure can be possible only when top politicians or Chief Minister/Prime Minister or a group of powerful politicians assert their interests. It is complicated, but not unfeasible. 82.2% of the All India Services Officers do not consider it an important mode of pressure. This mode of pressure has been ranked at 15th overall rank, indicating low priority. 85.5% of the Indian Forest Service officers, 80.2% of the Indian Police Service officers, and 81.1% of the Indian Administrative Service officers do not think this an important mode of pressure. Pearson Chi-square results are significant with a 0.03, level of significance.

Exhibit Number 13.8: Political Pressure through Changing Service Conditions

Services Name	No Response		Ranking of the Mode/Form of Political Pressure						
	Freq.	%	1st	2nd	3rd	4th	5th	6th	7th
I.A.S.	60	81.1	0	0	0	4.1	6.8	6.8	1.4
I.P.S.	77	80.2	0	1	0	0	6.3	7.3	5.2
I.F.S.	71	85.5	1.2	2.4	2.4	0	7.2	1.2	0
Total %	208	82.2	0.4	1.2	0.8	1.2	6.7	5.1	2.4

13.2.1.5. Abuse of Position and Authority: Politicians are located on the top in our present democratic setup, which provides them tremendous power, authority, and control over the most powerful bureaucrats in the bureaucratic system. When the politicians occupy the top position in the hierarchy, chances are that they can abuse their position in case bureaucrats do not toe in their desired design of actions. Transfer and postings are the readily available weapon in their hands, which can be used the way politicians like it. Politicians can abuse their position in most of the areas/points described in Unit 12 of this book.

Abuse of position by politicians has been rated as 2nd most common and important mode of pressure on the decision-making process. 81.4% of the All India Services Officers think that politicians misuse their position and exert pressure in the decision. 93.7% of the Indian Police Service officers, 90.5% of the Indian Administrative Service officers, and 59% of the Indian Forest Service officers consider that politicians abuse their position and induce distortions in the decision-making process. 22.9% of the Indian Police Service officers, 20.3% of the Indian Administrative Service officers, and 9.6% of the Indian Forest Service officers have assigned it 1st rank in ranking the modes of pressure.

Exhibit Number 13.9: Political Pressure by Abuse of Position and Authority

Services Name	No Response		Ranking of the Mode/Form of Political Pressure						
	Freq.	%	1st	2nd	3rd	4th	5th	6th	7th
I.A.S.	7	9.5	20.3	2.7	8.1	9.5	18.9	13.5	17.6
I.P.S.	6	6.3	22.9	0	10.4	16.7	14.6	12.5	16.7
I.F.S.	34	41	9.6	7.2	4.8	7.2	10.8	9.6	9.6
Total %	47	18.6	17.8	3.2	7.9	11.5	14.6	11.9	14.6

Politician abuse of position and decision-making process shows a strong association, which is shown by the Pearson Chi-square results. Pearson Chi-square value of 55.77 with 14 degrees of freedom and with a level of significance at '0.000' indicate good relations. Pearson's correlation (R) value of 0.22 and Spearman correlation value (Rho) of 0.24, both at a level of significance with 0.000, demonstrate strong correlations of abuse of position by politicians with the decision.

Political pressure by abuse of position and authority variable relationship with a demographic variable attitude of members of family statistical analyses results placed at Exhibit 13.10. Results show that 62.9% of spouses influence the decision process among members of the family. These results are also shown in Chart 13.3, spouse influence shows the highest score for abuse of position and authority.

Exhibit Number 13.10: Pressure by Abuse of Authority versus Attitude of Family Members

Mode	Rank of Mode of Pressure		Attitude Family Members				Total
			Spouse	Children	Parents	Brother/Sister	
Political pressure by abuse of position and authority	Answer not required	Count	30	2			32
		% of Total	13.4	0.89			14.3

Mode	Rank of Mode of Pressure		Attitude Family Members				Total
			Spouse	Children	Parents	Brother/Sister	
	First most important mode of political pressure	Count	25	3	11	4	43
		% of Total	11.2	1.34	4.91	1.78	19.2
	Second important mode of political pressure	Count	6			1	7
		% of Total	2.68			0.45	3.125
	Third important mode of political pressure	Count	12	2	4		18
		% of Total	5.35	0.89	1.78		8.04
	Fourth important mode of political pressure	Count	16	4	7	2	29
		% of Total	7.15	1.78	3.125	0.89	12.9
	Fifth important mode of political pressure	Count	22	3	6	3	34
		% of Total	9.83	1.34	2.67	1.34	15.1
	Sixth important mode of political pressure	Count	12	4	6	3	25
		% of Total	5.36	1.78	2.67	1.34	11.1
	Seventh in order of importance mode of political pressure	Count	18	5	9	4	36
		% of Total	8.04	2.24	4.02	1.78	16.1
Total		Count	141	23	43	17	224
		% of Total	62.9	10.2	19.19	7.58	100

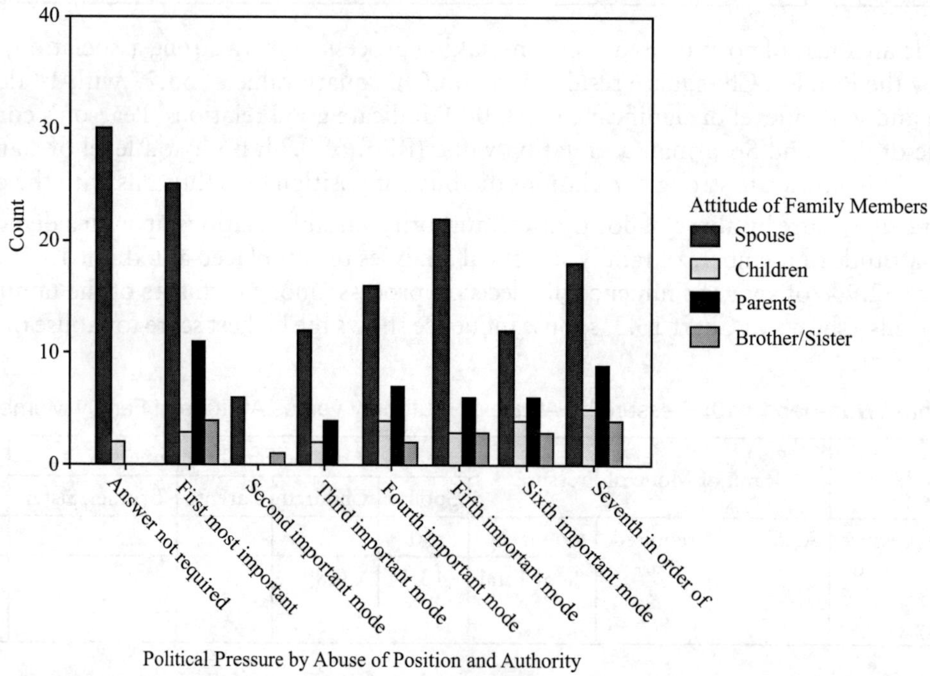

Chart No. 13.3: Family Member Attitude to Abuse Position and Authority

13.2.1.6. Grievance Redressing Mechanism: Politicians occupy the top position in the bureaucratic system and by virtue of being at the top position; they enjoy unlimited powers as the grievance redresser for the masses. In the name of public grievance, politicians can exert a tremendous amount of pressure on the All India Services Officers. Politicians' position is clear and authority effuse from them and their decision are ultimate and almost final. So, in the name of public grievances redressing, politicians pressurize the All India Services Officers and influence the decision-making process in their own favor.

73.5% of the All India Services Officers feel that the politicians do not misuse this mode. 80.7% of the Indian Forest Service officers, 70.8% of the Indian Police Service officers, and 68.9% of the Indian Administrative Service officers think that the grievance-redressing mechanism is not misused by the politicians. 16.2% of the Indian Administrative Service officers and 14.6% of the Indian Police Service officers have ranked it 6th and 4.8% of the Indian Forest Service officers ranked it 5th in the importance of this mode of pressure. 35.03 value of Pearson Chi-Square with 14 degree of freedom and with 0.001, level of significance, indicate a good association of this mode with the decision process.

Exhibit Number 13.11: Political Pressure through Grievance Redressal Mechanism

Services Name	No Response		Ranking of the Mode/Form of Political Pressure						
	Freq.	%	1st	2nd	3rd	4th	5th	6th	7th
I.A.S.	51	68.9	1.4	1.4	1.4	0	10.8	16.2	0
I.P.S.	68	70.8	0	0	1	0	13.5	14.6	0
I.F.S.	67	80.7	2.4	0	2.4	2.4	4.8	2.4	4.8
Total %	186	73.5	1.2	0.4	1.6	0.8	9.9	11.1	1.6

13.2.1.7. Performance Review: The politician is located at the top position, by virtue of his position he enjoys the overriding powers and, in many cases, and final authority to accept or reject the performance of any officer. Annual confidential reports/performance appraisal is the most crucial document for the All India Services Officers, for their career advancement and progression. Like any other service, the All India Services Officers also suffer due to groupism and in-service fighting, this makes them more vulnerable in front of politicians. They approach politicians for desired Annual Performance Review and manipulations in the review of their work. Politicians use this situation liberally for their own advantage and both are happy in a 'win-win' situation. This mode has been ranked at 13th in the overall ranking. 41.9% of the All India Services Officers consider it an important mode of pressure in the decision-making process. 66.3% of the Indian Forest Service officers, 58.3% of the Indian Police Service officers, and 49% of the Indian Administrative Service officers think that this mode is not important. The highest rank for the All India Services, 13.5% of the Indian Administrative Service officers ranked it at 5th rank, 9.4% of the Indian Police Service officers ranked it 6th rank and 8.4% of the Indian Forest Service officers ranked it at 7th rank in importance.

Exhibit Number 13.12: Political Pressure through Performance Review as Tool

Services Name	No Response		Ranking of the Mode/Form of Political Pressure						
	Freq.	%	1st	2nd	3rd	4th	5th	6th	7th
I.A.S.	36	48.6	1.4	8.1	8.1	0	13.5	12.2	8.1
I.P.S.	56	58.3	0	7.3	7.3	1	8.3	8.3	9.4
I.F.S.	55	66.3	1.2	6	6	4.8	3.6	8.4	3.6
Total %	147	58.1	0.8	7.1	7.1	2	8.3	9.5	7.1

13.2.1.8. Power of Promotions: Politicians' location at top of the bureaucratic system provides him power for appointment and promotions. Even in case, they do not have the real powers, files go through them and they enjoy complete regulatory powers. These powers make them highly powerful and the All India Services Officers develop close relations for sake of their promotions and prize postings. Even the topmost officers on verge of their retirement also move around politicians in search of post-retirement rehabilitations/appointments. This mode of pressure has been ranked as the 8th important mode of political pressure in the decision-making process. 64.8% of the All India Services Officers give it low consideration and do not consider it as the most important mode of pressure. 70.3% of the Indian Administrative Service officers, 69.8% of the Indian Police Service officers, and 54.2% of the Indian Forest Service officers have not considered this among the seven most important modes of pressure. Pearson Chi-square value of 24.99 with 14 degree of freedom and level of significance with 0.03 is significant and show good association with the decision.

Exhibit Number 13.13: Power of Appointment and Promotions by Politicians

Services Name	No Response		Ranking of the Mode/Form of Political Pressure						
	Freq.	%	1st	2nd	3rd	4th	5th	6th	7th
I.A.S.	52	70.3	1.4	8.1	9.5	0	1.4	8.1	1.4
I.P.S.	67	69.8	0	8.3	9.4	0	0	11.5	1
I.F.S.	45	54.2	6	10.8	9.6	4.8	4.8	9.6	0
Total %	164	64.8	2.4	9.1	9.5	1.6	2	9.9	0.8

13.2.1.9. Tours/Training: A bureaucratic system is such that politicians can get rid of undesirable officers in different ways and means, at the same time politician can reward them liberally by various methods. Foreign training, tours, and fellowships are one of such instruments in the hands of politicians. Politicians want that some decision is taken in his favor, he will tell concern officer that officer will be rewarded or penalized through sending them on training, tours, and visits abroad and within the country. Politicians use this as a mode of pressure, but our results indicate that this has very low priority and 21st rank. 92% of the All India Services Officers do not consider it an important mode of pressure in all the three services. The highest-ranking is the 7th for all the services with 8.3% for the Indian Police Service officers, 6.8% for the Indian Administrative Service officers, and 2.4% for the Indian Forest Service officers. Research results indicate that this is not an important mode of political pressure exerted in the decision-making process.

Exhibit Number 13.14: Politician Control over Foreign Tours/Training/Fellowships

Services Name	No Response		Ranking of the Mode/Form of Political Pressure						
	Freq.	%	1st	2nd	3rd	4th	5th	6th	7th
I.A.S.	68	91.9	0	0	1.4	0	0	0	6.8
I.P.S.	88	91.7	0	0	0	0	0	0	8.3
I.F.S.	76	91.6	0	0	0	1.2	2.4	2.4	2.4
Total %	232	91.7	0	0	0.4	0.4	0.8	0.8	5.9

13.2.2. Public and Social Power Groups

Pressure modes or forms commonly used by public and socially powerful groups are: (i) mobilize pressure through friends, relatives, and colleagues, (ii) use of communication media in different variations (print, audio, video, electronic and traditional) and related modes, (iii) public organize themselves in big groups as big rallies, delegations and community pressure, (iv) public mobilize prominent citizens, retired politicians and old guards of the system; and politicians, and (v) community raise demand for enhancing and protecting individual rights and freedom of people.

13.2.2.1. Friends/Relatives/Colleagues: Politicians use their friends, relatives, and colleagues to exert pressure on the decision-making process to get their objectives fulfilled in the desired manner. 37.9% of the All India Services Officers feel that politicians use their friends and relatives to exert political pressure. 41.75% of the Indian Police Service officers, 40.5% of the Indian Administrative Service officers, and 31.3% of the Indian Forest Service officers think that the politicians use this mode of political pressure in the decision-making process. The highest percentage of 12.6% has been in the 4th rank and no ranking for the first rank. The Indian Administrative Service officers and the Indian Police Service officers have encountered this model more than the Indian Forest Service officers have. This mode of political pressure has been assigned 10th overall rank.

Exhibit Number 13.15: Political Pressure through Friends/Relatives/Colleagues

Services Name	No Response		Ranking of the Mode/Form of Political Pressure						
	Freq.	%	1st	2nd	3rd	4th	5th	6th	7th
I.A.S.	44	59.5	0	6.8	8.1	17.6	0	6.8	1.4
I.P.S.	56	58.3	0	7.3	7.3	14.6	3.1	9.4	0
I.F.S.	57	68.7	0	2.4	8.4	6	4.8	6	3.6
Total %	157	62.1	0	5.5	7.9	12.6	2.8	7.5	1.6

13.2.2.2. Communication Media: Communication media in different forms and variations has also joined the race in the process of self-goal maximization. The All India Services Officers narrate numerous stories starting from pseudo-journalism to yellow journalism, how people chase them for petty gains. Communication media persons exert pressure on them for the small matter of transfer to allotment of resources and even cash benefits. Communication media watch that others are maximizing their own goals, why they should not chase their self-goals and interests. Prominent persons in communication media misuse their position to propagate their self-interests and number of times pressurize for the land, house, or other resource allocation for their individual use.

Exhibit Number 13.16: Political Pressure through Communication Media

Services Name		No Response		Ranking of the Mode/Form of Political Pressure						
		Freq.	%	1st	2nd	3rd	4th	5th	6th	7th
I.A.S.		67	90.5	0	0	6.8	0	1.4	1.4	0
I.P.S.		85	88.5	0	0	7.3	3.1	0	0	1
I.F.S.		60	72.3	0	3.6	3.6	3.6	6	4.8	6
Total	N	212			3	15	6	6	5	6
Total	%		83.8	0	1.2	5.9	2.4	2.4	2	2.4

This mode of pressure has been ranked at 14th. This has not been considered a very important mode of pressure. 83.8% of the All India Services Officers have denied that it is important for them. 90.5% of the Indian Administrative Service officers. 88.5% of the Indian Police Service officers and 72.3% of the Indian Forest Service officers feel that communication media is not an important mode of pressure for them. This indicates a very low percentage of officers, who have experienced pressure from the media people. Pearson Chi-square results show an association of this mode of pressure with the decision, the value of 31.63 with 12 degree of freedom and 0.002, level of significance. These relationships are strong and Pearson's correlation value of 0.23 with a level of significance at 0.000. Spearman correlation value of 0.2 is also significant with a level of significance at 0.001.

13.2.2.3. Organized Public: Politicians, when feeling that pressure has to be exerted at such a level or on such an officer, where individual politician stature is not enough to get things done in his favor, in such difficult situation's politician use the public as an instrument to meet own goals through the organized public pressure. This mode of pressure is rarely used and it has been ranked at overall 17th rank among the various modes used by the politicians. 87.45% of the All India Services Officers feel that this mode of pressure is not an important mode to exert pressure on them. 93.8% of the Indian Police Service officers, 91.9% of the Indian Administrative Service officers, and 75.9% of Indian Forest Service officers think that organized public is not an important mode of political pressure. Pearson Chi-square results show a good association between this mode with the decision-making process. Pearson Chi-square value of 30.75 with 12 degrees of freedom and level of significance at 0.002 indicates that results are significant. To know the strength of these relationships, we have a Spearman correlation value of 0.2 with a level of significance at 0.003. However, our statistical analysis shows an association and significant relationship with the decision-making process, but this is not a very popular mode of pressure and is only used in exigencies conditions. A very high percentage of the AISO has not bothered to reply to this variable, this indicates very low importance of this mode of pressure.

Exhibit Number 13.17: Political Pressure through Organised Public

	No Response		Ranking of the Mode/Form of Political Pressure						
Services Name	Freq.	%	1st	2nd	3rd	4th	5th	6th	7th
I.A.S.	68	91.9	0	0	0	0	0	8.1	0
I.P.S.	90	93.8	0	0	0	0	0	6.3	0
I.F.S.	63	75.9	0	3.6	3.6	2.4	4.8	7.2	2.4
Total N	221			3	3	2	4	18	2
Total %		87.4		1.2	1.2	0.8	1.6	7.1	0.8

13.2.2.4. Member of Citizenry: All India Services Officers narrated some instances of pressure coming through prominent citizens, such as retired highly placed bureaucrat or politician or persons who have excelled in one's own area at the national level or the concerned person acknowledges such prominence. 98% of the All India Services Officers do not consider it as a mode of pressure. This mode is ranked at the last rank and cannot be considered as a mode of pressure as proved by results. We can safely exclude it from its importance. Only a few IFS officers have considered this mode of pressure.

Exhibit Number 13.18: Political Pressure through Members of Citizenry

Services Name	No Response		Ranking of the Mode/Form of Political Pressure						
	Freq.	%	1st	2nd	3rd	4th	5th	6th	7th
I.A.S.	74	100	0	0	0	0	0	0	0
I.P.S.	96	100	0	0	0	0	0	0	0
I.F.S.	78	94	0	0	1.2	1.2	1.2	2.4	0
Total N	248		0	0	1	1	1	2	0
Total %		98	0	0	0.4	0.4	0.4	0.8	0

13.2.2.5. Individual Rights and Freedom: Politicians are the representatives of the public; they can always raise demand for enhancing the freedom and protecting the rights of the individual citizens. Politicians can always raise a banner for the emancipation of the public from the exploitation of the bureaucratic system, can even fight for higher freedom and a more liberal outlook from the officers. This is being used as one of the modes of political pressure. In our study results, this has not come out as an important mode of pressure in the decision. 96.8% of the All India Services Officers do not consider it an important mode of pressure. This has been ranked 20th in the overall ranking. The value of Pearson Chi-square is 17.12 with 8 degree of freedom and with a level of significance at 0.02, indicates a good association with the decision. Pearson's correlation and Spearman correlation value of 0.2 are significant and show good strength of this relationship.

Exhibit Number 13.19: Pressure through Demand for Enhancing and Protecting Individual Rights

Services Name	No Response		Ranking of the Mode/Form of Political Pressure						
	Freq.	%	1st	2nd	3rd	4th	5th	6th	7th
I.A.S.	73	98.6	0	1.4	0	0	0	0	0
I.P.S.	96	100	0	0	0	0	0	0	0
I.F.S.	76	91.6	0	0	0	3.6	2.4	2.4	0
Total %	245	96.8	0	0.4	0	1.2	0.8	0.8	0

13.2.3. Political Parties

Political parties use different modes to mobilize pressure are pressure through (i) political groups and activist; (ii) politician insistence for open and accountable government; (iii) politician supremacy in democratic decision-making process; (iv) politician enjoy full control over public servants; (v) and politician can use his discretionary power in decision-making process and authority over them.

13.2.3.1. Political Groups and Activist: It is commonly said that workers of the political party in power and their activists mobilize pressure to get their things done, in case they feel that concerned officer is not yielding under their pressure, then they form group/s and exert pressure in-group to get the desired outcome from the decision. It has been observed that on many occasions one or more ministers join together to exert pressure on decision. If they visualize that small group may not be effective to get thing moved according to own wishes, then they form bigger groups based on region, caste, religion, and political affiliations to a particular leader. To show their strength on occasions, they mobilize huge gatherings to pressurize Chief Minister/Prime Minister or power holders, so that they present their own interests as the interests of the masses. These pressure tactics are dynamic with time and space.

In this mode of exerting political pressure through political groups and activists, 58.7% of the All India Services Officers feel that it is not crucial for the decision. As individual service, 59.5% of the Indian Forest Service officers have feeling that they exert political pressure on the decision-making process. But 29.7% of the Indian Administrative Service officers feel interference from political activist. 12.2% of the Indian Administrative Service officers have given it 5th rank and 7.3% of the Indian Police Service officers assigned 7th rank. 17.9% of the Indian Forest Service officers have assigned it 1st rank; due to this political groups and activists have got overall 5th rank among all 22 modes of pressure. Pearson Chi-square value of 39.744, with 14 degree of freedom and a significance level of 0.000, shows a good relationship of this mode of political pressure with the decision. The strength of this correlation is shown by the Spearman correlation (Rho) value of 0.2 with a 0.002, level of significance.

Exhibit Number 13.20: Political Pressure through Political Activist and Political Groups

Services Name	No Response		Ranking of the Mode/Form of Political Pressure						
	Freq.	%	1st	2nd	3rd	4th	5th	6th	7th
I.A.S.	52	70.3	1.4	1.4	0	6.8	12.2	6.8	1.4
I.P.S.	63	65.6	8.3	1	3.1	8.3	6.3	7.3	0

Services Name		No Response		Ranking of the Mode/Form of Political Pressure						
		Freq.	%	1st	2nd	3rd	4th	5th	6th	7th
I.F.S.		34	40.5	17.9	6	8.3	3.6	9.5	9.5	4.8
Total	N	149		24	7	10	16	23	20	5
Total	%		58.7	9.4	2.8	3.9	6.3	9.1	7.9	2

13.2.3.2. Open and Accountable Government: Bureaucratic system working is such that officers like to take decisions and do not like to share with others. Under the garb of secrecy, bureaucrats cultivate their own interests and goals, this gives rise to suspicion. Politicians raise the banner for open and accountable government. They more often use this mode of pressure when politicians are out of power. This mode has been ranked 19th in the overall ranking. 96.1% of the All India Services Officers do not consider it an important mode of pressure. 99% of the Indian Police Service officers, 94.7% of the Indian Administrative Service officers, and 94% of the Indian Forest Service officers do not consider it an important mode of pressure. Our results indicate that insistence for open and accountable government cannot be considered an important mode of pressure.

Exhibit Number 13.21: Pressure through Insistence for Open and Accountable Government

Services Name		No Response		Ranking of the Mode/Form of Political Pressure						
		Freq.	%	1st	2nd	3rd	4th	5th	6th	7th
I.A.S.		71	94.7	0	1.3	1.3	1.3	0	1.3	0
I.P.S.		95	99	0	0	0	0	0	0	1
I.F.S.		79	94	0	0	2.4	1.2	2.4	0	0
Total	%	245	96.1	0	0.4	1.2	0.8	0.8	0.4	0.4

13.2.3.3. Supremacy in Decision Process: Politicians occupy the top position; hence enjoy supremacy in the decision-making process. This mode of pressure is more pronounced in policy-related decisions. Routine decisions are taken by the All India Services Officers from the lowest level to the secretariat level, where politicians do not have much say. In such cases, politicians approach the head of the department and other senior officers and indirect pressure is exerted on the All India Services Officers.

59.1% of the All India Services Officers realize this mode of pressure as an important mode of pressure and ranked it at 6th overall rank. 60% of the Indian Administrative Service officers, 59.5% of the Indian Forest Service officers, and 58.3% of the Indian Police Service officers realize that politician supremacy over them influence their decisions. The highest ranking in the mode is 13.3% with 2nd rank for the Indian Administrative Service officers, 12.5% with 2nd rank for the Indian Police Service officers, and 11.9% with 4th rank for the Indian Forest Service officers. Our research results indicate that this is one of the very important modes of political pressure in the decision-making process.

Exhibit Number 13.22: Political Pressure through Politician Supremacy in Decision Making

Services Name	No Response		Ranking of the Mode/Form of Political Pressure						
	Freq.	%	1st	2nd	3rd	4th	5th	6th	7th
I.A.S.	30	40	4	13.3	12	12	6.7	0	12
I.P.S.	40	41.7	8.3	12.5	13.5	7.3	8.3	0	8.3
I.F.S.	34	40.5	10.7	6	15.5	11.9	4.8	3.6	7.1
Total %	104	40.8	7.8	10.6	13.7	10.2	6.7	1.2	9

Exhibit Number 13.23: Politician Supremacy in Decision versus Educational Background of Officer

Mode	Rank of Mode of Pressure		Educational Background of Officer					Total
			Graduate	Engineer/ B.Tech./ Technology	P.G.	MBA/ CA/CW	Ph.D.	
Political pressure through politician supermacy in decision making	Answer not required	Count	25	20	34	13	5	97
		% of Total	10.33	8.26	14.04	5.37	2.06	40.08
	First most important mode of political pressure	Count	3	4	7		3	17
		% of Total	1.23	1.65	2.89		1.23	7.02
	Second important mode of political pressure	Count	8	5	9	4	1	27
		% of Total	3.3	2.06	3.71	1.65	0.41	11.15
	Third important mode of political pressure	Count	12	9	8	3	3	35
		% of Total	4.95	3.71	3.3	1.23	1.23	14.46
	Fourth important mode of political pressure	Count	8	5	8	3		24
		% of Total	3.3	2.06	3.3	1.23		9.91
	Fifth important mode of political pressure	Count	4	5	6	2		17
		% of Total	1.65	2.06	2.47	0.82		7.02
	Sixth important mode of political pressure	Count	1		2			3
		% of Total	0.41		0.82			1.23
	Seventh in order of importance mode of political pressure	Count	5	4	7	4	2	22
		% of Total	2.06	1.65	2.89	1.65	0.82	9.09
Total		Count	66	52	81	29	14	242
		% of Total	27.27	21.48	33.47	11.98	5.78	100

Politicians' supremacy in decision making a variable relationship with the demographic variable of the educational background of the officer analyses results are placed at Exhibit 13.23 indicate that 33.47% with postgraduate and 27.27% with a graduate qualification are amenable to this mode of pressure. Chart 13.4 shows this on the chart.

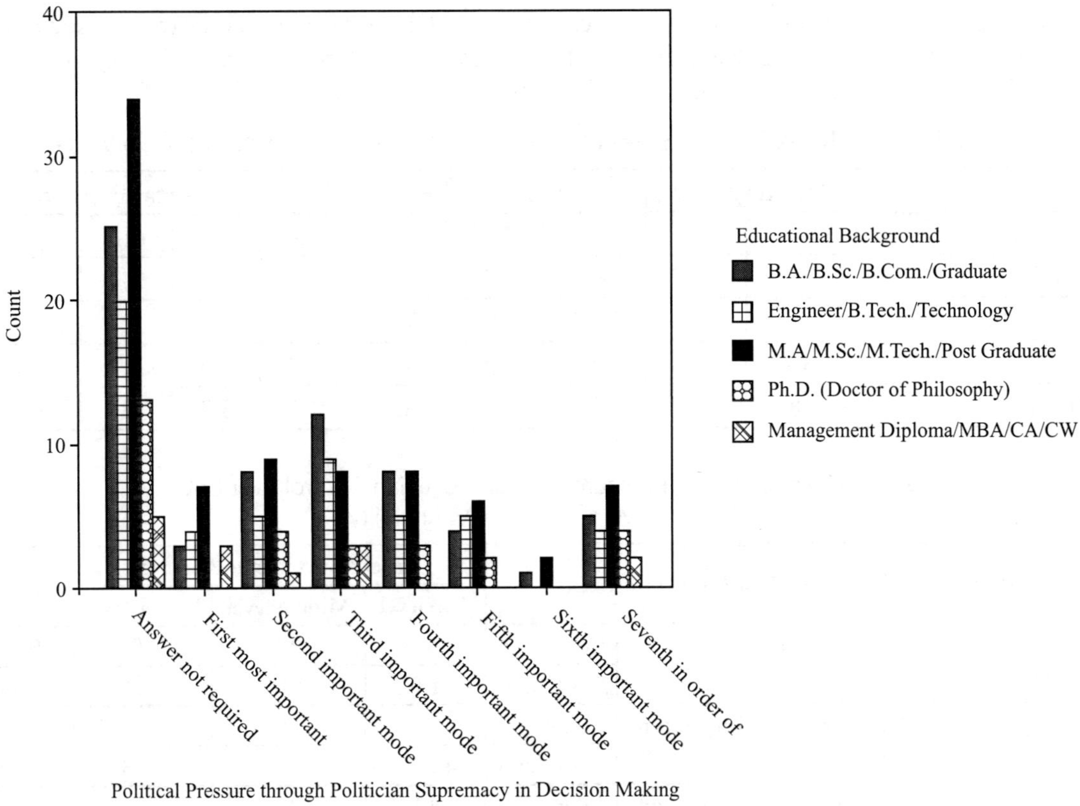

Chart No.13.4: Educational Background and Decision Supremacy of Politicians

13.2.3.4. Control over Public Servants: Politicians occupy the top position in the bureaucratic system and they enjoy control over the All India Services Officers and other public servants. This control over public servants provides politicians enormous power and authority, public servants, in turn, look for their own interests and try to develop strong relations with the politicians for the achievement of their own goals and interests. Politicians are not familiar with the internal intricacies of the bureaucratic system, so they are in search of such officers who can tell their inner stories, so that, they exercise complete and fuller control to enhance bargaining power. This develops a vicious circle of self-goals and interests, which is mutually gainful for both politicians and officers both.

Our results indicate that this mode of pressure is the first and most important mode of pressure commonly used by politicians. 61.3% of the All India Services Officers have ranked it an important mode of pressure in the decision-making process. 62.7% of the Indian Administrative Service officers, 62.5% of the Indian Police Service officers, and 58.5% of the Indian Forest Service officers have assigned importance to politician control over them as the major source of political pressure. 1st ranking in the mode is also very high with 29.3% for the Indian Administrative Service officers, 27.1% for the Indian Police Service officers, and 19.5% for the Indian Forest Service officers; clearly establish the importance of political control as the most crucial mode of political pressure in the decision-making process. Pearson Chi-square results show the association of political control with the decision by the All India Services Officers. Pearson Chi-square value is 27.75 with 14 degree of freedom and with a 0.01, level of significance.

Exhibit Number 13.24: Political Pressure through Politician Control over Public Servants

Services Name	No Response		Ranking of the Mode/Form of Political Pressure						
	Freq.	%	1st	2nd	3rd	4th	5th	6th	7th
I.A.S.	28	37.3	29.3	2.7	8	13.3	1.3	1.3	6.7
I.P.S.	36	37.5	27.1	13.5	7.3	6.3	0	1	7.3
I.F.S.	34	41.5	19.5	9.8	4.9	9.8	8.5	3.7	2.4
Total %	98	38.7	15.3	9.1	6.7	9.5	3.2	2	5.5

Exhibit Number 13.25: Pressure through Politician Control over Public Servants versus Levels Amenability

Mode	Rank of Mode of Pressure		Level Amenable to Pressure			Total
			Top level	Middle level	Lower level	
Political pressure through politician control over public servants	Answer not required	Count	55	23	19	97
		% of Total	21.91	9.16	7.56	38.69
	First most important mode of political pressure	Count	39	16	9	64
		% of Total	15.53	6.37	3.58	25.49
	Second important mode of political pressure	Count	12	8	1	21
		% of Total	4.78	3.18	0.39	8.36
	Third important mode of political pressure	Count	12	5	1	18
		% of Total	4.78	1.99	0.39	7.17
	Fourth important mode of political pressure	Count	17	4	3	24
		% of Total	6.77	1.59	1.19	9.56
	Fifth important mode of political pressure	Count	6	2		8
		% of Total	2.39	0.79		3.18
	Sixth important mode of political pressure	Count	4		1	5
		% of Total	1.59		0.39	1.99
	Seventh in order of importance mode of political pressure	Count	5	7	2	14
		% of Total	1.99	2.78	0.79	5.57
Total		Count	150	65	36	251
		% of Total	59.76	25.89	14.34	100

Politician control over public servants' variable relationship with bureaucratic levels amenable to pressure acceptance the data analyses results are placed in Exhibit 13.25. Results show 59.76%

of the AISO at the top level are amenable to accept pressure from this mode of pressure. 25.89% of middle-level officers are amenable to accept pressure. Chart 13.5 also show the relation of different level of bureaucracy amenable to accept pressure due to politicians' control over public servants.

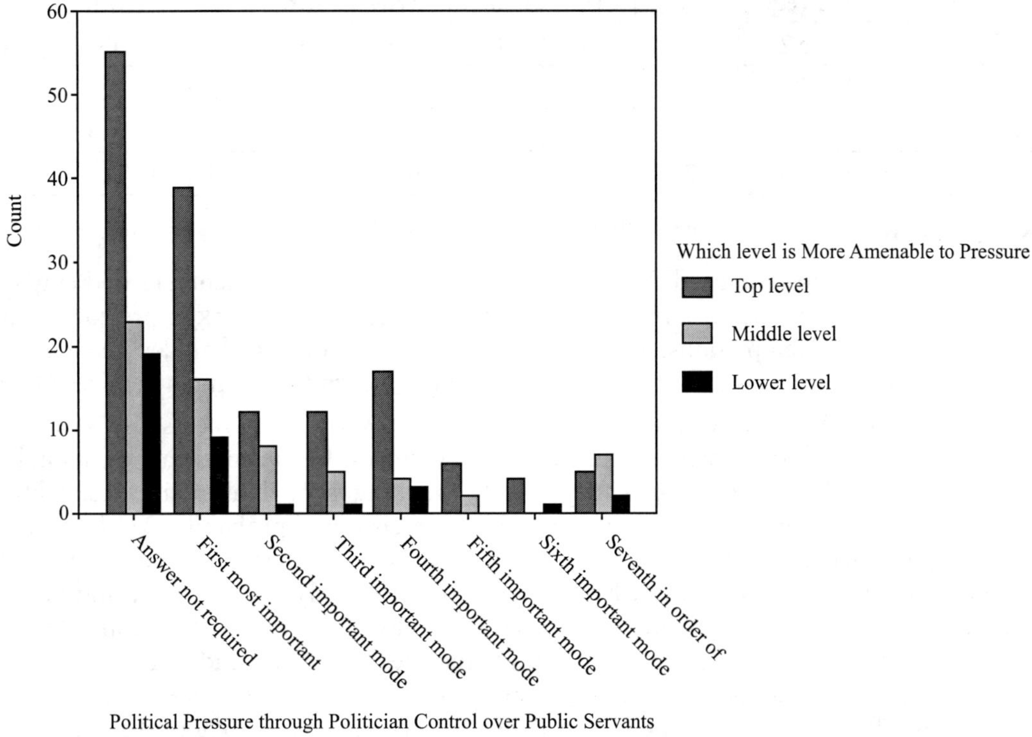

Chart No. 13.5: Political Pressure through Control over Public Servant and Level Amenable to Pressure

13.2.3.5. Authority: Politicians' top position in public administration provides him discretion and authority, which he can exercise over the decision-making process. 67.7% of the All India Services Officers feel that discretionary powers of the politicians are not an important mode of pressure as most of the decisions are taken below in the districts. 75% of the Indian Police Service officers, 69.3% of the Indian Administrative Service officers, and 57.8% of the Indian Forest Service officers assign a low priority to this mode of pressure. In overall ranking politician discretion has been ranked at 12th rank. Ranking in the present mode is 4th for 13.5% of the Indian Police Service officers and 13.3% for the Indian Administrative Service officers. 9.6% of the Indian Forest Service officers have considered it at 7th rank. Pearson Chi-square value is 43.95, with 14 degrees of freedom, and a level of significance with 0.000. Pearson Chi-square results show a good association of politician authority with the decision and results are significant.

Exhibit Number 13.26: Pressure through Use of Discretionary Authority by Politician

Services Name		No Response		Ranking of the Mode/Form of Political Pressure						
		Freq.	%	1st	2nd	3rd	4th	5th	6th	7th
I.A.S.		52	69.3	0	0	9.3	13.3	2.7	1.3	4
I.P.S.		72	75	0	0	8.3	13.5	3.1	0	0
I.F.S.		48	57.8	3.6	6	2.4	8.4	3.6	8.4	9.6
Total	%	172	67.7	1.2	2	6.7	11.8	3.1	3.1	4.3

13.2.4. Power Brokers

The pressure is also mobilized through: (i) power brokers, touts, agents, retired employees and officers work as conduits; (ii) musclemen and underworld people work as pressure point by issuing threatening and temptations; (iii) widespread networks of open and hidden financiers, who mobilize funds for politicians also work as modes of pressure on the All India Services Officers.

13.2.4.1. Power Brokers: Whenever, most of the All India Services Officers discuss about the frequent use of political pressure in the decision-making process by the politician, on a number of occasions they think that power brokers are probably operating through the politicians. Politicians are highly mobile and availability at times of need is the question of probability? Otherwise, also mostly many politicians like to operate through such brokers so that they continue to enjoy a clean image among the masses. Power brokers and touts are easily approachable and in case of hue and cry, politicians can use them as sacrificial goats also. Even many of the top bureaucrats also operate through such power brokers to evade the eyes of the law and to make the process simple to extract maximum out of the bureaucratic system in the shortest time. 65.2% of the All India Services Officers, 71.1% of the Indian Forest Service officers, 65.6% of the Indian Police Service officers, and 58.1% of the Indian Administrative Service officers do not realize this as a serious problem. This is having been considered as the 4th most important mode of political pressure exerted on the decision-making process.

Exhibit Number 13.27: Political Pressure through Power Brokers

Services Name		No Response		Ranking of the Mode/Form of Political Pressure						
		Freq.	%	1st	2nd	3rd	4th	5th	6th	7th
I.A.S.		43	58.1	14.9	0	1.4	1.4	8.1	0	16.2
I.P.S.		63	65.6	6.3	4.2	0	0	8.3	0	15.6
I.F.S.		59	71.1	8.4	4.8	2.4	2.4	4.8	1.2	4.8
Total	N	185		24	8	3	3	18	1	31
Total	%		65.2	9.5	3.2	1.2	1.2	7.1	0.4	12.3

The Indian Administrative Service officers maintain comparatively more distance from the real sufferers, so for them, power brokers are a grave problem. 41.9% of the Indian Administrative Service officers have ranked this problem in seven important ranks, 14.9% in the first rank. Chi-square value is 25.79, with a degree of freedom of 14 and a level of significance at 0.02.

Pearson's correlation value of –0.13 with a level of significance of 0.04, show correlation with the decision-making process.

13.2.4.2. Musclemen and Underworld: The problem of musclemen and underworld exerting political pressure is limited to some pockets in the country; it is not an extensive and widespread problem. In many States, such a mode of pressure is not common but, in some States, the All India Services Officers consider it as the most dangerous mode of pressure. Officers from Bihar, Madhya Pradesh, Uttar Pradesh, Kerala, Jharkhand, Chhattisgarh, and Maharashtra told that they do face pressure in the decision-making process from such modes.

Exhibit Number 13.28: Political Pressure through Musclemen and Underworld

Services Name		No Response		Ranking of the Mode/Form of Political Pressure						
		Freq.	%	1st	2nd	3rd	4th	5th	6th	7th
I.A.S.		64	86.5	0	0	6.8	0	0	0	6.8
I.P.S.		67	69.8	0	0	7.3	1	3.1	10.4	8.3
I.F.S.		71	85.5	0	2.4	3.6	1.2	1.2	1.2	4.8
Total	N	202		0	2	15	2	4	11	17
Total	%		79.8	0	0.8	5.9	0.8	1.6	4.3	6.7

79.8% of the All India Services Officers do not feel the importance of this mode of pressure. 86.5% of the Indian Administrative Service officers, 85.5% of the Indian Forest Service officers, and 69.8% of the Indian Police Service officers think that musclemen and underworld are not the important mode of pressure. The highest percentage of this rank is in the 7th rank, which again indicates low priority. Pearson Chi-square results are significant with a level of significance at 0.01.

13.2.4.3. Open and Hidden Financiers: Open and hidden financiers are the persons who finance the political activities, political parties, and politicians by direct or indirect manner, means, and methods to derive gains for their own interests in lieu of this. Such finance is common during elections and after elections, they organize events/political rallies for the ruling party, groups of politicians, and individual politicians. They carry out such activities as a business and earn fortunes by garnering undue benefits from the politicians. Their proximity to politicians saves them from a lot of inconvenient problems and bureaucratic hassles. In due course of time through political conduits, they develop relations in the bureaucratic system and connection with the top power holder in the hierarchy.

Exhibit Number 13.29: Political Pressure through Open and Hidden Financiers

Services Name		No Response		Ranking of the Mode/Form of Political Pressure						
		Freq.	%	1st	2nd	3rd	4th	5th	6th	7th
I.A.S.		41	55.4	0	28.4	1.4	8.1	0	1.4	5.4
I.P.S.		46	47.9	1	28.1	0	8.3	1	3.1	10.4
I.F.S.		63	75.9	0	9.6	1.2	3.6	2.4	2.4	4.8
Total	N	150		1	56	2	17	3	6	18
Total	%		59.3	0.4	22.1	0.8	6.7	1.2	2.4	7.1

40.7% of the All India Services Officers consider it an important mode of pressure in the decision-making process. 24.1% of the Indian Forest Service officers, 44.6% of the Indian Administrative Service officers, and 52.1% of the Indian Police Service officers consider it an important mode of pressure in the decision. Most of the All India Services Officers have given it 2nd rank with 22.1%. 28.4% of the Indian Administrative Service officers, 28.1% of the Indian Police Service officers, and 9.6% of the Indian Forest Service officers have assigned it the highest rank of 2nd in importance. Pearson Chi-square results show an association with the decision-making process with the value of 24.39 with 14 degree of freedom and with an acceptable level of significance of 0.04.

ANNEXURE 13.A: QUESTIONNAIRE ON MODES AND FORMS OF POLITICAL PRESSURE

Indirect political pressure is managed through various pressure groups. Such pressure is exerted on the officers of All India Services in various modes and forms. We have listed 22 modes of pressure. Kindly, write seven most important mode of political pressure in their order of importance as 1 to 7.

(208)	Pressure through power to correct the mistakes in the process of administration.	
(209)	Pressure through power brokers.	
(210)	Political pressure through political groups and political activist.	
(211)	Pressure through known/friendly bureaucrats.	
(212)	Pressure through bureaucratic system/seniors.	
(213)	Pressure through friends/relatives/colleagues.	
(214)	Pressure through communication media.	
(215)	Pressure through organized public.	
(216)	Pressure through member of citizenry.	
(217)	Pressure through musclemen and underworld.	
(218)	Pressure through open and hidden financiers.	
(219)	Pressure by changing the service conditions/rules.	
(220)	Political pressure by abuse of position and authority.	
(221)	Pressure through grievance redresser mechanism.	
(222)	Pressure through performance review as a tool.	
(223)	Pressure through demand for enhancing and protecting individual rights and freedom.	
(224)	Pressure through insistence of public for open and accountable government.	
(225)	Political pressure through politician supremacy in decision-making.	
(226)	Political pressure through control over public servants.	
(227)	Power of appointment and promotions by politicians.	
(228)	Political pressure through use of discretionary decision-making authority by politician.	
(229)	Politician control over foreign tours/training/fellowship.	

Unit 14

Reasons for Accepting Pressure

"Power doesn't corrupt people, people corrupt power."—William Gaddis

"Men are more often bribed by their loyalties and ambitions than by money." —Robert H. Jackson

- *Concept of causational factors to accept pressure*
- *Concept of values influence in accepting pressure*
- *Why the AISO go to politicians?*
- *Bureaucratic system propels*
- *Due to political reasons*
- *Individual reasons, technical or social*
- *Research analyses result for reasons*
- *Power & status reasons*
- *Professions related reasons*
- Decision conflict-related reasons
- *Family-related reasons*
- *Personal behaviour related reasons*
- *Control related reasons*
- *Ten-fold path of effectiveness*

Prevalent borderless global dynamism continuously restructures the goals and responsibilities of the All India Services in India also. Changes in politics and bureaucracy are more or less linear in India. The All India Services Officers shift in fundamental assumptions of politicians and that of the public has been mentioned in this unit. 15 major reasons for acceptance of political pressure in the decision have been studied and research analyses result presented in this unit.

14.1. Concept of Causational Factors for Accepting Pressure

Reasons for accepting political pressure are invariably dynamically associated with the position and posting of the individual All India Services Officer in government administration. Different reasons for accepting political pressure are also variable according to respective services environment related to IAS, IPS, and IFS cadre cultures and conditions prevalent in respective services at any given space, time, and place. Among the Indian Administrative Service officers due to their large cadre strength, there is neck-to-neck and stiffest competition for the prize (wet) postings. This is the reason that immediately after any change of any political leadership, a transfer list for the Indian Administrative Service officers is brought out and most pliable officers with situational choice are posted in all key positions. For the All India Services, transfers and postings are the single most important reason for accepting political pressure. Personality traits and value analysis of individual officers influence the acceptance of political pressure.

The All India Services Officers have to traverse through an ocean of uncertainty and discontinuities with ever-changing technology. Competition for retention and sustenance of power is becoming stiffer to unmanageable day by day or with every change of wind direction. Fellow colleagues use newer innovative tricks and methods to defend their position, power, and status. Ethics and values have evaporated from the bureaucratic system. The All India Services Officers are bound to adopt a new flexible and responsive approach to retain power. Social values had metamorphosed under the pressure of lulls and lusts. Faith, bondage, family institution, and social set up showing new facets. Food habits, dressing codes, rituals, code of conduct, the definition of love and respect have changed from home to house and office to personal fiefdom. World politics have undergone a sea change, so as domestic political leadership has changed, cheap politics have shaded off all values and norms exposed to nudeness and drought for values.

In the process of change and uncertainty, politicians change parties like changing clothes. So as voter perceptions have changed the electoral calculations and process. These continuous changes have left the All India Services Officers under tremendous multidirectional pressure. Some self-goal-oriented All India Services Officers are devoid of values and fight for self-needs, all the time waiting for fish like a goose on the bank of a pond. Such opportunist All India Services Officers eagerly wait for the right moments to strike at the door of a politician to win over their confidence to meet self-needs. Ever-available politicians, who are invariably interested in self-goals, readily enter into a bargaining process with such All India Services Officers. The process of mutual understanding has become the process of plundering government resources; they rinse the last drop of blood from the bureaucratic system. Self-goals motivate both parties; time is not far off when they will kill the hen laying golden eggs.

The ever-changing borderless world continuously redefines the goals and responsibilities. Changes in Indian politics and bureaucracy after independence up to late seventies were more or less linear. It was the initiation of a shift in fundamental assumptions of politicians, that of the All India Services Officers and public. Through the eighties multidimensional multilevel radical reforming of assumptions took place. Who changed whom, it is like which came first hen or egg? Through the nineties social assumptions have changed to a new public, politician and All India Services Officers, all are highly self-centered. Self-goals have replaced social and national goals. During the 21st century, we are relying more on external solutions (outside the system), rather than analyzing deep-rooted problems inside the bureaucratic system. It is normal that social behavior patterns change with the passage of time in any given society. In India, we have a fast pace of development after independence, newer technology replaced earlier one, means and methods of livelihood, development, and education also underwent changes, and lifestyle and urbanization pattern all-round changes necessitated the changes in human behavior also. Changes in perception patterns, thinking, and lifestyle also moved with the passage of time among the All India Services officer.

Opening of the market, globalization of borderless world of information and technology, invasion of multinationals is reflected in the behavior of the All India Services Officers. We have started feeling that external intervention can improve the situation. Political authority relations, power holder behavior, job structure, work environment variables are changing to force the modification of the system vis-à-vis All India Services Officers. Responsibilities and spans of control are under attack, which induces flattery and uncertainty in the decision-making process.

14.2. Concept of Values in Acceptance of Political Pressure

The All India Services Officers with cultural backgrounds from underdeveloped areas may put maximum emphasis on security and safety values. The All India Services Officers with upper-middle-class background and urban outlook may show higher concern for status and power-related values. The All India Services Officers from eastern and southern India desire for autonomy and loyalty are more directed towards self rather than department or public administration and more amenable to pressure acceptance. Individuals, who entered service up to late seventies showed more concern for traditional values, lesser friendly towards the computer and high technology. Those who joined during the eighties and early nineties are more inclined towards achievement, material success and no blockage to accept computer and modern technology. The All India Services Officers nineties onwards show strong feelings towards self-goals, material success, belief in ends to justify means, and computer friendly. Information boom, satellite communication, TV, Internet, online education, wi-fi, Bluetooth technology explosion of online audio and video streaming, social grouping and chatting (smartphones, etc.), globalization has been in their mind all the time. Flexibility in thinking and achievement of job satisfaction is on the decline in these young All India Services Officers. Nuclear family relationships and money are important for them, demand more leisure time, expanding lifestyle can cutthroat to near dear ones. Chances of pressure acceptance are higher with the coming time when these officers will occupy a higher position in the hierarchy.

To fulfill terminal values (desirable end-states of existence, goals that a person likes to achieve during lifetime) the All India Services Officers have certain goals hovering over one's mind that one likes to achieve during his service career. The All India Services Officers ever multiplying desires to attain those goals (terminal values), adopt a situational and preferable mode of behavior (instrumental values). Officers across the services and cadres hold different values, these values do change with time and space, i.e. place of posting and location in the hierarchy. The same officer as Deputy Commissioner/Collector and Chief Secretary, behave in different ways and manners for the same types and intensity of political pressure.

"The administrator/manager influenced by positive ethics would prove to be not only wise but also potent, vigorous, decisive, efficient, even for the affairs of the world. One who is influenced by negative ethical considerations would prove to be an indecisive, inefficient, ineffective, and corrupt public official. However, it must be noted that the socio-economic conditions and the nature of political culture prevailing in the larger society at a particular point of time are also responsible for producing its own appropriate type of public servant," Asok Kumar Mukhopadhyay, 2013. The All India Services officer values in governance or arriving at public-related decisions have also become dynamic with inbuilt dynamism in socio-economic conditions and political life of the nation. The concept of values in government administration has become rolling stone and that rolling stone has lost its momentum of own mass and volume, rather it is moved by demand of lust, goals, time, and prevailing situations.

Terminal and instrumental values are associated with different reasons for accepting pressure in the decision-making process as shown in Exhibit 14.1. These values provide basic convictions to an officer that specific mode of conduct, end-state of existence is personally or departmentally, or service wise preferred to particular modes or forms of political pressure in the decision-making process. Individual officer instantly carries out the ranking of different modes of political pressure in terms of intensity of pressure and individual values, prevalent bureaucratic system norms and goals achieved. Individual values provide him the judgmental element for what is right or desirable in the decision-making process. Exhibit 14.1 is very important to visualize the psychology of different reasons for the acceptance of political pressure in the decision and in-built behavioral science responses of the individual officer for that. How any reason (fifteen reasons studied during research in the questionnaire) mentioned in the first column will have a relation with terminal values (end-state of existence, goals to be achieved) in column two, instrumental values (a preferable type of behavior in achieving goals) are mentioned in the third column and resultant personality traits (what goal achieved) are shown in the fourth column?

Exhibit Number 14.1: Personality Traits and Values Relations with Reasons for Accepting Pressure

Reasons for accepting political pressure by the AISO	*Terminal values*. End state of existence. Goals to be achieved	*Instrumental values*. Preferable mode of behavior in achieving goals	*Personality Traits* of the AISO
Lust to grab power	Self-respect and esteem	obedient, devoted, faithful	Power
Career advancement	attention, appreciation, respect	polished, mannerly, courtecious	Growth
Security & stability	Security, protection from pressure	Creative, intelligent, reflective	Security
Enhancement of status	Sagacity, understanding	Self-control, discipline, restrained	Status
Avoid humiliation for self and family	Family protection against pressure	Exonerate, pardon others	Stress
Extract favors or ACR or PAR	Enjoyment, leisure in life	Coherent, reasonable, rational	Standards
Avoid conflict in decision	Peace, free from uncertainty/conflict	Joyfull, cheerful	Conflicts avoidance
Secure political patronage	Agreeable, conforming, free from inner conflict	Innovative, creative, daring	Confirmity

Recognition of own work	Sense of achievement, success, fulfilment	Competent, effective, capable	Warmth & Support
Safeguard incompetence	Coalition, close relations with politician	Reliable, dependable, obliged	Decision
Earn money, enhance resources	Relaxed, satisfied, rich and prosperous life	Ambitious, aspiring, chasing	Rewards
Proximity to politician generate information	Brotherhood, sharing, concern	Moving out for beliefs, audacity	Communication
Control over resources	Liberation, emancipation, salvation	Affectionate, loving	Control
Persue goals for self and family	Stimulating, active life	Broad outook, openness	Goals
Freedom in goal achievement/funds misuse	Freedom, independence, liberty in options	Helpful, working for number of persons	Immoral behavior

14.3. Why All India Services Officers Go to Politicians?

Ambiguity and changing environment motivate All India Services Officers to search for political pressure. Ever-changing technology enlists fear of loss of power among power holders; compel the All India Services Officers to approach for shelter behind the politicians. The All India Services Officers with high cultural diversity, increasing professionalism, politically directed/aligned workforce aligning thinking in the line with politicians. Shrinking security in decision fluctuations in government, short tenure of political parties in power, mobility of politician in different parties, entry of multinationals, have enhanced and multiplied the reasons for accepting more and more political pressure. Information technology and changing new approach to business have globalized the competition, where the All India Services Officers show concern for the growth and consolidate their position. The webs of some factors have been shown in the fireball model of Figure 14.1. These factors can be classified according to individual officer related, bureaucratic system related, political or politicians related, social, and pertaining to technical aspects. Important aspects have been described and elaborated further.

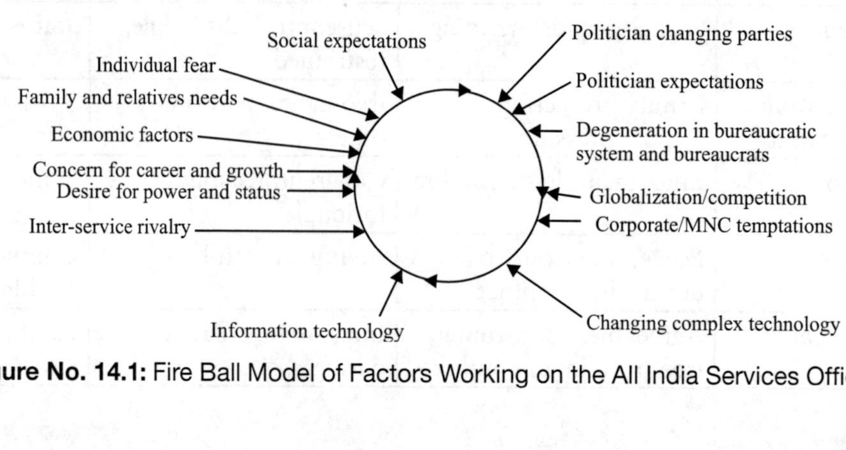

Figure No. 14.1: Fire Ball Model of Factors Working on the All India Services Officers

14.3.1. Bureaucratic System

The power holders have monopolized government administration. The colonial outlook of power holders has shattered the respect for people. Some of the All India Services Officers do not care about others; they consciously harm the dignity of other people and harm the society, where other officers are forced to go in a shelter of politicians. The IAS at the top, invariably busy with self-goals, effectively removed trust, openness, and supportive climate from the Indian bureaucracy. Some of the self-goal-centered Indian Administrative Service officers are continuously running after authority to misuse it for the effectiveness of delivery of illegal gratification only. Large numbers of decisions are taken in violation of law; after-effects have to be faced by other officers, but those IAS only maximize self-interests for a particular time. Who cares for the long-term impact on society and the system? Colonially created the All India Services have been highly subjective and against the principle of equity in power. The Indian Administrative Service officers have grabbed whole power in the hierarchy. Masses have lost faith in the All India Services because these officers have adopted conflicting approaches that have been against the interests of poor people. As other officers live under a tension of inequality and are victimized by favoritism, and turned to politicians for relief. When officers join All India Services, they are committed to fairness and participation, but in the due process the IAS denies them participation in the system, so slowly they develop a feeling of alienation and approach politicians for equity restitution.

Political pressure in the bureaucratic system has initiated the erosion of state power. Collectives' bargaining in the bureaucratic system serves self-goals and objectives. Under political pressure bureaucratic system pay a relative price to explain resource allocation in the market. The power and control relationship of politicians and bureaucrats is working as a cause for political pressure acceptance. Enormity in the size of public administration itself is the cause of generation for political pressure. Every political pressure is dealt with in isolation and even illegal actions taken under pressure or distribution of benefits get lost in the largeness of the department. Vastness encourages favoritism and lack of transparency covers it. Government culture of use of immoral power itself promotes the mobilization of political pressure.

Government culture of non-accountability, expenditure-oriented targets, prevalent mistrust among the All India Services Officers, frequent dislocations related with role ambiguity, biased and motivated review system, lack of transparency, ambiguity in policy and rules, the concentration of excessive decision making with the All India Services Officers, ever-changing performance criteria, high pressure on the All India Services Officers for delivery of results, self-seeking seniors, goal-motivated hierarchy, the All India Services Officers discretion in resource allocation, large-scale disparities in use of power by officers of various levels, monopolization of closeness of politicians by one service induce others to mobilize political pressure. Employees lose nothing if political pressure is not materialized but gain from pressure are enormous. Autocratic behavior of the All India Services Officers, misuse of position by the All India Services Officers, use of political power by the top officer is the greatest motivating factors for approaching political pressure. Individual All India Services Officer likes to be perceived by others as powerful and the person with influence motivates them to accept political pressure. In our research, fifteen major areas/types have been discussed with 76 pressure points in Unit 12, all these pressure points are breeding ground for political pressure acceptance in the bureaucratic system.

14.3.2. Political Reasons

The All India Services Officers and politicians both have developed the attitudes of appeasement and bargaining towards pressure in the decision-making process. Politicians are aware that individual All India Services Officer behavior towards political pressure will be full of compromises and choices. Politicians have done legitimization their power in the decision-making process. Political authority remains popular with masses and decision-makers both with the same intensity, which causes acceptance of political pressure. The bureaucratic system has accepted the political control and misuse of power through politicians. Political domination in the decision-making process influences the acceptance of political pressure in it. The strong desire for domination in the decision is prevalent among the All India Services Officers, which influence them to accept political pressure.

Political pressure is exerted due to rampant corruption in political parties at different levels. Politicians develop political *gangerism* to pressurize the All India Services Officers in the decision-making process. Politicians use repression as a tool for political pressure acceptance. Bureaucratic institutions are in decay, politicians know that system boundaries have faded; in such situations, officers do not have much scope except accepting political pressure. Individual officers also play politics of survival and accept pressure in the decision-making process to create breathing space for them. Individualism in services has drastically reduced the number of individuals with high moral standards, present personality cult is devoid of principles, and so the pressure is accepted in the first instance. The continuous rise of fascism and the dominant role of political mafias influence the All India Services Officers to accept political pressure.

"Civil servants have become pliable and they acquiesce in nefarious activities of the political leaders and take the plea of obeying the political leadership, whatever their own opinion may be", K. Seshadri (1994). Politicians have specialized in process of exchange with the All India Services Officers. Political economy in the decision has become the study of the interplay of power wielders and productive exchanges in the system (Zold, 1970). Differential means are used through which bargaining and political struggles over goal determination take place in the decision-making process (P.M. Jackson, 1983).

The politician makes appointments at the highest levels, which influences the All India Services Officers' perceptions to accept political pressure in the decision. The All India Services Officers frequently complained about intrigue and jealousy among other service officers, who are in the race for such posts, which influence them to accept political pressure. It is difficult to find any extraordinary All India Service Officer, who is free from sensational appetites, biases, and personal ambitions. Political authorities exploit the self-seeking behavior of the All India Service Officers.

Different services groups are more aligned towards political parties will be more amenable to political pressure. After the change of every government, the first thing politicians do is to transfer District Magistrate/Deputy Commissioners and other Indian Administrative Service officers. This establishes beyond an iota of doubt that these are the officers, who succumb under political pressure at first instance and help politicians for mutual aggrandizement of goals for each other. These elite members' desire for extending their own influence over colleagues and the social system, makes them most vulnerable to political pressure. Financial resources and command over them are crucial for the retention of the rein of power. Information is a big power; they develop a relationship with all the potential political parties to gather information for the extension of their power base. In the process of bargaining, various groups sustain their liaison with all the persons, who matter in the process of decision.

"Senior bureaucrats are known to have forged alliance with politician not only to brighten their own career prospectus but also articulate political views and gain a greater share of social and government resources", C.P. Bhambhri (1986).

14.3.3. Individual Reasons

The individual officer with a high internal locus of control with high self-monitors feel a high need for power, they are more likely to approach political power and succumb to pressure. Such officers feel they can manipulate their surrounding environment and, in a bid, to take control of situations in their own favor they accept political pressure. Officers sensitive towards family, relatives, and social norms, will be well versed in the management of surrounding social environment and exhibit better skills in handling political pressure.

Invariably concerned service and department expectations, individual officer perceptions about the influence of pressure motivate him to mobilize political pressure. As more and more merit is ignored in departments, real work is not respected, seniors are weak, top becomes indecisive, frequent violation of rules and favoritism by top brasses motivate individual officers to approach and accept political pressure. Slowly, more and more officers start investing in political pressure for encashment of future benefits and career advancement. In case officers do not get undue benefits or achieve self-goals/interests through political pressure, low expectations level will discourage the use of illegitimate political pressure. Individual officers attempt to build his own impression in their department to control the impression of others forms about the officer. In these attempts, many All India Services Officers make fraudulent claims or misrepresent their decisions to retain their position and power at the same time maintain proximity to politicians.

"There is a growing trend of selfish lobbying by public officials, social activists, and agents of the corporate sector for immoral considerations, plum postings, post-retirement rehabilitation, and economic gains. Upright and dedicated persons are occasionally punished for refusing to budge from the right path. Upcoming young generation naturally gives in to despair and cynicism. It is a common experience that influencing in the right quarters, one can commit even heinous crimes with impunity. Surely this tendency in the governance process will have a disastrous effect on discipline and morale in every field of human activities," Asok Kumar Mukhopodhyay, 2013.

"They (the AISO) have made it into a fine art anticipating the wishes of the political masters and delivering unasked whatever is necessary for their personal and political welfare", K. Mathur (1991). How a service culture has its impact on the members of family and society is "the valuation placed on the service (ICS) also tended to accentuate a featureless noticeable at home: racial superiority (now happening in Indian Society). Its breeding ground was a very superior position that ICS European (now IAS) did in fact have in India. As contrasted with their private position in England", Kathleen Griffiths w/o Percival Griffiths ICS, narrated an instance back home in England in 1930, when she got into train at Plymouth, her younger son asked: "Mummy, why has not the guard come along and asked your permission to start the train", she replied, "We are not in daddy's district now". "British rule in India was jolly good for India, but it was not always good for the British, because we did not doubt tend to get aloof and perhaps a little bit conceited," D.C. Potter.

A "large number of government employees at middle and lower levels also indulge in corruption by demanding bribe from the common citizens for doing their normal officials' duties, like the issue of passports, driving licenses, registration of land, conversion of leasehold houses to freeholds, approval of building plans, issuing various types of certificates, e.g. birth, death, marriage, caste, etc. There are hundreds of day-to-day works where common citizens come in contact with officials of the central and state government and also of local bodies. The general impression is that only a few public officials do their legitimate work for the people with speed and without demanding bribe," U.C. Agarwal, 2011.

14.3.4. Technical and Social Reasons

New technological innovations forced bureaucrats to change the system in the light of fresh researches and products. Technological innovations have shifted emphasis from person orientation to machine orientation. Power holders remain busy buttering the politicians to retain their positions, so they are not left with any time to learn new technology. The bureaucratic system cultivates inbuilt fear of losing power in the name of new research and new technology. So, bureaucrats keep the system under their own control and in the process, bureaucrats kill future research and technological innovations. Whole system and society get frustrated and in turn, start accepting the bureaucratic leadership.

14.4. Pressure Influences in Decision and Research Analyses

In this research instrument, 15 factors or reasons for acceptance of political pressure have been studied, which may influence the pressure acceptance behavior of the All India Services Officers in any decision-making process; these 15 reasons have been grouped into six subgroups for explaining statistical data research results. Results for each variable are discussed in respective groups and related variable heading.

Results: Statistical data research results for 15 reasons towards acceptance of political pressure in the decision process are placed at Exhibits 14.2 and 14.3 indicate that the lowest mean value of 1.89 with lowest standard deviation value of 1.16 show enhancement of status influenced by the dominance of extension motives is the most important reason for accepting the political pressure in the decision-making process. Our analysis from cross tabs in SPSS also has shown status at number one rank among the reasons studied for accepting the political pressure in the decision, which indicate that self-goals and family goals dominate over them. The All India Services Officers are the most competent persons and to safeguard the incompetence has been ranked at the last and lowest rank with the highest mean value of 3.02. While ranking the different reasons for accepting political pressure, we have taken into consideration the percentage score of the first rank and with due weightage to the highest score of that reason. Our analyses on Pearson Chi-square indicate that all the reasons studied by us have a good association with the decision-making process. Our results are highly significant with all values of significance are less than 0.05 (except two, all values are 0.000). The strength of associations for different reasons towards accepting political pressure with the decision-making process is established by the Rho and R-values, which are highly significant except in the case of three items, where the significance level is higher. Enhancement of status by accepting political pressure got the highest correlation value of 0.5, establishing its strong relation with the decision.

Exhibit Number 14.2: Reasons for Accepting Political Pressure—Statistical Analysis

Variable Name	Frequency = N		M	S.D.	Chi-square			Pearson R		Rho		Rk
	Total	Valid			Value	d.f.	Sif.	Value	Sif.	Value	Sif.	
Lust to grab power	280	258	2.20	1.33	49.69	8	0.000	0.3	0.000	0.2	0.000	3
Career advancement	280	261	1.96	1.04	39.8	8	0.000	0.2	0.004	0.1	0.09	4
Security & stability	280	253	2.11	1.17	30.8	8	0.000	0.2	0.002	0.15	0.01	6
Status enhancement	280	248	1.89	1.16	71.4	8	0.000	0.5	0.000	0.5	0.000	1
Avoid humiliation	280	255	2.87	1.26	74.4	8	0.000	....	...	.....	.....	13
Extract favor/ACR	280	260	2.52	1.32	34.4	8	0.000	0.14	0.02	0.2	0.01	8
Avoid conflicts	280	258	2.36	1.32	29.9	8	0.000	0.2	0.000	0.2	0.000	7
Political patronage	280	259	2.37	1.37	31.3	8	0.000	0.2	0.000	0.3	0.000	5
Appreciation of work	280	254	2.91	1.33	49.1	8	0.000	0.1	0.2	0.1	0.3	14
Hide incompetence	280	258	3.02	1.43	49.4	8	0.000	0.3	0.000	0.3	0.000	15
Earn money	280	256	2.66	1.36	16.5	8	0.04	...	....	....	...	12
Generate information	280	256	2.15	1.27	56.7	8	0.000	0.4	0.000	0.4	0.000	2
Resource control	280	258	2.69	1.36	51.7	8	0.000	0.3	0.000	0.3	0.000	9
Pursue self-goals	280	260	2.64	1.34	27.8	8	0.001	0.2	0.000	0.2	0.000	10
Immoral behaviour	280	233	2.87	1.51	32.8	8	0.000	0.2	0.001	0.2	0.000	11
mis = missing frequencies. M = mean value. Sif = significance level. Rk = rank among the reasons												

Exhibit Number 14.3: Reasons for Accepting Political Pressure—Highest Score of the Evaluation

Reason Name	I.A.S.			I.P.S.			I.F.S.			Total	
	N	Scl	%	N	Scl	%	N	Scl	%	Scl	%
230. Lust to grab power	71	1	53.5	90	1	36.7	91	1	40.7	1	42.9
231. Career advancement	75	2	44	96	1	47.9	90	1	38.9	1	42.1
232. Security & stability	74	2	47.3	91	2	33	88	1	40.9	1	38.3
233. Status enhancement	69	1	73.9	96	1	64.6	83	2	26.5	1	53.2
234. Avoid humiliation	74	1	36.5	91	4	39.6	90	2	40	2	24.3
235. Extract favor/ACR	74	1	45.9	96	3	33.3	90	2	32.2	1	31.2
236. Avoid conflicts	74	1	48.6	96	1	44.8	88	3	31.8	1	38
237. Political patronage	75	1	48	96	1	56.3	88	3	31.8	1	41.7
238. Appreciation of own	71	2	38	96	5	29.2	87	2	29.9	2	29.1
239. Hide incompetece	75	1	42.7	95	4	30.5	88	5	36.5	4	22.5
240. Earn money	75	1	29.3	91	3	36.3	90	1	27.8	1	28.9
241. Information	75	1	56	98	1	58.3	85	3	25.9	1	43
242. Resource control	74	1	47.3	96	4	26	88	2	33	2	30.2

Reason Name	I.A.S.			I.P.S.			I.F.S.			Total	
	N	Scl	%	N	Scl	%	N	Scl	%	Scl	%
243. Pursue self-goals	74	1	47.3	96	3	26	90	2	25.6	1	28.1
244. Immoral behaviour	63	1	50.8	84	2	27.4	86	5	23.3	1	26.2
N = Total frequency of a service in that reason. Scl = Evaluation on scale											

Results mentioned in Exhibit 14.3 will be discussed in detail under respective variables while describing the respective reason for political pressure in preceding paragraphs. These results also indicate that status enhancement is the most accepted ranked as the 'most important' reason in accepting the political pressure in the decision-making process. Among 15 reasons the variable relating to safeguarding own incompetence, the All India Services Officers accept political pressure got the last priority among all the items of study.

14.4.1. Power and Status

Reasons and factors related to power and status include two items: (i) lust to grab power and (ii) enhancement of status.

In Indian bureaucracy, the IAS enjoys maximum power and acts as a power center. "The main puppet-master in the IAS is the Establishment Officer (EO) in the Ministry of Personnel, about whom most people do not the slightest clue. The EO's sole purpose is to defend (and expand—to the extent possible) the powers that Patel gave to the IAS. The EO operates behind the scenes, manipulating and controlling (mainly frustrating) the elected government. He dramatically reduces options for the elected representatives on almost all major appointments. And of course, the Cabinet Secretary plays a crucial role in defending the IAS empire directly at the Cabinet. This itself is a huge anomaly. In genuine democracies, a bureaucrat must not have a seat at the political table. In Victoria, an elected MP serves as Cabinet Secretary," *The Times of India*, June 1, 2019 (TOI. website).

14.4.1.1. Lust to Grab Power: "Power tends to corrupt, and absolute power corrupts absolutely."—John Acton.

Power induces officers to control resources that are valued by others. The All India Services Officers use different strategies (dimensions) for this (power) variable to individual and situations. The All India Services Officers manipulate available data and facts to influence the power holders to retain power in their favor. The All India Services Officers enter into bargaining or negotiations by process of exchange of bureaucratic favors or government largess's or resources or postings with the politicians. The All India Services Officers assess the person who matters for retention of power, develop friendliness, use all methods of flattery, will visit politicians frequently to generate goodwill, pose themselves as a highly considerate officer and behave in a very humble way.

In case individual officers find it difficult to approach a particular politician, they try to win the support of friendly officers and develop a coalition in service. If the need arises, they try to win the support of their higher authorities (or subordinates) for retention of power. When they are well entrenched in their position, feel safe then they demand full compliance, order individuals with assertiveness, and exploit power to their full advantage. Rewards, punishments, transfer, posting, promotions, and resource allocation are frequently used as a powerful strategy. The

All India Services Officers play with the demands and expectations of the stakeholders in public administration.

Every department and service work in their own culture and discipline, the All India Services Officers assess that obedience and sincerity are exploited to their advantage. The Indian Administrative Service officers use directive power strategies and in case of resistance, they behave more assertively. The Indian Forest Service officers, when encountering resistance and perceive uncertainties, they stop trying. The All India Services Officers feeling for increasing their individual power induce them to accept political pressure. Among the three All India Services, the IAS tries their best to influence politicians successfully to remain as power holders and continuously expand their power base. In case of problems or resistance, they develop coalitions with politicians. Inter-service and intra-service coalitions are common to retain and widen the power base. Individual officer, who find it difficult to develop direct relations with politicians; they use an intermediary or combine their resources with other officers or power brokers or touts or various other sources to develop coalition with politicians. Power holders in Indian bureaucracy convert their power to rule the system to their own advantage.

Power has killing potency higher than any poison, ever known to a human being. Intoxicated with high doses of power, the All India Services Officers feel that everyone else must behave according to their desire's directions only. Any effort by any individuals to deviate from the All India Services Officers' power influence becomes suicidal for that person in the bureaucratic system. The All India Services Officers like to ensure that the entire societal system must remain dependent on them only. This is reasoning that politicians hanker after the All India Services Officers and the IAS in particular, who has monopolized every available power in the system. Even if Indian Administrative Service officers do not have a particular power, they always feel that they are the creator of this whole system; the destiny of the nation is always in their fist. Every business house, corporate, institution and any department have to accept the hegemony of the All India Services officers accordingly, in case of any dissent power is mobilized to crush them.

The only person, who appears to overrule or control the power of almighty All India Services Officers, is the politicians in the government power hierarchy. Power is the mechanism through which the All India Services Officers and politicians attain and fulfill their personal goals, needs, and interests. Power is a facilitator for goal achievement. Retention of crucial locations in hierarchy and control over policy process is the tool to concentrate power with the elite group only. Exclusive monopoly cultivates a feeling of prestige in power. If everyone has the power to arrest, who will respect the police? As service elites continue to expand their options overpower and starve and stifle others from power. Scarcity of power creates importance for the All India Services Officers.

The All India Services officers motivate politicians to create more and more uncertainty, which will lead to higher dependency on All India Services Officers; it will rate them consistently powerful. The only threat to the Indian Administrative Service officers' power is the technological innovations, so they keep consistent tab through the position of Secretary/Chief Secretary/Cabinet Secretary, which provide them absolute power. Scarcity and non-substitutability are buzzwords for the power of the All India Services Officers. In case any other officer is posted on such locations, the All India Services Officers ensure the failure of that person, so that message clear goes out that no substitute for the All India Services Officers is viable. Power makes individual All India

Services Officers aggressive and reduces concern for others, power only cultivate concern for self. Power becomes a tool for self-maximization.

Exhibit Number 14.4: Lust to Grab Power as Reason for Accepting Political Pressure

Other Details & Service		Score on Five Point Scale					Total
		Most Imp.	Very Imp.	Important	Least Imp. Not	Not Imp.	
I.A.S.	N	38	22	8	2	1	71
% of score		53.5	31	11.3	2.9	1.4	28.2
I.P.S.	N	33	25	23	7	2	90
% of score		36.7	27.8	25.6	7.9	2.2	35.7
I.F.S.	N	37	13	8	13	20	91
% of score		40.7	14.3	8.8	14.9	22	36.1
Total	N	108	60	39	22	23	252
% of score		42.9	23.8	15.5	8.7	9.1	100

Exhibit Number 14.5: Lust to Grab Power and Attitude of Family Members

Reason	Intensity of Pressure		Attitude of Family Members				Total
			Spouse	Children	Parents	Brother/Sister	
Lust to grab power	'Most important'	Count	55	12	14	6	87
		% of Total	25.23	5.5	6.42	2.75	39.9
	'Very important'	Count	38	4	11	4	57
		% of Total	17.43	1.83	5.04	1.83	26.14
	'Important'	Count	18	4	10	4	36
		% of Total	8.25	1.83	4.58	1.83	16.51
	'Least important'	Count	13	2	3	1	19
		% of Total	5.96	0.91	1.37	0.45	8.71
	'Not important'	Count	19				19
		% of Total	8.71				8.71
Total		Count	143	22	38	15	218
		% of Total	65.59	10.09	17.43	6.88	100

Pearson Chi-square results show a good association of lust for power with the decision and the results are significant with a level of significance at 0.000. Such a relationship is strong and R and Rho values of 0.3 and 0.225 are significant with a level of significance of 0.000. 42.9% of the All India Services Officers consider power lust as 'most important' in accepting political pressure. 53.5% of the Indian Administrative Service officers, 40.7% of the Indian Forest Service officers, and 36.7% of the Indian Police Service officers think that lust to grab power is the 'most important' in accepting the political pressure in the decision-making process. If we combine the 'most important' and 'very important' evaluation; 84.5% of the Indian Administrative Service officers, 64.5% of the Indian Police Service officers, and 55% of the Indian Forest Service officers score for the lust for power as a factor influencing the acceptance of political pressure. Among the All India Services, the Indian Administrative Service officers are the highest power-oriented and show the highest desire for the retention of power and the Indian Forest Service officers with least. If we look at the score of lust for power is 'not important' for them; 22% of the Indian Forest Service officers, 2.2% of the Indian Police Service officers, and 1.4% of the Indian Administrative Service officers scored here, which clearly indicates that due to pervasive powerlessness among the Indian Forest Service officers, at least 22% of them are not influenced by the power temptations.

Relation of lust to grab power with the demographic variable attitude of family members analyses results are placed at Exhibit 14.5 and indicate that 65.59% spouse of the All India Services Officers influences the decision-making process in the power-conscious variable. These results are also shown in Chart 14.1 showing the importance of power for the spouse of the All India Services Officer.

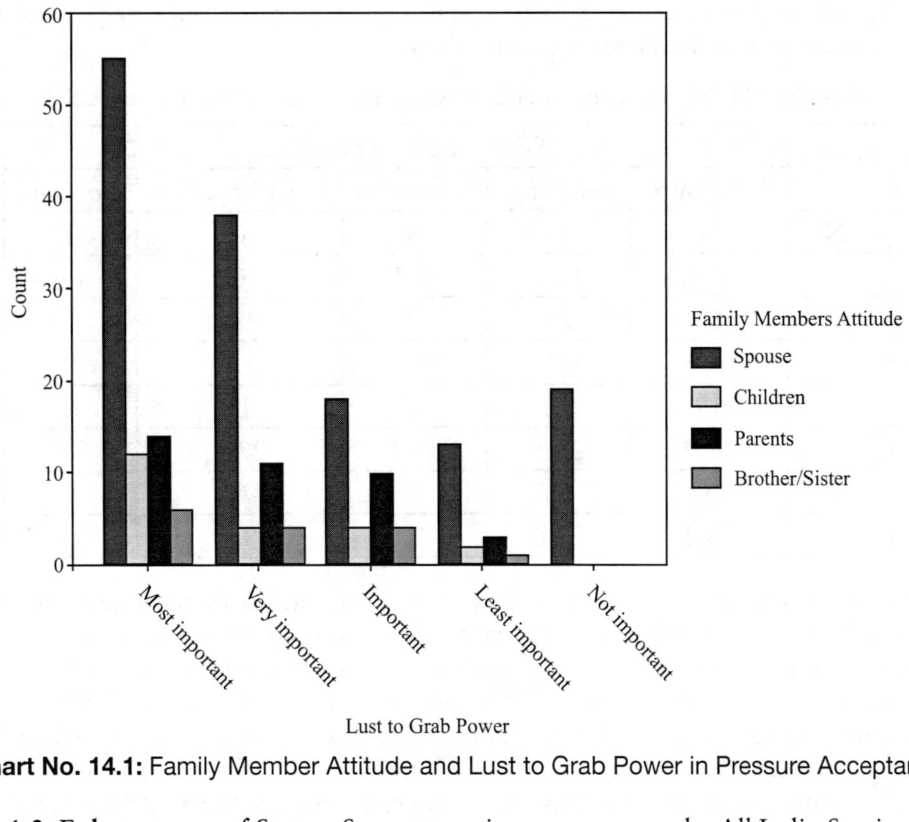

Chart No. 14.1: Family Member Attitude and Lust to Grab Power in Pressure Acceptance

14.4.1.2. Enhancement of Status: Status consciousness among the All India Services Officers exerts pressure on an individual officer for power norms to conform to political pressure. The All India Services Officers enjoy the highest status and exploit freedom and flexibility in a decision to deviate from standardized norms/rules/regulations/law. Individual officers with a strong desire for maintaining status motivate them to approach politicians and willfully they invite political pressure. The All India Services Officers, who do not care much about social rewards, such officers can withstand the political pressure with firm determinations. In the All India Services Officers hierarchy, as they climb up towards the top, status consciousness increases with an unlimited open spectrum of discretion in the decision.

Status equity creates problems among three services (IAS with IPS and IFS). The IPS and the IFS perceive a great amount of inequity, which create disequilibria in their behavior and relations (Greenberg, 1988). The All India Services Officers feel they are enjoying decreasing status; the IPS and the IFS have the feeling of losing the equity in status. Colonialist elite theory of the IAS originates from feeling that others do not deserve any kind of status at par with them or comparable with them. Due to the perceived ranking of status among the All India Services Officers, status incongruence is felt and experienced by them. This forces every individual All India Services Officer to run after politicians, who like to enjoy temporary gained status (five-year term). Politicians desire to maximize their own gains; motivate politicians to exercise differential pressure on a different member of the All India Services, who are related to goals/interests. The IAS, the IPS, and the IFS officers have different status criteria, create conflicting situations. Status differences initiate conflict in the service hierarchies.

Exhibit Number 14.6: Enhancement of Status as Reason for Accepting Political Pressure

Other Details & Service		Score on Five Point Scale					Total
		Most Imp.	Very Imp.	Important	Least Imp. Not	Not Imp.	
I.A.S.	N	51	11	6	0	1	69
% of score		73.9	15.9	8.7	0	1.4	27.8
I.P.S.	N	62	23	9	2	0	96
% of score		64.6	24	9.4	2.1	0	38.7
I.F.S.	N	19	22	15	19	8	83
% of score		22.9	26.5	18.1	22.9	9.6	33.5
Total	N	132	56	30	21	9	248
% of score		53.2	22.6	12.1	8.5	3.6	100

73.9% of the Indian Administrative Service officers, 64.6% of the Indian Police Service officers, and 22.9% of the Indian Forest Service officers consider the enhancement of status as the 'most important' factor in accepting political pressure. If we combine the first three score of 'most important', 'very important', and 'important' then the results are: 98.5% of the Indian Administrative Service officers, 98% of the Indian Police Service officers, and 67.5% of the Indian Forest Service officers think that enhancement of status is 'important' and above in acceptance of political pressure in the decision. This clearly indicates that the Indian Administrative Service officers are the highest status-conscious and to enjoy status and maintain their position, they easily accept the political pressure in the decision-making process.

Exhibit Number 14.7: Enhancement of Status and Profession of the Spouse

Reason	Frequency of Pressure		Profession of the Spouse				Total
			House Keeping	Services	Entrepreneur	Business	
Enhancement of status	'Most important'	Count	24	22	49	34	129
		% of Total	10.12	9.28	20.6	14.35	54.43
	'Very important'	Count	17	12	14	8	51
		% of Total	7.17	5.06	5.9	3.37	21.51
	'Important'	Count	8	4	11	3	26
		% of Total	3.37	1.68	4.6	1.26	10.97
	'Least important'	Count	15	3		4	22
		% of Total	6.32	1.26		1.68	9.28
	'Not important'	Count	7	1	1		9
		% of Total	2.95	0.42	0.4		3.79
Total		Count	71	42	75	49	237
		% of Total	29.96	17.73	31.65	20.68	100

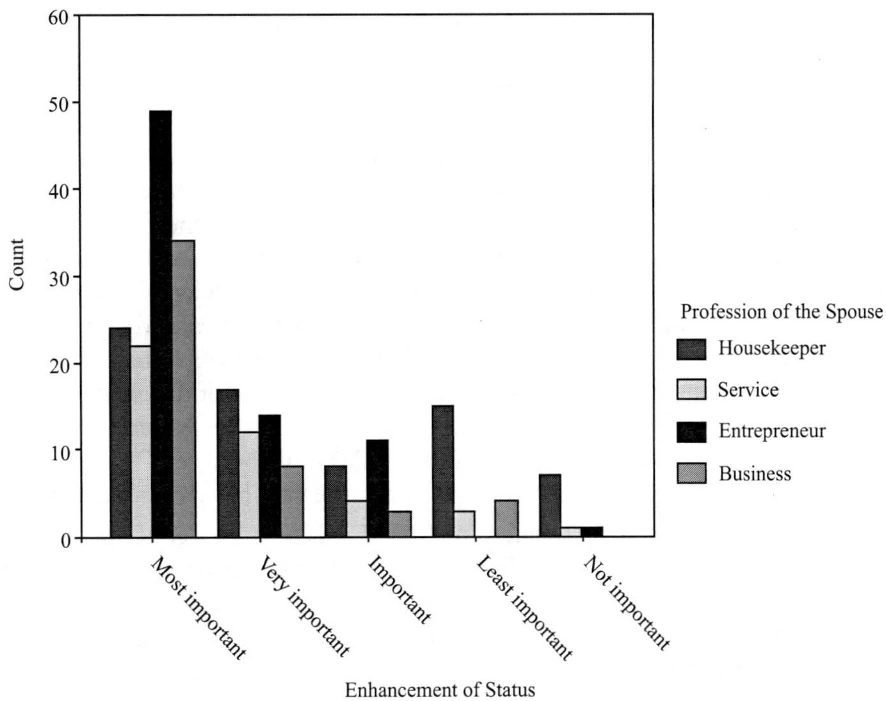

Chart No. 14.2: Acceptance of Pressure for Enhancement of Status and Profession of Spouse

Association of status with the decision-making process is established by the Pearson Chi-square results, which are highly significant, with a level of significance at 0.000. Pearson's correlation and Spearman correlation values of 0.5 with a level of significance of 0.000 indicate very strong correlationship with the decision. Enhancement of the status has been considered as the 'most important' factor and ranked as 1st rank among the various factors. A very high score establishes that this is the most crucial factor in the acceptance of political pressure, which is in turn influenced by the extension motive of these All India Services Officers. The alternate hypothesis is accepted that desire for enhancement of status increases the amenability towards political pressure and leads to higher acceptance of political pressure in the decision-making process.

Exhibit 14.7 shows results for the relation of enhancement of status variable with the profession of the spouse and 31.65% of entrepreneur spouse and 29.96% of housekeeping spouse influence the decision-making process in this variable. Chart 14.2 shows these results, where entrepreneur spouse is 'most important' category for status.

14.4.2. Profession-Related Reasons

We have studied four items related to the job: (i) career advancement, (ii) security and stability in the job, (iii) extract favors and desired annual appraisal/confidential report, and (iv) appreciation and recognition of own work.

14.4.2.1. Career Advancement: The All India Services Officers consider career advancement to enjoy higher responsibilities, independence in decision-making, higher control over resources, and more power to influence the system and leadership command over a bigger team of juniors. Advancement in career provides professional satisfaction to learn and update their own expertise in functional areas. Higher positions in the hierarchy enhance security through compliance with government prescriptions. A higher position in career to All India Services Officers provides increased opportunities for innovations and entrepreneurial skills. Higher career to All India Services Officers provides freedom of actions and independence in the decision. Advancement in career enables more supporting subordinates, demonstrating the loyalty of more employees. Career advancement improves the marketability of the All India Services Officers, enhances self-reliance, more chances to attain future goals, more growth opportunities, and reposition own future strategies for development. The All India Services Officers see advancement as an accomplishment of reputation, higher mobility help in developing better contacts/relations for future advancement. Advancement is the way to demonstrate strengths and hide weaknesses, and the opportunity to emphasize achievements. New opportunities motivate All India Services Officers to accept more and more political pressure for the cultivation of self at the cost of system security and stability.

Career advancement is the most crucial thing for the All India Services Officers in their career. Throughout their service only they nourish their career, they compromise for almost everything for the sake of their own career. Career advancement shows good association with the decision as demonstrated by the Pearson Chi-square analysis and the alternate hypothesis is accepted that the All India Services Officers accept political pressure for the advancement of their career. Pearson's correlation value of 0.2 with a 0.004, level of significance indicates significant strength in this relation. The All India Services Officers have ranked it as the 4th most important factor in accepting political pressure.

Exhibit Number 14.8: Career Advancement as Reason for Accepting Political Pressure

Other Details & Service		Score on Five Point Scale					Total
		Most Imp.	Very Imp.	Important	Least Imp. Not	Not Imp.	
I.A.S.	N	29	33	12	1	0	75
% of score		38.7	44	16	1.3	0	28.7
I.P.S.	N	48	28	21	1	0	96
% of score		47.9	29.2	21.9	1	0	36.8
I.F.S.	N	35	25	10	13	7	90
% of score		38.9	27.8	11.1	14.4	7.8	34.5
total	N	110	86	43	15	7	261
% of score		42.1	33	16.5	5.7	2.7	100

Exhibit 14.8 shows 42.1% of the All India Services Officers consider career advancement as the 'most important' factor in accepting political pressure in the decision-making process. 47.9% of the Indian Police Service officers and 38.9% of the Indian Forest Service officers think that career advancement is the 'most important' reason for accepting political pressure. But 44% of the Indian Administrative Service officers consider career advancement as a 'very important' factor in accepting political pressure. Among the All India Services, the Indian Administrative Service officers have shown the lowest temptation towards career advancement, this may be due to the reason that they have assured career and politicians are unable to harm their career largely. If we combine the 'most important', 'very important', and 'important' scores together; 98.7% of the Indian Administrative Service officers, 99% of the Indian Police Service officers, and 77.8% of the Indian Forest Service officers consider career advancement as a reason for accepting political pressure. Length of service relation with career advancement in Exhibit 14.9 shows that officers more than 24 years of service are most amenable to pressure acceptance. These results shown in Chart 14.3 show that All India Services officers with more than 24 years of service are more amenable to pressure than youngers.

Exhibit Number 14.9: Career Advancement and Length of Service Amenability to Pressure

Reason	Frequency of Pressure		Length of Service and Amenable to Pressure					Total
			1 to 4 years of service	5 to 10 years of service	11 to 17 years of service	18 to 23 years of service	> 24 years	
For career advancement	'Most important'	Count	5	10	14	19	53	101
		% of Total	2	4	5.6	7.6	21.2	40.4
	'Very important'	Count	12	10	11	13	39	85
		% of Total	4.8	4	4.4	5.2	15.6	34
	'Important'	Count	3	5	8	14	13	43
		% of Total	1.2	2	3.2	5.6	5.2	17.2

Reason	Frequency of Pressure		Length of Service and Amenable to Pressure					Total
			1 to 4 years of service	5 to 10 years of service	11 to 17 years of service	18 to 23 years of service	> 24 years	
	'Least important'	Count			7	2	7	16
		% of Total			2.8	0.8	2.8	6.4
	'Not important'	Count			1		4	5
		% of Total			0.4		1.6	2
Total		Count	20	25	41	48	116	250
		% of Total	8	10	16.4	19.2	46.4	100

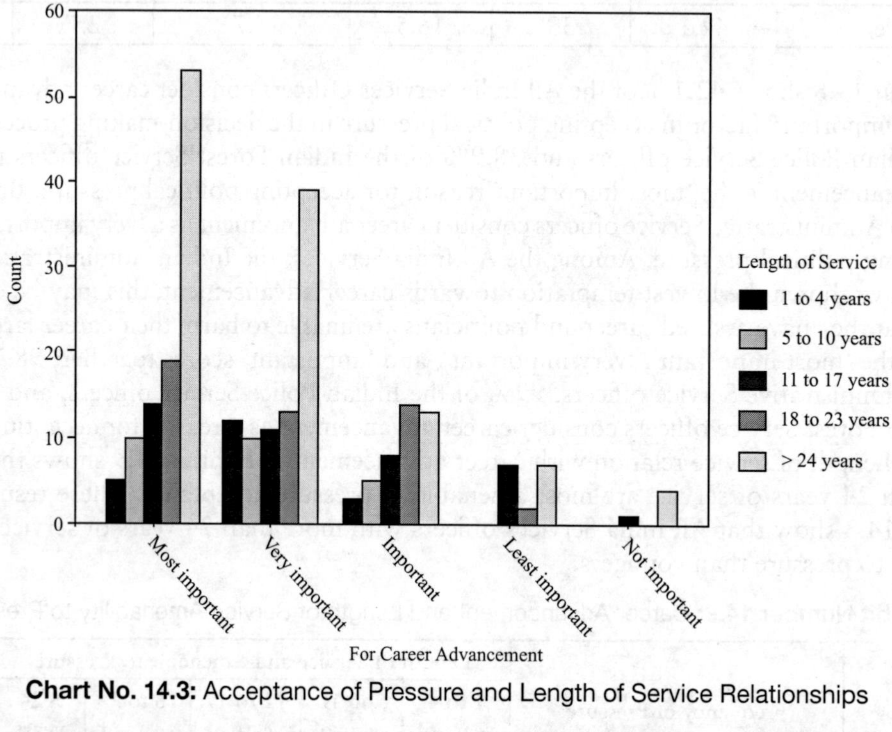

Chart No. 14.3: Acceptance of Pressure and Length of Service Relationships

14.4.2.2. Security Stability in Job: Least disturbances with security and stability in service postings are also assumed as one of the factors for accepting the political pressure in the decision-making process. The All India Services Officers are allocated to different state cadres and at present 66.6% of direct recruited are allocated to other than home state. The All India Services Officers have to work in diverse cultures and ever-changing highly stressful working conditions; they feel rootless and align with the new culture of cadre state. When they are transferred to a place, they show as if they like that, and the administrative system demands that they must continue at the same place for a minimum of two years to deliver goods to the public. Old literature is full of narrations mentioning frequent dislocations to destabilize them so that All India Services

Officers do not develop any relations with the local people. To avoid frequent dislocations, the All India Services Officers try to develop a relationship with the politicians of the ruling party in the state, and in turn, they oblige politicians in their day-to-day working decisions, to barter stability of tenure.

Exhibit Number 14.10: Security and Stability as Reason for Accepting Political Pressure

Other Details & Service	Score on Five Point Scale					
	Most Imp.	Very Imp.	Important	Least Imp. Not	Not Imp.	Total
I.A.S. N	34	35	5	0	0	74
% of score	45.9	47.3	6.8	0	0	29.2
I.P.S. N	27	30	14	13	7	91
% of score	29.7	33	15.4	14.3	7.7	36
I.F.S. N	36	20	17	8	7	88
% of score	40.9	22.7	19.3	9.1	8	34.8
Total N	97	85	36	21	14	253
% of score	38.3	33.6	14.2	8.3	5.5	100

The All India Services Officers have ranked security and stability at 6th rank among different factors influencing the acceptability of political pressure in the decision. Results placed at Exhibit 14.10 show that 71.9% of the All India Services Officers consider security and stability in their job influencing the acceptance of political pressure in the decision as 'very important' and 'most important'. 93.2% of the Indian Administrative Service officers, 63.6% of the Indian Forest Service officers, and 62.7% of the Indian Police Service officers consider security and stability in their job as 'very important' and above in accepting political pressure in the decision. This clearly indicates that the Indian Administrative Service officers give the highest priority to stability and disturbances in the job for acceptance of political pressure. They are highly mobile and most disturbed, so they approach politicians for protection of their posting and barter with the politician. Pearson Chi-square results are highly significant and show good strength of correlations. The alternate hypothesis is accepted that the higher the disturbances in the job, the All India Services Officers will be more amenable to acceptance of political pressure in the decision-making process.

Security and stability in job variable relationship with the demographic variable community background of the officers' analyses results are placed at Exhibit 14.11 and show that 42.72% officers from the general background are amenable to accept pressure in this variable. Chart 14.4 also displays these results by the bar graph.

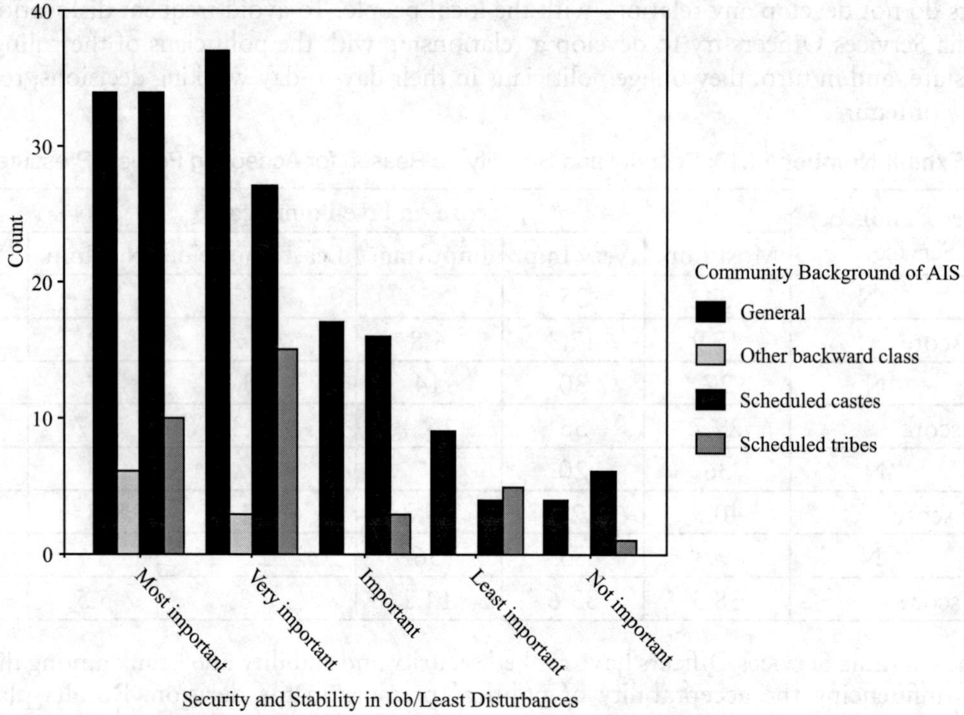

Chart No. 14.4: Acceptance of Pressure for Security and Stability in Job & Community Background of the Officer

Exhibit Number 14.11: Security and Stability in Job with Community Background

Reason	Frequency of Pressure		Community Background				Total
			General	OBC	SC	ST	
Security and stability in job/ least disturbances	'Most important'	Count	34	6	34	10	84
		% of Total	14.71	2.59	14.71	4.32	36.36
	'Very important'	Count	37	3	27	15	82
		% of Total	16.01	1.29	11.68	6.49	35.49
	'Important'	Count	17		16	3	36
		% of Total	7.35		6.92	1.29	15.58
	'Least important'	Count	9		4	5	18
		% of Total	3.89		1.73	2.16	7.79
	'Not important'	Count	4		6	1	11
		% of Total	1.73		2.59	0.43	4.76
Total		Count	101	9	87	34	231
		% of Total	42.72	3.89	37.66	14.71	100

14.4.2.3. Extract Favors: The All India Services Officers working environment is full of uncertainties and inbuilt conflicts. Politicians enjoy the top position in the bureaucratic system, have control over the All India Services Officers, individual officer desire to extract favors from the politicians cannot be free from pressure. Nothings are free in this system of temptations and lusts. It works like a mutual exchange or barter system, politicians provide protection to the All India Services Officers and officers deliver the politically desired decisions, both are in a win-win situation and relation goes happily. Truth, equity, law, legality is relegated to nowhere or forced causality.

Exhibit Number 14.12: Extract Favors/Desired Performance Appraisal Report as Reason for Accepting Political Pressure

Other Details & Service		Score on Five Point Scale					Total
		Most Imp.	Very Imp.	Important	Least Imp.	Not Imp.	
I.A.S.	N	34	17	10	6	7	74
% of score		45.9	23	13.5	8.1	9.5	28.5
I.P.S.	N	31	7	32	14	12	96
% of score		32.3	7.3	33.3	14.6	12.5	36.9
I.F.S.	N	16	29	28	8	9	90
% of score		17.8	32.2	31.1	8.9	10	34.6
Total	N	81	53	70	28	28	260
% of score		31.2	20.4	26.9	10.8	10.8	100

Exhibit Number 14.13: Extract Favours and Family Economic Background

Reason	Frequency of Pressure		Family Economic Background					Total
			Rich class	Upper middle class	Middle class	Lower middle class	Poor class	
Extract favours OR desired ACR/ performance appraisal	'Most important'	Count	27	26	7	11	6	77
		% of Total	10.75	10.35	2.78	4.38	2.39	30.67
	'Very important'	Count	14	10	11	10	5	50
		% of Total	5.57	3.98	4.38	3.98	1	19.93
	'Important'	Count	25	14	13	11	99	67
		% of Total	9.96	5.57	5.17	4.38	1.59	26.69
	'Least important'	Count	17	3	5	3	1	29
		% of Total	6.77	1.95	1.99	1.19	0.39	11.55
	'Not important'	Count	9	7	7	1	4	28
		% of Total	3.58	2.78	2.78	0.39	1.59	11.15
Total		Count	92	60	43	36	20	251
		% of Total	36.65	23.9	17.13	14.34	7.96	100

"Politicians continue to seek the assistance of the local police officer to promote their self or party interests, and in doing so it is inevitable that some of the demands made are, strictly speaking, not legal or they are at least against propriety," Dr. R. Prasher (1986). Some of the All India Services Officers do not like to annoy the political leadership for the sake of earning the desired annual appraisal/confidential report. Results shown in Exhibit 14.12 indicate that 45.9% of the Indian Administrative Service officers and 31.2% of total the All India Services Officers consider it 'most important' for getting favors/ACR/APA from a politician as a reason for acceptance of political pressure.

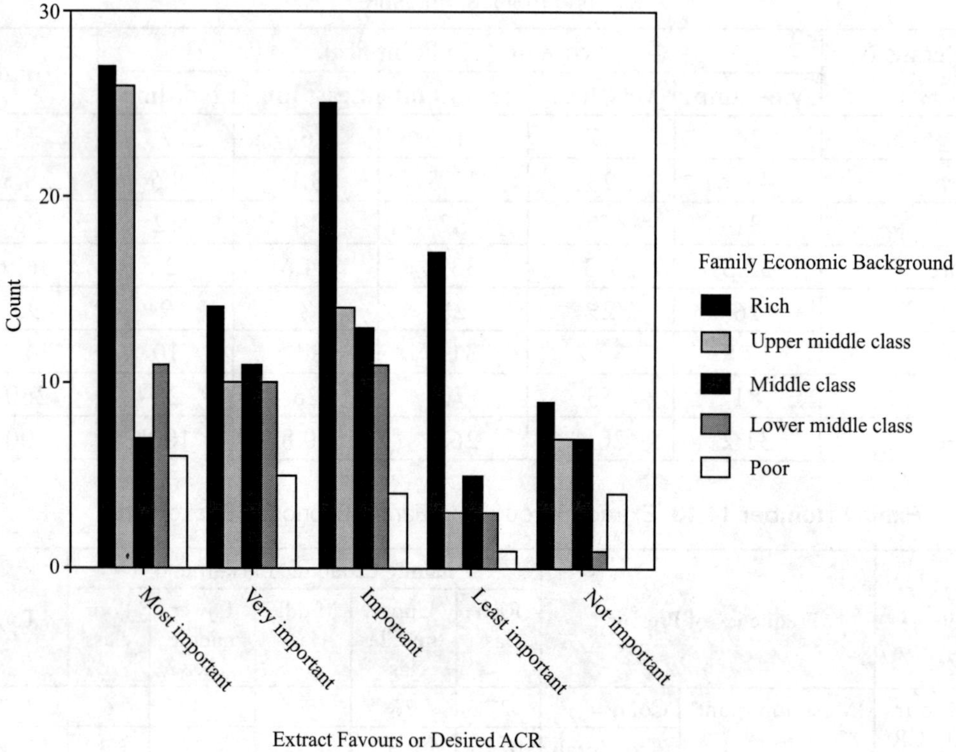

Chart No. 14.5: Accept Pressure for Favours versus Economic Background

Bureaucrats and politicians' relations are beyond favor seeking and are complex in nature. "Widespread political meddling has fuelled the notion that malicious politicians stand in the way of honest, hardworking bureaucrats who seek to implement key government policies. The relationship between politicians and the bureaucracy is far more complicated," *The Hindustan Times*, September 22, 2016.

Results placed at Exhibit 14.12 show that 32.2% of the Indian Forest Service officers consider it 'very important' and 33.3% of the Indian Police Service officers consider it 'important' towards acceptance of political pressure. 82.4% of the Indian Administrative Service officers, 81.1% of the Indian Forest Service officers, and 72.9% of the Indian Police Service officers think that the desired ACR/performance appraisal report/favor is an 'important' factor in the acceptance of political pressure in the decision. Good association or extracting favors from politicians and decision is established by the Pearson Chi-square results, which are highly significant with significance at 0.000, level. Spearman correlation value of 0.2 with a level of significance of 0.01, indicates significant strength of such a relationship. Our alternate hypothesis is accepted that a higher desire for getting favors from politicians enhances the chances of higher acceptance of political pressure in the decision-making process.

Exhibit 14.13 and Chart 14.5 show the relation of extracting favors from politicians' variable relationship with the economic background of the AISO. Results show 36.7% of the AISO from the rich economic background and 23.9% from the upper-middle class with a total of 60.6% officers from the well-off economic background are amenable to accept pressure in the decision.

14.4.2.4. Appreciation/Recognition of Own Work: While discussing reasons for acceptance of political pressure, many All India Services Officers told us that if we do not develop good relations with the politicians, they do not appreciate even good work done by us. Those officers who have good relations with the politicians, even they do not carry out good work, politicians appreciate them openly and publicly. Politician criticism in public destroys the innovations; good spirit and desire to continue good work, even this adversely affect the efficiency of the officer concerned. Even if individual officers, who do not like to accept political pressure, they do accept it for the improved projection of their name and work in the department and public. Good relations with the politicians facilitate the individual officer to make a quicker decision and the public develop faith in such decisions due to closeness to power holders. That desire for appreciation ultimately destroys the fairness in the decision.

Exhibit Number 14.14: Appreciation of Own Work as Reason for Accepting Pressure

Other Details & Service		Score on Five Point Scale					Total
		Most Imp.	Very Imp.	Important	Least Imp. Not	Not Imp.	
I.A.S.	N	20	27	12	4	8	71
% of score		28.2	38	16.9	5.6	11.3	28
I.P.S.	N	0	21	27	20	28	96
% of score		0	21.9	28.1	20.8	29.2	37.8
I.F.S.	N	18	26	24	7	12	87
% of score		20.7	29.9	27.6	8	13.8	34.3
Total	N	38	74	63	31	48	254
% of score		15	29.1	24.8	12.2	18.9	100

This factor has not been considered as very important by the All India Services Officers in acceptance of political pressure and has been ranked at 14th. Exhibit 14.14 shows that 29.1% of total All India Services Officers, 38% of the Indian Administrative Service officers, and 29.9% of the Indian Forest Service officers consider recognition of their own work as a 'very important' factor in the acceptance of political pressure in the decision-making process. 29.2% of the Indian Police Service officers do not consider the appreciation of their own work in acceptance of political pressure. Very low consideration by the Indian Police Service officers may be due to the fact that most of the time the politicians do not discuss police actions in the public. Pearson Chi-square results are highly significant with a 0.000, level of significance. This shows the good association of the factor, recognition of own work through politician in acceptance of political pressure.

Appreciation or recognitions of own work desires are inbuilt in a large number of persons, that is, an inbuilt part of the personality, such feelings work as motivating factor at the workplace. Such inner motivation propels any individual officer to arrive at decisions to expand those inner cognitions and feelings.

14.4.3. Decision Conflict-Related

Bureaucratic system is full of conflicts, the All India Services Officers like to avoid conflicts in the decision, and we have studied two items: (i) avoid humiliation for self and family and (ii) avoid conflicts in the decision process.

14.4.3.1. Stress/Avoid Humiliation: Stress has been viewed as an external force or characteristic that induces strain or threat, whereas others see it as a response of a person [Kahn (1964), Miller (1971), French et al. (1975), Selye (1974), and Mclean (1976)]. Stress is a perceived imbalance between demand and response capability, under conditions of failure to meet demand has perceived consequences. Humiliation for self and family is the consequence of the decision for the All India Services Officers. Here it is important that individual All India Services Officer perceive political pressure in different ways and appraise differentially to arrive at decision. End action or result or decision outcome is related to the individual officer's perceptions. Stress has a dynamic interaction between the person and environment when confronted with threats and challenges. It is manifested by changes in the psychological subsystem (inner state and behavior) and/or physical subsystem of the person, Asha Bhandarker (1985).

The All India Services Officers experience embarrassment, when they find that they are unable to interfere in the process of the decision-making process, they are signing according to the desires of the politicians. When they realized that external forces determine the decisions and seniors or other persons are making decisions, which was supposed to be taken by him. The All India Services Officers are confronted with shrinking opportunities, increasing constraints, exaggerating demands, and desires from the system for uncertain outcomes. Political and economic uncertainties enhance stress among All India Services Officers. The individual officer does not like to increase problems for himself and his family. It induces changes in individual All India Services Officer perceptions, attitudes, beliefs, hostility, social support, and work experiences. The All India Services Officer finds himself to cope with demands from the decision and his highly demanding roles.

The position of a politician in government hierarchy and structure is such that he exercises effective control over various stages in the departmental working of the All India Services Officers. The All India Services Officers experience that seniors, colleagues, and even subordinates do not provide desire support in the hours of need. One has to defend one's decisions oneself or face the consequences. In case decisions are overruled, individual officers feel utterly humiliated. He loses interest in work and belief from the merit. When merit begets distress, fairness humiliates self and family; then All India Services Officers' only option left is to accept the political pressure. "The overwhelming perceptions [that] corrupt bureaucrats are despised but thrive; the honest are respected but do not rise; idealists end up in the boondocks". Indeed, many observers believe that the excesses of India's political executive are in large part to blame for the troubled state of the

Indian bureaucracy, not least it's hobbled "steel frame"—the elite Indian Administrative Service (IAS). As reported in *The Hindustan Times*, September 22, 2016 (the HT website).

Exhibit Number 14.15: Avoid Humiliation for Self and Family as Reason for Accepting Pressure

Other Details & Service	Score on Five Point Scale					Total
	Most Imp.	Very Imp.	Important	Least Imp. Not	Not Imp.	
I.A.S. N	27	17	14	12	4	74
% of score	36.5	23	18.9	16.2	5.4	29
I.P.S. N	1	9	26	36	19	91
% of score	1.1	9.9	28.6	39.6	20.9	35.7
I.F.S. N	17	36	18	14	5	90
% of score	18.9	40	20	15.6	5.6	35.3
Total N	45	62	58	62	28	255
% of score	17.6	24.3	22.7	24.3	11	100

As far as the highest score is concerned, 24.3% of the All India Services Officers and 40% of the Indian Forest Service officers consider avoidance of humiliation as 'very important' as shown in Exhibit 14.15. 36% of the Indian Administrative Service officers consider it 'most important' and 39.6% of the Indian Police Service officers consider it 'least important'. The lowest score of the Indian Police Service officers may be due to fact that they are in commanding position with full control over police forces, so they feel that political pressure cannot humiliate them (being uniformed service) or they live in complete protection (by armed constabulary) and insulation. So, avoidance of humiliation for self and family does not work as a political pressure acceptance factor for the Indian Police Service officers. The Indian Administrative Service officers consider it as the 'most important' factor, which is supported by the highest score in this category. If we combine three scores above 'important' to 'most important' results are; 64.6% of the All India Services Officers, 78.9% of the Indian Forest Service officers, 78.4% of the Indian Administrative Service officers, and 39.6% of the Indian Police Service officers consider it an 'important' factor in the acceptance of political pressure in the decision-making process. Pearson Chi-square analyses establish a good relationship with the decision with a 0.00, level of significance.

14.4.3.2. Avoid Conflict: The decision-making process in government bureaucratic system is full of uncertainties and conflicts. These conflicts in process of decision generate tension, worry, stress, and adversely affect the outcome of the decision. As chances of conflict increase in the decision, the uncertainty-generated conflicts influence the outcome of decision quality. People may have beliefs and faith in the All India Services, but as an individual officer, it works in a different way with respect to political relations. "The people perceive the IAS to be incompetent, self-interested, and arrogant but they trust their political leaders even less. Further, many honest IAS officers, in their genuine concern for India, want the IAS to continue so it can block corrupt politicians. But their remedy does not address the cause of the problem. Fixing the problem of corrupt politicians requires a different approach (which I've elaborated elsewhere) and we should not use the existence of bad politicians to justify the world's most powerful but incompetent bureaucracy," *The Times of India*, June 1, 2019.

Exhibit Number 14.16: Avoid Conflict in Decision Process as Reason for Accepting Pressure

Other Details & Service		Score on Five Point Scale					Total
		Most Imp.	Very Imp.	Important	Least Imp. Not	Not Imp.	
I.A.S.	N	36	15	10	8	5	74
% of score		48.6	20.3	13.5	10.8	6.8	28.7
I.P.S.	N	43	22	9	15	7	96
% of score		44.8	22.9	9.4	15.6	7.3	37.2
I.F.S.	N	19	14	28	21	6	88
% of score		21.6	15.9	31.8	23.9	6.8	34.1
Total	N	98	51	47	44	18	258
% of score		38	19.8	18.2	17.1	7	100

Pearson Chi-square analyses indicate that there is a good association between decision and avoidance of conflict by the All India Services Officers. Results are significant with a level of significance at 0.000. The significance of good strength of these relations is demonstrated by Pearson's correlation and Spearman correlation values, which are highly significant with the level of significance of 0.000. This indicates that conflict avoidance is strongly related to the decision-making process by the All India Services Officers.

Exhibit Number 14.17: Avoid Conflicts in Decision and Officer Regional Background

Reason	Frequency of Pressure		Officer Regional Background						Total
			North Eastern	Eastern Part	Western Part	Northern Part	Southern Part	Central Part	
Avoid conflicts in decision process	'Most important'	Count	14	16	9	20	34	4	97
		% of Total	5.46	6.25	3.51	7.81	13.28	1.56	37.89
	'Very important'	Count	6	10	6	10	12	6	50
		% of Total	2.34	3.9	2.34	3.9	4.68	2.34	19.53
	'Important'	Count	7	10	1	13	12	6	49
		% of Total	2.73	3.9	0.39	5.07	4.68	2.34	19.14
	'Least important'	Count	8	3	3	14	9	6	43
		% of Total	3.12	1.17	1.17	5.46	3.51	2.34	16.79
	'Not important'	Count	1	2	3	5	4	2	17
		% of Total	0.39	0.78	1.17	1.95	1.56	0.78	6.64
Total		Count	36	41	22	62	71	24	256
		% of Total	14.06	16.01	8.59	24.21	27.73	9.37	100

38% of the All India Services Officers, 48.6% of the Indian Administrative Service officers, and 44.8% of the Indian Police Service officers consider conflict avoidance as 'most important' for the acceptance of political pressure as displayed in Exhibit 14.16. 31.8% of the Indian Forest Service officers consider avoidance of conflict as 'important' for decision. Among All India Services, the Indian Forest Service officers are least affected by the problem of conflict may be due to the higher technical nature of their job or comparatively lesser amount political pressure exerted on them or may some other reasons.

Variable to avoid conflicts in decision-making process relationship with the demographic variable of the AISO regional background data analyses results are placed at Exhibit 14.17 and also shown in Chart 14.6. 27.7% of the AISO with Southern India background and 24.2% of the Northern India regional background shows amenability to accept pressure in this variable.

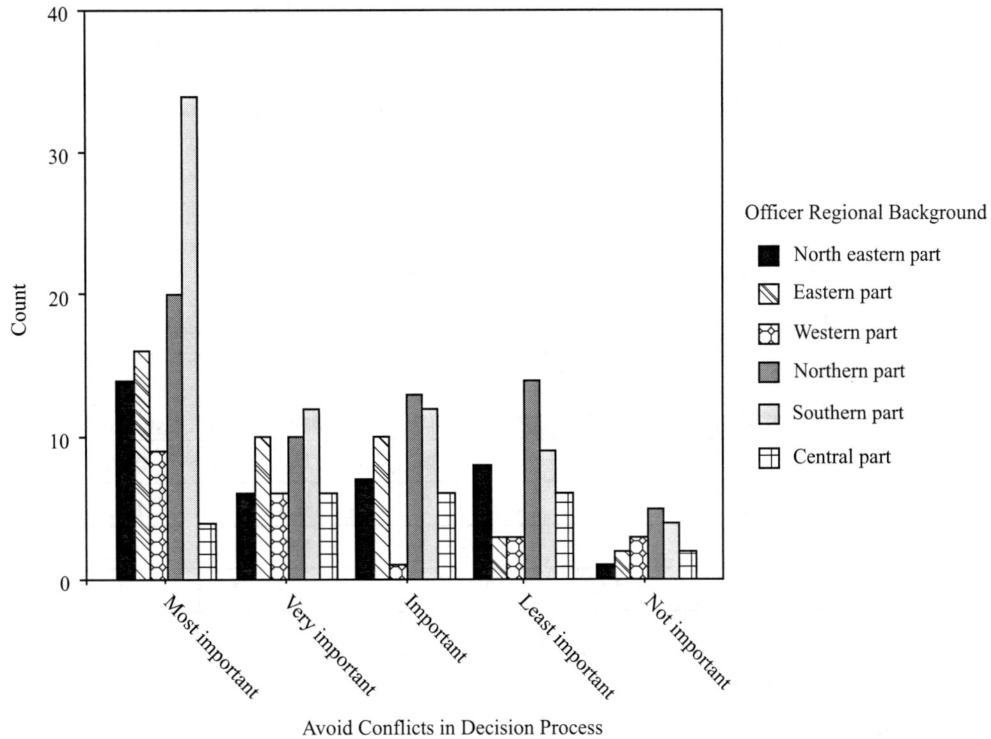

Chart No. 14.6: Acceptance of Pressure to Avoid Conflicts in Decision and Officer Regional Background

14.4.4. Family Related

We have studied three items pertaining to the future financial security of family: (i) to earn money/property to increase own resources, (ii) pursue goals for self and family, and (iii) immoral behavior for freedom in goal achievement or misuse of funds.

14.4.4.1. Enhance Resources: Some of the All India Services Officers earn money, acquire property, and enhance their resources by adopting various undesirable ways and means in violation of established norms. When the All India Services Officers amass resources and enhance own monetary power by adopting illegal and unfair methods, they are fully aware that there are possibilities of departmental action against them or maybe public complaints against them, in such situations only politicians can provide them shelter and can save them against legal actions. Such officers develop nexus with the politicians for their own safety and continue to misuse government resources in collusion with politicians. Both parties amass disproportionate wealth through unfair means and methods.

28.95 of the All India Services Officers, 29.3% of the Indian Administrative Service officers, and 27.8% of the Indian Forest Service officers consider earning money and enhancement of own resources as a 'most important' factor in the acceptance of political pressure as shown in Exhibit 14.18. Whereas 36.3% of the Indian Police Service officers think that money earning and accumulating resources is the 'important' factor in accepting the political pressure. If we add up the first three valuations together then 77% of the Indian Police Service officers, 73.3% of the Indian Administrative Service officers, and 66.7% of the Indian Forest Service officers consider resource accumulation and earning money as 'important' factor towards acceptance of political pressure. Pearson Chi-square results are significant with a level of significance of 0.04. The All India Services Officers have assigned earning money and resource enhancement at overall 9th rank, which shows that individual officers put importance to this factor.

Exhibit Number 14.18: Earn Property and Enhance Resources as Reason for Accepting Pressure

Other Details & Service		Score on Five Point Scale					Total
		Most Imp.	Very Imp.	Important	Least Imp. Not	Not Imp.	
I.A.S.	N	22	15	18	11	9	75
% of score		29.3	20	24	14.7	12	29.3
I.P.S.	N	27	10	33	15	6	91
% of score		29.7	11	36.3	16.5	6.6	35.5
I.F.S.	N	25	20	15	13	17	90
% of score		27.8	22.2	16.7	14.4	18.9	35.2
Total	N	74	45	66	39	32	256
% of score		28.9	17.6	25.8	15.2	12.5	100

Exhibit Number 14.19: Scope for Control over Resources and Place of Birth of an Officer

Reason	Frequency of Pressure		Birthplace of Officer			Total
			Rural	Urban	Semi-Urban	
Scope for control over resources	'Most important'	Count	9	30	14	53
		% of Total	3.67	12.24	5.71	21.63
	'Very important'	Count	18	38	20	76
		% of Total	7.34	15.51	8.16	31.02
	'Important'	Count	10	22	9	41
		% of Total	4.08	8.97	3.67	16.73
	'Least important'	Count	14	19	9	42
		% of Total	5.71	7.75	3.67	17.14
	'Not important'	Count	10	15	8	33
		% of Total	4.08	6.12	3.26	13.46
Total		Count	61	124	60	245
		% of Total	24.89	50.61	24.48	100

"All civil servants are in some position of authority and there are temptations. But it is not only power that corrupts. Weakness, too, corrupts," Pulok Chatterji, *The India Today*, August 14, 2012.

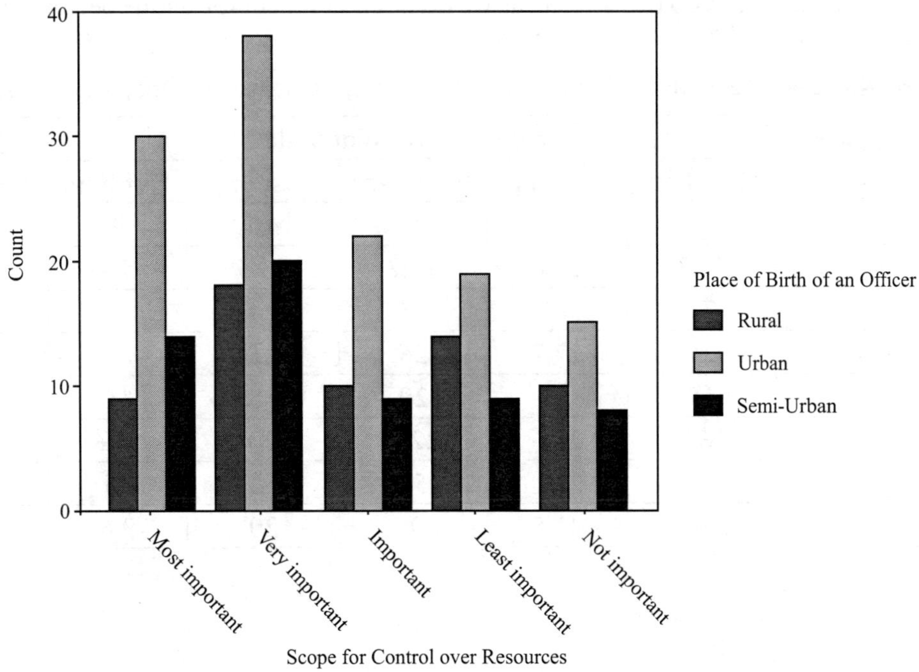

Chart No. 14.7: Acceptance of Pressure to Gain Control over Resources versus Place of Birth of an Officer

Data analysis results placed at Exhibit 14.19 and graphic representation at Chart 14.7 show the All India Services officers' effort to gain control over resources and its relation with the demographic variable place of birth of an officer. Results indicate that 50.61% of the AISO from an urban background, 24.89% from a rural, and 24.48% from a semi-urban background are amenable to accept pressure in a decision in this variable.

14.4.4.2. Pursue Goals for Self and Family: The All India Services Officers pursue self-goals and high self-goal orientation forces them to accept political pressure in the decision-making process. Achievement of goals for self and family is one of the critical factors in mobilizing political support, which induces the All India Services Officers slowly under political pressure. "Functioning of UP police is vitiated by political interference and willingness of some police officers to oblige the politician to fulfill their personal interests. Because of mutual accommodation of the officers and the politicians, many malpractices, and irregularities creep into the police functioning. The impression is that, because of vested interests, neither the politicians nor the police officers are seriously interested in removing these evils. In fact, both of them profit by the continuance of such evils," Dr. R. Parshar (1986).

Individual, "values are norms, which hold and sustain life and society and establish a symbol and interdependent relationship between humankind and the ecosystem. Values denote a fundamental category: in a common understanding this corresponds to what we mean when it is said that truth, beauty, and goodness are supreme values of life," S.L. Goel, 2013. Some ex-bureaucrats see politician bureaucrats' relation with different angle after retirement and advocated political pressure acceptance beyond self-goals also. "Our role is to strengthen the hands of the political leadership by giving them sound, objective advice and respecting their decision so long as it is legitimate. And we can do this so long as we do not go to them for undue personal favours," Pulok Chatterji, *The India Today*, August 14, 2012.

Exhibit Number 14.20: Pursue Goals for Self and Family as Reason for Accepting Pressure

Other Details & Service		Score on Five Point Scale					Total
		Most Imp.	Very Imp.	Important	Least Imp.	Not Imp.	
I.A.S.	N	35	16	9	10	4	74
% of score		47.3	21.6	12.2	13.5	5.4	28.5
I.P.S.	N	23	17	25	24	7	96
% of score		24	17.7	26	25	7.3	36.9
I.F.S.	N	15	23	20	18	14	90
% of score		16.7	25.6	22.2	20	15.6	34.6
Total	N	73	56	54	52	25	260
% of score		28.1	21.5	20.8	20	9.6	100

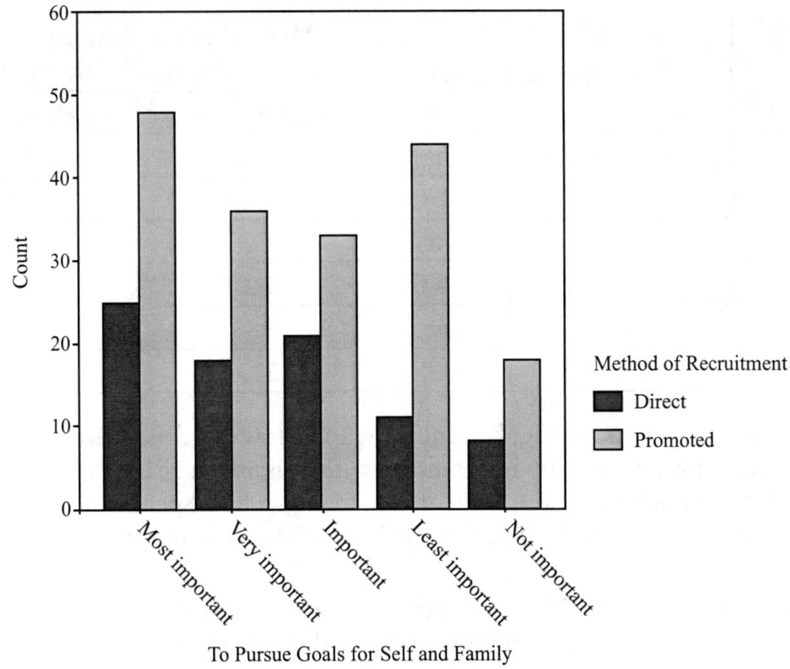

Chart No. 14.8: Acceptance of Pressure to Pursue Goals for Self and Family versus Method of Recruitment

Results placed at Exhibit 14.20 show that 28.1% of the All India Services Officers and 47.3% of the Indian Administrative Service officers consider the desire to pursue goals make them to accept political pressure as the 'most important' factor. 25.6% of the Indian Forest Service officers think that self-goal pursuance is 'very important' for the acceptance of political pressure. 26% of the Indian Police Service officers consider goal orientation only 'important' in acceptance of political pressure.

Exhibit Number 14.21: Pursue Goals for Self and Family versus Method of Recruitment

Reason	Frequency of Pressure		Method of Recruitment More Amenable to the Political Pressure		Total
			Direct Recruit	Promoted	
To pursue goals for self and family	'Most important'	Count	25	48	73
		% of Total	9.54	18.3	27.86
	'Very important'	Count	18	36	54
		% of Total	6.87	13.7	20.61
	'Important'	Count	21	33	54
		% of Total	8.01	12.6	20.61

Reason	Frequency of Pressure		Method of Recruitment More Amenable to the Political Pressure		Total
			Direct Recruit	Promoted	
	'Least important'	Count	11	44	55
		% of Total	4.19	16.8	20.99
	'Not important'	Count	8	18	26
		% of Total	3.05	6.8	9.92
Total		Count	83	179	262
		% of Total	31.67	68.3	100

Pearson Chi-square results are highly significant and show good association with the decision and goal pursuance. This relationship is significant with a significance level of 0.001. The strength of the relationship is indicated by the Pearson's correlation and Spearman correlation, both of which are significant with a significance level at 0.000. This factor has been considered at 10th rank in importance.

Results placed at Exhibit 14.21 and Chart 14.8 show the relationship of pursuing goals for self and family relationship with the demographic variable method of recruitment. 69.08% of All India Services officers consider self-goals pursuing from 'important' to 'most important' category for acceptance of pressure in the decision-making process, and 44.3% promoted officer consider this in this intensity of pressure.

14.4.4.3. Freedom in Goal Achievements: Bureaucratic systems are functioning through well-laid down rules, regulations, and procedures. These procedures and rules work as a hindrance in the way of officers, who have a strong yearning to misuse government resources. Politicians occupy the top position in the bureaucratic system, if an individual officer can have excellent access to politicians, then that politician can influence the senior officers of that department for providing the freedom to such officer towards the aggrandizement of self-goals. Some individual officers manipulate power through the politicians, they develop sharing arrangements with the top politicians, in place of cash or kind gains politician provide protection to such officers, who make money or achieve their self-goals freely without hindrance from the seniors. In some States some bureaucrats like to ensure their continuity in wet posting for long periods, they make payment to politicians on a quarterly or yearly basis also. Some bureaucrats transfer property in the name of politicians for wet/plumb posting or some other work, with changing time and technology innovations means and methods of bribe payments are also changing.

Exhibit Number 14.22: Freedom in Goals Achievement as Reason for Accepting Pressure

Service	Score on Five Point Scale					Total
	Most Imp.	Very Imp.	Important	Least Imp.	Not Imp.	
I.A.S. N	32	9	7	3	12	63
% of score	50.8	14.3	11.1	4.8	19	27
I.P.S. N	16	23	9	17	19	84
% of score	19	27.4	10.7	20.2	22.6	36.1

Service	Score on Five Point Scale					Total
	Most Imp.	Very Imp.	Important	Least Imp.	Not Imp.	
I.F.S. N	13	19	16	18	20	86
% of score	15.1	22.1	18.6	20.9	23.3	36.9
Total N	61	51	32	38	51	233
% of score	26.2	21.9	13.7	16.3	21.9	100

Statistical analyses result placed at Exhibit 14.22 show that 26.2% of the total All India Services Officers and 50.8% of the Indian Administrative Service officers consider immoral behavior as the 'most important' factor in accepting political pressure. 27.4% of the Indian Police Service officers think that immoral behavior is 'very important' factor in accepting the political pressure. 23.3% of the Indian Forest Service officers consider that immoral behavior is 'not important' in acceptance of political pressure. Scores are distributed across all the intensity of valuations in this factor. Pearson Chi-square results are highly significant with a 0.000, level of significance. Pearson Chi-square indicates a good association of immoral behavior with the decision. This association strength is shown by Pearson's correlation and Spearman correlation values, which are significant with 0.001 and '0.000' level of significance. The All India Services Officers have ranked immoral behavior at 11th rank among all the factors studied by us.

14.4.5. Personal Behavior Related

Two factors are relating to individual officer behavior: (i) secure political patronage for conformity and (ii) safeguard own incompetence in the decision.

14.4.5.1. Political Patronage: Politicians occupy the top position in the hierarchy of public administration in our democratic setup. Not only legislatures make the law and are the supreme in the bureaucratic system, where All India Services Officers try to secure their patronage for individual interests. Those All India Services Officers, who engage in self-goals maximization and cause distortion in the decision-making process, willfully or unknowingly commit a lot of mistakes in the process of harvesting the crop of the self-goals. So, such officers initiate the process of flattery or sycophancy towards the politicians and slowly majority of the officers get entrapped in that vicious cycle, politician find such situations conducive for them and exploit the officers to the fullest extent. Bureaucrats and politicians both remain busy in illegal benefits maximization, politician power is for short term and bureaucrat exploit that time thinking that next political incumbent will also be managed like this as word spread in public. In many cases, the new incumbent politician also collects information regarding such pliable officers and after coming to power they call such officers for bargaining and mutual benefits extractions. Invariably, such officers are well known in bureaucracy. Such pliable bureaucrats search political patronage for career security and protection of illegally accumulated wealth.

Some pliable officers seek political patronage even after retirement for seeking post-retirement rehabilitation. "The Election Commission, in the national interest, had recommended the government in 2012 to amend the service rules and set a cooling-off period before civil servants can join a political party and contest polls. This was with an object to prevent those with political ambition from favoring a particular party in their final years of service. But the Department of

Personnel and Training was of the view that debarring ex-bureaucrats from joining electoral politics immediately upon exit from service may violate the right to equality, enshrined in Article 14 of the Constitution," K.V. Chandra Mouli, *The Deccan Herald*, March 22, 2019. There is a strong need to debar all kinds of post-retirement rehabilitation.

Exhibit Number 14.23: Secure Political Patronage as Reason for Accepting Pressure

Other Details & Service		Score on Five Point Scale					Total
		Most Imp.	Very Imp.	Important	Least Imp. Not	Not Imp.	
I.A.S.	N	36	14	13	7	5	75
% of score		48	18.7	17.3	9.3	6.7	29
I.P.S.	N	54	7	16	13	6	96
% of score		56.3	7.3	16.7	13.5	6.3	37.1
I.F.S.	N	18	14	28	16	12	88
% of score		20.5	15.9	31.8	18.2	13.6	34
Total	N	108	35	57	36	23	259
% of score		41.7	13.5	22	13.9	8.9	100

Exhibit Number 14.24: Secure Political Patronage and Level Amenable to Pressure

Reason	Frequency of Pressure		Level More Amenable to Pressure			Total
			Top Level	Middle Level	Lower Level	
To secure political patronage	'Most important'	Count	62	35	10	107
		% of Total	24.03	13.56	3.87	41.47
	'Very important'	Count	20	10	4	34
		% of Total	7.75	3.87	1.56	13.17
	'Important'	Count	37	7	12	56
		% of Total	14.34	2.71	4.65	21.7
	'Least important'	Count	18	7	12	37
		% of Total	6.97	2.71	4.65	14.34
	'Not important'	Count	16	5	3	24
		% of Total	6.2	1.93	1.16	9.3
Total		Count	153	64	41	258
		% of Total	59.3	24.8	15.89	100

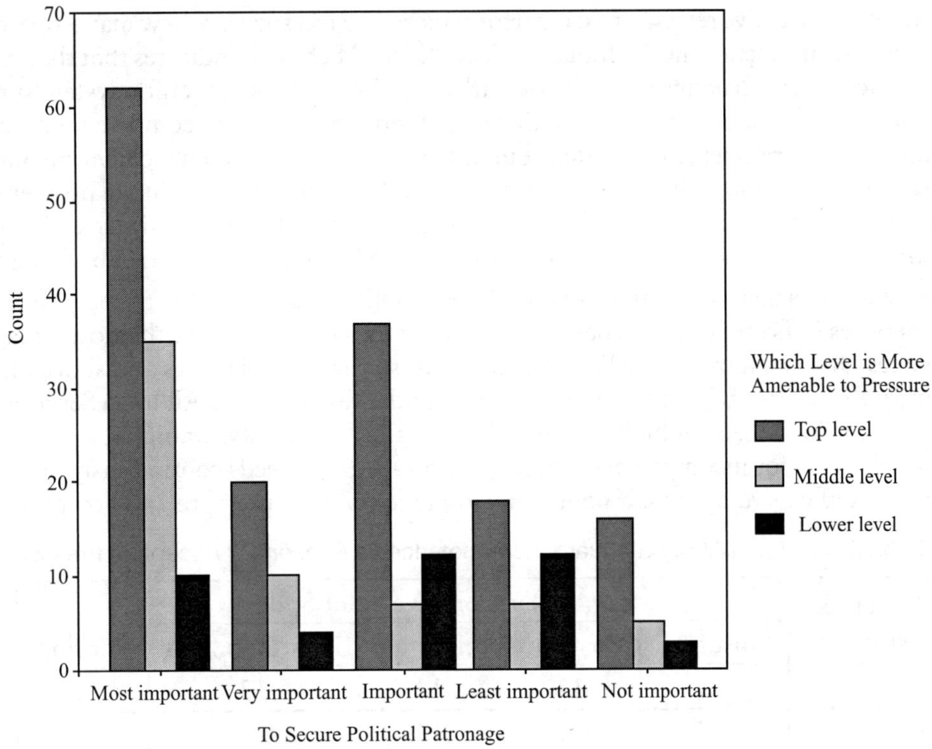

Chart No.14.9: Acceptance of Pressure to Secure Political Patronage and Level Amenable to Pressure

Results placed at Exhibit 14.23 show that 41.7% of the All India Services Officers, 48% of the Indian Administrative Service officers, and 56.3% of the Indian Police Service officers consider political patronage as the 'most important' factor for acceptance of political pressure in the decision-making process. 31.8% of the Indian Forest Service officers think that political patronage is an 'important' factor for acceptance of political pressure. Results are highly significant and the association of political patronage with the decision-making process is indicated by the Pearson Chi-square values. Pearson's correlation and Spearman correlation values are significant with 0.000, level of significance, and show good relation with the decision. The research variable to 'secure political patronage' is relationship with 'which level of bureaucracy is amenable to accept political pressure' in the decision-making process. Results are shown in Exhibit 14.24 and also presented in Chart 14.9. Results indicate that 59.3% of top level show interest in seeking political patronage in the decision process and every fourth top level officer considers it as 'most important' for them.

14.4.5.2. Safeguard Incompetence: The tendency to avoid and ignore the responsibility to circumvent administrative controls is the common problem of the Indian bureaucracy. The All India Services Officers are highly conscious to share their weaknesses and show high concern that may not be reflected in the performance review. The All India Services Officers demonstrate tremendous confrontation to a negative review of their performance; they feel such a review may jeopardize their future career advancement. The All India Services Officers' behavior indicates that they are highly defensive to accept constructive feedback or criticism. The entire bureaucratic system survives on inflated annual performance assessments. Eleven potential blockages to competence described by Dave Francis et al. are relevant to Indian bureaucracy also: (i) self-management incompetence, (ii) unclear personal values, (iii) stunning personal development, (iv) inadequate problem-solving skills, (v) unclear personal goals, (vi) low creativity, (vii) low influence, (viii) lack of managerial insights, (ix) poor supervisory skills, (x) low trainer capability, and (xi) low team building capacity.

Public start asserting in review system with local politicians and end with top politicians, the All India Services Officers view own performance as all the best. To achieve their own goals the All India Services Officers, move in the line of politicians, so that, own failures and shortcomings are hidden under the layers of the bureaucratic system. Under that urge, the All India Services Officers satisfy the politicians' needs. A high amount of uncertainty, flexibility, ambiguous policy, and law create enough space for incompetence. So, lust for future goals/needs continuously pressurize All India Services Officers to approach politicians to invite political pressure and accept it.

Exhibit Number 14.25: Safeguard Incompetence as Reason for Accepting Pressure

Other Details & Service		Score on Five Point Scale					Total
		Most Imp.	Very Imp.	Important	Least Imp. Not	Not Imp.	
I.A.S.	N	32	11	12	12	8	75
% of score		42.7	14.7	16	16.3	107	29.1
I.P.S.	N	12	25	17	29	12	95
% of score		12.6	26.3	17.9	30.5	12.6	36.8
I.F.S.	N	10	15	14	17	32	88
% of score		11.4	17	15.9	19.3	36.4	34.1
Total	N	54	51	43	58	52	258
% of score		20.9	19.8	16.7	22.5	20.2	100

The All India Services Officers consider them 'most competent', hence this item has received last and 15th ranking. Only 42.7% of the Indian Administrative Service officers consider acceptance of political pressure 'most important' as a safeguard to incompetence. Exhibit 14.25 shows that 22.5% of the All India Services Officers and 30.5% of Indian Police Service officers consider acceptance of political pressure 'least important' as a safeguard to incompetence. 36.4% of the Indian Forest Service officers think that acceptance of political pressure, as a safeguard to incompetence is 'not important' for them. Pearson Chi-square results indicate that acceptance of political pressure to safeguard the incompetence of the All India Services Officers has good association and association is significant with 0.000, level of significance. The strength of relations is shown by Pearson's correlation and Spearman correlation values with 0.000, level of significance.

14.4.6. Control-Related Reasons

Two factors are related to control feelings: All India Services Officers think that (i) proximity to politicians generates information, which makes individual officer powerfuls, and political association help in (ii) retention of control over the resources.

14.4.6.1. Proximity to Politicians Generate Information (**Communication**): Control over information or access to information influence the All India Services Officers' behavior in different ways. The All India Services Officers derive information on what is going on in and around top authorities and layers of hierarchy. The All India Services Officers try to gather information about grievances related to him or his colleagues, attitudes and behavior of senior bosses, and disposition of juniors towards him. From such information individual, the All India Services Officer can draw inferences about his future strategies, present performance evaluation, and implementation of government policies. From politicians, the All India Services Officers try to retrieve what control functions are going to be used and what are the outcomes of the monitoring results. The right information at right time motivates the All India Services Officers to control his subordinates and system both. Timings of information retrieval are highly crucial for government administration decisions.

Even there are All India Services Officers who en-cash the information. In government administration, advance information about new decisions can command a great premium. Information regarding transfers, postings, and promotions is in evergreen great demand and commands a high premium, which helps in the attainment of self-goals. During service, we observed that some officers used advanced information regarding transfer and posting as industry to earn money and blackmailing juniors and seniors both. Some unscrupulous elements in bureaucracy develop close relations in Chief Minister Office (or other power centers) and gather advance information regarding new selections/appointments and then they collect money from those selected candidates saying that they will get him selected/appointed for a job, and this information becomes money-minting industry for some people. The information helps in releasing the emotional expression of feelings and fulfillment of needs. Politicians in the power seat, their attitudes, policy decisions, and information about such vital inputs help in making decisions. The All India Services Officers like to derive information regarding implications of political pressure exerted on them, so accordingly can change their behavior and approach in decision towards pressure and pressure groups.

The information helps individual All India Services Officers to reduce ambiguity and clarify the decision behavior. The vital importance of information to reduce uncertainty, improve decision performance, and satisfaction in the decision. The All India Services Officers information from a politician is crucial to know about public opinion, public mood, public expectations, and reactions to the decision. Ever-changing policies, political leadership, make it more important to share information with the politicians in power to attune decision delivery towards political commitments. Many All India Services Officers are new to the culture of the district, they are posted, and they share information with politicians to work with public expectations. Lusts for gathering information from politicians work as a constant reason for working for acceptance of political pressure.

Exhibit Number 14.26: Proximity to Politicians Generate Information for Accepting Pressure

Other Details & Service		Score on Five Point Scale					Total
		Most Imp.	Very Imp.	Important	Least Imp. Not	Not Imp.	
I.A.S.	N	42	21	6	4	2	75
% of score		56	28	8	5.3	2.7	29.3
I.P.S.	N	56	19	12	7	2	96
% of score		58.3	19.8	12.5	7.3	2.1	37.5
I.F.S.	N	12	25	22	11	15	85
% of score		14.1	29.4	25.9	12.9	17.5	33.2
Total	N	110	65	40	22	19	258
% of score		43	25.4	15.6	8.6	7.4	100

Exhibit Number 14.27: Proximity to Politician Generate Information and Educational Background of the Officer

Reason	Frequency of Pressure		Educational Background of the Officer					Total
			Graduate	Engineer/ B.Tech./ Technology	P.G.	MBA/ CA/CW	Ph.D.	
Proximity to politician generate information	'Most important'	Count	29	23	32	18	5	107
		% of Total	11.93	9.46	13.17	7.4	2.05	44.03
	'Very important'	Count	15	14	22	5	4	60
		% of Total	6.17	5.76	9.05	2.05	1.64	24.69
	'Important'	Count	9	6	16	3	3	37
		% of Total	3.7	2.46	6.58	1.23	1.23	15.23
	'Least important'	Count	4	7	6	3	1	21
		% of Total	1.64	2.88	2.46	1.23	0.42	8.64
	'Not important'	Count	8	1	8		1	18
		% of Total	3.29	0.41	3.29		0.41	7.4
Total		Count	65	51	84	29	14	243
		% of Total	26.74	20.98	34.57	11.93	5.76	100

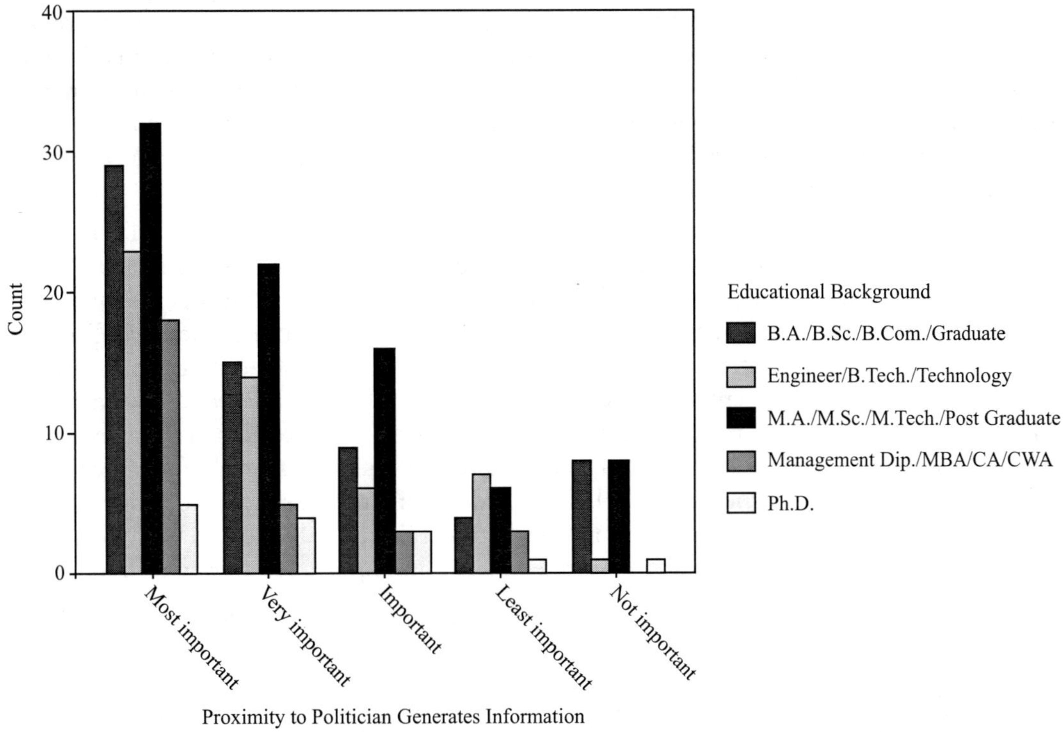

Chart No. 14.10: Educational Background and Proximity to Politician Generate Information

Results of Exhibit 14.26 indicate that 43% of the All India Services Officers use communications by developing proximity to politicians gather information, this desire for information motivates them to accept political pressure in the decision-making process. 58.3% of the Indian Police Service officers and 56% of the Indian Administrative Service officers think that access to political information is 'most important' for acceptance of political pressure in the decision. 25.9% of the Indian Forest Service officers consider information power in accepting political pressure as 'important' category. The very low score of the Indian Forest Service officers indicates that either they do not have access to information or they have not tasted the power of information. Our results for Pearson Chi-square indicate that proximity to politicians generate information has a good association with the decision-making process. These relationships are very strong as indicated by Pearson's correlation value of 0.4 and Spearman's correlation value of 0.4, both with a level of significance at 0.000. Information generation has been rated as 2nd rank by the All India Services Officers. Results placed at Exhibit 14.27 and Chart 14.10 show results for a relation of this variable with an educational background of the All India Services officer and 34.57% officers with post-graduate qualification indicate highest score and Ph.D. 5.79% lowest score for gathering information from politicians.

14.4.6.2. Scope for Control Over Resources: In the present-day bureaucratic system, those who control the resources are the most powerful persons in the bureaucratic system. Resource control makes them powerful, by virtue of such control, all resource users run after the controller.

Persons who control resources can force all others to obey their command because there is stiff competition for scarce resources. Resource controller enjoys the power to induce manipulations and distortions in future planning, through such long-term planning, persons who make noise can be destroyed and persons, who sing songs for the controller are rewarded. In our bureaucratic system, the Indian Administrative Service officers exercise complete control over the resources to sustain their overriding power and supreme position.

Exhibit 14.28 results show that 47.3% of the Indian Administrative Service officers consider resource control as the 'most important' factor in accepting the political pressure. 30.2% of the All India Services Officers and 33% of the Indian Forest Service officers consider resource control as a 'very important' factor in accepting the political pressure. 26% of the Indian Police Service officers assessed resource control as 'least important' for acceptance of political pressure in the decision. Low score for the IPS may be due to the reason that they are related to law enforcement mainly and in general budgetary or land or development-related resources are not managed by them. Pearson Chi-square results are highly significant with the 0.000, level of significance. This indicates an association of resource control with the decision and the strength of this relationship is indicated by the Pearson's correlation and Spearman correlation values of 0.3 with a 0.000, level of significance. Resource control has been ranked at 12th in importance among different factors.

Exhibit Number 14.28: Scope for Control Over Resources as Reason for Accepting Pressure

Other Details & Service		Score on five Point Scale					Total
		Most Imp.	Very Imp.	Important	Least Imp. Not	Not Imp.	
I.A.S.	N	35	26	4	4	5	74
% of score		47.3	35.1	5.4	5.4	6.8	28.7
I.P.S.	N	16	23	19	25	13	96
% of score		16.7	24	19.8	26	13.5	37.2
I.F.S.	N	9	29	19	14	17	88
% of score		10.2	33	21.6	15.9	19.3	34.1
Total	N	60	78	42	43	35	258
% of score		23.3	30.2	16.3	16.7	13.6	1000

14.5. Ten-Fold Path of the AISO for Political Effectiveness

(i) Resource Captivity: Controlling style for self-promotions/resource captivity by the All India Services Officers had mobilized and manipulated full control over government resources, from top-level to down to district level all resources are used as power by these officers. Resource allocation provides them pushbutton for knowledge and expertise, which make them well sought after by political power holders also. Resource pushbuttons provide them a commanding position in society and government hierarchy.

(ii) Powerful Lobby/Associations: The All India Services Officers develop a powerful lobby with potential powerful persons, maybe politicians, bureaucrats, or any other person coalition of support required for retention and use of power.

(iii) **Camouflaging:** The All India Services Officers have specialized in hiding their real goals and interests in the garb of public interest. They garner a host of benefits on the name interest of the political party, voter interest, and politician interest. But the ultimate gainer in the game is the officer who manages it through politicians.

(iv) **Indispensable by Excuses:** The All India Services Officers' coalition manipulates their power in such a way that politician feels that the bureaucratic system cannot survive without these All India Services Officers. In case someone else occupies their position, their coalition surrogate the system and presents decisions in such a manner to convince politicians that without All India Services Officers politicians cannot function effectively.

(v) **Image Building:** The All India Services Officers propagate that only they are protector and custodian of the cultural heritage of India. Only they are honest, respect values; understand the feeling of the public, and right decision taker. In the Indian bureaucratic system, no one else can assess and evaluate their performance, hence they are the supreme leader.

(vi) **Elitist:** The All India Services Officers propagate only the elite can rule Indian society; they are born elite in their service hence they have full right to misrule.

(vii) **Sycophancy, Flattery and Hypocrisy:** Colonial origin of the All India Services is based on premises of hypocrisy and sycophancy to the Viceroy. All India Services Officers devote full time to telling their political masters and senior bosses regarding their own pseudo achievements. Their achievements are visible to an immediate boss and political master only, others do not know or do not have any access for evaluation, so powerful lobby at the top feel individual All India Services Officer at the top is the person who matters, ignore all others in the system.

(viii) **Misuse of Power as Deterrent:** The All India Services Officers are habitual in the manipulation of power to their own advantage. They develop syndicate/coalition for retention of power if anyone speaks against their interests they all misuse power as a deterrent or pre-emptive strike to crush the first voice against them.

(ix) **Conformity, Boss is Always Right:** The All India Services Officers always support their boss in case the boss is from their own service. They believe what so ever the boss desires, it should be complied with so that they earn the desired annual performance review report and meet their own goals with the least resistance. Enjoy yourself and let the boss also enjoy at the same time, there is enough in the system.

(x) **Deny Access Others:** The All India Services Officers believe that their loyalty should not be doubtful, if this belief is maintained they meet their goals easily. In case they suspect an individual is not of much use or is tainted, they keep their distance from such persons. They do not believe in friends and relations, they worship power. Power must be retained at any cost by them exclusively.

ANNEXURE 14.A: QUESTIONNAIRE, REASONS FOR ACCEPTING POLITICAL PRESSURE

Acceptance of political pressure by any individual officers of the All India Services may be situational and influenced by numerous factors/reasons accordingly. We have listed 15 such reasons/factors, which may influence the acceptance of political pressure. Kindly, evaluate these items on the five point scale, 1 being the most important, 2 very important, 3 important, 4 least important, 5 not being important.

Reasons for Accepting the Political Pressure	Evaluation Score				
(230) Lust to grab power	1	2	3	4	5
(231) For career advancement	1	2	3	4	5
(232) Security and stability in job/least disturbances	1	2	3	4	5
(233) Enhancement of status	1	2	3	4	5
(234) Avoid humiliation for self and family	1	2	3	4	5
(235) Extract favours OR desired ACR/APA	1	2	3	4	5
(236) Avoid conflicts in decision process	1	2	3	4	5
(237) To secure political patronage	1	2	3	4	5
(238) Appreciation/recognition of own work	1	2	3	4	5
(239) To safeguard the incompetence	1	2	3	4	5
(240) Earn money/property and enhance resources	1	2	3	4	5
(241) Proximity to politician generate information	1	2	3	4	5
(242) Scope for control over resources	1	2	3	4	5
(243) To pursue goals for self and family	1	2	3	4	5
(244) Freedom in goal achievement/funds misuse	1	2	3	4	5

Unit 15

Role of Culture in Acceptance of Pressure

"Cherishing insatiable desires and embracing false doctrines through ignorance, such person of adulterated behavior move in this world, full of hypocrisy, pride, and arrogance," *The Bhagavad Gita* 16.10

"Nearly all men can stand adversity, but if you want to test a man's character, give him power."—Abraham Lincoln

"If something can corrupt you, you're corrupted already."—Bob Marley

- *Role of culture in acceptance of pressure*
- *The All India Services cultural dimensions*
- *The structural characteristic of bureaucracy*
- *Bureaucratic culture model*
- *Research analyses result for culture impact*
- *Salary, Nepotism, Arrogance, Security*
- *Careerism, Status, Self-goals, Power*
- *Political interventions. Devotion to work*
- *Discriminations, Opportunism*
- *Immoral behavior*

The All India Services Officer 11 cultural dimensions have been described along with 11 structural characteristics of the Indian bureaucracy keeping in mind its historical perspectives. The bureaucratic culture model has been described in a conceptual framework. Research outcomes for 13 cultural variables of Indian bureaucracy have been evaluated through ranking as well on a five-point scale and research data analyses results presented in this unit make it more interesting to read and visualize about bureaucratic culture in India.

15.1. The AISO Cultural Dimensions in Decision

The All India Services Officers violate normative aspects of socially desirable behavior and people attribute it as a total loss of ethics from the All India Services. Values, beliefs, attitudes, and norms are the greatest casualty in the present-day administration system. Continuous erosion and interaction between beliefs and values under pressure have produced selfish and self-goal-oriented attitudes with resulting in total evaporation of ethical norms among the All India Services Officers. Goal or self-interest norms have been institutionalized in government administration. Spatial openness, information sharing, and free flow of feedback in government hierarchy are not encouraged, which cultivate growing acceptance of pressure for individual goal-oriented survival by the All India Services Officers. Nolan Seven principles of public life implementation need to be made part of the bureaucratic culture, which are selflessness, integrity, objectivity, accountability, openness, honesty, and good leadership (R. Ravikiran et al., 2013).

Indian bureaucratic colonial culture is continuing but considered obstructive in development by many people. "If something is simple, it's made more complicated in India. The system (bureaucratic) does not seem to allow simplicity. If you are trying to do something from a business standpoint, it is very frustrating." Indian bureaucracy legacy and culture are frustrating to new entrepreneurs as reported in the same article. "India is one place where you can never separate the regulatory from reality," Nicolas Berggruen, *The Economic Times*, 25.11.2015. The cultural milieu of Indian bureaucracy is complex, colonial cultural evolution raises many questions, and such questions will continue to arise in the future also. "How should our bureaucracy evolve to navigate the challenge this creates?, J. Sinha, *The India Express*, 6.10.2017. Indian bureaucracy colonial culture has been a debatable issue since independence.

15.1.1. Working Autonomy

The All India Services Officers rarely work jointly with others to explore solutions for problems confronting them. In the name of confidentiality mutual commitment and obligation have reduced empathy and accumulated stress in the system. The proactively driven initiative has been on the wane from the All India Services Officers under pressure culture. **Working autonomy** was inherent in the All India Services Officers, which induced most people to join these services, but it is on the decline in the decision under pressure in geometrical progression. Lack of collaboration in the All India Services Officers has induced non-sharing of experience, blockage of communication channels, devoid of team spirit, and monopolization of resources. Prevalent political pressure has surrogated the innovations from the administration. "Values and beliefs contribute significantly to the socio-economic-political modernization," P. Singh et al. (1979).

15.1.2. Monopolization of Power and Resources

The All India Services Officers' beliefs in the **monopolization of power** and resources are the root cause for comprehensive degradation culture. The All India Services Officers' assumptions about political power in the decision are that it is unavoidable, so enjoy it. The All India Services Officers are entrenched deep in a concentration of power for their services and individuals. The process of power distribution has intensified the power struggle among them. The All India Services Officers culture of concentration and centralization of power is a reminiscence of the colonial character of feudal and autocratic behavior. Barnard (1946) wrote about the All India Service, "the system of status is a strong and probably an indispensable developer of sense of responsibility and therefore of stability and reliability." The All India Services Officers autocratic and feudal culture is dominant by the observance of proper protocol and their dependency on their subordinates.

15.1.3. Feudalism

Feudal All India Services Officers select their trusted subordinates based on past relationships and deploy these loyal persons to crucial locations to meet self-seeking goals. The bureaucratic culture of the primacy of rules, regulations, procedures, unmanageable porous hierarchy, and goal-oriented power is the continuation of lineage from exploitative and barbaric colonial rule. Knowledge and merit have been surrogated by the goal-oriented selfish power. The process of retention and monopolization of power to perpetuate self have destroyed the technical skills and professionalism from bureaucracy.

15.1.4. Control over Other Services

Cultures of **retention of control over other services** have destroyed the slightest development of excellence and expert knowledge. Culture of elitist, overlords, unmindful of others, authoritarian, power monopolizer, unresponsive, negative orientation, status hungry, manipulative, play safe, suspicious, conflict milling, decision dodger and empire builder for self have surrogated entire public administration. "Public government (in India) has become so pervasive and powerful that it penetrates every facet of life...becomes increasingly defined and regulated within the political arena," A. Holtzman (1966).

15.1.5. Personal Conflicts

Inferior status gives rise to **personal conflicts** among competitors for status. Barnard further observed, "Premium on routine qualities has a depressing effect on creative and innovative leadership." Status anxieties develop a feeling of keen competition among the All India Services and create bitter rivalry among officers. This generates a feeling of putting individual against individual and service class against service class. The feeling of competition has been aggravated by virtue of IAS occupying a monolithic position in hierarchy over IPS and IFS including other organized services. This has induced the feeling of every individual officer magnifying his duties and work. Such feelings obliterated the relationship among services. Rivalry for promotion and career progression had been generic to these services. Lack of everlasting contacts with vide spectrum of public and apprehensions among the member of the All India Service officers are hampering the progress and sustainability of the system.

15.1.6. Interests-Oriented Culture

Interests-oriented culture in the All India Services Officers causes cumulative preferences for self-goals and dominance over public interests. Ego and arrogance dominance culture of the All India Services Officers pervades through hierarchical levels in bureaucracy, which is reflected in society in turn. Colonial culture of keeping distance and aloofness from the public is still pervasive among the All India Services Officers. Individual officers' power orientation culture induces them to see power as a target and worship power for survival and sustenance. Individual Indian Administrative Service officers are seen as more powerful than the collective bureaucratic system, collectivism has become subordinate to individuals giving rise to particularistic orientation.

15.1.7. Individualistic Culture

In an **individualistic culture**, the All India Services Officers pursue their own goals and purposes. Individuals develop strong obligations, relationships, and loyalty to political masters. Such relations take precedence towards personal obligations over collective purposes; decisions are influenced by individualistic goals. Norms decide the behavior and norms are decoded by the individuals (the IAS), who judge their own actions, giving rise to inner-directed orientation. Individualism (IAS) induces strong group identities, which is reflected in the form of service, caste, and interests subgroups' culture among All India Services Officers. A serious problem of individualism is inner-directed orientation. Individual officer behavior is directed by internal standards, which in turn is guided by inner worth and sin, where the All India Services Officers neglect their reputation and honor. Individualism culture has killed the feeling of shame, humiliation, a consciousness of guilt, and disgrace among many All India Services Officers. But still few officers are left in these services, who survive to save their reputation. This culture of individual services orientation and individual goal orientation does not allow growth and innovation in the bureaucratic system. One nation and one service culture need to be brought in through restructuring the entire system.

15.1.8. Decentralization

Employees have high morale and experience better job satisfaction in smaller departments (Cummings and Elsalmi, 1970). Sizes of the department have an impact on the behavior, beliefs, perceptions, and attitudes of the individuals' officers. **Decentralization** causes less work alienation, greater satisfaction from work, increased performance, and improved communication as studied by Cummings and Berger (1976). Bureaucracy continuously decentralizes departments to create new departments by creating higher posts for themselves. The culture of decentralization is used as a tool for self-goals maximization.

15.1.9. Unequal Distribution of Power

Unequal distribution of power is associated with emotional and assertive culture. Initially, the All India Services Officers feel uncomfortable with ambiguity, try to avoid uncertainty, but in due course of time develop tolerance to ambiguity. The Indian Administrative Service officers occupy the position of power other two All India Services (IPS and IFS) have not reconciled for this distribution of power and strive for power equalization, in this process they put forward various justifications to remove inequalities. The All India Services Officers believe that persons with higher status in the hierarchy and their service seniors can help them in enhancing their status. This culture is more or less prevalent in all three All India Services. The All India Services Officers strengthen themselves on the ladder of power by retaining and maximizing power sources. The All India Services Officers are vigorous exhibitionistic in asserting their power in the social system. This cultivates the culture of a demoralized societal system and breeds powerlessness and frustration among the masses. The expanding culture of the IAS emphasized the creation and consolidation of their position in every institution in the country. Empire building culture of the Indian Administrative Service officers has paralyzed and destroyed societal self-confidence, morals, innovations, desires, and feeling to come up.

15.1.10. Social Systems Culture

Indian **social system**, religion, and family set up teach and condition the growing child to respect the authority. In joint family respect for the head of the family and his authority is inherent and children learn to wait for their turn in the hierarchy. Present-day nuclear family concepts breed the individualistic approach and inculcate disrespect for the authority. The pluralistic conception of society has replaced the idea of the individual citizen faced by the monolithic sovereign state (L.P. Misquitta, 1991). Social structuring along caste lines, low political awakening, and fragmentation of society into regions provide leverage for the All India Services Officers to sustain their own system. In the present system of conflicting and layered societal setup public school background mobile neo-rich extract maximum benefit from the government. Such an unstable position induces them to compromise behavior and believes in the position of least disturbances. The fundamental assumption of neo-rich doctrine is the self-goal maximizations. Sense of goal achievement culture induces them for indiscriminate obligations of political pressure meet their needs. The disproportionate distribution of resources and benefit maximization by a few privileged persons generate restlessness in the social culture.

Bureaucrats, "organise themselves into lobbies and pressure groups to ward off any threat to their hegemony and the 'Networking' pays. Those citizens who have the paying capacity are ready to exchange money for the benefits. State can bestow through manipulations of the fallible lot. A win-win situation indeed! Who will complain and who will rectify? Not all officers are corrupt but they are too weak to either withstand the pressure for unreasonable actions or act against them," Shalini Rajneesh, 2013.

15.1.11. Elitist Culture

The All India Services Officers with a foundation of **elitist** thoughts reflect the concern of potential obstruction from political authority, but it is not substantiated through the passage of time. Political authority manipulates through a handful of the All India Service Officers to control 130 crores hands in India. The politicians at the top and members of the Indian Administrative Service control government administration to coordinate and enjoy authority over all other services. This propagates the culture of self-goal attainment. Political authority, by and large, is used by the IAS power holders, so the IAS group only determines the horizontal and vertical relationship with the political authority. Work culture, behavior, attitude, and perceptions in public administration are largely controlled and regulated by the Indian Administrative Service officers in India.

15.2. Structural Characteristic of Bureaucracy

The structural characteristic of the Indian bureaucratic system determines the roles assigned to members of various services and in turn regulate the lives of others. The origin monopolistic culture of dominance got its roots from the colonial period. Basic attitude and perceptions, the behavior of bureaucrat has been continuously imitating the behavior of *Bara Sahib* of the colonial English rule. We can explain and assign various logics, but the real notion dominating among the All India Services Officers is that of cruel, self-goal oriented, crusher, exploiter, benefit maximizer, and parasitical behavior only. The Englishmen left India but the *Bara Sahib* culture left behind has weakened the societal system got multiplied and grown out of proportion under the new name of elite All India Services. When we go through the old memoirs and records, we can say colonial bureaucrats have been better than the present generation of ruling elite bureaucrats. At least, they have openly acknowledged and practiced their alien culture. The public was fully aware of their game plan and objectives. Public perception about present-day All India Services Officers as bloodsucking dishonesty cheat, and exploiting own fellow citizens in most hypocrite manners. The All India Services Officers only propagate a culture of self-maximization.

15.2.1. Exploiters

Present-day adopted approaches by the All India Services Officers are worse than the Dark Age landlords and **exploiters**, they smile and exploit the whole resources of government and in turn retard the progress of the country. The present-day culture of these elites grab every opening and surrogate all others until they crumble down. The All India Services Officers occupy and control policy in such a way that none other than them can work successfully to fulfill the aspirations of the country. Hard workers, independent thinkers, innovative and creative officers are relegated to backbenches and ultimately forced out of the policy process. Only sycophant servicing to each other's interest perpetuate and grow to reach the top. These elites All India Services Officers have imposed a culture of exclusive All India Services slavery in India.

15.2.2. Institutionalization

These elites All India Services officers have institutionalized the goods and services for themselves only. Entire bureaucratic system productivity is valued in favor of self. The All India Services Officers are producers and consumers at the same time. Immorality doesn't allow any leftover for the others. Public welfare goals have been made redundant and irrelevant and replaced by self-goals. Resources allocated in the name of the poor public are essential resources created for benefit of their own service benefit maximization. A high degree of **institutionalization** has created a common understanding among members of elite service, resource lust dominated by immoral behavior fundamentally cultivates a culture of self-propagation. In a system as a member of elite service, they accept immoral behavior as the most commonly accepted mode of work.

15.2.3. Shared Service Orientations

The government administrative culture is the commonly acceptable perception that is shared by members of these services with the shared meaning of it. As immorality in self-seeking goals maximization is shared by all of them as a moral right in the interest of own service. In comparison to interests of own service, the interests of the country and public are relegated to nowhere in such shared perceptions. Abuse of power and authority by elite officers is only the shear indicative of **shared orientations** culture of that service. The welfare of the public and country has been replaced by self-goals; such consciousness is shared and accepted by most of the members of that elite service. No one shows serious concern for the long-term outcome in such a culture, the All India Services Officers only think to cultivate their own service interests. Team cultures across the departmental lines have been replaced by a culture of individuals or individual service only. Zeal, enthusiasm, and assertiveness in the process for the welfare of the nation have been eaten away by the culture of self-cultivation. In the present scenario, the All India Services Officers never bother with precision detailed analysis, innovation, and risk-taking in the process of decision.

15.2.4. Favoritism and Nepotism

A culture of frequent transfers provides opportunities to the All India Services Officers to hide all failures and create room for passing on the blame on someone else or the system itself. **Favoritism and nepotism** culture propagate careerism among members of the public administration system. The All India Services Officers are obsessed with the status and like to live in the den of ego and arrogance. These elite officers never bother to think that ego and arrogance sustained by them have destroyed the innovation, creativity, freethinking, and fairness from the bureaucratic system as well as from social systems. All failures caused by the All India Services Officers are covered under the excuse of excessive political interference. They forget that the All India Services Officers themselves are responsible for cultivating the culture of these external interferences. Individual officer lusts for abuse of power and authority to propagate own immoral behavior has evaporated the devotion for duty among these All India Services Officers. The culture of political opportunism has collapsed the decision process, eroded the faith of the masses in the bureaucratic system and its operators both. A culture of distrust is bound to bounce back and will destroy the immoral custodian of the system in due course of time.

15.2.5. Self-seeking Goals

The majority of the All India Services Officers share the core value of **self-seeking goals.** Even the sub-cultures of different departments are forced to share the same values due to the system coercing them. Acceptance of political pressure has become the core of the government system of administration. The dominant culture of self-seeking goals spread across the geographical length and breadth, motivate the All India Services Officers to align them with the direction of political pressure. The All India Services Officers' strong concern and commitment towards self-needs have influenced the behavior of other members, created the internal strong culture of own service welfare and individual needs attainment. This has seriously impaired and punctured the decision-making process.

15.2.6. Cultural Diversity

The All India Services Officers comprising officers from different cultural backgrounds tend to produce a better solution to the problem faced in the decision. **Cultural diversity** among the All India Services Officers helps them and advantageous to them. Researches demonstrate that heterogeneity among members of service increase the creativity, improve the quality of decision and facilitate change by enhancing member flexibility (Robins, 1998; Cox and Black, 1991; Medeod and Lebel, 1992). Present research results analyses under Unit 3 demographic characters of the All India Services Officer also indicate that the AISO with different cultural backgrounds shows a difference towards amenability to accept pressure in the decision-making process. Cultural diversity helps in improving bureaucratic efficacy.

15.2.7. Formalization

Elite officers invariably accelerate the effort to formalize the regulations to regulate the behavior of all others. Such **formalization** has ensured safety, consistency, and orderliness culture for the elites. Others are forced to accept that top slots are exclusively for the elite, then the same elite propagates that others are not working or competent. First, destroy the system with a target to crumble delivery mechanism, and then blame the system that targets have not been achieved, and ultimately usurp control over the system. Whereas the elite is always safe, credit for all the system success is taken by the elites, elite's assigns any kind of failure to others. The All India Services Officers sharing of such values in a subculture has taken the shape of national culture; as All India Services Officers are spread over the whole Union of India.

15.2.8. National Culture

Politicians and the public both have been forced to accept the dominance of the elite All India Services Officers as national culture. This is because we have continued and sustained **colonial culture** through All India Services Officers. Continuity of the same service all the times at top propagate, sustain and strengthen the one service-oriented culture, which sustains the immoral behavior with a sense of security, the feather of the same flock fly together. Members of the same services have institutionalized immoral behavior due to predictability, connectivity, and consistency of position. Such a chain continues to survive, no one likes to disturb the system, as the system ensures delivery of goods to that service, in turn to individual members. The chain of immoral behavior persistently saves one another immoral behavior.

15.2.9. Commitment to Own Service

Separate service cultures define the boundary role for its member and enhance the distributions and differences among different services. Service members identify themselves with their own, such a culture creates unity among those service members. Such unity culture cultivates **commitment towards their own service** groups to cultivate individual members' interests/needs in the future. Due to the cultivation of a particular service at the expense of others, ensure the stability of elite service in society. In the long-run social system readily accepts the leadership of elite service members. So, it makes it easy to sustain control over the whole machinery by members of that service. Members of one service assured continuance at the top position, guide help in shaping the perception, attitude, beliefs, and behavior of public and other officers of the government administration. Culture of sustenance on position reduces the dynamism from the system. Commitment towards their own service ultimately damage the uniformity in national progress and ultimately cultivate individualistic orientation behavior among officers.

15.2.10. Dynamic Political Pressures

Dynamic political pressures influence the performance of the system and effectiveness of the All India Services Officers. Strong service culture dominating over Indian bureaucracy is the greatest barrier to incorporate any change. Strong elite service culture asserts/exerts considerable pressure on other services to conform to elite wishes. Dominating service members engage in disparaging others in front of a politician, sustain the culture of self-survival, and condone others with prejudices to harm the culture of services diversity. Strong culture of power holders inclined in favor of elite service; Indian Administrative Service officers effectively use it to eliminate unique strength of other services in winning the support of the politicians to propagate for the sustenance of institutional bias to own advantage. Different services cultural identity and compatibility have become the topic of hot discussion and primary concern for the development of the country. Strong service cultures hindered the re-engineering and restructuring of the government administration. Strong service-oriented culture enhances the conflicts in the public work culture.

15.2.11. Historical Colonial Traditions

Present public administration culture is the outcome of the sustenance of the colonial culture, which is exploitative in its origin and approach. Surrogating and suffocative culture of the All India Services getting recurring strength from **historical traditions**, service customs, and ideologies, where elite impose own thinking and interests on the bureaucratic system. System of recruitment, transfers, postings, promotions, resource allocation, rewards distribution, control on punishments, policy decision finalizing, and performance evaluation, career progression are important elements, which sustain the present exploitative culture. Power occupancy by elite service for continuous selection and recruitment sustain the culture of elite service. Senior officers groom juniors in the light of their own experiences, newly recruit imbibe the culture of elite dominance over others at the cost of the future progress of the nation.

15.3. Bureaucratic Culture Impact Model

As officers grow in their careers, perceptions about the role of a politician and political pressure also grow simultaneously. The role of politics in the decision process can be understood by the All India Services Officers from the prevalent departmental culture. The All India Services Officers' socialization as a learning experience formulates their attitudes, thinking, and beliefs towards service culture. With the entry into service, the All India Services Officers socialization process starts and continues to grow with experience in encounters political pressure, towards the end of career assumed as metamorphosed. **The repetitive sequence of pressure activities**, which express and reinforce the central values in the department, which goals are important, which people are crucial, which are expandable, R. Kamoche (1995) and Robins (1998). Repetitive political pressure events ritualize the pressure culture in the decision. The All India Services Officers' perception about pressure in government administrative culture related to the extent of uncertainty tolerance, risk-taking behavior, conflict management, and support from seniors and behavior of the politician itself, variables operating in this process have been depicted in Figure 15.1. "Rampant and mounting corruption, especially among the political class, i.e. Ministers and MPs, who exercise real power in a democracy," U.C. Agarwal, 2013. Prevalent culture in bureaucratic system work as a cementing factor towards modified behaviour orientation of individual officers and slowly officers develop tolerance towards pervading immorality in the administration of decision. Ultimately, everybody become sufferer from the system including the outcomes of decision churned out from the system as well as bureaucrats.

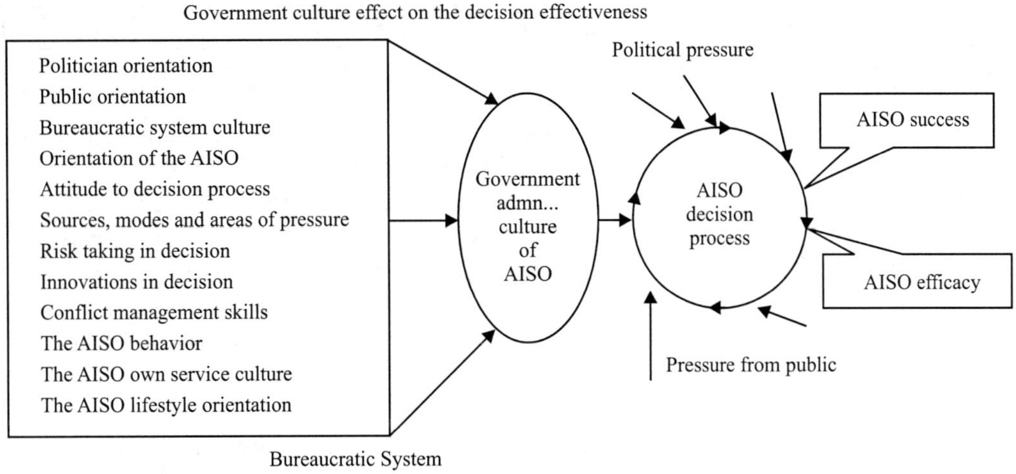

Figure No. 15.1: Bureaucratic Culture Impact on Decision Performance

Government culture for the decision-making process is related to the factors mentioned on the left-hand side of Figure 15.1, which are influenced by the continuous pressure from the bureaucratic system, pressure from the public, political pressure, and culture of that department/service. The All India Services Officers' success and efficacy in the decision-making process are always influenced by these factors and the outcome is related to them. Based on our model, we can say that outcome of any decision in government administration, where the All India Services Officers occupy the pivotal positions is related to the prevalent government culture and cultures of that the All India Services in that environment.

15.4. Research Analyses of AISO Culture and Pressure in Decision

Exhibit Number 15.1: Statistical Analyses: Culture of the All India Services Officers

Item Name	Total Cases		Valid Cases		Pearson Chi-square			Rank
	Freq.	%	Freq.	%	Value	df	Sgnf.	
140. Low salaries	281	100	249	88.6	18.186	6	0.006	13
141. Favouritism & nepotism	281	100	246	87.5	55.09	6	0.000	10
142. Ego & arrogance	281	100	246	87.5	17.298	6	0.008	1
143. Frequent transfers	281	100	246	87.5	17.311	6	0.008	9
144. Too much careerism	281	100	246	87.5	19.079	6	0.004	6
145. Obsession with status	281	100	246	87.5	26.885	6	0.000	2
146. Self-seeking goals	281	100	246	87.5	74.517	6	0.000	3
147. Political interference in work	281	100	246	87.5	34.644	6	0.000	5
148. Lack of devotion to work	281	100	246	87.5	11.835	6	0.06	7
149. Abuse of power & authority	281	100	246	87.5	11.3	6	0.07	4
150. Discrimination obustraction	281	100	246	87.5	26.614	6	0.001	8
151. Political opportunism	281	100	246	87.5	33.29	6	0.000	12
152. Immoral behavior	281	100	246	87.5	26.29	6	0.000	11

We have tried to study, what are the most common problems in government bureaucratic culture, which have a direct impact on the decision-making process. After discussion with the All India Services Officers, politicians, businesspersons, and public persons, we retained 13 items, which are pervasive in the bureaucratic culture across the ranks and files. It is really difficult to assign or fix up malicious part of such a huge system, which has spread over the length and breadth of the country. Every individual enumerates different reasons according to their own wisdom and experience. How these elites All India Services Officers think about the bureaucratic cultural problems? What are their perceptions about the malady in the system, which they are controlling, and must own responsibility for such a passé?

During an analysis of results, it is observed that the All India Services Officers have tried to evade the evaluation to this question and mainly officers have not marked options properly. The most important aspect of the study is that all the issues under study are widely accepted and spread across all the respondents. This is the reason that no single item has been assigned a high percentage. A low score for every rank indicates that these problems are pervasive all over the system and are inseparable; officers from different regions/cadres have different perceptions about cultural problems. We ranked these items for the whole country (Exhibit 15.1); regional and cadre variations have to be accepted with different modifications with respect to their own culture.

Exhibit Number 15.2: The All India Services Officers Culture-Ranking of Three Most Disliked Items

Variable Name	A.I.S. Total				I.A.S., N = 73				I.P.S., N = 92				I.F.S., N = 81			
	Anr.	I%	II%	III%	Anr.	I%	II%	III%	Anr.	I%	II%	III%	Anr.	I%	II%	III%
Low salaries	90.4	8.4	0.4	0.8	100	0	0	0	84.8	15.2	0	0	88.1	8.3	1.2	2.4
Favouritism & nepotism	82.9	6.9	7.7	2.4	84.9	12.3	0	2.7	97.8	2.2	0	0	64.2	7.4	23.5	4.9
Ego & arrogance	60.2	19.1	10.6	10.2	52.1	30.1	12.3	5.5	59.8	15.2	15.2	9.8	67.9	13.6	3.7	14.8
Frequent transfers	81.7	8.1	8.1	2.0	80.8	9.6	6.8	2.7	92.4	1.1	6.5	0	70.4	14.8	11.1	3.7
Too much careerism	74.	5.7	5.7	14.6	69.9	4.1	11.0	15.1	68.5	7.6	1.1	22.8	84	4.9	6.2	4.9
Obsession with status by them	62.6	14.2	13.4	9.8	58.9	6.8	24.7	9.6	57.6	26.1	8.7	7.6	71.6	7.4	8.6	12.3
Self-seeking goals	56.9	4.9	24.4	13.8	31.8	4.1	26	38.4	56.5	7.6	34.8	1.1	80.2	2.5	11.1	6.2
Political interference in their work	72	9.8	8.1	10.2	80.8	15.1	0	4.1	68.5	0	13.0	18.5		16.0	9.9	6.2
Lack of devotion to work	78.9	1.6	17.9	1.6	72.6	1.4	24.7	1.4	81.5	0	18.5	0	81.5	3.7	11.1	3.7
Abuse of power & authority by them	70.7	8.1	3.7	17.5	71.2	5.5	2.7	20.5	72.8	8.7	0	18.5	67.9	9.9	8.6	13.6
Discrimination & obustraction by them	82.5	5.3	0.4	11.8	93.2	5.5	1.4	0	70.7	7.6	0	21.7	86.4	2.5	0	11.1
Political opportunism by them	91.1	2.4	4.5	2	100	0	0	0	90.2	0	9.8	0	84	7.4	2.5	6.2
Retension of immoral behavior	91.9	4.5	1.6	2.0	100	0	0	0	91.3	8.7	0	0	85.2	3.7	4.9	6.2

Anr. = % of the respondent not ranked variable among first three disliked items.

Exhibits 15.1 and 15.2 results show that 19.1% of the All India Services Officers have ranked dominant ego and arrogance as pervasive across the cadres as the greatest enemy of the All India Services at 1st rank. Second rank obsession with status has been hotly contested, based on the weighted percentage it is ranked 2nd, 14.2% of the All India Services Officers have assigned obsession with status as of 1st rank and a cumulative score of 3rd ranks is assigned by 37.4%. The dominance of self-seeking goals among the All India Services Officers has been totaled at 43.1%, but only 4.9% of officers have assigned it 1st rank, so this item has been ranked 3rd most important problem of the bureaucratic system. Pearson Chi-square results indicate that obsession with status, self-seeking goals, political interference in their work, favoritism and nepotism adopted by them, common retention of immoral behavior by them, and political opportunism by them have been highly significant at '0.000' significance level. Pearson Chi-square values for ego and arrogance, frequent transfers, too much careerism, discrimination and obstruction by them, and low salaries are significant, where values range from '0.001' to '0.008', i.e. less than the well-accepted value of 0.05. Pearson Chi-square values for lack of devotion to work and abuse of power and authority by them are slightly more than '0.05' indicate that it can be independent of the decision also.

The All India Services Officers' high obsession with status is a serious problem for the decision, development, and equity. It slowly erodes and destroys the merit, efficiency, and work culture of the government, 26.1% of the Indian Police Service officers ranked its first problem of the system. The Indian Police Service officers are showing the highest consciousness regarding their status, among the All India Services Officers. Excessive ego and arrogance create distance from reality and the All India Services Officers live under the illusion of colonial *Bura Sahib* away from the masses. 30.1% of the Indian Administrative Service officers have ranked it at 1st level. The Indian Administrative Service officers have realized that other persons related to the system, commonly affected by the high ego and arrogance shown by them. 16% of the Indian Forest Service officers have ranked abuse of power and authority by the All India Services Officers at 1st rank. This indicates that they themselves are the sufferer and abused by the officers occupying the top position in the hierarchy.

Real degeneration of the All India Services and whole government bureaucratic system has caused by adoption and fulfillment of the self-seeking goals, and every stakeholder tries to extract maximum for self at the expense of others. 24.4% of the All India Services Officers feel that officers are serving their own goals from the decision outcome and ranked it at 2nd. 34.8% of the Indian Police Service officers and 26.0% of the Indian Administrative Service officers have ranked self-seeking goals at 2nd rank. Among the Indian Administrative Service officers, 38.0% have assigned it 3rd rank also. In a true sense, self-seeking goals are the first and foremost reason for immoral behavior, which is eating away the entire societal and governance system.

Results for the Indian Forest Service officers are different from the Indian Police Service officers and the Indian Police Service officers in all three ranks. 23% of the Indian Forest Service officers suffer from the favoritism and nepotism prevalent in the government system. Because the Indian Administrative Service officers are occupying all the key positions above them, these power holders show bias in the decision; this has changed the psychology of the Indian Forest Service officers and generated frustration in them. 22.8% of the Indian Police Service officers have ranked too much careerism by the All India Services Officers at 3rd rank. This indicates the aggravation commonly dominant among them against the Indian Administrative Service officers, who have occupied their top slots. In 3rd rank, 14% of the Indian Forest Service officers have shown their sufferance due to the ego and arrogance of the power holders. 17.5% of the All India Services Officers have ranked abuse of power and authority by them at 3rd rank. All these ranking exercises indicate that ego and arrogance, obsession with status, abuse of power and authority, too much careerism, self-seeking goals, favoritism and nepotism, and political opportunism adopted by the All India Services Officers are causing problems and creating a blockage in the decision-making process.

Statistical evaluation of dominating culture prevalent in government bureaucracy indicates that our results are highly significant in respect of most of the items. Pearson Chi-square values except for salaries and obsession with status are highly significant with '0.000', significance level. Pearson Chi-square values for low salaries and obsession with status are significant, where significance level values are '0.008' and '0.007' respectively. Except for item lack of devotion to duty, Pearson's R-values for correlation show that each variable is correlated with itself and other items. The probabilities of correlation occurring by chance are very slim, less than '0.000' in eight items, and less than '0.006' in the other four items. All the items show a negative correlation. We can say with confidence that the relationship between political pressure in the decision and dominant bureaucratic culture is genuine. Spearman's correlation results are similar to Pearson values and also indicate a similar outcome, reconfirm the validity of our findings.

Exhibit Number 15.3: All India Services—Cultural Milieu, Statistical Analysis

Item Name	Cases (Frequency) N		Pearson Chi-square			Correlation			
	Total	Valid	Value	df	Sigf.	R	Sigf.	Rho	Sigf.
Low salaries	281	244	27.05	8	0.001	–0.2	0.006	–0.2	0.002
Favouritism and nepotism	281	253	64.78	8	0.000	–0.4	0.000	–0.3	0.000
Ego and arrogance	281	253	40.25	8	0.000	–0.3	0.000	–0.3	0.000
Frequent transfers	281	250	58.4	8	0.000	–0.2	0.002	–0.2	0.010
Too much careerism	281	243	67.22	8	0.000	–0.4	0.000	–0.3	0.000
Obsession with status	281	243	21.45	8	0.007	–0.3	0.000	–0.3	0.000
Self-seeking goals	281	242	28.75	8	0.000	–0.4	0.000	–0.4	0.000
Political interference in work	281	254	59.72	8	0.000	–0.2	0.01	–0.1	0.07
Lack of devotion to work	281	243	62..17	8	0.000	–0.1	0.1	–0.1	0.2
Abuse of power and authority	281	253	67.25	8	0.000	–0.4	0.000	–0.3	0.000
Discrimination obstruction	281	244	30.09	8	0.000	–0.3	0.000	–0.3	0.000
Political opportunism	281	246	67.34	8	0.000	–0.3	0.000	–0.2	0.000
Immoral behavior	281	242	49.96	8	0.000	–0.2	0.002	–0.2	0.001
R = Pearson's R correlation values. Rho = Spearman correlation value. df = degree of freedom. Sigf. = Significance value.									

We have studied the results for respective All India Services also, 56.5% of the Indian Administrative Service officers think that self-seeking goals orientation among the All India Services Officers, is the biggest evil prevalent in these services. They ranked it at 1st rank. Subsequent common problems are an obsession with status, favoritism, and nepotism approach adopted by officers, political influence in their day-to-day work, high ego and arrogance displayed by officers, and political opportunism adopted by officers respectively in descending order.

74.5% of the Indian Police Service officers have indicated the dominance of status consciousness among them is the 1st rank problem. Police work being uniformed and highly disciplined and continuous dominance of the Indian Administrative Service officers over them had made them highest status-conscious even more than the Indian Administrative Service officers. Subsequent problems in descending order as visualized by the Indian Police Service officers are, political interference in their daily work, high ego and arrogance prevalent in the system, too much career consciousness approach adopted by officers, common retention of immoral behavior by officers and officers adopting highly political opportunist path in the decision-making process.

Exhibit Number 15.4: All India Services, Evaluation of Prevalent Culture

Item Name	I.A.S. Valid N = 69			I.P.S. Valid N = 94			I.F.S. Valid N = 99		
	Strongly Agree	Agree	Rk	Strongly Agree	Agree	Rk	Strongly Agree	Agree	Rank
154. Low salaries	37.7	24.6	11	26.6	41.5	12	16.3	21.3	13
155. Favouritism and nepotism	50.7	29.6	3	51.1	34	8	31	25.3	3
156. Ego and arrogance	47.8	44.9	5	65.3	26.3	3	30.7	26.1	4
157. Frequent transfers	43.7	39.4	8	48.9	34	9	35.7	28.6	2
158. Too much careerism	44.9	31.9	7	61.3	31.2	4	16.3	31.3	12
159. Obsession with status	52.2	33.3	2	74.5	19.1	1	29.1	31.6	6
160. Self-seeking goals	56.5	36.2	1	52.1	45.7	7	17.9	46.2	7
161. Political interference in work	50.7	26.8	4	70.2	19.1	2	42	29.5	1
162. Lack of devotion to work	17.4	26.1	13	16	33	13	17.7	26.6	11
163. Abuse of power and authority	42%	36.20%	9	46.8	34	10	24.7	25.8	8
164. Discrimination obstruction	33.3	43.5	12	26.6	62.8	11	18.8	28.8	10
165 Political opportunism	44.9	46.4	6	53.7	44.2	6	29.6	32.1	5
166 Immoral behavior	40.6	21.7	10	56.4	25.5	5	19.2	20.5	9
S. Agree = % of officers strongly agree. Agree = % of officers agree. Rk = Ranking of item.									
Rank = Ranking among item 154 to 166.									

42% of the Indian Forest Service officers have felt political interference in their daily work as a 1st rank problem. Other problems visualized by them in descending order are frequent transfers, prevalent favoritism, and nepotism in bureaucracy, ego, and arrogance shown by officers in their dealings, political opportunism followed by officers, and high reliance on obsession with status feeling.

Comparatively, all three services have visualized different problems related to their own work culture and experience. Data inferences indicate that powerlessness among the Indian Forest Service officers is the highest and status orientation among the Indian Police Service officers is higher. The Indian Administrative Service officers are highly self-goals oriented, this approach of self-propagation is at the expense of others and the system.

15.4.1. Low Salary

We have been hearing enormous hue and cry for higher and better salaries at the time of pay commission. Salary structure is the symbol of inequality between the 'heaven-born' and other services. Present salary structure also creates distance between the power elite and other services, vis-à-vis with subordinates. Higher pay differential among bureaucracy successfully induce a feeling of alienation among various groups and are reflected in the decision-making process. Further perquisites and facilities made available to the All India Services and other services are also a matter of serious concern and reflect the mental frame of the colonial exploitative era. Why we should have different houses for different officers, some of the All India Services Officers are living in houses spread over more than 2 to 10 acres complex, whereas others are not getting any house to live in. Imperialistic inequalities also induce behavioral distance and alienation from other officers of the district. The entire district officers must have the same houses with the same design and must live together in the same complex, with 100% similar living facilities for the sake of uniformity and equality.

Our study results show different inference and the All India Services Officers have ranked low salary problem at last 13th rank. 90.4% of the All India Services Officers have considered low salary as their problem in the system. 100% of the Indian Administrative Service officers' respondents have not considered low salaries as a problem and ignored it in the ranking, indicate competition for satisfaction with their status-quo position. 15.2% of the Indian Police Service officers and 12% of the Indian Forest Service officers have reflected low salary as a problem in ranking, i.e. dissatisfaction from the present salaries in comparison to other problems.

Same cultural items, we have evaluated on a five-point scale also, 37.7% of the Indian Administrative Service officers ranked it 11th, 26.6% of the Indian Police Service officers ranked it 12th and 16.3% of the Indian Forest Service officers ranked it 13th among other listed items. This difference in preferences while evaluating every item individually and ranking the three most disliked issues indicate perception and attitude differences prevailing in that culture. Low ranking in comparison indicates largely satisfaction from the existing salary structure.

Exhibit Number 15.5: Low Salaries versus 'I can largely Determine what Matters me in Department'

	Value	df	Asymp. Sig. (2-sided)
Pearson Chi-Square	28.832a	16	0.025
Likelihood Ratio	27.898	16	0.033
N of Valid Cases	236		

Chi-square results placed at Exhibit 15.5 with 0.025 significance value show good relation of variables under study. Whereas, data evaluation results placed at Exhibit 15.6 regarding variable 'low salaries culture' relation with the variable of the locus that 'I can largely determine what matters me in department' among three AIS show that 30% in 'agree' and 25.30% in 'strongly agree' with a total of 55.30% of the AISO feel even with the low salary they are the master in the decision-making process in their department. In the locus parameter, 65% of the AISO feel 'strongly' plus 'generally' feel that way category. The low score in 'hardly feel' that way and completely 'disagree' indicate that in the present salary structure the AISO is capable to deliver decisions in their own way.

Exhibit Number 15.6: Low Salaries Culture with Variable 'I can Largely Determine what Matters me in Department'

In Low Salaries	I can Largely Determine what Matters me in Department					Total
	Hardly feel this way	Slightly feel this way	Some what feel this way	Generally feel this way	Strongly feel this way	
'Completely disagree'	1.30%	2.10%	3.80%	3.00%	5.10%	15.20%
'Disagree'	0.80%	1.30%	3.40%	5.10%	3.40%	13.90%
'Undecided'	1.30%	0.00%	2.10%	8.40%	3.80%	15.60%
'Agree'	2.50%	0.40%	8.00%	9.30%	9.70%	30.00%
'Strongly agree'	3.00%	0.00%	5.10%	8.00%	9.30%	25.30%
Total in low salaries	8.90%	3.80%	22.40%	33.80%	31.20%	100.00%

15.4.2. Favoritism and Nepotism

Favoritism and nepotism are the cancer of the bureaucratic system in India. Multitudes, extent, and variance of favoritism and nepotism are insurmountable and innumerable. Repercussions of favoritism and nepotism are everlasting and uncontrollable. In the ranking, 17% of the All India Services Officers have ranked it 10th rank. 84.9% of the Indian Administrative Service officers and 97.8% of the Indian Police Service officers have not considered it a problem. 35.8% of the Indian Forest Service officers have shown concern for this problem. 82.9% of the All India Services Officers have not included this item in the ranking.

In an evaluation exercise for different services, 50.7% of the Indian Administrative Service officers have ranked it 3rd most common irritating item in administration with 'strongly agrees' scoring. 51.1% of the Indian Police Service officers in the 'strongly agree' category have ranked it at 8th place. The Indian Forest Service officers have assigned it 3rd rank with 31% in the 'strongly agree' category. Pearson Chi-square establishes that favoritism and nepotism have a strong relationship with the decision-making process. R correlation value and Rho correlation value with the significance of 0.000, level indicate our results are truly representative of the population.

Exhibit Number 15.7: Favouritism and Nepotism versus 'I Largely Determine what Matters me in Department'

	Value	df	Asymp. Sig. (2-sided)
Pearson Chi-Square	54.462a	16	0.0001
Likelihood Ratio	39.963	16	0.001
Linear-by-Linear Association	5.539	1	0.019
N of Valid Cases	244		

Data analyses for Chi-square in Exhibit 15.7 show a very good association of two variables with a significance of 0.0001 levels. Results placed at Exhibit 15.8 regarding variable favoritism and nepotism culture in bureaucracy relation with locus 'I can largely determine what matters me in department' and 44.30% 'strongly agree' plus 30.0% 'agree' make it 74.60% of the AISO agree with the issue of favoritism and nepotism in the decision-making process. Locus of the individual AISO analysis shows 63.10% of the AISO feel that that they are master of what they decide in their department or location.

Exhibit Number 15.8: Favouritism and Nepotism versus 'I Largely Determine what Matters me in Department'

Favouritism and Nepotism	I can Largely Determine what Matters me in Department					Total
	Hardly feel this way	Slightly feel this way	Some what feel this way	Generally feel this way	Strongly feel this way	
'Completely disagree'	0.00%	1.60%	1.60%	0.00%	0.80%	4.10%
'Disagree'	1.60%	0.00%	2.00%	2.50%	0.40%	6.60%
'Undecided'	1.60%	0.40%	1.20%	5.30%	6.10%	14.80%
'Agree'	2.90%	0.80%	7.40%	11.10%	8.20%	30.30%
'Strongly agree'	2.90%	1.20%	11.50%	13.50%	15.20%	44.30%
Total	9.00%	4.10%	23.80%	32.40%	30.70%	100.00%

15.4.3. Ego and Arrogance

All India Services Officers (39%) have ranked at number one the ego and arrogance as the biggest problem of the bureaucratic system. Every All India Services Officers feel that he is the best officer on the earth, by chance if someone tells them that their first priority is God, invariably concerned officer will never forgive that person who has relegated the All India Services Officers after God. Then the All India Services Officers will mobilize earth and heaven to penalize such a person who has evaluated All India Services officer less than the GOD. The dominant ego and arrogance of these officers always prevail over the decision. In the elite concept, their exclusiveness has damaged administrative initiative and activity. Under the ego and arrogance of the elite, they blame others for their failures and always exclude themselves from the position of failures.

Pearson Chi-square results indicate a significant association of ego and arrogance with the decision. Results are highly significant with a 0.000, level of significance. Pearson's correlation and Spearman's correlation value show high significance and correlation of ego and arrogance with a decision. 47.9% of the Indian Administrative Service officers realize that ego and arrogance adopted by them is the torturing issue for them. Now their own arrows have wounded them, yes, it is near the proverb; as you sow so shall you reap. 40.2% of the Indian Police Service officers assess this item as a serious problem, but still, continue to cultivate the bumper crop of same ego and arrogance. The Indian Forest Service officers are also not far behind in the race and 30.1% of them harvest the crop of ego and arrogance.

The same item in ranking evaluation, 47.8% of the Indian Administrative Service officers ranked it at 5th rank in the 'strongly agree' category. 65.3% of the Indian Police Service officers 'strongly agree' that ego and arrogance are related to the decision-making process, and ranked it at 3rd rank. 30.7% of the Indian Forest Service officers show an association of ego with the decision and have ranked it at 4th rank. The problem of ego and arrogance is twice higher among the Indian Police Service officers in comparison to the Indian Forest Service officers. Results indicate that ego, arrogance is highest among the Indian Police Service officers (maybe due to being uniform service), and it is seriously hampering the decision by them.

Exhibit Number 15.9: Chi-square: Ego and Arrogance versus 'Success of Person Depends upon the Chances one Gets'

	Value	df	Asymp. Sig. (2-sided)
Pearson Chi-Square	63.333a	16	'0.000'
Likelihood Ratio	59.587	16	'0.000'
Linear-by-Linear Association	16.361	1	'0.000'
N of Valid Cases	247		

Relation of ego and arrogance of the individual AISO with locus variable 'success of a person depends upon the chances one gets' in results placed at Exhibit 15.9 show 0.000 significance level showing very high association of two variables. Evaluation results in Exhibit 15.10 regarding 'ego and arrogance of individual All India Services Officer' in decision-making process relation with locus variable 'success of a person depend upon the chances one gets' show 79% 'strongly agree' with 'agree' category and in locus category, 55.10% 'slightly feel' plus 'somehow' feel ranking show that the AISO does not believe in chance factor, rather they feel they are the master of the situation in the decision-making process.

Exhibit Number 15.10: Ego and Arrogance versus 'Success of Person Depends upon the Chances one Gets'

Ego and Arrogance	Success of Person Depends upon the Chances one Gets					Total
	Hardly feel this way	Slightly feel this way	Somewhat feel this way	Generally feel this way	Strongly feel this way	
'Completely disagree'	0.00%	0.00%	1.20%	0.40%	2.00%	3.60%
'Disagree'	0.00%	0.40%	3.20%	2.00%	0.00%	5.70%
'Undecided'	1.60%	2.00%	2.00%	5.30%	0.80%	11.70%
'Agree'	4.00%	8.50%	11.70%	2.80%	4.00%	31.20%
'Strongly agree'	10.90%	14.60%	11.30%	4.00%	6.90%	47.80%
Total	16.60%	25.50%	29.60%	14.60%	13.80%	100.00%

15.4.4. Dislocations/Tenure Security

Frequent transfers are the greatest weapon used by politicians and bureaucrats both to victimize the real workers and propagate the breed of sycophants and incompetent officers to spread the virus of self-goal aggrandizement culture. The All India Services Officers themselves, motivated by self-goals use different pretexts or cover stories to mobilize political pressure to grab the choicest postings. When they join service, they are fully aware that they have to work in remote areas and live in inhospitable conditions, but very soon after the probation period, they forget, what they have promised in the UPSC interview room, lusts and lulls motivate individual to harness maximum benefits for self from the system. When the very same officer moves ahead by illegal and unfair means, how, that officer can provide justice to the public, which is expected from them that they will deliver. Whatsoever variations and sophisticated cover-up stories or arguments, frequent transfers have immobilized the bureaucratic system.

18.3% of the All India Services Officers have assigned 9th rank to their frequent transfers. Low ranking indicates that officers have realized that they themselves are responsible for this impasse and they compromised and attuned with the system. 19.1% of the Indian Administrative Service officers, 7.6% of the Indian Police Service officers, and 29.6% of the Indian Forest Service officers have shown concern in ranking this problem. Pearson Chi-square results are significant with a 0.008, level of significance.

Detailed evaluation results of Pearson Chi-square indicate frequent transfers and decisions are related to a lesser level of significance of 0.007, i.e. 0.7% chances that decision and transfer are independent of each other. Again, comparatively lower Rho and R-values for correlation with lower significance level also indicate lower correlations of two variables. However, 35.7% of the Indian Forest Service officers have evaluated this as a second problem in the 'strongly agree' category. 43.7% of the Indian Administrative Service officers and 48.9% of the Indian Police Service officers have 'strongly agreed' that (8th and 9th ranking) transfer frequency impairs the decision.

Exhibit Number 15.11: Chi-square: Frequent Transfers versus 'Seniors Person's Preference Determines who would be Rewarded in the Department'

	Value	df	Asymp. Sig. (2-sided)
Pearson Chi-Square	36.983	16	0.002
Likelihood Ratio	38.566	16	0.001
Linear-by-Linear Association	10.767	1	0.001
N of Valid Cases	240		

Exhibit Number 15.12: Frequent Transfers versus 'Seniors Person's Preference Determines who would be Rewarded in the Department'

Their Frequent Transfers	Seniors Person's Preference Determines who would be Rewarded in the Department					Total
	Hardly feel this way	Slightly feel this way	Somewhat feel this way	Generally feel this way	Strongly feel this way	
'Completely disagree'	0.80%	0.00%	0.40%	1.70%	0.00%	2.90%
'Disagree'	0.80%	2.90%	5.40%	3.30%	0.00%	12.50%
'Undecided'	0.00%	1.70%	2.10%	3.30%	0.80%	7.90%
'Agree'	1.70%	8.80%	6.30%	12.10%	5.00%	33.80%
'Strongly agree'	0.80%	3.80%	13.80%	17.50%	7.10%	42.90%
Total	4.20%	17.10%	27.90%	37.90%	12.90%	100.00%

Statistical analysis results placed at Exhibit 15.11 for Chi-square values of '0.002' significance level indicates a very good association of two variables. Results placed at Exhibit 15.12 regarding variable frequent transfers of the AISO relation with locus variable of 'seniors person's preference determines who would be rewarded in the department' show 76.70% 'strongly agree' and 'agree' category added together with, this culture of the department means that seniors play a decisive role in the transfer of individual officer-related his decision-making process. Evaluation results in the locus of control show 50.8% feel 'generally' + 'strongly' and if we add 'somewhat way' category, then 78.7% that show seniors preferences determine who would be rewarded in the department, this also indicates a senior role in the decision-making process. Among the All India Services Officer, seniors are respected and obeyed by junior officers.

15.4.5. Careerism

Why people join the All India Services? Mostly for the best, career available in the country. When rules and procedures are violated in favor of incompetent and inefficient the All India Services Officers; innovative, sincere, hard-working officers see that the right connections at right time are only helpful in the advancement of career, as a result of this, they also start mobilizing such forces, which can help them for their advancement. Resource crunch, fast-moving time, globalization of information has made major concern for the career conscious the All India Services Officers. Another important aspect is that with the passage of time administrative powers of All India Services Officers are reduced or clipped and most of the powers, which were enjoyed at the district level, have been taken away by top bureaucrats or politicians. This reduction in administrative powers makes promotions more relevant in the present time. It pertains to focusing on the opportunities and openings available in the government administrative ladders.

Excessive careerism has forced high corporatization of the bureaucratic system. Sophisticated hidden replacement path and garnering promotions by highly pliable All India Services Officers, induce to change in the path of other officer's career chart also. The Indian Administrative Service officers at the top continuously re-engineer, restructure the bureaucratic system to enhance career flexibility for them, which forces others to mobilize political pressure to induce concern for self-career. In the process rest of the services, mobilize career development for various groups and services. Excessive career emphasis by the All India Services Officers is cancer for the system, which enhances and accelerates the realistic expectations from the job.

Though the Indian Administrative Service officers enjoy the best career management in the country, yet their lusts and temptations are unlimited continue to pressurize political leadership to snatch more and higher positions from other services. Excessive career consciousness forces them to oblige the politicians at the cost of quality and equity in the decision. Ultimately, the Indian Administrative Service officer as an individual is the gainer but the country at large is the enormous loser. The system of growth of self at the cost of others has killed the feeling for work, concern for the country, and patriotism. Ultimately, elite service behavior produces frustration among other services.

26% of the All India Services Officers have ranked it 6th problem of the system. Pearson Chi-square results are significant and the alternate hypothesis is accepted that too much career consciousness adversely affects the decision-making process. 30.1% of the Indian Administrative Service officers, 31.5% of the Indian Police Service officers, and 16% of the Indian Forest Service officers realize that feeling too much careerism is a serious problem in the system. The Indian Forest Service officers have the least career consciousness, which may be indicative of blockage of all the channels by the Indian Administrative Service officers, so they have compromised with their luck and destiny.

Our evaluation of each item/variable indicates that 44.9% of the Indian Administrative Service officers with a rank of 8th, and 61.4% of the Indian Police Service officers with 4th rank have 'strongly agreed' that excessive career consciousness is the serious problem causing manipulations in the decision under political pressure. 16.3% of the Indian Forest Service officers have 'strongly agreed' with the 12th rank regarding this problem. Pervasive powerlessness among the Indian Forest Service officers has killed any expectation from the career. Our analyses on Pearson Chi-square are highly significant with '0.000', level of significance under two-tailed test. Pearson's correlation and Spearman's correlation values show a good correlation between too much careerism and the decision-making process under political pressure.

Exhibit Number 15.13: Chi-square: Too much Careerism versus 'My Success or Failure Depends mostly on those who Work with me'

	Value	df	Asymp. Sig. (2-sided)
Pearson Chi-Square	38.052	16	'0.001'
Likelihood Ratio	41.808	16	'0.000'
Linear-by-Linear Association	12.906	1	'0.000'
N of Valid Cases	215		

Statistical analysis for variable too much careerism culture of the AISO relation with locus variable of 'my success or failure depends mostly on those who work with me' results are placed at Exhibit 15.13 show very good association of two variable at '0.001' significance level. Results placed at Exhibit 15.14 for variable 'too much careerism culture' of the AISO and locus of control that 'my success or failure depends mostly on those who work with me' show that 72.10% 'agree' + 'strongly agree' with this culture prevalent in their career. Whereas locus of control in this variable show the 60.90% of the AISO 'hardly feel' + 'slightly feel' category indicate that individual officer does not feel that his success or failure in the decision-making process depends on those who work with him. These results for the locus of control show independence of the AISO in the decision-making process and not influenced by the person working with them.

Exhibit Number 15.14: Too much Careerism versus 'My Success or Failure Depends mostly on those who Work with me'

Too Much Careerism	My Success or Failure Depends Mostly on those who Work with Me					Total
	Hardly feel this way	Slightly feel this way	Somewhat feel this way	Generally feel this way	Strongly feel this way	
'Completely disagree'	0.90%	0.00%	2.70%	0.00%	0.50%	4.10%
'Disagree'	0.50%	0.90%	2.30%	0.50%	0.50%	4.70%
'Undecided'	4.20%	5.60%	6.50%	1.90%	0.90%	19.10%
'Agree'	7.40%	8.80%	8.80%	4.20%	2.80%	32.10%
'Strongly agree'	13.50%	19.10%	5.60%	0.50%	1.40%	40.00%
Total	26.50%	34.40%	26.00%	7.00%	6.00%	100.00%

15.4.6. Status Culture

Cunnings and Berger's (1976) findings indicate that position in hierarchy contributes towards job satisfaction, which is related to attitudes and behavior of the individual (Rousseau, 1978) job perceptions. Status is related to the position in the hierarchy and departmental structure vis-à-vis the location of a member of a particular service in that cadre. These colonially created All India Services Officers are highly status-oriented culturally and historically. High-status consciousness creates distances from the masses, which obliterates the decision ultimately. The All India Services Officer status consciousness and self-orientation delays in decisions is a serious issue for Indian bureaucracy. "What is holding the economy back? Several instances indicate execution and implementation—where bureaucracy plays a pivotal role—have been one of the key reasons that have failed to provide timely intervention, aggravating the crisis. From telecom to highways to financial services to oil, a large part of the problem would have been addressed if *babus* had intervened in time," Gaurie Dwivedi, *The Sunday Guardian*, 16.11.2019. Excessive status consciousnesses pervasive among the All India Services Officers kill and destroy the innovations and causes a delay in the decision process.

Obsession with status has a strong association with political pressure in the decision-making process as indicated by Pearson Chi-square results with '0.000' significance level significance value. 37.4% of the All India Services Officers have ranked obsession with status at 2nd. 41.1% of the Indian Administrative Service officers, 42.4% of the Indian Police Service officers, and 28.4% of the Indian Forest Service officers have shown serious concern for the obstruction of the decision by status obsession. As per common perception, the Indian Forest Service officers show the least concern, and the Indian Police Service officers show the highest concern for the status in ranking exercise.

Results for individual item evaluation indicate a strong association of status and acceptance of political pressure in the decision-making process in Pearson Chi-square results with '0.000', significance. The strength of this correlation was studied with Pearson's correlation and Spearman correlation, which show good correlation with 0.000, significance. Our results indicate that analyses are truly representative of the whole population. 52.2% of the Indian Administrative Service officers and 74.5% of the Indian Police Service officers (1st rank) have 'strongly agreed' that status is related to the decision. 29.1% of the Indian Forest Service officers have 'strongly agreed' with the 6th rank that status influences the decision. The Indian Police Service officers are highly obsessed with the feeling of status, anyhow this motivates them to accept political pressure in the decision-making process.

Exhibit Number 15.15: Chi-Square: Obsession with Status versus 'Being liked by Seniors or Making Good Impression usually Influence Promotion Decision'

	Value	df	Asymp. Sig. (2-sided)
Pearson Chi-Square	33.538	12	'0.001'
Likelihood Ratio	26.263	12	'0.001'
Linear-by-Linear Association	18.25	1	'0.000'
N of Valid Cases	242		

Statistical analysis of variable obsession with the status of the AISO relation with the locus of control variable 'being liked by seniors or making good impression usually influence promotion decision' are placed at Exhibit 15.15 and show very good association with a significance value of 0.001 level. Results placed at Exhibit 15.16 regarding 'obsession with the status of the individual All India Services Officer' correlation with the locus of control variable indicates that 66.10% of AISO in 'generally' + 'strongly feel' category that 'being liked by seniors or making good impression usually influence promotion decision' and 80.60% of the AISO 'strongly' + 'agree' intensity with this prevalent culture in the system that their senior liking will influence their promotion decisions.

Exhibit Number 15.16: Obsession with Status versus 'Being liked by Seniors or Making Good Impression usually Influence Promotion Decision'

Obsession with Status	Being Liked by Seniors or Making Good Impression Usually Influence Promotion Decision					Total
	Hardly feel this way	Slightly feel this way	Somewhat feel this way	Generally feel this way	Strongly feel this way	
'Disagree'	1.20%	1.70%	2.50%	1.70%	0.40%	7.40%
'Undecided'	0.40%	0.80%	2.50%	5.40%	2.90%	12.00%
'Agree'	0.40%	2.10%	8.70%	9.50%	6.60%	27.30%
'Strongly agree'	0.80%	1.20%	11.60%	23.60%	16.10%	53.30%
Total	2.90%	5.80%	25.20%	40.10%	26.00%	100.00%

15.4.7. Self-Goals Culture

Since the inception of the All India Services, self-goals have been the consistent and single utmost important cause of deterioration of decision. It is true that no bureaucracy can be free from self-goals, but the extent of self-goals fulfillment jeopardizes the decision and system itself in a long run. A goal is some future state of the world, which the members of an organization try to bring about by the application of a set of means. A time-dependent means-end sequence implies, therefore, the existence of a series of intermediate states, which may or may not be emphasized, P.M. Jackson 1983, Simon 1958. To extent that they are, they become themselves goals and might be called intermediate goals, with reference being made to some global or end state which is the primary goal of the system. Individual officer goal orientation seriously impairs the delivery of the decision. "Source of corruption in the All India Services, is the vast powers vested in its personnel, especially their power to interfere with the life of the citizens", R. Prasher (1986). Continuous enjoyment of uninterrupted power and position by officers of same service ensure the protection in illegal gratification of goals. "The goals, norms and structure of authority both limit and validate political actions and in this way provide what tends to become a context for political interactions", B.B. Khare (1974).

43.1% of the All India Services Officers have ranked 3rd, that individual goals gratification is the problem in the bureaucracy. Pearson Chi-square results significance is validated by 0.000, significance values. Alternate hypothesis is accepted that self-goals influence the All India Services Officers to accept political pressure in the decision-making process. 68.5% of the Indian Administrative Service officers, 43.5% of the Indian Police Service officers, and 19.8% of the Indian Forest Service officers are influenced by self-goals in the decision-making process.

We have evaluated all the items/variables individually, results indicate that in the 'strongly agree' category; 17.9% of the Indian Forest Service officers with 7th rank, 52.1% of the Indian Police Service officers also with 7th rank, and 56.5% of the Indian Administrative Service officers with 5th rank have been antagonized by the dominance of self-seeking goals in the decision. Pearson Chi-square value is 59.715, with 6 degree of freedom showing 0.000, significance value. The strength of this good association is also supported by the good correlation values of Rho and R at 0.000 significance. This indicates that almost all the influence of political pressure in the decision-making process and self-seeking goals are highly correlated with each other.

Exhibit Number 15.17: Chi-Square: Self-Seeking of Goals versus 'Success of Person Depends upon the Chances one Gets'

	Value	df	Asymp. Sig. (2-sided)
Pearson Chi-Square	48.562	12	'0.000'
Likelihood Ratio	48.606	12	'0.000'
Linear-by-Linear Association	21.075	1	'0.000'
N of Valid Cases	234		

The statistical analysis placed at Exhibit 15.17 for variable self-seeking of goals and locus variable 'success of a person depends upon the chances one gets' show a very strong association of variables with 0.000 level of significance. Results placed at Exhibit 15.18 regarding self-seeking of goals of the individual AISO relation with the locus of control variable 'success of a person depends upon the chances one gets' show that 85% of the officers 'strongly agree' + 'agree' category believe in this culture of the bureaucratic system. Our locus of control results shows that 43.60% of the AISO 'slightly' and 'hardly' feel the intensity that success depends on self-seeking goals in the decision. If we add the 'somewhat feel' category it makes 74.40% of the AISO feel that success only does not depends upon chance one gets but that have to create chances for them.

Exhibit Number 15.18: Self-Seeking of Goals versus 'Success of Person Depends upon the Chances one Gets'

Self-Seeking of Goals	Success of Person Depends upon the Chances one Gets					Total
	Hardly feel this way	Slightly feel this way	Somewhat feel this way	Generally feel this way	Strongly feel this way	
'Disagree'	0.00%	0.90%	2.10%	3.00%	2.60%	8.50%
'Undecided'	0.90%	0.00%	2.10%	3.00%	0.40%	6.40%
'Agree'	8.50%	11.10%	13.70%	4.70%	6.40%	44.40%
'Strongly agree'	8.10%	14.10%	12.80%	1.30%	4.30%	40.60%
Total	17.50%	26.10%	30.80%	12.00%	13.70%	100.00%

15.4.8. Culture of Political Interferences

Political interference in the decision-making process is a serious problem of the bureaucracy, but it is equally important to know how such interferences are surviving in the bureaucratic system. One-way force cannot sustain for a long period, only collaborative forces can survive for a long period. If political interference is surviving in the bureaucratic system, then it is surely both sided affairs. The All India Services Officers look for their own interests, to protect such interests individual officer accept political interference, if one officer accepts it others follow it, no one is blamed for it. This process continues with mutual understanding and mutual gains. The All India Services Officers feel that there is too much political interference in their day-to-day works. 28% of the All India Services Officers ranked it 5th in ranking the problems of the system. Pearson Chi-square analysis shows a significant association of political interference in their work and decision-making process, results show '0.000' significance level.

Political interference in the All India Services Officers work was studied concerning the decision-making process of respective services. 50.7% of the Indian Administrative Service officers evaluated it 4th problem, 70.2% of the Indian Police Service officers ranked it 2nd, and 42% of the Indian Forest Service officers ranked it 1st problem of the system. The Indian Police Service officers are feeling that excessive political interference in their work seriously blockades the decision. This also reflects political interference in the day-to-day law implementation process and administration of justice to the public. Under political interference how the public can expect fair deal and justice, it means a person with political connections influence legal matters to their own advantage.

Exhibit Number 15.19: Chi-Square: Political Interference in their Work versus 'How much I am Liked in the Department Depends upon my Seniors'

	Value	df	Asymp. Sig. (2-sided)
Pearson Chi-Square	43.931	16	'0.0000'
Likelihood Ratio	44.479	16	'0.000'
Linear-by-Linear Association	10.551	1	'0.001'
N of Valid Cases	252		

Exhibit Number 15.20: Political Interference in their Work versus 'How much I am Liked in the Department Depends upon my Seniors'

Political interference in their work	How much I am Liked in the Department Depends upon my Seniors					Total
	Hardly feel this way	Slightly feel this way	Somewhat feel this way	Generally feel this way	Strongly feel this way	
'Completely disagree'	1.60%	0.40%	0.80%	0.40%	0.00%	3.20%
'Disagree'	0.00%	0.80%	0.00%	0.80%	0.00%	1.60%
'Undecided'	2.80%	4.80%	2.40%	3.60%	1.20%	14.70%
'Agree'	6.00%	2.00%	9.10%	7.90%	0.40%	25.40%
'Strongly agree'	5.60%	6.70%	23.40%	12.30%	7.10%	55.20%
Total	15.90%	14.70%	35.70%	25.00%	8.70%	100.00%

Exhibit 15.18 Chi-square results with '0.000' level of significance show very good association of variable political interference in the AISO work with the locus of control variable 'how much I am liked in the department depends upon my seniors'. Data analysis results placed at Exhibit 15.20

regarding political interference in the AISO work relation with the locus of control variable 'how much I am liked in the department depends upon my seniors' show that 80.60% of the officers 'strongly agree' + 'agree' intensity with this culture of the system indicates a very high-level culture of political interferences in the decision-making process. How much individual officer is liked in the department under political interference show that 33.70% of officers 'generally' + 'strongly feel' intensity this way means every third officer feel that individual liking in the department is related to political interferences in the decision.

15.4.9. Culture of Lack of Devotion to Work

Lack of devotion to work issue looks like irrelevant when we are studying the acceptance of political pressure in the decision-making process for the All India Services. Everyone will think that they are officers of the highest caliber and are of the highest level. There cannot be any kind of laxity. It looks insignificant to study an issue for such senior and responsible officers, who are running the nation according to their whims and fancies. 78.9% of the All India Services Officers have not considered this item in the ranking. The All India Services Officers assigned 7th rank in ordering problems. 6% chances are that decision and political pressure acceptance may be independent of each other. Our results are significant at a 0.06, level of significance. 81.5% of the Indian Police Service officers and the Indian Forest Service officers and 72.6% of the Indian Administrative Service officers do not consider it a problem while ranking all of them.

17.4 % of the Indian Administrative Service officers have 'strongly agreed' that lack of devotion to work is the problem and it got 13th lowest rank. 16% of the Indian Police Service officers and 17.4% of the Indian Forest Service officers have also ranked it very low.

Exhibit Number 15.21: Chi-Square: Lack of Devotion to Work versus 'My Success or Failure Depends mostly on those who Work with Me'

	Value	df	Asymp. Sig. (2-sided)
Pearson Chi-Square	35.217	16	0.004
Likelihood Ratio	34.203	16	0.005
Linear-by-Linear Association	3.288	1	0.07
N of Valid Cases	216		

Statistical results for Chi-square analysis placed at Exhibit 15.21 show a very good association of two variables lack the devotion to work by the AISO and locus of control 'my success or failure depends mostly on those who work with me' with Chi-square significance value of 0.004. Locus of control variable 'my success or failure depends mostly on those who work with me' relation with the AISO 'lack of devotion to work' analyses results placed at Exhibit 15.22 and show that 61.20% of the AISO 'hardly feel' this way + 'slightly feel' this that individual officer success or failure depends upon those who work with them, indicate that the AISO believe on their own work. Regarding culture of lack of devotion to work by an individual officer and locus of control in this variable show that 53.70% of AISO completely 'disagree' to 'undecided' category, indicate that the AISO does not accept that there is a lack of devotion to work by these officers.

Exhibit Number 15.22: Lack of Devotion to Work versus 'My Success or Failure Depends mostly on those who Work with Me'

Lack of Devotion to Work	My Success or Failure Depends Mostly on those who Work with Me					Total
	Hardly feel this way	Slightly feel this way	Somewhat feel this way	Generally feel this way	Strongly feel this way	
'Completely disagree'	0.50%	1.40%	4.20%	2.30%	0.00%	8.30%
'Disagree'	6.00%	6.50%	5.60%	0.00%	2.30%	20.40%
'Undecided'	7.40%	8.80%	6.00%	1.40%	1.40%	25.00%
'Agree'	6.50%	12.50%	7.40%	0.90%	0.90%	28.20%
'Strongly agree'	6.50%	5.10%	3.20%	1.90%	1.40%	18.10%
Total	26.90%	34.30%	26.40%	6.50%	6.00%	100.00%

15.4.10. Abuse of Power and Authority Culture

Abuse of power and authority by power holders is a serious problem since time immemorial. Absolute power corrupts absolutely. To meet the desire to dominate in the department, the power elite outflanked and oppressed their subordinate officers. They manipulate in such a way that ignorance and absence of knowledge pervade in the system so that strategically powerless remain without power forever. Rules, regulations, and procedures are doctored in a manner that style and substance of power remain out of their reach. Even if they know about the rules, regulations, and procedures, they are forced not to use it and power is un-interrupted enjoyed by the power elite. Power elites crush any kind of resistance or such resistance remains isolated, so that can be controlled easily. Power elite minimizes subordinate interactions to keep them in isolation, introduce competition among them to retain what they have so, whole energy is spent on retaining and no time is left for consolidation and fight for power. Even if subordinate consolidates, chances of success remain lower than the cost/efforts required for fighting out for power. Keep them busy in work, pressure, worries for livelihood, and a lot of exertion will leave no time for thinking for power.

Power is frequently used to defeat any kind of conflict in administration and individual officers preserve their interests and goals in the process. Structures of power have been designed in such a way that authority, position, ideology, culture, and expert knowledge is imbued with top elite power dominancy. Elite services use power in hidden ways and behind the scene through subordinate officers to meet their own goals and give it form, where legitimacy, values, technical information, and departmental rules are excluded from the computation.

The All India Services Officers power holders attempt to influence target persons through different tactics. The All India Services Officers from their position influence others under cover of rational thinking and reasoning. For their own sustainability, the All India Services Officers believe in creating a culture of power, where everyone accepts them as power holders. The Indian Administrative Service officers retain full control over resources; all others including politicians and the public accept the dominance of the Indian Administrative Service officers in the system. To abuse power to own advantage, the culture of dominance prevails among the Indian Administrative Service officers like any other bureaucratic system. In any case, reluctance by the target groups perceive the cost they have to pay for it. The Indian Police Service officers and the

Indian Forest Service officers are forced to survive in the culture, where they strive to develop pleasant relationships with the Indian Administrative Service officers, others develop a friendship with the Indian Administrative Service officers, in turn, IAS exploit them to meet own goals.

The Indian Administrative Service officers use coalition with people and politicians to exercise power and retain power-holder-ship. When the Indian Police Service officers, the Indian Forest Service officers, masses, other politicians, and other officers develop a close relationship with the powerful politician, the Indian Administrative Service officers enter into bargaining undercover to protect their power. The All India Services Officers never miss using higher authority and sanctions to retention the power for their exclusive misuse. The All India Services Officers show stiff competition to enhance and increase their own service power; glorify individual power to remain power holders. The All India Services Officers develop any type of coalition to abuse power in the process politician start exerting pressure to meet their goals.

Culture of abusing power invite pressure on the decision-making process. When the All India Services Officers' chances to retain power are reduced, then they approach politicians power brokers, hidden financiers, media persons, and various pressure groups to remain power holders. The Indian Administrative Service officers never like to implement such a decision, which endanger their power holder position. Government bureaucracy tends to develop autocratic behavior, power elites controlling the hierarchy maximize own service utility. Various service groups try to attain their tasks from small coalitions. The Indian Administrative Service officers' location and position successfully substitute such dependence of politician with own service members, which help in successfully abusing power by them. This enhances the competition among all the officers of public administration to maximize power for their own advantage. Power abuse remains accepted as norms and politician enjoy on the top of it, which cultivate sustenance of culture of power abuse.

In the ranking exercise, 31.3% of the All India Services Officers have ranked abuse of power as the 4th problem. Results for respective services are: 32.1% for the Indian Forest Service officers, 28.8 % for the Indian Administrative Service officers, and 27.2% for the Indian Police Service officers are seized with this issue. In individual item evaluation for the 'strongly agree' category, 24.7% of the Indian Forest Service officers, 36.2% of the Indian Administrative Service officers, and 46.8% of the Indian Police Service officers feel that abuse of power is the problem. Pearson Chi-square value of 67.249 is significant with '0.000', level of significance. Rho and R correlation values show a significant correlation with the decision-making process.

Exhibit Number 15.23: Chi-Square—Abuse of Power and Authority by them versus 'I can Largely Determine what Matters me in Department'

	Value	df	Asymp. Sig. (2-sided)
Pearson Chi-Square	25.353	16	0.064
Likelihood Ratio	26.373	16	0.049
Linear-by-Linear Association	0.375	1	0.54
N of Valid Cases	246		

Pearson Chi-square results placed at Exhibit 15.23 show association two variables and Chi-square significance value of 0.064 show abuse of power and authority by the AISO and locus of the control variable that 'I can largely determine what matters me in department'. Results placed at Exhibit 15.24 show that 'abuse of power and authority by the All India Services Officer' culture relationship with the locus of the control variable that 'I can largely determine what matters me in the department; 69.50% of the All India Services Officer 'strongly agree' + 'agree' category to this culture and in the locus of control and 63.40% of the All India Services Officer 'generally feet' this way + 'strongly feel' that the All India Services Officer control the decisions of department, where they work.

Exhibit Number 15.24: Abuse of Power and Authority by them versus 'I can Largely Determine what Matters me in Department'

Abuse of Power & Authority by Them	I can Largely Determine what Matters me in Department					Total
	Hardly feel this way	Slightly feel this way	Somewhat feel this way	Generally feel this way	Strongly feel this way	
'Completely disagree'	0.80%	1.20%	0.00%	3.30%	0.80%	6.10%
'Disagree'	0.40%	0.40%	2.00%	3.30%	1.20%	7.30%
'Undecided'	1.60%	0.00%	2.80%	6.50%	6.10%	17.10%
'Agree'	2.40%	1.20%	8.50%	10.60%	8.90%	31.70%
'Strongly agree'	3.70%	1.20%	10.20%	9.80%	13.00%	37.80%
Total	8.90%	4.10%	23.60%	33.30%	30.10%	100.00%

15.4.11. Discrimination and Obstruction Culture

People are heard saying frequently that these All India Services Officers are the greatest obstructionist. Discrimination is the compulsive evil of any bureaucratic system, so the All India Services are not the exception. In our ranking of variables, 17.5% of the All India Services Officers have ranked it 8th problem of the system. The Indian Administrative Service officers have no problem, as they are the head everywhere, 6.8% ignore it as a problem. 13.6% of the Indian Forest Service officers and 29.3% of the Indian Police Service officers feel this as a problem. Pearson Chi-square results are significant with a 0.001, level of significance.

Individual item evaluation indicates that 33.3% of the Indian Administrative Service officers, 26.6% of the Indian Police Service officers, and 18.8% of the Indian Forest Service officers are obstructionist and use a discriminatory method in the decision. Pearson Chi-square values of 62.169 show good association at 0.000, significance level. Rho and R correlation value show good strength of association and good correlation between the decision-making process and obstructionist and discriminatory attitude of All India Services Officers.

Exhibit Number 15.25: Chi-Square—Discrimination and Obstruction versus 'Large Extent my Career Depends on my Seniors'

	Value	df	Asymp. Sig. (2-sided)
Pearson Chi-Square	57.062	16	0.001

Chi-square results placed at Exhibit 15.25 show a very good association of two variables discrimination and obstruction by the AISO and locus of control variable 'to a large extent my career depends on my seniors' with a significance value of 0.001. Results placed at Exhibit 15.26 regarding the culture of discrimination and obstruction used by the AISO with the locus of control variable 'to a large extent my career depends on my seniors' show that 70.80% of the AISO 'strongly agree' + 'agree' category observed that seniors play a crucial role in discrimination and obstruction in the decision-making process. In the culture of discrimination and obstruction the career of officers largely depends upon seniors 65% of the AISO 'feel that way', if we add the 'somewhat' category then 91.10% of the AISO feel that seniors hold the key for their career with the culture of discrimination and obstruction in the decision.

Exhibit Number 15.26: Discrimination and Obstruction versus 'Large Extent my Career Depends on my Seniors'

Discrimination and Obstruction by Them	To Large Extent My Career Depends on My Seniors					Total
	Hardly feel this way	Slightly feel this way	Somewhat feel this way	Generally feel this way	Strongly feel this way	
'Completely disagree'	0.90%	1.80%	1.80%	0.00%	0.90%	5.30%
'Disagree'	0.00%	0.40%	3.50%	2.20%	0.00%	6.20%
'Undecided'	1.80%	1.30%	4.00%	6.60%	4.00%	17.70%
'Agree'	1.30%	1.30%	10.20%	25.20%	7.50%	45.60%
'Strongly agree'	0.00%	0.00%	6.60%	11.10%	7.50%	25.20%
% of Total	4.00%	4.90%	26.10%	45.10%	19.90%	100.00%

15.4.12. Political Opportunism Culture

When we discuss the individual All India Services Officers privately, they acknowledge that a large number of officers are highly opportunist to fulfill their self-goals, they develop a strong association with the politicians. Political opportunism dominant among the All India Services Officers is a problem of serious proportions. "Commitment of civil servants to the values of the constitution by false commitment to the power that changed emphasis and bread sycophancy", A. Mukopadhyay (1994).

Only 8.9% of the All India Services Officers acknowledge this issue at the lowest rank of 12th with 0.000, level of significance, Pearson Chi-square results are significant. The Indian Administrative Service Officers do not consider it a problem for ranking. 9.8% of the Indian Police Service officers and 16% of the Indian Forest Service officers view it as a problem.

Individual item evaluation results indicate that 44.9% of the Indian Administrative Service officers have assigned it 6th rank, which is contrary to the above ranking. 53.7% of the Indian Police Service officers have evaluated it at 6th rank. 29.6% of the Indian Forest Service officers have ranked it at 5th rank. Political opportunism is highest among the Indian Administrative Service officers and least among the Indian Forest Service officers in all the three All India Services. Pearson Chi-square results are highly significant showing a good association of political opportunism and decision process, with a 0.000, level of significance. Rho and R values for correlations of two variables show good strength with a 0.000, level of significance.

Exhibit Number 15.27: Chi-Square—Political Opportunism by them versus 'Usually I am Responsible for Getting/not Getting Rewards'

	Value	df	Asymp. Sig. (2-sided)
Pearson Chi-Square	29.691	16	0.02
Likelihood Ratio	33.397	16	0.007
Linear-by-Linear Association	4.2	1	0.04
N of Valid Cases	246		

Chi-square results placed at Exhibit 15.27 show a good association of two variables political opportunism by the AISO and locus of control 'usually I am responsible for getting/not getting rewards' with '0.02' level of significance. Data analysis placed at Exhibit 15.28 related to political opportunism used by the AISO in decision relation with the locus of control variable 'usually I am responsible for getting/not getting rewards' show that 84.20% of the AISO ranked it 'strongly agree' + 'agree' category. Are the AISO responsible for getting or not getting rewards in the decision-making process, 78.90% of the AISO feel among 'somewhat way' category + 'strongly feel' that way category, this show political opportunism culture is pervasive in the decision-making process.

Exhibit Number 15.28: Political Opportunism by them versus 'Usually I am Responsible for Getting/not Getting Rewards'

Political Opportunism by Them	Usually I am Responsible for Getting/Not Getting Rewards					Total
	Hardly feel this way	Slightly feel this way	Somewhat feel this way	Generally feel this way	Strongly feel this way	
'Completely disagree'	0.00%	0.00%	0.80%	1.20%	0.00%	2.00%
'Disagree'	1.20%	1.60%	1.20%	1.60%	0.40%	6.10%
'Undecided'	0.00%	1.60%	0.80%	2.40%	2.80%	7.70%
'Agree'	4.10%	6.90%	11.00%	14.20%	4.90%	41.10%
'Strongly agree'	3.70%	2.00%	9.80%	16.70%	11.00%	43.10%
% of Total	8.90%	12.20%	23.60%	36.20%	19.10%	100.00%

15.4.13. Immoral Behavior Culture

We have been reading frequently the various stories about corruption and immoral behavior demonstrated by the All India Services Officers. "Lack of material resources, but also a backwardness of the human element, which is exhibited besides other things in poor standards of honesty in people," S.C. Mishra (1973). He further elucidated, "When power changes hands, the new officials, bureaucrats, and politicians are all quick to exploit the situation for their own benefit because of political uncertainty and past poverty of those who come to power. Corruption like a cancerous growth trickles down from the highest official level to the lower ranks due to bad example set by those at the top." The public is not sure that the guilty officers would be punished. On the contrary, there is widespread feeling (and maybe without foundation) that, if a corrupt official is caught, it is due to chance or ill luck, and that a large number of corrupt officials continue to flourish. Besides the bribe givers, they gain considerable advantage by paying bribes, and therefore they are more anxious to conceal rather than reveal corruption. The collusive type of corruption, which brings both to the official and bribe giver, will always remain underground", R. Prasher (1986).

"Corruption starts from the top, rapidly contaminating the lower levels of our social and political life that is why we find it corroding and eating into the vitals of almost every phase of our social and political structure. It is common knowledge that despite the law limiting the expenses of the election, people have to spend huge amounts on their elections propaganda and for feeding and maintaining vast machinery for that purpose. That is inevitable because of the big constituencies from which they seek elections and collecting funds in the name of the party, the temptation to fill their coffers is not easily avoidable" due to uncertainty of future. (Justice Sarjoo Prasad, Report of Sarjoo Prasad Commission', Orissa Govt.).

Pearson Chi-square values show a very strong association between immoral behavior and decision-making process, with '0.000', level of significance. In ranking of this issue, 8.1% of the All India Services Officers acknowledge this problem. 100% of the Indian Administrative Service officers, 91.3% of the Indian Police Service officers, and 85.2% of the Indian Forest Service officers do not consider it as a problem within the All India Services. The All India Services Officers with ranks and files deny the problem of immoral behavior at the lowest level.

An evaluation of each item, Pearson Chi-square significance level of '0.000', demonstrates a good association between immoral behavior and the decision-making process. Rho and R correlation values show a good relationship with a 0.001, level of significance. 40.6% of the Indian Administrative Service officers' value it at 10th rank, 56.4% of the Indian Police Service officers' rank it at 5th, and 19.2% of the Indian Forest Service officers rank it at 9th rank as part of the bureaucratic culture.

"The gentlemanly code and the traditional service values that went with it were no longer relevant in that one does not use these ideas in conversation or as a defense of action because doing makes you look like ridiculous. Political corruption and black money loomed very largely in this explanation of these developments. Most administrators had become part of this corrupt scene, either becoming actually involved or passively winking at such practices because they had no power to control them. Top administrator as a class had become the link between politician and business class," D.C. Potter.

Exhibit Number 15.29: Chi-square—Retention of Immoral Behaviour versus 'My Acceptability to others will Depend on my Behaviour with them'

	Value	df	Asymp. Sig. (2-sided)
Pearson Chi-Square	36.887	16	0.002
Likelihood Ratio	38.11	16	0.001
Linear-by-Linear Association	8.644	1	0.003
N of Valid Cases	215		

One former Chief Secretary of UP expressed like this, "previously civil servants had clear ideas about the type of behavior that would be rewarded or punished; furthermore, control over that judgment about it were in the hands of civil servants itself. Now increasingly these standards for rewards or punishment can no longer be identified-lip service is still paid to the old conventions and values but they no longer provide working criteria." Acceptable and unacceptable immoral behavior has no boundaries. Political accommodation, flexibility, loyalty are the criteria for the decision, D.C. Potter.

Chi-square value of 0.002 shown in Exhibit 15.29 show a good association of variable retention of immoral behaviour by the AISO with a variable in the locus of control 'my acceptability to others will depend on my behaviour with them'. Data analysis results placed at Exhibit 15.30 regarding the AISO retention of immoral behaviour in the decision-making process related with the locus of control variable 'my acceptability to others will depend on my behaviour with them' show that 60% of the AISO rank this culture in 'strongly agree' + 'agree' with category, so immorality culture of bureaucracy is indicated by results. Locus of control variable 'my acceptability to others will depend on my behaviour with them' show 80.90% of the AISO 'generally feel this way' + 'strongly feel this way' that in the culture of immoral behaviour individual officer acceptability will depend upon individual behaviour with the system. This indicates the concept of survival in the system of immorality in the decision-making process.

Exhibit Number 15.30: Retention of Immoral Behaviour versus 'My Acceptability to others will Depend on my Behaviour with them'

Retention of Immoral Behaviour	My Acceptability to Others will Depend on My Behaviour with Them					Total
	Hardly feel this way	Slightly feel this way	Somewhat feel this way	Generally feel this way	Strongly feel this way	
'Completely disagree'	0.00%	0.50%	3.30%	5.10%	4.70%	13.50%
'Disagree'	0.90%	0.50%	0.00%	3.70%	3.30%	8.40%
'Undecided'	0.90%	1.40%	4.20%	4.70%	7.00%	18.10%
'Agree'	0.00%	0.50%	1.40%	10.70%	9.80%	22.30%
'Strongly agree'	0.00%	0.00%	5.60%	10.70%	21.40%	37.70%
Total %	1.90%	2.80%	14.40%	34.90%	46.00%	100.00%

ANNEXURE 15.A: QUESTIONNAIRE ON THE AISO CULTURE IN DECISION

What things in All India Services people dislike most? Please rank three most disliked items in left hand side. Kindly, read these items again and evaluate them on five-point scale in right hand side. Mark 1, in case completely disagrees. Mark 2, in case disagrees. Mark 3, in case undecided. Mark 4, in case agrees. Mark 5, in case strongly agrees.

Code No.	Ranking	Disliked Items		Score				
				1	2	3	4	5
(141)		Low salaries	(154)					
(142)		Favoritism and nepotism	(155)					
(143)		Ego and arrogance	(156)					
(144)		Their frequent transfers	(157)					
(145)		Too much careerism	(158)					
(146)		Obsession with status	(159)					
(147)		Self-seeking of goals	(160)					
(148)		Political interference in their work	(161)					
(149)		Lack of devotion to work	(162)					
(150)		Abuse of power & authority by them	(163)					
(151)		Discrimination and obstruction by them	(164)					
(152)		Political opportunism by them	(165)					
(153)		Retention of immoral behavior	(166)					

Unit 16

Workplace Environment Orientation in Decision

"Cheerfulness of mind, placidity, a habit of contemplation on the Supreme, control of the mind, and perfect purity of inner feelings...all this is called austerity of the mind." *The Bhagavad Gita* 17.16.

"If your actions inspire others to dream more, learn more, do more, and become more, you are a leader."—John Quincy Adams.

"Hypocrisy is the audacity to preach integrity from a den of corruption."—Wes Fesler.

- *Workplace environment impact on decision behaviour*
- *Workplace environment process*
- *Workplace design and layout*
- *Research analyses result for the prevalent environment in decision*

Public administration is also a living organization. Workplace environmental constraints depend upon the values, attitudes, and beliefs of All India Services Officer individually and collectively they hold. In this unit, environmental association with some fundamental consistencies in the behaviour of individual officers of respective services, which are modified to reflect individual service differences are studied. The workplace design layout model and process with reference to the All India Service has been described conceptually. Analyses results for workplace-related variables are presented here.

16.1. Workplace Environment Impact on Decision Behaviour

The All India Services Officers' perception regarding the effectiveness of the public administration environment is related to their working efficiency in a given environmental setup. Functional aspects of work are related to the effectiveness of the motivational environment prevalent in a particular department and a given place and time. The All India Services Officers under achievement motive avail success and like to avoid failures at their workplace. The All India Services Officers' desires for career growth motivate them to avoid loneliness and aloofness in their working environment. Individual officer desires to be included in the decision-making process force them to avoid an exclusive environment. In avoidance behaviour the All India Services Officers feel frozen due to a pressure anxiety environment.

In the workplace, how seniors show interest in the juniors to build their capacities and grooming? In many services junior respect seniors and repose faith in them or feel protected under them. In any service work environment, hierarchical relations are necessary for their survival and sustenance. Any service can retain and preserve knowledge and power only through an atmosphere of unity and harmony. In case of low tolerance for power, service members question their seniors and develop a critical attitude towards them.

"Ability of organic system to cope with various environmental constraints depends upon the values, attitude and beliefs its members individually and collectively hold," P. Singh et al. (1979). In case of faith in seniors, procedures are faithfully carried out and seniors are sincerely followed. In an environment of faith and belief in seniors, service members believe in acquired status through the hierarchy.

The departmental environment is associated with some fundamental consistencies in the behaviour of an individual member of service that can be modified to reflect individual service member differences. In the workplace environment, what motivates the All India Services Officers, and do they feel comfortable to work? The workplace environment motivates them or they feel suffocated to work. Political pressure and politician location in public administration provide them opportunities to influence the work environment. There is tremendous competition for power among the All India Services Officers, this makes politicians' word more crucial for the growth of any service. With the passage of time, politicians are getting more awareness and higher pressure from voters in the direction of their goals and interests. Awakened people mobilize direct pressure on the All India Services Officers. Slowly, they are realizing the power of pressure groups to get things done in their favour.

"Work means something more to man than economic compensation. It has a major influence on men's self-concept or self-identity (Miller, 1963; Erikson, 1956; and Super, 1931). It is the primary source of meaning and self-worth in life (Kierkegaard, 1960; Franki, 1955); gives a purpose in life and a feeling of being unified into the larger society (Morse and Weiss, 1955). Hartley (1980) cited a number of studies, which indicates that lack of work leads to loss of self-esteem (Tausky and Piedmont, 1967 and Koarovsky, 1940), damaged ego (Levine, 1975), loss of self-worth (Harrison, 1976), loss of self-respect (Daniel, 1972), loss of self-confidence (Weddurburn, 1964), and loss of personal identity (Hill, 1976). Thus, highlighting the importance of work for positive mental health...in all cultures, work has a significance, beyond money, although cultures vary a good deal in the extent to which they value work," Asha Bhandarker, 1985. The author further elaborates, "Work fulfills a number of human needs and allows individual development along certain channels. When work does not fulfill man's needs, it can affect his self-esteem and morals, and thus his total being, behaviour and productivity. Negative emotional reactions can occur and impair normal judgment and thinking capacity."

Any happening at the workplace and its environment has a direct relationship with the All India Services Officers' self-worth and happiness. Negative political pressure and its negative consequences are manifested through poor job satisfaction, which in turn leads to low performance and negative emotional attitudes towards the decision process. Ever-increasing and goals-oriented political pressure has crumbled and toppled the service norms. A goal-oriented work environment has an impact on the structure, hierarchy, promotions, postings, policies, and career progression of the All India Services and process of decision, thereupon. Bureaucratic processes and hierarchy have an impact on individual officers' psychological needs and expectations. The same work environment produces a different degree of impact on the decision among different officers depending upon individual officers' values, beliefs, and perceptions.

Rapid information flow through the Internet, online working (audio and video), and satellite communication (5G network) through various fast and easily available media have changed the whole environment of the workplace. Now the public administrator cannot hide his incompetence's under the garb of secrecy after the Right to Information Act. Transparency has to come with more demand for information sharing by stakeholders. With the blast of information, the technology world has become a global village. Colonially perpetuated All India Services Officers control and regulations have to go sooner or later. Lack of information induces helplessness and withdrawal behaviour (Weiss, 1972). Sharing and flow of information are invariably related to individual behaviour to cope with the uncertainty.

Power-centered All India Services Officers cannot afford to exploit the whole nation to their advantage for a long time in the coming future. Regarding the elite approach of the All India Services Officers, a serious debate is brewing up. Monopoly in ruling by the elite at the workplace has been challenged by the sufferers and public at large. It is a question of time when the All India Services Officers will be overthrown or working style is changed. And the stakeholders will share power.

The All India Services Officers are allocated to the cadre of different states are supposed to adopt the culture and environment of that cadre State, but this has not happened in practice after more than a century time period. Most of them do not feel comfortable in a new environment and throughout their career, they behave in a remorseful manner. Outside cadre has only helped the All India Services Officers to hide their disproportionate assets back in-home state and immoral behaviour. Assimilation in the culture and environment of the cadre state has not worked well as envisaged by the framers of the Constitution.

Globalization in the corporate sector will have an impact on the All India Services Officers work environment also. The demand has already been raised for transparency and openness in administration. Recently, some joint secretaries in the Government of India were recruited (on contract basis) directly from the open market. There was a time when the IAS (EO, DoP&T Office) was not allowing members of other services for empanelment to the Joint Secretary post. The All India Services Officers have to work with bosses, seniors, peers, politicians, subordinates, and masses, who are born and raised in different environments and cultures. Environment and individual cause-effect relationship molds the social character (Fromm, 1976). In a public bureaucracy, officers are passive, conformist, and follow rules, regulations, and procedures blindly. Obedience to procedures is the most convenient ploy to escape from environmental hazards.

The All India Services Officers needs, values, beliefs, past experience in handling the political pressure, capabilities and personality interact with the workplace environment, their position in the departmental hierarchy (location in the bureaucratic system), service officer belongs to and support he is getting from the officers in the hierarchy (colleagues, juniors, seniors and fellow friends). These factors in turn interact with the family, friends, social and economic factors. All of these factors interact with each other on three sides of the triangle (Figure 16.1) and the outcome invariably related to the perception of the All India Services Officers about the political pressure.

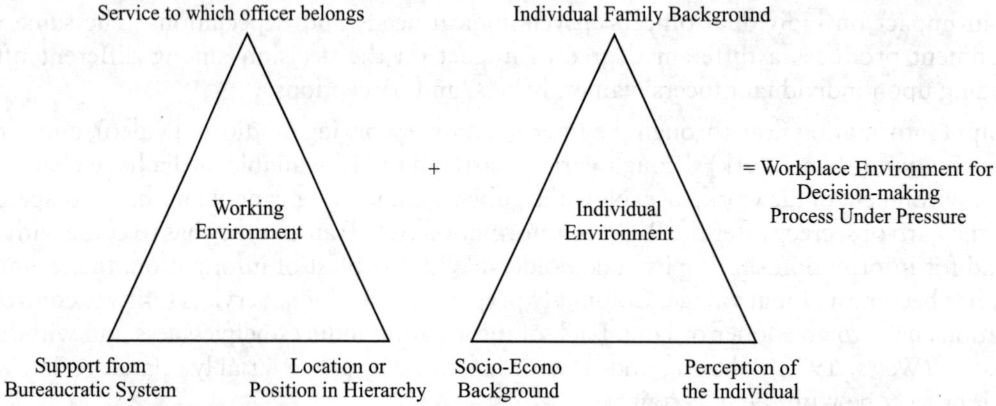

Figure No. 16.1: Workplace Environment Impact on Decision

Perceptions of the All India Services Officers comprise the service demand, threat from the decision outcome, new challenges in the work environment. These interactions generate conflict in the decision process for the All India Services Officers. Workplace conflicts have a serious effect on the All India Services Officers and decision process, which may be related to the individual officer's personality. The All India Services Officers may adopt short-term or temporary or long-term pressure management tricks or adjustment to local conditions to get a temporary reprieve. The outcome will be reflected in the behavior of the officer through a change in his habits and work style, the All India Services Officers decision-making process will be related to such outcomes. This will have bearing on the family life and in turn the decision process also. Continuous pressure and conflict may be manifested through psychological diseases as depression, tension, hypertension, and sudden outburst of emotions.

Cadre state workforce diversity, enviro-cultural differences, and ethnic diversity pose a serious challenge to the All India Services Officers in their daily management. The All India Services Officers have to accommodate their cadre state subordinates regional thinking bias, values, preferences, lifestyle, and social attitudes in the decision process, which is not available in any textbook. This in turn forces them to re-evaluate their own lifestyle, family needs, social perceptions and reconsider/refurbish attitudes to cadre state social milieu or in tune with the social need and cultural environment of the posting area. In the work environment, the All India Services

Officers have to treat alike the interests of the minority, women, and disadvantaged groups and underprivileged, at the same time maintain the efficacy of the administrative system/machinery.

The All India Services Officers have to infuse creativity and innovation in cultural diversity for effective delivery of the decision and solve the problems in proper perspectives. The All India Services Officers face the Herculean task of overall improvement and deliver goods and services from huge unmanageable hierarchies. Successive changes of political leadership at the top throw onerous task of managing new challenges and reengineering the policy procedure at short intervals. Frequent mobility of the All India Services Officers hampers the speed and control in decision delivery. The All India Services Officers have to accommodate in decision ever-changing contrasting interests and goals of different people, with an ever-demanding environment of political uncertainty.

The All India Services Officers have to sustain continuous improvement, streamline the process of service delivery, avoid wasteful public expenses, make administration accessible to all, win the confidence of the masses, inculcate a sense of justice and constant satisfaction of the public at the workplace. The All India Services Officers have to assess performance variables and compared them against the departmental standards to identify the root of the problem and eliminate causes. Within limited resources, the All India Services Officers have to keep pace with ever-changing job skills in their work.

The All India Services Officers have to carry out skill up-gradation among the working force with limited resources. The All India Services Officers have to work in the roles of coach, adviser, sponsor, facilitator, associate, teammate, friend, and harsh boss, as demanded by the workplace situations. Decision making has gone down to lower level across the hierarchy, lower level functionaries are in full control of their work, they operate at will due to erosion of the power of the All India Services Officers from the administration, in turn, grabbed by a politician. Employees, who are remotely controlled by the political leadership, decide on behalf of the All India Services Officers, for their actions the All India Services Officers are often held accountable.

The environment of change is prevalent in the country. With little stability of tenure at the workplace, resource constraints, unmanageable subordinate, and political control, the All India Services Officers have to steer the change, multi-skilling, and job rotation place of work. The All India Services Officers have to deliver results in the environment, where government policies are in a state of flux, army of poor performing subordinates, decreasing government interventions, increasing privatization, downsizing the government operations, huge lethargic establishment, the rigidity of procedures and uncertainty on their heads loom at large at the workplace. The decision process environment is bound to be full of flexibility, spontaneity, unpredictability, and temporariness.

The environment of ethical dilemmas is pervasive in public administration. No one has enough courage to blow the whistle for uncovering unethical and illegal activities in the governance of public administration. Every individual employee plays dirty politics for the advancement own career. No one is willing to evaluate oneself for their own goals and interests. Boundaries between right and wrong have blurred by one to all in the mad race of vested self-interests. Line of command in government hierarchy has melted away and evaporated under pressure of unethical temptations and self-goals.

Top bureaucrats incite, induce, and educate top politicians regarding misuse of government machinery and rigging of rules and law. It is a misconception that politicians use pressure to meet their own goals, politicians are taught and educated by these powers greedy individual All India Services Officers to distort the whole system to their own advantage. Politicians are used as a pawn in the hands of the All India Services Officers, once individual All India Services Officers get confidence and control over the politician, then the politician has to dance in tune with individual officer desires and whims. In the long-run decision by the All India Services Officers used to be devoid of code of ethics and honesty, public perceptions and opinions remain molded that the All India Services Officers are highly unfair and prejudice in nature. There is a prevailing environment of a total loss of faith from the All India Services Officer's decisions taken under pressure from different sources.

16.2. Workplace Environment Processes

The All India Services Officers face the challenge to manage working force diversity and ethnic-cultural diversity. The All India Services Officers have to accommodate subordinates, regional value preferences, lifestyle, and social attitudes. This forces them to consider their lifestyle, family needs, social perceptions, adjusted attitudes to cadre state, or posting area social needs. In the work environment, the All India Services Officers have to treat alike the interests of minorities, women, disadvantaged groups, and the underprivileged at the same time maintain the efficiency of the administration. The All India Services Officers have to infuse creativity and innovation in cultural diversity for effective decisions and solve the problem in proper perspectives as shown in Figure 16.2.

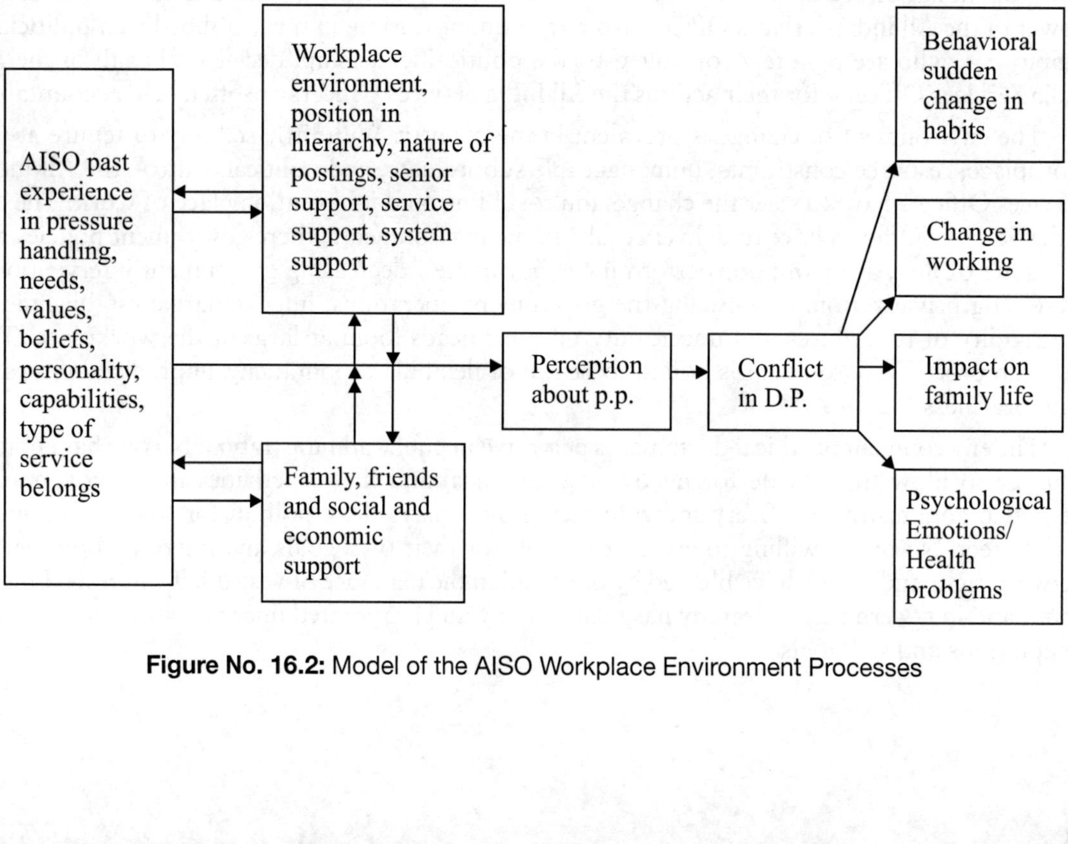

Figure No. 16.2: Model of the AISO Workplace Environment Processes

The All India Services Officers face the Herculean task of improvement and deliver goods and services from an enormous unmanageable hierarchy. Successive changes of political leadership at the top, throw the onerous task of managing new challenges and reengineering the policy at a short interval. Frequent mobility of the All India Services Officers hampers the speed and control in decision delivery. Changing political goals and interests create a contradiction in an ever-demanding environment of politics.

When we discuss the environment for a particular service, we mean that it comprises the forces outside that service or other services or institutions, potentiality affecting the performance of that service. In the case of the Indian Police Service officers and the Indian Forest Service officers' political parties, institutions, the public, and the Indian Administrative Service cadres all determine the performance of these services. In the case of the Indian Administrative Service cadres, politicians and the publics affect their performance. Environment for the All India Services as one unit comprises political and public forces affecting their performance.

Politicians and the Indian Administrative Service officers infuse uncertainty to induce dynamic character in the All India Services environment. Government administration ever remains dynamic as every change of political leadership and change of government has its own agenda and to full that on changing government law, rules, regulations, and procedures. These goals directed uncertainty induce adjustment in the government hierarchy and structure, which continuously hamper the performance of government bureaucracy. In such an environment of uncertainty, every service and individual officer seeks adjustments that increase the complexity dimension of the environment.

Every system has a certain capacity beyond buffer limits; government resources got strained and impaired. Growth and performance remain hindered. The environment of high degrees of uncertainty just makes it impossible for the All India Services Officers to compute continually changing probabilities for the options available in the decision. Ever-changing leadership and increasing demand from government resources enhance the environmental complexities. Individual All India Services Officers are competing among themselves with power holders and political authority; no one knows what to do at what time. This type of environment has highly vitiated the decision process. A higher degree of uncertainty will induce higher structural arrangements in the public administration.

Efforts, goals, and needs are the basic elements in work, which motivate the All India Services Officers' work environment. Satisfying outcomes appear attractive and unsatisfied outcomes create tensions and stimulate drives within individual All India Services Officers. The All India Services Officers exert efforts to relieve tension and achieve satisfaction. Hertzberg (1959) researched on what people look into a work or a job; achievement, reorganization, responsibility, advancement, career growth, and work itself constitute the intrinsic factors. Policy, supervision, interpersonal relations with satisfaction, and working conditions are extrinsic factors related to the dissatisfaction.

Aldefer (1969) worked on the core needs of existence, relatedness, and growth of a person. David McClelland (1961, 1974, 1975) looked into achievement, power, and affiliation in the work. Lawrence (1960) predicted that people prefer complex and challenging work. The person looks for variety, autonomy, responsibility, knowledge, and social interactions in the workplace. Hackman and Oldham (1976) described workplace in the dimensions that a person searches a variety of activities, identifiable pieces of work to complete, work has an impact on other people, work must provide. Independence and discretion available to the individual, direct and clear information about performance is related to the workplace environment.

Ever-changing technology has an impact on the workplace environment. The computer has invaded and replaced the typewriter; changing the perception of the All India Services Officers that now they themselves can type confidential letters. With smart mobile phones, WhatsApp on cell phones, laptops, most of the young All India Services Officers are keen to use it in the workplace. The All India Services Officers' workplace environment is also related to the social response and feedback they receive. Earlier sitting on the high dais has been reacted and denounced by the societal system. Colonially imbibed attitudes and behavior environment of All India Services Officers is under attack from all social segments. The workplace environment is under continuous change under the need and demand for changing times.

Politicians and public pressure forced the All India Services Officers to eliminate the variations and increase the uniformity in the decision. Continuous improvement in the workplace environment has increased the functional conflicts in the working style. Rethinking, redesigning, and reengineering the workplace improve the output in the decision process. Political pressure has enhanced flexibility at the work. The All India Services Officers movements with the politicians have an impact on the public, and in turn, inflate the decision process. Political leadership regulates the salary and perks for the All India Services Officers; inequalities in salaries make-work less attractive. Higher equity in salary motivates to work and mesmerize the work environment. Career progression and promotions are invariably and essentially related to the workplace. Increased equity and fairness in chances of promotions motivate the All India Services Officers to work in less conducive and difficult situations.

Interpersonal relationships and departmental web of relationships are directly related to the performance at the workplace. Deterioration in relationships decreases the performance at decision and interests in work. Ambiguous and flexible working time, the All India Services Officers has to work day and night, almost no quality in family life. Most of their time is spent on traveling and meetings, very little time is left for working in an office and thinks about any problems. But this flexibility and freedom in work still motivate them to work day and night. Worldly physical temptations may lie somewhere else.

16.3. Workplace Design and Layout

The physical environment of the workplace and conditions are invariably dynamic and most of the All India Services Officers continue to modify it. The All India Services Officers workplace can be located anywhere from State secretariat/capital/New Delhi down to district and subdivisions locations. Across the breadth and length of the country, they have to work in the geographical variables of their cadre. Extreme weather vagaries are not considered by them as a distraction to work. In metropolitan cities, the All India Services Officers have to work in highly polluted locations also, which is beyond the scope of the present work to describe.

Mostly workplace physical set up are considered conducive. On many occasions, the All India Services Officers have to work in highly problematic places also. Interior countryside locations do decrease the performance of the All India Services Officers. The All India Services Officers are used to work with human noise in their surroundings. In the countryside interiors, where electricity, roads, and means of communications are straining and limiting factors for the workplace, an individual officer posted there have to deliver results in those limitations only. Workplace design, arrangement, layout, and degree of privacy do provide a sense of satisfaction to the officers. Most of the buildings are constructed and maintained by the Centre/State public works department. The All India Services Officers enjoy limited autonomy for making changes and alterations in workplace design. However, they appreciate much cannot be done in this aspect. At the same time, they enjoy a luxurious office space with comfortable fittings. The influence of workplace design and setting on the individual has been shown in Figure 16.3.

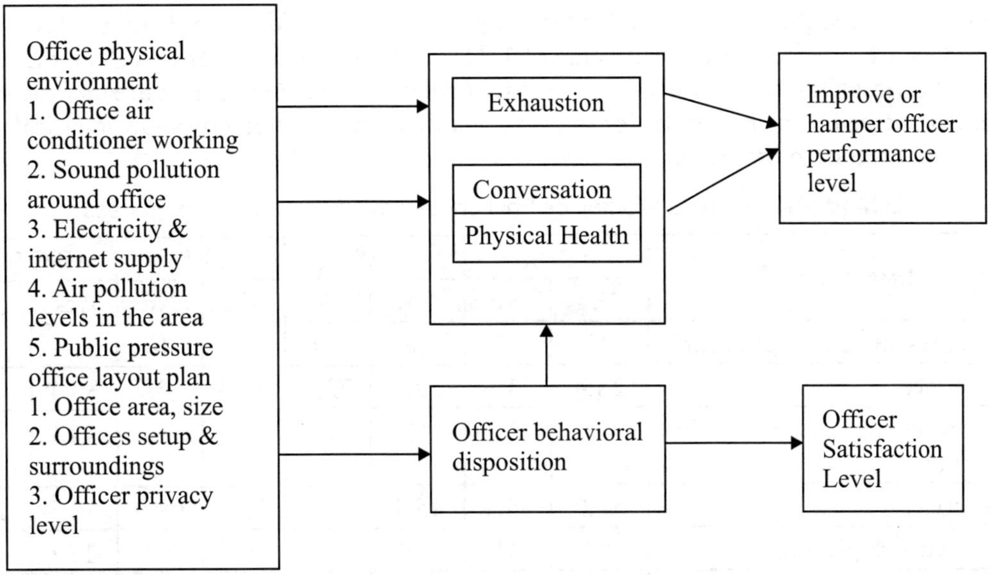

Figure No. 16.3: Influence of Physical Working Conditions and Work Space Design[1]

16.4. Research Analyses of Prevalent Environment in Decision

Exhibit Number 16.1: Working Environment—Statistical Results

Variable Name	Frequency (N)					AIS Mean Value			Mean Value	Standard Deviation
	Total	Missing	%	Valid	%	I.A.S.	I.P.S.	I.F.S.		
Is present salary sufficient?	280	7	2.5	273	97.5	1.65	1.69	1.5	1.61	0.49
Are chances of promotion sufficient?	280	15	5.4	265	94.6	1.61	1.54	1.52	1.57	0.5
Is work satisfying?	280	17	6.1	263	93.9	1.5	1.47	1.43	1.47	0.5
Are interpersonal relations sufficient?	280	23	8.2	257	91.8	1.57	1.45	1.44	1.5	0.5
Are rules for work & conduct satisfactory?	280	16	5.7	264	943	1.35	1.29	1.28	1.31	0.46

1. Adapted and modified from *Organization Behavior*, Stephen P. Robins, p. 533, 1998.

Variable Name	Frequency (N)					AIS Mean Value			Mean Value	Standard Deviation
	Total	Missing	%	Valid	%	I.A.S.	I.P.S.	I.F.S.		
Workplace and work environment conducive?	280	17	6.1	263	93.9	1.51	1.4	1.45	1.47	0.5
Written instructions be taken for decisions?	280	7	2.5	273	97.5	1.49	1.57	1.35	1.48	0.5

In our analyses, the lowest score for 'no' response is in the fifth variable that rules of work and conduct are satisfactory, a mean value of 1.31 and standard deviation of 0.46 indicate that All India Services Officers are fully convinced that rules for working in the bureaucratic system are not conducive for them. Results for the most of other items understudy show identical values for mean and standard deviation.

Exhibit Number 16.2: Workplace Environment in Decision-making Process

Item Name	I.A.S.		I.P.S.		I.F.S.		AISO Total	
	Yes	No	Yes	No	Yes	No	Yes	No
201. Is present salary sufficient?	21	53	26	70	57	46	104	169
% in service	28.4	71.6	27.1	72.9	55.3	44.7	38.1	61.9
202. Are chances of promotion sufficient?	39	32	41	50	32	71	112	153
% in service	54.9	45.1	45.1	54.9	31.1	68.9	42.3	57.7
203. Is work satisfying?	40	31	47	43	52	50	139	124
% in service	56.3	43.7	52.2	47.8	51	49	52.9	47.1
204. Are interpersonal relations sufficient?	37	30	41	46	51	52	129	128
% in service	55.2	44.8	47.1	52.9	49.5	50.5	50.2	49.8
205. Are rules for work and conduct satisfactory?	55	17	69	21	60	42	184	80
% in service	76.4	23.6	76.7	23.3	58.8	41.2	69.7	30.3
206. Workplace and work environment conducive?	42	29	57	35	43	57	142	121
% in service	59.2	40.8	62	38	43	57	54	46
207. Written instructions be taken for decisions?	27	47	38	58	77	26	142	131
% in service	36.5	63.5	39.6	60.4	74.8	25.2	52	48

Satisfaction for rules for work and conduct among the All India Services indicate that the Indian Administrative Service officers, the Indian Police Service officers are almost equally and highly satisfied with the present working procedures prevalent in the bureaucratic system. Mean values are 1.31 to 1.61 and standard deviation from 0.46 to 0.5, this indicates that the maximum the All India Services Officers are not satisfied with the workplace environment.

16.4.1. Salary

Salary is the most important motivator in the work. Among factors of dissatisfaction in work, excellent salaries stimulate the decision-making process. 61.9% of the All India Services Officers are not satisfied with the present salary structure. 72.9% of the Indian Police Service officers and 71.6% of the Indian Administrative Service officers are not satisfied with the present salary. 55.3% of the Indian Forest Service officers have indicated satisfaction from the present salary. This marginal improvement in perceptions of the Indian Forest Service officers may be due to expectations from re-structuring exercises in their respective cadres. Pearson's correlation (R) negative value of –0.25 with a level of significance at 0.000, and similar values for the Spearman correlation (Rho), indicate good strength of correlation of salary with the political pressure in the decision-making process.

Statistical analysis results placed at Exhibit 16.3 for this variable 'is the present salary of the AISO sufficient' relation with the locus of control variable 'success of a person depends upon the chances one gets' with a significance level of 0.016 for the AIS show the good relationship of variables. Results for the respective three services show some variations, 0.056 for IAS show a good association but the value of 0.121 for IPS and 0.218 for IFS are more than 0.05 indicating independence of two variables for IPS and IFS. Likelihood ratio and linear-by-linear relation show a good correlation of two variables among the three services. Data analysis results at Exhibit 16.4 show 62.1% of the AISO evaluated that the present salary is not sufficient with locus variable success of a person depends upon the chances one gets. Results for IAS 71.2% with a score of 35.6% 'feel somewhat way' category, in IPS 71.9% with 37.10% 'slightly feel that way' and in IFS 46.5% 'generally feel that way' indicated that present salary is not sufficient.

Exhibit Number 16.3: Chi-Square—Is Present Salary Sufficient versus 'Success of Person Depends upon the Chances one Gets'

AIS Name		Value	df	Asymp. Sig. (2-sided)
Indian Administrative Service	Pearson Chi-Square	9.228b	4	0.056
	Likelihood Ratio	11.055	4	0.026
	Linear-by-Linear Association	3.45	1	0.063
	N of Valid Cases	73		
Indian Police Service	Pearson Chi-Square	7.301c	4	0.121
	Likelihood Ratio	9.672	4	0.046
	Linear-by-Linear Association	5.55	1	0.018
	N of Valid Cases	89		
Indian Forest Service	Pearson Chi-Square	5.763d	4	0.218
	Likelihood Ratio	5.85	4	0.211
	Linear-by-Linear Association	0.358	1	0.549
	N of Valid Cases	99		

AIS Name		Value	df	Asymp. Sig. (2-sided)
Total AIS	Pearson Chi-Square	12.234a	4	0.016
	Likelihood Ratio	12.03	4	0.017
	Linear-by-Linear Association	0.057	1	0.811
	N of Valid Cases	261		

Exhibit Number 16.4: Is Present Salary Sufficient versus 'Success of Person Depends upon the Chances one Gets'

Service Name	Present Salary Sufficient	Success of Person Depends upon the Chances One Gets					Total
		Hardly feel this way	Slightly feel this way	Somewhat feel this way	Generally feel this way	Strongly feel this way	
IAS	'YES'	6.80%	13.70%	6.80%	1.30%	0.00%	28.80%
	'NO'	16.40%	13.70%	28.80%	1.40%	11.00%	71.20%
	Total	23.30%	27.40%	35.60%	2.70%	11.00%	100.00%
IPS	'YES'	7.90%	14.60%	5.60%	0.00%	0.00%	28.10%
	'NO'	14.60%	22.50%	24.70%	2.20%	7.90%	71.90%
	Total	22.50%	37.10%	30.30%	2.20%	7.90%	100.00%
IFS	'YES'	1.00%	4.00%	16.20%	21.20%	11.10%	53.50%
	'NO'	3.00%	7.10%	11.10%	11.10%	14.10%	46.50%
	Total	4.00%	11.10%	27.30%	32.30%	25.30%	100.00%
Total AIS	'YES'	5.00%	10.30%	10.00%	8.40%	4.20%	37.90%
	'NO'	10.70%	14.20%	20.70%	5.40%	11.10%	62.10%
	Total	15.70%	24.50%	30.70%	13.80%	15.30%	100.00%

16.4.2. Chances for Promotions

Stagnation in the career destroys the feelings to work hard and struggle in the decision-making process. At the same time, excessive and assured promotions equally destroy the innovations and creativity from the decision-making process. 57.7% of the All India Services Officers are not satisfied with the present chances of promotions. Among All India Services, only 54.9% of the Indian Administrative Service officers are satisfied with the present chances of the promotions. 68.9% of the Indian Forest Service officers and 54.9% of the Indian Police Service officers are not satisfied with the present chances of promotions. Among All India Services, the Indian Forest Service officers are the least satisfied with the promotion avenues available for them. This may be due to widespread stagnation across the cadres all over in India. The strength of the relationship with the decision-making process represented by Spearman correlation and Pearson's correlation with the value of 0.2 at a level of significance 0.001, is highly significant.

Exhibit Number 16.5: Chi-Square: Are Present Chances of Promotion Sufficient versus 'I can Largely Determine what Matters me in Department'

Pearson Chi-Square	11.839	4	0.019
Likelihood Ratio	15.94	4	0.003
Linear-by-Linear Association	2.921	1	0.087
N of Valid Cases	254		

Statistical analysis for Chi-square at Exhibit 16.5 with a significance value of 0.019 shows good relation of two variables namely are present chances of promotion sufficient to AISO and variable of locus of control 'I can largely determine what matters me in department' with which service amenable to political pressure. Data analysis results placed at Exhibit 16.6 for three services regarding 'chances of promotion in the AIS are sufficient' relation with the locus of control variable 'AISO can largely determine what matters in the department' show that 43.30% of the AISO said 'yes' to this variable and (31.1 + 31.1) 62.20% of the AISO in locus variable 'generally feel' plus 'strongly felt' this way category.

Exhibit Number 16.6: Are Present Chances of Promotion Sufficient versus 'I can Largely Determine what Matters me in Department'

Name of Service	Answer	I can Largely Determine what Matters me in Department					Total
		Hardly feel this way	Slightly feel this way	Somewhat feel this way	Generally feel this way	Strongly feel this way	
IAS	'Yes'	1.70%	0.00%	12.80%	12.80%	11.10%	38.50%
	'No'	4.30%	3.40%	9.40%	23.90%	20.50%	61.50%
	Total	6.00%	3.40%	22.20%	36.80%	31.60%	100.00%
IPS	'Yes'	2.60%	0.00%	3.90%	17.10%	21.10%	44.70%
	'No'	7.90%	2.60%	15.80%	15.80%	13.20%	55.30%
	Total	10.50%	2.60%	19.70%	32.90%	34.20%	100.00%
IFS	'Yes'	4.90%	0.00%	23.00%	8.20%	14.80%	50.80%
	'No'	6.60%	8.20%	13.10%	9.80%	11.50%	49.20%
	Total	11.50%	8.20%	36.10%	18.00%	26.20%	100.00%
AIS Total	'Yes'	2.80%	0.00%	12.60%	13.00%	15.00%	43.30%
	'No'	5.90%	4.30%	12.20%	18.10%	16.10%	56.70%
	Total	8.70%	4.30%	24.80%	31.10%	31.10%	100.00%

16.4.3. Nature of Work

The All India Services Officers' daily work is brimming with challenges and risks. These inbuilt unreliable and different types of challenges in work stimulate the All India Services Officers to work with changing pressure in a decision at work. The All India Services Officers have learned to enjoy frequently job changing variations and mobility in their services. This provides All India Services Officers marvelous exposure to different problems prevalent in diverse cultural and geographical variations. Changing work conditions reduces the boredom and monotony of work. The All India Services Officers have to handle diversifying activities of employees, the public, or stakeholders. The All India Services Officers' nature of work cannot be confined to any working hours, they work 24 hours, so continuous rescheduling of work instills in them the flexibility to adapt to new changes and challenges. Every posting provide them something new and different, so they gain rich experience in due course of a career. "Though India is one of the worst governed countries in the world, cracking at its scams in just about every area, from social welfare, food distribution, to environment and riddled with rampant shameless corruption, it is clear that the Indian media does not take the issue of governance seriously," Anil Agarwal, Down to Earth, 11.6.2015. The working environment of Indian bureaucracy is observed to be riddled with corruption and inefficiency by some people.

Exhibit Number 16.7: Chi-Square: Nature of Work Done by the AISO is Satisfying versus 'the Course of my Career Largely Depends upon me'

	Value	df	Asymp. Sig. (2-sided)
Pearson Chi-Square	9.851	4	0.043
Likelihood Ratio	10.06	4	0.039
Linear-by-Linear Association	7.263	1	0.007
N of Valid Cases	262		

52.9% of the All India Services Officers think that the nature of work done by them is 'satisfying'. Among the three services with the majority of them 'feel satisfied' with work done by them. Services wise, 56.3% of the Indian Administrative Service officers, 52.2% of the Indian Police Service officers, and 51% of the Indian Forest Service officers 'feel satisfied' with present work done by them. This variable shows a good correlation with the decision-making process. Analyses results indicate –0.32 values for Pearson's correlation and –0.33 value of Spearman correlation, both with the level of significance at 0.000, are highly significant.

Exhibit Number 16.8: Nature of Work Done by the AISO is Satisfying versus 'the Course of my Career Largely Depends upon me'

Nature of Work Done by the AISO is Satisfying	The Course of My Career Largely Depends upon Me					Total
	Hardly feel this way	Slightly feel this way	Somewhat feel this way	Generally feel this way	Strongly feel this way	
'Yes'	0.40%	4.60%	10.30%	18.30%	18.70%	52.30%
'No'	1.50%	8.40%	8.40%	18.30%	11.10%	47.70%
AIS total	1.90%	13.00%	18.70%	36.60%	29.80%	100.00%

Chi-square results at Exhibit 16.7 for variable 'nature of work done by the All India Services Officer is satisfying' relationship with the locus of control variable 'the course of my career largely depends upon me' show good association with a significance value of 0.043. 'Nature of work done by the AISO is satisfying', 52.30% officers responded in 'yes' and 47.70% officers 'disagreed' with this. Relationship results of locus of control show that 'the course of the AISO career largely depends on them' with 36.60% score of 'generally feel that way' and 29.80% of the AISO 'strongly feel this way' intensity.

16.4.4. Interpersonal Relations

Interpersonal relationships with juniors, seniors, and colleagues stimulate the workplace environment and better relations motivate them to assert in the decision-making process. "Managerial beliefs are correlated with the process of organizational adaptation of new environmental constraints", P. Singh et al. (1979). Interpersonal relations among the All India Services Officers attract each other and motivate them to stay together in their respective service. The All India Services Officer and politicians' relations remain a topic for discussion and many raise figures on their relationships. "Take any minister who gets appointed to head a ministry. Since most of our ministers are clueless about what needs to be done with the department under their charge, they listen carefully to their guardian officials and within a few months, you can see a dramatic change in them. Even the most open-minded critic becomes a fervent defender of past and present government policies. There is no question of change, no question even of keeping the promises, however banal; they made before taking over the chair. Change is now mired in complex procedures and there is always a problem for every solution. The result is almost always the same—confronted with the articulate and intelligent class of our generalist super managers our clueless politicians soon become the biggest agents of the *status quo*. There is, therefore, no scope for imagination and innovation left in the governance of the country," Anil Agarwal, Down to Earth, 11.6.2015.

Our results have provided marginal replies with 50.2% of the All India Services Officers are 'satisfied' with the present situations of relationships. 52.9% of the Indian Administrative Service officers and 50.5% of the Indian Police Service officers are 'not satisfied' with the present interpersonal relations. However, 55.2% of the Indian Forest Service officers 'feel satisfied' with the present state of the interpersonal relationship web.

Results placed at Exhibit 16.9 for Chi-square analyses show good association with a significance value of 0.034 of two variables present interpersonal relation with juniors/seniors/colleagues are sufficient with the locus of control variable 'seniors person's preference determines who would be rewarded in the department'. Data analysis results placed at Exhibit 16.10 regarding present 'interpersonal relation with juniors/seniors/colleagues are sufficient' show that 50.20% of the AISO marked 'yes' and its correlation with the locus of the control variable that 'seniors person's preference determines who would be rewarded in the department' show that 37.50% of the AISO 'generally feel this way' and 14.70% 'strongly felt this way' intensity score.

Exhibit Number 16.9: Chi-Square—Present Interpersonal Relation with Juniors/Seniors/Colleagues are Sufficient versus 'Seniors Person's Preference Determines who would be Rewarded in the Department'

	Value	df	Asymp. Sig. (2-sided)
Pearson Chi-square	10.381	4	0.034
Likelihood Ratio	10.689	4	0.03
Linear-by-Linear Association	2.739	1	0.098

Exhibit Number 16.10: Present Interpersonal Relation with Juniors/Seniors/Colleagues are Sufficient versus 'Seniors Person's Preference Determines who would be Rewarded in the Department'

Present Intrepresonal Relation with Juniors/Seniors/ Colleagues are Sufficient	Seniors Person's Preference Determines who would be Rewarded in the Department					Total
	Hardly feel this way	Slightly feel this way	Somewhat feel this way	Generally feel this way	Strongly feel this way	
'Yes'	3.20%	6.40%	17.10%	17.90%	5.60%	50.20%
'No'	0.80%	9.20%	11.20%	19.50%	9.20%	49.80%
% AIS Total	4.00%	15.50%	28.30%	37.50%	14.70%	100.00%

16.4.5. Rules of Work

The All India Services Officers have to work in diverse working conditions and rules for work and conduct are ever-changing. Flexibility in rules and situational interpretation of rules and decisions pose the greatest challenge in the decision-making process. In our research, we have tried to study this aspect and 69.7% of the All India Services Officers feel 'satisfied' with the present work and conduct in the office. 76.7% of the Indian Police Service officers, 76.4% of the Indian Administrative Service officers, and 58.8% of the Indian Forest Service officers feel 'satisfied' with the rules of work and conduct in office. Indian Forest Service officers are least satisfied with prevalent rules of work and conduct.

Exhibit Number 16.11: Chi-Square—Rules of Work and Conduct are Satisfactory in the Office versus 'Successful Completion of Assignments is Mainly due to my Detailed Planning and Hardwork'

	Value	df	Asymp. Sig. (2-sided)
Pearson Chi-Square	8.359	3	0.039
Likelihood Ratio	8.585	3	0.035
Linear-by-Linear Association	4.486	1	0.034
N of Valid Cases	257		

Exhibit Number 16.12: Rules of Work and Conduct are Satisfactory in the Office versus 'Successful Completion of Assignments is Mainly due to my Detailed Planning and Hardwork'

Rules of Work and Conduct are Satisfactory in the Office	Successful Completion of Assignments is Mainly due to my Detailed Planning and Hardwork				Total
	Hardly feel this way	Somewhat feel this way	Generally feel this way	Strongly feel this way	
'Yes'	0.00%	13.20%	21.80%	35.00%	70.00%
'No'	1.20%	7.00%	9.30%	12.50%	30.00%
% of total AIS	1.20%	20.20%	31.10%	47.50%	100.00%

Results for Chi-square placed at Exhibit 16.11 for variable rules of work and conduct are satisfactory in the office relation with the locus of control variable 'successful completion of assignments is mainly due to my detailed planning and hard work' show good association and relation with a significance value of 0.039. Statistical analysis results shown at Exhibit 16.12 towards the correlation of the AISO rules of work and conduct are satisfactory in the office 70% of the AISO said 'yes' and 30% 'disagreed' with keeping in view the relationship with the locus of control that 'successful completion of assignments is mainly due to my detailed planning and hard work. Results show that the 47.50% 'strongly feel this way' category. It can be inferred that the majority of the AISO are satisfied with the working environment in the office or system.

16.4.6. Workplace

Workplace setting and working environment have a great impact on the decision-making process. The All India Services Officers' workplace setting and working environment are highly variable and invariably influence the decision. Data analysis results show that 54% of the All India Services Officers have 'agreed' that they are satisfied with the workplace and working environment. 59.2% of the Indian Administrative Service officers and 62% of the Indian Police Service officers are 'feeling satisfied' with the environment and workplace ambiance. But 57% of the Indian Forest Service officers are 'not satisfied' with the working environment and workplace setting. These results indicate that only the Indian Forest Service officers are not feeling satisfied and not get thrilled in the present office setting, this may due to the fact that their offices are located in far-flung areas and most remote locations. There is a strong need to improve their environment and workplace for improvement in the decision-making process.

Exhibit Number 16.13: Chi-Square—Workplace and Working Environment is Conducive versus 'my Experience is that most Things in Department are Beyond one's Control'

	Value	df	Asymp. Sig. (2-sided)
Pearson Chi-Square	10.788	4	0.029
Likelihood Ratio	10.978	4	0.027
Linear-by-Linear Association	0.561	1	0.454
N of Valid Cases	215		

Workplace and working environment is conducive relation with the variable of locus 'my experience is that most things in the department are beyond one's control' in Chi-square (Exhibit 16.13) show significance value of 0.029 as a good association of variables and good correlation of two variables. Statistical analysis results placed in Exhibit 16.14 show a relationship of the 49.80% of the 'AISO workplace and working environment is conducive' correlation with the locus of the control variable that 'individual AISO experience that most things in the department are beyond one's control' score is distributed across columns, even we total the 'somehow feel this way' to 'strongly feel this way' it comes 54.40%, it indicates that things are beyond the control of the AISO in the decision-making process. This may be due to prevalent political pressure in the system.

Exhibit Number 16.14: Workplace and Working Environment is Conducive versus 'my Experience is that most Things in Department are Beyond one's Control'

Workplace and Working Environment is Conducive	My Experience is that Most Things in Department are Beyond One's Control					Total
	Hardly feel this way	Slightly feel this way	Somewhat feel this way	Generally feel this way	Strongly feel this way	
'Yes'	7.90%	14.90%	8.80%	17.20%	0.90%	49.80%
'No'	10.20%	12.60%	14.90%	9.80%	2.80%	50.20%
% AIS Total	18.10%	27.40%	23.70%	27.00%	3.70%	100.00%

16.4.7. Conformity to Orders

The All India Services Officers have to work under high uncertainty and mostly verbal orders are given for most of the decisions. Political pressure in the decision-making process is mostly an outcome of verbal orders; even the senior officers pass on most of the illegal orders verbally. If the All India Services Officers do not comply with the verbal instructions, they land in serious trouble. In case they implement verbal orders, they land in serious trouble for violation of procedures. The tradition of issuing verbal orders is highest among the Indian Administrative Service officers and is the creation and gift by them to the entire bureaucratic system. Politicians do not know the rules and politicians are always amenable to reasoning, but it is the Indian Administrative Service officers, who are most arrogant in case of passing illegal verbal orders.

52% of the All India Services Officers like to get confirmation of verbal orders in writings; this high percentage is due to the high score of the Indian Forest Service officers in this item. 63.5% of the Indian Administrative Service officers and 60.4% of the Indian Police Service officers do not want confirmation for verbal orders issued by another end. But 74.8% of the Indian Forest Service officers want that the superior officer or politicians must confirm any verbal order in writing. This indicates that the Indian Forest Service officers have a low reliance on their seniors or the top brasses or another way there are getting maximum verbal orders which are against rules and law. Prevalent high powerlessness among the Indian Forest Service officers and higher concern for rules and law also dominate on them for issuing written instructions. The strength of this item correlation with the decision-making process is indicated by Pearson's correlation value of 0.15 with a level of significance at 0.02 and Spearman correlation value of 0.15 with a level of significance 0.01.

Exhibit Number 16.15: Chi-square—While Taking any Decision Written Instruction be Taken versus 'If my Seniors do not like me, I Probably would not Succeed in this Department'

	Value	df	Asymp. Sig. (2-sided)
Pearson Chi-Square	11.924	4	0.018
Likelihood Ratio	12.181	4	0.016
Linear-by-Linear Association	9.318	1	0.002
N of Valid Cases	271		

The AISO feeling that while taking any decision written instruction to be taken and its relation with the locus variable that 'if my seniors do not like me, I probably would not succeed in this department' in Chi-square show good association with 0.018 (Exhibit 16.15) significance level and also show good correlation values. Statistical analysis results placed at the Exhibit 16.16 show correlation of the AISO workplace environment that 'while taking any decision written instruction to be taken from concerned authority', 52.80% gave 'yes' answer and its relation with the locus of the control variable that 'if my seniors do not like me, I probably would not succeed in this department' show majority of the AISO 'disagreed' with this, 59.40% giving it 'hardly feel this way' with 'slightly feel this way'. This indicates self-confidence of the AISO is high that they take decisions independent of their seniors.

Exhibit Number 16.16: While Taking any Decision Written Instruction be Taken versus 'If my Seniors do not like me, I Probably would not Succeed in this Department'

While Taking any Decision Written Instruction be Taken	If my Seniors do not like me, I Probably would not Succeed in this Department					Total
	Hardly feel this way	Slightly feel this way	Somewhat feel this way	Generally feel this way	Strongly feel this way	
'Yes'	14.80%	11.80%	17.00%	6.60%	2.60%	52.80%
'No'	19.90%	12.90%	8.90%	4.80%	0.70%	47.20%
% AIS Total	34.70%	24.70%	25.80%	11.40%	3.30%	100.00%

ANNEXURE 16.A: QUESTIONNAIRE FOR WORKPLACE ENVIRONMENT

Kindly, mark 'yes', if you agree with the statement and mark 'no' if you do not agree with it

(201)	Is the present salary sufficient?	(1) Yes (2) No
(202)	Are present chances of promotion sufficient?	(1) Yes (2) No
(203)	Nature of work done by the AISO is satisfying	(1) Yes (2) No
(204)	Present interpersonal relation with juniors/seniors/colleagues are sufficient	(1) Yes (2) No
(205)	Rules of work and conduct are satisfactory in the office	(1) Yes (2) No
(206)	Workplace and working environment is conducive	(1) Yes (2) No
(207)	While taking any decision written instruction by taken	(1) Yes (2) No

The knower, knowledge, and object of knowledge—these three motivate actions. Even so, the doer, the organs, and activity—these are three ingredients of action. *The Bhagavad Gita* 18.18

The world will not be destroyed by those who do evil, but by those who watch them without doing anything.—Albert Einstein

Part–Five
Future Strategy for Managing Bureaucracy in India

What people fail to appreciate is that the currency of corruption in elective office is, not money, but votes.—James L. Buckley

Unit 17

Future Strategy for Managing Bureaucracy in India

The truth about action (*karma*) must be known and the truth of inaction also must be known; even so, the truth about prohibited action (bad action or *vikrama*) must be known. Mysterious are ways of action. *The Bhagavad Gita* 4.17.

The world will not be destroyed by those who do evil, but by those who watch them without doing anything.—Albert Einstein

There is no more dangerous menace to civilization than a government of incompetent, corrupt, or vile men.—Ludwig von Mises

- *Review, Views, and Implications of Present System*
- *Research Observations and Propositions*
- *Future Strategy for Managing Bureaucratic Decisions*
- *Restructuring of Bureaucracy & All India Services*
- *Recruitment Process (one nation one exam)*
- *Bureaucracy Training*
- *Career Progression and Seniority*
- *Pay Scales and Hierarchical Levels*
- *Rules, Regulations, and Procedures*
- *Improvement in Individual Parameters*

In this unit, the present bureaucratic system review has been presented. Future changes and the need for changes in different areas has been suggested. Based on research observation new propositions have been proposed for restructuring the entire bureaucratic system. A new system of recruitment, reorganization of the All India Service, and the need for new rules for promotion and career progression with behaviour modification have been proposed.

समानो मन्त्रः समितिः समानी समानं मनः सह चित्तमेषाम।
समानं मन्त्रमभि मन्त्रये वः समानेन वोहविषा जुहोमि।।

(ऋग्वेद 10.191.3)

समानी व आकूतिः समाना हृदयानि वः।
समानमस्तु वोमनो यथा वः सुसहासति।।

(ऋग्वेद 10.191.4)

"Assemble, speak together; let your minds be all of one accord,
As ancient gods unanimous and sit down to their appointed share.
The place is common, common the assembly, common the mind, so be your thoughts united.
A common purpose do I lay before you, and worship with your general oblation.
One and same be your resolve and be your minds of one accord.
United be the thoughts of all that all may happily agree."

[Rig Veda X. 191.3 and 4]

17.1. Review, Views, and Implications of Present System

The Vedic literature mentions that *Bharatavarsh* was administrated through the system of (Council) *Samitis*[1] (and *Sabha*[1]) through management council. They were answerable for every kind of commissions and omissions in their jurisdiction. Such a council of eminent persons managed the entire public administration during that period. Council members had to carry out their routine work to earn their livelihood as ordinary citizens and at the same time chairing the meetings of the council as and when required. The decision of the majority used to prevail in the *samiti*[1], *sabha*[1], and *Mantri Parishad* during that early period. These decision-making bodies had powers to overrule the chairperson. Everyone was conscious of truth and justice in the decision. Management of affairs in the society was contractual in those Contract States, complete your assigned job, deliver a decision, and go back to your original profession. Such a decision process was in partnership with independent and neutral organizations and each decision was issue-based. Issues under discussions were thoroughly dealt with at length and hair's breadth. In case council member standards were not up to expectations, they were liable to be changed. Instances had been quoted where decisions were also taken on a piecemeal basis. In the decision-making process, an intermediate layer of governance comprised of ad-hoc bodies, which had no scope for partiality.

During the Medieval period, some sort of deficiencies crept in due to emphasis on the individual (emperor), and later on, the colonial rulers started their own system of administration through Convented Servants to perpetuate their selfish interests. The civil administration, policing, and maintenance of village resources had been sustained through centuries and centuries together by the village committee/councils until imperialists occupied the throne of the land. Community-oriented administration was the time-tested solution and sustainable to perpetuity. Imperialistic All India Services were created to discipline and change the public opinion mindset. Let All India Services

1. *Samiti* defined as Assembly of *Rastra* (national) whole community or people and *Sabha* as association of Ruling folk or advisory body to rule. There are variations of views regarding this.

Officers change and amend themselves and their mindset first. The All India Services Officers have injured the competencies of local people. Government law and policy for governance is framed in such a way that masses look towards bureaucrats or politicians, and ultimately become dependent on them. Law of dependency ensures continuity of weakness among the subjects, week people will always depend upon others or power holders, ultimately destroy the sense of nationalism.

These highly ego-centered powerful All India Services elites certainly do not match with the Gandhian ideology of equality. "Roughly three million colonial officials who were working for British at the time of independence had been asked to stay at their posts", D.C. Potter. Entire colonial structure and colonial culture from lowest level to highest remained intact in India. Colonial administrative mechanism of self-maximization continued to grow with every new entrant in the government services and as a result of this public continued to suffer. Sufferance and corruption multiplied at all levels unhindered and unbridled. Now after no work is expected to be done without money or power intervention. New Indian bureaucracy reassured capitalists, decisions have been continuously in favor of businesspersons, and political leadership has been the approver of that.

At the time of independence, it was a compulsion of the time and necessity to use known inherited instrument to control the political uncertainty, instead of experimenting with a new system or experimenting with uncertainties. That could have been the compulsion that Sardar Vallabhbhai Patel throws himself fully and asserted tireless efforts to save the Indian Administrative Service officers and Indian Police Service officers at the time of debate in the Constituent Assembly. "If you are to be held responsible for law and order, you simply must have the power to enforce your authority. The fact that you have this power and are prepared to use it will mean that it will seldom be used. If you don't have the power, this will quickly become known and you may expect widespread disorders with which you will be enabled to cope."[2] The All India Services Officers are no exception, "after all, public bureaucracies everywhere are notoriously slow to change, if left to their own devices", D.C. Potter (1986).

"Jawaharlal Nehru was 'quite sure' in 1934 that 'no new order can be built in India so long as the spirit of Indian Civil Service pervades our administration and our public services'. It is therefore 'essential that the ICS and similar services must disappear completely", D.C. Potter. When the British left India, a journalist remarked, that we like to 'build a new India, a more egalitarian society, through the agency of those who had been the trained servants of imperialism'. In 1964, Prime Minister of India, Jawaharlal Nehru, considered his greatest failure that, "I could not change the administration, it is still a colonial administration, was one of main causes of India's inability to solve the problem of poverty."[3]

The All India Services Officers continuously managed political support to survive in the continual opposition from other services; in the process, Indian Administrative Service officers excluded the others. The Indian Administrative Service officers took the opportunity to develop nexus with politicians to retain its exclusive top position in administration at central, state, and district levels. In spite of opposition from other services and numerous periodic attempts made through administrative reforms, cultivation of a broad political support structure to introduce

2. 15.02.1946, as in Haig Paper as cited by D.C. Potter.
3. *The Guardian*, 10.4.1978, London.

radical administrative reforms, any move to undermine the Indian Administrative Service was shown the dustbin.

Reforms suggested by different Reforms Committees were implemented halfway. Tottenham Report on the Reorganization of Central Government of 1946 supported a sleek and streamlined secretariat. He was against the post of deputy secretary and recommended waiving the tenure system of staffing after fifteen- or twenty-years' service, N. Gopalaswami Ayyangar (a civil servant) "Report on Reorganization of the Government Machinery", recommended for grouping of central governmental ministries into four bureaus: Bureau of Natural Resources & Agriculture, Bureau of Industry & Commerce, Bureau of Transport & Communications and Bureau of Labor & Social Services.

A.D. Gorwala, a retired civil servant submitted two reports in 1950—Report on Public Administration and Report on the Efficient Conduct of State Enterprises. Paul H. Appleby an American expert on public administration submitted a report in 1953 and 1956. Asoka Chanda submitted his report in 1954, entitled "Notes on Changes Necessary in the System of Budgetary and Financial Control and in Other Matters to Eliminate Delays in Execution of Projects". During 1960, the Planning Commission asked V.T. Krishnamachari to study the questions relating to administrative personnel at different levels in the states, and the issues arising from the introduction of democratic institutions at the district and block levels, and suggestions for improvements. The report was submitted in 1962.

The government appointed a high-power Administrative Reform Commission (ARC) in 1966, with Morarji Desai as its chairman. Under the leadership of late Prime Minister Rajiv Gandhi, the government relied heavily on in-service training to strengthen the administrative capabilities of its public functionaries. 'Administrative Reform through Training' became a new concept, L.K. Jha Economic-Administrative Reforms Commission for the economy. The most notable contribution of this commission's report was the recommendation to shift the governmental emphasis from regulation to development. The Action Plan for Effective and Responsive Administration at the Central and a State level was discussed in the conference of Chief Ministers held in May 1997 under the Chairmanship of the then Prime Minister. The Government of India constituted a Core Group to evaluate the steps on administration Reforms in November 2001. A large number of committees and commission reports were related to improvement in the existing administrative system. New experimentation of inducting Joint Secretary level persons from the public on some identified posts carried out during NDA regime 2014 to 2019, which invited a lot of criticism from experts that this experiment may lead to corporate people encroaching on civil servant merit and intellect.

The principle of **equity and equality** of all citizens have been undermined in a democratic set up by these elites in collusion with political support. Political leaders remain bogged down in the districts and the secretariat attempting to find solutions for difficulties faced by their public and themselves. Emergent political situations compelled politicians to accept colonial bureaucratic structure unwillingly and bureaucrats continued to extend them selective help and information, so that, they continue to live in such a mental frame, where they give high priority to Indian Administrative Service officers only.

The feelings of one Chief Minister were "You may think you are doing your duty, but if I think you are going beyond it, remember I am the judge" (L.M. Bhatia, 1974). All India Services

Officers slowly learned how to survive under adverse political situations and manage politicians in their own direction. "Politics influenced the administration and administrator learned to be sensitive to politics", Mangat Rai, 1976. The politician was compelled to realize that without the Indian Administrative Service officer's support it is difficult to rule. Even politicians felt surrogated under the excessive hegemony of the Indian Administrative Service officers. One minister resigned on 09.11.1966 protesting that his secretary had been insubordinate and uncooperative, C.P. Bhambri, 1971. Even another minister protested that IAS doesn't allow them to choose their advisor from an expert, Indian Administrative Service officers force us to choose from ranks of Indian Administrative Service officers only, Subramaniam, 1966.

"If we have not modernized the administration, if we have to start using modern tools and techniques, if we haven't had a sufficiently enquiring mind, if we haven't be sufficiently critical and analytical, if we have taken far too many things for granted, and if we have never tried to calculate the cost of various operations and think of doing things more economically or more speedily, let's be honest, we have to blame ourselves, not ministers, not politicians, not legislators. To my mind, this preoccupation with political and comparative neglect of professional problems of administration has been greatest single failure of the civil services in independent India", L.P. Singh, 1970.

Late Jagjivan Ram, in his presidential address to the Bombay session of All India Congress Committee, 1969, declared that 'the so-called neutral administrative machinery is a hindrance, not a help...and is hardly relevant to Indian conditions'. Later Congress party agreed that "the present bureaucracy under the orthodox and conservative leadership of the ICS with upper-class prejudices can hardly be expected to meet the requirement of social and economic change along socialist lines. The creation of an administrative cadre committed to national objectives and responsive to our social needs is an urgent necessity," S.P. Aiyar, 1971 and D.C. Potter, 1986.

"Shah Commission of Inquiry Report after Emergency suggested that most Indian Administrative Service officers in secretariats and districts, who were responsible for advising on, and implementing MISA, accepted orders they believed to be improper and politically motivated. "Even the cream of the talent of the country in the administrative field often collapse at the slightest pressure," Shah Commission Interim Report, 1978. It further observed that "IAS officers engaged in forging of records, fabrication of ground of detention, ante-dating of detention orders, and callous disregarded of the rights of the detainees as regards revocation, parole, etc."

H.K. Paranjape (1966) charged that ICS/IAS represent casteism to the extent that it has created a caste/class within government services. Perhaps there is "no other single group of civil servants in the world holding such an in-creditable array of administrative posts. Young IAS direct recruits were moving all over the places after only a few years in service," D.C. Potter. In a case father has been very intelligent, became a doctor/engineer, if his son happens to be less intelligent and become an IAS, and posted in the same district, the IAS son will be commanding over his father with full impunity and unbridled powers oozing from arrogance. This is the imperial system, where chance success overrules the proved competence and intelligence. In Haryana, it was whispered that a person with a criminal background, with manipulated doubtful qualifications with money power stage-managed entry into provincial service. Such persons in the bureaucratic system will also occupy the chair of power (DC/DM), at that time, what they can deliver except arrogance and absolute corruption. But institutions provide them unlimited powers to exploit the system to the advantage of elite exploiters. Even Indian Administrative Service officers themselves agree that "it is neither desirable nor easy for [the IAS] to fit from one kind of job to another without being specialized in any."[4]

In the Federal structure of the Union of India, many people raise the question of how to exercise responsibilities without the All India Services. "Such an all-India administrative arrangement, appropriate for a colonial regime, was hardly likely to delight political leaders in the state governments. In effect, what the central government was doing to recruit a group of administrators and send them into the states to hold the key administrative posts there. State Ministers, in consequence, were severely restricted in their choice of whom they could appoint to be responsible for the implementation of their policies. When, for example, a new Chief Minister took office and found that he could not work well with the existing Chief Secretary, his range of choices for a successor was limited to only a few individuals—the men who happened at that time to be at the very top of the IAS cadre in that state. If he liked none of these individuals, he was struck", D.C. Potter, 1986.

"We must strive to find out administrators processing the following values to ensure ethical governance; competence, missionary zeal, the capacity to motivate other people, the capacity to communicate with others, the ability to get along with colleagues and the people, cultural adaptability, and manage, the capacity to inspire confidence, patience, and dignity in others. Besides, they must have faith in the ideal of their work, be willing to accept hardships. Their ambition and enthusiasm should not be dampened by local conditions, which may not provide them with the necessary facilities. Unfortunately, the sense of dedication has been the crassest causality of the prevailing atmosphere of cynicism bred by increasing propensity towards expediency," S.L. Goel, 2013.

The higher the choice more will be merit and intelligence. There should be higher and wider options and such posts are given based on competence not on a particular service. This very position of exclusiveness makes bureaucrats more important than politicians. The All India Services Officers impress upon other services that politicians come and go; ultimate power is with them only. Most of the politicians are being fooled by indulging them in rules and procedures, in case a politician is intelligent, these bureaucrats slowly poison the ears of Prime Minister/Chief Minister to create distance from the head of power and any such assertive Minister find his way out of power. Then the Indian Administrative Service officers celebrate such ouster by impressing on incoming Minister to toe-in with them and their desires. "It did not help that ICS/IAS officers were frequently perceived by politicians as confident and rather arrogant agents from Delhi." In A.N. Jha (ICS, UP) words, "Tended to think out problems on their own on an all-India scale and have tended to assume that deviations from their way of thinking are acts of sacrilege". He further elaborated, "the bureaucracy in India is united in doing wrong, and no one can actually bring a successful action against an IAS officer". It is like a dictatorship.[5]

"It has been complained that bureaucrats are rigid, delay things, are reluctant to delegate authority, develop sycophancy towards superiors, insist on prestige and status symbols, and have tendency to politicization. All these maladies can be overcome if the ministers exhort their subordinates in right directions, effectively control them, segregate them from old-timers, and

4. LBSNAA, Conference, 21-23, Sept. 1982.
5. As cited by D.C. Potter, 1986.

accordingly arrange their training. The fearless, honest, and hardworking officers be identified and suitably rewarded. They should discourage the subordinates from seeking their support, favor, and blessings through their kith and kin. Political leaders should keep the undisciplined employees at a distance", Basudev Panda, 1978.

In the present system of bureaucracy, these powerful power elites start their post-retirement rehabilitation towards the end of their career, and that needs to be curtailed or stopped. "The Election Commission, in the national interest, had recommended the government in 2012 to amend the service rules and set a cooling-off period before civil servants can join a political party and contest polls. This was with an object to prevent those with political ambition from favoring a particular party in their final years of service. But the Department of Personnel and Training was of the view that debarring ex-bureaucrats from joining electoral politics immediately upon exit from service may violate the right to equality, enshrined in Article 14 of the Constitution," K.V. Chandra Mouli, *The Deccan Herald*, March 22, 2019.

17.2. Research Observations and Propositions

In the present research, we have studied 262 variables, structuring around different questionnaires. Research observations and propositions are presented considering one instrument as one unit, which has been succinctly presented in the following paragraphs.

INDIVIDUAL VARIABLES (PART II)

17.2.1. Demographic Characters (Unit 3)

Results analyses of demographic individual variables of our study indicate that Indian Administrative Service officers are comparatively more amenable to political pressure acceptance than other services, equitable distribution of power may help in the reduction of this pressure. The All India Services Officers promoted from feeder services are more amenable to political pressure acceptance than directly recruited officers, this indicates that there is a need to change induction of feeder services officers to the All India Services. Introduction of written examination followed by interview through UPSC with a small weightage to the length of service may help in solving this issue. In bureaucratic system, officers occupying top positions are more amenable to political pressure acceptance in the decision-making process than young junior officers. In the length of service category, officers with more than 24 years of service are the highest amenable to political pressure acceptance, and officers with less than five years' service are the least amenable to political pressure acceptance. This also indicates that there is a strong need to decentralize power and more powers may be given to lower and middle-level bureaucracy. Excessive senior-centric powers need to be changed to a wide base at lower and middle levels.

Regional background of the All India Services Officers from southern India showed more amenability towards political pressure acceptance in the decision-making process and officers from western India showed the least amenability. This may be related to the cultural background of different regions and behavioural modification during training can help to address this issue. The All India Services Officers allocated to outside cadre showed more amenability to political pressure acceptance than officers in home state cadre, tenure postings, and security mechanism for transfer can help to improve the system. Community background and economic background analyses show differential amenability to political pressure acceptance in the decision and the All India Services Officers feel that officers from the upper-middle class and rich economic background are more amenable to political pressure acceptance. Union of India and States have to intensify and restructure their efforts to remove socio-economic inequalities during the selection process. Social structural layering has to be removed from our social system. The syllabus for the UPSC competition examination may be designed in such a way that more and more persons from suppressed rural and poor backgrounds can compete successfully for selection.

The All India Services Officers with post-graduation/Bachelor of Arts qualifications showed maximum amenability to political pressure acceptance and officers with Ph.D. qualifications showed least. Results indicate that professional qualifications perhaps make officers more confident and higher confidence to compete; so lesser immorality. The UPSC may think seriously about making postgraduate qualification essential for entry into the All India Service and group 'A' services. Behavioural training can help in confidence-building and psychological remolding of the AISO during training programs. Postgraduate qualification of parents and spouse influence individual All India Services Officers with higher intensity for political pressure acceptance than lesser qualified parents and spouse. An entrepreneur spouse makes individual All India Services Officers more amenable for political pressure acceptance than a serving spouse. In the early background of an individual officer, parents, spouse, and place of education after high school, on all these scores urban background officers are more amenable for political pressure acceptance in the decision-making process than the rural background. This may be related to the desires expectation level of individuals. The UPSC recruitment process may lay more emphasis on recruiting persons from a rural culture so that persons from rural and poor backgrounds can compete reasonably to join the AIS. In an attitude of members of the family, spouse influence, maximum individual All India Services Officers for political pressure acceptance and brother/sister are the least influencer. Specialized experts relate all these variables to officer background and behaviour modification training at regular intervals.

17.2.2. Locus of Control (Unit 4)

The All India Services Officers show internality to a large extent, but it shows a declining trend among the Indian Forest Service officers. The All India Services Officers have shown concern for the politicians and seniors. Research results indicate that their amenability to pressure in the decision is higher due to this locus of control. A high score for externality indicates dysfunctional dependence on seniors and politicians. This issue can be addressed by relaxing rules and regulation adherence and open and participatory performance review. There is a need to give more powers to junior officers. Our bureaucratic system needs more and more innovations at the district level. The AISO are effective performers and high self-confidence is a good indicator for bureaucracy, at the same time enhance the status and power orientation. The mean internality score of 38 indicates that the AISO is not realistic regarding the problem faced by them. Internality related to locus of control can be improved after assessing individual officers' needs and necessary training imparted for improvement of that. The Indian Administrative Service officers show higher externality than the other two services. In the score for the externality for the chance all, the services show comparable results and low externality for the chance or luck factor. Positive stimulator and motivation enhancers through behavioural training can address this. During the recruitment process also there is a need to assess the locus of control of the person to be recruited and based on that record during training behaviour modifications need to be incorporated.

17.2.3. Bureaucracy Motivation (Unit 5)

Many motivational factors operate on the AISO decision behavior and our research has observed covariance matrices of the dependable variable are equal across the groups of the AISO. Status, power, and influence variable showed the highest motivator, and prestige and reputation in society variable ranked as the second motivator. There is a strong need for incorporating changes and restructuring the bureaucratic system to reduce the status and power orientation. Variable less work, little responsibility, and no risk was ranked last, which showed that the AISO work with full responsibilities. High status and prestige consciousness since the origin of the AIS create distance from the ground realities and masses. There is a strong need for reorganization, restructuring the bureaucratic system, and reduction of power base orientation to make the AIS welfare-oriented towards equity and equality principles for the development of the nation. This also indicates a strong need for behavioural training for changing power motivator orientation. There is a need to enhance public orientation through training interventions.

17.2.4. Lifestyle Orientation (Unit 6)

The AISO lifestyle orientation showed a healthy trend and the AISO indicated their activities related to family and relatives as a first priority activity, recreational activities at the second rank, and religious activities, at last, research indicate the secular outlook of the AISO and family orientation. But low ranking is reading and writing variable and self-improvement variables is not a good indicator in their lifestyle orientation better workplace management such that some spare time is at the disposal of the AISO to pursue their interest, which will help them to improve and rejuvenate their professional skills. A sound mind in sound health, some regular doses of physical exercises and a daily yoga routine may help them. In lifestyle orientation, there is a need to streamline the entire system, so that bureaucrats can essentially spare some time reading and learning new technology to introduce innovation and improvement in the system. Regular upgradation of the knowledge base (online learning, exploration and updating of self) will certainly help in introducing creativity and new ideas.

GROUP VARIABLES (PART III)

17.2.5. Behavioural Orientation (Unit 7)

The AISO has ranked devotion to duty as 1st quality and honesty and integrity as 2nd most important behavioral quality for the AISO. This is a good indicator, but at the same time emphasis on other behavioural parameters needs urgent attention for the efficiency of the bureaucratic system. Professional competence needs to be improved by more exposure to training by their respective academies or elsewhere. Good mannerism, sympathetic and human nature, helping attitude and conduct and behaviour with others are the important variables, where the AISO have shown deficiencies and these behavioural aspects are very important and crucial for the public dealing decision process. Perhaps respective departmental working culture and power enjoyed by these super elites AISO alter their behaviour and there is an urgent need to reclaim and reform these variables of behaviour. Perhaps there is a need for exposure to self-introspection psychological instruments to these power elites for self-assessment and then behaviour modification process through training sessions. Modification in these variables will make the AISO more responsible towards the public and repetitive doses of training by behavioural trainer/psychologist will improve their decision delivery system. Perhaps behavioural training exposures at regular intervals will help in improving these variables, otherwise, excessive power orientation inculcate complacency, and that self-maximization hamper the decision process. This area needs maximum behavioural scientist expert attention for improving the system and officers both.

17.2.6. Risk Management (Unit 8)

Research results indicated that in case of any risky situations the All India Services Officers show the highest reliance on their immediate seniors and demonstrate high dependency behaviour in risk management. At the same time, the All India Services Officers showed the lowest extension behaviour and low concern for their subordinate staff in risk management. This situation demand solution for risk management, in our bureaucratic system, no one can remove risk from the decision-making process in the AISO working. The only solution is to impart training to enhance capability and capacity building in these officers to manage risk in the decision, at the same time need for bringing changes in the bureaucratic decision process by bringing transparency in the decision process. The probabilities of individual choices in the decision must be reduced to a bare minimum level, so that outcome of decisions must be predictable in given parameters. Rules, regulations, and procedures must be well defined to avoid risky decisions. The risk management system needs the introduction of a transparent online computer-aided decision-making system, where every single action point at every stage are enumerated (with accountability and responsibility well defined) and decision feedback is instantly available online for continuous rectification and improvement of the information-driven online system supported by artificial intelligence system.

17.2.7. Innovations in System (Unit 9)

Research data analysis indicated that the All India Services Officers before taking any decisions, they consult their immediate seniors and showed a lack of innovations in decisions. This locus of control behavior needs regular specialized training to modify such behavior. The All India Services Officers showed low concern for the innovations and scarcity of the new ideas or use of new methods to handle pressure in decision, rather old imperial culture is continuing and suppressing innovations in bureaucratic decision processes. The AISO extension motive indicates a very low ranking for innovations and the least concern for bringing out any changes in the decision process. Specialized behavior training measures can infuse new ideas to bring innovations to the decision-making process. A strong need is felt for bringing changes and restructuring our bureaucratic system to reduce dependence on the hierarchies. There is a strong need that the AISO use innovations in their decision by introducing an online system of feedback and restricting the entire system. In the present system, individual officers have not been left with any choices and time for incorporating innovations due to fear of failure or recoiling back of such an idea on the officer.

17.2.8. Conflicts Management (Unit 10)

Our analysis indicates that most of the All India Services Officers think that in due course of time conflicting issues will be resolved automatically, lack of will to solve the conflict in the decision due to pressure is not good for our decision delivery bureaucratic system. In case of difficult situations under pressure, the All India Services Officers adopt the approach of resignation in conflicting situations; running away from pressure is not healthy for the bureaucracy and that goes against disadvantaged people. The AISO resigning under pressure indicates that powerful and resourceful persons will usurp the public resources and the persons not having access to power will be deprived of public resources. The All India Services Officer's efforts to manage conflict in the decision-making process by resorting to mutually acceptable solutions with politicians generate more conflict in the bureaucratic resource crunch system. What motivates politicians towards continuity of such pressure on the bureaucrats. In due course of time, the less privileged people are bound to loosen faith in the system. The All India Services Officers have lost the initiatives, unable to confront pressure in the decision, and then they deliver tailor-made decisions under pressure according to politician's needs. Research results showed that the feeling of fighting out for the right things or merit in the decision has disappeared from the system. The public thinks that the All India Services Officers will try hard to implement merit-based correct and fair decisions. The All India Services Officers' highest preference for conflict management is that they allow a situation to be resolved automatically in due course of time. Lack of conflict management skills in the decision process is causing serious damage and inculcating stress and strain among the AISO. By changing rules and laws now the government must incorporate transparency in the decision-making process. The introduction of transparency and fixing up accountability at various levels will help in reducing the conflict in the decision. The politicians and the officer must be held responsible for their transparently defined areas and levels. To cope with conflict the AISO must be imparted training for how to manage unexpected conflict in the decision. Specialized training courses for conflict management techniques are essential for the AISO.

SYSTEM RELATED (PART IV)

17.2.9. Sources of Political Pressure (Unit 11)

In the present research study, the ten most important sources of political pressure (Annexure 11.A) have been studied. Political pressures from the Member Legislative Assembly/MLC and Centre/State Ministers have been raked as the highest intensity pressure exertion on the All India Services Officers in the decision-making process. Intensity measurements of political pressure indicate that different sources of pressure exert a different level of pressure on the decision with variable intensity. How to manage or reduce political pressure from the decision process is a complex problem and no way is visible in near sight to solve this. A commonly proposed approach can be introducing transparency in the bureaucratic decision process, where predictability of every decision-making process is based on given parameters and where there is no scope for personal bias of the AISO in decision-making. Well-defined decision stages and well-defined parameters required for any e-decision (Internet-based electronic decision) can help in reducing pressure from different sources. Transparency will reduce corruption and bias, but politicians and bureaucrats both will not like to introduce transparency, because that will make them redundant. Most of the decision process should be made online Internet-based to reduce interaction between bureaucrats and decision seekers (e-administration). Make every decision time based and notify the whole decision process in advance, chance factors or arbitrary powers must be reduced to zero. Let the public apply online every stage of file movement must be informed to the applicant and supply decision copy online. The present system of bureaucracy is full of uncertainties and bias; things with biased origins are bound to produce a biased outcome. We have to change, restructure and reorganize the whole bureaucratic system of India, after that only can reduce the political pressure from the decision.

17.2.10. Areas/Types of Political Pressure (Unit 12)

Research results for 15 pressure areas/types on 76 pressure points (Annexure 12.A) indicate that different sources of pressure exert pressure with variable intensity on different points/types in the decision process. The All India Services Officers get the high intensity of political pressure to get wet and plumb postings. The AISO likes to ensure continuity on plum posting on the basis of their pliability and they serve political goals and in turn, serve their own goals also. Research results clearly indicate that the All India Services Officers approach politicians on maximum occasions to get desired postings. It is very difficult to find solutions for this. There is an urgent need to restructure the whole bureaucratic system, remove the difference between various postings, powers enjoyed on wet postings need to be diluted and reduced, tenure for plumb postings must be reduced and the rule is changed that and same officers must not be provided any plum posting as the second tenure during the whole career. Plumb postings in ministries and locations need to be categorized and norms must be made for postings at such places. Fix tenure for posting and transfers with defining transparent rules and procedures for plumb posting and difficult postings. Bureaucratic norms need to be fixed that how not more than one tenure on plumb posting can be avoided and categorization of the category of different posts for different length of service. Similarly, one stint of difficult posting be defined and a similar procedure for deputation must be made transparent.

The All India Services Officers get very high political pressure for recruitment on basis of petty considerations and decide rewards for future benefits for their career growth. Reduce our whole recruitment procedure need to be restructured and marks for an interview to a bare minimum (2% of the written examination). Examination procedure, method, subjects, the system need to be changed, and online procedure must be devised. Psychosomatic and behavioural aspects (instruments) can be made part of the selection procedure. Recruitment procedure must be made transparent, time-bound, and merit-oriented and recruiting agencies must be made neutral and completion examination procedure and papers evaluation must be made open and transparent (maybe online) removing all chances of subjectivity.

The issues related to crime, politicians use government machinery to settle scores, and misuse of law in registration/cancellation of reports for the crime (FIR). The whole justice delivery system needs to be made transparent and time-bound. Reporting and inquiry of crime-related issues must be made transparent, online recording of statements, every stage of inquiry outcome made public by sharing information online and time-bound. Personal bias must remove by video recording of all statements. On this variable large-scale exploitation of the poor must be stopped. Variables related to crime, law/acts involve multiple agencies, difficult to solve this issue, but transparency, e-based procedure, and timely proper implementation can help to solve the problem.

Politicians exert political pressure rarely for the general welfare of public and social issues. Maximum political pressure is exerted to maximize individual gains. What can be solutions for these issues related and spread over the whole bureaucracy? Resource allocation, rewards, punishments, promotions, policy matters, developmental issues, demure in decision, rules, and regulations must be based on well-defined parameters, so that, everyone is aware who will get what and bureaucrats' options are left to a minimum in the decision. There is a need for developing computer-based software (with artificial intelligence) that can be used for this purpose towards the implementation of these variables. The system must be developed, where any violation or deviation from well-defined rules is detected automatically in the online information environment and known to the public and entire bureaucratic system.

The AISO carried out a ranking of priorities of different sources (Annexure 12.B) and intensity of political pressure they receive in the decision process. Center/State Ministers and MLA/MLC exert the highest intensity of pressure, but the AISO ranked their priority to accept different sources of political pressure differentially in the decision process. In some areas/types, the AISO considers pressure for the same area with a different level of acceptance. Research results for ranking of different sources of political pressure can help us to reduce the intensity of pressure by educating the pressure inducer and accepter at both ends. There is a need to remove subjectivity from the decision process. The politicians and bureaucrats both intervention areas and steps must be well defined and for any violation respective person be held responsible and accountable.

17.2.11. Modes of Political Pressure (Unit 13)

Different modes and forms are used for exerting political pressure on the All India Services Officers to get tailor-made decisions. In present study, 22 (Annexure 13.A) most commonly used modes/forms have been studied. Politicians' control over public servants is the most frequently used mode of political pressure in the decision-making process. Second commonly used mode is the abuse of political position and authority by them. Other mostly used modes are the seniors in the bureaucratic system and power brokers along with political groups and political activists. Member citizenry and training tours are the least used modes to exert political pressure in the decision-making process. What propositions can be made to reduce the use of different modes of pressure in the decision process? The present bureaucratic system is secrecy and power-oriented, may be changed towards complete transparency, openness, and decentralization of power across different levels and services starting top at the CS level down to village level. There is need to remove or reduce political control from the system and make it rule-based and open transparent, discretionary powers at different level must be removed/reduced, file movement need to be reduced to only three levels transparently and full accountability and responsibility must be fixed at every level in bureaucracy. Performance review tools must be made participatory, open and transparent manner to remove personal bias/likings. More power is given to the public by awareness making transparently and entry of hidden financiers, power brokers, etc. must be reduced to a bare minimum by an online recording of every interaction/entry in public offices, rest houses, and public officers' residences or at any other place with bureaucrats and politicians.

17.2.12. Reasons for Accepting Political Pressure (Unit 14)

Why the All India Services Officers accept political pressure in the decision-making process, what are the reasons for accepting political pressure? Research results indicate that desire for enhancement of status is the most important reason for the acceptance of political pressure in the decision-making process, so the bureaucratic system has to reduce this status consciousness from the bureaucrats. Excessive power concentration in few services elites is the root cause of problems; introduce equidistribution of power and aura of such posts among all the services. Remove power base orientation from different services. Other important reasons for pressure acceptance are;

individual officer thinking that proximity to a politician will generate information, which can be used for propagation of self-interests; this is due to inbuilt secrecy and different layerings in a bureaucratic system, remove all those levels and introduce rule-based information, so for every file outcome of the decision must be predictable and transparent. The All India Services Officers lust to grab power and to meet the desire for career advancement in service, merit-based, work quality-based, responsibility and accountability-based, career advancement can help in improving this variable. The Indian Administrative Service officers accept the higher intensity of political pressure for status enhancement and to grab power in the bureaucratic system, all the services must be given equal chances and opportunities to perform and occupy different positions/postings in the bureaucratic system. No posts/postings are kept exclusive for one service, include every department for manning positions on the basis of training imparted, merit and performance. The Indian Police Service officers accept political pressure for status enhancement, gathering information from politicians for self-use, the present culture of the rod must go away, police are for the public, and public participation with dignity must be a system of management. The Indian Forest Service officers accept political pressure to ensure stability, security in job and to grab power for self-use, tenure posting in a transparent manner. The forests must be saved through public participation. It is never possible to improve or remove all the reasons because new situations will breed new reasons for pressure acceptance, certainly, transparency, accountability, and adherence to well-specified parameters for every bureaucratic decision can help in reducing the pressure acceptance in the decision.

17.2.13. Bureaucratic Culture (Unit 15)

The dominance of ego and arrogance observed pervasive across the cadres and that is the greatest enemy of the All India Services in the decision process. These power elites never try to come out of self-ego and arrogance of one's service. They deviate from transparency and merit in the decision. There is a strong need to dilute this, how it can be done. Only by changing and restructuring the entire bureaucratic system and the new system must be reconstituted based on equity and equality for all. The All India Services Officers obsession with status is a serious problem of our bureaucratic system. Inequalities and colonial origin inbuilt status need to be removed. Then the AISO will say they joined the AIS for status only. We must strive towards equality and equity and dedicated services for the masses. The All India Services aura needs to be reduced by giving equal powers to all services at that level irrespective of the service name. Nomenclature of departments must be harmonized and changed with the working of the related different department must be made performance and accountability-oriented not service-oriented. The dominance of self-seeking goals among the All India Services Officers is the liability of the bureaucratic system, transparency, and use of information technology by making most of the public works on line and transparent parameters based can help in improving the delivery system in the decision. The dominance of political interference in their work, favoritism and nepotism adopted by them, common retention of immoral behavior by them, and political opportunism by them have been highly prevalent in the bureaucratic system. Frequent transfers, too much careerism, discrimination, and obstruction by them and low salaries, lack of devotion to work, and abuse of power and authority by them are the cultural problems of the system. This colonial culture and imperial origin-based deficiencies can only be removed by complete reorganization and restructuring of all the services and department in India, otherwise somewhere hidden problems will remain unless and until present system is not changed, by solving one problem present system create another problem in renamed another form, name, and shape. Solutions can be incorporated by complete restructuring imperial origin bureaucracy.

17.2.14. Bureaucracy Workplace Environment Orientation (Unit 16)

Research results indicate that the All India Services Officers are fully convinced that rules for working in a bureaucratic system are not conducive for them. There is a need to improve the present rules for their work. There is a need for improving interpersonal relations vertically, horizontally, and down below them at their workplace. Verbal orders are a serious issue; every level in bureaucracy must confirm every verbal instruction followed by written instruction. There is a need for conducting more training programs to improve interpersonal relations at the workplace. Improvements in the workplace environment will also improve the efficiency of the bureaucracy and the quality of the decision process. Every person visiting the public office must feel at ease while dealing with public servants. When a person moves out of public office, that person must be feeling happy and satisfied and that must have no hesitation in visiting again if the need arises.

The All India Services Officers are highly self-goal oriented and to perpetuate self-interests and needs. They grossly and thoroughly misuse their positions in the hierarchy at every level. In the process, these officers befool both politicians and the public to sustain their own goals at the cost of others. The All India Services Officers are highly self-goal oriented in behaviour and approach.

17.3. Future Strategy for Managing the Bureaucracy in India

Based on our research results and findings, we have proposed some hard-core recommendations to reorganize and restructure the colonially created imperialistic and exploitative bureaucratic system. To bring any meaningful change, entire bureaucratic systems have to be reorganized and restructured in new form and shape; cosmetic changes or curative changes in the present system will never change its original exploitative characteristics of the inbuilt system. Aesthetic changes cannot provide desired results without holistic changes at all levels by changing the present bureaucratic system. Such changes must be directed towards the mind and psychology of the public servants and public both at the same time. We have to come out of individual service orientation and forego feeling of self-cultivation or self-glorification at the cost of others. Such thinking is highly harmful and detrimental to national progress and all-around psycho-socio development. Parasitic behaviours have to be removed from the bureaucratic system. The culture of inclusiveness and participation has to replace the culture of exclusiveness and an individualistic approach. The government officers and employees have to work on the concept that they are equal, one among others, and part and parcel of the public decision system. Present concepts that they are above others have to be dispensed with and brought to an end at any cost or circumstances. The principle of equity and equality has to be the foundation of public administration.

"There is an urgent need to control the post-retirement conduct also of all public servants. The highest among them must be insulated from any temptations of likely post-retirement benefits from the corporate sector or political establishment," J.S. Verma, 2011. Bureaucrats' adherence to the following norms will facilitate administration work. People should get timely and prompt service with good ethical values shown by bureaucracy. Bureaucrats must show courteous behaviour with the public with a bare minimum waiting time. The number of visits to government office is reduced, form filling to be reduced to bare minimum and eliminate red tap-ism. Online prompt information to be provided with a quick disposal of matter without any intermediaries or arbitrator. Propagate ethics and value-based efficiency to transform the system. Good governance must develop ethical selfless service traditions and love for citizens with effective interpersonal relations (*IJPA*, Vol. LIX, 2013).

17.3.1. Restructuring of Bureaucracy and All India Services

During the colonial period, excessive powers were provided to one service and few positions as District Magistrate/Deputy Commissioner/Collector and Chief Secretary to develop power centers to control the Indian public and strengthen the alien power grip in the hands few Englishmen remotely regulated from England. Deputy Commissioners/Collectors were provided luxurious lifestyles, so that, they can develop a superiority complex over local rulers/kings in the surrounding areas. That excessive power and luxurious lifestyle provided to them was required at that time to inculcate confidence in them for exploiting Indian masses ruthlessly at that time of slavery. That arrangement provided motivation back home in England to the Britishers, so that, more Englishmen can join this process of exploitation towards strengthening their suzerainty and imperialism. Excessive powers were centralized to avoid (exclude) the participation of Indians in the decision-making process. At the present time this exploitation and suppression of masses is not required and this urgently deserves a complete change. Indian Administrative Service has introduced inequality among the state services also. In some states, Provincial Civil Services and their feeder services have been provided undue pay advantages in pay scales and overriding powers vis-à-vis other provincial services. At the same time, other state services have been denied their due scales or pay scales have been lowered and powers have been reduced/taken away slowly. Structural layering among All India Services is propagating layering in other services to further own advantage only.

Structural layering in the bureaucratic system among the different services is the reflection of the prevalent caste system in India. The inclusion of the All India Services for state affairs has further strengthened this structural caste system. We have to combine the entire group 'A' services in one category and with one pay scale and similar opportunities for career progressions. This is easy to say and difficult to implement. The complete proposed process is explained briefly.

17.3.1.1. Restructuring and Regrouping of Services: Numbers of administrative reforms were suggested to improve the existing bureaucratic system, but system boundaries absorbed every suggestion to own advantage. One has to go out of the box to bring major changes in the colonially created system. Restructuring and reorganizing all existing services necessarily to be carried out and all the services of Government of India and respective States may be regrouped and restructured into maximum ten service groups to reduce redundancy and repetition. The respective States may prefix name own state in place of word 'Bharat', e.g. 'Bharat Financial Services' can be named as/ Haryana Financial Services' (HFS) by Haryana State Government and so on.

(i) **Bharat Financial Services** ***(include every finance-related works)***: Bharat Financial Services (BFS) may comprise all the services dealing with finance, financial matters, financial planning, and implementation in the Government of India. Indian P&T Accounts & Finance Service, Indian Audit & Accounts Service, Indian Defence Accounts Service, Indian Revenue Service, Indian Customs Service, Central Excise Service, Indian Civil Accounts Service, Indian Railway Accounts Service, all other Service working with various department/Ministries related to Accounts and Finance in the country and States be merge into one service. There is a need for using the same training, the same accounting procedure, and similar working norms for all reorganizations and services.

(ii) Bharat Development and Social Services *(every aspect of societal development)*: Bharat Development and Social Services (BDSS) may comprise all services related to societal development, food and civil supply, administration of justice, socio-economic-cultural issues, development planning and works, information and communication related, mass communication, rural development, planning and program implementation, program implementation, social welfare, housing development sectors, urban development, labor-related issues, and employment, etc. works, and issues. Services such as Indian Economic Service, Indian Statistical Service, Indian Information Service, all the services related to Legal and Judicial Services, Indian Salt Service, Archaeological Service, Central Legal Service, Indian Supply Service, Company Law Board Service, Labour Related Services and All other Services related with social and cultural developmental works.

(iii) Bharat Scientific Research Services *(all science and research works)*: Bharat Scientific Research Services (BSRS) may comprise the services exclusively engaged in all types of scientific and industrial research activities. The Bharat Technical Services all those researches findings in the field will implement researches done by this service. The Council of Scientific and Industrial, Department of Atomic Energy, Department of Space, Defence Research and Development Organization, Department of Biotechnology, Department of Science & Industrial Research, Survey of India, Department of Science & Technology, Indian Meteorological Service, Indian Council of Agricultural Research, Department of Ocean Development, and Indian Council Medical Research, etc. Every research-based work and activity must be placed in one place and a single service to manage all research activities.

(iv) Bharat Technical Services *(all technical, scientific work implementation)*: Bharat Technical Services (BTS) may comprise different services engaged in the implementation of scientific, industrial research and technical programs in the field. All Services related to technical programs and where the implementation of works comprises scientific and technology-based. This may include services such as; Indian Forest Service, Agriculture Services, Transport related services, housing infrastructure creation related, technical services wings in different ministries, non-conventional energy, energy- and power-related services, water resources, and other Technical Services., Botanical Survey of India, Zoological Survey of India, Central Water Engineering Service, Central Power Engineering Service, Geological Survey of India and all other services carrying out technical and scientific work implementation in the field.

(v) Bharat Engineering Services *(all engineering works)*: Bharat Engineering Services (BES) will comprise all the engineering services working with different ministries and may be brought to one place. Engineering works such as Railways, Telecommunications, National Highway Authority of India, CPWD, Department of Electronics, Indian Engineering Services and other Engineers working at different places like Overseas Communications Service, Central Engineering Services of all wings and Indian Telecommunication Service, etc.

(vi) Bharat Medical Services *(Medical and health-related)*: Bharat Medical Services (BMS) will comprise all services related to allopathic, homeopathic, ayurvedic, unani, and all other alternative systems of medicine, CGHS, all doctors in PSU, health and family welfare, and all veterinary doctors (animals' welfare) engaged in the field including Central Health Service.

(vii) **Bharat Commercial Services** *(all commerce, commercial & production activities)*: Bharat Commercial Services (BCS) will comprise all services related to commercial activities, banking service, industrial production and management, commerce ministry works, all public sector undertakings, production and marketing-related services, Railways commercial activities, tourism, coal, ordinance factories civilian organization. Included services may be such as Indian Ordnance Factories Service, Indian Foreign Service (international dealings), Indian Trade Service, and Indian Railway Traffic Service, etc. Indian Postal Service, Mercantile Marine Training Ship Service, Central Trade Service, Department of Posts & Telegraphs, etc.

(viii) **Bharat Personnel Services** *(human resource management)*: Bharat Personnel Services (BPS) may comprise all services handling the personnel job or personnel management and human resource management at various levels and locations. Central Secretariat Service, Indian Administrative Service, Indian Railway Personnel Service, Indian Defence Estate Service, Railway Board Secretariat Service, Armed Forces Headquarter Civil Services, Delhi and Andaman and the Nicobar Islands Civil Service, and Indian Frontier Administrative Service and any other service related to human resource management.

(ix) **Bharat Education Service** *(complete education and training)*: Bharat Education Service (BES) will comprise all services related to education, cultural education, and sports, this includes every kind of teaching staff in all the universities, training institutions, technical and engineering institutions, colleges, schools, and activities related to imparting any kind of education, training programs. All institutions and organizations related to cultural education; sports may be included in this. All training institutes for different services may be included in one place. Central Secretariat Official Language Service, Rajyabhasa, etc. and other languages related works will come under education.

(x) **Bharat Defence and Security Services** *(internal and external security)*: Bharat Defence and Security Services (BDSS) may include all services related to the external and internal security of the country. All Armed Forces (Army, Navy and Air Force), Para-military police as BSF, CRPF, ITBP, Central Industrial Security Force, State Police organizations including Indian Police Service and Railway Protection Force in Government of India, Delhi and Andaman and Nicobar Islands Police Service, Armed Forces Headquarters Civil Services any other policing service and intelligence gathering-related works.

17.3.2. Recruitment Process (One Nation One Exam)

Union Public Service Commission to conduct a single examination for recruitment after graduation and post-graduation qualifications entry into services for the entire group 'A' and group 'B', 'C' posts for all the services for the Central Government and State Governments. (i) Screening test essentially comprising general knowledge, aptitude testing, mathematics, language proficiency reasoning, computational skills testing, Intelligence Quotient (IQ) and Emotional Quotient (EQ), etc. The qualifying percentage may be fixed like university examinations. One/two elective subject score to be included with above-mentioned general knowledge paper/s. This examination may be conducted in three stages: (i) screening (preliminary, objective type may be online), (ii) main descriptive examination with emphasis on elective and specialized subjects like science, engineering and medical, etc. (according to job requirement of different services), and (iii) third stage in two parts: (a) specialization and behaviour assessment through established scientific methods and (b) interview by using established scientific methods.

The Union Public Service Commission will conduct recruitment for the Government of India, which may include an interview (two stages of behaviour test + interview) and a final selection process. For group 'C' posts based on qualifying score screening recruitment can be made and special skills tests can be conducted for job-specific requirements, like a shorthand or computer proficiency or any other technical/special skill test for any specific job like scientific/engineering/ technician test, etc. This will require the segregation of different subjects and skills needed for a particular job to be completed by the Staff Selection Board (group 'C' is not dealt with further).

Possibilities may be explored (wheresoever possible) to constitute state cadres and central cadres in these services. Officers allotted to state cadres may be assigned to state cadres to serve in the states. After UPSC (one nation one examination) examinations respective State Public Service Commission will conduct stage three process of behavioural assessment + interview for respective vacant posts for that State on the basis of choice of the applicant. Similarly, for group 'C' posts persons will be selected by respective State Staff Selection Boards from common merit-based on candidate choice and merit of that person in 'one nation one exam'. Further process of selection will be completed by respective State Governments.

Before nomination from the State Government to the central services, all the State Public Service Commissions can notify their vacancies, one examination for all the States and UTs may be conducted by UPSC. Moreover, based on such merit respective State Public Service Commissions, then can conduct interviews for 5 to 2% of examination marks, and final results can be published accordingly.

Another option is that for preliminary screening online tests (maybe on fixed dates twice or thrice a year) can be carried out all over the Union of India for all types of graduate entry and based on that computerized scores next stage of examination can be conducted. Special physical requirements (or any other specific job requirement) for defense, police, forests, and some other services may be tested after main examinations during behaviour assessment slot before an interview. This will ensure merit and eliminate the subjectivity of States to avoid all types of political pressure in recruitment.

17.3.3. Bureaucracy Training

After selection by the Union Public Service Commission, all the officers must be provided training for six to eight (?) months in general management in different management institutions. Then officers must go to respective services specialization training institutes for nine months (?) or whatsoever period required for a particular service including on the job training for three to six months. After job training during the final three months of training, they may be trained in a training institute of that service. After 10-, 17- and 24-years next scale examinations; every officer must get one to three months of training before taking a new assignment as promotion linked training. Every year one/two-week period multi-skilling training courses must be linked with the career progression and made mandatory for every officer. All training programs are to be conducted through Bharat Education Service.

17.3.4. Career Progression and Seniority

Based on the performance in the Union Public Service Commission examinations combined seniority may be managed centrally and for respective services for that service also. The nodal ministries may keep respective service seniority list, the Government of India will maintain combined seniority of all the services. Employees at every level must be provided equal opportunities and equity in career management for all the services at all levels. Every employee may be compulsorily asked to appear in competitive examinations conducted by the Union Public Service Commission for gazetted officers and Staff Selection for other than gazetted posts. Such examinations may be conducted every year on a fixed time schedule and employees who have completed 10, 17, and 24 years of service may be allowed to appear in that year's examination. Any employee/officer, who has completed a minimum of 10 years' service in that level, may be allowed to appear in that level for the next scale examination.

As feeder services to the central services, state services may be allowed to compete to fill up 33.3% in promotion quota at level-IV examinations for entry in level-V. Once any state officers qualify for central services, that person may be sent compulsorily outside the native state. Equity at all levels must be maintained to increase the competence and capability of the individuals. Those who do not perform well have to be relegated to last and performers have to be provided chances to progress and override in seniority. Pay scale must be such that no one will stagnate throughout one's career, but higher positions must only be available to competent persons. Merit must allow competence to grow and sycophants to decay. If someone fails to qualify in 10, 17, 24 years competition examinations that officer will remain in that old stage only, next stage promotion only to be made after qualifying examinations at three-level to sustain merit in bureaucracy. Lateral shift among ten services may be allowed based on merit-cum-choice in these 10, 17, 24 years examinations.

Multi-skilling at all levels through job rotation; job enlargement and job enrichment will look after all the problems pertaining to excessive cadres, redeployment, and retrenchment. Reengineering and restructuring will be inbuilt in the bureaucratic system to infuse the innovations. Diversity will be a part of the bureaucratic system. Reduction in levels will remove the necessary required choking/blockage in the decision-making process.

17.3.4.1. Integration of States Services in Union of India: All the States Government can also classify their services into ten groups parallel to the Government of India. 33% posts at level-IV and level-V may be kept for the exchange program. Such exchange may be based on the written examination conducted by the Union Public Service Commission to join the Government of India and State Public Service Commission to join a State Government at the same level of examination. This exchange may be allowed only after 10 and 17 years of examination only. This 33% will be similar to what is available in the All India Services at present but extended to all the ten services. Any person, who fails to qualify examinations regularly for four years in the next level, such officers may be debarred for a period of five years to compete in Union Public Service Commission examinations, as a penalty for inefficiency. Such persons may be compulsorily posted out of parent department, region, or the State, and posted on difficult postings as a penalty. Those who stand high in merit may be given choice for a change of service according to their position in merit. After examinations of every level, a fresh seniority list may be prepared for the next level according to their standing in merit in Union Public Service Commission performance.

Level-VII, all posts may be filled on the basis of equity and merit. Topmost positions may be made available to all the officers from ten services, who have qualified for the 24 years examinations. From this list according to merit fresh empanelment may be drawn, this will provide wider options to the Chief Minister and Prime Minister for selection of officers for Chief Secretary and Cabinet Secretary level.

At present, the post of the secretary to any department does not serve any purpose and it is not required at all. Where the head of the department is posted, another level of secretary or special secretary makes no sense, so it may be merged with the head of the department. Similarly, posts of additional secretary and joint secretary be merged into one level after 17 years of examinations, in states these officers may be posted at regional levels. Similarly, Deputy Secretary and the Director's posts are one and the same; all the officers after 10 years examination may be in one rank. Only officers from this rank may be posted as head of the districts.

After independence, the post of the District Magistrate/Deputy Commissioner/Collector is redundant and serves little purpose. However, to suit our psychological needs for coordination senior-most officers in that district among all ten services, the officer who have passed 10 years examination and highest score in the UPSC examination may be assigned the job. Grievances redressing mechanism may be completely handed over to the elected representatives in all situations and circumstances. Given a chance, bureaucrats only misuse this process to their own advantage.

For commercial services examinations after 10 and 17 years, persons from the private sector may be allowed to sit in the examination to get the best talent for commercial purposes. 10% of persons may be taken from the private sector and a similar number of the officer must go to the private sector as a sharing mechanism.

On a similar pattern, examinations may be conducted for the level-I to level-III employees after 10, 17, and 24 years of service in respective levels.

17.3.5. Pay Scales and Hierarchical Levels

Equity in pay scales, equity in chances of promotions, and equity in career progression must be adhered to keep alive the merit. Objective merit must prevail over in career management. Every Indian citizen must be provided with equal opportunities to reach the top. There should not be any kind of exclusiveness. The exclusiveness of service and exclusive career in one department or service is the basic and root cause of immoral behaviour. Every government employee has to perform at every level otherwise, one has to suffer and go out of the system. Everyone has to keep one's knowledge and skills updated to the tune with time, only after qualifying in examinations person will go to the next stage of career and pay scale. Pay scale and promotions have to be de-linked. Pay scales are made such that one can survive to the maximum level of one's incompetence. Promotion or no promotion you are getting your pay scale of that level.

For the entire country and all the services may be placed in only seven pay scales with seven levels in hierarchy be retained, rest be abolished. Excessive protection and exclusiveness of a career in one service have developed the feelings of class and connections in every service. Persons start cultivating relations with individual officers for self-goals attainment in the future, so this service-certainty factor has to be eliminated. All the subordinates start behaving in a sycophant manner with officers, so that, in case of need, they can seek help from the officer of that service in the future. Grooming and growth of an employee in a particular service or department have become the cause of corruption. People/public start cultivating relations with persons of a particular service or department in hope that in future that person services can be utilized for own benefit maximization, concerned service person continue such relations for own advantage and benefits.

Similarly, everyone wants a promotion, under individual pressure number of posts has been increased to an undesirable level in every department, which has become a burden on the system.

Exhibit Number 17.1: Proposed Pay Scales for the Services

Sr.	Qualifications	Level	Proposed Pay Scale	7th Pay Scale/6th Pay Scales
1	10+2 pass, 18 years of age & 12 years of education	I, Worker	18000-92300	18000-92300
2	Graduation, 21 years age and 15 years of education, 10 years service in level-I plus graduation degree	II, Front Staff/ Supervisor	21000-97300	18000-92300/5200-20000
3	Graduation/postgraduation, 21 years age, 10 years service in level-II	III, executive	35400-167800	35400-167800/9300-34800
4	Graduation/postgraduation, 21 years age and 15 years of education, 10 years service in level-III	IV, Senior executive	56100-209200	56100-209200/15600-39100
5	UPSC examination after 10 years of level IV officers	V, Divisional Heads, JAG	118500-218200	118500-218200/37400-67000
6	UPSC examination after 17 years of level V officers	VI, Regional Heads	182200-224100	182200-224100/67000-79000
7	UPSC examination after 24 years of level VI officers	VII, Dept. Heads	205600-250000 including fix 225000 & 250000 merged in one scale	205600-224400/7550-80000/80000 fixed/90000 fixed

Present proposals will involve a large-scale reduction in unnecessary ranks and redundant levels in the hierarchy. Power holders will feel an uncomfortable due loss of their hegemony over the bureaucratic system. If the food chain is disturbed, occupants with parasite behaviour will feel uncomfortable for any change. The complete reorganization is essential to remove redundancy and immorality from the bureaucracy.

Level-I, Workers: This level may comprise all workers; persons who carry out work at the end level. Now the question will be raised at the same pay level, who will agree to do the Peon/Chowkidar level job when the pay scale is the same. It is one's position in merit, which will decide the job content of an individual person. This worker 10+2 qualification level is kept keeping in view the rural population of India (but need to be considered graduate) where education network is week. The pay scale for this level may be ₹ 18000-92300.

Level-II, Front-Staff (Graduate Entry): According to a position in merit for respective examinations (National Exam results followed by State Staff Selection Boards skill need-based selection), Front Staff will look after initiation of work in front office or field. The largest strength and number of employees falls on this level. The pay scale for Front Staff may be as ₹ 21000-97300. A large number of job classification in this level of present group 'C' jobs, different types of skills are needed for various jobs and that can be done on the basis of personal preferences cum merit on the basis of individual qualifications and rank in merit in 'one nation one exam'.

Level-III, Executives: All the positions in this level will be either from promotion from level-II or direct recruitment. Professional qualifications, personal choice cum merit may be used for segregating postings on different posts. This also comprises gazetted class-II posts. Persons at this level will be empowered to take limited independent decisions. This may the first level, where decision-making may be allowed. It will be on a pay scale of ₹ 35400 to 167800.

Level-IV, Senior Executives: This may be gazetted class-I and equivalent posts, officers' level, and recruitment through both direct entries and by promotion from level-III officers. Classification for various services may be based on the personal choice cum merit position in examinations and professional qualifications. Pay scale may be kept at ₹ 56100-209200.

Level-V, District/Divisional Heads: This level may also be called junior administrative grade. All district heads and divisional heads may be posted from this level. This will be the first promotion stage for level-IV officers after 10 years of examinations and also for officers from the State Governments. Pay scale may be kept at ₹ 118500 to 218200.

Level-VI, Regional Heads: This level officer may hold the positions at a regional level like Commissioners, Inspector General of Police, and Chief Conservator of Forests, Heads of Regional Institutions, Regional officers in Government of India, and any other position at the regional level. This may be the first super time selection scale with ₹ 182200 to 224100 and after 17 years examinations of level-IV.

Level-VII, Departmental Heads: In this top scale of pay of ₹ 205600 to 250000 including present posts with 225000 fixed and 250000 fixed, all the departmental heads in the states and Government of India may be kept in this pay scale. Persons for top posts may be based on merit and competence, i.e. based on the written test and interviews both, after 24 years examination of level-IV.

All the examinations and interviews for induction from level-IV to level-VII including career progression and promotion to the next level may be conducted through the Union Public Service Commission for the Government of India officers and after feedback from State Public Service Commission for State Government officers. The Staff Selection Boards in the States and Government of India may conduct all the examinations and interviews for level-I to level-III, along with All India Written Test (one nation one exam).

17.3.6. Rules, Regulations, and Procedures

All the ten services must have similar basic rules, with the flexibility to have additional rules required for a particular service, like defense, police, scientist and engineers, etc. In the decision-making process, no file must be allowed to go beyond three levels in the hierarchy. If any officer in the hierarchy is unable to take a decision within one's competencies, and with given time frame and parameters, such officers may be held responsible for that. Individual officers may be held accountable for every decision taken by them. No file must start below level-II. A case initiated by level-II must end at level-IV and a similar case initiated by a level-IV officer must end up at level-

VII. File initiated at level-VII must go to the concerned minister or maximum at Chief Minister in the State or Prime Minister level at the Centre.

No one is allowed to occupy any position in any organization after 60 years of age in the whole country. Consultancy, engagement, or association of any kind with any organization after retirement from any service in the country should not be permitted. This may be applicable from peon, the lowest level to the highest office in the country. No politicians may be allowed to occupy any public office after 65 years of age. This will improve the working of the political parties and create space for equity, growth, and certainty in minds of junior politicians. No bureaucrats may be allowed to occupy public office (ministerial) with the support of any political party after retirement. Efforts will be made to fix a uniform retirement age for the private sector also; otherwise, after retirement bureaucrats will try to occupy positions in the private sector. Retirement age may be reviewed to lower it (58 or 55 years) to create jobs for younger generations, behavioural sciences studies results indicate efficiency goes down with higher age. Political pressure acceptance has been highest with a higher length of service.

In the present system, when a person joins a particular service, that employee or officer will work in a particular department or position. So public and persons in any department start cultivating relations for future utilities. They start providing facilities and bribes even if they are transferred out with the hope that the person will be of some use in case of emergency or need in the future. If a person is not directly dealing with your case, then at least the cultivated officer will steer the way out or arrange a meeting with some other person in the department. This excessive job service surety, certainty, and security of being in the same service throughout career breeds immoral behaviour and creates power brokers in the bureaucratic system. This has to be abolished from all levels otherwise things will not improve.

In rules, it must be ensured that all the ten services are provided same housing facilities, same type of construction on same design, same transport facility, and same staff is posted for similar work, similar hierarchical structure, similar power (financial and administrative and others), responsibilities and accountabilities for a similar type of work. Present systems of differential treatment to different services have intensified the competition for self-benefit maximization. The few-privileged one in the bureaucratic system enjoys major resources of the country and others look towards them with a feeling of powerlessness. Psychological this system creates dissent in society. Those who do not have access to perks and benefits, develop frustration. Those who have exclusive control over resources and means stop working on merit. They remain busy in devising ways and means to retain those perquisites and benefits. The system of government vehicles needs to be reviewed. All government staff cars deserve to be withdrawn up to Ministers levels, only the PM/CM and the Chief Justices be allowed government cars with drivers, rest all be provided vehicle allowance with one basic pay for a driver, so that, the officer may hire a driver of own choice and pay from transport allowance provided by the government. Liberal loan for car purchasing may be provided at all levels.

17.3.7. Improvement in Individual Parameters

Research results indicate that due to excessive concentration of powers and controls in the hands of the Indian Administrative Service officers, desire to continue such powers, and such officers accept political pressure in undesirable proportions. Time has come; whole powers have to be decentralized to different levels. Respective services officer may be allowed to take decision up to top levels and interference of the one service deserve to be removed from the bureaucratic system.

Promoted officers are more amenable to political pressure acceptance, promotion process deserves to make more rigorous and merit-based. After promotion to All India Services, every such officer may be provided training to equip them with new skills and improving the existing skills. A rigorous evaluation process may be introduced to monitor and evaluate such officer works on a half-yearly basis. Similarly, the age factor is crucial for political pressure acceptance; a person with higher age becomes emotionally weak, reducing retirement age can check this. The social security system may be provided after retirement and possibilities may be explored by settling officers in clusters to provide support to each other. Any kind of after retirement assignment may be banned and prohibited from all levels, lust for post-retirement benefits make individual officers weak to develop a relationship with politicians. After retirement housing clusters may be developed and according to choose the type of house to be allotted to retired employees and cost may be covered during the service period and if any balance that may be recovered from the pension of the retiree. Community living of pensioners will provide them mental peace and security.

Most of the biographic characters are highly private in nature it is difficult to manipulate due to the emotional sensitivity associated with such characters. In locus of control, an effort may be made to increase the internality of the All India Services Officers and externality for chance or luck and externality for others may be reduced to appropriate levels through well-organized training programs and improving the work culture and environment.

17.3.7.1. Change in Behaviour: The All India Services Officers are located in crucial and highly important positions, immediate need for change in behaviour by changing and remolding the individual officers' perceptions, attitudes, values, and beliefs during the process of career progression. This is possible only after incorporating restructuring of the entire bureaucratic system from the bottom to the top level. Basic concepts and philosophy of administration have to be changed to bring any change. One cannot expect any change with the present colonial imperialistic bureaucratic system. Present motivation levels and motivating factors are negative, self-centered, and full of colonial ego and arrogance; these are the basic cause of prevalent immoral behaviour in the bureaucratic system. We have to induce equity-based motivation, motivation for posterity, and welfare of all. Chain saw model motivation has to be removed and forces operating in the orbital path of the decision have to be reduced to the lowest level. The coercive power base has to reduce to participative and equity, prestige, and status need to be removed from the services. Concepts of elite and exclusiveness have to be removed from the bureaucratic system. Public servants have to change their orientation from self-centered to public-centered. Present cultures of immoral decisions and self-maximization at the cost of others have to be removed. We have to allow equal growth of all the services and all the persons engaged in public administration. The AISO bureaucratic mistrust and fear need to be changed to trust.

Organization of hierarchy in the bureaucratic system need to be changed to teamwork.

17.3.7.2. Bureaucratic Culture and Motivation: Now the time has come to review the present culture of a multiplicity of application forms moving from desk to desk (multiplicity of forms and returns need to be designed in minimum forms) itself, need to be changed and the possibility of making whole transaction paperless and online transactions may be brought in the system. Our present bureaucratic system of extremely tight culture of boundaries has lost the ability to change and adapt new things; new blood had to be infused in this culture by changing it. Government employee's orientation of lordship, the culture of power ingrained with status need an appropriate reorientation of employees and officers changed to how to deals with the public with a behavioural change in that culture. Our bureaucratic system is unable to change with rapidly changing and self-restructuring civil society state formerly, interventionist, producer, regulator, and seller need now changed to be a facilitator, promoter, partner, and arbitrator. The reorganized bureaucratic system must be much more concerned about their performance, profitability, and ethics in the decision. Behavioural scientist says everything in learning organization must be more responsive to the public, focused on the issue, fast in solving a problem or providing solutions, friendly towards the public, flexible in decision approach. Thus, fast and responsible All India Services Officers need to merge one's individuality with duty. In changing bureaucracy discrimination and obstruction culture needs to be changed to equality and fast decisions. Political opportunism culture needs to be removed and changed to fairness.

17.3.7.3. Risk Management and Innovations in Bureaucracy: Bureaucracy exclusiveness and secrecy need to ensure the ever-increasing involvement of citizens in the decision process by opening up a bureaucracy to openness. Once citizens are involved and considered part of the system that will consolidate democracy. Bureaucracy must endeavor to stabilize societies through innovations. Bureaucratic system riddled with conflicts, the system must adapt to resolve conflicts peacefully to support the building of the peace, in a bid to accelerate the progress of the nation. Status and position orientation have brought in false satisfaction and loss of innovations, urgent need to improve the system to bring competitiveness in the decision process. Conflicts have reduced innovation in the system and hampered the development process; changes need to be made for effective management of the development process with innovative thinking. Individual bureaucrats lost innovations in the surrogating atmosphere. There is a need to institute a conducive atmosphere for individual creativity and innovation in the decision delivery system. Most of the administrative reforms are about problem-solving on a piecemeal basis, we have to think about out of box innovative solutions. We may use total quality management as a holistic approach to problem-solving and risk management. Some components of the total quality management approach may include customer focus, stakeholder involvement, empowerment of employees, teamwork orientation, data-driven decision making, benchmarking of best practices in the system. The bureaucratic system is highly conservative inflexible needs to be made more creative, higher flexible and introducing innovations in the decision. Present bureaucratic system of repetition seeking orientation need to be changed and made creative, efficiently orientated. To ensure the ever-increasing involvement of citizens, we have to introduce system innovation to institute a favorable atmosphere for individual creativity in the decision. We have to reintroduce innovations and creativity in the bureaucratic decision-making system. Only chance to allow the growth of innovations is possible after a complete change of present bureaucratic system as a present system by its origin during the colonial period was devoid of innovations.

17.3.7.4. Bureaucratic System: Excessive conflict, uncertainty, and risk have to be reduced from the bureaucratic system. Bureaucracy contradictions and risks have to be managed within permissible limits, so that; it works as constructive and energizing to the decision-making process in the bureaucratic system. The decision-making process in public administration has been hijacked by self-goals and individual interests' orientation, it deserves to be changed towards merit, equity, objectivity, fairness, and justice. The decision-making environment needs to be changed towards mutual trust, inter-service beliefs, participation, and teamwork. A new bureaucratic system has to be innovation and creativity oriented. Our local bureaucratic services standards may be repositioned to excellent standards. Speedy and easy access to information must be essentially ensured to the public regarding every decision process. There is a widespread consensus on the need to assure the public regarding free access and freedom of information. There is a need to amend such laws that stipulate unnecessary restrictions on free access of the public to information in the bureaucratic system. The bureaucratic system may be changed such that quick, speedy and easy access to information can be provided to the public regarding services and activities of the government.

There is a strong need for the development of appropriate management information systems in bureaucracy to share information with the public. Centre and State Governments must facilitate the public through facilitation centers at every level of bureaucracy and for every department/ local bodies/PSUs. Rather village-level government employees may work as facilitators for the whole village community. There is a need for developing an appropriate information management system with transparency and openness by defining time limits for every work in bureaucracy and transparency, every such information must be displayed on the website and display boards at every level. The AISO must be responsive to public needs, to be held responsible for their decisions, accountable for every act done by them, provisions for removing them for their lapses, and recallable by the public for their failures. There is a need for government to reinvent their delivery systems and the whole bureaucracy to be re-positioned to serve the public. The whole society is suffering due to the present bureaucratic system imperial outlook, need those government business sectors to be re-invigorated with a social motive. Bureaucrats' status-specific, stable roles need to be changed to open, transparent, and with full rights to information to the public.

17.3.8. Political Pressure Sources

Our research results indicate that Member Legislative Assembly, Ministers, and district-level politicians are the greatest source of political pressure in the decision-making process. In a new bureaucratic system, care must be taken to look after merit and transparency. Lack of transparency, clarity, and objectivity in the rules, regulations, and law has forced these sources of political pressure to exert political pressure in the decision. The present system of providing control and powers to the Secretary and Deputy Commissioner/Collector level has enhanced temptation to the sources of political pressures to exert pressure in the decision to get desired outcomes. Colonially created a power base of Deputy Commissioner/Collector and the Secretary has to be abolished in the interest of the country. These two levels are solely responsible to change the whole psychological framework of the whole public and exclusively responsible for immoral behaviour. If public servants take decisions based on merit, fairness, equity, impartiality, objectivity, and transparency, rest assured no one is going to pressurize them for tailor-made decisions. Public servants have to live like a saint of the Vedic period, free from all lusts and temptations. It is the other way round, not that political sources exert political pressure rather colonially created bureaucratic positions/ posts are such that bureaucrats posted on such positions oblige politicians for the attainment of their own self-goals and sustenance.

17.3.9. Types/Areas of Pressure

Present bureaucratic system working is such that only selfish and sycophants' flourishes and hardworking intelligent honest persons are sidelined to an insignificant death knell. Boiling points in the bureaucratic system are the transfers, postings, recruitment, promotions, resource allocations, and crime-related issues (Unit 12). Research results indicate that the present system is outdated immorality is driven and that causes of immoral behaviour located inside the bureaucratic system. Let us have a transparent and clear policy for these aspects; transfers may be made on a tenure basis by participative and impartial boards based on merit. All the posts may be classified into work-related groups and certain weightage may be assigned to each post/position, according to the Union Public Service Commission performance and merit (initially, the UPSC merit, thereafter 10-, 17- and 24-years examinations), persons may be posted on these positions. Reduction in hierarchical levels and only seven pay scales will reduce a lot of subjectivity from the bureaucratic system. The concept of the promotion will undergo a sea change and the rat race for the creation of new posts will be stopped as a person will remain in the same pay and workload level. Present hierarchical structure and excessive orientation towards specific services have created a whole web of problems. First officers of specific service distort the whole system to their own advantage then others approach politicians to extend the same manipulations for their service also. An administrative person located at control has no reply and has to bend the rules under political pressure, thus the process of distortion in the form of a chain reaction continues to infinity with respect to time and space. Firm policy relating to all the 15 areas/types/76 points (or any other such area/type/point left out from research) of the bureaucratic system be declared and made fully transparent and equity-based, which only can remove immoral behaviour of public servants.

The Central and State Governments have to work together for the simplification of existing laws, regulations, and procedures as well as the repeal of obsolete rules/laws and reform of Laws/Acts/Rules. The Central and State Governments may open computerized information and facilitation counters in all their offices with a large public interface. People-friendly and effective administration depends on the cleansing of civil services at all levels, adherence to ethical standards, and commitment to basic principles of the Constitution regarding equity and equality. The existing rules and legal provisions in Central and State Governments need to be amended to make them public centric.

The existing procedures for departmental inquiries and vigilance proceedings of government employees need to be revamped making space for specialization and transparency. The areas of discretion available to various levels of bureaucracy need to be reduced to the bare minimum, along with steps to prevent their arbitrary use or misuse. Responsive bureaucracy requires that service delivery and administration of income support schemes/programs are decentralized through the elected local bodies in rural and urban areas. Problems of reforms were that solutions were sought within existing bureaucratic system boundaries and not going out of present administrative system boundaries, we have to go outside the boundaries of a closed system to make it open and transparent. Various State Governments have undertaken detailed exercises to simplify and liberalize various rules and regulations during the passage of time. Many Central Ministries have also been addressing the administrative issues seriously and a major exercise for amending various laws affecting economic reforms, but ultimately that process was used for enhancing the powers of elites and diluting powers of other bureaucrats and technocrats.

The AISO regulator and controller working behaviour in the system needs to be changed as an enabler of development. Existing fat complacent bureaucracy needs to be changed to slender and alert with openness. Bureaucratic system customer hostility needs to be changed towards customer empathy. The present system of rule/regulation/procedures driven may be changed to public need driven decisions. Public services in the bureaucratic system lack adequate arrangement for immediate and efficient grievance redressal mechanism need to set up public facilitation centers or online solutions by providing information on respective departments/public offices web sites. The government must provide all forms on a single-window system of the NIC website or Internet for every kind of application/grievance with full details. Such as how and where paper/file will be moving, every step of file movement needs to be displayed on the web portal and facility for the applicant to track that mobiles/WhatsApp type system needs to be developed by NIC/email, etc.

17.3.10. Reasons and Modes of Pressure

Research results analyses for the modes (Unit 13) of the political pressure and reasons for accepting political pressure (Unit 14) in the decision-making process indicate that the whole bureaucratic system is self-goal directed and based on a faulty concept of exclusiveness. Excessive powers given to specific services and particular positions or locations in the hierarchy have created a web of all these problems. If the public is aware that tomorrow anyone can occupy the position of prominence/power, they will continue to cultivate future-oriented relations with that person. In the present system people know that Specific Service officers will continue to occupy the position of prominence in a particular cadre, people start paying them or start investing in them for future utilities. An officer of income tax (IRS) will remain in income tax throughout one's career, so the chartered accountant can safely cultivate and invest for long-term relations with officers of that department; similarly, a contractor with CPWD/telecommunication can invest for long-term relations with persons of that department, the present system encourages the nexus development. Prevalent situations encourage pressure group formation, thus different modes of political pressure continue to take different shapes and forms. Similarly, reasons for accepting political pressure in the decision-making process continue to multiply and slowly individual people become highly self-centered. Modes (Unit 13) and reasons (Unit 14) mentioned (any other mode of pressure or reason for accepting pressure) are dynamic and the bureaucratic system itself is responsible for multiplying these factors. The bureaucratic system provides authority and a particular position full of status or rank at various levels of hierarchy needs to be changed towards personal expertise or relationships.

Any efforts to reduce or remove these factors from the decision-making process require wholehearted efforts to change the very basis of the cause of the origin of these factors so that in the future external causes of political pressure are reduced or eliminated. Complete elimination of these factors is not possible in any bureaucratic system, but subjectivity can be reduced to such a low level that it does not hamper the decision-making process and cause loss to any individuals. In this process, we have to reduce individual-based factors and increase social participation with equity and transparency.

Power and status orientation have to be removed from the public administration. Career progression has to be equity and merit-based with the reduction of so many levels from the hierarchy. Stability and security have to be incorporated in the individual tenure to avoid disturbances. Politician roles and bureaucratic roles have to be clearly defined and ambiguities have to be removed from the decision-making process in the bureaucratic system.

Excessive emphases from the Annual Performance/Confidential Reports have to be removed and the Annual Confidential/Performance Report deserves to be made the participative process of evaluation, let subordinates also evaluate the seniors in a joint meeting of all the concerned persons. The evaluation may be made both way assessment participatory process. Uncertainties and conflicts from the decision-making process may be reduced to a productive level. Incompetent persons may be identified and continuously separated from the decision-making process. To regulate the lust for higher and higher money, property, and resources, checks, and strict regulations may be introduced for *Benami* property/shares/stock owners in urban/other areas. In country like India expenditure-oriented regulation may work to rein persons with immoral behaviour. Clearly defined demarcations may be drawn for politician interventions and accountability at every level be fixed for decision.

"The need for an independent informal and speedy citizens' grievance redressal machinery was thought to be a *sine qua non* by the ARC in our democratic form of government," U.C. Agarwal, 2013. Grievance handling and sound complaints handling system should ideally be created, which is accessible to all, simple to follow, provide quick results with complete fairness, and showing respect for every individual citizen. Excessive confidentiality clauses of the bureaucratic system may be changed to responsive bureaucracy. Bureaucratic system delivery mechanism must be effective and accountable providing feedback towards management systemic reforms. Guidelines for public grievances redressing system must be made simple and effective. The designated senior officer in every office should strengthen internal grievance redressing machinery in every sector to observe a fixed day once a week to receive and hear public grievances. To look after grievances handling, we must ensure that every grievance is processed in a fair, objective, and just manner. Public grievances received and solved data must be analyzed regularly towards the identification of the problem areas, which will help in indicating the right authority for contracting for services pertaining to a particular office. Efforts must be made to pick up grievances appearing in newspaper columns and remedial actions to be taken on them in a time-bound manner. Fix time limit for disposal of work relating to public grievances help in public confidence building. The system must acknowledge each grievance indicating the name, designation and telephone number and email of the official who is processing the case. This will work as public confidence-building and improve the justice delivery system. Any bureaucratic system should not be stable with fixed notions/norms, it must have inbuilt dynamism for change and repositioning according to changing time, space, and technology.

The attempt has been made to include a proposal to streamline and improve our imperial bureaucratic system. There can be numerous means and methods to address any issue; there cannot be one fixed solution to eradicate all prevailing problems. Some may like some method and others may suggest another method, it does not matter which method one adopts, but results must be sustainable with equity and equality. Our objective is our national welfare; our public and every citizen's comfort and dignity have been our mission while making proposals and propositions.

The All India Services Officers are the best, well trained, and most competent bureaucrats in India. The All India Services are functioning in its best way. The All India Service cannot be compared with any other services with respect to their job contents and results delivered by them. Corporate sector arrogance is very high, corporate executive behaviour and handlings of the public issue have been worst. The All India Services Officer even after so much power even the poorest of the poor can approach them and they listen to them patiently also. The author has been a scientist and worked with scientists, once power is attained, our people behave in the most arrogant manner. it was observed that in India power given to anyone, they also work in a similar manner, rather than behave in a more arrogant manner. Power must be distributed in such a manner that it does not cultivate arrogance in the system. Restructuring of entire civil services is essential and a need of the time for equity and equal development of our society.

"He who give up all desires, and moves free from attachments, egoism and thirst for enjoyment attain peace" *Bhagwat Gita*, Chap. 2. 71.

Bibliography

Abraham, Holtzman, *Interest Group and Lobbying*; MacMillan, New York, 1966.

Ackerman, S.R., *Corruption, A Study in Political Economy*; Academic Press, New York, 1978.

Adams, J.S., "Inequity in Social Exchange", *Advances in Experimental Social Psychology*, Academic Press, New York, 1965.

Agor, W.H., *Introduction in Organization*; Sage Publications, New Burry Park, CA, 1989.

Aiyar, S.P., "Political Context of Indian Administration", *Indian Journal of Public Administration*, xvii. 3, New Delhi, 1971.

Akhilesh, K.B., L. Parsad and P. Singh, *Evolving Performing Organization through People: A Global Agenda*; New Age International, New Delhi, 1995.

Alexander, H.M.L., *Discarding "Steel Frames"—Changing Images among ICS in Early Twentieth Century*, 1982.

All India Service Manual, Government of India, Publication Division, New Delhi, 1984.

Anderson, G., *British Administration in India*; MacMillan, London, 1920.

Anthony, R., Ciminera, K.S. Calhoun and H.E. Adams, *Handbook of Behavioural Assessment*; John Willey & Sons, New York, 1986.

Argyris, C. *Integrating the Individual and the Organisation*, John Wiley & Sons Inc., New York 1964.

Armstrong, J., *The European Administrative Elite*; Princeton, 1973.

Atheeq, L.K. et al., Economic Restructuring and the I.A.S.; *The Administrator*, 37(1), Jan-March 92.

Backer, C.J., A. Seal, *Power, Profit and Politics: Essay on Imperialism, Nationalism and Change in Twentieth-Centaury in India*, Cambridge, 1981.

Bailey, Stephen K., "Ethics in Public Services" in *Public Administration and Democracy*, Edited by Roscoe C.M., Syracuse, University Press, 1965.

Bakshi, R.S., *Politicians, Bureaucrats and the Development Process*; Radiant Pub. New Delhi, 1986.

Banerjea, Pramathanath, *Public Administration in Ancient India*; Indian Reprints Pub. Co. New Delhi, 1973.

Banorjee, N.B., *Under Two Masters*, Oxford University Press, Calcutta, 1970.

Bansal, P.L., *Administrative Development in India*, New Delhi, 1974.

Baron, Robert A. and Donn Byrne, *Social Psychology*; 8th Edition Prentice Hall of India, New Delhi, 2001.

Bayley, David H., *The Police and Political Development in India*; Princeton University, Princeton, 1969.

Bentley, A.F., *The Process of Government—A Study of Social Pressures*, The Principal Press Inc. Bhoomington, 1949.

Berger, Charles R. and Steven H.C., *Handbook of Communication Science*; Sage Pub. Inc. California, USA, 1987.

Beveridge, Henry, *The District of Backerganj, its History and Statistics*; Trubner & Co. London, 1876.

Bhambhri, C.P., *Bureaucracy and Politics in India*, New Delhi, 1971.

——, "Bureaucracy in India", an Article in *A Survey of Research in Public Administration, 1970-1979*. Editor K. Mathur, Indian Council of Social Science Research, New Delhi, 1986.

Bhandarkar, Asha, Managerial Stress with Special Reference to Public Enterprise, Ph.D., Thesis, Osmania University, Hyderabad, 1985.

Bhardwaj, R.K., *Indian Police Administration*; National Publishing House, New Delhi, 1978.

Bhartiya Yogi, *Kautilaya Arthshashtra*; Sanskriti Sansthan, Bareli, UP, India, 1988.

Bhatia, L.M., "Public Service Ethics", *Administrator*, LBSNAA, Mussorie, xix. 3, 1974.

Blau, G.J., "Locus of Control as Potential Moderator of turnover Process". *Journal of Occupational Psychology*. Fall, 1987, pp. 21-29.

Blau, P.M. and W.R. Scott. *Formal Organisations: A Comparative Analysis*, Chandler Pub. Com. San Francisco, 1962.

Bradford Spangberg, *British Bureaucracy in India*, Manohar Book Service, Delhi, 1976.

Buras, Oskar Krisen, *The Mental Measurement Year Book*; Highland Park, NJ, USA, 1978.

Burns, Allan C., *Colonial Civil Servant*; George Allen & Urwin Ltd. London, UK, 1949.

Calder, B.J. and B.M. Staw, "Self Perception of Intrinsic and Extrinsic Motivation", *Journal of Personality and Social Psychology*, April 1975.

Chanda, Ashok, *Indian Administration*, George Allen & Unwin, London, 1958.

Charles, A. Hollowing, *Decision Making Under Uncertainty: Models and Choices*; Prentice Hall Inc. New Jersey, 1979.

Chaturvedi, Anil, *District Administration—The Dynamics of Discord*; Sage Pub. New Delhi, 1988.

Chaturvedi, T.N., *Contemporary Administrative Culture of India*; I.I.P.A. New Delhi, 1996.

Chaturvedi, T.N., "Value Orientation in Human Problem Solving"; *Management in Government*, Vol. 15, July-Sept. 1981, pp. 107-16

Cohen, Allan R. and D.L. Bradferd, *Influence Without Authority*; John Wiley & Sons, New York, 1990.

Cook, Fred J., *Corrupted Land: The Social Morality of Modern America*; London Jonathan Cape, 1967.

Dalton, M., *Men Who Manage*; John & Willey, Inc., New York, 1959.

Dar, R.K., *Governance and the I.A.S. in Search of Resilience*; Tata McGraw-Hill Pub. Co. Ltd. New Delhi, 1999.

Das, S.K., *Civil Service Reform and Structural Adjustment*; Oxford University Press, New Delhi, 1998.

Das, S.K., *Public Office, Private Interest: Bureaucracy and Corruption in India*; Oxford University Press, New Delhi, 2001.

Davis, Kerth, *Human Behaviour at Work*; Tata McGraw-Hill Pub. Co. Ltd., New Delhi, 1977.

Dayal, I. and K. Mathur, *Dynamics of Formulating Policy in Government of India*; New Delhi, 1976.

Dayal, I.M. et al. *Dynamics of Formulating Policy in Government of India*, New Delhi, 1976.

Desai, Uday C., "Bureaucracy's Autocratic and Democratic Tendencies: A Brief Survey"; *Management in Government*, Vol. xxi, Nos. 1-3, April-Dec. 1989.

Deshpande, R.A., "Bureaucracy and Civil Service"; *Civic Affairs*, 6:10, May 1959.

Dey, Bata K., "Beyond Bureaucracy: Beyond Hierarchy", *Management in Government*, Department of Administrative Reforms and Public Grievances, Government of India, New Delhi, July 1992.

——, *Bureaucracy, Development and Public Management in India*; Uppal Pub. House, New Delhi, 1978.

——, "Elites and Masses in Development Paradigms" in *Indian Journal of Public Administration*, New Delhi, Vol. xxxvii No. 4, 1991, pp. 649-53.

Dhakha, R.N., *The All India Services—A Study of their Origin and Growth*, Bharti Bhawan, Patna, 1969.

Dilks, David, *Curzon in India*, Vol. I (Achievements), Rupert Hart-Davis, London, 1969.

——, *Curzon in India*, Vol. II (Frustration), Rupert Hart-Davis, London, 1970.

Dwivedi, O.P. and R.B. Jain, *India's Administrative State*; Gitanjali Pub. House, New Delhi, 1985.

Doctorates in Social Sciences Up to 1967; ICSSR, New Delhi, 1971.

Douglas, N.J. and Samuel Messick, *Problems in Human Assessment*, McGraw Hill Book Co., New York, 1967.

Dubhashi, P.R., *The Process of Public Administration*, Pune, 1980.

——, *Recent Trends in Public Administration*, Kaveri Books, New Delhi, 1995.

Dubin, R. Robert, *Human Relations in Administrating*, Prentice-Hall of India, New Delhi, 1974.

Duck, Steve, Danniel and Amy Starch, *Handbook of Personal Relationships: Theory, Research and Interventions*; John Wiley & Sons Ltd. Essex. UK, 1988.

Durhane, W.R. and Fritz Rieger, *International Management Research—Looking to Future*; Walter de Gruyter & Co. Berlin, 1993.

Dwarkadas, R., *Role of Higher Civil Service in India*, Popular Book Depot, Bombay, 1958.

Einspruch, Eric L., *An Introductory Guide to SPSS for Windows*; Sage Publications, London, 1998.

Elihu, Kalz and Brenda, D., *Bureaucracy and the Public*; Basic Books Inc. Pub., New York, 1973.

Etzioni, A., *Modern Organisation*, Prentice-Hall of India, New Delhi, 1972.

Everett, M. Ragers, *Diffusion of Innovations*, The Free Press, London, 1983.

Field, Andy, *Discovering Statistics Using SPSS for Windows*; Sage Publications, London, 2000.

Francis, Dave and M. Woodcock, *Activities for Self-Development*; Grower Publishing Co. Ltd. Aldershot, Hants, England, 1982.

Frasher, Report on Indian Police Commission, 1902-1903.

Friedman, M.R.H. Rosenman, "Type 'A' Behaviour and Your Heart", Alfred A. Knopf; New York, 1974.

Fritz, Robert, *The Path of Least Resistance*; Butterworth-Heonemann Ltd., Oxford, UK, 1994.

Gerald, R.F., S.D. Rosen and D.T. Barnum, *Hand Book of Human Resource Management*; Blackwell Pub. Marsathuselt, USA, 1995.

Ghoshal, A.K., *Civil Service in India*; University Press, Calcutta, 1941.

Goel, S.L., *International Civil Service: Principles, Practice and Prospectus*; Sterling Pub. Pvt. Ltd. New Delhi, 1984.

Gorwala, A.D., Report on Public Administration, Government of India, Planning Commission, New Delhi, 1951.

Government of India, 'Report Personnel Administration', Administrative Reforms Commission, New Delhi, 1969.

——, Gradation List, IAS, New Delhi, 1998, 2018.

——, Gradation List, IFS, New Delhi, 1998, 2018.

——, Gradation List, IPS, New Delhi, 1998, 2018.

——, National Police Commission, 6th Report, March 1981.

Greenberg, J. "Equity & Workplace Status, A Field Experiment"; *Journal of Applied Psychology*, Nov. 1988.

Gregory, B.N. and Margaret A.N., *Organisation Behaviour: A Management Challenge*, The Dryden Press, Orlando, Florida, 1990.

Gupta, A.S., *Police in British India*, 1861-1947; Concept Publishing Co. New Delhi, 1979.

Guy Peters, B., *The Politics of Bureaucracy*; Longman Inc. New York, 1988.

Hackman, J.R. et al., "Motivation Through the Design of Work: Text of a Theory", *Organisation Behaviour and Human Performance*, August, 1976.

Heginbotham, S.J., *Cultures in Conflict: The Four Faces of Indian Bureaucracy*, New York, 1975.

ICSSR, New Delhi, A Survey of Research in Public Administration; Vol. I, Allied Publisher, New Delhi, 1973.

ICSSR, New Delhi, A Survey of Research in Public Administration; Vol. II, Allied Publisher, New Delhi, 1975.

Indian Journal of Public Administration, Volume XLI, July-Sept. (3)1995; XXXIX, July-Sept (3), 1993; July-Sept, 1961, July-Sept Supplementary, 1963; July-Sept, 1965; July-Sept, 1966; July-Sept, 1971, July-Sept, 1975, July-Sept, 1976, Jan.-March, 1978, July-Sept, 1978; July-Sept, 1980, July-Sept, 1982, July-Sept, 1983, July-Sept, 1985, July-Sept, 1990, July-Sept,

1994, Volume LVII, July- September 2011 and Volume LIX, July-September 2013; by Indian Institute of Public Administration, New Delhi.

Jackson, J.H. and C.P. Morgan, *Organisation Theory*, Prentice Hall Inc. New Jersey, 1978.

Jackson, N., Douglas and Messick, Samuel, *Problems in Human Assessment.*

Jackson, P.M., *The Political Economy of Bureaucracy Theories of Bureaucratic Behavior*, Heritage Pub., New Delhi, 1983.

Jagdishwaranand Saraswati, *Sukraniti Saar*; Rishidev Rooplal Trust, Bahalgarh, Haryana, 1983.

Jain, R.B., *Public Services in a Democratic Context*, I.I.P.A. New Delhi, 1983.

Jusim, L., "Self Fulfilling Prophecies: A Theoretical & Integrative Review"; *Psychological Review*, Oct. 1986, pp. 429-45.

Kamoche, K., "Rhetoric Ritualism, and Totemism in Human Resource Management"; *Human Relations*, April 1995.

Katz, D. and R.L. Kalin, The Social Psychology of Organisations, John Willey & Sons, Inc. New York, 1978.

Kaw, M.K. *Bureaucrazy, Indian Administrative Service officers Unmasked*, Konark Pub. New Delhi, 1993.

Keller, L.M., et al., "Work Values: Genetic and Environmental Influences". *Journal of Applied Psychology*, February 1992, pp. 79-88.

Kelly, J., *Organisational Behaviour*, Richard, D. Brown Inc. Homewood Illinois, 1974.

Kerlinger, Fred N., *Foundation of Behavioral Research*; Surjeet Pub. New Delhi, 1983.

Khair, Tabish, Babu Fictions; Oxford University Press, New Delhi, 2001.

Khandwall, Pradip N., *Fourth Eye: An Excellence Through Creativity*; A.H. Wheeler & Co. Pvt. Ltd. New Delhi, 1988.

——, *Organisation Design for Excellence*; Tata McGraw-Hill Pub. Co. Ltd. New Delhi, 1993.

Khare, Brij B., *India, Political Attitude and Social Change*, Light and Life Publishers, New Delhi, 1974.

Kogan, Nathan and M.A. Wallach, *Risk Taking—A Study in Cognition and Personality*; Holt Rinerhart and Winston, New York, 1964.

Kothari, C.R., *Research Methodology—Methods and Techniques*; Wishwa Prakashan, New Delhi, 1995.

Kothari, Shanti and Ramashray Ray, *Relation Between Politician & Administrator at District Level*, Indian Institute of Public Administration New Delhi; 1981.

Kripalani, S.K., *Fifty Years with British*, Orient Longman, New Delhi, 1993.

Kriplani, B., Corruption in Indian Politics, *Bhavans Journal*, Vol. 25, No.1, Aug. 13, 1978, pp. 156-69.

Krishanamachari, V.T., Report on Indian and State Administrative Services and Problems of District Administration, Government of India, Planning Commission, New Delhi, 1962.

Kumar, Arun, *Public Administration: Today and Tomorrow*; Vols. I & II, Anmol Publications Pvt. Ltd., New Delhi, 2000.

Lake, Dale G., Mathew B.M. and Ralph, B.E. *Measuring Human Behavior*, New York, Teacher College Press, 1973.

Lambert, Tom E., *The Power of Influence*; Nicholas Brealley Publishing, London. 1996.

Lasswell, H. and A. Kaplan, *Power and Society*, Yale Univ. Press, New Haven, 1950.

Leonora D'Souza, "Coping with Bureaucrats and Technocrats", in *Management in Government*, Vol. Xxiii, No. 3, Oct-Dec, 1991.

Limmaye, Madhu, *Why Samyukata Socialist?*, New Delhi, 1967.

Luthans, Fred, *Organisation Behaviour*; McGraw-Hill Inc., Singapore, 1992.

Lynton, Rolf P. and Udai Pareek, *Training for Development*, Vistaar Publi. New Delhi, 1990.

M., Webr, *The Theory of Social & Economic Organisation*, Translated by Henderson T. Parsous, New York, Oxford Univ. Press Inc. 1947.

Maconochie, Sir Evan, *Life in Indian Civil Service*; Chapman & Hall Ltd. London, 1926.

Madhok, B., *Why Jana Sangh?*, New Delhi, 1967.

Mahaeshwari, S., *The Administrative Reform Commission*, Agra, 1972.

——, "Constituency Linkage of National Legislature in India", *Legislative Studies Quarterly*, 1.3, 1976.

Maheshwari, S.K., *The Evolution of Indian Administration*, Lakshmi Narain Agarwal, Agra, 1970.

Maheshwari, S.R., *The Indian Administrative Year Book*, 1990.

Maheshwari, Shriram, *The Indian Administrative System*; Jawahar Publishers and Distributors, New Delhi, 1994.

Maltz, Maxwell, *Psycho-Cybernetics*; Pocket Books, New York. 1973.

Mamoria, C.B., *Personnel Management*, Himalaya Pub. House, New Delhi, 1989.

Mandal, U.C., *Bureaucracy: Growth and Development*; Sarup & Sons, New Delhi. 1997.

Maslow, A.H., *Motivation and Personality*, Harperr Row Ind. New York, 1970.

Mathur, Krishan Mohan, *The Problems of Police in Democratic Society*; R.B.S.A. Jaipur, 1987.

Mathur, Kuldeep, "Bureaucracy in India: Development and Pursuit of Self-interest", in *Indian Journal of Public Administration*, New Delhi, Vol. xxxvii, No. 4, 1991, pp. 637-48.

McConnell, James V., *Understanding Human Behaviour—An Introduction to Psychology*; Holt, Rinechart and Winston, New York, 1986.

Miller, D.C., *Handbook of Research Design and Social Measurement*, Sage Pub. Newbury Pack, USA, 1991.

Miller, David W. and Martin, K.S., *The Structure of Human Decisions*; Prentice Hall, Inc. New Jersay, 1967.

Miller, Debert C., *Handbook of Research Design and Social Measurement*; Sage Pub., London.

Miner, J.B., *Theories of Organizational Behavior*, Dryden Press, Hinsdal, IL, 1980.

Mishra, B.B., *Government and Bureaucracy in India, 1947-1976*, Oxford Univ. Press, New Delhi; 1986.

Mishra, B.B., *The Bureaucracy in India, An Historical Analysis of Development up to 1947*, Oxford Univ. Press, New Delhi, 1977.

Mishra, Sharad Chander, *Police Administration in India*; National Police Academy, Mt. Abu. Rajasthan, 1973.

Misquitta, L.P., *Pressure Groups and Democracy in India*; Sterling Publishers Pvt. Ltd. New Delhi, 1991.

Mitchell, Garry, *The Trainer's Handbook—The AMA Guide to Effective Training*, AMACOM, American Management Association, New York, 1987.

Mohanlal, Acharya, A Study of Civil Services in Madhya Pradesh; Ph.D. Thesis, Indore University. 1977.

Mohanty, N., "Administrative Reform Commission on Personnel Administration: A Study in Bias", *Indian Journal of Public Administration*, xv. 4, 1969, IIPA, New Delhi.

Morris, C.G., *Psychology: An Introduction*; 9th Edition, Prentice Hall, Upper Saddle R.N. 1996.

Mullick, B.N., *My Years With Nehru*, Bombay, 1971.

Murray J. Horn, *The Political Economy of Public Administration*; Cambridge University, Press. 1995.

Muttalib, M.A., *Democracy, Bureaucracy and Technocracy: Assumptions of Public Management Theory*; Concept Pub. New Delhi, 1980.

Nandy, Raj, *Perceptions or Reality—A Study Job Attitudes of Delhi Traffic Police*; I.I.P.A. New Delhi, 1982.

Nayak, Radhakant, *Administrative Justice in India*; The Sage Pub. New Delhi, 1989.

Nigam, S.R., *Scotland Yard and the Indian Police*; Kitab Mahal Pvt. Ltd. Allahabad, 1963.

O. Malley, L.S.S. The Indian Civil Service, 1601-1930; John Murry, Albemarle St. London, 1931.

Orwell, George, *Burmese Day's*; New American Librans, New York, 1963.

P.M. Davies and A.P.M. Coxon, *Key Texts in Multidimensional Scaling*; Heinemann Educational Books Ltd., London, 1982.

Panandikar, V.A. Pai, *Problems of Governance in South Asia*; Konark Publishers Pvt. Ltd. New Delhi, 2000.

Panda, Basudev, *Indian Bureaucracy: An Inside Story*; Uppal Publishing House, New Delhi, 1978.

Panikar, K.M., *Civil Service, History and Problems*, University of Madras, 1955.

Pareek, Udai and T.V. Rao, *First Handbook of Psychological and Social Instruments*, Samashti, B-2 Chamelibagh, Baroda, 1992.

Pareek, Udai, T.V. Rao and M.K. Singhvi, *Behavioural Processes in Organisations*; Oxford & IBH, New Delhi, 1985.

Pareek, Udai, *Training Instruments for Human Resource Development*; Tata McGraw Hill Pub. New Delhi; 1997.

Paul, Appleby, *Public Administration in India*, Report of a Survey, Cabinet Secretariat, New Delhi, 1953.

Paul, F. Lazarsfeld and Morris Rasenberg, *Language of Social Research*; The Free Press, MAC Million C., New York, 1955.

Pavarala, Vinod, *Interpreting Corruption*, Elite Perspective in India; Sage Pub. New Delhi. 1996.

Pease, Allan, *Body Language*; Sudha Publications Pvt. Ltd., New Delhi, 1998.

Percival, Griffiths, *The British Impact on India*, MacDonald, London, 1952.

Pfeiffer and Ballow, A.C., *Using Instruments in Human Resource Development*, University Associates, San Diego, 1988.

Pfeiffer, William J., 'The 1982 Annual', Pfeiffer & Company, San Diego, Canada; 1982.

Pfeiffer, William J., 'The 1983 Annual', Pfeiffer & Company, San Diego, Canada; 1983.

Pfeiffer, William J., 'The 1994 Annual', Pfeiffer & Company, San Diego, Canada; 1994.

Pfeiffer, William J., 'The 1995 Annual', Pfeiffer & Company, San Diego, Canada; 1995.

Pfeiffer, William J., 'The 1996 Annual', Vols. I & II, Pfeiffer & Company, San Diego, Canada; 1996.

Pfeiffer, William J., et al. 'Instrumentation in Human Relations', University Associates, Inc. California, 1976.

Pfeiffer, William J., Hustin, R. and John E., J.; *Instrumentation in Human Relation Training*; University Associates, Inc. California, USA, 1976.

Pfeiffer, William J., *Instrumentation Kit*, University Associates, San Diego, 1988.

Pfeiffer, William J., *Theories & Models in Applied Behavioural Science*; Vols. I & II, Vanity Book International, New Delhi, 1996.

Pfeiffer, William J., 'The 1993 Annual', Pfeiffer & Company, San Diego, Canada; 1993.

Phillip, Jack J., *Training Evaluation and Measurement Methods*; Gulf Pub. Company, Houstan, Texas.

Pinto, Marina, *Administrative Behaviour*, in Konark Publications, New Delhi.

Piskurich, George M., *The ASTD Handbook of Instructional Technology*; McGraw-Hill Inc. New York, 1993.

Pistonjee, D.M., *Handbook of Psychological and Social Instruments*, Concept Publishing Company, New Delhi, 1988.

Potter, David C., *India's Political Administrators—1919-1983*, Clarendon Press, Oxford, UK, 1986.

Prachypruit, T., "Administrative Practices and Development Orientedness of Civil Servants"; *The Asian Journal of Public Administration*, Vol. 7, No. 1, June 1985, pp. 36-54.

Prashar, Rajinder, *Police Administration*; Deep & Deep Publications Co. New Delhi, 1979.

Price, James L. *Handbook of Organisation Measurement*, 1992.

Punjabi, K.L., *The Civil Servant in India*, Bhartiya Vidya Bhavan, Bombay, 1965.

Punnett, Betty Jane and O. Shenkar, *Handbook for International Management Research*; Blackwell Publishers Ltd., USA, 1996.

Putt, Allen D. and J.F. Springer, *Policy Research Concepts, Methods and Applications*; Prentice Hall, New Jersey, 1989.

Ractham, Arun, "Political Behavior in Organisation: A Thai Perspective"; *Indian Journal of Public Administration*, xxxv, Oct-Dec, 1989.

Rai, Mangat E.N., *Commitment My Style: Career in the Indian Civil Service*, New Delhi, 1973.

Ram, N.V.R., *Games Bureaucrats Play*, New Delhi, 1978.

Rao, S.L., *Successful Negotiations: Strategies and Tactics for Mutual Gains*; Wheeler Publishing, New Delhi, 1999.

Report of Fifth Pay Commission, Ministry of Finance, Government of India, India, New Delhi, 1994.

Report of Fourth Pay Commission, Ministry of Finance, Government of India, New Delhi.

Report of Seventh Pay Commission, Ministry of Finance, Government of India, New Delhi, India.

Report of Sixth Pay Commission, Ministry of Finance, Government of India, New Delhi, India.

Report on the National Police Commission (8 Vols.), Govt. of India, New Delhi, 1979.

Report: Personnel Administration, Administrative Reform Commission, New Delhi, 1969.

Richard, L.L. and David, S.R., *Statistics for Management*, Prentice Hall of India, New Delhi, 1994.

Robbins, Stephen P., *Managing Organizational Conflicts: A Non-traditional Approach*, Prentice Hall, Englewood Cliffs, New York, 1974.

Robbins, Stephen P., *Organization Behavior*; Prentice Hall of India Pvt. Ltd., New Delhi, 1996.

Robinson, John P. and Phillip R. Shaver, Measures of Social Psychological Attitudes, University of Michigan, Institute of Social Research, 1973.

Robinson, John P., Jerarrold, G.R. and Kendra, B.H., *Measures of Political Attitudes*, University of Michigan, Institute of Social Research, 1969.

Robinson, John P., Robert, A. and Kendra, B.H., *Measure of Occupational Attitudes and Occupational Characters*; Ann. Arbor University of Michigan, Institute of Social Research, 1969.

Rokeach, Milton, *The Nature of Human Values*; The Free Press, New York, 1973.

Ronen, S., "Equity Perception in Multiple Comparisons: A Field Study", *Human Relations*, April 1986.

Roy, Jaytilak Guha, *Policing a District*, Indian Institute of Public Administration, New Delhi, 1992.

Roy, Naresh Chander, *The Civil Services in India*, K.L. Mukhopadhya, Calcutta, 1960.

Sachin, E.H., *Organisational Psychology*, Prentice Hall of India, New Delhi, 1968.

Saxena, N.C., *Administration and the People: Higher Bureaucracy Needs Radical Reforms*; 1999 (Private Communication).

Saxena, N.S., *Law and Order in India*; Abhinav Publications, New Delhi, 1987.

Seshmodh, Satish Kumar, Strategic Change Process and Politicality of Decision Making; in *ASCI Journal of Management*, Hyderabad. 26(1&2), 1997.

Shanna, Subhash, Decision Styles: Conceptual Models and an Empirical Study of IAS Officers, in *Indian Journal of Public Administration*, New Delhi, vol. xxxviii, No. 2, 1992, pp. 95-108.

Sharma, B.R., *Motivational Crisis in Indian Administration*; I.I.P.A. New Delhi. 1986.

Shaw, Marvin E. and J.W. Wright, *Scales of Measurement of Attitudes*, 1967.

Sheppard, B.H. et al. *Organization Justice: The Search for Fairness in the Workplace*, Lexington Books, New York, 1992.

Shivaraman, B., *Bitter Sweet: Governance of India in Transition*, Ashish Publishing House, New Delhi; 1991.

Shukla, J.D., *Indianisation of All India Services and Its Impact on Administration*; Allied Publishers Pvt. Ltd. New Delhi, 1982.

Simon, Herbert A. *Administrative Behaviour*; Free Press, New York, 1945.

Simon, Herbert A., "Making Management Decisions: The Role of Intuition and Emotions", in *Academy of Management Executives*, Feb. 1987.

Singh, P. and Asha Bhandarkar, Corporate Success Transformational Leadership, Willey Eastern Ltd. New Delhi; 1990.

Singh, P. and Asha Bhandarkar, *IAS Profile: Myths and Realities*; Wiley Eastern, New Delhi, 1994.

Singh, P. and Asha Bhandarkar, Paradigm Shifts in the Indian Industry: The Need for Tolerance of Ambiguity; *MDI Management Journal*, Vol. 9, No. 2, July 1996.

Singh, P., "A Matter of Ambiguity", Indian Book Croncile, 16.31981, as cited in Laporte, R., *Public Administration Review*, 41.5, 1981, p. 588.

Singh, P., *Human Growth Through Self-Awareness*; Himalaya Publishing House, Bombay, 1982.

Singh, P., *Occupational Values and Style of Indian Managers*, Wiley Eastern, New Delhi; 1979.

Singh, P., Performance Appraisal Systems: A Critical Analysis; *Indian Journal of Industrial Relations*, Vol. 16, No. 3, Jan. 1981.

Sinha, Navnit, *Role and Rationale of All India Services*; IJPA, New Delhi, Vol. xxxvii, No. 1, Jan.-March, 1991.

Sliarnia, R.A., *Organisational Theory Behaviour*, Tata McGraw Hill Pub. Co. Ltd. New Delhi, 1973.

Spector, P.E., "Behaviour in Organisation as a Function of Employee's Locus of Control" *Psychological Bulletin*, May 1982, pp. 482-97.

Srivastava, C.P., *Corruption, India's Enemy Within*; MacMillion India Ltd., New Delhi, 2001.

Steward, R.C., Cynthia H. and W.R. Nord, *Hand Book of Organization Studies*; Sage Publications, New Delhi, 1996.

Suri, S.S., Corruption of Political Life—Lack of Public Philosophy Main Course, *The Times of India*, New Delhi, 23.2.1981.

Tayal, H., General & Industrial Administration, Translated by Costance Storrs, Sir lssac Pitman & Sons Ltd., 1949.

Taylor, F.W., *Scientific Management*, Harper & Row, New York, 1947.

Tenbrunsel, A.E. et al. Cognitions in Organizations; in *Handbook of Organization Studies*, Sage, New Delhi, 1996.

Terry & Franklin, *Principles of Management*, All India Traveler Bookseller, New Delhi, 1991.

Terry, Larry D., *Leadership of Public Bureaucracies*; Sage Publisher, New Delhi.

Thakur, R.N., *The All India Services, A Study of Their Origin and Growth*, Bharti Bhawan, Patna, 1969.

Thakur, Upender, *Corruption in Ancient India*; Abhinav Pub. New Delhi, 1979.

Thimmiah, G., *Power, Politics and Social Justice*; Sage Pub. New Delhi, 1993.

Thomas, Harns, *I am OK—You're OK*, Pan Books London, 1978.

Thurstone, L.L., *The Measurement of Values*; The University Chicago Press, Chicago, 1959.

Truman, D.B., *The Governmental Process—Political Interests and Public Opinion*; Alfred A. Knopf. Inc. New York, 1962.

Tumala, Krishna K., *Public Administration in India Times Academic Press*, Singapore; 1994.

Vajpayi, S.C. and P.K. Kaul, Politician-Civil Servant Relationship; *IJPA*, New Delhi, Vol. xxxix, No. 1, Jan-March, 1993.

Vajpeyi, S.C. and P.X. Kaul, Politician-Civil Servant Relationship, in *Indian Journal of Public Administration*, New Delhi, Vol. xxxix, No. 1, 1993, pp. 29-45.

Varma, R.S., *Bureaucracy in India*; Progress Pub., Bhopal, 1973.

Varma, S.P., Corruption and Political Development in India, *Political Science Review*, Vol. 13, Vols. 1-4, Jan.-Dec. 1974, pp. 157-79.

Verrey, Levet, *A History of Indian Nationalist Movement*; John Murry, London, 1920.

Vittachi, T., Bureaucrats Who Won't Lie Down, *the Guardian*, London, 10.4.1978.

Vittal, N. and S. Mahalingam, *Fighting Corruption and Restructuring Governance*; Manas Publications, New Delhi. 2000.

Vroom, V.H., *Work and Motivation*, John Wiley, New York, 1964.

Waston, W.E., K. Kumar and L.K. Michaelsen, "Cultural Diversity & Impact on Interaction Process and Performance: Comparing Homogeneous & Diverse Table Group", *Academy of Management Journal*, June 1993, pp. 590-602.

Wamsley, Gary L. et al., *Refounding Public Administration*; Sage Pub. New Delhi, 1990.

Watton, R.E. and R.B. McKerbie, *A Behavioural Theory of Labor Negotiation: An Analysis of Social Interactive System*; McGraw Hill, New York, 1965.

White, J.D. and G.B. Adams, *Research in Public Administration—Reflection on Theory and Practice*, Sage Publications India Pvt. Ltd., New Delhi, 1994.

Whitemore, D.A., *Management for Administrators*; William Heinemann Ltd., London, 1985.

Winston, Wayne L., Introduction to Mathematical Programming; *Applications and Algorithms*; Duxbury Press, California. 1995.

William, J. Gore, *Administrative Decision Making: A Heuristic Model*, John Wiley & Sons, Inc., New York, 1964.

Wolfe, D.M. Power, Authority in the Family, in D. Cartwright (ed.), *Studies in Social Power*, Institute for Social Research, Michigan 1959.

Woodruff, P., *The Men Who Ruled India*, Vols. I & II, Jonathan Cape, London, 1953.

Index